Data Structures & Algorithm Analysis in C++

THIRD EDITION

Clifford A. Shaffer

Department of Computer Science
Virginia Tech

Dover Publications, Inc.
Mineola, New York

Bibliographical Note

This Dover edition, first published in 2011, is the first publication in book form of the revised and updated Third Edition of *A Practical Introduction to Data Structures and Algorithm Analysis*, which is available from the author's website at: http://people.cs.vt.edu/~shaffer/Book/

Library of Congress Cataloging-in-Publication Data

Shaffer, Clifford A.
    Data structures and algorithm analysis in C++ / Clifford A. Shaffer. — 3rd ed.
        p. cm.
    Rev. ed. of: A practical introduction to data structures and algorithm analysis / Clifford A. Shaffer. 2001.
    Includes bibliographical references and index.
    ISBN-13: 978-0-486-48582-9 (pbk.)
    ISBN-10: 0-486-48582-X
    1. Data structures (Computer science) 2. Computer algorithms. I. Shaffer, Clifford A. Practical introduction to data structures and algorithm analysis. II. Title.

QA76.9.D35S45 2011
005.13'3—dc23

                                                                        2011020251

Manufactured in the United States by LSC Communications
4500057301
www.doverpublications.com

Contents

Preface

We study data structures so that we can learn to write more efficient programs. But why must programs be efficient when new computers are faster every year? The reason is that our ambitions grow with our capabilities. Instead of rendering efficiency needs obsolete, the modern revolution in computing power and storage capability merely raises the efficiency stakes as we attempt more complex tasks.

The quest for program efficiency need not and should not conflict with sound design and clear coding. Creating efficient programs has little to do with "programming tricks" but rather is based on good organization of information and good algorithms. A programmer who has not mastered the basic principles of clear design is not likely to write efficient programs. Conversely, concerns related to development costs and maintainability should not be used as an excuse to justify inefficient performance. Generality in design can and should be achieved without sacrificing performance, but this can only be done if the designer understands how to measure performance and does so as an integral part of the design and implementation process. Most computer science curricula recognize that good programming skills begin with a strong emphasis on fundamental software engineering principles. Then, once a programmer has learned the principles of clear program design and implementation, the next step is to study the effects of data organization and algorithms on program efficiency.

Approach: This book describes many techniques for representing data. These techniques are presented within the context of the following principles:

1. Each data structure and each algorithm has costs and benefits. Practitioners need a thorough understanding of how to assess costs and benefits to be able to adapt to new design challenges. This requires an understanding of the principles of algorithm analysis, and also an appreciation for the significant effects of the physical medium employed (e.g., data stored on disk versus main memory).

2. Related to costs and benefits is the notion of tradeoffs. For example, it is quite common to reduce time requirements at the expense of an increase in space requirements, or vice versa. Programmers face tradeoff issues regularly in all

phases of software design and implementation, so the concept must become deeply ingrained.

3. Programmers should know enough about common practice to avoid reinventing the wheel. Thus, programmers need to learn the commonly used data structures, their related algorithms, and the most frequently encountered design patterns found in programming.

4. Data structures follow needs. Programmers must learn to assess application needs first, then find a data structure with matching capabilities. To do this requires competence in Principles 1, 2, and 3.

As I have taught data structures through the years, I have found that design issues have played an ever greater role in my courses. This can be traced through the various editions of this textbook by the increasing coverage for design patterns and generic interfaces. The first edition had no mention of design patterns. The second edition had limited coverage of a few example patterns, and introduced the dictionary ADT and comparator classes. With the third edition, there is explicit coverage of some design patterns that are encountered when programming the basic data structures and algorithms covered in the book.

Using the Book in Class: Data structures and algorithms textbooks tend to fall into one of two categories: teaching texts or encyclopedias. Books that attempt to do both usually fail at both. This book is intended as a teaching text. I believe it is more important for a practitioner to understand the principles required to select or design the data structure that will best solve some problem than it is to memorize a lot of textbook implementations. Hence, I have designed this as a teaching text that covers most standard data structures, but not all. A few data structures that are not widely adopted are included to illustrate important principles. Some relatively new data structures that should become widely used in the future are included.

Within an undergraduate program, this textbook is designed for use in either an advanced lower division (sophomore or junior level) data structures course, or for a senior level algorithms course. New material has been added in the third edition to support its use in an algorithms course. Normally, this text would be used in a course beyond the standard freshman level "CS2" course that often serves as the initial introduction to data structures. Readers of this book should typically have two semesters of the equivalent of programming experience, including at least some exposure to C++. Readers who are already familiar with recursion will have an advantage. Students of data structures will also benefit from having first completed a good course in Discrete Mathematics. Nonetheless, Chapter 2 attempts to give a reasonably complete survey of the prerequisite mathematical topics at the level necessary to understand their use in this book. Readers may wish to refer back to the appropriate sections as needed when encountering unfamiliar mathematical material.

A sophomore-level class where students have only a little background in basic data structures or analysis (that is, background equivalent to what would be had from a traditional CS2 course) might cover Chapters 1-11 in detail, as well as selected topics from Chapter 13. That is how I use the book for my own sophomore-level class. Students with greater background might cover Chapter 1, skip most of Chapter 2 except for reference, briefly cover Chapters 3 and 4, and then cover chapters 5-12 in detail. Again, only certain topics from Chapter 13 might be covered, depending on the programming assignments selected by the instructor. A senior-level algorithms course would focus on Chapters 11 and 14-17.

Chapter 13 is intended in part as a source for larger programming exercises. I recommend that all students taking a data structures course be required to implement some advanced tree structure, or another dynamic structure of comparable difficulty such as the skip list or sparse matrix representations of Chapter 12. None of these data structures are significantly more difficult to implement than the binary search tree, and any of them should be within a student's ability after completing Chapter 5.

While I have attempted to arrange the presentation in an order that makes sense, instructors should feel free to rearrange the topics as they see fit. The book has been written so that once the reader has mastered Chapters 1-6, the remaining material has relatively few dependencies. Clearly, external sorting depends on understanding internal sorting and disk files. Section 6.2 on the UNION/FIND algorithm is used in Kruskal's Minimum-Cost Spanning Tree algorithm. Section 9.2 on self-organizing lists mentions the buffer replacement schemes covered in Section 8.3. Chapter 14 draws on examples from throughout the book. Section 17.2 relies on knowledge of graphs. Otherwise, most topics depend only on material presented earlier within the same chapter.

Most chapters end with a section entitled "Further Reading." These sections are not comprehensive lists of references on the topics presented. Rather, I include books and articles that, in my opinion, may prove exceptionally informative or entertaining to the reader. In some cases I include references to works that should become familiar to any well-rounded computer scientist.

Use of C++: The programming examples are written in C++, but I do not wish to discourage those unfamiliar with C++ from reading this book. I have attempted to make the examples as clear as possible while maintaining the advantages of C++. C++ is used here strictly as a tool to illustrate data structures concepts. In particular, I make use of C++'s support for hiding implementation details, including features such as classes, private class members, constructors, and destructors. These features of the language support the crucial concept of separating logical design, as embodied in the abstract data type, from physical implementation as embodied in the data structure.

To keep the presentation as clear as possible, some important features of **C**++ are avoided here. I deliberately minimize use of certain features commonly used by experienced **C**++ programmers such as class hierarchy, inheritance, and virtual functions. Operator and function overloading is used sparingly. **C**-like initialization syntax is preferred to some of the alternatives offered by **C**++.

While the **C**++ features mentioned above have valid design rationale in real programs, they tend to obscure rather than enlighten the principles espoused in this book. For example, inheritance is an important tool that helps programmers avoid duplication, and thus minimize bugs. From a pedagogical standpoint, however, inheritance often makes code examples harder to understand since it tends to spread the description for one logical unit among several classes. Thus, my class definitions only use inheritance where inheritance is explicitly relevant to the point illustrated (e.g., Section 5.3.1). This does not mean that a programmer should do likewise. Avoiding code duplication and minimizing errors are important goals. Treat the programming examples as illustrations of data structure principles, but do not copy them directly into your own programs.

One painful decision I had to make was whether to use templates in the code examples. In the first edition of this book, the decision was to leave templates out as it was felt that their syntax obscures the meaning of the code for those not familiar with **C**++. In the years following, the use of **C**++ in computer science curricula has greatly expanded. I now assume that readers of the text will be familiar with template syntax. Thus, templates are now used extensively in the code examples.

My implementations are meant to provide concrete illustrations of data structure principles, as an aid to the textual exposition. Code examples should not be read or used in isolation from the associated text because the bulk of each example's documentation is contained in the text, not the code. The code complements the text, not the other way around. They are not meant to be a series of commercial-quality class implementations. If you are looking for a complete implementation of a standard data structure for use in your own code, you would do well to do an Internet search.

For instance, the code examples provide less parameter checking than is sound programming practice, since including such checking would obscure rather than illuminate the text. Some parameter checking and testing for other constraints (e.g., whether a value is being removed from an empty container) is included in the form of a call to **Assert**. The inputs to **Assert** are a Boolean expression and a character string. If this expression evaluates to **false**, then a message is printed and the program terminates immediately. Terminating a program when a function receives a bad parameter is generally considered undesirable in real programs, but is quite adequate for understanding how a data structure is meant to operate. In real programming applications, **C**++'s exception handling features should be used to deal with input data errors. However, assertions provide a simpler mechanism for indicating required conditions in a way that is both adequate for clarifying how a data structure is meant to operate, and is easily modified into true exception handling. See the Appendix for the implementation of **Assert**.

I make a distinction in the text between "C++ implementations" and "pseudocode." Code labeled as a C++ implementation has actually been compiled and tested on one or more C++ compilers. Pseudocode examples often conform closely to C++ syntax, but typically contain one or more lines of higher-level description. Pseudocode is used where I perceived a greater pedagogical advantage to a simpler, but less precise, description.

Exercises and Projects: Proper implementation and analysis of data structures cannot be learned simply by reading a book. You must practice by implementing real programs, constantly comparing different techniques to see what really works best in a given situation.

One of the most important aspects of a course in data structures is that it is where students really learn to program using pointers and dynamic memory allocation, by implementing data structures such as linked lists and trees. It is often where students truly learn recursion. In our curriculum, this is the first course where students do significant design, because it often requires real data structures to motivate significant design exercises. Finally, the fundamental differences between memory-based and disk-based data access cannot be appreciated without practical programming experience. For all of these reasons, a data structures course cannot succeed without a significant programming component. In our department, the data structures course is one of the most difficult programming course in the curriculum.

Students should also work problems to develop their analytical abilities. I provide over 450 exercises and suggestions for programming projects. I urge readers to take advantage of them.

Contacting the Author and Supplementary Materials: A book such as this is sure to contain errors and have room for improvement. I welcome bug reports and constructive criticism. I can be reached by electronic mail via the Internet at **shaffer@vt.edu**. Alternatively, comments can be mailed to

> Cliff Shaffer
> Department of Computer Science
> Virginia Tech
> Blacksburg, VA 24061

The electronic posting of this book, along with a set of lecture notes for use in class can be obtained at

http://www.cs.vt.edu/~shaffer/book.html.

The code examples used in the book are available at the same site. Online Web pages for Virginia Tech's sophomore-level data structures class can be found at `http://courses.cs.vt.edu/~cs3114.`

This book was typeset by the author using LATEX. The bibliography was prepared using BIBTEX. The index was prepared using **makeindex**. The figures were mostly drawn with **Xfig**. Figures 3.1 and 9.10 were partially created using Mathematica.

Acknowledgments: It takes a lot of help from a lot of people to make a book. I wish to acknowledge a few of those who helped to make this book possible. I apologize for the inevitable omissions.

Virginia Tech helped make this whole thing possible through sabbatical research leave during Fall 1994, enabling me to get the project off the ground. My department heads during the time I have written the various editions of this book, Dennis Kafura and Jack Carroll, provided unwavering moral support for this project. Mike Keenan, Lenny Heath, and Jeff Shaffer provided valuable input on early versions of the chapters. I also wish to thank Lenny Heath for many years of stimulating discussions about algorithms and analysis (and how to teach both to students). Steve Edwards deserves special thanks for spending so much time helping me on various redesigns of the C++ and Java code versions for the second and third editions, and many hours of discussion on the principles of program design. Thanks to Layne Watson for his help with Mathematica, and to Bo Begole, Philip Isenhour, Jeff Nielsen, and Craig Struble for much technical assistance. Thanks to Bill McQuain, Mark Abrams and Dennis Kafura for answering lots of silly questions about C++ and Java.

I am truly indebted to the many reviewers of the various editions of this manuscript. For the first edition these reviewers included J. David Bezek (University of Evansville), Douglas Campbell (Brigham Young University), Karen Davis (University of Cincinnati), Vijay Kumar Garg (University of Texas – Austin), Jim Miller (University of Kansas), Bruce Maxim (University of Michigan – Dearborn), Jeff Parker (Agile Networks/Harvard), Dana Richards (George Mason University), Jack Tan (University of Houston), and Lixin Tao (Concordia University). Without their help, this book would contain many more technical errors and many fewer insights.

For the second edition, I wish to thank these reviewers: Gurdip Singh (Kansas State University), Peter Allen (Columbia University), Robin Hill (University of Wyoming), Norman Jacobson (University of California – Irvine), Ben Keller (Eastern Michigan University), and Ken Bosworth (Idaho State University). In addition, I wish to thank Neil Stewart and Frank J. Thesen for their comments and ideas for improvement.

Third edition reviewers included Randall Lechlitner (University of Houstin, Clear Lake) and Brian C. Hipp (York Technical College). I thank them for their comments.

Prentice Hall was the original print publisher for the first and second editions. Without the hard work of many people there, none of this would be possible. Authors simply do not create printer-ready books on their own. Foremost thanks go to Kate Hargett, Petra Rector, Laura Steele, and Alan Apt, my editors over the years. My production editors, Irwin Zucker for the second edition, Kathleen Caren for the original C++ version, and Ed DeFelippis for the Java version, kept everything moving smoothly during that horrible rush at the end. Thanks to Bill Zobrist and Bruce Gregory (I think) for getting me into this in the first place. Others at Prentice Hall who helped me along the way include Truly Donovan, Linda Behrens, and Phyllis Bregman. Thanks to Tracy Dunkelberger for her help in returning the copyright to me, thus enabling the electronic future of this work. I am sure I owe thanks to many others at Prentice Hall for their help in ways that I am not even aware of.

I am thankful to Shelley Kronzek at Dover publications for her faith in taking on the print publication of this third edition. Much expanded, with both Java and C++ versions, and many inconsistencies corrected, I am confident that this is the best edition yet. But none of us really knows whether students will prefer a free online textbook or a low-cost, printed bound version. In the end, we believe that the two formats will be mutually supporting by offering more choices. Production editor James Miller and design manager Marie Zaczkiewicz have worked hard to ensure that the production is of the highest quality.

I wish to express my appreciation to Hanan Samet for teaching me about data structures. I learned much of the philosophy presented here from him as well, though he is not responsible for any problems with the result. Thanks to my wife Terry, for her love and support, and to my daughters Irena and Kate for pleasant diversions from working too hard. Finally, and most importantly, to all of the data structures students over the years who have taught me what is important and what should be skipped in a data structures course, and the many new insights they have provided. This book is dedicated to them.

Cliff Shaffer
Blacksburg, Virginia

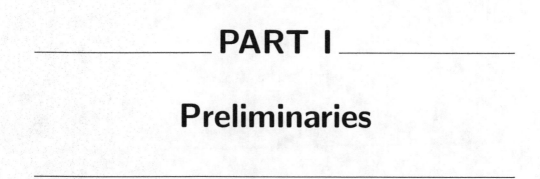

PART I

Preliminaries

1

Data Structures and Algorithms

How many cities with more than 250,000 people lie within 500 miles of Dallas, Texas? How many people in my company make over $100,000 per year? Can we connect all of our telephone customers with less than 1,000 miles of cable? To answer questions like these, it is not enough to have the necessary information. We must organize that information in a way that allows us to find the answers in time to satisfy our needs.

Representing information is fundamental to computer science. The primary purpose of most computer programs is not to perform calculations, but to store and retrieve information — usually as fast as possible. For this reason, the study of data structures and the algorithms that manipulate them is at the heart of computer science. And that is what this book is about — helping you to understand how to structure information to support efficient processing.

This book has three primary goals. The first is to present the commonly used data structures. These form a programmer's basic data structure "toolkit." For many problems, some data structure in the toolkit provides a good solution.

The second goal is to introduce the idea of tradeoffs and reinforce the concept that there are costs and benefits associated with every data structure. This is done by describing, for each data structure, the amount of space and time required for typical operations.

The third goal is to teach how to measure the effectiveness of a data structure or algorithm. Only through such measurement can you determine which data structure in your toolkit is most appropriate for a new problem. The techniques presented also allow you to judge the merits of new data structures that you or others might invent.

There are often many approaches to solving a problem. How do we choose between them? At the heart of computer program design are two (sometimes conflicting) goals:

1. To design an algorithm that is easy to understand, code, and debug.
2. To design an algorithm that makes efficient use of the computer's resources.

Ideally, the resulting program is true to both of these goals. We might say that such a program is "elegant." While the algorithms and program code examples presented here attempt to be elegant in this sense, it is not the purpose of this book to explicitly treat issues related to goal (1). These are primarily concerns of the discipline of Software Engineering. Rather, this book is mostly about issues relating to goal (2).

How do we measure efficiency? Chapter 3 describes a method for evaluating the efficiency of an algorithm or computer program, called **asymptotic analysis**. Asymptotic analysis also allows you to measure the inherent difficulty of a problem. The remaining chapters use asymptotic analysis techniques to estimate the time cost for every algorithm presented. This allows you to see how each algorithm compares to other algorithms for solving the same problem in terms of its efficiency.

This first chapter sets the stage for what is to follow, by presenting some higher-order issues related to the selection and use of data structures. We first examine the process by which a designer selects a data structure appropriate to the task at hand. We then consider the role of abstraction in program design. We briefly consider the concept of a design pattern and see some examples. The chapter ends with an exploration of the relationship between problems, algorithms, and programs.

1.1   A Philosophy of Data Structures

1.1.1   The Need for Data Structures

You might think that with ever more powerful computers, program efficiency is becoming less important. After all, processor speed and memory size still continue to improve. Won't any efficiency problem we might have today be solved by tomorrow's hardware?

As we develop more powerful computers, our history so far has always been to use that additional computing power to tackle more complex problems, be it in the form of more sophisticated user interfaces, bigger problem sizes, or new problems previously deemed computationally infeasible. More complex problems demand more computation, making the need for efficient programs even greater. Worse yet, as tasks become more complex, they become less like our everyday experience. Today's computer scientists must be trained to have a thorough understanding of the principles behind efficient program design, because their ordinary life experiences often do not apply when designing computer programs.

In the most general sense, a data structure is any data representation and its associated operations. Even an integer or floating point number stored on the computer can be viewed as a simple data structure. More commonly, people use the term "data structure" to mean an organization or structuring for a collection of data items. A sorted list of integers stored in an array is an example of such a structuring.

Given sufficient space to store a collection of data items, it is always possible to search for specified items within the collection, print or otherwise process the data items in any desired order, or modify the value of any particular data item. Thus, it is possible to perform all necessary operations on any data structure. However, using the proper data structure can make the difference between a program running in a few seconds and one requiring many days.

A solution is said to be **efficient** if it solves the problem within the required **resource constraints**. Examples of resource constraints include the total space available to store the data — possibly divided into separate main memory and disk space constraints — and the time allowed to perform each subtask. A solution is sometimes said to be efficient if it requires fewer resources than known alternatives, regardless of whether it meets any particular requirements. The **cost** of a solution is the amount of resources that the solution consumes. Most often, cost is measured in terms of one key resource such as time, with the implied assumption that the solution meets the other resource constraints.

It should go without saying that people write programs to solve problems. However, it is crucial to keep this truism in mind when selecting a data structure to solve a particular problem. Only by first analyzing the problem to determine the performance goals that must be achieved can there be any hope of selecting the right data structure for the job. Poor program designers ignore this analysis step and apply a data structure that they are familiar with but which is inappropriate to the problem. The result is typically a slow program. Conversely, there is no sense in adopting a complex representation to "improve" a program that can meet its performance goals when implemented using a simpler design.

When selecting a data structure to solve a problem, you should follow these steps.

1. Analyze your problem to determine the basic operations that must be supported. Examples of basic operations include inserting a data item into the data structure, deleting a data item from the data structure, and finding a specified data item.
2. Quantify the resource constraints for each operation.
3. Select the data structure that best meets these requirements.

This three-step approach to selecting a data structure operationalizes a data-centered view of the design process. The first concern is for the data and the operations to be performed on them, the next concern is the representation for those data, and the final concern is the implementation of that representation.

Resource constraints on certain key operations, such as search, inserting data records, and deleting data records, normally drive the data structure selection process. Many issues relating to the relative importance of these operations are addressed by the following three questions, which you should ask yourself whenever you must choose a data structure:

- Are all data items inserted into the data structure at the beginning, or are insertions interspersed with other operations? Static applications (where the data are loaded at the beginning and never change) typically require only simpler data structures to get an efficient implementation than do dynamic applications.
- Can data items be deleted? If so, this will probably make the implementation more complicated.
- Are all data items processed in some well-defined order, or is search for specific data items allowed? "Random access" search generally requires more complex data structures.

1.1.2 Costs and Benefits

Each data structure has associated costs and benefits. In practice, it is hardly ever true that one data structure is better than another for use in all situations. If one data structure or algorithm is superior to another in all respects, the inferior one will usually have long been forgotten. For nearly every data structure and algorithm presented in this book, you will see examples of where it is the best choice. Some of the examples might surprise you.

A data structure requires a certain amount of space for each data item it stores, a certain amount of time to perform a single basic operation, and a certain amount of programming effort. Each problem has constraints on available space and time. Each solution to a problem makes use of the basic operations in some relative proportion, and the data structure selection process must account for this. Only after a careful analysis of your problem's characteristics can you determine the best data structure for the task.

Example 1.1 A bank must support many types of transactions with its customers, but we will examine a simple model where customers wish to open accounts, close accounts, and add money or withdraw money from accounts. We can consider this problem at two distinct levels: (1) the requirements for the physical infrastructure and workflow process that the bank uses in its interactions with its customers, and (2) the requirements for the database system that manages the accounts.

The typical customer opens and closes accounts far less often than he or she accesses the account. Customers are willing to wait many minutes while accounts are created or deleted but are typically not willing to wait more than a brief time for individual account transactions such as a deposit or withdrawal. These observations can be considered as informal specifications for the time constraints on the problem.

It is common practice for banks to provide two tiers of service. Human tellers or automated teller machines (ATMs) support customer access to account balances and updates such as deposits and withdrawals. Special service representatives are typically provided (during restricted hours) to handle opening and closing accounts. Teller and ATM transactions are expected to take little time. Opening or closing an account can take much longer (perhaps up to an hour from the customer's perspective).

From a database perspective, we see that ATM transactions do not modify the database significantly. For simplicity, assume that if money is added or removed, this transaction simply changes the value stored in an account record. Adding a new account to the database is allowed to take several minutes. Deleting an account need have no time constraint, because from the customer's point of view all that matters is that all the money be returned (equivalent to a withdrawal). From the bank's point of view, the account record might be removed from the database system after business hours, or at the end of the monthly account cycle.

When considering the choice of data structure to use in the database system that manages customer accounts, we see that a data structure that has little concern for the cost of deletion, but is highly efficient for search and moderately efficient for insertion, should meet the resource constraints imposed by this problem. Records are accessible by unique account number (sometimes called an **exact-match query**). One data structure that meets these requirements is the hash table described in Chapter 9.4. Hash tables allow for extremely fast exact-match search. A record can be modified quickly when the modification does not affect its space requirements. Hash tables also support efficient insertion of new records. While deletions can also be supported efficiently, too many deletions lead to some degradation in performance for the remaining operations. However, the hash table can be reorganized periodically to restore the system to peak efficiency. Such reorganization can occur offline so as not to affect ATM transactions.

Example 1.2 A company is developing a database system containing information about cities and towns in the United States. There are many thousands of cities and towns, and the database program should allow users to find information about a particular place by name (another example of an exact-match query). Users should also be able to find all places that match a particular value or range of values for attributes such as location or population size. This is known as a **range query**.

A reasonable database system must answer queries quickly enough to satisfy the patience of a typical user. For an exact-match query, a few seconds is satisfactory. If the database is meant to support range queries that can return many cities that match the query specification, the entire operation may be allowed to take longer, perhaps on the order of a minute. To meet this requirement, it will be necessary to support operations that process range queries efficiently by processing all cities in the range as a batch, rather than as a series of operations on individual cities.

The hash table suggested in the previous example is inappropriate for implementing our city database, because it cannot perform efficient range queries. The B^+-tree of Section 10.5.1 supports large databases, insertion and deletion of data records, and range queries. However, a simple linear index as described in Section 10.1 would be more appropriate if the database is created once, and then never changed, such as an atlas distributed on a CD or accessed from a website.

1.2   Abstract Data Types and Data Structures

The previous section used the terms "data item" and "data structure" without properly defining them. This section presents terminology and motivates the design process embodied in the three-step approach to selecting a data structure. This motivation stems from the need to manage the tremendous complexity of computer programs.

A **type** is a collection of values. For example, the Boolean type consists of the values **true** and **false**. The integers also form a type. An integer is a **simple type** because its values contain no subparts. A bank account record will typically contain several pieces of information such as name, address, account number, and account balance. Such a record is an example of an **aggregate type** or **composite type**. A **data item** is a piece of information or a record whose value is drawn from a type. A data item is said to be a **member** of a type.

A **data type** is a type together with a collection of operations to manipulate the type. For example, an integer variable is a member of the integer data type. Addition is an example of an operation on the integer data type.

A distinction should be made between the logical concept of a data type and its physical implementation in a computer program. For example, there are two traditional implementations for the list data type: the linked list and the array-based list. The list data type can therefore be implemented using a linked list or an array. Even the term "array" is ambiguous in that it can refer either to a data type or an implementation. "Array" is commonly used in computer programming to mean a contiguous block of memory locations, where each memory location stores one fixed-length data item. By this meaning, an array is a physical data structure. However, array can also mean a logical data type composed of a (typically homogeneous) collection of data items, with each data item identified by an index number. It is possible to implement arrays in many different ways. For example, Section 12.2 describes the data structure used to implement a sparse matrix, a large two-dimensional array that stores only a relatively few non-zero values. This implementation is quite different from the physical representation of an array as contiguous memory locations.

An **abstract data type** (ADT) is the realization of a data type as a software component. The interface of the ADT is defined in terms of a type and a set of operations on that type. The behavior of each operation is determined by its inputs and outputs. An ADT does not specify *how* the data type is implemented. These implementation details are hidden from the user of the ADT and protected from outside access, a concept referred to as **encapsulation**.

A **data structure** is the implementation for an ADT. In an object-oriented language such as **C++**, an ADT and its implementation together make up a **class**. Each operation associated with the ADT is implemented by a **member function** or **method**. The variables that define the space required by a data item are referred to as **data members**. An **object** is an instance of a class, that is, something that is created and takes up storage during the execution of a computer program.

The term "data structure" often refers to data stored in a computer's main memory. The related term **file structure** often refers to the organization of data on peripheral storage, such as a disk drive or CD.

Example 1.3 The mathematical concept of an integer, along with operations that manipulate integers, form a data type. The **C++** `int` variable type is a physical representation of the abstract integer. The `int` variable type, along with the operations that act on an `int` variable, form an ADT. Unfortunately, the `int` implementation is not completely true to the abstract integer, as there are limitations on the range of values an `int` variable can store. If these limitations prove unacceptable, then some other representation for the ADT "integer" must be devised, and a new implementation must be used for the associated operations.

Example 1.4 An ADT for a list of integers might specify the following operations:

- Insert a new integer at a particular position in the list.
- Return `true` if the list is empty.
- Reinitialize the list.
- Return the number of integers currently in the list.
- Delete the integer at a particular position in the list.

From this description, the input and output of each operation should be clear, but the implementation for lists has not been specified.

One application that makes use of some ADT might use particular member functions of that ADT more than a second application, or the two applications might have different time requirements for the various operations. These differences in the requirements of applications are the reason why a given ADT might be supported by more than one implementation.

Example 1.5 Two popular implementations for large disk-based database applications are hashing (Section 9.4) and the B^+-tree (Section 10.5). Both support efficient insertion and deletion of records, and both support exact-match queries. However, hashing is more efficient than the B^+-tree for exact-match queries. On the other hand, the B^+-tree can perform range queries efficiently, while hashing is hopelessly inefficient for range queries. Thus, if the database application limits searches to exact-match queries, hashing is preferred. On the other hand, if the application requires support for range queries, the B^+-tree is preferred. Despite these performance issues, both implementations solve versions of the same problem: updating and searching a large collection of records.

The concept of an ADT can help us to focus on key issues even in non-computing applications.

Example 1.6 When operating a car, the primary activities are steering, accelerating, and braking. On nearly all passenger cars, you steer by turning the steering wheel, accelerate by pushing the gas pedal, and brake by pushing the brake pedal. This design for cars can be viewed as an ADT with operations "steer," "accelerate," and "brake." Two cars might implement these operations in radically different ways, say with different types of engine, or front- versus rear-wheel drive. Yet, most drivers can operate many different cars because the ADT presents a uniform method of operation that does not require the driver to understand the specifics of any particular engine or drive design. These differences are deliberately hidden.

The concept of an ADT is one instance of an important principle that must be understood by any successful computer scientist: managing complexity through abstraction. A central theme of computer science is complexity and techniques for handling it. Humans deal with complexity by assigning a label to an assembly of objects or concepts and then manipulating the label in place of the assembly. Cognitive psychologists call such a label a **metaphor**. A particular label might be related to other pieces of information or other labels. This collection can in turn be given a label, forming a hierarchy of concepts and labels. This hierarchy of labels allows us to focus on important issues while ignoring unnecessary details.

Example 1.7 We apply the label "hard drive" to a collection of hardware that manipulates data on a particular type of storage device, and we apply the label "CPU" to the hardware that controls execution of computer instructions. These and other labels are gathered together under the label "computer." Because even the smallest home computers today have millions of components, some form of abstraction is necessary to comprehend how a computer operates.

Consider how you might go about the process of designing a complex computer program that implements and manipulates an ADT. The ADT is implemented in one part of the program by a particular data structure. While designing those parts of the program that use the ADT, you can think in terms of operations on the data type without concern for the data structure's implementation. Without this ability to simplify your thinking about a complex program, you would have no hope of understanding or implementing it.

Example 1.8 Consider the design for a relatively simple database system stored on disk. Typically, records on disk in such a program are accessed through a buffer pool (see Section 8.3) rather than directly. Variable length records might use a memory manager (see Section 12.3) to find an appropriate location within the disk file to place the record. Multiple index structures (see Chapter 10) will typically be used to access records in various ways. Thus, we have a chain of classes, each with its own responsibilities and access privileges. A database query from a user is implemented by searching an index structure. This index requests access to the record by means of a request to the buffer pool. If a record is being inserted or deleted, such a request goes through the memory manager, which in turn interacts with the buffer pool to gain access to the disk file. A program such as this is far too complex for nearly any human programmer to keep all of the details in his or her head at once. The only way to design and implement such a program is through proper use of abstraction and metaphors. In object-oriented programming, such abstraction is handled using classes.

Data types have both a **logical** and a **physical** form. The definition of the data type in terms of an ADT is its logical form. The implementation of the data type as a data structure is its physical form. Figure 1.1 illustrates this relationship between logical and physical forms for data types. When you implement an ADT, you are dealing with the physical form of the associated data type. When you use an ADT elsewhere in your program, you are concerned with the associated data type's logical form. Some sections of this book focus on physical implementations for a

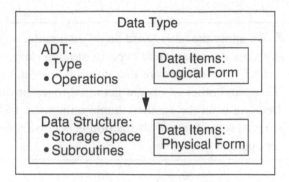

Figure 1.1 The relationship between data items, abstract data types, and data structures. The ADT defines the logical form of the data type. The data structure implements the physical form of the data type.

given data structure. Other sections use the logical ADT for the data structure in the context of a higher-level task.

Example 1.9 A particular C++ environment might provide a library that includes a list class. The logical form of the list is defined by the public functions, their inputs, and their outputs that define the class. This might be all that you know about the list class implementation, and this should be all you need to know. Within the class, a variety of physical implementations for lists is possible. Several are described in Section 4.1.

1.3   Design Patterns

At a higher level of abstraction than ADTs are abstractions for describing the design of programs — that is, the interactions of objects and classes. Experienced software designers learn and reuse patterns for combining software components. These have come to be referred to as **design patterns**.

A design pattern embodies and generalizes important design concepts for a recurring problem. A primary goal of design patterns is to quickly transfer the knowledge gained by expert designers to newer programmers. Another goal is to allow for efficient communication between programmers. It is much easier to discuss a design issue when you share a technical vocabulary relevant to the topic.

Specific design patterns emerge from the realization that a particular design problem appears repeatedly in many contexts. They are meant to solve real problems. Design patterns are a bit like templates. They describe the structure for a design solution, with the details filled in for any given problem. Design patterns are a bit like data structures: Each one provides costs and benefits, which implies that tradeoffs are possible. Therefore, a given design pattern might have variations on its application to match the various tradeoffs inherent in a given situation.

The rest of this section introduces a few simple design patterns that are used later in the book.

1.3.1 Flyweight

The Flyweight design pattern is meant to solve the following problem. You have an application with many objects. Some of these objects are identical in the information that they contain, and the role that they play. But they must be reached from various places, and conceptually they really are distinct objects. Because there is so much duplication of the same information, we would like to take advantage of the opportunity to reduce memory cost by sharing that space. An example comes from representing the layout for a document. The letter "C" might reasonably be represented by an object that describes that character's strokes and bounding box. However, we do not want to create a separate "C" object everywhere in the document that a "C" appears. The solution is to allocate a single copy of the shared representation for "C" objects. Then, every place in the document that needs a "C" in a given font, size, and typeface will reference this single copy. The various instances of references to a specific form of "C" are called flyweights.

We could describe the layout of text on a page by using a tree structure. The root of the tree represents the entire page. The page has multiple child nodes, one for each column. The column nodes have child nodes for each row. And the rows have child nodes for each character. These representations for characters are the flyweights. The flyweight includes the reference to the shared shape information, and might contain additional information specific to that instance. For example, each instance for "C" will contain a reference to the shared information about strokes and shapes, and it might also contain the exact location for that instance of the character on the page.

Flyweights are used in the implementation for the PR quadtree data structure for storing collections of point objects, described in Section 13.3. In a PR quadtree, we again have a tree with leaf nodes. Many of these leaf nodes represent empty areas, and so the only information that they store is the fact that they are empty. These identical nodes can be implemented using a reference to a single instance of the flyweight for better memory efficiency.

1.3.2 Visitor

Given a tree of objects to describe a page layout, we might wish to perform some activity on every node in the tree. Section 5.2 discusses tree traversal, which is the process of visiting every node in the tree in a defined order. A simple example for our text composition application might be to count the number of nodes in the tree that represents the page. At another time, we might wish to print a listing of all the nodes for debugging purposes.

We could write a separate traversal function for each such activity that we intend to perform on the tree. A better approach would be to write a generic traversal function, and pass in the activity to be performed at each node. This organization constitutes the visitor design pattern. The visitor design pattern is used in Sections 5.2 (tree traversal) and 11.3 (graph traversal).

1.3.3 Composite

There are two fundamental approaches to dealing with the relationship between a collection of actions and a hierarchy of object types. First consider the typical procedural approach. Say we have a base class for page layout entities, with a subclass hierarchy to define specific subtypes (page, columns, rows, figures, characters, etc.). And say there are actions to be performed on a collection of such objects (such as rendering the objects to the screen). The procedural design approach is for each action to be implemented as a method that takes as a parameter a pointer to the base class type. Each action such method will traverse through the collection of objects, visiting each object in turn. Each action method contains something like a switch statement that defines the details of the action for each subclass in the collection (e.g., page, column, row, character). We can cut the code down some by using the visitor design pattern so that we only need to write the traversal once, and then write a visitor subroutine for each action that might be applied to the collection of objects. But each such visitor subroutine must still contain logic for dealing with each of the possible subclasses.

In our page composition application, there are only a few activities that we would like to perform on the page representation. We might render the objects in full detail. Or we might want a "rough draft" rendering that prints only the bounding boxes of the objects. If we come up with a new activity to apply to the collection of objects, we do not need to change any of the code that implements the existing activities. But adding new activities won't happen often for this application. In contrast, there could be many object types, and we might frequently add new object types to our implementation. Unfortunately, adding a new object type requires that we modify each activity, and the subroutines implementing the activities get rather long switch statements to distinguish the behavior of the many subclasses.

An alternative design is to have each object subclass in the hierarchy embody the action for each of the various activities that might be performed. Each subclass will have code to perform each activity (such as full rendering or bounding box rendering). Then, if we wish to apply the activity to the collection, we simply call the first object in the collection and specify the action (as a method call on that object). In the case of our page layout and its hierarchical collection of objects, those objects that contain other objects (such as a row objects that contains letters)

will call the appropriate method for each child. If we want to add a new activity
with this organization, we have to change the code for every subclass. But this is
relatively rare for our text compositing application. In contrast, adding a new object
into the subclass hierarchy (which for this application is far more likely than adding
a new rendering function) is easy. Adding a new subclass does not require changing
any of the existing subclasses. It merely requires that we define the behavior of each
activity that can be performed on the new subclass.

This second design approach of burying the functional activity in the subclasses
is called the Composite design pattern. A detailed example for using the Composite
design pattern is presented in Section 5.3.1.

1.3.4 Strategy

Our final example of a design pattern lets us encapsulate and make interchangeable
a set of alternative actions that might be performed as part of some larger activity.
Again continuing our text compositing example, each output device that we wish
to render to will require its own function for doing the actual rendering. That is,
the objects will be broken down into constituent pixels or strokes, but the actual
mechanics of rendering a pixel or stroke will depend on the output device. We
don't want to build this rendering functionality into the object subclasses. Instead,
we want to pass to the subroutine performing the rendering action a method or class
that does the appropriate rendering details for that output device. That is, we wish
to hand to the object the appropriate "strategy" for accomplishing the details of the
rendering task. Thus, this approach is called the Strategy design pattern.

The Strategy design pattern will be discussed further in Chapter 7. There, a
sorting function is given a class (called a comparator) that understands how to
extract and compare the key values for records to be sorted. In this way, the sorting
function does not need to know any details of how its record type is implemented.

One of the biggest challenges to understanding design patterns is that sometimes one is only subtly different from another. For example, you might be con-
fused about the difference between the composite pattern and the visitor pattern.
The distinction is that the composite design pattern is about whether to give control
of the traversal process to the nodes of the tree or to the tree itself. Both approaches
can make use of the visitor design pattern to avoid rewriting the traversal function
many times, by encapsulating the activity performed at each node.

But isn't the strategy design pattern doing the same thing? The difference between the visitor pattern and the strategy pattern is more subtle. Here the difference
is primarily one of intent and focus. In both the strategy design pattern and the visitor design pattern, an activity is being passed in as a parameter. The strategy design
pattern is focused on encapsulating an activity that is part of a larger process, so
that different ways of performing that activity can be substituted. The visitor design pattern is focused on encapsulating an activity that will be performed on all

members of a collection so that completely different activities can be substituted within a generic method that accesses all of the collection members.

1.4   Problems, Algorithms, and Programs

Programmers commonly deal with problems, algorithms, and computer programs. These are three distinct concepts.

Problems: As your intuition would suggest, a **problem** is a task to be performed. It is best thought of in terms of inputs and matching outputs. A problem definition should not include any constraints on *how* the problem is to be solved. The solution method should be developed only after the problem is precisely defined and thoroughly understood. However, a problem definition should include constraints on the resources that may be consumed by any acceptable solution. For any problem to be solved by a computer, there are always such constraints, whether stated or implied. For example, any computer program may use only the main memory and disk space available, and it must run in a "reasonable" amount of time.

Problems can be viewed as functions in the mathematical sense. A **function** is a matching between inputs (the **domain**) and outputs (the **range**). An input to a function might be a single value or a collection of information. The values making up an input are called the **parameters** of the function. A specific selection of values for the parameters is called an **instance** of the problem. For example, the input parameter to a sorting function might be an array of integers. A particular array of integers, with a given size and specific values for each position in the array, would be an instance of the sorting problem. Different instances might generate the same output. However, any problem instance must always result in the same output every time the function is computed using that particular input.

This concept of all problems behaving like mathematical functions might not match your intuition for the behavior of computer programs. You might know of programs to which you can give the same input value on two separate occasions, and two different outputs will result. For example, if you type "`date`" to a typical UNIX command line prompt, you will get the current date. Naturally the date will be different on different days, even though the same command is given. However, there is obviously more to the input for the date program than the command that you type to run the program. The date program computes a function. In other words, on any particular day there can only be a single answer returned by a properly running date program on a completely specified input. For all computer programs, the output is completely determined by the program's full set of inputs. Even a "random number generator" is completely determined by its inputs (although some random number generating systems appear to get around this by accepting a random input from a physical process beyond the user's control). The relationship between programs and functions is explored further in Section 17.3.

Algorithms: An **algorithm** is a method or a process followed to solve a problem. If the problem is viewed as a function, then an algorithm is an implementation for the function that transforms an input to the corresponding output. A problem can be solved by many different algorithms. A given algorithm solves only one problem (i.e., computes a particular function). This book covers many problems, and for several of these problems I present more than one algorithm. For the important problem of sorting I present nearly a dozen algorithms!

The advantage of knowing several solutions to a problem is that solution A might be more efficient than solution B for a specific variation of the problem, or for a specific class of inputs to the problem, while solution B might be more efficient than A for another variation or class of inputs. For example, one sorting algorithm might be the best for sorting a small collection of integers (which is important if you need to do this many times). Another might be the best for sorting a large collection of integers. A third might be the best for sorting a collection of variable-length strings.

By definition, something can only be called an algorithm if it has all of the following properties.

1. It must be *correct*. In other words, it must compute the desired function, converting each input to the correct output. Note that every algorithm implements some function, because every algorithm maps every input to some output (even if that output is a program crash). At issue here is whether a given algorithm implements the *intended* function.

2. It is composed of a series of *concrete steps*. Concrete means that the action described by that step is completely understood — and doable — by the person or machine that must perform the algorithm. Each step must also be doable in a finite amount of time. Thus, the algorithm gives us a "recipe" for solving the problem by performing a series of steps, where each such step is within our capacity to perform. The ability to perform a step can depend on who or what is intended to execute the recipe. For example, the steps of a cookie recipe in a cookbook might be considered sufficiently concrete for instructing a human cook, but not for programming an automated cookie-making factory.

3. There can be *no ambiguity* as to which step will be performed next. Often it is the next step of the algorithm description. Selection (e.g., the **if** statement in **C**++) is normally a part of any language for describing algorithms. Selection allows a choice for which step will be performed next, but the selection process is unambiguous at the time when the choice is made.

4. It must be composed of a *finite* number of steps. If the description for the algorithm were made up of an infinite number of steps, we could never hope to write it down, nor implement it as a computer program. Most languages for describing algorithms (including English and "pseudocode") provide some

way to perform repeated actions, known as iteration. Examples of iteration in programming languages include the `while` and `for` loop constructs of C++. Iteration allows for short descriptions, with the number of steps actually performed controlled by the input.

5. It must *terminate*. In other words, it may not go into an infinite loop.

Programs: We often think of a **computer program** as an instance, or concrete representation, of an algorithm in some programming language. In this book, nearly all of the algorithms are presented in terms of programs, or parts of programs. Naturally, there are many programs that are instances of the same algorithm, because any modern computer programming language can be used to implement the same collection of algorithms (although some programming languages can make life easier for the programmer). To simplify presentation, I often use the terms "algorithm" and "program" interchangeably, despite the fact that they are really separate concepts. By definition, an algorithm must provide sufficient detail that it can be converted into a program when needed.

The requirement that an algorithm must terminate means that not all computer programs meet the technical definition of an algorithm. Your operating system is one such program. However, you can think of the various tasks for an operating system (each with associated inputs and outputs) as individual problems, each solved by specific algorithms implemented by a part of the operating system program, and each one of which terminates once its output is produced.

To summarize: A **problem** is a function or a mapping of inputs to outputs. An **algorithm** is a recipe for solving a problem whose steps are concrete and unambiguous. Algorithms must be correct, of finite length, and must terminate for all inputs. A **program** is an instantiation of an algorithm in a programming language.

1.5   Further Reading

An early authoritative work on data structures and algorithms was the series of books *The Art of Computer Programming* by Donald E. Knuth, with Volumes 1 and 3 being most relevant to the study of data structures [Knu97, Knu98]. A modern encyclopedic approach to data structures and algorithms that should be easy to understand once you have mastered this book is *Algorithms* by Robert Sedgewick [Sed11]. For an excellent and highly readable (but more advanced) teaching introduction to algorithms, their design, and their analysis, see *Introduction to Algorithms: A Creative Approach* by Udi Manber [Man89]. For an advanced, encyclopedic approach, see *Introduction to Algorithms* by Cormen, Leiserson, and Rivest [CLRS09]. Steven S. Skiena's *The Algorithm Design Manual* [Ski10] provides pointers to many implementations for data structures and algorithms that are available on the Web.

The claim that all modern programming languages can implement the same algorithms (stated more precisely, any function that is computable by one programming language is computable by any programming language with certain standard capabilities) is a key result from computability theory. For an easy introduction to this field see James L. Hein, *Discrete Structures, Logic, and Computability* [Hei09].

Much of computer science is devoted to problem solving. Indeed, this is what attracts many people to the field. *How to Solve It* by George Pólya [Pól57] is considered to be the classic work on how to improve your problem-solving abilities. If you want to be a better student (as well as a better problem solver in general), see *Strategies for Creative Problem Solving* by Folger and LeBlanc [FL95], *Effective Problem Solving* by Marvin Levine [Lev94], and *Problem Solving & Comprehension* by Arthur Whimbey and Jack Lochhead [WL99], and *Puzzle-Based Learning* by Zbigniew and Matthew Michaelewicz [MM08].

See *The Origin of Consciousness in the Breakdown of the Bicameral Mind* by Julian Jaynes [Jay90] for a good discussion on how humans use the concept of metaphor to handle complexity. More directly related to computer science education and programming, see "Cogito, Ergo Sum! Cognitive Processes of Students Dealing with Data Structures" by Dan Aharoni [Aha00] for a discussion on moving from programming-context thinking to higher-level (and more design-oriented) programming-free thinking.

On a more pragmatic level, most people study data structures to write better programs. If you expect your program to work correctly and efficiently, it must first be understandable to yourself and your co-workers. Kernighan and Pike's *The Practice of Programming* [KP99] discusses a number of practical issues related to programming, including good coding and documentation style. For an excellent (and entertaining!) introduction to the difficulties involved with writing large programs, read the classic *The Mythical Man-Month: Essays on Software Engineering* by Frederick P. Brooks [Bro95].

If you want to be a successful **C++** programmer, you need good reference manuals close at hand. The standard reference for **C++** is *The C++ Programming Language* by Bjarne Stroustrup [Str00], with further information provided in *The Annotated C++ Reference Manual* by Ellis and Stroustrup [ES90]. No **C++** programmer should be without Stroustrup's book, as it provides the definitive description of the language and also includes a great deal of information about the principles of object-oriented design. Unfortunately, it is a poor text for learning how to program in **C++**. A good, gentle introduction to the basics of the language is Patrick Henry Winston's *On to C++* [Win94]. A good introductory teaching text for a wider range of **C++** is Deitel and Deitel's *C++ How to Program* [DD08].

After gaining proficiency in the mechanics of program writing, the next step is to become proficient in program design. Good design is difficult to learn in any discipline, and good design for object-oriented software is one of the most difficult of arts. The novice designer can jump-start the learning process by studying well-known and well-used design patterns. The classic reference on design patterns is *Design Patterns: Elements of Reusable Object-Oriented Software* by Gamma, Helm, Johnson, and Vlissides [GHJV95] (this is commonly referred to as the "gang of four" book). Unfortunately, this is an extremely difficult book to understand, in part because the concepts are inherently difficult. A number of Web sites are available that discuss design patterns, and which provide study guides for the *Design Patterns* book. Two other books that discuss object-oriented software design are *Object-Oriented Software Design and Construction with C++* by Dennis Kafura [Kaf98], and *Object-Oriented Design Heuristics* by Arthur J. Riel [Rie96].

1.6 Exercises

The exercises for this chapter are different from those in the rest of the book. Most of these exercises are answered in the following chapters. However, you should *not* look up the answers in other parts of the book. These exercises are intended to make you think about some of the issues to be covered later on. Answer them to the best of your ability with your current knowledge.

1.1 Think of a program you have used that is unacceptably slow. Identify the specific operations that make the program slow. Identify other basic operations that the program performs quickly enough.

1.2 Most programming languages have a built-in integer data type. Normally this representation has a fixed size, thus placing a limit on how large a value can be stored in an integer variable. Describe a representation for integers that has no size restriction (other than the limits of the computer's available main memory), and thus no practical limit on how large an integer can be stored. Briefly show how your representation can be used to implement the operations of addition, multiplication, and exponentiation.

1.3 Define an ADT for character strings. Your ADT should consist of typical functions that can be performed on strings, with each function defined in terms of its input and output. Then define two different physical representations for strings.

1.4 Define an ADT for a list of integers. First, decide what functionality your ADT should provide. Example 1.4 should give you some ideas. Then, specify your ADT in C++ in the form of an abstract class declaration, showing the functions, their parameters, and their return types.

1.5 Briefly describe how integer variables are typically represented on a computer. (Look up one's complement and two's complement arithmetic in an introductory computer science textbook if you are not familiar with these.)

Why does this representation for integers qualify as a data structure as defined in Section 1.2?

1.6 Define an ADT for a two-dimensional array of integers. Specify precisely the basic operations that can be performed on such arrays. Next, imagine an application that stores an array with 1000 rows and 1000 columns, where less than 10,000 of the array values are non-zero. Describe two different implementations for such arrays that would be more space efficient than a standard two-dimensional array implementation requiring one million positions.

1.7 Imagine that you have been assigned to implement a sorting program. The goal is to make this program general purpose, in that you don't want to define in advance what record or key types are used. Describe ways to generalize a simple sorting algorithm (such as insertion sort, or any other sort you are familiar with) to support this generalization.

1.8 Imagine that you have been assigned to implement a simple sequential search on an array. The problem is that you want the search to be as general as possible. This means that you need to support arbitrary record and key types. Describe ways to generalize the search function to support this goal. Consider the possibility that the function will be used multiple times in the same program, on differing record types. Consider the possibility that the function will need to be used on different keys (possibly with the same or different types) of the same record. For example, a student data record might be searched by zip code, by name, by salary, or by GPA.

1.9 Does every problem have an algorithm?

1.10 Does every algorithm have a **C++** program?

1.11 Consider the design for a spelling checker program meant to run on a home computer. The spelling checker should be able to handle quickly a document of less than twenty pages. Assume that the spelling checker comes with a dictionary of about 20,000 words. What primitive operations must be implemented on the dictionary, and what is a reasonable time constraint for each operation?

1.12 Imagine that you have been hired to design a database service containing information about cities and towns in the United States, as described in Example 1.2. Suggest two possible implementations for the database.

1.13 Imagine that you are given an array of records that is sorted with respect to some key field contained in each record. Give two different algorithms for searching the array to find the record with a specified key value. Which one do you consider "better" and why?

1.14 How would you go about comparing two proposed algorithms for sorting an array of integers? In particular,

    (a) What would be appropriate measures of cost to use as a basis for comparing the two sorting algorithms?

(b) What tests or analysis would you conduct to determine how the two algorithms perform under these cost measures?

1.15 A common problem for compilers and text editors is to determine if the parentheses (or other brackets) in a string are balanced and properly nested. For example, the string "((())()()" contains properly nested pairs of parentheses, but the string ")()(" does not; and the string "())" does not contain properly matching parentheses.

(a) Give an algorithm that returns **true** if a string contains properly nested and balanced parentheses, and **false** if otherwise. *Hint*: At no time while scanning a legal string from left to right will you have encountered more right parentheses than left parentheses.

(b) Give an algorithm that returns the position in the string of the first offending parenthesis if the string is not properly nested and balanced. That is, if an excess right parenthesis is found, return its position; if there are too many left parentheses, return the position of the first excess left parenthesis. Return -1 if the string is properly balanced and nested.

1.16 A graph consists of a set of objects (called vertices) and a set of edges, where each edge connects two vertices. Any given pair of vertices can be connected by only one edge. Describe at least two different ways to represent the connections defined by the vertices and edges of a graph.

1.17 Imagine that you are a shipping clerk for a large company. You have just been handed about 1000 invoices, each of which is a single sheet of paper with a large number in the upper right corner. The invoices must be sorted by this number, in order from lowest to highest. Write down as many different approaches to sorting the invoices as you can think of.

1.18 How would you sort an array of about 1000 integers from lowest value to highest value? Write down at least five approaches to sorting the array. Do not write algorithms in **C++** or pseudocode. Just write a sentence or two for each approach to describe how it would work.

1.19 Think of an algorithm to find the maximum value in an (unsorted) array. Now, think of an algorithm to find the second largest value in the array. Which is harder to implement? Which takes more time to run (as measured by the number of comparisons performed)? Now, think of an algorithm to find the third largest value. Finally, think of an algorithm to find the middle value. Which is the most difficult of these problems to solve?

1.20 An unsorted list allows for constant-time insert by adding a new element at the end of the list. Unfortunately, searching for the element with key value X requires a sequential search through the unsorted list until X is found, which on average requires looking at half the list element. On the other hand, a sorted array-based list of n elements can be searched in $\log n$ time with a binary search. Unfortunately, inserting a new element requires a lot of time because many elements might be shifted in the array if we want to keep it sorted. How might data be organized to support both insertion and search in $\log n$ time?

2

Mathematical Preliminaries

This chapter presents mathematical notation, background, and techniques used throughout the book. This material is provided primarily for review and reference. You might wish to return to the relevant sections when you encounter unfamiliar notation or mathematical techniques in later chapters.

Section 2.7 on estimation might be unfamiliar to many readers. Estimation is not a mathematical technique, but rather a general engineering skill. It is enormously useful to computer scientists doing design work, because any proposed solution whose estimated resource requirements fall well outside the problem's resource constraints can be discarded immediately, allowing time for greater analysis of more promising solutions.

2.1 Sets and Relations

The concept of a set in the mathematical sense has wide application in computer science. The notations and techniques of set theory are commonly used when describing and implementing algorithms because the abstractions associated with sets often help to clarify and simplify algorithm design.

A **set** is a collection of distinguishable **members** or **elements**. The members are typically drawn from some larger population known as the **base type**. Each member of a set is either a **primitive element** of the base type or is a set itself. There is no concept of duplication in a set. Each value from the base type is either in the set or not in the set. For example, a set named **P** might consist of the three integers 7, 11, and 42. In this case, **P**'s members are 7, 11, and 42, and the base type is integer.

Figure 2.1 shows the symbols commonly used to express sets and their relationships. Here are some examples of this notation in use. First define two sets, **P** and **Q**.

$$\mathbf{P} = \{2, 3, 5\}, \qquad \mathbf{Q} = \{5, 10\}.$$

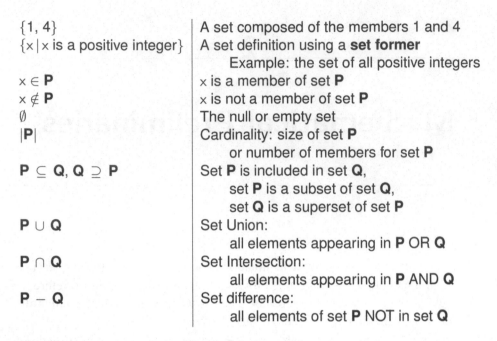

$\{1, 4\}$	A set composed of the members 1 and 4
$\{x \mid x \text{ is a positive integer}\}$	A set definition using a **set former**
	Example: the set of all positive integers
$x \in \mathbf{P}$	x is a member of set **P**
$x \notin \mathbf{P}$	x is not a member of set **P**
$\emptyset$	The null or empty set
$\mid \mathbf{P} \mid$	Cardinality: size of set **P**
	or number of members for set **P**
$\mathbf{P} \subseteq \mathbf{Q}, \mathbf{Q} \supseteq \mathbf{P}$	Set **P** is included in set **Q**,
	set **P** is a subset of set **Q**,
	set **Q** is a superset of set **P**
$\mathbf{P} \cup \mathbf{Q}$	Set Union:
	all elements appearing in **P** OR **Q**
$\mathbf{P} \cap \mathbf{Q}$	Set Intersection:
	all elements appearing in **P** AND **Q**
$\mathbf{P} - \mathbf{Q}$	Set difference:
	all elements of set **P** NOT in set **Q**

Figure 2.1 Set notation.

$|\mathbf{P}| = 3$ (because **P** has three members) and $|\mathbf{Q}| = 2$ (because **Q** has two members). The union of **P** and **Q**, written $\mathbf{P} \cup \mathbf{Q}$, is the set of elements in either **P** or **Q**, which is $\{2, 3, 5, 10\}$. The intersection of **P** and **Q**, written $\mathbf{P} \cap \mathbf{Q}$, is the set of elements that appear in both **P** and **Q**, which is $\{5\}$. The set difference of **P** and **Q**, written $\mathbf{P} - \mathbf{Q}$, is the set of elements that occur in **P** but not in **Q**, which is $\{2, 3\}$. Note that $\mathbf{P} \cup \mathbf{Q} = \mathbf{Q} \cup \mathbf{P}$ and that $\mathbf{P} \cap \mathbf{Q} = \mathbf{Q} \cap \mathbf{P}$, but in general $\mathbf{P} - \mathbf{Q} \neq \mathbf{Q} - \mathbf{P}$. In this example, $\mathbf{Q} - \mathbf{P} = \{10\}$. Note that the set $\{4, 3, 5\}$ is indistinguishable from set **P**, because sets have no concept of order. Likewise, set $\{4, 3, 4, 5\}$ is also indistinguishable from **P**, because sets have no concept of duplicate elements.

The **powerset** of a set **S** is the set of all possible subsets for **S**. Consider the set $\mathbf{S} = \{a, b, c\}$. The powerset of **S** is

$$\{\emptyset, \{a\}, \{b\}, \{c\}, \{a, b\}, \{a, c\}, \{b, c\}, \{a, b, c\}\}.$$

A collection of elements with no order (like a set), but with duplicate-valued elements is called a **bag**.[1] To distinguish bags from sets, I use square brackets [] around a bag's elements. For example, bag [3, 4, 5, 4] is distinct from bag [3, 4, 5], while set $\{3, 4, 5, 4\}$ is indistinguishable from set $\{3, 4, 5\}$. However, bag [3, 4, 5, 4] is indistinguishable from bag [3, 4, 4, 5].

---

[1]The object referred to here as a bag is sometimes called a **multilist**. But, I reserve the term multilist for a list that may contain sublists (see Section 12.1).

A **sequence** is a collection of elements with an order, and which may contain duplicate-valued elements. A sequence is also sometimes called a **tuple** or a **vector**. In a sequence, there is a 0th element, a 1st element, 2nd element, and so on. I indicate a sequence by using angle brackets $\langle \rangle$ to enclose its elements. For example, $\langle 3, 4, 5, 4 \rangle$ is a sequence. Note that sequence $\langle 3, 5, 4, 4 \rangle$ is distinct from sequence $\langle 3, 4, 5, 4 \rangle$, and both are distinct from sequence $\langle 3, 4, 5 \rangle$.

A **relation** R over set **S** is a set of ordered pairs from **S**. As an example of a relation, if **S** is $\{a, b, c\}$, then

$$\{\langle a, c \rangle, \langle b, c \rangle, \langle c, b \rangle\}$$

is a relation, and

$$\{\langle a, a \rangle, \langle a, c \rangle, \langle b, b \rangle, \langle b, c \rangle, \langle c, c \rangle\}$$

is a different relation. If tuple $\langle x, y \rangle$ is in relation R, we may use the infix notation xRy. We often use relations such as the less than operator ($<$) on the natural numbers, which includes ordered pairs such as $\langle 1, 3 \rangle$ and $\langle 2, 23 \rangle$, but not $\langle 3, 2 \rangle$ or $\langle 2, 2 \rangle$. Rather than writing the relationship in terms of ordered pairs, we typically use an infix notation for such relations, writing $1 < 3$.

Define the properties of relations as follows, with R a binary relation over set **S**.

- R is **reflexive** if aRa for all $a \in$ **S**.
- R is **symmetric** if whenever aRb, then bRa, for all $a, b \in$ **S**.
- R is **antisymmetric** if whenever aRb and bRa, then $a = b$, for all $a, b \in$ **S**.
- R is **transitive** if whenever aRb and bRc, then aRc, for all $a, b, c \in$ **S**.

As examples, for the natural numbers, $<$ is antisymmetric (because there is no case where aRb and bRa) and transitive; $\leq$ is reflexive, antisymmetric, and transitive, and $=$ is reflexive, symmetric (and antisymmetric!), and transitive. For people, the relation "is a sibling of" is symmetric and transitive. If we define a person to be a sibling of himself, then it is reflexive; if we define a person not to be a sibling of himself, then it is not reflexive.

R is an **equivalence relation** on set **S** if it is reflexive, symmetric, and transitive. An equivalence relation can be used to partition a set into **equivalence classes**. If two elements a and b are equivalent to each other, we write $a \equiv b$. A **partition** of a set **S** is a collection of subsets that are disjoint from each other and whose union is **S**. An equivalence relation on set **S** partitions the set into subsets whose elements are equivalent. See Section 6.2 for a discussion on how to represent equivalence classes on a set. One application for disjoint sets appears in Section 11.5.2.

Example 2.1 For the integers, $=$ is an equivalence relation that partitions each element into a distinct subset. In other words, for any integer a, three things are true.

   1. $a = a$,

2. if $a = b$ then $b = a$, and

3. if $a = b$ and $b = c$, then $a = c$.

Of course, for distinct integers a, b, and c there are never cases where $a = b$, $b = a$, or $b = c$. So the claims that $=$ is symmetric and transitive are vacuously true (there are never examples in the relation where these events occur). But because the requirements for symmetry and transitivity are not violated, the relation is symmetric and transitive.

Example 2.2 If we clarify the definition of sibling to mean that a person is a sibling of him- or herself, then the sibling relation is an equivalence relation that partitions the set of people.

Example 2.3 We can use the modulus function (defined in the next section) to define an equivalence relation. For the set of integers, use the modulus function to define a binary relation such that two numbers x and y are in the relation if and only if $x \bmod m = y \bmod m$. Thus, for $m = 4$, $\langle 1, 5 \rangle$ is in the relation because $1 \bmod 4 = 5 \bmod 4$. We see that modulus used in this way defines an equivalence relation on the integers, and this relation can be used to partition the integers into m equivalence classes. This relation is an equivalence relation because

1. $x \bmod m = x \bmod m$ for all x;

2. if $x \bmod m = y \bmod m$, then $y \bmod m = x \bmod m$; and

3. if $x \bmod m = y \bmod m$ and $y \bmod m = z \bmod m$, then $x \bmod m = z \bmod m$.

A binary relation is called a **partial order** if it is antisymmetric and transitive.[2] The set on which the partial order is defined is called a **partially ordered set** or a **poset**. Elements x and y of a set are **comparable** under a given relation if either xRy or yRx. If every pair of distinct elements in a partial order are comparable, then the order is called a **total order** or **linear order**.

Example 2.4 For the integers, relations $<$ and $\leq$ define partial orders. Operation $<$ is a total order because, for every pair of integers x and y such that $x \neq y$, either $x < y$ or $y < x$. Likewise, $\leq$ is a total order because, for every pair of integers x and y such that $x \neq y$, either $x \leq y$ or $y \leq x$.

---

[2]Not all authors use this definition for partial order. I have seen at least three significantly different definitions in the literature. I have selected the one that lets $<$ and $\leq$ both define partial orders on the integers, because this seems the most natural to me.

Example 2.5 For the powerset of the integers, the subset operator defines
a partial order (because it is antisymmetric and transitive). For example,
$\{1,2\} \subseteq \{1,2,3\}$. However, sets $\{1,2\}$ and $\{1,3\}$ are not comparable by
the subset operator, because neither is a subset of the other. Therefore, the
subset operator does not define a total order on the powerset of the integers.

2.2   Miscellaneous Notation

Units of measure: I use the following notation for units of measure. "B" will
be used as an abbreviation for bytes, "b" for bits, "KB" for kilobytes ($2^{10} =$
1024 bytes), "MB" for megabytes (2^{20} bytes), "GB" for gigabytes (2^{30} bytes), and
"ms" for milliseconds (a millisecond is $\frac{1}{1000}$ of a second). Spaces are not placed between the number and the unit abbreviation when a power of two is intended. Thus
a disk drive of size 25 gigabytes (where a gigabyte is intended as 2^{30} bytes) will be
written as "25GB." Spaces are used when a decimal value is intended. An amount
of 2000 bits would therefore be written "2 Kb" while "2Kb" represents 2048 bits.
2000 milliseconds is written as 2000 ms. Note that in this book large amounts of
storage are nearly always measured in powers of two and times in powers of ten.

Factorial function: The **factorial** function, written $n!$ for n an integer greater
than 0, is the product of the integers between 1 and n, inclusive. Thus, $5! =$
$1 \cdot 2 \cdot 3 \cdot 4 \cdot 5 = 120$. As a special case, $0! = 1$. The factorial function grows
quickly as n becomes larger. Because computing the factorial function directly
is a time-consuming process, it can be useful to have an equation that provides a
good approximation. Stirling's approximation states that $n! \approx \sqrt{2\pi n}(\frac{n}{c})^n$, where
$e \approx 2.71828$ (e is the base for the system of natural logarithms).[3] Thus we see that
while $n!$ grows slower than n^n (because $\sqrt{2\pi n}/e^n < 1$), it grows faster than c^n for
any positive integer constant c.

Permutations: A **permutation** of a sequence **S** is simply the members of **S** arranged in some order. For example, a permutation of the integers 1 through n
would be those values arranged in some order. If the sequence contains n distinct
members, then there are $n!$ different permutations for the sequence. This is because
there are n choices for the first member in the permutation; for each choice of first
member there are $n - 1$ choices for the second member, and so on. Sometimes
one would like to obtain a **random permutation** for a sequence, that is, one of the
$n!$ possible permutations is selected in such a way that each permutation has equal
probability of being selected. A simple **C++** function for generating a random permutation is as follows. Here, the n values of the sequence are stored in positions 0

---

[3]The symbol "$\approx$" means "approximately equal."

through $n-1$ of array **A**, function **swap(A, i, j)** exchanges elements **i** and **j** in array **A**, and **Random(n)** returns an integer value in the range 0 to $n-1$ (see the Appendix for more information on **swap** and **Random**).

```
// Randomly permute the "n" values of array "A"
template<typename E>
void permute(E A[], int n) {
  for (int i=n; i>0; i--)
    swap(A, i-1, Random(i));
}
```

Boolean variables: A **Boolean variable** is a variable (of type **bool** in C++) that takes on one of the two values **true** and **false**. These two values are often associated with the values 1 and 0, respectively, although there is no reason why this needs to be the case. It is poor programming practice to rely on the correspondence between 0 and **false**, because these are logically distinct objects of different types.

Logic Notation: We will occasionally make use of the notation of symbolic or Boolean logic. $A \Rightarrow B$ means "A implies B" or "If A then B." $A \Leftrightarrow B$ means "A if and only if B" or "A is equivalent to B." $A \vee B$ means "A or B" (useful both in the context of symbolic logic or when performing a Boolean operation). $A \wedge B$ means "A and B." $\sim A$ and $\overline{A}$ both mean "not A" or the negation of A where A is a Boolean variable.

Floor and ceiling: The **floor** of x (written $\lfloor x \rfloor$) takes real value x and returns the greatest integer $\leq x$. For example, $\lfloor 3.4 \rfloor = 3$, as does $\lfloor 3.0 \rfloor$, while $\lfloor -3.4 \rfloor = -4$ and $\lfloor -3.0 \rfloor = -3$. The **ceiling** of x (written $\lceil x \rceil$) takes real value x and returns the least integer $\geq x$. For example, $\lceil 3.4 \rceil = 4$, as does $\lceil 4.0 \rceil$, while $\lceil -3.4 \rceil = \lceil -3.0 \rceil = -3$.

Modulus operator: The **modulus** (or **mod**) function returns the remainder of an integer division. Sometimes written $n \bmod m$ in mathematical expressions, the syntax for the C++ modulus operator is **n % m**. From the definition of remainder, $n \bmod m$ is the integer r such that $n = qm + r$ for q an integer, and $|r| < |m|$. Therefore, the result of $n \bmod m$ must be between 0 and $m-1$ when n and m are positive integers. For example, $5 \bmod 3 = 2$; $25 \bmod 3 = 1$, $5 \bmod 7 = 5$, and $5 \bmod 5 = 0$.

There is more than one way to assign values to q and r, depending on how integer division is interpreted. The most common mathematical definition computes the mod function as $n \bmod m = n - m\lfloor n/m \rfloor$. In this case, $-3 \bmod 5 = 2$. However, Java and C++ compilers typically use the underlying processor's machine instruction for computing integer arithmetic. On many computers this is done by truncating the resulting fraction, meaning $n \bmod m = n - m(\mathrm{trunc}(n/m))$. Under this definition, $-3 \bmod 5 = -3$.

Unfortunately, for many applications this is not what the user wants or expects. For example, many hash systems will perform some computation on a record's key value and then take the result modulo the hash table size. The expectation here would be that the result is a legal index into the hash table, not a negative number. Implementers of hash functions must either insure that the result of the computation is always positive, or else add the hash table size to the result of the modulo function when that result is negative.

2.3 Logarithms

A **logarithm** of base b for value y is the power to which b is raised to get y. Normally, this is written as $\log_b y = x$. Thus, if $\log_b y = x$ then $b^x = y$, and $b^{\log_b y} = y$. Logarithms are used frequently by programmers. Here are two typical uses.

Example 2.6 Many programs require an encoding for a collection of objects. What is the minimum number of bits needed to represent n distinct code values? The answer is $\lceil \log_2 n \rceil$ bits. For example, if you have 1000 codes to store, you will require at least $\lceil \log_2 1000 \rceil = 10$ bits to have 1000 different codes (10 bits provide 1024 distinct code values).

Example 2.7 Consider the binary search algorithm for finding a given value within an array sorted by value from lowest to highest. Binary search first looks at the middle element and determines if the value being searched for is in the upper half or the lower half of the array. The algorithm then continues splitting the appropriate subarray in half until the desired value is found. (Binary search is described in more detail in Section 3.5.) How many times can an array of size n be split in half until only one element remains in the final subarray? The answer is $\lceil \log_2 n \rceil$ times.

In this book, nearly all logarithms used have a base of two. This is because data structures and algorithms most often divide things in half, or store codes with binary bits. Whenever you see the notation $\log n$ in this book, either $\log_2 n$ is meant or else the term is being used asymptotically and so the actual base does not matter. Logarithms using any base other than two will show the base explicitly.

Logarithms have the following properties, for any positive values of m, n, and r, and any positive integers a and b.

1. $\log(nm) = \log n + \log m$.
2. $\log(n/m) = \log n - \log m$.
3. $\log(n^r) = r \log n$.
4. $\log_a n = \log_b n / \log_b a$.

The first two properties state that the logarithm of two numbers multiplied (or divided) can be found by adding (or subtracting) the logarithms of the two numbers.[4] Property (3) is simply an extension of property (1). Property (4) tells us that, for variable n and any two integer constants a and b, $\log_a n$ and $\log_b n$ differ by the constant factor $\log_b a$, regardless of the value of n. Most runtime analyses in this book are of a type that ignores constant factors in costs. Property (4) says that such analyses need not be concerned with the base of the logarithm, because this can change the total cost only by a constant factor. Note that $2^{\log n} = n$.

When discussing logarithms, exponents often lead to confusion. Property (3) tells us that $\log n^2 = 2\log n$. How do we indicate the square of the logarithm (as opposed to the logarithm of n^2)? This could be written as $(\log n)^2$, but it is traditional to use $\log^2 n$. On the other hand, we might want to take the logarithm of the logarithm of n. This is written $\log\log n$.

A special notation is used in the rare case when we need to know how many times we must take the log of a number before we reach a value ≤ 1. This quantity is written $\log^* n$. For example, $\log^* 1024 = 4$ because $\log 1024 = 10$, $\log 10 \approx 3.33$, $\log 3.33 \approx 1.74$, and $\log 1.74 < 1$, which is a total of 4 log operations.

2.4 Summations and Recurrences

Most programs contain loop constructs. When analyzing running time costs for programs with loops, we need to add up the costs for each time the loop is executed. This is an example of a **summation**. Summations are simply the sum of costs for some function applied to a range of parameter values. Summations are typically written with the following "Sigma" notation:

$$\sum_{i=1}^{n} f(i).$$

This notation indicates that we are summing the value of $f(i)$ over some range of (integer) values. The parameter to the expression and its initial value are indicated below the $\sum$ symbol. Here, the notation $i = 1$ indicates that the parameter is i and that it begins with the value 1. At the top of the $\sum$ symbol is the expression n. This indicates the maximum value for the parameter i. Thus, this notation means to sum the values of $f(i)$ as i ranges across the integers from 1 through n. This can also be

---

[4]These properties are the idea behind the slide rule. Adding two numbers can be viewed as joining two lengths together and measuring their combined length. Multiplication is not so easily done. However, if the numbers are first converted to the lengths of their logarithms, then those lengths can be added and the inverse logarithm of the resulting length gives the answer for the multiplication (this is simply logarithm property (1)). A slide rule measures the length of the logarithm for the numbers, lets you slide bars representing these lengths to add up the total length, and finally converts this total length to the correct numeric answer by taking the inverse of the logarithm for the result.

written $f(1) + f(2) + \cdots + f(n-1) + f(n)$. Within a sentence, Sigma notation is typeset as $\sum_{i=1}^{n} f(i)$.

Given a summation, you often wish to replace it with an algebraic equation with the same value as the summation. This is known as a **closed-form solution**, and the process of replacing the summation with its closed-form solution is known as **solving** the summation. For example, the summation $\sum_{i=1}^{n} 1$ is simply the expression "1" summed n times (remember that i ranges from 1 to n). Because the sum of n 1s is n, the closed-form solution is n. The following is a list of useful summations, along with their closed-form solutions.

$$\sum_{i=1}^{n} i = \frac{n(n+1)}{2}. \tag{2.1}$$

$$\sum_{i=1}^{n} i^2 = \frac{2n^3 + 3n^2 + n}{6} = \frac{n(2n+1)(n+1)}{6}. \tag{2.2}$$

$$\sum_{i=1}^{\log n} n = n \log n. \tag{2.3}$$

$$\sum_{i=0}^{\infty} a^i = \frac{1}{1-a} \text{ for } 0 < a < 1. \tag{2.4}$$

$$\sum_{i=0}^{n} a^i = \frac{a^{n+1} - 1}{a - 1} \text{ for } a \neq 1. \tag{2.5}$$

As special cases to Equation 2.5,

$$\sum_{i=1}^{n} \frac{1}{2^i} = 1 - \frac{1}{2^n}, \tag{2.6}$$

and

$$\sum_{i=0}^{n} 2^i = 2^{n+1} - 1. \tag{2.7}$$

As a corollary to Equation 2.7,

$$\sum_{i=0}^{\log n} 2^i = 2^{\log n + 1} - 1 = 2n - 1. \tag{2.8}$$

Finally,

$$\sum_{i=1}^{n} \frac{i}{2^i} = 2 - \frac{n+2}{2^n}. \tag{2.9}$$

The sum of reciprocals from 1 to n, called the **Harmonic Series** and written $\mathcal{H}_n$, has a value between $\log_e n$ and $\log_e n + 1$. To be more precise, as n grows, the summation grows closer to

$$\mathcal{H}_n \approx \log_e n + \gamma + \frac{1}{2n}, \tag{2.10}$$

where γ is Euler's constant and has the value $0.5772...$

Most of these equalities can be proved easily by mathematical induction (see Section 2.6.3). Unfortunately, induction does not help us derive a closed-form solution. It only confirms when a proposed closed-form solution is correct. Techniques for deriving closed-form solutions are discussed in Section 14.1.

The running time for a recursive algorithm is most easily expressed by a recursive expression because the total time for the recursive algorithm includes the time to run the recursive call(s). A **recurrence relation** defines a function by means of an expression that includes one or more (smaller) instances of itself. A classic example is the recursive definition for the factorial function:

$$n! = (n-1)! \cdot n \text{ for } n > 1; \quad 1! = 0! = 1.$$

Another standard example of a recurrence is the Fibonacci sequence:

$$\text{Fib}(n) = \text{Fib}(n-1) + \text{Fib}(n-2) \text{ for } n > 2; \quad \text{Fib}(1) = \text{Fib}(2) = 1.$$

From this definition, the first seven numbers of the Fibonacci sequence are

$$1, 1, 2, 3, 5, 8, \text{ and } 13.$$

Notice that this definition contains two parts: the general definition for $\text{Fib}(n)$ and the base cases for $\text{Fib}(1)$ and $\text{Fib}(2)$. Likewise, the definition for factorial contains a recursive part and base cases.

Recurrence relations are often used to model the cost of recursive functions. For example, the number of multiplications required by function **fact** of Section 2.5 for an input of size n will be zero when $n = 0$ or $n = 1$ (the base cases), and it will be one plus the cost of calling **fact** on a value of $n - 1$. This can be defined using the following recurrence:

$$\mathbf{T}(n) = \mathbf{T}(n-1) + 1 \text{ for } n > 1; \quad \mathbf{T}(0) = \mathbf{T}(1) = 0.$$

As with summations, we typically wish to replace the recurrence relation with a closed-form solution. One approach is to **expand** the recurrence by replacing any occurrences of $\mathbf{T}$ on the right-hand side with its definition.

Example 2.8 If we expand the recurrence $\mathbf{T}(n) = \mathbf{T}(n-1) + 1$, we get

$$\begin{aligned} \mathbf{T}(n) &= \mathbf{T}(n-1) + 1 \\ &= (\mathbf{T}(n-2) + 1) + 1. \end{aligned}$$

We can expand the recurrence as many steps as we like, but the goal is to detect some pattern that will permit us to rewrite the recurrence in terms of a summation. In this example, we might notice that

$$(\mathbf{T}(n-2)+1)+1 = \mathbf{T}(n-2)+2$$

and if we expand the recurrence again, we get

$$\mathbf{T}(n) = \mathbf{T}(n-2)+2 = \mathbf{T}(n-3)+1+2 = \mathbf{T}(n-3)+3$$

which generalizes to the pattern $\mathbf{T}(n) = \mathbf{T}(n-i)+i$. We might conclude that

$$
\begin{aligned}
\mathbf{T}(n) &= \mathbf{T}(n-(n-1))+(n-1) \\
&= \mathbf{T}(1)+n-1 \\
&= n-1.
\end{aligned}
$$

Because we have merely guessed at a pattern and not actually proved that this is the correct closed form solution, we should use an induction proof to complete the process (see Example 2.13).

Example 2.9 A slightly more complicated recurrence is

$$\mathbf{T}(n) = \mathbf{T}(n-1)+n; \quad T(1) = 1.$$

Expanding this recurrence a few steps, we get

$$
\begin{aligned}
\mathbf{T}(n) &= \mathbf{T}(n-1)+n \\
&= \mathbf{T}(n-2)+(n-1)+n \\
&= \mathbf{T}(n-3)+(n-2)+(n-1)+n.
\end{aligned}
$$

We should then observe that this recurrence appears to have a pattern that leads to

$$
\begin{aligned}
\mathbf{T}(n) &= \mathbf{T}(n-(n-1))+(n-(n-2))+\cdots+(n-1)+n \\
&= 1+2+\cdots+(n-1)+n.
\end{aligned}
$$

This is equivalent to the summation $\sum_{i=1}^{n} i$, for which we already know the closed-form solution.

Techniques to find closed-form solutions for recurrence relations are discussed in Section 14.2. Prior to Chapter 14, recurrence relations are used infrequently in this book, and the corresponding closed-form solution and an explanation for how it was derived will be supplied at the time of use.

2.5   Recursion

An algorithm is **recursive** if it calls itself to do part of its work. For this approach to be successful, the "call to itself" must be on a smaller problem then the one originally attempted. In general, a recursive algorithm must have two parts: the **base case**, which handles a simple input that can be solved without resorting to a recursive call, and the recursive part which contains one or more recursive calls to the algorithm where the parameters are in some sense "closer" to the base case than those of the original call. Here is a recursive C++ function to compute the factorial of n. A trace of **fact**'s execution for a small value of n is presented in Section 4.2.4.

```
long fact(int n) {          // Compute n! recursively
  // To fit n! into a long variable, we require n <= 12
  Assert((n >= 0) && (n <= 12), "Input out of range");
  if (n <= 1)  return 1; // Base case: return base solution
  return n * fact(n-1);  // Recursive call for n > 1
}
```

The first two lines of the function constitute the base cases. If $n \leq 1$, then one of the base cases computes a solution for the problem. If $n > 1$, then **fact** calls a function that knows how to find the factorial of $n - 1$. Of course, the function that knows how to compute the factorial of $n - 1$ happens to be **fact** itself. But we should not think too hard about this while writing the algorithm. The design for recursive algorithms can always be approached in this way. First write the base cases. Then think about solving the problem by combining the results of one or more smaller — but similar — subproblems. If the algorithm you write is correct, then certainly you can rely on it (recursively) to solve the smaller subproblems. The secret to success is: Do not worry about *how* the recursive call solves the subproblem. Simply accept that it *will* solve it correctly, and use this result to in turn correctly solve the original problem. What could be simpler?

Recursion has no counterpart in everyday, physical-world problem solving. The concept can be difficult to grasp because it requires you to think about problems in a new way. To use recursion effectively, it is necessary to train yourself to stop analyzing the recursive process beyond the recursive call. The subproblems will take care of themselves. You just worry about the base cases and how to recombine the subproblems.

The recursive version of the factorial function might seem unnecessarily complicated to you because the same effect can be achieved by using a **while** loop. Here is another example of recursion, based on a famous puzzle called "Towers of Hanoi." The natural algorithm to solve this problem has multiple recursive calls. It cannot be rewritten easily using **while** loops.

The Towers of Hanoi puzzle begins with three poles and n rings, where all rings start on the leftmost pole (labeled Pole 1). The rings each have a different size, and

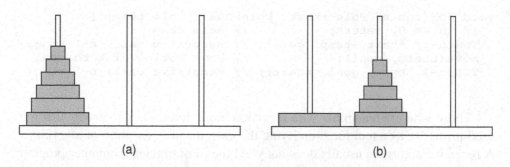

Figure 2.2 Towers of Hanoi example. (a) The initial conditions for a problem with six rings. (b) A necessary intermediate step on the road to a solution.

are stacked in order of decreasing size with the largest ring at the bottom, as shown in Figure 2.2(a). The problem is to move the rings from the leftmost pole to the rightmost pole (labeled Pole 3) in a series of steps. At each step the top ring on some pole is moved to another pole. There is one limitation on where rings may be moved: A ring can never be moved on top of a smaller ring.

How can you solve this problem? It is easy if you don't think too hard about the details. Instead, consider that all rings are to be moved from Pole 1 to Pole 3. It is not possible to do this without first moving the bottom (largest) ring to Pole 3. To do that, Pole 3 must be empty, and only the bottom ring can be on Pole 1. The remaining $n - 1$ rings must be stacked up in order on Pole 2, as shown in Figure 2.2(b). How can you do this? Assume that a function X is available to solve the problem of moving the top $n - 1$ rings from Pole 1 to Pole 2. Then move the bottom ring from Pole 1 to Pole 3. Finally, again use function X to move the remaining $n - 1$ rings from Pole 2 to Pole 3. In both cases, "function X" is simply the Towers of Hanoi function called on a smaller version of the problem.

The secret to success is relying on the Towers of Hanoi algorithm to do the work for you. You need not be concerned about the gory details of *how* the Towers of Hanoi subproblem will be solved. That will take care of itself provided that two things are done. First, there must be a base case (what to do if there is only one ring) so that the recursive process will not go on forever. Second, the recursive call to Towers of Hanoi can only be used to solve a smaller problem, and then only one of the proper form (one that meets the original definition for the Towers of Hanoi problem, assuming appropriate renaming of the poles).

Here is an implementation for the recursive Towers of Hanoi algorithm. Function **move(start, goal)** takes the top ring from Pole **start** and moves it to Pole **goal**. If **move** were to print the values of its parameters, then the result of calling **TOH** would be a list of ring-moving instructions that solves the problem.

```
void TOH(int n, Pole start, Pole goal, Pole temp) {
  if (n == 0) return;        // Base case
  TOH(n-1, start, temp, goal); // Recursive call: n-1 rings
  move(start, goal);         // Move bottom disk to goal
  TOH(n-1, temp, goal, start); // Recursive call: n-1 rings
}
```

Those who are unfamiliar with recursion might find it hard to accept that it is used primarily as a tool for simplifying the design and description of algorithms. A recursive algorithm usually does not yield the most efficient computer program for solving the problem because recursion involves function calls, which are typically more expensive than other alternatives such as a **while** loop. However, the recursive approach usually provides an algorithm that is reasonably efficient in the sense discussed in Chapter 3. (But not always! See Exercise 2.11.) If necessary, the clear, recursive solution can later be modified to yield a faster implementation, as described in Section 4.2.4.

Many data structures are naturally recursive, in that they can be defined as being made up of self-similar parts. Tree structures are an example of this. Thus, the algorithms to manipulate such data structures are often presented recursively. Many searching and sorting algorithms are based on a strategy of **divide and conquer**. That is, a solution is found by breaking the problem into smaller (similar) subproblems, solving the subproblems, then combining the subproblem solutions to form the solution to the original problem. This process is often implemented using recursion. Thus, recursion plays an important role throughout this book, and many more examples of recursive functions will be given.

2.6   Mathematical Proof Techniques

Solving any problem has two distinct parts: the investigation and the argument. Students are too used to seeing only the argument in their textbooks and lectures. But to be successful in school (and in life after school), one needs to be good at both, and to understand the differences between these two phases of the process. To solve the problem, you must investigate successfully. That means engaging the problem, and working through until you find a solution. Then, to give the answer to your client (whether that "client" be your instructor when writing answers on a homework assignment or exam, or a written report to your boss), you need to be able to make the argument in a way that gets the solution across clearly and succinctly. The argument phase involves good technical writing skills — the ability to make a clear, logical argument.

Being conversant with standard proof techniques can help you in this process. Knowing how to write a good proof helps in many ways. First, it clarifies your thought process, which in turn clarifies your explanations. Second, if you use one of the standard proof structures such as proof by contradiction or an induction proof, then both you and your reader are working from a shared understanding of that structure. That makes for less complexity to your reader to understand your proof, because the reader need not decode the structure of your argument from scratch.

This section briefly introduces three commonly used proof techniques: (i) deduction, or direct proof; (ii) proof by contradiction, and (iii) proof by mathematical induction.

2.6.1 Direct Proof

In general, a **direct proof** is just a "logical explanation." A direct proof is sometimes referred to as an argument by deduction. This is simply an argument in terms of logic. Often written in English with words such as "if ... then," it could also be written with logic notation such as "$P \Rightarrow Q$." Even if we don't wish to use symbolic logic notation, we can still take advantage of fundamental theorems of logic to structure our arguments. For example, if we want to prove that P and Q are equivalent, we can first prove $P \Rightarrow Q$ and then prove $Q \Rightarrow P$.

In some domains, proofs are essentially a series of state changes from a start state to an end state. Formal predicate logic can be viewed in this way, with the various "rules of logic" being used to make the changes from one formula or combining a couple of formulas to make a new formula on the route to the destination. Symbolic manipulations to solve integration problems in introductory calculus classes are similar in spirit, as are high school geometry proofs.

2.6.2 Proof by Contradiction

The simplest way to *disprove* a theorem or statement is to find a counterexample to the theorem. Unfortunately, no number of examples supporting a theorem is sufficient to prove that the theorem is correct. However, there is an approach that is vaguely similar to disproving by counterexample, called Proof by Contradiction. To prove a theorem by contradiction, we first *assume* that the theorem is *false*. We then find a logical contradiction stemming from this assumption. If the logic used to find the contradiction is correct, then the only way to resolve the contradiction is to recognize that the assumption that the theorem is false must be incorrect. That is, we conclude that the theorem must be true.

Example 2.10 Here is a simple proof by contradiction.

Theorem 2.1 *There is no largest integer.*
Proof: Proof by contradiction.

   Step 1. Contrary assumption: Assume that there *is* a largest integer. Call it B (for "biggest").

   Step 2. Show this assumption leads to a contradiction: Consider $C = B + 1$. C is an integer because it is the sum of two integers. Also,

$C > B$, which means that B is not the largest integer after all. Thus, we have reached a contradiction. The only flaw in our reasoning is the initial assumption that the theorem is false. Thus, we conclude that the theorem is correct.   □

A related proof technique is proving the contrapositive. We can prove that $P \Rightarrow Q$ by proving $(\text{not } Q) \Rightarrow (\text{not } P)$.

2.6.3 Proof by Mathematical Induction

Mathematical induction can be used to prove a wide variety of theorems. Induction also provides a useful way to think about algorithm design, because it encourages you to think about solving a problem by building up from simple subproblems. Induction can help to prove that a recursive function produces the correct result.. Understanding recursion is a big step toward understanding induction, and vice versa, since they work by essentially the same process.

Within the context of algorithm analysis, one of the most important uses for mathematical induction is as a method to test a hypothesis. As explained in Section 2.4, when seeking a closed-form solution for a summation or recurrence we might first guess or otherwise acquire evidence that a particular formula is the correct solution. If the formula is indeed correct, it is often an easy matter to prove that fact with an induction proof.

Let **Thrm** be a theorem to prove, and express **Thrm** in terms of a positive integer parameter n. Mathematical induction states that **Thrm** is true for any value of parameter n (for $n \geq c$, where c is some constant) if the following two conditions are true:

1. **Base Case: Thrm** holds for $n = c$, and
2. **Induction Step:** If **Thrm** holds for $n - 1$, then **Thrm** holds for n.

Proving the base case is usually easy, typically requiring that some small value such as 1 be substituted for n in the theorem and applying simple algebra or logic as necessary to verify the theorem. Proving the induction step is sometimes easy, and sometimes difficult. An alternative formulation of the induction step is known as **strong induction**. The induction step for strong induction is:

2a. Induction Step: If **Thrm** holds for all k, $c \leq k < n$, then **Thrm** holds for n.

Proving either variant of the induction step (in conjunction with verifying the base case) yields a satisfactory proof by mathematical induction.

The two conditions that make up the induction proof combine to demonstrate that **Thrm** holds for $n = 2$ as an extension of the fact that **Thrm** holds for $n = 1$. This fact, combined again with condition (2) or (2a), indicates that **Thrm** also holds for $n = 3$, and so on. Thus, **Thrm** holds for all values of n (larger than the base cases) once the two conditions have been proved.

What makes mathematical induction so powerful (and so mystifying to most people at first) is that we can take advantage of the *assumption* that **Thrm** holds for all values less than n as a tool to help us prove that **Thrm** holds for n. This is known as the **induction hypothesis**. Having this assumption to work with makes the induction step easier to prove than tackling the original theorem itself. Being able to rely on the induction hypothesis provides extra information that we can bring to bear on the problem.

Recursion and induction have many similarities. Both are anchored on one or more base cases. A recursive function relies on the ability to call itself to get the answer for smaller instances of the problem. Likewise, induction proofs rely on the truth of the induction hypothesis to prove the theorem. The induction hypothesis does not come out of thin air. It is true if and only if the theorem itself is true, and therefore is reliable within the proof context. Using the induction hypothesis it do work is exactly the same as using a recursive call to do work.

Example 2.11 Here is a sample proof by mathematical induction. Call the sum of the first n positive integers $\mathbf{S}(n)$.

Theorem 2.2 $\mathbf{S}(n) = n(n+1)/2$.

Proof: The proof is by mathematical induction.

1. **Check the base case.** For $n = 1$, verify that $\mathbf{S}(1) = 1(1+1)/2$. $\mathbf{S}(1)$ is simply the sum of the first positive number, which is 1. Because $1(1+1)/2 = 1$, the formula is correct for the base case.

2. **State the induction hypothesis.** The induction hypothesis is

$$\mathbf{S}(n-1) = \sum_{i=1}^{n-1} i = \frac{(n-1)((n-1)+1)}{2} = \frac{(n-1)(n)}{2}.$$

3. **Use the assumption from the induction hypothesis for $n-1$ to show that the result is true for n.** The induction hypothesis states that $\mathbf{S}(n-1) = (n-1)(n)/2$, and because $\mathbf{S}(n) = \mathbf{S}(n-1) + n$, we can substitute for $\mathbf{S}(n-1)$ to get

$$\sum_{i=1}^{n} i = \left(\sum_{i=1}^{n-1} i \right) + n = \frac{(n-1)(n)}{2} + n$$

$$= \frac{n^2 - n + 2n}{2} = \frac{n(n+1)}{2}.$$

Thus, by mathematical induction,

$$\mathbf{S}(n) = \sum_{i=1}^{n} i = n(n+1)/2.$$

□

Note carefully what took place in this example. First we cast $\mathbf{S}(n)$ in terms of a smaller occurrence of the problem: $\mathbf{S}(n) = \mathbf{S}(n-1) + n$. This is important because once $\mathbf{S}(n-1)$ comes into the picture, we can use the induction hypothesis to replace $\mathbf{S}(n-1)$ with $(n-1)(n)/2$. From here, it is simple algebra to prove that $\mathbf{S}(n-1) + n$ equals the right-hand side of the original theorem.

Example 2.12 Here is another simple proof by induction that illustrates choosing the proper variable for induction. We wish to prove by induction that the sum of the first n positive odd numbers is n^2. First we need a way to describe the nth odd number, which is simply $2n - 1$. This also allows us to cast the theorem as a summation.

Theorem 2.3 $\sum_{i=1}^{n}(2i-1) = n^2$.
Proof: The base case of $n = 1$ yields $1 = 1^2$, which is true. The induction hypothesis is

$$\sum_{i=1}^{n-1}(2i-1) = (n-1)^2.$$

We now use the induction hypothesis to show that the theorem holds true for n. The sum of the first n odd numbers is simply the sum of the first $n - 1$ odd numbers plus the nth odd number. In the second line below, we will use the induction hypothesis to replace the partial summation (shown in brackets in the first line) with its closed-form solution. After that, algebra takes care of the rest.

$$\begin{aligned}
\sum_{i=1}^{n}(2i-1) &= \left[\sum_{i=1}^{n-1}(2i-1)\right] + 2n - 1 \\
&= [(n-1)^2] + 2n - 1 \\
&= n^2 - 2n + 1 + 2n - 1 \\
&= n^2.
\end{aligned}$$

Thus, by mathematical induction, $\sum_{i=1}^{n}(2i-1) = n^2$.   □

Example 2.13 This example shows how we can use induction to prove that a proposed closed-form solution for a recurrence relation is correct.

Theorem 2.4 *The recurrence relation* $\mathbf{T}(n) = \mathbf{T}(n-1)+1; \quad \mathbf{T}(1) = 0$ *has closed-form solution* $\mathbf{T}(n) = n - 1$.

Proof: To prove the base case, we observe that $\mathbf{T}(1) = 1 - 1 = 0$. The induction hypothesis is that $\mathbf{T}(n - 1) = n - 2$. Combining the definition of the recurrence with the induction hypothesis, we see immediately that

$$\mathbf{T}(n) = \mathbf{T}(n - 1) + 1 = n - 2 + 1 = n - 1$$

for $n > 1$. Thus, we have proved the theorem correct by mathematical induction.   □

Example 2.14 This example uses induction without involving summations or other equations. It also illustrates a more flexible use of base cases.

Theorem 2.5 *2¢ and 5¢ stamps can be used to form any value (for values* ≥ 4).

Proof: The theorem defines the problem for values ≥ 4 because it does not hold for the values 1 and 3. Using 4 as the base case, a value of 4¢ can be made from two 2¢ stamps. The induction hypothesis is that a value of $n - 1$ can be made from some combination of 2¢ and 5¢ stamps. We now use the induction hypothesis to show how to get the value n from 2¢ and 5¢ stamps. Either the makeup for value $n - 1$ includes a 5¢ stamp, or it does not. If so, then replace a 5¢ stamp with three 2¢ stamps. If not, then the makeup must have included at least two 2¢ stamps (because it is at least of size 4 and contains only 2¢ stamps). In this case, replace two of the 2¢ stamps with a single 5¢ stamp. In either case, we now have a value of n made up of 2¢ and 5¢ stamps. Thus, by mathematical induction, the theorem is correct.   □

Example 2.15 Here is an example using strong induction.

Theorem 2.6 *For* n > 1, n *is divisible by some prime number.*

Proof: For the base case, choose $n = 2$. 2 is divisible by the prime number 2. The induction hypothesis is that *any* value a, $2 \leq a < n$, is divisible by some prime number. There are now two cases to consider when proving the theorem for n. If n is a prime number, then n is divisible by itself. If n is not a prime number, then $n = a \times b$ for a and b, both integers less than n but greater than 1. The induction hypothesis tells us that a is divisible by some prime number. That same prime number must also divide n. Thus, by mathematical induction, the theorem is correct.   □

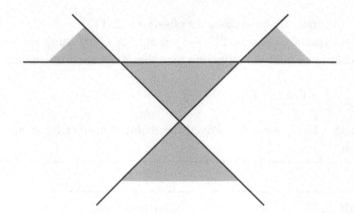

Figure 2.3 A two-coloring for the regions formed by three lines in the plane.

Our next example of mathematical induction proves a theorem from geometry. It also illustrates a standard technique of induction proof where we take n objects and remove some object to use the induction hypothesis.

Example 2.16 Define a **two-coloring** for a set of regions as a way of assigning one of two colors to each region such that no two regions sharing a side have the same color. For example, a chessboard is two-colored. Figure 2.3 shows a two-coloring for the plane with three lines. We will assume that the two colors to be used are black and white.

Theorem 2.7 *The set of regions formed by* n *infinite lines in the plane can be two-colored.*

Proof: Consider the base case of a single infinite line in the plane. This line splits the plane into two regions. One region can be colored black and the other white to get a valid two-coloring. The induction hypothesis is that the set of regions formed by $n - 1$ infinite lines can be two-colored. To prove the theorem for n, consider the set of regions formed by the $n - 1$ lines remaining when any one of the n lines is removed. By the induction hypothesis, this set of regions can be two-colored. Now, put the nth line back. This splits the plane into two half-planes, each of which (independently) has a valid two-coloring inherited from the two-coloring of the plane with $n - 1$ lines. Unfortunately, the regions newly split by the nth line violate the rule for a two-coloring. Take all regions on one side of the nth line and reverse their coloring (after doing so, this half-plane is still two-colored). Those regions split by the nth line are now properly two-colored, because the part of the region to one side of the line is now black and the region to the other side is now white. Thus, by mathematical induction, the entire plane is two-colored. $\square$

Compare the proof of Theorem 2.7 with that of Theorem 2.5. For Theorem 2.5, we took a collection of stamps of size $n - 1$ (which, by the induction hypothesis, must have the desired property) and from that "built" a collection of size n that has the desired property. We therefore proved the existence of *some* collection of stamps of size n with the desired property.

For Theorem 2.7 we must prove that *any* collection of n lines has the desired property. Thus, our strategy is to take an *arbitrary* collection of n lines, and "reduce" it so that we have a set of lines that must have the desired property because it matches the induction hypothesis. From there, we merely need to show that reversing the original reduction process preserves the desired property.

In contrast, consider what is required if we attempt to "build" from a set of lines of size $n - 1$ to one of size n. We would have great difficulty justifying that *all* possible collections of n lines are covered by our building process. By reducing from an arbitrary collection of n lines to something less, we avoid this problem.

This section's final example shows how induction can be used to prove that a recursive function produces the correct result.

Example 2.17 We would like to prove that function **fact** does indeed compute the factorial function. There are two distinct steps to such a proof. The first is to prove that the function always terminates. The second is to prove that the function returns the correct value.

Theorem 2.8 *Function* **fact** *will terminate for any value of n.*
Proof: For the base case, we observe that **fact** will terminate directly whenever $n \leq 0$. The induction hypothesis is that **fact** will terminate for $n - 1$. For n, we have two possibilities. One possibility is that $n \geq 12$. In that case, **fact** will terminate directly because it will fail its assertion test. Otherwise, **fact** will make a recursive call to **fact(n-1)**. By the induction hypothesis, **fact(n-1)** must terminate.   □

Theorem 2.9 *Function* **fact** *does compute the factorial function for any value in the range 0 to 12.*
Proof: To prove the base case, observe that when $n = 0$ or $n = 1$, **fact(n)** returns the correct value of 1. The induction hypothesis is that **fact(n-1)** returns the correct value of $(n-1)!$. For any value n within the legal range, **fact(n)** returns $n * $ **fact(n-1)**. By the induction hypothesis, **fact(n-1)** $= (n-1)!$, and because $n * (n-1)! = n!$, we have proved that **fact(n)** produces the correct result.   □

We can use a similar process to prove many recursive programs correct. The general form is to show that the base cases perform correctly, and then to use the induction hypothesis to show that the recursive step also produces the correct result.

Prior to this, we must prove that the function always terminates, which might also be done using an induction proof.

2.7 Estimation

One of the most useful life skills that you can gain from your computer science training is the ability to perform quick estimates. This is sometimes known as "back of the napkin" or "back of the envelope" calculation. Both nicknames suggest that only a rough estimate is produced. Estimation techniques are a standard part of engineering curricula but are often neglected in computer science. Estimation is no substitute for rigorous, detailed analysis of a problem, but it can serve to indicate when a rigorous analysis is warranted: If the initial estimate indicates that the solution is unworkable, then further analysis is probably unnecessary.

Estimation can be formalized by the following three-step process:

1. Determine the major parameters that affect the problem.
2. Derive an equation that relates the parameters to the problem.
3. Select values for the parameters, and apply the equation to yield an estimated solution.

When doing estimations, a good way to reassure yourself that the estimate is reasonable is to do it in two different ways. In general, if you want to know what comes out of a system, you can either try to estimate that directly, or you can estimate what goes into the system (assuming that what goes in must later come out). If both approaches (independently) give similar answers, then this should build confidence in the estimate.

When calculating, be sure that your units match. For example, do not add feet and pounds. Verify that the result is in the correct units. Always keep in mind that the output of a calculation is only as good as its input. The more uncertain your valuation for the input parameters in Step 3, the more uncertain the output value. However, back of the envelope calculations are often meant only to get an answer within an order of magnitude, or perhaps within a factor of two. Before doing an estimate, you should decide on acceptable error bounds, such as within 25%, within a factor of two, and so forth. Once you are confident that an estimate falls within your error bounds, leave it alone! Do not try to get a more precise estimate than necessary for your purpose.

Example 2.18 How many library bookcases does it take to store books containing one million pages? I estimate that a 500-page book requires one inch on the library shelf (it will help to look at the size of any handy book), yielding about 200 feet of shelf space for one million pages. If a shelf is 4 feet wide, then 50 shelves are required. If a bookcase contains

5 shelves, this yields about 10 library bookcases. To reach this conclusion, I estimated the number of pages per inch, the width of a shelf, and the number of shelves in a bookcase. None of my estimates are likely to be precise, but I feel confident that my answer is correct to within a factor of two. (After writing this, I went to Virginia Tech's library and looked at some real bookcases. They were only about 3 feet wide, but typically had 7 shelves for a total of 21 shelf-feet. So I was correct to within 10% on bookcase capacity, far better than I expected or needed. One of my selected values was too high, and the other too low, which canceled out the errors.)

Example 2.19 Is it more economical to buy a car that gets 20 miles per gallon, or one that gets 30 miles per gallon but costs $3000 more? The typical car is driven about 12,000 miles per year. If gasoline costs $3/gallon, then the yearly gas bill is $1800 for the less efficient car and $1200 for the more efficient car. If we ignore issues such as the payback that would be received if we invested $3000 in a bank, it would take 5 years to make up the difference in price. At this point, the buyer must decide if price is the only criterion and if a 5-year payback time is acceptable. Naturally, a person who drives more will make up the difference more quickly, and changes in gasoline prices will also greatly affect the outcome.

Example 2.20 When at the supermarket doing the week's shopping, can you estimate about how much you will have to pay at the checkout? One simple way is to round the price of each item to the nearest dollar, and add this value to a mental running total as you put the item in your shopping cart. This will likely give an answer within a couple of dollars of the true total.

2.8 Further Reading

Most of the topics covered in this chapter are considered part of Discrete Mathematics. An introduction to this field is *Discrete Mathematics with Applications* by Susanna S. Epp [Epp10]. An advanced treatment of many mathematical topics useful to computer scientists is *Concrete Mathematics: A Foundation for Computer Science* by Graham, Knuth, and Patashnik [GKP94].

See "Technically Speaking" from the February 1995 issue of *IEEE Spectrum* [Sel95] for a discussion on the standard for indicating units of computer storage used in this book.

Introduction to Algorithms by Udi Manber [Man89] makes extensive use of mathematical induction as a technique for developing algorithms.

For more information on recursion, see *Thinking Recursively* by Eric S. Roberts [Rob86]. To learn recursion properly, it is worth your while to learn the programming languages LISP or Scheme, even if you never intend to write a program in either language. In particular, Friedman and Felleisen's "Little" books (including *The Little LISPer*[FF89] and *The Little Schemer*[FFBS95]) are designed to teach you how to think recursively as well as teach you the language. These books are entertaining reading as well.

A good book on writing mathematical proofs is Daniel Solow's *How to Read and Do Proofs* [Sol09]. To improve your general mathematical problem-solving abilities, see *The Art and Craft of Problem Solving* by Paul Zeitz [Zei07]. Zeitz also discusses the three proof techniques presented in Section 2.6, and the roles of investigation and argument in problem solving.

For more about estimation techniques, see two Programming Pearls by John Louis Bentley entitled *The Back of the Envelope* and *The Envelope is Back* [Ben84, Ben00, Ben86, Ben88]. *Genius: The Life and Science of Richard Feynman* by James Gleick [Gle92] gives insight into how important back of the envelope calculation was to the developers of the atomic bomb, and to modern theoretical physics in general.

2.9   Exercises

2.1 For each relation below, explain why the relation does or does not satisfy each of the properties reflexive, symmetric, antisymmetric, and transitive.

(a) "isBrotherOf" on the set of people.
(b) "isFatherOf" on the set of people.
(c) The relation $R = \{\langle x, y\rangle \mid x^2 + y^2 = 1\}$ for real numbers x and y.
(d) The relation $R = \{\langle x, y\rangle \mid x^2 = y^2\}$ for real numbers x and y.
(e) The relation $R = \{\langle x, y\rangle \mid x \bmod y = 0\}$ for $x, y \in \{1, 2, 3, 4\}$.
(f) The empty relation $\emptyset$ (i.e., the relation with no ordered pairs for which it is true) on the set of integers.
(g) The empty relation $\emptyset$ (i.e., the relation with no ordered pairs for which it is true) on the empty set.

2.2 For each of the following relations, either prove that it is an equivalence relation or prove that it is not an equivalence relation.

(a) For integers a and b, $a \equiv b$ if and only if $a + b$ is even.
(b) For integers a and b, $a \equiv b$ if and only if $a + b$ is odd.
(c) For nonzero rational numbers a and b, $a \equiv b$ if and only if $a \times b > 0$.
(d) For nonzero rational numbers a and b, $a \equiv b$ if and only if a/b is an integer.

     (e) For rational numbers a and b, $a \equiv b$ if and only if $a - b$ is an integer.

     (f) For rational numbers a and b, $a \equiv b$ if and only if $|a - b| \le 2$.

2.3 State whether each of the following relations is a partial ordering, and explain why or why not.

     (a) "isFatherOf" on the set of people.

     (b) "isAncestorOf" on the set of people.

     (c) "isOlderThan" on the set of people.

     (d) "isSisterOf" on the set of people.

     (e) $\{\langle a, b\rangle, \langle a, a\rangle, \langle b, a\rangle\}$ on the set $\{a, b\}$.

     (f) $\{\langle 2, 1\rangle, \langle 1, 3\rangle, \langle 2, 3\rangle\}$ on the set $\{1, 2, 3\}$.

2.4 How many total orderings can be defined on a set with n elements? Explain your answer.

2.5 Define an ADT for a set of integers (remember that a set has no concept of duplicate elements, and has no concept of order). Your ADT should consist of the functions that can be performed on a set to control its membership, check the size, check if a given element is in the set, and so on. Each function should be defined in terms of its input and output.

2.6 Define an ADT for a bag of integers (remember that a bag may contain duplicates, and has no concept of order). Your ADT should consist of the functions that can be performed on a bag to control its membership, check the size, check if a given element is in the set, and so on. Each function should be defined in terms of its input and output.

2.7 Define an ADT for a sequence of integers (remember that a sequence may contain duplicates, and supports the concept of position for its elements). Your ADT should consist of the functions that can be performed on a sequence to control its membership, check the size, check if a given element is in the set, and so on. Each function should be defined in terms of its input and output.

2.8 An investor places \$30,000 into a stock fund. 10 years later the account has a value of \$69,000. Using logarithms and anti-logarithms, present a formula for calculating the average annual rate of increase. Then use your formula to determine the average annual growth rate for this fund.

2.9 Rewrite the factorial function of Section 2.5 without using recursion.

2.10 Rewrite the **for** loop for the random permutation generator of Section 2.2 as a recursive function.

2.11 Here is a simple recursive function to compute the Fibonacci sequence:

```
long fibr(int n) { // Recursive Fibonacci generator
  // fibr(46) is largest value that fits in a long
  Assert((n > 0) && (n < 47), "Input out of range");
  if ((n == 1) || (n == 2)) return 1; // Base cases
  return fibr(n-1) + fibr(n-2);        // Recursion
}
```

This algorithm turns out to be very slow, calling **Fibr** a total of Fib(n) times. Contrast this with the following iterative algorithm:

```
long fibi(int n) { // Iterative Fibonacci generator
  // fibi(46) is largest value that fits in a long
  Assert((n > 0) && (n < 47), "Input out of range");
  long past, prev, curr;  // Store temporary values
  past = prev = curr = 1;     // initialize
  for (int i=3; i<=n; i++) { // Compute next value
    past = prev;             // past holds fibi(i-2)
    prev = curr;             // prev holds fibi(i-1)
    curr = past + prev;      // curr now holds fibi(i)
  }
  return curr;
}
```

Function **Fibi** executes the **for** loop $n - 2$ times.

   (a) Which version is easier to understand? Why?

   (b) Explain why **Fibr** is so much slower than **Fibi**.

2.12 Write a recursive function to solve a generalization of the Towers of Hanoi problem where each ring may begin on any pole so long as no ring sits on top of a smaller ring.

2.13 Revise the recursive implementation for Towers of Hanoi from Section 2.5 to return the list of moves needed to solve the problem.

2.14 Consider the following function:

```
void foo (double val) {
  if (val != 0.0)
    foo(val/2.0);
}
```

This function makes progress towards the base case on every recursive call. In theory (that is, if **double** variables acted like true real numbers), would this function ever terminate for input **val** a nonzero number? In practice (an actual computer implementation), will it terminate?

2.15 Write a function to print all of the permutations for the elements of an array containing n distinct integer values.

2.16 Write a recursive algorithm to print all of the subsets for the set of the first n positive integers.

2.17 The Largest Common Factor (LCF) for two positive integers n and m is the largest integer that divides both n and m evenly. LCF(n, m) is at least one, and at most m, assuming that $n \geq m$. Over two thousand years ago, Euclid provided an efficient algorithm based on the observation that, when $n \bmod m \neq 0$, LCF(n, m) = LCF($m, n \bmod m$). Use this fact to write two algorithms to find the LCF for two positive integers. The first version should compute the value iteratively. The second version should compute the value using recursion.

2.18 Prove by contradiction that the number of primes is infinite.

2.19 (a) Use induction to show that $n^2 - n$ is always even.

(b) Give a direct proof in one or two sentences that $n^2 - n$ is always even.

(c) Show that $n^3 - n$ is always divisible by three.

(d) Is $n^5 - n$ aways divisible by 5? Explain your answer.

2.20 Prove that $\sqrt{2}$ is irrational.

2.21 Explain why

$$\sum_{i=1}^{n} i = \sum_{i=1}^{n}(n - i + 1) = \sum_{i=0}^{n-1}(n - i).$$

2.22 Prove Equation 2.2 using mathematical induction.

2.23 Prove Equation 2.6 using mathematical induction.

2.24 Prove Equation 2.7 using mathematical induction.

2.25 Find a closed-form solution and prove (using induction) that your solution is correct for the summation

$$\sum_{i=1}^{n} 3^i.$$

2.26 Prove that the sum of the first n even numbers is $n^2 + n$

(a) by assuming that the sum of the first n odd numbers is n^2.

(b) by mathematical induction.

2.27 Give a closed-form formula for the summation $\sum_{i=a}^{n} i$ where a is an integer between 1 and n.

2.28 Prove that $\text{Fib}(n) < (\frac{5}{3})^n$.

2.29 Prove, for $n \geq 1$, that

$$\sum_{i=1}^{n} i^3 = \frac{n^2(n + 1)^2}{4}.$$

2.30 The following theorem is called the **Pigeonhole Principle**.

Theorem 2.10 *When* n + 1 *pigeons roost in* n *holes, there must be some hole containing at least two pigeons.*

(a) Prove the Pigeonhole Principle using proof by contradiction.

(b) Prove the Pigeonhole Principle using mathematical induction.

2.31 For this problem, you will consider arrangements of infinite lines in the plane such that three or more lines never intersect at a single point and no two lines are parallel.

(a) Give a recurrence relation that expresses the number of regions formed by n lines, and explain why your recurrence is correct.

(b) Give the summation that results from expanding your recurrence.

(c) Give a closed-form solution for the summation.

2.32 Prove (using induction) that the recurrence $\mathbf{T}(n) = \mathbf{T}(n-1) + n$; $\mathbf{T}(1) = 1$ has as its closed-form solution $\mathbf{T}(n) = n(n+1)/2$.

2.33 Expand the following recurrence to help you find a closed-form solution, and then use induction to prove your answer is correct.

$$\mathbf{T}(n) = 2\mathbf{T}(n-1) + 1 \text{ for } n > 0; \ \mathbf{T}(0) = 0.$$

2.34 Expand the following recurrence to help you find a closed-form solution, and then use induction to prove your answer is correct.

$$\mathbf{T}(n) = \mathbf{T}(n-1) + 3n + 1 \text{ for } n > 0; \ \mathbf{T}(0) = 1.$$

2.35 Assume that an n-bit integer (represented by standard binary notation) takes any value in the range 0 to $2^n - 1$ with equal probability.

(a) For each bit position, what is the probability of its value being 1 and what is the probability of its value being 0?

(b) What is the average number of "1" bits for an n-bit random number?

(c) What is the expected value for the position of the leftmost "1" bit? In other words, how many positions on average must we examine when moving from left to right before encountering a "1" bit? Show the appropriate summation.

2.36 What is the total volume of your body in liters (or, if you prefer, gallons)?

2.37 An art historian has a database of 20,000 full-screen color images.

(a) About how much space will this require? How many CDs would be required to store the database? (A CD holds about 600MB of data). Be sure to explain all assumptions you made to derive your answer.

(b) Now, assume that you have access to a good image compression technique that can store the images in only 1/10 of the space required for an uncompressed image. Will the entire database fit onto a single CD if the images are compressed?

2.38 How many cubic miles of water flow out of the mouth of the Mississippi River each day? DO NOT look up the answer or any supplemental facts. Be sure to describe all assumptions made in arriving at your answer.

2.39 When buying a home mortgage, you often have the option of paying some money in advance (called "discount points") to get a lower interest rate. Assume that you have the choice between two 15-year fixed-rate mortgages: one at 8% with no up-front charge, and the other at $7\frac{3}{4}\%$ with an up-front charge of 1% of the mortgage value. How long would it take to recover the 1% charge when you take the mortgage at the lower rate? As a second, more precise estimate, how long would it take to recover the charge plus the interest you would have received if you had invested the equivalent of the 1% charge in the bank at 5% interest while paying the higher rate? DO NOT use a calculator to help you answer this question.

2.40 When you build a new house, you sometimes get a "construction loan" which is a temporary line of credit out of which you pay construction costs as they occur. At the end of the construction period, you then replace the construction loan with a regular mortgage on the house. During the construction loan, you only pay each month for the interest charged against the actual amount borrowed so far. Assume that your house construction project starts at the beginning of April, and is complete at the end of six months. Assume that the total construction cost will be $300,000 with the costs occurring at the beginning of each month in $50,000 increments. The construction loan charges 6% interest. Estimate the total interest payments that must be paid over the life of the construction loan.

2.41 Here are some questions that test your working knowledge of how fast computers operate. Is disk drive access time normally measured in milliseconds (thousandths of a second) or microseconds (millionths of a second)? Does your RAM memory access a word in more or less than one microsecond? How many instructions can your CPU execute in one year if the machine is left running at full speed all the time? DO NOT use paper or a calculator to derive your answers.

2.42 Does your home contain enough books to total one million pages? How many total pages are stored in your school library building?

2.43 How many words are in this book?

2.44 How many hours are one million seconds? How many days? Answer these questions doing all arithmetic in your head.

2.45 How many cities and towns are there in the United States?

2.46 How many steps would it take to walk from Boston to San Francisco?

2.47 A man begins a car trip to visit his in-laws. The total distance is 60 miles, and he starts off at a speed of 60 miles per hour. After driving exactly 1 mile, he loses some of his enthusiasm for the journey, and (instantaneously) slows down to 59 miles per hour. After traveling another mile, he again slows to 58 miles per hour. This continues, progressively slowing by 1 mile per hour for each mile traveled until the trip is complete.

  (a) How long does it take the man to reach his in-laws?

  (b) How long would the trip take in the continuous case where the speed smoothly diminishes with the distance yet to travel?

3

Algorithm Analysis

How long will it take to process the company payroll once we complete our planned merger? Should I buy a new payroll program from vendor X or vendor Y? If a particular program is slow, is it badly implemented or is it solving a hard problem? Questions like these ask us to consider the difficulty of a problem, or the relative efficiency of two or more approaches to solving a problem.

This chapter introduces the motivation, basic notation, and fundamental techniques of algorithm analysis. We focus on a methodology known as **asymptotic algorithm analysis**, or simply **asymptotic analysis**. Asymptotic analysis attempts to estimate the resource consumption of an algorithm. It allows us to compare the relative costs of two or more algorithms for solving the same problem. Asymptotic analysis also gives algorithm designers a tool for estimating whether a proposed solution is likely to meet the resource constraints for a problem before they implement an actual program. After reading this chapter, you should understand

- the concept of a growth rate, the rate at which the cost of an algorithm grows as the size of its input grows;
- the concept of upper and lower bounds for a growth rate, and how to estimate these bounds for a simple program, algorithm, or problem; and
- the difference between the cost of an algorithm (or program) and the cost of a problem.

The chapter concludes with a brief discussion of the practical difficulties encountered when empirically measuring the cost of a program, and some principles for code tuning to improve program efficiency.

3.1 Introduction

How do you compare two algorithms for solving some problem in terms of efficiency? We could implement both algorithms as computer programs and then run them on a suitable range of inputs, measuring how much of the resources in question each program uses. This approach is often unsatisfactory for four reasons. First, there is the effort involved in programming and testing two algorithms when at best you want to keep only one. Second, when empirically comparing two algorithms there is always the chance that one of the programs was "better written" than the other, and therefor the relative qualities of the underlying algorithms are not truly represented by their implementations. This can easily occur when the programmer has a bias regarding the algorithms. Third, the choice of empirical test cases might unfairly favor one algorithm. Fourth, you could find that even the better of the two algorithms does not fall within your resource budget. In that case you must begin the entire process again with yet another program implementing a new algorithm. But, how would you know if any algorithm can meet the resource budget? Perhaps the problem is simply too difficult for any implementation to be within budget.

These problems can often be avoided by using asymptotic analysis. Asymptotic analysis measures the efficiency of an algorithm, or its implementation as a program, as the input size becomes large. It is actually an estimating technique and does not tell us anything about the relative merits of two programs where one is always "slightly faster" than the other. However, asymptotic analysis has proved useful to computer scientists who must determine if a particular algorithm is worth considering for implementation.

The critical resource for a program is most often its running time. However, you cannot pay attention to running time alone. You must also be concerned with other factors such as the space required to run the program (both main memory and disk space). Typically you will analyze the *time* required for an *algorithm* (or the instantiation of an algorithm in the form of a program), and the *space* required for a *data structure*.

Many factors affect the running time of a program. Some relate to the environment in which the program is compiled and run. Such factors include the speed of the computer's CPU, bus, and peripheral hardware. Competition with other users for the computer's (or the network's) resources can make a program slow to a crawl. The programming language and the quality of code generated by a particular compiler can have a significant effect. The "coding efficiency" of the programmer who converts the algorithm to a program can have a tremendous impact as well.

If you need to get a program working within time and space constraints on a particular computer, all of these factors can be relevant. Yet, none of these factors address the differences between two algorithms or data structures. To be fair, programs derived from two algorithms for solving the same problem should both be compiled with the same compiler and run on the same computer under the same conditions. As much as possible, the same amount of care should be taken in the programming effort devoted to each program to make the implementations "equally efficient." In this sense, all of the factors mentioned above should cancel out of the comparison because they apply to both algorithms equally.

If you truly wish to understand the running time of an algorithm, there are other factors that are more appropriate to consider than machine speed, programming language, compiler, and so forth. Ideally we would measure the running time of the algorithm under standard benchmark conditions. However, we have no way to calculate the running time reliably other than to run an implementation of the algorithm on some computer. The only alternative is to use some other measure as a surrogate for running time.

Of primary consideration when estimating an algorithm's performance is the number of **basic operations** required by the algorithm to process an input of a certain **size**. The terms "basic operations" and "size" are both rather vague and depend on the algorithm being analyzed. Size is often the number of inputs processed. For example, when comparing sorting algorithms, the size of the problem is typically measured by the number of records to be sorted. A basic operation must have the property that its time to complete does not depend on the particular values of its operands. Adding or comparing two integer variables are examples of basic operations in most programming languages. Summing the contents of an array containing n integers is not, because the cost depends on the value of n (i.e., the size of the input).

Example 3.1 Consider a simple algorithm to solve the problem of finding the largest value in an array of n integers. The algorithm looks at each integer in turn, saving the position of the largest value seen so far. This algorithm is called the *largest-value sequential search* and is illustrated by the following function:

```
// Return position of largest value in "A" of size "n"
int largest(int A[], int n) {
  int currlarge = 0; // Holds largest element position
  for (int i=1; i<n; i++)    // For each array element
    if (A[currlarge] < A[i]) // if A[i] is larger
      currlarge = i;         //    remember its position
  return currlarge;          // Return largest position
}
```

Here, the size of the problem is **A.length**, the number of integers stored in array **A**. The basic operation is to compare an integer's value to that of the largest value seen so far. It is reasonable to assume that it takes a fixed amount of time to do one such comparison, regardless of the value of the two integers or their positions in the array.

Because the most important factor affecting running time is normally size of the input, for a given input size n we often express the time $\mathbf{T}$ to run the algorithm as a function of n, written as $\mathbf{T}(n)$. We will always assume $\mathbf{T}(n)$ is a non-negative value.

Let us call c the amount of time required to compare two integers in function **largest**. We do not care right now what the precise value of c might be. Nor are we concerned with the time required to increment variable i because this must be done for each value in the array, or the time for the actual assignment when a larger value is found, or the little bit of extra time taken to initialize **currlarge**. We just want a reasonable approximation for the time taken to execute the algorithm. The total time to run **largest** is therefore approximately cn, because we must make n comparisons, with each comparison costing c time. We say that function **largest** (and by extension ,the largest-value sequential search algorithm for any typical implementation) has a running time expressed by the equation

$$\mathbf{T}(n) = cn.$$

This equation describes the growth rate for the running time of the largest-value sequential search algorithm.

Example 3.2 The running time of a statement that assigns the first value of an integer array to a variable is simply the time required to copy the value of the first array value. We can assume this assignment takes a constant amount of time regardless of the value. Let us call c_1 the amount of time necessary to copy an integer. No matter how large the array on a typical computer (given reasonable conditions for memory and array size), the time to copy the value from the first position of the array is always c_1. Thus, the equation for this algorithm is simply

$$\mathbf{T}(n) = c_1,$$

indicating that the size of the input n has no effect on the running time. This is called a **constant** running time.

Example 3.3 Consider the following code:

```
sum = 0;
for (i=1; i<=n; i++)
   for (j=1; j<=n; j++)
      sum++;
```

What is the running time for this code fragment? Clearly it takes longer to run when n is larger. The basic operation in this example is the increment

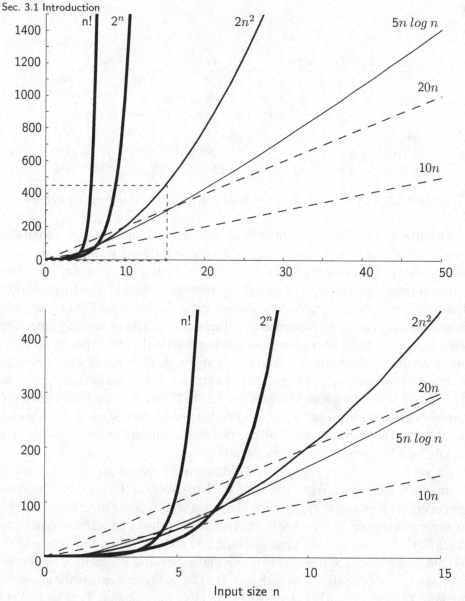

Figure 3.1 Two views of a graph illustrating the growth rates for six equations. The bottom view shows in detail the lower-left portion of the top view. The horizontal axis represents input size. The vertical axis can represent time, space, or any other measure of cost.

operation for variable *sum*. We can assume that incrementing takes constant time; call this time c_2. (We can ignore the time required to initialize *sum*, and to increment the loop counters i and j. In practice, these costs can safely be bundled into time c_2.) The total number of increment operations is n^2. Thus, we say that the running time is $\mathbf{T}(n) = c_2 n^2$.

n	log log n	log n	n	n log n	n^2	n^3	2^n
16	2	4	2^4	$2 \cdot 2^4 = 2^5$	2^8	2^{12}	2^{16}
256	3	8	2^8	$8 \cdot 2^8 = 2^{11}$	2^{16}	2^{24}	2^{256}
1024	≈ 3.3	10	2^{10}	$10 \cdot 2^{10} \approx 2^{13}$	2^{20}	2^{30}	2^{1024}
64K	4	16	2^{16}	$16 \cdot 2^{16} = 2^{20}$	2^{32}	2^{48}	2^{64K}
1M	≈ 4.3	20	2^{20}	$20 \cdot 2^{20} \approx 2^{24}$	2^{40}	2^{60}	2^{1M}
1G	≈ 4.9	30	2^{30}	$30 \cdot 2^{30} \approx 2^{35}$	2^{60}	2^{90}	2^{1G}

Figure 3.2 Costs for growth rates representative of most computer algorithms.

The **growth rate** for an algorithm is the rate at which the cost of the algorithm grows as the size of its input grows. Figure 3.1 shows a graph for six equations, each meant to describe the running time for a particular program or algorithm. A variety of growth rates representative of typical algorithms are shown. The two equations labeled $10n$ and $20n$ are graphed by straight lines. A growth rate of cn (for c any positive constant) is often referred to as a **linear** growth rate or running time. This means that as the value of n grows, the running time of the algorithm grows in the same proportion. Doubling the value of n roughly doubles the running time. An algorithm whose running-time equation has a highest-order term containing a factor of n^2 is said to have a **quadratic** growth rate. In Figure 3.1, the line labeled $2n^2$ represents a quadratic growth rate. The line labeled 2^n represents an **exponential** growth rate. This name comes from the fact that n appears in the exponent. The line labeled $n!$ is also growing exponentially.

As you can see from Figure 3.1, the difference between an algorithm whose running time has cost $\mathbf{T}(n) = 10n$ and another with cost $\mathbf{T}(n) = 2n^2$ becomes tremendous as n grows. For $n > 5$, the algorithm with running time $\mathbf{T}(n) = 2n^2$ is already much slower. This is despite the fact that $10n$ has a greater constant factor than $2n^2$. Comparing the two curves marked $20n$ and $2n^2$ shows that changing the constant factor for one of the equations only shifts the point at which the two curves cross. For $n > 10$, the algorithm with cost $\mathbf{T}(n) = 2n^2$ is slower than the algorithm with cost $\mathbf{T}(n) = 20n$. This graph also shows that the equation $\mathbf{T}(n) = 5n \log n$ grows somewhat more quickly than both $\mathbf{T}(n) = 10n$ and $\mathbf{T}(n) = 20n$, but not nearly so quickly as the equation $\mathbf{T}(n) = 2n^2$. For constants $a, b > 1$, n^a grows faster than either $\log^b n$ or $\log n^b$. Finally, algorithms with cost $\mathbf{T}(n) = 2^n$ or $\mathbf{T}(n) = n!$ are prohibitively expensive for even modest values of n. Note that for constants $a, b \geq 1$, a^n grows faster than n^b.

We can get some further insight into relative growth rates for various algorithms from Figure 3.2. Most of the growth rates that appear in typical algorithms are shown, along with some representative input sizes. Once again, we see that the growth rate has a tremendous effect on the resources consumed by an algorithm.

3.2 Best, Worst, and Average Cases

Consider the problem of finding the factorial of n. For this problem, there is only one input of a given "size" (that is, there is only a single instance for each size of n). Now consider our largest-value sequential search algorithm of Example 3.1, which always examines every array value. This algorithm works on many inputs of a given size n. That is, there are many possible arrays of any given size. However, no matter what array of size n that the algorithm looks at, its cost will always be the same in that it always looks at every element in the array one time.

For some algorithms, different inputs of a given size require different amounts of time. For example, consider the problem of searching an array containing n integers to find the one with a particular value K (assume that K appears exactly once in the array). The **sequential search** algorithm begins at the first position in the array and looks at each value in turn until K is found. Once K is found, the algorithm stops. This is different from the largest-value sequential search algorithm of Example 3.1, which always examines every array value.

There is a wide range of possible running times for the sequential search algorithm. The first integer in the array could have value K, and so only one integer is examined. In this case the running time is short. This is the **best case** for this algorithm, because it is not possible for sequential search to look at less than one value. Alternatively, if the last position in the array contains K, then the running time is relatively long, because the algorithm must examine n values. This is the **worst case** for this algorithm, because sequential search never looks at more than n values. If we implement sequential search as a program and run it many times on many different arrays of size n, or search for many different values of K within the same array, we expect the algorithm on average to go halfway through the array before finding the value we seek. On average, the algorithm examines about $n/2$ values. We call this the **average case** for this algorithm.

When analyzing an algorithm, should we study the best, worst, or average case? Normally we are not interested in the best case, because this might happen only rarely and generally is too optimistic for a fair characterization of the algorithm's running time. In other words, analysis based on the best case is not likely to be representative of the behavior of the algorithm. However, there are rare instances where a best-case analysis is useful — in particular, when the best case has high probability of occurring. In Chapter 7 you will see some examples where taking advantage of the best-case running time for one sorting algorithm makes a second more efficient.

How about the worst case? The advantage to analyzing the worst case is that you know for certain that the algorithm must perform at least that well. This is especially important for real-time applications, such as for the computers that monitor an air traffic control system. Here, it would not be acceptable to use an algorithm that can handle n airplanes quickly enough *most of the time*, but which fails to perform quickly enough when all n airplanes are coming from the same direction.

For other applications — particularly when we wish to aggregate the cost of running the program many times on many different inputs — worst-case analysis might not be a representative measure of the algorithm's performance. Often we prefer to know the average-case running time. This means that we would like to know the *typical* behavior of the algorithm on inputs of size n. Unfortunately, average-case analysis is not always possible. Average-case analysis first requires that we understand how the actual inputs to the program (and their costs) are distributed with respect to the set of all possible inputs to the program. For example, it was stated previously that the sequential search algorithm on average examines half of the array values. This is only true if the element with value K is equally likely to appear in any position in the array. If this assumption is not correct, then the algorithm does *not* necessarily examine half of the array values in the average case. See Section 9.2 for further discussion regarding the effects of data distribution on the sequential search algorithm.

The characteristics of a data distribution have a significant effect on many search algorithms, such as those based on hashing (Section 9.4) and search trees (e.g., see Section 5.4). Incorrect assumptions about data distribution can have disastrous consequences on a program's space or time performance. Unusual data distributions can also be used to advantage, as shown in Section 9.2.

In summary, for real-time applications we are likely to prefer a worst-case analysis of an algorithm. Otherwise, we often desire an average-case analysis if we know enough about the distribution of our input to compute the average case. If not, then we must resort to worst-case analysis.

3.3   A Faster Computer, or a Faster Algorithm?

Imagine that you have a problem to solve, and you know of an algorithm whose running time is proportional to n^2. Unfortunately, the resulting program takes ten times too long to run. If you replace your current computer with a new one that is ten times faster, will the n^2 algorithm become acceptable? If the problem size remains the same, then perhaps the faster computer will allow you to get your work done quickly enough even with an algorithm having a high growth rate. But a funny thing happens to most people who get a faster computer. They don't run the same problem faster. They run a bigger problem! Say that on your old computer you were content to sort 10,000 records because that could be done by the computer during your lunch break. On your new computer you might hope to sort 100,000 records in the same time. You won't be back from lunch any sooner, so you are better off solving a larger problem. And because the new machine is ten times faster, you would like to sort ten times as many records.

f(n)	n	n'	Change	n'/n
10n	1000	10,000	$n' = 10n$	10
20n	500	5000	$n' = 10n$	10
5n log n	250	1842	$\sqrt{10}n < n' < 10n$	7.37
$2n^2$	70	223	$n' = \sqrt{10}n$	3.16
2^n	13	16	$n' = n + 3$	--

Figure 3.3 The increase in problem size that can be run in a fixed period of time on a computer that is ten times faster. The first column lists the right-hand sides for each of five growth rate equations from Figure 3.1. For the purpose of this example, arbitrarily assume that the old machine can run 10,000 basic operations in one hour. The second column shows the maximum value for n that can be run in 10,000 basic operations on the old machine. The third column shows the value for n', the new maximum size for the problem that can be run in the same time on the new machine that is ten times faster. Variable n' is the greatest size for the problem that can run in 100,000 basic operations. The fourth column shows how the size of n changed to become n' on the new machine. The fifth column shows the increase in the problem size as the ratio of n' to n.

If your algorithm's growth rate is linear (i.e., if the equation that describes the running time on input size n is $\mathbf{T}(n) = cn$ for some constant c), then 100,000 records on the new machine will be sorted in the same time as 10,000 records on the old machine. If the algorithm's growth rate is greater than cn, such as $c_1 n^2$, then you will *not* be able to do a problem ten times the size in the same amount of time on a machine that is ten times faster.

How much larger a problem can be solved in a given amount of time by a faster computer? Assume that the new machine is ten times faster than the old. Say that the old machine could solve a problem of size n in an hour. What is the largest problem that the new machine can solve in one hour? Figure 3.3 shows how large a problem can be solved on the two machines for five of the running-time functions from Figure 3.1.

This table illustrates many important points. The first two equations are both linear; only the value of the constant factor has changed. In both cases, the machine that is ten times faster gives an increase in problem size by a factor of ten. In other words, while the value of the constant does affect the absolute size of the problem that can be solved in a fixed amount of time, it does not affect the *improvement* in problem size (as a proportion to the original size) gained by a faster computer. This relationship holds true regardless of the algorithm's growth rate: Constant factors never affect the relative improvement gained by a faster computer.

An algorithm with time equation $\mathbf{T}(n) = 2n^2$ does not receive nearly as great an improvement from the faster machine as an algorithm with linear growth rate. Instead of an improvement by a factor of ten, the improvement is only the square root of that: $\sqrt{10} \approx 3.16$. Thus, the algorithm with higher growth rate not only solves a smaller problem in a given time in the first place, it *also* receives less of a speedup from a faster computer. As computers get ever faster, the disparity in problem sizes becomes ever greater.

The algorithm with growth rate $\mathbf{T}(n) = 5n \log n$ improves by a greater amount than the one with quadratic growth rate, but not by as great an amount as the algorithms with linear growth rates.

Note that something special happens in the case of the algorithm whose running time grows exponentially. In Figure 3.1, the curve for the algorithm whose time is proportional to 2^n goes up very quickly. In Figure 3.3, the increase in problem size on the machine ten times as fast is shown to be about $n + 3$ (to be precise, it is $n + \log_2 10$). The increase in problem size for an algorithm with exponential growth rate is by a constant addition, not by a multiplicative factor. Because the old value of n was 13, the new problem size is 16. If next year you buy another computer ten times faster yet, then the new computer (100 times faster than the original computer) will only run a problem of size 19. If you had a second program whose growth rate is 2^n and for which the original computer could run a problem of size 1000 in an hour, than a machine ten times faster can run a problem only of size 1003 in an hour! Thus, an exponential growth rate is radically different than the other growth rates shown in Figure 3.3. The significance of this difference is explored in Chapter 17.

Instead of buying a faster computer, consider what happens if you replace an algorithm whose running time is proportional to n^2 with a new algorithm whose running time is proportional to $n \log n$. In the graph of Figure 3.1, a fixed amount of time would appear as a horizontal line. If the line for the amount of time available to solve your problem is above the point at which the curves for the two growth rates in question meet, then the algorithm whose running time grows less quickly is faster. An algorithm with running time $\mathbf{T}(n) = n^2$ requires $1024 \times 1024 = 1,048,576$ time steps for an input of size $n = 1024$. An algorithm with running time $\mathbf{T}(n) = n \log n$ requires $1024 \times 10 = 10,240$ time steps for an input of size $n = 1024$, which is an improvement of much more than a factor of ten when compared to the algorithm with running time $\mathbf{T}(n) = n^2$. Because $n^2 > 10n \log n$ whenever $n > 58$, if the typical problem size is larger than 58 for this example, then you would be much better off changing algorithms instead of buying a computer ten times faster. Furthermore, when you do buy a faster computer, an algorithm with a slower growth rate provides a greater benefit in terms of larger problem size that can run in a certain time on the new computer.

3.4   Asymptotic Analysis

Despite the larger constant for the curve labeled $10n$ in Figure 3.1, $2n^2$ crosses it at the relatively small value of $n = 5$. What if we double the value of the constant in front of the linear equation? As shown in the graph, $20n$ is surpassed by $2n^2$ once $n = 10$. The additional factor of two for the linear growth rate does not much matter. It only doubles the x-coordinate for the intersection point. In general, changes to a constant factor in either equation only shift *where* the two curves cross, not *whether* the two curves cross.

When you buy a faster computer or a faster compiler, the new problem size that can be run in a given amount of time for a given growth rate is larger by the same factor, regardless of the constant on the running-time equation. The time curves for two algorithms with different growth rates still cross, regardless of their running-time equation constants. For these reasons, we usually ignore the constants when we want an estimate of the growth rate for the running time or other resource requirements of an algorithm. This simplifies the analysis and keeps us thinking about the most important aspect: the growth rate. This is called **asymptotic algorithm analysis**. To be precise, asymptotic analysis refers to the study of an algorithm as the input size "gets big" or reaches a limit (in the calculus sense). However, it has proved to be so useful to ignore all constant factors that asymptotic analysis is used for most algorithm comparisons.

It is not always reasonable to ignore the constants. When comparing algorithms meant to run on small values of n, the constant can have a large effect. For example, if the problem is to sort a collection of exactly five records, then an algorithm designed for sorting thousands of records is probably not appropriate, even if its asymptotic analysis indicates good performance. There are rare cases where the constants for two algorithms under comparison can differ by a factor of 1000 or more, making the one with lower growth rate impractical for most purposes due to its large constant. Asymptotic analysis is a form of "back of the envelope" estimation for algorithm resource consumption. It provides a simplified model of the running time or other resource needs of an algorithm. This simplification usually helps you understand the behavior of your algorithms. Just be aware of the limitations to asymptotic analysis in the rare situation where the constant is important.

3.4.1   Upper Bounds

Several terms are used to describe the running-time equation for an algorithm. These terms — and their associated symbols — indicate precisely what aspect of the algorithm's behavior is being described. One is the **upper bound** for the growth of the algorithm's running time. It indicates the upper or highest growth rate that the algorithm can have.

Because the phrase "has an upper bound to its growth rate of $f(n)$" is long and often used when discussing algorithms, we adopt a special notation, called **big-Oh notation**. If the upper bound for an algorithm's growth rate (for, say, the worst case) is $f(n)$, then we would write that this algorithm is "in the set $O(f(n))$ in the worst case" (or just "in $O(f(n))$ in the worst case"). For example, if n^2 grows as fast as $\mathbf{T}(n)$ (the running time of our algorithm) for the worst-case input, we would say the algorithm is "in $O(n^2)$ in the worst case."

The following is a precise definition for an upper bound. $\mathbf{T}(n)$ represents the true running time of the algorithm. $f(n)$ is some expression for the upper bound.

> For $\mathbf{T}(n)$ a non-negatively valued function, $\mathbf{T}(n)$ is in set $O(f(n))$ if there exist two positive constants c and n_0 such that $\mathbf{T}(n) \leq cf(n)$ for all $n > n_0$.

Constant n_0 is the smallest value of n for which the claim of an upper bound holds true. Usually n_0 is small, such as 1, but does not need to be. You must also be able to pick some constant c, but it is irrelevant what the value for c actually is. In other words, the definition says that for *all* inputs of the type in question (such as the worst case for all inputs of size n) that are large enough (i.e., $n > n_0$), the algorithm *always* executes in less than $cf(n)$ steps for some constant c.

Example 3.4 Consider the sequential search algorithm for finding a specified value in an array of integers. If visiting and examining one value in the array requires c_s steps where c_s is a positive number, and if the value we search for has equal probability of appearing in any position in the array, then in the average case $\mathbf{T}(n) = c_s n/2$. For all values of $n > 1$, $c_s n/2 \leq c_s n$. Therefore, by the definition, $\mathbf{T}(n)$ is in $O(n)$ for $n_0 = 1$ and $c = c_s$.

Example 3.5 For a particular algorithm, $\mathbf{T}(n) = c_1 n^2 + c_2 n$ in the average case where c_1 and c_2 are positive numbers. Then, $c_1 n^2 + c_2 n \leq c_1 n^2 + c_2 n^2 \leq (c_1 + c_2) n^2$ for all $n > 1$. So, $\mathbf{T}(n) \leq c n^2$ for $c = c_1 + c_2$, and $n_0 = 1$. Therefore, $\mathbf{T}(n)$ is in $O(n^2)$ by the second definition.

Example 3.6 Assigning the value from the first position of an array to a variable takes constant time regardless of the size of the array. Thus, $\mathbf{T}(n) = c$ (for the best, worst, and average cases). We could say in this case that $\mathbf{T}(n)$ is in $O(c)$. However, it is traditional to say that an algorithm whose running time has a constant upper bound is in $O(1)$.

If someone asked you out of the blue "Who is the best?" your natural reaction should be to reply "Best at what?" In the same way, if you are asked "What is the growth rate of this algorithm," you would need to ask "When? Best case? Average case? Or worst case?" Some algorithms have the same behavior no matter which input instance they receive. An example is finding the maximum in an array of integers. But for many algorithms, it makes a big difference, such as when searching an unsorted array for a particular value. So any statement about the upper bound of an algorithm must be in the context of some class of inputs of size n. We measure this upper bound nearly always on the best-case, average-case, or worst-case inputs. Thus, we cannot say, "this algorithm has an upper bound to its growth rate of n^2." We must say something like, "this algorithm has an upper bound to its growth rate of n^2 *in the average case*."

Knowing that something is in $O(f(n))$ says only how bad things can be. Perhaps things are not nearly so bad. Because sequential search is in $O(n)$ in the worst case, it is also true to say that sequential search is in $O(n^2)$. But sequential search is practical for large n, in a way that is not true for some other algorithms in $O(n^2)$. We always seek to define the running time of an algorithm with the tightest (lowest) possible upper bound. Thus, we prefer to say that sequential search is in $O(n)$. This also explains why the phrase "is in $O(f(n))$" or the notation "$\in O(f(n))$" is used instead of "is $O(f(n))$" or "$= O(f(n))$." There is no strict equality to the use of big-Oh notation. $O(n)$ is in $O(n^2)$, but $O(n^2)$ is not in $O(n)$.

3.4.2 Lower Bounds

Big-Oh notation describes an upper bound. In other words, big-Oh notation states a claim about the greatest amount of some resource (usually time) that is required by an algorithm for some class of inputs of size n (typically the worst such input, the average of all possible inputs, or the best such input).

Similar notation is used to describe the least amount of a resource that an algorithm needs for some class of input. Like big-Oh notation, this is a measure of the algorithm's growth rate. Like big-Oh notation, it works for any resource, but we most often measure the least amount of time required. And again, like big-Oh notation, we are measuring the resource required for some particular class of inputs: the worst-, average-, or best-case input of size n.

The lower bound for an algorithm (or a problem, as explained later) is denoted by the symbol Ω, pronounced "big-Omega" or just "Omega." The following definition for Ω is symmetric with the definition of big-Oh.

> For $\mathbf{T}(n)$ a non-negatively valued function, $\mathbf{T}(n)$ is in set $\Omega(g(n))$
> if there exist two positive constants c and n_0 such that $\mathbf{T}(n) \geq cg(n)$
> for all $n > n_0$.[1]

---

[1] An alternate (non-equivalent) definition for Ω is

Example 3.7 Assume $\mathbf{T}(n) = c_1 n^2 + c_2 n$ for c_1 and $c_2 > 0$. Then,

$$c_1 n^2 + c_2 n \geq c_1 n^2$$

for all $n > 1$. So, $\mathbf{T}(n) \geq cn^2$ for $c = c_1$ and $n_0 = 1$. Therefore, $\mathbf{T}(n)$ is in $\Omega(n^2)$ by the definition.

It is also true that the equation of Example 3.7 is in $\Omega(n)$. However, as with big-Oh notation, we wish to get the "tightest" (for Ω notation, the largest) bound possible. Thus, we prefer to say that this running time is in $\Omega(n^2)$.

Recall the sequential search algorithm to find a value K within an array of integers. In the average and worst cases this algorithm is in $\Omega(n)$, because in both the average and worst cases we must examine *at least* cn values (where c is $1/2$ in the average case and 1 in the worst case).

3.4.3 Θ Notation

The definitions for big-Oh and Ω give us ways to describe the upper bound for an algorithm (if we can find an equation for the maximum cost of a particular class of inputs of size n) and the lower bound for an algorithm (if we can find an equation for the minimum cost for a particular class of inputs of size n). When the upper and lower bounds are the same within a constant factor, we indicate this by using Θ (big-Theta) notation. An algorithm is said to be $\Theta(h(n))$ if it is in $\mathrm{O}(h(n))$ *and*

$\mathbf{T}(n)$ is in the set $\Omega(g(n))$ if there exists a positive constant c such that $\mathbf{T}(n) \geq cg(n)$ for an infinite number of values for n.

This definition says that for an "interesting" number of cases, the algorithm takes at least $cg(n)$ time. Note that this definition is *not* symmetric with the definition of big-Oh. For $g(n)$ to be a lower bound, this definition *does not* require that $\mathbf{T}(n) \geq cg(n)$ for all values of n greater than some constant. It only requires that this happen often enough, in particular that it happen for an infinite number of values for n. Motivation for this alternate definition can be found in the following example. Assume a particular algorithm has the following behavior:

$$\mathbf{T}(n) = \begin{cases} n & \text{for all odd } n \geq 1 \\ n^2/100 & \text{for all even } n \geq 0 \end{cases}$$

From this definition, $n^2/100 \geq \frac{1}{100}n^2$ for all even $n \geq 0$. So, $\mathbf{T}(n) \geq cn^2$ for an infinite number of values of n (i.e., for all even n) for $c = 1/100$. Therefore, $\mathbf{T}(n)$ is in $\Omega(n^2)$ by the definition.

For this equation for $\mathbf{T}(n)$, it is true that all inputs of size n take at least cn time. But an infinite number of inputs of size n take cn^2 time, so we would like to say that the algorithm is in $\Omega(n^2)$. Unfortunately, using our first definition will yield a lower bound of $\Omega(n)$ because it is not possible to pick constants c and n_0 such that $\mathbf{T}(n) \geq cn^2$ for all $n > n_0$. The alternative definition does result in a lower bound of $\Omega(n^2)$ for this algorithm, which seems to fit common sense more closely. Fortunately, few real algorithms or computer programs display the pathological behavior of this example. Our first definition for Ω generally yields the expected result.

As you can see from this discussion, asymptotic bounds notation is not a law of nature. It is merely a powerful modeling tool used to describe the behavior of algorithms.

it is in $\Omega(h(n))$. Note that we drop the word "in" for Θ notation, because there is a strict equality for two equations with the same Θ. In other words, if $f(n)$ is $\Theta(g(n))$, then $g(n)$ is $\Theta(f(n))$.

Because the sequential search algorithm is both in $O(n)$ and in $\Omega(n)$ in the average case, we say it is $\Theta(n)$ in the average case.

Given an algebraic equation describing the time requirement for an algorithm, the upper and lower bounds always meet. That is because in some sense we have a perfect analysis for the algorithm, embodied by the running-time equation. For many algorithms (or their instantiations as programs), it is easy to come up with the equation that defines their runtime behavior. Most algorithms presented in this book are well understood and we can almost always give a Θ analysis for them. However, Chapter 17 discusses a whole class of algorithms for which we have no Θ analysis, just some unsatisfying big-Oh and Ω analyses. Exercise 3.14 presents a short, simple program fragment for which nobody currently knows the true upper or lower bounds.

While some textbooks and programmers will casually say that an algorithm is "order of" or "big-Oh" of some cost function, it is generally better to use Θ notation rather than big-Oh notation whenever we have sufficient knowledge about an algorithm to be sure that the upper and lower bounds indeed match. Throughout this book, Θ notation will be used in preference to big-Oh notation whenever our state of knowledge makes that possible. Limitations on our ability to analyze certain algorithms may require use of big-Oh or Ω notations. In rare occasions when the discussion is explicitly about the upper or lower bound of a problem or algorithm, the corresponding notation will be used in preference to Θ notation.

3.4.4 Simplifying Rules

Once you determine the running-time equation for an algorithm, it really is a simple matter to derive the big-Oh, Ω, and Θ expressions from the equation. You do not need to resort to the formal definitions of asymptotic analysis. Instead, you can use the following rules to determine the simplest form.

1. If $f(n)$ is in $O(g(n))$ and $g(n)$ is in $O(h(n))$, then $f(n)$ is in $O(h(n))$.
2. If $f(n)$ is in $O(kg(n))$ for any constant $k > 0$, then $f(n)$ is in $O(g(n))$.
3. If $f_1(n)$ is in $O(g_1(n))$ and $f_2(n)$ is in $O(g_2(n))$, then $f_1(n) + f_2(n)$ is in $O(\max(g_1(n), g_2(n)))$.
4. If $f_1(n)$ is in $O(g_1(n))$ and $f_2(n)$ is in $O(g_2(n))$, then $f_1(n)f_2(n)$ is in $O(g_1(n)g_2(n))$.

The first rule says that if some function $g(n)$ is an upper bound for your cost function, then any upper bound for $g(n)$ is also an upper bound for your cost function. A similar property holds true for Ω notation: If $g(n)$ is a lower bound for your cost function, then any lower bound for $g(n)$ is also a lower bound for your cost function. Likewise for Θ notation.

The significance of rule (2) is that you can ignore any multiplicative constants in your equations when using big-Oh notation. This rule also holds true for Ω and Θ notations.

Rule (3) says that given two parts of a program run in sequence (whether two statements or two sections of code), you need consider only the more expensive part. This rule applies to Ω and Θ notations as well: For both, you need consider only the more expensive part.

Rule (4) is used to analyze simple loops in programs. If some action is repeated some number of times, and each repetition has the same cost, then the total cost is the cost of the action multiplied by the number of times that the action takes place. This rule applies to Ω and Θ notations as well.

Taking the first three rules collectively, you can ignore all constants and all lower-order terms to determine the asymptotic growth rate for any cost function. The advantages and dangers of ignoring constants were discussed near the beginning of this section. Ignoring lower-order terms is reasonable when performing an asymptotic analysis. The higher-order terms soon swamp the lower-order terms in their contribution to the total cost as n becomes larger. Thus, if $\mathbf{T}(n) = 3n^4 + 5n^2$, then $\mathbf{T}(n)$ is in $O(n^4)$. The n^2 term contributes relatively little to the total cost for large n.

Throughout the rest of this book, these simplifying rules are used when discussing the cost for a program or algorithm.

3.4.5 Classifying Functions

Given functions $f(n)$ and $g(n)$ whose growth rates are expressed as algebraic equations, we might like to determine if one grows faster than the other. The best way to do this is to take the limit of the two functions as n grows towards infinity,

$$\lim_{n \to \infty} \frac{f(n)}{g(n)}.$$

If the limit goes to ∞, then $f(n)$ is in $\Omega(g(n))$ because $f(n)$ grows faster. If the limit goes to zero, then $f(n)$ is in $O(g(n))$ because $g(n)$ grows faster. If the limit goes to some constant other than zero, then $f(n) = \Theta(g(n))$ because both grow at the same rate.

Example 3.8 If $f(n) = 2n \log n$ and $g(n) = n^2$, is $f(n)$ in $O(g(n))$, $\Omega(g(n))$, or $\Theta(g(n))$? Because

$$\frac{n^2}{2n \log n} = \frac{n}{2 \log n},$$

we easily see that

$$\lim_{n \to \infty} \frac{n^2}{2n \log n} = \infty$$

because n grows faster than $2 \log n$. Thus, n^2 is in $\Omega(2n \log n)$.

3.5   Calculating the Running Time for a Program

This section presents the analysis for several simple code fragments.

Example 3.9 We begin with an analysis of a simple assignment to an integer variable.

```
a = b;
```

Because the assignment statement takes constant time, it is $\Theta(1)$.

Example 3.10 Consider a simple **for** loop.

```
sum = 0;
for (i=1; i<=n; i++)
   sum += n;
```

The first line is $\Theta(1)$. The **for** loop is repeated n times. The third line takes constant time so, by simplifying rule (4) of Section 3.4.4, the total cost for executing the two lines making up the **for** loop is $\Theta(n)$. By rule (3), the cost of the entire code fragment is also $\Theta(n)$.

Example 3.11 We now analyze a code fragment with several **for** loops, some of which are nested.

```
sum = 0;
for (i=1; i<=n; i++)       // First for loop
   for (j=1; j<=i; j++)    //    is a double loop
      sum++;
for (k=0; k<n; k++)        // Second for loop
   A[k] = k;
```

This code fragment has three separate statements: the first assignment statement and the two **for** loops. Again the assignment statement takes constant time; call it c_1. The second **for** loop is just like the one in Example 3.10 and takes $c_2 n = \Theta(n)$ time.

The first **for** loop is a double loop and requires a special technique. We work from the inside of the loop outward. The expression **sum++** requires constant time; call it c_3. Because the inner **for** loop is executed i times, by simplifying rule (4) it has cost $c_3 i$. The outer **for** loop is executed n times, but each time the cost of the inner loop is different because it costs $c_3 i$ with i changing each time. You should see that for the first execution of the outer loop, i is 1. For the second execution of the outer loop, i is 2. Each time through the outer loop, i becomes one greater, until the last time through the loop when $i = n$. Thus, the total cost of the loop is c_3 times the sum of the integers 1 through n. From Equation 2.1, we know that

$$\sum_{i=1}^{n} i = \frac{n(n+1)}{2},$$

which is $\Theta(n^2)$. By simplifying rule (3), $\Theta(c_1 + c_2 n + c_3 n^2)$ is simply $\Theta(n^2)$.

Example 3.12 Compare the asymptotic analysis for the following two code fragments:

```
sum1 = 0;
for (i=1; i<=n; i++)        // First double loop
   for (j=1; j<=n; j++)     //    do n times
      sum1++;

sum2 = 0;
for (i=1; i<=n; i++)        // Second double loop
   for (j=1; j<=i; j++)     //    do i times
      sum2++;
```

In the first double loop, the inner **for** loop always executes n times. Because the outer loop executes n times, it should be obvious that the statement **sum1++** is executed precisely n^2 times. The second loop is similar to the one analyzed in the previous example, with cost $\sum_{j=1}^{n} j$. This is approximately $\frac{1}{2}n^2$. Thus, both double loops cost $\Theta(n^2)$, though the second requires about half the time of the first.

Example 3.13 Not all doubly nested **for** loops are $\Theta(n^2)$. The following pair of nested loops illustrates this fact.

```
sum1 = 0;
for (k=1; k<=n; k*=2)       // Do log n times
   for (j=1; j<=n; j++)     // Do n times
      sum1++;

sum2 = 0;
for (k=1; k<=n; k*=2)       // Do log n times
   for (j=1; j<=k; j++)     // Do k times
      sum2++;
```

When analyzing these two code fragments, we will assume that n is a power of two. The first code fragment has its outer **for** loop executed $\log n + 1$ times because on each iteration k is multiplied by two until it reaches n. Because the inner loop always executes n times, the total cost for the first code fragment can be expressed as $\sum_{i=0}^{\log n} n$. Note that a variable substitution takes place here to create the summation, with $k = 2^i$. From Equation 2.3, the solution for this summation is $\Theta(n \log n)$. In the second code fragment, the outer loop is also executed $\log n + 1$ times. The inner loop has cost k, which doubles each time. The summation can be expressed as $\sum_{i=0}^{\log n} 2^i$ where n is assumed to be a power of two and again $k = 2^i$. From Equation 2.8, we know that this summation is simply $\Theta(n)$.

What about other control statements? **While** loops are analyzed in a manner similar to **for** loops. The cost of an **if** statement in the worst case is the greater of the costs for the **then** and **else** clauses. This is also true for the average case, assuming that the size of n does not affect the probability of executing one of the clauses (which is usually, but not necessarily, true). For **switch** statements, the worst-case cost is that of the most expensive branch. For subroutine calls, simply add the cost of executing the subroutine.

There are rare situations in which the probability for executing the various branches of an **if** or **switch** statement are functions of the input size. For example, for input of size n, the **then** clause of an **if** statement might be executed with probability $1/n$. An example would be an **if** statement that executes the **then** clause only for the smallest of n values. To perform an average-case analysis for such programs, we cannot simply count the cost of the **if** statement as being the cost of the more expensive branch. In such situations, the technique of amortized analysis (see Section 14.3) can come to the rescue.

Determining the execution time of a recursive subroutine can be difficult. The running time for a recursive subroutine is typically best expressed by a recurrence relation. For example, the recursive factorial function **fact** of Section 2.5 calls itself with a value one less than its input value. The result of this recursive call is then multiplied by the input value, which takes constant time. Thus, the cost of the factorial function, if we wish to measure cost in terms of the number of multiplication operations, is one more than the number of multiplications made by the recursive call on the smaller input. Because the base case does no multiplications, its cost is zero. Thus, the running time for this function can be expressed as

$$\mathbf{T}(n) = \mathbf{T}(n-1) + 1 \text{ for } n > 1; \quad T(1) = 0.$$

We know from Examples 2.8 and 2.13 that the closed-form solution for this recurrence relation is $\Theta(n)$.

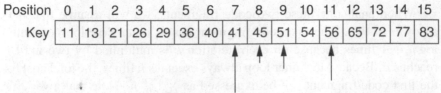

Figure 3.4 An illustration of binary search on a sorted array of 16 positions. Consider a search for the position with value $K = 45$. Binary search first checks the value at position 7. Because $41 < K$, the desired value cannot appear in any position below 7 in the array. Next, binary search checks the value at position 11. Because $56 > K$, the desired value (if it exists) must be between positions 7 and 11. Position 9 is checked next. Again, its value is too great. The final search is at position 8, which contains the desired value. Thus, function **binary** returns position 8. Alternatively, if K were 44, then the same series of record accesses would be made. After checking position 8, **binary** would return a value of n, indicating that the search is unsuccessful.

The final example of algorithm analysis for this section will compare two algorithms for performing search in an array. Earlier, we determined that the running time for sequential search on an array where the search value K is equally likely to appear in any location is $\Theta(n)$ in both the average and worst cases. We would like to compare this running time to that required to perform a **binary search** on an array whose values are stored in order from lowest to highest.

Binary search begins by examining the value in the middle position of the array; call this position mid and the corresponding value k_{mid}. If $k_{mid} = K$, then processing can stop immediately. This is unlikely to be the case, however. Fortunately, knowing the middle value provides useful information that can help guide the search process. In particular, if $k_{mid} > K$, then you know that the value K cannot appear in the array at any position greater than mid. Thus, you can eliminate future search in the upper half of the array. Conversely, if $k_{mid} < K$, then you know that you can ignore all positions in the array less than mid. Either way, half of the positions are eliminated from further consideration. Binary search next looks at the middle position in that part of the array where value K may exist. The value at this position again allows us to eliminate half of the remaining positions from consideration. This process repeats until either the desired value is found, or there are no positions remaining in the array that might contain the value K. Figure 3.4 illustrates the binary search method. Figure 3.5 shows an implementation for binary search.

To find the cost of this algorithm in the worst case, we can model the running time as a recurrence and then find the closed-form solution. Each recursive call to **binary** cuts the size of the array approximately in half, so we can model the worst-case cost as follows, assuming for simplicity that n is a power of two.

$$\mathbf{T}(n) = \mathbf{T}(n/2) + 1 \text{ for } n > 1; \quad \mathbf{T}(1) = 1.$$

```
// Return the position of an element in sorted array "A" of
// size "n" with value "K".  If "K" is not in "A", return
// the value "n".
int binary(int A[], int n, int K) {
  int l = -1;
  int r = n;                  // l and r are beyond array bounds
  while (l+1 != r) {  // Stop when l and r meet
    int i = (l+r)/2;   // Check middle of remaining subarray
    if (K < A[i]) r = i;       // In left half
    if (K == A[i]) return i; // Found it
    if (K > A[i]) l = i;       // In right half
  }
  return n; // Search value not in A
}
```

Figure 3.5 Implementation for binary search.

If we expand the recurrence, we find that we can do so only $\log n$ times before we reach the base case, and each expansion adds one to the cost. Thus, the closed-form solution for the recurrence is $\mathbf{T}(n) = \log n$.

Function **binary** is designed to find the (single) occurrence of K and return its position. A special value is returned if K does not appear in the array. This algorithm can be modified to implement variations such as returning the position of the first occurrence of K in the array if multiple occurrences are allowed, and returning the position of the greatest value less than K when K is not in the array.

Comparing sequential search to binary search, we see that as n grows, the $\Theta(n)$ running time for sequential search in the average and worst cases quickly becomes much greater than the $\Theta(\log n)$ running time for binary search. Taken in isolation, binary search appears to be much more efficient than sequential search. This is despite the fact that the constant factor for binary search is greater than that for sequential search, because the calculation for the next search position in binary search is more expensive than just incrementing the current position, as sequential search does.

Note however that the running time for sequential search will be roughly the same regardless of whether or not the array values are stored in order. In contrast, binary search requires that the array values be ordered from lowest to highest. Depending on the context in which binary search is to be used, this requirement for a sorted array could be detrimental to the running time of a complete program, because maintaining the values in sorted order requires to greater cost when inserting new elements into the array. This is an example of a tradeoff between the advantage of binary search during search and the disadvantage related to maintaining a sorted array. Only in the context of the complete problem to be solved can we know whether the advantage outweighs the disadvantage.

3.6   Analyzing Problems

You most often use the techniques of "algorithm" analysis to analyze an algorithm, or the instantiation of an algorithm as a program. You can also use these same techniques to analyze the cost of a problem. It should make sense to you to say that the upper bound for a problem cannot be worse than the upper bound for the best algorithm that we know for that problem. But what does it mean to give a lower bound for a problem?

Consider a graph of cost over all inputs of a given size n for some algorithm for a given problem. Define $\mathcal{A}$ to be the collection of all algorithms that solve the problem (theoretically, there are an infinite number of such algorithms). Now, consider the collection of all the graphs for all of the (infinitely many) algorithms in $\mathcal{A}$. The worst case lower bound is the *least* of all the *highest* points on all the graphs.

It is much easier to show that an algorithm (or program) is in $\Omega(f(n))$ than it is to show that a problem is in $\Omega(f(n))$. For a problem to be in $\Omega(f(n))$ means that *every* algorithm that solves the problem is in $\Omega(f(n))$, even algorithms that we have not thought of!

So far all of our examples of algorithm analysis give "obvious" results, with big-Oh always matching Ω. To understand how big-Oh, Ω, and Θ notations are properly used to describe our understanding of a problem or an algorithm, it is best to consider an example where you do not already know a lot about the problem.

Let us look ahead to analyzing the problem of sorting to see how this process works. What is the least possible cost for any sorting algorithm in the worst case? The algorithm must at least look at every element in the input, just to determine that the input is truly sorted. Thus, any sorting algorithm must take at least cn time. For many problems, this observation that each of the n inputs must be looked at leads to an easy $\Omega(n)$ lower bound.

In your previous study of computer science, you have probably seen an example of a sorting algorithm whose running time is in $O(n^2)$ in the worst case. The simple Bubble Sort and Insertion Sort algorithms typically given as examples in a first year programming course have worst case running times in $O(n^2)$. Thus, the problem of sorting can be said to have an upper bound in $O(n^2)$. How do we close the gap between $\Omega(n)$ and $O(n^2)$? Can there be a better sorting algorithm? If you can think of no algorithm whose worst-case growth rate is better than $O(n^2)$, and if you have discovered no analysis technique to show that the least cost for the problem of sorting in the worst case is greater than $\Omega(n)$, then you cannot know for sure whether or not there is a better algorithm.

Chapter 7 presents sorting algorithms whose running time is in $O(n \log n)$ for the worst case. This greatly narrows the gap. With this new knowledge, we now have a lower bound in $\Omega(n)$ and an upper bound in $O(n \log n)$. Should we search for a faster algorithm? Many have tried, without success. Fortunately (or perhaps unfortunately?), Chapter 7 also includes a proof that any sorting algorithm must have running time in $\Omega(n \log n)$ in the worst case.[2] This proof is one of the most important results in the field of algorithm analysis, and it means that no sorting algorithm can possibly run faster than $cn \log n$ for the worst-case input of size n. Thus, we can conclude that the problem of sorting is $\Theta(n \log n)$ in the worst case, because the upper and lower bounds have met.

Knowing the lower bound for a problem does not give you a good algorithm. But it does help you to know when to stop looking. If the lower bound for the problem matches the upper bound for the algorithm (within a constant factor), then we know that we can find an algorithm that is better only by a constant factor.

3.7 Common Misunderstandings

Asymptotic analysis is one of the most intellectually difficult topics that undergraduate computer science majors are confronted with. Most people find growth rates and asymptotic analysis confusing and so develop misconceptions about either the concepts or the terminology. It helps to know what the standard points of confusion are, in hopes of avoiding them.

One problem with differentiating the concepts of upper and lower bounds is that, for most algorithms that you will encounter, it is easy to recognize the true growth rate for that algorithm. Given complete knowledge about a cost function, the upper and lower bound for that cost function are always the same. Thus, the distinction between an upper and a lower bound is only worthwhile when you have incomplete knowledge about the thing being measured. If this distinction is still not clear, reread Section 3.6. We use Θ-notation to indicate that there is no meaningful difference between what we know about the growth rates of the upper and lower bound (which is usually the case for simple algorithms).

It is a common mistake to confuse the concepts of upper bound or lower bound on the one hand, and worst case or best case on the other. The best, worst, or average cases each give us a concrete input instance (or concrete set of instances) that we can apply to an algorithm description to get a cost measure. The upper and lower bounds describe our understanding of the *growth rate* for that cost measure. So to define the growth rate for an algorithm or problem, we need to determine what we are measuring (the best, worst, or average case) and also our description for what we know about the growth rate of that cost measure (big-Oh, Ω, or Θ).

The upper bound for an algorithm is not the same as the worst case for that algorithm for a given input of size n. What is being bounded is not the actual cost (which you can determine for a given value of n), but rather the *growth rate* for the

---

[2]While it is fortunate to know the truth, it is unfortunate that sorting is $\Theta(n \log n)$ rather than $\Theta(n)$!

cost. There cannot be a growth rate for a single point, such as a particular value of n. The growth *rate* applies to the *change* in cost as a *change* in input size occurs. Likewise, the lower bound is not the same as the best case for a given size n.

Another common misconception is thinking that the best case for an algorithm occurs when the input size is as small as possible, or that the worst case occurs when the input size is as large as possible. What is correct is that best- and worse-case instances exist for each possible size of input. That is, for all inputs of a given size, say i, one (or more) of the inputs of size i is the best and one (or more) of the inputs of size i is the worst. Often (but not always!), we can characterize the best input case for an arbitrary size, and we can characterize the worst input case for an arbitrary size. Ideally, we can determine the growth rate for the characterized best, worst, and average cases as the input size grows.

Example 3.14 What is the growth rate of the best case for sequential search? For any array of size n, the best case occurs when the value we are looking for appears in the first position of the array. This is true regardless of the size of the array. Thus, the best case (for arbitrary size n) occurs when the desired value is in the first of n positions, and its cost is 1. It is *not* correct to say that the best case occurs when $n = 1$.

Example 3.15 Imagine drawing a graph to show the cost of finding the maximum value among n values, as n grows. That is, the x axis would be n, and the y value would be the cost. Of course, this is a diagonal line going up to the right, as n increases (you might want to sketch this graph for yourself before reading further).

Now, imagine the graph showing the cost for *each* instance of the problem of finding the maximum value among (say) 20 elements in an array. The first position along the x axis of the graph might correspond to having the maximum element in the first position of the array. The second position along the x axis of the graph might correspond to having the maximum element in the second position of the array, and so on. Of course, the cost is always 20. Therefore, the graph would be a horizontal line with value 20. You should sketch this graph for yourself.

Now, let us switch to the problem of doing a sequential search for a given value in an array. Think about the graph showing all the problem instances of size 20. The first problem instance might be when the value we search for is in the first position of the array. This has cost 1. The second problem instance might be when the value we search for is in the second position of the array. This has cost 2. And so on. If we arrange the problem instances of size 20 from least expensive on the left to most expensive on the right, we see that the graph forms a diagonal line from lower left (with value 0) to upper right (with value 20). Sketch this graph for yourself.

Finally, let us consider the cost for performing sequential search as the size of the array n gets bigger. What will this graph look like? Unfortunately, there's not one simple answer, as there was for finding the maximum value. The shape of this graph depends on whether we are considering the best case cost (that would be a horizontal line with value 1), the worst case cost (that would be a diagonal line with value i at position i along the x axis), or the average cost (that would be a a a diagonal line with value $i/2$ at position i along the x axis). This is why we must always say that function $f(n)$ is in $O(g(n))$ in the best, average, or worst case! If we leave off which class of inputs we are discussing, we cannot know which cost measure we are referring to for most algorithms.

3.8 Multiple Parameters

Sometimes the proper analysis for an algorithm requires multiple parameters to describe the cost. To illustrate the concept, consider an algorithm to compute the rank ordering for counts of all pixel values in a picture. Pictures are often represented by a two-dimensional array, and a pixel is one cell in the array. The value of a pixel is either the code value for the color, or a value for the intensity of the picture at that pixel. Assume that each pixel can take any integer value in the range 0 to $C - 1$. The problem is to find the number of pixels of each color value and then sort the color values with respect to the number of times each value appears in the picture. Assume that the picture is a rectangle with P pixels. A pseudocode algorithm to solve the problem follows.

```
for (i=0; i<C; i++)    // Initialize count
   count[i] = 0;
for (i=0; i<P; i++)    // Look at all of the pixels
   count[value(i)]++;  // Increment a pixel value count
sort(count, C);        // Sort pixel value counts
```

In this example, **count** is an array of size C that stores the number of pixels for each color value. Function **value(i)** returns the color value for pixel i.

The time for the first **for** loop (which initializes **count**) is based on the number of colors, C. The time for the second loop (which determines the number of pixels with each color) is $\Theta(P)$. The time for the final line, the call to **sort**, depends on the cost of the sorting algorithm used. From the discussion of Section 3.6, we can assume that the sorting algorithm has cost $\Theta(P \log P)$ if P items are sorted, thus yielding $\Theta(P \log P)$ as the total algorithm cost.

Is this a good representation for the cost of this algorithm? What is actually being sorted? It is not the pixels, but rather the colors. What if C is much smaller than P? Then the estimate of $\Theta(P \log P)$ is pessimistic, because much fewer than P items are being sorted. Instead, we should use P as our analysis variable for steps that look at each pixel, and C as our analysis variable for steps that look at colors. Then we get $\Theta(C)$ for the initialization loop, $\Theta(P)$ for the pixel count loop, and $\Theta(C \log C)$ for the sorting operation. This yields a total cost of $\Theta(P + C \log C)$.

Why can we not simply use the value of C for input size and say that the cost of the algorithm is $\Theta(C \log C)$? Because, C is typically much less than P. For example, a picture might have 1000×1000 pixels and a range of 256 possible colors. So, P is one million, which is much larger than $C \log C$. But, if P is smaller, or C larger (even if it is still less than P), then $C \log C$ can become the larger quantity. Thus, neither variable should be ignored.

3.9   Space Bounds

Besides time, space is the other computing resource that is commonly of concern to programmers. Just as computers have become much faster over the years, they have also received greater allotments of memory. Even so, the amount of available disk space or main memory can be significant constraints for algorithm designers.

The analysis techniques used to measure space requirements are similar to those used to measure time requirements. However, while time requirements are normally measured for an algorithm that manipulates a particular data structure, space requirements are normally determined for the data structure itself. The concepts of asymptotic analysis for growth rates on input size apply completely to measuring space requirements.

Example 3.16 What are the space requirements for an array of n integers? If each integer requires c bytes, then the array requires cn bytes, which is $\Theta(n)$.

Example 3.17 Imagine that we want to keep track of friendships between n people. We can do this with an array of size $n \times n$. Each row of the array represents the friends of an individual, with the columns indicating who has that individual as a friend. For example, if person j is a friend of person i, then we place a mark in column j of row i in the array. Likewise, we should also place a mark in column i of row j if we assume that friendship works both ways. For n people, the total size of the array is $\Theta(n^2)$.

A data structure's primary purpose is to store data in a way that allows efficient access to those data. To provide efficient access, it may be necessary to store additional information about where the data are within the data structure. For example, each node of a linked list must store a pointer to the next value on the list. All such information stored in addition to the actual data values is referred to as **overhead**. Ideally, overhead should be kept to a minimum while allowing maximum access. The need to maintain a balance between these opposing goals is what makes the study of data structures so interesting.

One important aspect of algorithm design is referred to as the **space/time tradeoff** principle. The space/time tradeoff principle says that one can often achieve a reduction in time if one is willing to sacrifice space or vice versa. Many programs can be modified to reduce storage requirements by "packing" or encoding information. "Unpacking" or decoding the information requires additional time. Thus, the resulting program uses less space but runs slower. Conversely, many programs can be modified to pre-store results or reorganize information to allow faster running time at the expense of greater storage requirements. Typically, such changes in time and space are both by a constant factor.

A classic example of a space/time tradeoff is the **lookup table**. A lookup table pre-stores the value of a function that would otherwise be computed each time it is needed. For example, 12! is the greatest value for the factorial function that can be stored in a 32-bit **int** variable. If you are writing a program that often computes factorials, it is likely to be much more time efficient to simply pre-compute and store the 12 values in a table. Whenever the program needs the value of $n!$ it can simply check the lookup table. (If $n > 12$, the value is too large to store as an **int** variable anyway.) Compared to the time required to compute factorials, it may be well worth the small amount of additional space needed to store the lookup table.

Lookup tables can also store approximations for an expensive function such as sine or cosine. If you compute this function only for exact degrees or are willing to approximate the answer with the value for the nearest degree, then a lookup table storing the computation for exact degrees can be used instead of repeatedly computing the sine function. Note that initially building the lookup table requires a certain amount of time. Your application must use the lookup table often enough to make this initialization worthwhile.

Another example of the space/time tradeoff is typical of what a programmer might encounter when trying to optimize space. Here is a simple code fragment for sorting an array of integers. We assume that this is a special case where there are n integers whose values are a permutation of the integers from 0 to $n - 1$. This is an example of a Binsort, which is discussed in Section 7.7. Binsort assigns each value to an array position corresponding to its value.

```
for (i=0; i<n; i++)
   B[A[i]] = A[i];
```

This is efficient and requires $\Theta(n)$ time. However, it also requires two arrays of size n. Next is a code fragment that places the permutation in order but does so within the same array (thus it is an example of an "in place" sort).

```
for (i=0; i<n; i++)
    while (A[i] != i)
        swap(A, i, A[i]);
```

Function `swap(A, i, j)` exchanges elements `i` and `j` in array `A`. It may not be obvious that the second code fragment actually sorts the array. To see that this does work, notice that each pass through the `for` loop will at least move the integer with value i to its correct position in the array, and that during this iteration, the value of `A[i]` must be greater than or equal to i. A total of at most n `swap` operations take place, because an integer cannot be moved out of its correct position once it has been placed there, and each swap operation places at least one integer in its correct position. Thus, this code fragment has cost $\Theta(n)$. However, it requires more time to run than the first code fragment. On my computer the second version takes nearly twice as long to run as the first, but it only requires half the space.

A second principle for the relationship between a program's space and time requirements applies to programs that process information stored on disk, as discussed in Chapter 8 and thereafter. Strangely enough, the disk-based space/time tradeoff principle is almost the reverse of the space/time tradeoff principle for programs using main memory.

The **disk-based space/time tradeoff** principle states that the smaller you can make your disk storage requirements, the faster your program will run. This is because the time to read information from disk is enormous compared to computation time, so almost any amount of additional computation needed to unpack the data is going to be less than the disk-reading time saved by reducing the storage requirements. Naturally this principle does not hold true in all cases, but it is good to keep in mind when designing programs that process information stored on disk.

3.10 Speeding Up Your Programs

In practice, there is not such a big difference in running time between an algorithm with growth rate $\Theta(n)$ and another with growth rate $\Theta(n \log n)$. There is, however, an enormous difference in running time between algorithms with growth rates of $\Theta(n \log n)$ and $\Theta(n^2)$. As you shall see during the course of your study of common data structures and algorithms, it is not unusual that a problem whose obvious solution requires $\Theta(n^2)$ time also has a solution requiring $\Theta(n \log n)$ time. Examples include sorting and searching, two of the most important computer problems.

Example 3.18 The following is a true story. A few years ago, one of my graduate students had a big problem. His thesis work involved several intricate operations on a large database. He was now working on the final step. "Dr. Shaffer," he said, "I am running this program and it seems to be taking a long time." After examining the algorithm we realized that its running time was $\Theta(n^2)$, and that it would likely take one to two weeks to complete. Even if we could keep the computer running uninterrupted for that long, he was hoping to complete his thesis and graduate before then. Fortunately, we realized that there was a fairly easy way to convert the algorithm so that its running time was $\Theta(n \log n)$. By the next day he had modified the program. It ran in only a few hours, and he finished his thesis on time.

While not nearly so important as changing an algorithm to reduce its growth rate, "code tuning" can also lead to dramatic improvements in running time. Code tuning is the art of hand-optimizing a program to run faster or require less storage. For many programs, code tuning can reduce running time by a factor of ten, or cut the storage requirements by a factor of two or more. I once tuned a critical function in a program — without changing its basic algorithm — to achieve a factor of 200 speedup. To get this speedup, however, I did make major changes in the representation of the information, converting from a symbolic coding scheme to a numeric coding scheme on which I was able to do direct computation.

Here are some suggestions for ways to speed up your programs by code tuning. The most important thing to realize is that most statements in a program do not have much effect on the running time of that program. There are normally just a few key subroutines, possibly even key lines of code within the key subroutines, that account for most of the running time. There is little point to cutting in half the running time of a subroutine that accounts for only 1% of the total running time. Focus your attention on those parts of the program that have the most impact.

When tuning code, it is important to gather good timing statistics. Many compilers and operating systems include profilers and other special tools to help gather information on both time and space use. These are invaluable when trying to make a program more efficient, because they can tell you where to invest your effort.

A lot of code tuning is based on the principle of avoiding work rather than speeding up work. A common situation occurs when we can test for a condition that lets us skip some work. However, such a test is never completely free. Care must be taken that the cost of the test does not exceed the amount of work saved. While one test might be cheaper than the work potentially saved, the test must always be made and the work can be avoided only some fraction of the time.

Example 3.19 A common operation in computer graphics applications is to find which among a set of complex objects contains a given point in space. Many useful data structures and algorithms have been developed to deal with variations of this problem. Most such implementations involve the following tuning step. Directly testing whether a given complex object contains the point in question is relatively expensive. Instead, we can screen for whether the point is contained within a **bounding box** for the object. The bounding box is simply the smallest rectangle (usually defined to have sides perpendicular to the x and y axes) that contains the object. If the point is not in the bounding box, then it cannot be in the object. If the point is in the bounding box, only then would we conduct the full comparison of the object versus the point. Note that if the point is outside the bounding box, we saved time because the bounding box test is cheaper than the comparison of the full object versus the point. But if the point is inside the bounding box, then that test is redundant because we still have to compare the point against the object. Typically the amount of work avoided by making this test is greater than the cost of making the test on every object.

Example 3.20 Section 7.2.3 presents a sorting algorithm named Selection Sort. The chief distinguishing characteristic of this algorithm is that it requires relatively few swaps of records stored in the array to be sorted. However, it sometimes performs an unnecessary swap operation where it tries to swap a record with itself. This work could be avoided by testing whether the two indices being swapped are the same. However, this event does not occurr often. Because the cost of the test is high enough compared to the work saved when the test is successful, adding the test typically will slow down the program rather than speed it up.

Be careful not to use tricks that make the program unreadable. Most code tuning is simply cleaning up a carelessly written program, not taking a clear program and adding tricks. In particular, you should develop an appreciation for the capabilities of modern compilers to make extremely good optimizations of expressions. "Optimization of expressions" here means a rearrangement of arithmetic or logical expressions to run more efficiently. Be careful not to damage the compiler's ability to do such optimizations for you in an effort to optimize the expression yourself. Always check that your "optimizations" really do improve the program by running the program before and after the change on a suitable benchmark set of input. Many times I have been wrong about the positive effects of code tuning in my own programs. Most often I am wrong when I try to optimize an expression. It is hard to do better than the compiler.

The greatest time and space improvements come from a better data structure or algorithm. The final thought for this section is

First tune the algorithm, then tune the code.

3.11 Empirical Analysis

This chapter has focused on asymptotic analysis. This is an analytic tool, whereby we model the key aspects of an algorithm to determine the growth rate of the algorithm as the input size grows. As pointed out previously, there are many limitations to this approach. These include the effects at small problem size, determining the finer distinctions between algorithms with the same growth rate, and the inherent difficulty of doing mathematical modeling for more complex problems.

An alternative to analytical approaches are empirical ones. The most obvious empirical approach is simply to run two competitors and see which performs better. In this way we might overcome the deficiencies of analytical approaches.

Be warned that comparative timing of programs is a difficult business, often subject to experimental errors arising from uncontrolled factors (system load, the language or compiler used, etc.). The most important point is not to be biased in favor of one of the programs. If you are biased, this is certain to be reflected in the timings. One look at competing software or hardware vendors' advertisements should convince you of this. The most common pitfall when writing two programs to compare their performance is that one receives more code-tuning effort than the other. As mentioned in Section 3.10, code tuning can often reduce running time by a factor of ten. If the running times for two programs differ by a constant factor regardless of input size (i.e., their growth rates are the same), then differences in code tuning might account for any difference in running time. Be suspicious of empirical comparisons in this situation.

Another approach to analysis is simulation. The idea of simulation is to model the problem with a computer program and then run it to get a result. In the context of algorithm analysis, simulation is distinct from empirical comparison of two competitors because the purpose of the simulation is to perform analysis that might otherwise be too difficult. A good example of this appears in Figure 9.10. This figure shows the cost for inserting or deleting a record from a hash table under two different assumptions for the policy used to find a free slot in the table. The y axes is the cost in number of hash table slots evaluated, and the x axes is the percentage of slots in the table that are full. The mathematical equations for these curves can be determined, but this is not so easy. A reasonable alternative is to write simple variations on hashing. By timing the cost of the program for various loading conditions, it is not difficult to construct a plot similar to Figure 9.10. The purpose of this analysis is not to determine which approach to hashing is most efficient, so we are not doing empirical comparison of hashing alternatives. Instead, the purpose is to analyze the proper loading factor that would be used in an efficient hashing system to balance time cost versus hash table size (space cost).

3.12   Further Reading

Pioneering works on algorithm analysis include *The Art of Computer Programming* by Donald E. Knuth [Knu97, Knu98], and *The Design and Analysis of Computer Algorithms* by Aho, Hopcroft, and Ullman [AHU74]. The alternate definition for Ω comes from [AHU83]. The use of the notation "$\mathbf{T}(n)$ is in $\mathrm{O}(f(n))$" rather than the more commonly used "$\mathbf{T}(n) = \mathrm{O}(f(n))$" I derive from Brassard and Bratley [BB96], though certainly this use predates them. A good book to read for further information on algorithm analysis techniques is *Compared to What?* by Gregory J.E. Rawlins [Raw92].

Bentley [Ben88] describes one problem in numerical analysis for which, between 1945 and 1988, the complexity of the best known algorithm had decreased from $\mathrm{O}(n^7)$ to $\mathrm{O}(n^3)$. For a problem of size $n = 64$, this is roughly equivalent to the speedup achieved from all advances in computer hardware during the same time period.

While the most important aspect of program efficiency is the algorithm, much improvement can be gained from efficient coding of a program. As cited by Frederick P. Brooks in *The Mythical Man-Month* [Bro95], an efficient programmer can often produce programs that run five times faster than an inefficient programmer, even when neither takes special efforts to speed up their code. For excellent and enjoyable essays on improving your coding efficiency, and ways to speed up your code when it really matters, see the books by Jon Bentley [Ben82, Ben00, Ben88]. The situation described in Example 3.18 arose when we were working on the project reported on in [SU92].

As an interesting aside, writing a correct binary search algorithm is not easy. Knuth [Knu98] notes that while the first binary search was published in 1946, the first bug-free algorithm was not published until 1962! Bentley ("Writing Correct Programs" in [Ben00]) has found that 90% of the computer professionals he tested could not write a bug-free binary search in two hours.

3.13   Exercises

3.1 For each of the six expressions of Figure 3.1, give the range of values of n for which that expression is most efficient.

3.2 Graph the following expressions. For each expression, state the range of values of n for which that expression is the most efficient.

$$4n^2 \qquad \log_3 n \qquad 3^n \qquad 20n \qquad 2 \qquad \log_2 n \qquad n^{2/3}$$

3.3 Arrange the following expressions by growth rate from slowest to fastest.

$$4n^2 \qquad \log_3 n \qquad n! \qquad 3^n \qquad 20n \qquad 2 \qquad \log_2 n \qquad n^{2/3}$$

See Stirling's approximation in Section 2.2 for help in classifying $n!$.

3.4 **(a)** Suppose that a particular algorithm has time complexity $\mathbf{T}(n) = 3 \times 2^n$, and that executing an implementation of it on a particular machine takes t seconds for n inputs. Now suppose that we are presented with a machine that is 64 times as fast. How many inputs could we process on the new machine in t seconds?

(b) Suppose that another algorithm has time complexity $\mathbf{T}(n) = n^2$, and that executing an implementation of it on a particular machine takes t seconds for n inputs. Now suppose that we are presented with a machine that is 64 times as fast. How many inputs could we process on the new machine in t seconds?

(c) A third algorithm has time complexity $\mathbf{T}(n) = 8n$. Executing an implementation of it on a particular machine takes t seconds for n inputs. Given a new machine that is 64 times as fast, how many inputs could we process in t seconds?

3.5 Hardware vendor XYZ Corp. claims that their latest computer will run 100 times faster than that of their competitor, Prunes, Inc. If the Prunes, Inc. computer can execute a program on input of size n in one hour, what size input can XYZ's computer execute in one hour for each algorithm with the following growth rate equations?

$$n \qquad n^2 \qquad n^3 \qquad 2^n$$

3.6 **(a)** Find a growth rate that squares the run time when we double the input size. That is, if $\mathbf{T}(n) = X$, then $\mathbf{T}(2n) = x^2$

(b) Find a growth rate that cubes the run time when we double the input size. That is, if $\mathbf{T}(n) = X$, then $\mathbf{T}(2n) = x^3$

3.7 Using the definition of big-Oh, show that 1 is in $O(1)$ and that 1 is in $O(n)$.

3.8 Using the definitions of big-Oh and Ω, find the upper and lower bounds for the following expressions. Be sure to state appropriate values for c and n_0.

(a) $c_1 n$
(b) $c_2 n^3 + c_3$
(c) $c_4 n \log n + c_5 n$
(d) $c_6 2^n + c_7 n^6$

3.9 **(a)** What is the smallest integer k such that $\sqrt{n} = O(n^k)$?
(b) What is the smallest integer k such that $n \log n = O(n^k)$?

3.10 **(a)** Is $2n = \Theta(3n)$? Explain why or why not.
(b) Is $2^n = \Theta(3^n)$? Explain why or why not.

3.11 For each of the following pairs of functions, either $f(n)$ is in $O(g(n))$, $f(n)$ is in $\Omega(g(n))$, or $f(n) = \Theta(g(n))$. For each pair, determine which relationship is correct. Justify your answer, using the method of limits discussed in Section 3.4.5.

    (a) $f(n) = \log n^2$; $g(n) = \log n + 5$.
    (b) $f(n) = \sqrt{n}$; $g(n) = \log n^2$.
    (c) $f(n) = \log^2 n$; $g(n) = \log n$.
    (d) $f(n) = n$; $g(n) = log^2 n$.
    (e) $f(n) = n \log n + n$; $g(n) = \log n$.
    (f) $f(n) = \log n^2$; $g(n) = (\log n)^2$.
    (g) $f(n) = 10$; $g(n) = \log 10$.
    (h) $f(n) = 2^n$; $g(n) = 10n^2$.
    (i) $f(n) = 2^n$; $g(n) = n \log n$.
    (j) $f(n) = 2^n$; $g(n) = 3^n$.
    (k) $f(n) = 2^n$; $g(n) = n^n$.

3.12 Determine Θ for the following code fragments in the average case. Assume that all variables are of type **int**.

    (a)
```
a = b + c;
d = a + e;
```

    (b)
```
sum = 0;
for (i=0; i<3; i++)
    for (j=0; j<n; j++)
        sum++;
```

    (c)
```
sum=0;
for (i=0; i<n*n; i++)
    sum++;
```

    (d)
```
for (i=0; i < n-1; i++)
    for (j=i+1; j < n; j++) {
      tmp = A[i][j];
      A[i][j] = A[j][i];
      A[j][i] = tmp;
    }
```

    (e)
```
sum = 0;
for (i=1; i<=n; i++)
    for (j=1; j<=n; j*=2)
      sum++;
```

    (f)
```
sum = 0;
for (i=1; i<=n; i*=2)
    for (j=1; j<=n; j++)
      sum++;
```

    (g) Assume that array **A** contains n values, **Random** takes constant time, and **sort** takes $n \log n$ steps.

```
for (i=0; i<n; i++) {
  for (j=0; j<n; j++)
    A[i] = Random(n);
  sort(A, n);
}
```

(h) Assume array **A** contains a random permutation of the values from 0 to $n - 1$.

```
sum = 0;
for (i=0; i<n; i++)
  for (j=0; A[j]!=i; j++)
    sum++;
```

(i)
```
sum = 0;
if (EVEN(n))
  for (i=0; i<n; i++)
    sum++;
else
  sum = sum + n;
```

3.13 Show that big-Theta notation (Θ) defines an equivalence relation on the set of functions.

3.14 Give the best *lower* bound that you can for the following code fragment, as a function of the initial value of n.

```
while (n > 1)
  if (ODD(n))
    n = 3 * n + 1;
  else
    n = n / 2;
```

Do you think that the upper bound is likely to be the same as the answer you gave for the lower bound?

3.15 Does every algorithm have a Θ running-time equation? In other words, are the upper and lower bounds for the running time (on any specified class of inputs) always the same?

3.16 Does every problem for which there exists some algorithm have a Θ running-time equation? In other words, for every problem, and for any specified class of inputs, is there some algorithm whose upper bound is equal to the problem's lower bound?

3.17 Given an array storing integers ordered by value, modify the binary search routine to return the position of the first integer with value K in the situation where K can appear multiple times in the array. Be sure that your algorithm is $\Theta(\log n)$, that is, do *not* resort to sequential search once an occurrence of K is found.

3.18 Given an array storing integers ordered by value, modify the binary search routine to return the position of the integer with the greatest value less than K when K itself does not appear in the array. Return **ERROR** if the least value in the array is greater than K.

3.19 Modify the binary search routine to support search in an array of infinite size. In particular, you are given as input a sorted array and a key value K to search for. Call n the position of the smallest value in the array that is equal to or larger than X. Provide an algorithm that can determine n in $O(\log n)$ comparisons in the worst case. Explain why your algorithm meets the required time bound.

3.20 It is possible to change the way that we pick the dividing point in a binary search, and still get a working search routine. However, where we pick the dividing point could affect the performance of the algorithm.

  (a) If we change the dividing point computation in function **binary** from $i = (l + r)/2$ to $i = (l + ((r - l)/3))$, what will the worst-case running time be in asymptotic terms? If the difference is only a constant time factor, how much slower or faster will the modified program be compared to the original version of **binary**?

  (b) If we change the dividing point computation in function **binary** from $i = (l + r)/2$ to $i = r - 2$, what will the worst-case running time be in asymptotic terms? If the difference is only a constant time factor, how much slower or faster will the modified program be compared to the original version of **binary**?

3.21 Design an algorithm to assemble a jigsaw puzzle. Assume that each piece has four sides, and that each piece's final orientation is known (top, bottom, etc.). Assume that you have available a function

```
bool compare(Piece a, Piece b, Side ad)
```

that can tell, in constant time, whether piece a connects to piece b on a's side ad and b's opposite side bd. The input to your algorithm should consist of an $n \times m$ array of random pieces, along with dimensions n and m. The algorithm should put the pieces in their correct positions in the array. Your algorithm should be as efficient as possible in the asymptotic sense. Write a summation for the running time of your algorithm on n pieces, and then derive a closed-form solution for the summation.

3.22 Can the average case cost for an algorithm be worse than the worst case cost? Can it be better than the best case cost? Explain why or why not.

3.23 Prove that if an algorithm is $\Theta(f(n))$ in the average case, then it is $\Omega(f(n))$ in the worst case.

3.24 Prove that if an algorithm is $\Theta(f(n))$ in the average case, then it is $O(f(n))$ in the best case.

3.14 Projects

3.1 Imagine that you are trying to store 32 Boolean values, and must access them frequently. Compare the time required to access Boolean values stored alternatively as a single bit field, a character, a short integer, or a long integer. There are two things to be careful of when writing your program. First, be sure that your program does enough variable accesses to make meaningful measurements. A single access takes much less time than a single unit of measurement (typically milliseconds) for all four methods. Second, be sure that your program spends as much time as possible doing variable accesses rather than other things such as calling timing functions or incrementing **for** loop counters.

3.2 Implement sequential search and binary search algorithms on your computer. Run timings for each algorithm on arrays of size $n = 10^i$ for i ranging from 1 to as large a value as your computer's memory and compiler will allow. For both algorithms, store the values 0 through $n - 1$ in order in the array, and use a variety of random search values in the range 0 to $n - 1$ on each size n. Graph the resulting times. When is sequential search faster than binary search for a sorted array?

3.3 Implement a program that runs and gives timings for the two Fibonacci sequence functions provided in Exercise 2.11. Graph the resulting running times for as many values of n as your computer can handle.

PART II

Fundamental Data Structures

4

Lists, Stacks, and Queues

If your program needs to store a few things — numbers, payroll records, or job descriptions for example — the simplest and most effective approach might be to put them in a list. Only when you have to organize and search through a large number of things do more sophisticated data structures usually become necessary. (We will study how to organize and search through medium amounts of data in Chapters 5, 7, and 9, and discuss how to deal with large amounts of data in Chapters 8–10.) Many applications don't require any form of search, and they do not require that any ordering be placed on the objects being stored. Some applications require processing in a strict chronological order, processing objects in the order that they arrived, or perhaps processing objects in the reverse of the order that they arrived. For all these situations, a simple list structure is appropriate.

This chapter describes representations for lists in general, as well as two important list-like structures called the stack and the queue. Along with presenting these fundamental data structures, the other goals of the chapter are to: (1) Give examples of separating a logical representation in the form of an ADT from a physical implementation for a data structure. (2) Illustrate the use of asymptotic analysis in the context of some simple operations that you might already be familiar with. In this way you can begin to see how asymptotic analysis works, without the complications that arise when analyzing more sophisticated algorithms and data structures. (3) Introduce the concept and use of dictionaries.

We begin by defining an ADT for lists in Section 4.1. Two implementations for the list ADT — the array-based list and the linked list — are covered in detail and their relative merits discussed. Sections 4.2 and 4.3 cover stacks and queues, respectively. Sample implementations for each of these data structures are presented. Section 4.4 presents the Dictionary ADT for storing and retrieving data, which sets a context for implementing search structures such as the Binary Search Tree of Section 5.4.

4.1   Lists

We all have an intuitive understanding of what we mean by a "list." Our first step is
to define precisely what is meant so that this intuitive understanding can eventually
be converted into a concrete data structure and its operations. The most important
concept related to lists is that of **position**. In other words, we perceive that there
is a first element in the list, a second element, and so on. We should view a list as
embodying the mathematical concepts of a sequence, as defined in Section 2.1.

We define a **list** to be a finite, ordered sequence of data items known as **elements**. "Ordered" in this definition means that each element has a position in the
list. (We will not use "ordered" in this context to mean that the list elements are
sorted by value.) Each list element has a data type. In the simple list implementations discussed in this chapter, all elements of the list have the same data type,
although there is no conceptual objection to lists whose elements have differing
data types if the application requires it (see Section 12.1). The operations defined
as part of the list ADT do not depend on the elemental data type. For example, the
list ADT can be used for lists of integers, lists of characters, lists of payroll records,
even lists of lists.

A list is said to be **empty** when it contains no elements. The number of elements currently stored is called the **length** of the list. The beginning of the list is
called the **head**, the end of the list is called the **tail**. There might or might not be
some relationship between the value of an element and its position in the list. For
example, **sorted lists** have their elements positioned in ascending order of value,
while **unsorted lists** have no particular relationship between element values and
positions. This section will consider only unsorted lists. Chapters 7 and 9 treat the
problems of how to create and search sorted lists efficiently.

When presenting the contents of a list, we use the same notation as was introduced for sequences in Section 2.1. To be consistent with **C++** array indexing,
the first position on the list is denoted as 0. Thus, if there are n elements in the
list, they are given positions 0 through $n - 1$ as $\langle a_0, a_1, ..., a_{n-1} \rangle$. The subscript
indicates an element's position within the list. Using this notation, the empty list
would appear as $\langle \rangle$.

Before selecting a list implementation, a program designer should first consider
what basic operations the implementation must support. Our common intuition
about lists tells us that a list should be able to grow and shrink in size as we insert
and remove elements. We should be able to insert and remove elements from anywhere in the list. We should be able to gain access to any element's value, either to
read it or to change it. We must be able to create and clear (or reinitialize) lists. It
is also convenient to access the next or previous element from the "current" one.

The next step is to define the ADT for a list object in terms of a set of operations
on that object. We will use the **C++** notation of anabstract class to formally define

the list ADT. An abstract class is one whose member functions are all declared to be "pure virtual" as indicated by the "**=0**" notation at the end of the member function declarations. Class **List** defines the member functions that any list implementation inheriting from it must support, along with their parameters and return types. We increase the flexibility of the list ADT by writing it as a **C++** template.

True to the notion of an ADT, anabstract class does not specify how operations are implemented. Two complete implementations are presented later in this section, both of which use the same list ADT to define their operations, but they are considerably different in approaches and in their space/time tradeoffs.

Figure 4.1 presents our list ADT. Class **List** is a template of one parameter, named **E** for "element". **E** serves as a placeholder for whatever element type the user would like to store in a list. The comments given in Figure 4.1 describe precisely what each member function is intended to do. However, some explanation of the basic design is in order. Given that we wish to support the concept of a sequence, with access to any position in the list, the need for many of the member functions such as **insert** and **moveToPos** is clear. The key design decision embodied in this ADT is support for the concept of a **current position**. For example, member **moveToStart** sets the current position to be the first element on the list, while methods **next** and **prev** move the current position to the next and previous elements, respectively. The intention is that any implementation for this ADT support the concept of a current position. The current position is where any action such as insertion or deletion will take place.

Since insertions take place at the current position, and since we want to be able to insert to the front or the back of the list as well as anywhere in between, there are actually $n + 1$ possible "current positions" when there are n elements in the list.

It is helpful to modify our list display notation to show the position of the current element. I will use a vertical bar, such as $\langle 20,\ 23\ |\ 12,\ 15 \rangle$ to indicate the list of four elements, with the current position being to the right of the bar at element 12. Given this configuration, calling **insert** with value 10 will change the list to be $\langle 20,\ 23\ |\ 10,\ 12,\ 15 \rangle$.

If you examine Figure 4.1, you should find that the list member functions provided allow you to build a list with elements in any desired order, and to access any desired position in the list. You might notice that the **clear** method is not necessary, in that it could be implemented by means of the other member functions in the same asymptotic time. It is included merely for convenience.

Method **getValue** returns a pointer to the current element. It is considered a violation of **getValue**'s preconditions to ask for the value of a non-existent element (i.e., there must be something to the right of the vertical bar). In our concrete list implementations, assertions are used to enforce such preconditions. In a commercial implementation, such violations would be best implemented by the **C++** exception mechanism.

```
template <typename E> class List { // List ADT
private:
  void operator =(const List&) {}        // Protect assignment
  List(const List&) {}                   // Protect copy constructor
public:
  List() {}              // Default constructor
  virtual ~List() {} // Base destructor

  // Clear contents from the list, to make it empty.
  virtual void clear() = 0;

  // Insert an element at the current location.
  // item: The element to be inserted
  virtual void insert(const E& item) = 0;

  // Append an element at the end of the list.
  // item: The element to be appended.
  virtual void append(const E& item) = 0;

  // Remove and return the current element.
  // Return: the element that was removed.
  virtual E remove() = 0;

  // Set the current position to the start of the list
  virtual void moveToStart() = 0;

  // Set the current position to the end of the list
  virtual void moveToEnd() = 0;

  // Move the current position one step left. No change
  // if already at beginning.
  virtual void prev() = 0;

  // Move the current position one step right. No change
  // if already at end.
  virtual void next() = 0;

  // Return: The number of elements in the list.
  virtual int length() const = 0;

  // Return: The position of the current element.
  virtual int currPos() const = 0;

  // Set current position.
  // pos: The position to make current.
  virtual void moveToPos(int pos) = 0;

  // Return: The current element.
  virtual const E& getValue() const = 0;
};
```

Figure 4.1 The ADT for a list.

A list can be iterated through as shown in the following code fragment.

```
for (L.moveToStart(); L.currPos()<L.length(); L.next()) {
  it = L.getValue();
  doSomething(it);
}
```

In this example, each element of the list in turn is stored in **it**, and passed to the **doSomething** function. The loop terminates when the current position reaches the end of the list.

The declaration for abstract class **List** also makes private the class copy constructor and an overloading for the assignment operator. This protects the class from accidentally being copied. This is done in part to simplify the example code used in this book. A full-featured list implementation would likely support copying and assigning list objects.

The list class declaration presented here is just one of many possible interpretations for lists. Figure 4.1 provides most of the operations that one naturally expects to perform on lists and serves to illustrate the issues relevant to implementing the list data structure. As an example of using the list ADT, we can create a function to return **true** if there is an occurrence of a given integer in the list, and **false** otherwise. The **find** method needs no knowledge about the specific list implementation, just the list ADT.

```
// Return true if "K" is in list "L", false otherwise
bool find(List<int>& L, int K) {
  int it;
  for (L.moveToStart(); L.currPos()<L.length(); L.next()) {
    it = L.getValue();
    if (K == it) return true;   // Found K
  }
  return false;                 // K not found
}
```

While this implementation for **find** could be written as a template with respect to the element type, it would still be limited in its ability to handle different data types stored on the list. In particular, it only works when the description for the object being searched for (**k** in the function) is of the same type as the objects themselves, and that can meaningfully be compared when using the **==** comparison operator. A more typical situation is that we are searching for a record that contains a key field who's value matches **k**. Similar functions to find and return a composite element based on a key value can be created using the list implementation, but to do so requires some agreement between the list ADT and the **find** function on the concept of a key, and on how keys may be compared. This topic will be discussed in Section 4.4.

4.1.1   Array-Based List Implementation

There are two standard approaches to implementing lists, the **array-based** list, and the **linked** list. This section discusses the array-based approach. The linked list is presented in Section 4.1.2. Time and space efficiency comparisons for the two are discussed in Section 4.1.3.

Figure 4.2 shows the array-based list implementation, named **AList**. **AList** inherits from abstract class **List** and so must implement all of the member functions of **List**.

Class **AList**'s private portion contains the data members for the array-based list. These include **listArray**, the array which holds the list elements. Because **listArray** must be allocated at some fixed size, the size of the array must be known when the list object is created. Note that an optional parameter is declared for the **AList** constructor. With this parameter, the user can indicate the maximum number of elements permitted in the list. The phrase "**=defaultSize**" indicates that the parameter is optional. If no parameter is given, then it takes the value **defaultSize**, which is assumed to be a suitably defined constant value.

Because each list can have a differently sized array, each list must remember its maximum permitted size. Data member **maxSize** serves this purpose. At any given time the list actually holds some number of elements that can be less than the maximum allowed by the array. This value is stored in **listSize**. Data member **curr** stores the current position. Because **listArray**, **maxSize**, **listSize**, and **curr** are all declared to be **private**, they may only be accessed by methods of Class **AList**.

Class **AList** stores the list elements in the first **listSize** contiguous array positions. Array positions correspond to list positions. In other words, the element at position i in the list is stored at array cell i. The head of the list is always at position 0. This makes random access to any element in the list quite easy. Given some position in the list, the value of the element in that position can be accessed directly. Thus, access to any element using the **moveToPos** method followed by the **getValue** method takes $\Theta(1)$ time.

Because the array-based list implementation is defined to store list elements in contiguous cells of the array, the **insert**, **append**, and **remove** methods must maintain this property. Inserting or removing elements at the tail of the list is easy, so the **append** operation takes $\Theta(1)$ time. But if we wish to insert an element at the head of the list, all elements currently in the list must shift one position toward the tail to make room, as illustrated by Figure 4.3. This process takes $\Theta(n)$ time if there are n elements already in the list. If we wish to insert at position i within a list of n elements, then $n - i$ elements must shift toward the tail. Removing an element from the head of the list is similar in that all remaining elements must shift toward the head by one position to fill in the gap. To remove the element at position

```
template <typename E> // Array-based list implementation
class AList : public List<E> {
private:
  int maxSize;         // Maximum size of list
  int listSize;        // Number of list items now
  int curr;            // Position of current element
  E* listArray;        // Array holding list elements

public:
  AList(int size=defaultSize) { // Constructor
    maxSize = size;
    listSize = curr = 0;
    listArray = new E[maxSize];
  }

  ~AList() { delete [] listArray; } // Destructor

  void clear() {                       // Reinitialize the list
    delete [] listArray;               // Remove the array
    listSize = curr = 0;               // Reset the size
    listArray = new E[maxSize];  // Recreate array
  }

  // Insert "it" at current position
  void insert(const E& it) {
    Assert(listSize < maxSize, "List capacity exceeded");
    for(int i=listSize; i>curr; i--) // Shift elements up
      listArray[i] = listArray[i-1]; //   to make room
    listArray[curr] = it;
    listSize++;                              // Increment list size
  }

  void append(const E& it) {         // Append "it"
    Assert(listSize < maxSize, "List capacity exceeded");
    listArray[listSize++] = it;
  }

  // Remove and return the current element.
  E remove() {
    Assert((curr>=0) && (curr < listSize), "No element");
    E it = listArray[curr];              // Copy the element
    for(int i=curr; i<listSize-1; i++)  // Shift them down
      listArray[i] = listArray[i+1];
    listSize--;                               // Decrement size
    return it;
  }
```

Figure 4.2 An array-based list implementation.

```
void moveToStart() { curr = 0; }          // Reset position
void moveToEnd() { curr = listSize; }      // Set at end
void prev() { if (curr != 0) curr--; }       // Back up
void next() { if (curr < listSize) curr++; } // Next

// Return list size
int length() const  { return listSize; }

// Return current position
int currPos() const { return curr; }

// Set current list position to "pos"
void moveToPos(int pos) {
  Assert ((pos>=0)&&(pos<=listSize), "Pos out of range");
  curr = pos;
}

const E& getValue() const { // Return current element
  Assert((curr>=0)&&(curr<listSize),"No current element");
  return listArray[curr];
}
};
```

Figure 4.2 (continued)

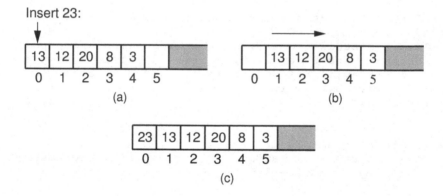

Figure 4.3 Inserting an element at the head of an array-based list requires shifting all existing elements in the array by one position toward the tail. (a) A list containing five elements before inserting an element with value 23. (b) The list after shifting all existing elements one position to the right. (c) The list after 23 has been inserted in array position 0. Shading indicates the unused part of the array.

i, $n - i - 1$ elements must shift toward the head. In the average case, insertion or removal requires moving half of the elements, which is $\Theta(n)$.

Most of the other member functions for Class **AList** simply access the current list element or move the current position. Such operations all require $\Theta(1)$ time. Aside from **insert** and **remove**, the only other operations that might require

```
// Singly linked list node
template <typename E> class Link {
public:
  E element;          // Value for this node
  Link *next;         // Pointer to next node in list
  // Constructors
  Link(const E& elemval, Link* nextval =NULL)
    { element = elemval;  next = nextval; }
  Link(Link* nextval =NULL) { next = nextval; }
};
```

Figure 4.4 A simple singly linked list node implementation.

more than constant time are the constructor, the destructor, and **clear**. These three member functions each make use of the system free-storeoperators **new** and **delete**. As discussed further in Section 4.1.2, system free-store operations can be expensive. In particular, the cost to delete **listArray** depends in part on the type of elements it stores, and whether the **delete** operator must call a destructor on each one.

4.1.2 Linked Lists

The second traditional approach to implementing lists makes use of pointers and is usually called a **linked list**. The linked list uses **dynamic memory allocation**, that is, it allocates memory for new list elements as needed.

A linked list is made up of a series of objects, called the **nodes** of the list. Because a list node is a distinct object (as opposed to simply a cell in an array), it is good practice to make a separate list node class. An additional benefit to creating a list node class is that it can be reused by the linked implementations for the stack and queue data structures presented later in this chapter. Figure 4.4 shows the implementation for list nodes, called the **Link** class. Objects in the **Link** class contain an **element** field to store the element value, and a **next** field to store a pointer to the next node on the list. The list built from such nodes is called a **singly linked list**, or a **one-way list**, because each list node has a single pointer to the next node on the list.

The **Link** class is quite simple. There are two forms for its constructor, one with an initial element value and one without. Because the **Link** class is also used by the stack and queue implementations presented later, its data members are made public. While technically this is breaking encapsulation, in practice the **Link** class should be implemented as a private class of the linked list (or stack or queue) implementation, and thus not visible to the rest of the program.

Figure 4.5(a) shows a graphical depiction for a linked list storing four integers. The value stored in a pointer variable is indicated by an arrow "pointing" to something. C++ uses the special symbol **NULL** for a pointer value that points nowhere, such as for the last list node's **next** field. A **NULL** pointer is indicated graphically

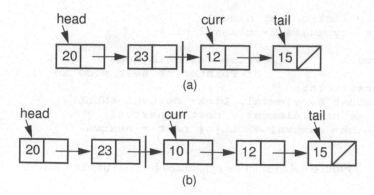

Figure 4.5 Illustration of a faulty linked-list implementation where **curr** points directly to the current node. (a) Linked list prior to inserting element with value 10. (b) Desired effect of inserting element with value 10.

by a diagonal slash through a pointer variable's box. The vertical line between the nodes labeled 23 and 12 in Figure 4.5(a) indicates the current position (immediately to the right of this line).

The list's first node is accessed from a pointer named **head**. To speed access to the end of the list, and to allow the **append** method to be performed in constant time, a pointer named **tail** is also kept to the last link of the list. The position of the current element is indicated by another pointer, named **curr**. Finally, because there is no simple way to compute the length of the list simply from these three pointers, the list length must be stored explicitly, and updated by every operation that modifies the list size. The value **cnt** stores the length of the list.

Class **LList** also includes private helper methods **init** and **removeall**. They are used by **LList**'s constructor, destructor, and **clear** methods.

Note that **LList**'s constructor maintains the optional parameter for minimum list size introduced for Class **AList**. This is done simply to keep the calls to the constructor the same for both variants. Because the linked list class does not need to declare a fixed-size array when the list is created, this parameter is unnecessary for linked lists. It is ignored by the implementation.

A key design decision for the linked list implementation is how to represent the current position. The most reasonable choices appear to be a pointer to the current element. But there is a big advantage to making **curr** point to the element preceding the current element.

Figure 4.5(a) shows the list's **curr** pointer pointing to the current element. The vertical line between the nodes containing 23 and 12 indicates the logical position of the current element. Consider what happens if we wish to insert a new node with value 10 into the list. The result should be as shown in Figure 4.5(b). However, there is a problem. To "splice" the list node containing the new element into the list, the list node storing 23 must have its **next** pointer changed to point to the new

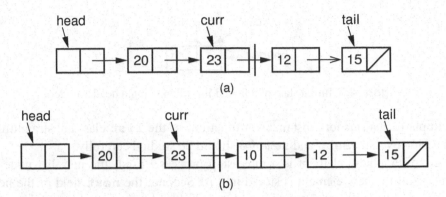

Figure 4.6 Insertion using a header node, with **curr** pointing one node head of the current element. (a) Linked list before insertion. The current node contains 12. (b) Linked list after inserting the node containing 10.

node. Unfortunately, there is no convenient access to the node preceding the one pointed to by **curr**.

There is an easy solution to this problem. If we set **curr** to point directly to the preceding element, there is no difficulty in adding a new element after **curr**. Figure 4.6 shows how the list looks when pointer variable **curr** is set to point to the node preceding the physical current node. See Exercise 4.5 for further discussion of why making **curr** point directly to the current element fails.

We encounter a number of potential special cases when the list is empty, or when the current position is at an end of the list. In particular, when the list is empty we have no element for **head**, **tail**, and **curr** to point to. Implementing special cases for **insert** and **remove** increases code complexity, making it harder to understand, and thus increases the chance of introducing a programming bug.

These special cases can be eliminated by implementing linked lists with an additional **header node** as the first node of the list. This header node is a link node like any other, but its value is ignored and it is not considered to be an actual element of the list. The header node saves coding effort because we no longer need to consider special cases for empty lists or when the current position is at one end of the list. The cost of this simplification is the space for the header node. However, there are space savings due to smaller code size, because statements to handle the special cases are omitted. In practice, this reduction in code size typically saves more space than that required for the header node, depending on the number of lists created. Figure 4.7 shows the state of an initialized or empty list when using a header node.

Figure 4.8 shows the definition for the linked list class, named **LList**. Class **LList** inherits from the abstract list class and thus must implement all of Class **List**'s member functions.

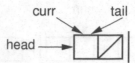

Figure 4.7 Initial state of a linked list when using a header node.

Implementations for most member functions of the **list** class are straightforward. However, **insert** and **remove** should be studied carefully.

Inserting a new element is a three-step process. First, the new list node is created and the new element is stored into it. Second, the **next** field of the new list node is assigned to point to the current node (the one *after* the node that **curr** points to). Third, the **next** field of node pointed to by **curr** is assigned to point to the newly inserted node. The following line in the **insert** method of Figure 4.8 does all three of these steps.

```
curr->next = new Link<E>(it, curr->next);
```

Operator **new** creates the new link node and calls the **Link** class constructor, which takes two parameters. The first is the element. The second is the value to be placed in the list node's **next** field, in this case"**curr->next**."   Figure 4.9 illustrates this three-step process. Once the new node is added, **tail** is pushed forward if the new element was added to the end of the list. Insertion requires $\Theta(1)$ time.

Removing a node from the linked list requires only that the appropriate pointer be redirected around the node to be deleted. The following lines from the **remove** method of Figure 4.8 do precisely this.

```
Link<E>* ltemp = curr->next;     // Remember link node
curr->next = curr->next->next;   // Remove from list
```

We must be careful not to "lose" the memory for the deleted link node. So, temporary pointer **ltemp** is first assigned to point to the node being removed. A call to **delete** is later used to return the old node to free storage.   Figure 4.10 illustrates the **remove** method.Assuming that the free-store **delete** operator requires constant time, removing an element requires $\Theta(1)$ time.

Method **next** simply moves **curr** one position toward the tail of the list, which takes $\Theta(1)$ time. Method **prev** moves **curr** one position toward the head of the list, but its implementation is more difficult. In a singly linked list, there is no pointer to the previous node. Thus, the only alternative is to march down the list from the beginning until we reach the current node (being sure always to remember the node before it, because that is what we really want). This takes $\Theta(n)$ time in the average and worst cases. Implementation of method **moveToPos** is similar in that finding the ith position requires marching down i positions from the head of the list, taking $\Theta(i)$ time.

Implementations for the remaining operations each require $\Theta(1)$ time.

```
// Linked list implementation
template <typename E> class LList: public List<E> {
private:
  Link<E>* head;        // Pointer to list header
  Link<E>* tail;        // Pointer to last element
  Link<E>* curr;        // Access to current element
  int cnt;              // Size of list

  void init() {         // Intialization helper method
    curr = tail = head = new Link<E>;
    cnt = 0;
  }

  void removeall() {    // Return link nodes to free store
    while(head != NULL) {
      curr = head;
      head = head->next;
      delete curr;
    }
  }

public:
  LList(int size=defaultSize) { init(); }     // Constructor
  ~LList() { removeall(); }                    // Destructor
  void print() const;                    // Print list contents
  void clear() { removeall(); init(); }      // Clear list

  // Insert "it" at current position
  void insert(const E& it) {
    curr->next = new Link<E>(it, curr->next);
    if (tail == curr) tail = curr->next;   // New tail
    cnt++;
  }

  void append(const E& it) { // Append "it" to list
    tail = tail->next = new Link<E>(it, NULL);
    cnt++;
  }

  // Remove and return current element
  E remove() {
    Assert(curr->next != NULL, "No element");
    E it = curr->next->element;          // Remember value
    Link<E>* ltemp = curr->next;         // Remember link node
    if (tail == curr->next) tail = curr; // Reset tail
    curr->next = curr->next->next;       // Remove from list
    delete ltemp;                        // Reclaim space
    cnt--;                               // Decrement the count
    return it;
  }
```

Figure 4.8 A linked list implementation.

```cpp
void moveToStart() // Place curr at list start
  { curr = head; }

void moveToEnd()    // Place curr at list end
  { curr = tail; }

// Move curr one step left; no change if already at front
void prev() {
  if (curr == head) return;           // No previous element
  Link<E>* temp = head;
  // March down list until we find the previous element
  while (temp->next!=curr) temp=temp->next;
  curr = temp;
}

// Move curr one step right; no change if already at end
void next()
  { if (curr != tail) curr = curr->next; }

int length() const   { return cnt; } // Return length

// Return the position of the current element
int currPos() const {
  Link<E>* temp = head;
  int i;
  for (i=0; curr != temp; i++)
    temp = temp->next;
  return i;
}

// Move down list to "pos" position
void moveToPos(int pos) {
  Assert ((pos>=0)&&(pos<=cnt), "Position out of range");
  curr = head;
  for(int i=0; i<pos; i++) curr = curr->next;
}

const E& getValue() const { // Return current element
  Assert(curr->next != NULL, "No value");
  return curr->next->element;
}
};
```

Figure 4.8 (continued)

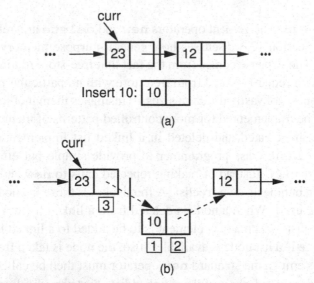

Figure 4.9 The linked list insertion process. (a) The linked list before insertion. (b) The linked list after insertion. $\boxed{1}$ marks the **element** field of the new link node. $\boxed{2}$ marks the **next** field of the new link node, which is set to point to what used to be the current node (the node with value 12). $\boxed{3}$ marks the **next** field of the node preceding the current position. It used to point to the node containing 12; now it points to the new node containing 10.

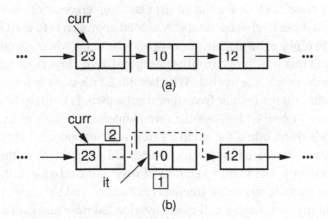

Figure 4.10 The linked list removal process. (a) The linked list before removing the node with value 10. (b) The linked list after removal. $\boxed{1}$ marks the list node being removed. **it** is set to point to the element. $\boxed{2}$ marks the **next** field of the preceding list node, which is set to point to the node following the one being deleted.

Freelists

The C++ free-store management operators **new** and **delete** are relatively expensive to use.   Section 12.3 discusses how general-purpose memory managers are implemented. The expense comes from the fact that free-store routines must be capable of handling requests to and from free store with no particular pattern, as well as memory requests of vastly different sizes. This makes them inefficient compared to what might be implemented for more controlled patterns of memory access.

List nodes are created and deleted in a linked list implementation in a way that allows the **Link** class programmer to provide simple but efficient memory management routines. Instead of making repeated calls to **new** and **delete**, the **Link** class can handle its own **freelist**. A freelist holds those list nodes that are not currently being used. When a node is deleted from a linked list, it is placed at the head of the freelist. When a new element is to be added to a linked list, the freelist is checked to see if a list node is available. If so, the node is taken from the freelist. If the freelist is empty, the standard **new** operator must then be called.

Freelists are particularly useful for linked lists that periodically grow and then shrink. The freelist will never grow larger than the largest size yet reached by the linked list. Requests for new nodes (after the list has shrunk) can be handled by the freelist. Another good opportunity to use a freelist occurs when a program uses multiple lists. So long as they do not all grow and shrink together, the free list can let link nodes move between the lists.

One approach to implementing freelists would be to create two new operators to use instead of the standard free-store routines **new** and **delete**. This requires that the user's code, such as the linked list class implementation of Figure 4.8, be modified to call these freelist operators. A second approach is to use C++ **operator overloading** to replace the meaning of **new** and **delete** when operating on **Link** class objects. In this way, programs that use the **LList** class need not be modified at all to take advantage of a freelist. Whether the **Link** class is implemented with freelists, or relies on the regular free-store mechanism, is entirely hidden from the list class user.   Figure 4.11 shows the reimplementation for the **Link** class with freelist methods overloading the standard free-store operators.   Note how simple they are, because they need only remove and add an element to the front of the freelist, respectively. The freelist versions of **new** and **delete** both run in $\Theta(1)$ time, except in the case where the freelist is exhausted and the **new** operation must be called.   On my computer, a call to the overloaded **new** and **delete** operators requires about one tenth of the time required by the system free-store operators.

There is an additional efficiency gain to be had from a freelist implementation. The implementation of Figure 4.11 makes a separate call to the system **new** operator for each link node requested whenever the freelist is empty. These link nodes tend to be small — only a few bytes more than the size of the **element** field. If at some point in time the program requires thousands of active link nodes, these will

```cpp
// Singly linked list node with freelist support
template <typename E> class Link {
private:
  static Link<E>* freelist; // Reference to freelist head
public:
  E element;                     // Value for this node
  Link* next;                    // Point to next node in list

  // Constructors
  Link(const E& elemval, Link* nextval =NULL)
    { element = elemval;  next = nextval; }
  Link(Link* nextval =NULL) { next = nextval; }

  void* operator new(size_t) {  // Overloaded new operator
    if (freelist == NULL) return ::new Link; // Create space
    Link<E>* temp = freelist; // Can take from freelist
    freelist = freelist->next;
    return temp;                   // Return the link
  }

  // Overloaded delete operator
  void operator delete(void* ptr) {
    ((Link<E>*)ptr)->next = freelist; // Put on freelist
    freelist = (Link<E>*)ptr;
  }
};

// The freelist head pointer is actually created here
template <typename E>
Link<E>* Link<E>::freelist = NULL;
```

Figure 4.11 Implementation for the **Link** class with a freelist. Note that the redefinition for **new** refers to `::new` on the third line. This indicates that the standard **C**++ **new** operator is used, rather than the redefined **new** operator. If the colons had not been used, then the **Link** class **new** operator would be called, setting up an infinite recursion. The **static** declaration for member **freelist** means that all **Link** class objects share the same freelist pointer variable instead of each object storing its own copy.

have been created by many calls to the system version of **new**. An alternative is to allocate many link nodes in a single call to the system version of **new**, anticipating that if the freelist is exhausted now, more nodes will be needed soon. It is faster to make one call to **new** to get space for 100 **link** nodes, and then load all 100 onto the freelist at once, rather than to make 100 separate calls to **new**. The following statement will assign **ptr** to point to an array of 100 link nodes.

```cpp
ptr = ::new Link[100];
```

The implementation for the **new** operator in the **link** class could then place each of these 100 nodes onto the freelist.

The **freelist** variable declaration uses the keyword **static**. This creates a single variable shared among all instances of the **Link** nodes. We want only a single freelist for all **Link** nodes of a given type. A program might create multiple lists. If they are all of the same type (that is, their element types are the same), then they can and should share the same freelist. This will happen with the implementation of Figure 4.11. If lists are created that have different element types, because this code is implemented with a template, the need for different list implementations will be discovered by the compiler at compile time. Separate versions of the list class will be generated for each element type. Thus, each element type will also get its own separate copy of the **Link** class. And each distinct **Link** class implementation will get a separate freelist.

4.1.3 Comparison of List Implementations

Now that you have seen two substantially different implementations for lists, it is natural to ask which is better. In particular, if you must implement a list for some task, which implementation should you choose?

Array-based lists have the disadvantage that their size must be predetermined before the array can be allocated. Array-based lists cannot grow beyond their predetermined size. Whenever the list contains only a few elements, a substantial amount of space might be tied up in a largely empty array. Linked lists have the advantage that they only need space for the objects actually on the list. There is no limit to the number of elements on a linked list, as long as there is free-store memory available. The amount of space required by a linked list is $\Theta(n)$, while the space required by the array-based list implementation is $\Omega(n)$, but can be greater.

Array-based lists have the advantage that there is no wasted space for an individual element. Linked lists require that an extra pointer be added to every list node. If the element size is small, then the overhead for links can be a significant fraction of the total storage. When the array for the array-based list is completely filled, there is no storage overhead. The array-based list will then be more space efficient, by a constant factor, than the linked implementation.

A simple formula can be used to determine whether the array-based list or linked list implementation will be more space efficient in a particular situation. Call n the number of elements currently in the list, P the size of a pointer in storage units (typically four bytes), E the size of a data element in storage units (this could be anything, from one bit for a Boolean variable on up to thousands of bytes or more for complex records), and D the maximum number of list elements that can be stored in the array. The amount of space required for the array-based list is DE, regardless of the number of elements actually stored in the list at any given time. The amount of space required for the linked list is $n(P + E)$. The smaller of these expressions for a given value n determines the more space-efficient implementation for n elements. In general, the linked implementation requires less space than the array-based implementation when relatively few elements are in the list. Conversely, the array-based implementation becomes more space efficient when the array is close to full. Using the equation, we can solve for n to determine the break-even point beyond which the array-based implementation is more space efficient in any particular situation. This occurs when

$$n > DE/(P + E).$$

If $P = E$, then the break-even point is at $D/2$. This would happen if the element field is either a four-byte **int** value or a pointer, and the next field is a typical four-byte pointer. That is, the array-based implementation would be more efficient (if the link field and the element field are the same size) whenever the array is more than half full.

As a rule of thumb, linked lists are more space efficient when implementing lists whose number of elements varies widely or is unknown. Array-based lists are generally more space efficient when the user knows in advance approximately how large the list will become.

Array-based lists are faster for random access by position. Positions can easily be adjusted forwards or backwards by the **next** and **prev** methods. These operations always take $\Theta(1)$ time. In contrast, singly linked lists have no explicit access to the previous element, and access by position requires that we march down the list from the front (or the current position) to the specified position. Both of these operations require $\Theta(n)$ time in the average and worst cases, if we assume that each position on the list is equally likely to be accessed on any call to **prev** or **moveToPos**.

Given a pointer to a suitable location in the list, the **insert** and **remove** methods for linked lists require only $\Theta(1)$ time. Array-based lists must shift the remainder of the list up or down within the array. This requires $\Theta(n)$ time in the average and worst cases. For many applications, the time to insert and delete elements dominates all other operations. For this reason, linked lists are often preferred to array-based lists.

When implementing the array-based list, an implementor could allow the size of the array to grow and shrink depending on the number of elements that are actually stored. This data structure is known as a **dynamic array**. Both the Java and C++/STL **Vector** classes implement a dynamic array. Dynamic arrays allow the programmer to get around the limitation on the standard array that its size cannot be changed once the array has been created. This also means that space need not be allocated to the dynamic array until it is to be used. The disadvantage of this approach is that it takes time to deal with space adjustments on the array. Each time the array grows in size, its contents must be copied. A good implementation of the dynamic array will grow and shrink the array in such a way as to keep the overall cost for a series of insert/delete operations relatively inexpensive, even though an occasional insert/delete operation might be expensive. A simple rule of thumb is to double the size of the array when it becomes full, and to cut the array size in half when it becomes one quarter full. To analyze the overall cost of dynamic array operations over time, we need to use a technique known as **amortized analysis**, which is discussed in Section 14.3.

4.1.4 Element Implementations

List users must decide whether they wish to store a copy of any given element on each list that contains it. For small elements such as an integer, this makes sense. If the elements are payroll records, it might be desirable for the list node to store a pointer to the record rather than store a copy of the record itself. This change would allow multiple list nodes (or other data structures) to point to the same record, rather than make repeated copies of the record. Not only might this save space, but it also means that a modification to an element's value is automatically reflected at all locations where it is referenced. The disadvantage of storing a pointer to each element is that the pointer requires space of its own. If elements are never duplicated, then this additional space adds unnecessary overhead.

The C++ implementations for lists presented in this section give the user of the list the choice of whether to store copies of elements or pointers to elements. The user can declare **E** to be, for example, a pointer to a payroll record. In this case, multiple lists can point to the same copy of the record. On the other hand, if the user declares **E** to be the record itself, then a new copy of the record will be made when it is inserted into the list.

Whether it is more advantageous to use pointers to shared elements or separate copies depends on the intended application. In general, the larger the elements and the more they are duplicated, the more likely that pointers to shared elements is the better approach.

A second issue faced by implementors of a list class (or any other data structure that stores a collection of user-defined data elements) is whether the elements stored are all required to be of the same type. This is known as **homogeneity** in a data structure. In some applications, the user would like to define the class of the data element that is stored on a given list, and then never permit objects of a different class to be stored on that same list. In other applications, the user would like to permit the objects stored on a single list to be of differing types.

For the list implementations presented in this section, the compiler requires that all objects stored on the list be of the same type. In fact, because the lists are implemented using templates, a new class is created by the compiler for each data type. For implementors who wish to minimize the number of classes created by the compiler, the lists can all store a **void*** pointer, with the user performing the necessary casting to and from the actual object type for each element. However, this approach requires that the user do his or her own type checking, either to enforce homogeneity or to differentiate between the various object types.

Besides **C++** templates, there are other techniques that implementors of a list class can use to ensure that the element type for a given list remains fixed, while still permitting different lists to store different element types. One approach is to store an object of the appropriate type in the header node of the list (perhaps an object of the appropriate type is supplied as a parameter to the list constructor), and then check that all insert operations on that list use the same element type.

The third issue that users of the list implementations must face is primarily of concern when programming in languages that do not support automatic garbage collection. That is how to deal with the memory of the objects stored on the list when the list is deleted or the **clear** method is called. The list destructor and the **clear** method are problematic in that there is a potential that they will bemisused, thus causing a memory leak. The type of the element stored determines whether there is a potential for trouble here. If the elements are of a simple type such as an **int**, then there is no need to delete the elements explicitly. If the elements are of a user-defined class, then their own destructor will be called. However, what if the list elements are pointers to objects? Then deleting **listArray** in the array-based implementation, or deleting a link node in the linked list implementation, might remove the only reference to an object, leaving its memory space inaccessible. Unfortunately, there is no way for the list implementation to know whether a given object is pointed to in another part of the program or not. Thus, the user of the list must be responsible for deleting these objects when that is appropriate.

4.1.5 Doubly Linked Lists

The singly linked list presented in Section 4.1.2 allows for direct access from a list node only to the next node in the list. A **doubly linked list** allows convenient access from a list node to the next node and also to the preceding node on the list. The doubly linked list node accomplishes this in the obvious way by storing two pointers: one to the node following it (as in the singly linked list), and a second pointer to the node preceding it. The most common reason to use a doubly linked list is because it is easier to implement than a singly linked list. While the code for the doubly linked implementation is a little longer than for the singly linked version, it tends to be a bit more "obvious" in its intention, and so easier to implement and debug. Figure 4.12 illustrates the doubly linked list concept. Whether a list implementation is doubly or singly linked should be hidden from the **List** class user.

Like our singly linked list implementation, the doubly linked list implementation makes use of a header node. We also add a tailer node to the end of the list. The tailer is similar to the header, in that it is a node that contains no value, and it always exists. When the doubly linked list is initialized, the header and tailer nodes

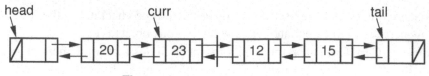

Figure 4.12 A doubly linked list.

are created. Data member **head** points to the header node, and **tail** points to the tailer node. The purpose of these nodes is to simplify the **insert**, **append**, and **remove** methods by eliminating all need for special-case code when the list is empty, or when we insert at the head or tail of the list.

For singly linked lists we set **curr** to point to the node preceding the node that contained the actual current element, due to lack of access to the previous node during insertion and deletion. Since we do have access to the previous node in a doubly linked list, this is no longer necessary. We could set **curr** to point directly to the node containing the current element. However, I have chosen to keep the same convention for the **curr** pointer as we set up for singly linked lists, purely for the sake of consistency.

Figure 4.13 shows the complete implementation for a **Link** class to be used with doubly linked lists. This code is a little longer than that for the singly linked list node implementation since the doubly linked list nodes have an extra data member.

Figure 4.14 shows the implementation for the **insert**, **append**, **remove**, and **prev** doubly linked list methods. The class declaration and the remaining member functions for the doubly linked list class are nearly identical to the singly linked list version.

The **insert** method is especially simple for our doubly linked list implementation, because most of the work is done by the node's constructor. Figure 4.15 shows the list before and after insertion of a node with value 10.

The three parameters to the **new** operator allow the list node class constructor to set the **element**, **prev**, and **next** fields, respectively, for the new link node. The **new** operator returns a pointer to the newly created node. The nodes to either side have their pointers updated to point to the newly created node. The existence of the header and tailer nodes mean that there are no special cases to worry about when inserting into an empty list.

The **append** method is also simple. Again, the **Link** class constructor sets the **element**, **prev**, and **next** fields of the node when the **new** operator is executed.

Method **remove** (illustrated by Figure 4.16) is straightforward, though the code is somewhat longer. First, the variable **it** is assigned the value being removed. Note that we must separate the element, which is returned to the caller, from the link object. The following lines then adjust the list.

```cpp
// Doubly linked list link node with freelist support
template <typename E> class Link {
private:
  static Link<E>* freelist; // Reference to freelist head

public:
  E element;         // Value for this node
  Link* next;        // Pointer to next node in list
  Link* prev;        // Pointer to previous node

  // Constructors
  Link(const E& it, Link* prevp, Link* nextp) {
    element = it;
    prev = prevp;
    next = nextp;
  }
  Link(Link* prevp =NULL, Link* nextp =NULL) {
    prev = prevp;
    next = nextp;
  }

  void* operator new(size_t) {  // Overloaded new operator
    if (freelist == NULL) return ::new Link; // Create space
    Link<E>* temp = freelist; // Can take from freelist
    freelist = freelist->next;
    return temp;                       // Return the link
  }

  // Overloaded delete operator
  void operator delete(void* ptr) {
    ((Link<E>*)ptr)->next = freelist; // Put on freelist
    freelist = (Link<E>*)ptr;
  }
};

// The freelist head pointer is actually created here
template <typename E>
Link<E>* Link<E>::freelist = NULL;
```

Figure 4.13 Doubly linked list node implementation with a freelist.

```cpp
// Insert "it" at current position
void insert(const E& it) {
  curr->next = curr->next->prev =
    new Link<E>(it, curr, curr->next);
  cnt++;
}

// Append "it" to the end of the list.
void append(const E& it) {
  tail->prev = tail->prev->next =
    new Link<E>(it, tail->prev, tail);
  cnt++;
}

// Remove and return current element
E remove() {
  if (curr->next == tail)          // Nothing to remove
    return NULL;
  E it = curr->next->element;      // Remember value
  Link<E>* ltemp = curr->next;     // Remember link node
  curr->next->next->prev = curr;
  curr->next = curr->next->next;   // Remove from list
  delete ltemp;                    // Reclaim space
  cnt--;                           // Decrement cnt
  return it;
}

// Move fence one step left; no change if left is empty
void prev() {
  if (curr != head)   // Can't back up from list head
    curr = curr->prev;
}
```

Figure 4.14 Implementations for doubly linked list **insert**, **append**, **remove**, and **prev** methods.

```cpp
Link<E>* ltemp = curr->next;     // Remember link node
curr->next->next->prev = curr;
curr->next = curr->next->next;   // Remove from list
delete ltemp;                    // Reclaim space
```

The first line sets a temporary pointer to the node being removed. The second line makes the next node's **prev** pointer point to the left of the node being removed. Finally, the **next** field of the node preceding the one being deleted is adjusted. The final steps of method **remove** are to update the listlength, return the deleted node to free store, and return the value of the deleted element.

The only disadvantage of the doubly linked list as compared to the singly linked list is the additional space used. The doubly linked list requires two pointers per node, and so in the implementation presented it requires twice as much overhead as the singly linked list.

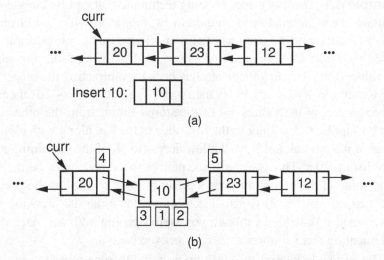

(a)

(b)

Figure 4.15 Insertion for doubly linked lists. The labels $\boxed{1}$, $\boxed{2}$, and $\boxed{3}$ correspond to assignments done by the linked list node constructor. $\boxed{4}$ marks the assignment to **curr->next**. $\boxed{5}$ marks the assignment to the **prev** pointer of the node following the newly inserted node.

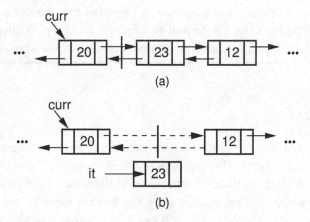

(a)

(b)

Figure 4.16 Doubly linked list removal. Element **it** stores the element of the node being removed. Then the nodes to either side have their pointers adjusted.

Example 4.1 There is a space-saving technique that can be employed to eliminate the additional space requirement, though it will complicate the implementation and be somewhat slower. Thus, this is an example of a space/time tradeoff. It is based on observing that, if we store the sum of two values, then we can get either value back by subtracting the other. That is, if we store $a + b$ in variable c, then $b = c - a$ and $a = c - b$. Of course, to recover one of the values out of the stored summation, the other value must be supplied. A pointer to the first node in the list, along with the value of one of its two link fields, will allow access to all of the remaining nodes of the list in order. This is because the pointer to the node must be the same as the value of the following node's **prev** pointer, as well as the previous node's **next** pointer. It is possible to move down the list breaking apart the summed link fields as though you were opening a zipper. Details for implementing this variation are left as an exercise.

The principle behind this technique is worth remembering, as it has many applications. The following code fragment will swap the contents of two variables without using a temporary variable (at the cost of three arithmetic operations).

```
a = a + b;
b = a - b; // Now b contains original value of a
a = a - b; // Now a contains original value of b
```

A similar effect can be had by using the exclusive-or operator. This fact is widely used in computer graphics. A region of the computer screen can be highlighted by XORing the outline of a box around it. XORing the box outline a second time restores the original contents of the screen.

4.2   Stacks

The **stack** is a list-like structure in which elements may be inserted or removed from only one end. While this restriction makes stacks less flexible than lists, it also makes stacks both efficient (for those operations they can do) and easy to implement. Many applications require only the limited form of insert and remove operations that stacks provide. In such cases, it is more efficient to use the simpler stack data structure rather than the generic list. For example, the freelist of Section 4.1.2 is really a stack.

Despite their restrictions, stacks have many uses. Thus, a special vocabulary for stacks has developed. Accountants used stacks long before the invention of the computer. They called the stack a "LIFO" list, which stands for "Last-In, First-

```
// Stack abtract class
template <typename E> class Stack {
private:
  void operator =(const Stack&) {}      // Protect assignment
  Stack(const Stack&) {}                // Protect copy constructor

public:
  Stack() {}                            // Default constructor
  virtual ~Stack() {}                   // Base destructor

  // Reinitialize the stack.  The user is responsible for
  // reclaiming the storage used by the stack elements.
  virtual void clear() = 0;

  // Push an element onto the top of the stack.
  // it: The element being pushed onto the stack.
  virtual void push(const E& it) = 0;

  // Remove the element at the top of the stack.
  // Return: The element at the top of the stack.
  virtual E pop() = 0;

  // Return: A copy of the top element.
  virtual const E& topValue() const = 0;

  // Return: The number of elements in the stack.
  virtual int length() const = 0;
};
```

Figure 4.17 The stack ADT.

Out." Note that one implication of the LIFO policy is that stacks remove elements in reverse order of their arrival.

The accessible element of the stack is called the **top** element. Elements are not said to be inserted, they are **pushed** onto the stack. When removed, an element is said to be **popped** from the stack. Figure 4.17 shows a sample stack ADT.

As with lists, there are many variations on stack implementation. The two approaches presented here are **array-based** and **linked stacks**, which are analogous to array-based and linked lists, respectively.

4.2.1 Array-Based Stacks

Figure 4.18 shows a complete implementation for the array-based stack class. As with the array-based list implementation, **listArray** must be declared of fixed size when the stack is created. In the stack constructor, **size** serves to indicate this size. Method **top** acts somewhat like a current position value (because the "current" position is always at the top of the stack), as well as indicating the number of elements currently in the stack.

```
// Array-based stack implementation
template <typename E> class AStack: public Stack<E> {
private:
  int maxSize;              // Maximum size of stack
  int top;                  // Index for top element
  E *listArray;             // Array holding stack elements

public:
  AStack(int size =defaultSize)    // Constructor
    { maxSize = size; top = 0; listArray = new E[size]; }

  ~AStack() { delete [] listArray; }   // Destructor

  void clear() { top = 0; }            // Reinitialize

  void push(const E& it) {             // Put "it" on stack
    Assert(top != maxSize, "Stack is full");
    listArray[top++] = it;
  }

  E pop() {                            // Pop top element
    Assert(top != 0, "Stack is empty");
    return listArray[--top];
  }

  const E& topValue() const {          // Return top element
    Assert(top != 0, "Stack is empty");
    return listArray[top-1];
  }

  int length() const { return top; }  // Return length
};
```

Figure 4.18 Array-based stack class implementation.

The array-based stack implementation is essentially a simplified version of the array-based list. The only important design decision to be made is which end of the array should represent the top of the stack. One choice is to make the top be at position 0 in the array. In terms of list functions, all **insert** and **remove** operations would then be on the element in position 0. This implementation is inefficient, because now every **push** or **pop** operation will require that all elements currently in the stack be shifted one position in the array, for a cost of $\Theta(n)$ if there are n elements. The other choice is have the top element be at position $n - 1$ when there are n elements in the stack. In other words, as elements are pushed onto the stack, they are appended to the tail of the list. Method **pop** removes the tail element. In this case, the cost for each **push** or **pop** operation is only $\Theta(1)$.

For the implementation of Figure 4.18, **top** is defined to be the array index of the first free position in the stack. Thus, an empty stack has **top** set to 0, the first available free position in the array. (Alternatively, **top** could have been defined to be the index for the top element in the stack, rather than the first free position. If this had been done, the empty list would initialize **top** as −1.) Methods **push** and **pop** simply place an element into, or remove an element from, the array position indicated by **top**. Because **top** is assumed to be at the first free position, **push** first inserts its value into the top position and then increments **top**, while **pop** first decrements **top** and then removes the top element.

```
// Linked stack implementation
template <typename E> class LStack: public Stack<E> {
private:
  Link<E>* top;                   // Pointer to first element
  int size;                       // Number of elements

public:
  LStack(int sz =defaultSize) // Constructor
    { top = NULL; size = 0; }

  ~LStack() { clear(); }                   // Destructor

  void clear() {                       // Reinitialize
    while (top != NULL) {              // Delete link nodes
      Link<E>* temp = top;
      top = top->next;
      delete temp;
    }
    size = 0;
  }

  void push(const E& it) { // Put "it" on stack
    top = new Link<E>(it, top);
    size++;
  }

  E pop() {                       // Remove "it" from stack
    Assert(top != NULL, "Stack is empty");
    E it = top->element;
    Link<E>* ltemp = top->next;
    delete top;
    top = ltemp;
    size--;
    return it;
  }

  const E& topValue() const { // Return top value
    Assert(top != 0, "Stack is empty");
    return top->element;
  }

  int length() const { return size; } // Return length
};
```

Figure 4.19 Linked stack class implementation.

4.2.2 Linked Stacks

The linked stack implementation is quite simple. The freelist of Section 4.1.2 is an example of a linked stack. Elements are inserted and removed only from the head of the list. A header node is not used because no special-case code is required for lists of zero or one elements. Figure 4.19 shows the complete linked stack

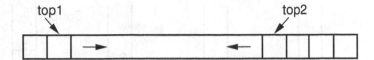

Figure 4.20 Two stacks implemented within in a single array, both growing toward the middle.

implementation. The only data member is **top**, a pointer to the first (top) link node of the stack. Method **push** first modifies the **next** field of the newly created link node to point to the top of the stack and then sets **top** to point to the new link node. Method **pop** is also quite simple. Variable **temp** stores the top nodes' value, while **ltemp** links to the top node as it is removed from the stack. The stack is updated by setting **top** to point to the next link in the stack. The old top node is then returned to free store (or the freelist), and the element value is returned.

4.2.3 Comparison of Array-Based and Linked Stacks

All operations for the array-based and linked stack implementations take constant time, so from a time efficiency perspective, neither has a significant advantage. Another basis for comparison is the total space required. The analysis is similar to that done for list implementations. The array-based stack must declare a fixed-size array initially, and some of that space is wasted whenever the stack is not full. The linked stack can shrink and grow but requires the overhead of a link field for every element.

When multiple stacks are to be implemented, it is possible to take advantage of the one-way growth of the array-based stack. This can be done by using a single array to store two stacks. One stack grows inward from each end as illustrated by Figure 4.20, hopefully leading to less wasted space. However, this only works well when the space requirements of the two stacks are inversely correlated. In other words, ideally when one stack grows, the other will shrink. This is particularly effective when elements are taken from one stack and given to the other. If instead both stacks grow at the same time, then the free space in the middle of the array will be exhausted quickly.

4.2.4 Implementing Recursion

Perhaps the most common computer application that uses stacks is not even visible to its users. This is the implementation of subroutine calls in most programming language runtime environments. A subroutine call is normally implemented by placing necessary information about the subroutine (including the return address, parameters, and local variables) onto a stack. This information is called an **activation record**. Further subroutine calls add to the stack. Each return from a subroutine pops the top activation record off the stack. Figure 4.21 illustrates the

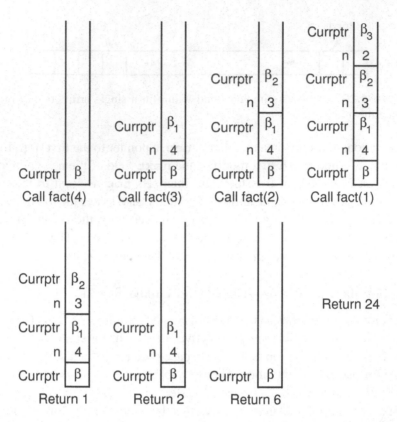

Figure 4.21 Implementing recursion with a stack. β values indicate the address of the program instruction to return to after completing the current function call. On each recursive function call to **fact** (as implemented in Section 2.5), both the return address and the current value of **n** must be saved. Each return from **fact** pops the top activation record off the stack.

implementation of the recursive factorial function of Section 2.5 from the runtime environment's point of view.

Consider what happens when we call **fact** with the value 4. We use β to indicate the address of the program instruction where the call to **fact** is made. Thus, the stack must first store the address β, and the value 4 is passed to **fact**. Next, a recursive call to **fact** is made, this time with value 3. We will name the program address from which the call is made β_1. The address β_1, along with the current value for n (which is 4), is saved on the stack. Function **fact** is invoked with input parameter 3.

In similar manner, another recursive call is made with input parameter 2, requiring that the address from which the call is made (say β_2) and the current value for n (which is 3) are stored on the stack. A final recursive call with input parameter 1 is made, requiring that the stack store the calling address (say β_3) and current value (which is 2).

At this point, we have reached the base case for **fact**, and so the recursion begins to unwind. Each return from **fact** involves popping the stored value for n from the stack, along with the return address from the function call. The return value for **fact** is multiplied by the restored value for n, and the result is returned.

Because an activation record must be created and placed onto the stack for each subroutine call, making subroutine calls is a relatively expensive operation. While recursion is often used to make implementation easy and clear, sometimes you might want to eliminate the overhead imposed by the recursive function calls. In some cases, such as the factorial function of Section 2.5, recursion can easily be replaced by iteration.

Example 4.2 As a simple example of replacing recursion with a stack, consider the following non-recursive version of the factorial function.

```
long fact(int n, Stack<int>& S) { // Compute n!
  // To fit n! in a long variable, require n <= 12
  Assert((n >= 0) && (n <= 12), "Input out of range");
  while (n > 1) S.push(n--);   // Load up the stack
  long result = 1;             // Holds final result
  while(S.length() > 0)
     result = result * S.pop();   // Compute
  return result;
}
```

Here, we simply push successively smaller values of n onto the stack until the base case is reached, then repeatedly pop off the stored values and multiply them into the result.

An iterative form of the factorial function is both simpler and faster than the version shown in Example 4.2. But it is not always possible to replace recursion with iteration. Recursion, or some imitation of it, is necessary when implementing algorithms that require multiple branching such as in the Towers of Hanoi algorithm, or when traversing a binary tree. The Mergesort and Quicksort algorithms of Chapter 7 are also examples in which recursion is required. Fortunately, it is always possible to imitate recursion with a stack. Let us now turn to a non-recursive version of the Towers of Hanoi function, which cannot be done iteratively.

Example 4.3 The **TOH** function shown in Figure 2.2 makes two recursive calls: one to move $n-1$ rings off the bottom ring, and another to move these $n-1$ rings back to the goal pole. We can eliminate the recursion by using a stack to store a representation of the three operations that **TOH** must perform: two recursive calls and a move operation. To do so, we must first come up with a representation of the various operations, implemented as a class whose objects will be stored on the stack.

```
// Operation choices: DOMOVE will move a disk
// DOTOH corresponds to a recursive call
enum TOHop { DOMOVE, DOTOH };
class TOHobj { // An operation object
public:
  TOHop op;              // This operation type
  int num;               // How many disks
  Pole start, goal, tmp; // Define pole order

  // DOTOH operation constructor
  TOHobj(int n, Pole s, Pole g, Pole t) {
    op = DOTOH; num = n;
    start = s; goal = g; tmp = t;
  }

  // DOMOVE operation constructor
  TOHobj(Pole s, Pole g)
    { op = DOMOVE; start = s; goal = g; }
};

void TOH(int n, Pole start, Pole goal, Pole tmp,
         Stack<TOHobj*>& S) {
  S.push(new TOHobj(n, start, goal, tmp)); // Initial
  TOHobj* t;
  while (S.length() > 0) {         // Grab next task
    t = S.pop();
    if (t->op == DOMOVE)    // Do a move
      move(t->start, t->goal);
    else if (t->num > 0) {
      // Store (in reverse) 3 recursive statements
      int num = t->num;
      Pole tmp = t->tmp;  Pole goal = t->goal;
      Pole start = t->start;
      S.push(new TOHobj(num-1, tmp, goal, start));
      S.push(new TOHobj(start, goal));
      S.push(new TOHobj(num-1, start, tmp, goal));
    }
    delete t; // Must delete the TOHobj we made
  }
}
```

Figure 4.22 Stack-based implementation for Towers of Hanoi.

Figure 4.22 shows such a class. We first define an enumerated type called **TOHop**, with two values MOVE and TOH, to indicate calls to the **move** function and recursive calls to **TOH**, respectively. Class **TOHobj** stores five values: an operation field (indicating either a move or a new TOH operation), the number of rings, and the three poles. Note that the move operation actually needs only to store information about two poles. Thus, there are two constructors: one to store the state when imitating a recursive call, and one to store the state for a move operation.

An array-based stack is used because we know that the stack will need to store exactly $2n+1$ elements. The new version of **TOH** begins by placing on the stack a description of the initial problem for n rings. The rest of the function is simply a **while** loop that pops the stack and executes the appropriate operation. In the case of a **TOH** operation (for $n > 0$), we store on the stack representations for the three operations executed by the recursive version. However, these operations must be placed on the stack in reverse order, so that they will be popped off in the correct order.

Recursive algorithms lend themselves to efficient implementation with a stack when the amount of information needed to describe a sub-problem is small. For example, Section 7.5 discusses a stack-based implementation for Quicksort.

4.3   Queues

Like the stack, the **queue** is a list-like structure that provides restricted access to its elements. Queue elements may only be inserted at the back (called an **enqueue** operation) and removed from the front (called a **dequeue** operation). Queues operate like standing in line at a movie theater ticket counter.[1] If nobody cheats, then newcomers go to the back of the line. The person at the front of the line is the next to be served. Thus, queues release their elements in order of arrival. Accountants have used queues since long before the existence of computers. They call a queue a "FIFO" list, which stands for "First-In, First-Out." Figure 4.23 shows a sample queue ADT. This section presents two implementations for queues: the array-based queue and the linked queue.

4.3.1   Array-Based Queues

The array-based queue is somewhat tricky to implement effectively. A simple conversion of the array-based list implementation is not efficient.

Assume that there are n elements in the queue. By analogy to the array-based list implementation, we could require that all elements of the queue be stored in the first n positions of the array. If we choose the rear element of the queue to be in position 0, then **dequeue** operations require only $\Theta(1)$ time because the front element of the queue (the one being removed) is the last element in the array. However, **enqueue** operations will require $\Theta(n)$ time, because the n elements currently in the queue must each be shifted one position in the array. If instead we chose the rear element of the queue to be in position $n - 1$, then an **enqueue** operation is equivalent to an **append** operation on a list. This requires only $\Theta(1)$ time. But now, a **dequeue** operation requires $\Theta(n)$ time, because all of the elements must be shifted down by one position to retain the property that the remaining $n - 1$ queue elements reside in the first $n - 1$ positions of the array.

---

[1] In Britain, a line of people is called a "queue," and getting into line to wait for service is called "queuing up."

```
// Abstract queue class
template <typename E> class Queue {
private:
  void operator =(const Queue&) {}      // Protect assignment
  Queue(const Queue&) {}                // Protect copy constructor

public:
  Queue() {}              // Default
  virtual ~Queue() {} // Base destructor

  // Reinitialize the queue.  The user is responsible for
  // reclaiming the storage used by the queue elements.
  virtual void clear() = 0;

  // Place an element at the rear of the queue.
  // it: The element being enqueued.
  virtual void enqueue(const E&) = 0;

  // Remove and return element at the front of the queue.
  // Return: The element at the front of the queue.
  virtual E dequeue() = 0;

  // Return: A copy of the front element.
  virtual const E& frontValue() const = 0;

  // Return: The number of elements in the queue.
  virtual int length() const = 0;
};
```

Figure 4.23 The C++ ADT for a queue.

A far more efficient implementation can be obtained by relaxing the requirement that all elements of the queue must be in the first n positions of the array. We will still require that the queue be stored be in contiguous array positions, but the contents of the queue will be permitted to drift within the array, as illustrated by Figure 4.24. Now, both the **enqueue** and the **dequeue** operations can be performed in $\Theta(1)$ time because no other elements in the queue need be moved.

This implementation raises a new problem. Assume that the front element of the queue is initially at position 0, and that elements are added to successively higher-numbered positions in the array. When elements are removed from the queue, the front index increases. Over time, the entire queue will drift toward the higher-numbered positions in the array. Once an element is inserted into the highest-numbered position in the array, the queue has run out of space. This happens despite the fact that there might be free positions at the low end of the array where elements have previously been removed from the queue.

The "drifting queue" problem can be solved by pretending that the array is circular and so allow the queue to continue directly from the highest-numbered position in the array to the lowest-numbered position. This is easily implemented

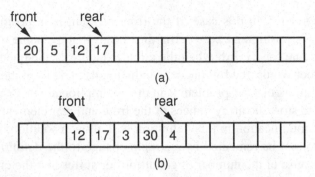

Figure 4.24 After repeated use, elements in the array-based queue will drift to the back of the array. (a) The queue after the initial four numbers 20, 5, 12, and 17 have been inserted. (b) The queue after elements 20 and 5 are deleted, following which 3, 30, and 4 are inserted.

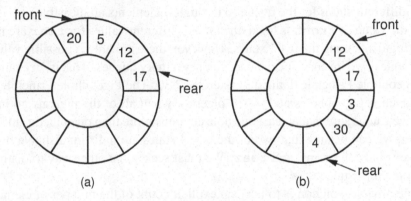

Figure 4.25 The circular queue with array positions increasing in the clockwise direction. (a) The queue after the initial four numbers 20, 5, 12, and 17 have been inserted. (b) The queue after elements 20 and 5 are deleted, following which 3, 30, and 4 are inserted.

through use of the modulus operator (denoted by `%` in **C++**). In this way, positions in the array are numbered from 0 through `size`−1, and position `size`−1 is defined to immediately precede position 0 (which is equivalent to position `size % size`). Figure 4.25 illustrates this solution.

There remains one more serious, though subtle, problem to the array-based queue implementation. How can we recognize when the queue is empty or full? Assume that **front** stores the array index for the front element in the queue, and **rear** stores the array index for the rear element. If both **front** and **rear** have the same position, then with this scheme there must be one element in the queue. Thus, an empty queue would be recognized by having **rear** be *one less* than **front** (taking into account the fact that the queue is circular, so position `size`−1 is actually considered to be one less than position 0). But what if the queue is completely full? In other words, what is the situation when a queue with n array positions available contains n elements? In this case, if the front element is in position 0, then the rear element is in position **size**-1. But this means that the value for **rear** is one less than the value for **front** when the circular nature of the queue is taken into account. In other words, the full queue is indistinguishable from the empty queue!

You might think that the problem is in the assumption about **front** and **rear** being defined to store the array indices of the front and rear elements, respectively, and that some modification in this definition will allow a solution. Unfortunately, the problem cannot be remedied by a simple change to the definition for **front** and **rear**, because of the number of conditions or **states** that the queue can be in. Ignoring the actual position of the first element, and ignoring the actual values of the elements stored in the queue, how many different states are there? There can be no elements in the queue, one element, two, and so on. At most there can be n elements in the queue if there are n array positions. This means that there are $n + 1$ different states for the queue (0 through n elements are possible).

If the value of **front** is fixed, then $n + 1$ different values for **rear** are needed to distinguish among the $n + 1$ states. However, there are only n possible values for **rear** unless we invent a special case for, say, empty queues. This is an example of the Pigeonhole Principle defined in Exercise 2.30. The Pigeonhole Principle states that, given n pigeonholes and $n + 1$ pigeons, when all of the pigeons go into the holes we can be sure that at least one hole contains more than one pigeon. In similar manner, we can be sure that two of the $n + 1$ states are indistinguishable by the n relative values of **front** and **rear**. We must seek some other way to distinguish full from empty queues.

One obvious solution is to keep an explicit count of the number of elements in the queue, or at least a Boolean variable that indicates whether the queue is empty or not. Another solution is to make the array be of size $n + 1$, and only allow n elements to be stored. Which of these solutions to adopt is purely a matter of the implementor's taste in such affairs. My choice is to use an array of size $n + 1$.

Figure 4.26 shows an array-based queue implementation. **listArray** holds the queue elements, and as usual, the queue constructor allows an optional parameter to set the maximum size of the queue. The array as created is actually large enough to hold one element more than the queue will allow, so that empty queues can be distinguished from full queues. Method **size** is used to control the circular motion of the queue (it is the base for the modulus operator). Method **rear** is set to the position of the rear element.

In this implementation, the front of the queue is defined to be toward the lower numbered positions in the array (in the counter-clockwise direction in Figure 4.25), and the rear is defined to be toward the higher-numbered positions. Thus, **enqueue** increments the rear pointer (modulus **size**), and **dequeue** increments the front pointer. Implementation of all member functions is straightforward.

```
// Array-based queue implementation
template <typename E> class AQueue: public Queue<E> {
private:
  int maxSize;                // Maximum size of queue
  int front;                  // Index of front element
  int rear;                   // Index of rear element
  E *listArray;               // Array holding queue elements

public:
  AQueue(int size =defaultSize) {  // Constructor
    // Make list array one position larger for empty slot
    maxSize = size+1;
    rear = 0;   front = 1;
    listArray = new E[maxSize];
  }

  ~AQueue() { delete [] listArray; } // Destructor

  void clear() { rear = 0; front = 1; } // Reinitialize

  void enqueue(const E& it) {        // Put "it" in queue
    Assert(((rear+2) % maxSize) != front, "Queue is full");
    rear = (rear+1) % maxSize;            // Circular increment
    listArray[rear] = it;
  }

  E dequeue() {              // Take element out
    Assert(length() != 0, "Queue is empty");
    E it = listArray[front];
    front = (front+1) % maxSize;    // Circular increment
    return it;
  }

  const E& frontValue() const {  // Get front value
    Assert(length() != 0, "Queue is empty");
    return listArray[front];
  }

  virtual int length() const          // Return length
    { return ((rear+maxSize) - front + 1) % maxSize; }
};
```

Figure 4.26 An array-based queue implementation.

4.3.2   Linked Queues

The linked queue implementation is a straightforward adaptation of the linked list. Figure 4.27 shows the linked queue class declaration. Methods **front** and **rear** are pointers to the front and rear queue elements, respectively. We will use a header link node, which allows for a simpler implementation of the enqueue operation by avoiding any special cases when the queue is empty. On initialization, the **front** and **rear** pointers will point to the header node, and front will always point to the header node while rear points to the true last link node in the queue. Method **enqueue** places the new element in a link node at the end of the linked list (i.e., the node that **rear** points to) and then advances **rear** to point to the new link node. Method **dequeue** removes and returns the first element of the list.

4.3.3   Comparison of Array-Based and Linked Queues

All member functions for both the array-based and linked queue implementations require constant time. The space comparison issues are the same as for the equivalent stack implementations. Unlike the array-based stack implementation, there is no convenient way to store two queues in the same array, unless items are always transferred directly from one queue to the other.

4.4   Dictionaries

The most common objective of computer programs is to store and retrieve data. Much of this book is about efficient ways to organize collections of data records so that they can be stored and retrieved quickly. In this section we describe a simple interface for such a collection, called a **dictionary**. The dictionary ADT provides operations for storing records, finding records, and removing records from the collection. This ADT gives us a standard basis for comparing various data structures.

Before we can discuss the interface for a dictionary, we must first define the concepts of a **key** and **comparable** objects. If we want to search for a given record in a database, how should we describe what we are looking for? A database record could simply be a number, or it could be quite complicated, such as a payroll record with many fields of varying types. We do not want to describe what we are looking for by detailing and matching the entire contents of the record. If we knew everything about the record already, we probably would not need to look for it. Instead, we typically define what record we want in terms of a key value. For example, if searching for payroll records, we might wish to search for the record that matches a particular ID number. In this example the ID number is the **search key**.

To implement the search function, we require that keys be comparable. At a minimum, we must be able to take two keys and reliably determine whether they

```
// Linked queue implementation
template <typename E> class LQueue: public Queue<E> {
private:
  Link<E>* front;          // Pointer to front queue node
  Link<E>* rear;           // Pointer to rear queue node
  int size;                // Number of elements in queue

public:
  LQueue(int sz =defaultSize) // Constructor
    { front = rear = new Link<E>(); size = 0; }

  ~LQueue() { clear(); delete front; }       // Destructor

  void clear() {                 // Clear queue
    while(front->next != NULL) { // Delete each link node
      rear = front;
      delete rear;
    }
    rear = front;
    size = 0;
  }

  void enqueue(const E& it) { // Put element on rear
    rear->next = new Link<E>(it, NULL);
    rear = rear->next;
    size++;
  }

  E dequeue() {                  // Remove element from front
    Assert(size != 0, "Queue is empty");
    E it = front->next->element;  // Store dequeued value
    Link<E>* ltemp = front->next; // Hold dequeued link
    front->next = ltemp->next;        // Advance front
    if (rear == ltemp) rear = front; // Dequeue last element
    delete ltemp;                     // Delete link
    size --;
    return it;                        // Return element value
  }

  const E& frontValue() const { // Get front element
    Assert(size != 0, "Queue is empty");
    return front->next->element;
  }

  virtual int length() const { return size; }
};
```

Figure 4.27 Linked queue class implementation.

are equal or not. That is enough to enable a sequential search through a database of records and find one that matches a given key. However, we typically would like for the keys to define a total order (see Section 2.1), which means that we can tell which of two keys is greater than the other. Using key types with total orderings gives the database implementor the opportunity to organize a collection of records in a way that makes searching more efficient. An example is storing the records in sorted order in an array, which permits a binary search. Fortunately, in practice most fields of most records consist of simple data types with natural total orders. For example, integers, floats, doubles, and character strings all are totally ordered. Ordering fields that are naturally multi-dimensional, such as a point in two or three dimensions, present special opportunities if we wish to take advantage of their multidimensional nature. This problem is addressed in Section 13.3.

Figure 4.28 shows the definition for a simple abstract dictionary class. The methods **insert** and **find** are the heart of the class. Method **insert** takes a record and inserts it into the dictionary. Method **find** takes a key value and returns some record from the dictionary whose key matches the one provided. If there are multiple records in the dictionary with that key value, there is no requirement as to which one is returned.

Method **clear** simply re-initializes the dictionary. The **remove** method is similar to **find**, except that it also deletes the record returned from the dictionary. Once again, if there are multiple records in the dictionary that match the desired key, there is no requirement as to which one actually is removed and returned. Method **size** returns the number of elements in the dictionary.

The remaining Method is **removeAny**. This is similar to **remove**, except that it does not take a key value. Instead, it removes an arbitrary record from the dictionary, if one exists. The purpose of this method is to allow a user the ability to iterate over all elements in the dictionary (of course, the dictionary will become empty in the process). Without the **removeAny** method, a dictionary user could not get at a record of the dictionary that he didn't already know the key value for. With the **removeAny** method, the user can process all records in the dictionary as shown in the following code fragment.

```
while (dict.size() > 0) {
  it = dict.removeAny();
  doSomething(it);
}
```

There are other approaches that might seem more natural for iterating though a dictionary, such as using a "first" and a "next" function. But not all data structures that we want to use to implement a dictionary are able to do "first" efficiently. For example, a hash table implementation cannot efficiently locate the record in the table with the smallest key value. By using **RemoveAny**, we have a mechanism that provides generic access.

```
// The Dictionary abstract class.
template <typename Key, typename E>
class  Dictionary {
private:
  void operator =(const Dictionary&) {}
  Dictionary(const Dictionary&) {}

public:
  Dictionary() {}              // Default constructor
  virtual ~Dictionary() {} // Base destructor

  // Reinitialize dictionary
  virtual void clear() = 0;

  // Insert a record
  // k: The key for the record being inserted.
  // e: The record being inserted.
  virtual void insert(const Key& k, const E& e) = 0;

  // Remove and return a record.
  // k: The key of the record to be removed.
  // Return: A maching record. If multiple records match
  // "k", remove an arbitrary one. Return NULL if no record
  // with key "k" exists.
  virtual E remove(const Key& k) = 0;

  // Remove and return an arbitrary record from dictionary.
  // Return: The record removed, or NULL if none exists.
  virtual E removeAny() = 0;

  // Return: A record matching "k" (NULL if none exists).
  // If multiple records match, return an arbitrary one.
  // k: The key of the record to find
  virtual E find(const Key& k) const = 0;

  // Return the number of records in the dictionary.
  virtual int size() = 0;
};
```

Figure 4.28 The ADT for a simple dictionary.

```
// A simple payroll entry with ID, name, address fields
class Payroll {
private:
  int ID;
  string name;
  string address;

public:
  // Constructor
  Payroll(int inID, string inname, string inaddr) {
    ID = inID;
    name = inname;
    address = inaddr;
  }

  ~Payroll() {}  // Destructor

  // Local data member access functions
  int getID() { return ID; }
  string getname() { return name; }
  string getaddr() { return address; }
};
```

Figure 4.29 A payroll record implementation.

Given a database storing records of a particular type, we might want to search for records in multiple ways. For example, we might want to store payroll records in one dictionary that allows us to search by ID, and also store those same records in a second dictionary that allows us to search by name.

Figure 4.29 shows an implementation for a payroll record. Class **Payroll** has multiple fields, each of which might be used as a search key. Simply by varying the type for the key, and using the appropriate field in each record as the key value, we can define a dictionary whose search key is the ID field, another whose search key is the name field, and a third whose search key is the address field. Figure 4.30 shows an example where **Payroll** objects are stored in two separate dictionaries, one using the ID field as the key and the other using the name field as the key.

The fundamental operation for a dictionary is finding a record that matches a given key. This raises the issue of how to extract the key from a record. We would like any given dictionary implementation to support arbitrary record types, so we need some mechanism for extracting keys that is sufficiently general. One approach is to require all record types to support some particular method that returns the key value. For example, in Java the **Comparable** interface can be used to provide this effect. Unfortunately, this approach does not work when the same record type is meant to be stored in multiple dictionaries, each keyed by a different field of the record. This is typical in database applications. Another, more general approach is to supply a class whose job is to extract the key from the record. Unfortunately,

```
int main() {
  // IDdict organizes Payroll records by ID
  UALdict<int, Payroll*> IDdict;
  // namedict organizes Payroll records by name
  UALdict<string, Payroll*> namedict;
  Payroll *foo1, *foo2, *findfoo1, *findfoo2;

  foo1 = new Payroll(5, "Joe", "Anytown");
  foo2 = new Payroll(10, "John", "Mytown");

  IDdict.insert(foo1->getID(), foo1);
  IDdict.insert(foo2->getID(), foo2);
  namedict.insert(foo1->getname(), foo1);
  namedict.insert(foo2->getname(), foo2);

  findfoo1 = IDdict.find(5);
  if (findfoo1 != NULL) cout << findfoo1;
  else cout << "NULL ";
  findfoo2 = namedict.find("John");
  if (findfoo2 != NULL) cout << findfoo2;
  else cout << "NULL ";
}
```

Figure 4.30 A dictionary search example. Here, payroll records are stored in two dictionaries, one organized by ID and the other organized by name. Both dictionaries are implemented with an unsorted array-based list.

this solution also does not work in all situations, because there are record types for which it is not possible to write a key extraction method.[2]

The fundamental issue is that the key value for a record is not an intrinsic property of the record's class, or of any field within the class. The key for a record is actually a property of the context in which the record is used.

A truly general alternative is to explicitly store the key associated with a given record, as a separate field in the dictionary. That is, each entry in the dictionary will contain both a record and its associated key. Such entries are known as key-value pairs. It is typical that storing the key explicitly duplicates some field in the record. However, keys tend to be much smaller than records, so this additional space overhead will not be great. A simple class for representing key-value pairs is shown in Figure 4.31. The **insert** method of the dictionary class supports the key-value pair implementation because it takes two parameters, a record and its associated key for that dictionary.

---

[2]One example of such a situation occurs when we have a collection of records that describe books in a library. One of the fields for such a record might be a list of subject keywords, where the typical record stores a few keywords. Our dictionary might be implemented as a list of records sorted by keyword. If a book contains three keywords, it would appear three times on the list, once for each associated keyword. However, given the record, there is no simple way to determine which keyword on the keyword list triggered this appearance of the record. Thus, we cannot write a function that extracts the key from such a record.

```
// Container for a key-value pair
template <typename Key, typename E>
class KVpair {
private:
  Key k;
  E e;
public:
  // Constructors
  KVpair() {}
  KVpair(Key kval, E eval)
    { k = kval; e = eval; }
  KVpair(const KVpair& o)   // Copy constructor
    { k = o.k; e = o.e; }

  void operator =(const KVpair& o) // Assignment operator
    { k = o.k; e = o.e; }

  // Data member access functions
  Key key() { return k; }
  void setKey(Key ink) { k = ink; }
  E value() { return e; }
};
```

Figure 4.31 Implementation for a class representing a key-value pair.

Now that we have defined the dictionary ADT and settled on the design approach of storing key-value pairs for our dictionary entries, we are ready to consider ways to implement it. Two possibilities would be to use an array-based or linked list. Figure 4.32 shows an implementation for the dictionary using an (unsorted) array-based list.

Examining class **UALdict** (UAL stands for "unsorted array-based list), we can easily see that **insert** is a constant-time operation, because it simply inserts the new record at the end of the list. However, **find**, and **remove** both require $\Theta(n)$ time in the average and worst cases, because we need to do a sequential search. Method **remove** in particular must touch every record in the list, because once the desired record is found, the remaining records must be shifted down in the list to fill the gap. Method **removeAny** removes the last record from the list, so this is a constant-time operation.

As an alternative, we could implement the dictionary using a linked list. The implementation would be quite similar to that shown in Figure 4.32, and the cost of the functions should be the same asymptotically.

Another alternative would be to implement the dictionary with a sorted list. The advantage of this approach would be that we might be able to speed up the **find** operation by using a binary search. To do so, first we must define a variation on the **List** ADT to support sorted lists.An implementation for the array-based sorted list is shown in Figure 4.33. A sorted list is somewhat different from an unsorted list in that it cannot permit the user to control where elements get inserted. Thus,

141

```
// Dictionary implemented with an unsorted array-based list
template <typename Key, typename E>
class UALdict : public Dictionary<Key, E> {
private:
  AList<KVpair<Key,E> >* list;
public:
  UALdict(int size=defaultSize)    // Constructor
    { list = new AList<KVpair<Key,E> >(size); }
  ~UALdict() { delete list; }            // Destructor
  void clear() { list->clear(); }        // Reinitialize

  // Insert an element: append to list
  void insert(const Key&k, const E& e) {
    KVpair<Key,E> temp(k, e);
    list->append(temp);
  }

  // Use sequential search to find the element to remove
  E remove(const Key& k) {
    E temp = find(k); // "find" will set list position
    if(temp != NULL) list->remove();
    return temp;
  }

  E removeAny() { // Remove the last element
    Assert(size() != 0, "Dictionary is empty");
    list->moveToEnd();
    list->prev();
    KVpair<Key,E> e = list->remove();
    return e.value();
  }

  // Find "k" using sequential search
  E find(const Key& k) const {
    for(list->moveToStart();
        list->currPos() < list->length(); list->next()) {
      KVpair<Key,E> temp = list->getValue();
      if (k == temp.key())
        return temp.value();
    }
    return NULL; // "k" does not appear in dictionary
  }
```

Figure 4.32 A dictionary implemented with an unsorted array-based list.

```
  int size() // Return list size
    { return list->length(); }
};
```

Figure 4.32 (continued)

```
// Sorted array-based list
// Inherit from AList as a protected base class
template <typename Key, typename E>
class SAList: protected AList<KVpair<Key,E> > {
public:
  SAList(int size=defaultSize) :
    AList<KVpair<Key,E> >(size) {}

  ~SAList() {}                        // Destructor

  // Redefine insert function to keep values sorted
  void insert(KVpair<Key,E>& it) { // Insert at right
    KVpair<Key,E> curr;
    for (moveToStart(); currPos() < length(); next()) {
      curr = getValue();
      if(curr.key() > it.key())
        break;
    }
    AList<KVpair<Key,E> >::insert(it); // Do AList insert
  }

  // With the exception of append, all remaining methods are
  // exposed from AList. Append is not available to SAlist
  // class users since it has not been explicitly exposed.
  AList<KVpair<Key,E> >::clear;
  AList<KVpair<Key,E> >::remove;
  AList<KVpair<Key,E> >::moveToStart;
  AList<KVpair<Key,E> >::moveToEnd;
  AList<KVpair<Key,E> >::prev;
  AList<KVpair<Key,E> >::next;
  AList<KVpair<Key,E> >::length;
  AList<KVpair<Key,E> >::currPos;
  AList<KVpair<Key,E> >::moveToPos;
  AList<KVpair<Key,E> >::getValue;
};
```

Figure 4.33 An implementation for a sorted array-based list.

the **insert** method must be quite different in a sorted list than in an unsorted list. Likewise, the user cannot be permitted to append elements onto the list. For these reasons, a sorted list cannot be implemented with straightforward inheritance from the **List** ADT.

Class **SAList** (SAL stands for "sorted array-based list") does inherit from class **AList**; however it does so using class **AList** as a protected base class. This means that **SAList** has available for its use any member functions of **AList**, but those member functions are not necessarily available to the user of **SAList**. However, many of the **AList** member functions are useful to the **SALlist** user. Thus, most of the **AList** member functions are passed along directly to the **SAList** user without change. For example, the line

```
AList<KVpair<Key,E> >::remove;
```

provides **SAList**'s clients with access to the **remove** method of **AList**. However, the original **insert** method from class **AList** is replaced, and the **append** method of **AList** is kept hidden.

The dictionary ADT can easily be implemented from class **SAList**, as shown in Figure 4.34. Method **insert** for the dictionary simply calls the **insert** method of the sorted list. Method **find** uses a generalization of the binary search function originally shown in Section 3.5. The cost for **find** in a sorted list is $\Theta(\log n)$ for a list of length n. This is a great improvement over the cost of **find** in an unsorted list. Unfortunately, the cost of **insert** changes from constant time in the unsorted list to $\Theta(n)$ time in the sorted list. Whether the sorted list implementation for the dictionary ADT is more or less efficient than the unsorted list implementation depends on the relative number of **insert** and **find** operations to be performed. If many more **find** operations than **insert** operations are used, then it might be worth using a sorted list to implement the dictionary. In both cases, **remove** requires $\Theta(n)$ time in the worst and average cases. Even if we used binary search to cut down on the time to find the record prior to removal, we would still need to shift down the remaining records in the list to fill the gap left by the **remove** operation.

Given two keys, we have not properly addressed the issue of how to compare them. One possibility would be to simply use the basic **==**, **<=**, and **>=** operators built into **C++**. This is the approach taken by our implementations for dictionaries shown inFigures 4.32 and 4.34. If the key type is **int**, for example, this will work fine. However, if the key is a pointer to a string or any other type of object, then this will not give the desired result. When we compare two strings we probably want to know which comes first in alphabetical order, but what we will get from the standard comparison operators is simply which object appears first in memory. Unfortunately, the code will compile fine, but the answers probably will not be fine.

In a language like **C++** that supports operator overloading, we could require that the user of the dictionary overload the **==**, **<=**, and **>=** operators for the given key type. This requirement then becomes an obligation on the user of the dictionary class. Unfortunately, this obligation is hidden within the code of the dictionary (and possibly in the user's manual) rather than exposed in the dictionary's interface. As a result, some users of the dictionary might neglect to implement the overloading, with unexpected results. Again, the compiler will not catch this problem.

The most general solution is to have users supply their own definition for comparing keys. The concept of a class that does comparison (called a **comparator**) is quite important. By making these operations be template parameters, the requirement to supply the comparator class becomes part of the interface. This design is an example of the Strategy design pattern, because the "strategies" for comparing and getting keys from records are provided by the client. In some cases, it makes

```cpp
// Dictionary implemented with a sorted array-based list
template <typename Key, typename E>
class SALdict : public Dictionary<Key, E> {
private:
  SAList<Key,E>* list;
public:
  SALdict(int size=defaultSize)    // Constructor
    { list = new SAList<Key,E>(size); }
  ~SALdict() { delete list; }          // Destructor
  void clear() { list->clear(); }      // Reinitialize

  // Insert an element: Keep elements sorted
  void insert(const Key&k, const E& e) {
    KVpair<Key,E> temp(k, e);
    list->insert(temp);
  }

  // Use sequential search to find the element to remove
  E remove(const Key& k) {
    E temp = find(k);
    if (temp != NULL) list->remove();
    return temp;
  }

  E removeAny() { // Remove the last element
    Assert(size() != 0, "Dictionary is empty");
    list->moveToEnd();
    list->prev();
    KVpair<Key,E> e = list->remove();
    return e.value();
  }

  // Find "K" using binary search
  E find(const Key& k) const {
    int l = -1;
    int r = list->length();
    while (l+1 != r) { // Stop when l and r meet
      int i = (l+r)/2; // Check middle of remaining subarray
      list->moveToPos(i);
      KVpair<Key,E> temp = list->getValue();
      if (k < temp.key()) r = i;          // In left
      if (k == temp.key()) return temp.value(); // Found it
      if (k > temp.key()) l = i;          // In right
    }
    return NULL; // "k" does not appear in dictionary
  }
```

Figure 4.34 Dictionary implementation using a sorted array-based list.

```
int size() // Return list size
   { return list->length(); }
};
```

Figure 4.34 (continued)

sense for for the comparator class to extract the key from the record type, as an alternative to storing key-value pairs.

Here is an example of the required class for comparing two integers.

```
class intintCompare { // Comparator class for integer keys
public:
   static bool lt(int x, int y) { return x < y; }
   static bool eq(int x, int y) { return x == y; }
   static bool gt(int x, int y) { return x > y; }
};
```

Class **intintCompare** provides methods for determining if two **int** variables are equal (**eq**), or if the first is less than the second (**lt**), or greater than the second (**gt**).

Here is a class for comparing two C-style character strings. It makes use of the standard library function **strcmp** to do the actual comparison.

```
class CCCompare { // Compare two character strings
public:
   static bool lt(char* x, char* y)
      { return strcmp(x, y) < 0; }
   static bool eq(char* x, char* y)
      { return strcmp(x, y) == 0; }
   static bool gt(char* x, char* y)
      { return strcmp(x, y) > 0; }
};
```

We will usea comparator in Section 5.5 to implement comparison in heaps, and in Chapter 7 to implement comparison in sorting algorithms.

4.5 Further Reading

For more discussion on choice of functions used to define the **List** ADT, see the work of the Reusable Software Research Group from Ohio State. Their definition for the **List** ADT can be found in [SWH93]. More information about designing such classes can be found in [SW94].

4.6 Exercises

4.1 Assume a list has the following configuration:

$$\langle \, | \, 2, \, 23, \, 15, \, 5, \, 9 \, \rangle.$$

Write a series of C++ statements using the **List** ADT of Figure 4.1 to delete the element with value 15.

4.2 Show the list configuration resulting from each series of list operations using the **List** ADT of Figure 4.1. Assume that lists **L1** and **L2** are empty at the beginning of each series. Show where the current position is in the list.

    (a) `L1.append(10);`
        `L1.append(20);`
        `L1.append(15);`

    (b) `L2.append(10);`
        `L2.append(20);`
        `L2.append(15);`
        `L2.moveToStart();`
        `L2.insert(39);`
        `L2.next();`
        `L2.insert(12);`

4.3 Write a series of C++ statements that uses the **List** ADT of Figure 4.1 to create a list capable of holding twenty elements and which actually stores the list with the following configuration:

$$\langle\, 2,\ 23 \mid 15,\ 5,\ 9 \,\rangle.$$

4.4 Using the list ADT of Figure 4.1, write a function to interchange the current element and the one following it.

4.5 In the linked list implementation presented in Section 4.1.2, the current position is implemented using a pointer to the element ahead of the logical current node. The more "natural" approach might seem to be to have **curr** point directly to the node containing the current element. However, if this was done, then the pointer of the node preceding the current one cannot be updated properly because there is no access to this node from **curr**. An alternative is to add a new node *after* the current element, copy the value of the current element to this new node, and then insert the new value into the old current node.

    (a) What happens if **curr** is at the end of the list already? Is there still a way to make this work? Is the resulting code simpler or more complex than the implementation of Section 4.1.2?

    (b) Will deletion always work in constant time if **curr** points directly to the current node? In particular, can you make several deletions in a row?

4.6 Add to the **LList** class implementation a member function to reverse the order of the elements on the list. Your algorithm should run in $\Theta(n)$ time for a list of n elements.

4.7 Write a function to merge two linked lists. The input lists have their elements in sorted order, from lowest to highest. The output list should also be sorted from lowest to highest. Your algorithm should run in linear time on the length of the output list.

4.8 A **circular linked list** is one in which the **next** field for the last link node of the list points to the first link node of the list. This can be useful when you wish to have a relative positioning for elements, but no concept of an absolute first or last position.

    (a) Modify the code of Figure 4.8 to implement circular singly linked lists.

    (b) Modify the code of Figure 4.14 to implement circular doubly linked lists.

4.9 Section 4.1.3 states "the space required by the array-based list implementation is $\Omega(n)$, but can be greater." Explain why this is so.

4.10 Section 4.1.3 presents an equation for determining the break-even point for the space requirements of two implementations of lists. The variables are D, E, P, and n. What are the dimensional units for each variable? Show that both sides of the equation balance in terms of their dimensional units.

4.11 Use the space equation of Section 4.1.3 to determine the break-even point for an array-based list and linked list implementation for lists when the sizes for the data field, a pointer, and the array-based list's array are as specified.

    (a) The data field is eight bytes, a pointer is four bytes, and the array holds twenty elements.

    (b) The data field is two bytes, a pointer is four bytes, and the array holds thirty elements.

    (c) The data field is one byte, a pointer is four bytes, and the array holds thirty elements.

    (d) The data field is 32 bytes, a pointer is four bytes, and the array holds forty elements.

4.12 Determine the size of an **int** variable, a **double** variable, and a pointer on your computer. (The **C++** operator **sizeof** might be useful here if you do not already know the answer.)

    (a) Calculate the break-even point, as a function of n, beyond which the array-based list is more space efficient than the linked list for lists whose elements are of type **int**.

    (b) Calculate the break-even point, as a function of n, beyond which the array-based list is more space efficient than the linked list for lists whose elements are of type **double**.

4.13 Modify the code of Figure 4.18 to implement two stacks sharing the same array, as shown in Figure 4.20.

4.14 Modify the array-based queue definition of Figure 4.26 to use a separate Boolean member to keep track of whether the queue is empty, rather than require that one array position remain empty.

4.15 A **palindrome** is a string that reads the same forwards as backwards. Using only a fixed number of stacks and queues, the stack and queue ADT functions, and a fixed number of **int** and **char** variables, write an algorithm to determine if a string is a palindrome. Assume that the string is read from standard input one character at a time. The algorithm should output **true** or **false** as appropriate.

4.16 Re-implement function **fibr** from Exercise 2.11, using a stack to replace the recursive call as described in Section 4.2.4.

4.17 Write a recursive algorithm to compute the value of the recurrence relation

$$\mathbf{T}(n) = \mathbf{T}(\lceil n/2 \rceil) + \mathbf{T}(\lfloor n/2 \rfloor) + n; \quad \mathbf{T}(1) = 1.$$

Then, rewrite your algorithm to simulate the recursive calls with a stack.

4.18 Let Q be a non-empty queue, and let S be an empty stack. Using only the stack and queue ADT functions and a single element variable X, write an algorithm to reverse the order of the elements in Q.

4.19 A common problem for compilers and text editors is to determine if the parentheses (or other brackets) in a string are balanced and properly nested. For example, the string "((())())()" contains properly nested pairs of parentheses, but the string ")()(" does not, and the string "())" does not contain properly matching parentheses.

   (a) Give an algorithm that returns **true** if a string contains properly nested and balanced parentheses, and **false** otherwise. Use a stack to keep track of the number of left parentheses seen so far. *Hint*: At no time while scanning a legal string from left to right will you have encountered more right parentheses than left parentheses.

   (b) Give an algorithm that returns the position in the string of the first offending parenthesis if the string is not properly nested and balanced. That is, if an excess right parenthesis is found, return its position; if there are too many left parentheses, return the position of the first excess left parenthesis. Return -1 if the string is properly balanced and nested. Use a stack to keep track of the number and positions of left parentheses seen so far.

4.20 Imagine that you are designing an application where you need to perform the operations **Insert**, **Delete_Maximum**, and **Delete_Minimum**. For this application, the cost of inserting is not important, because it can be done off-line prior to startup of the time-critical section, but the performance of the two deletion operations are critical. Repeated deletions of either kind must work as fast as possible. Suggest a data structure that can support this application, and justify your suggestion. What is the time complexity for each of the three key operations?

4.21 Write a function that reverses the order of an array of n items.

4.7 Projects

4.1 A **deque** (pronounced "deck") is like a queue, except that items may be added and removed from both the front and the rear. Write either an array-based or linked implementation for the deque.

4.2 One solution to the problem of running out of space for an array-based list implementation is to replace the array with a larger array whenever the original array overflows. A good rule that leads to an implementation that is both space and time efficient is to double the current size of the array when there is an overflow. Re-implement the array-based **List** class of Figure 4.2 to support this array-doubling rule.

4.3 Use singly linked lists to implement integers of unlimited size. Each node of the list should store one digit of the integer. You should implement addition, subtraction, multiplication, and exponentiation operations. Limit exponents to be positive integers. What is the asymptotic running time for each of your operations, expressed in terms of the number of digits for the two operands of each function?

4.4 Implement doubly linked lists by storing the sum of the **next** and **prev** pointers in a single pointer variable as described in Example 4.1.

4.5 Implement a city database using unordered lists. Each database record contains the name of the city (a string of arbitrary length) and the coordinates of the city expressed as integer x and y coordinates. Your database should allow records to be inserted, deleted by name or coordinate, and searched by name or coordinate. Another operation that should be supported is to print all records within a given distance of a specified point. Implement the database using an array-based list implementation, and then a linked list implementation. Collect running time statistics for each operation in both implementations. What are your conclusions about the relative advantages and disadvantages of the two implementations? Would storing records on the list in alphabetical order by city name speed any of the operations? Would keeping the list in alphabetical order slow any of the operations?

4.6 Modify the code of Figure 4.18 to support storing variable-length strings of at most 255 characters. The stack array should have type **char**. A string is represented by a series of characters (one character per stack element), with

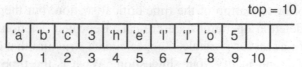

Figure 4.35 An array-based stack storing variable-length strings. Each position stores either one character or the length of the string immediately to the left of it in the stack.

the length of the string stored in the stack element immediately above the string itself, as illustrated by Figure 4.35. The **push** operation would store an element requiring i storage units in the i positions beginning with the current value of **top** and store the size in the position i storage units above **top**. The value of **top** would then be reset above the newly inserted element. The **pop** operation need only look at the size value stored in position **top** $- 1$ and then pop off the appropriate number of units. You may store the string on the stack in reverse order if you prefer, provided that when it is popped from the stack, it is returned in its proper order.

4.7 Define an ADT for a bag (see Section 2.1) and create an array-based implementation for bags. Be sure that your bag ADT does not rely in any way on knowing or controlling the position of an element. Then, implement the dictionary ADT of Figure 4.28 using your bag implementation.

4.8 Implement the dictionary ADT of Figure 4.28 using an unsorted linked list as defined by class **LList** in Figure 4.8. Make the implementation as efficient as you can, given the restriction that your implementation must use the unsorted linked list and its access operations to implement the dictionary. State the asymptotic time requirements for each function member of the dictionary ADT under your implementation.

4.9 Implement the dictionary ADT of Figure 4.28 based on stacks. Your implementation should declare and use two stacks.

4.10 Implement the dictionary ADT of Figure 4.28 based on queues. Your implementation should declare and use two queues.

5

Binary Trees

The list representations of Chapter 4 have a fundamental limitation: Either search or insert can be made efficient, but not both at the same time. Tree structures permit both efficient access and update to large collections of data. Binary trees in particular are widely used and relatively easy to implement. But binary trees are useful for many things besides searching. Just a few examples of applications that trees can speed up include prioritizing jobs, describing mathematical expressions and the syntactic elements of computer programs, or organizing the information needed to drive data compression algorithms.

This chapter begins by presenting definitions and some key properties of binary trees. Section 5.2 discusses how to process all nodes of the binary tree in an organized manner. Section 5.3 presents various methods for implementing binary trees and their nodes. Sections 5.4 through 5.6 present three examples of binary trees used in specific applications: the Binary Search Tree (BST) for implementing dictionaries, heaps for implementing priority queues, and Huffman coding trees for text compression. The BST, heap, and Huffman coding tree each have distinctive structural features that affect their implementation and use.

5.1 Definitions and Properties

A **binary tree** is made up of a finite set of elements called **nodes**. This set either is empty or consists of a node called the **root** together with two binary trees, called the left and right **subtrees**, which are disjoint from each other and from the root. (Disjoint means that they have no nodes in common.) The roots of these subtrees are **children** of the root. There is an **edge** from a node to each of its children, and a node is said to be the **parent** of its children.

If $n_1, n_2, ..., n_k$ is a sequence of nodes in the tree such that n_i is the parent of n_{i+1} for $1 \leq i < k$, then this sequence is called a **path** from n_1 to n_k. The **length** of the path is $k - 1$. If there is a path from node R to node M, then R is an **ancestor** of M, and M is a **descendant** of R. Thus, all nodes in the tree are descendants of the

151

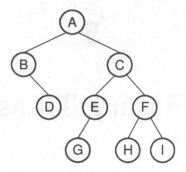

Figure 5.1 A binary tree. Node A is the root. Nodes B and C are A's children. Nodes B and D together form a subtree. Node B has two children: Its left child is the empty tree and its right child is D. Nodes A, C, and E are ancestors of G. Nodes D, E, and F make up level 2 of the tree; node A is at level 0. The edges from A to C to E to G form a path of length 3. Nodes D, G, H, and I are leaves. Nodes A, B, C, E, and F are internal nodes. The depth of I is 3. The height of this tree is 4.

root of the tree, while the root is the ancestor of all nodes. The **depth** of a node M in the tree is the length of the path from the root of the tree to M. The **height** of a tree is one more than the depth of the deepest node in the tree. All nodes of depth d are at **level** d in the tree. The root is the only node at level 0, and its depth is 0. A **leaf** node is any node that has two empty children. An **internal** node is any node that has at least one non-empty child.

Figure 5.1 illustrates the various terms used to identify parts of a binary tree. Figure 5.2 illustrates an important point regarding the structure of binary trees. Because *all* binary tree nodes have two children (one or both of which might be empty), the two binary trees of Figure 5.2 are *not* the same.

Two restricted forms of binary tree are sufficiently important to warrant special names. Each node in a **full** binary tree is either (1) an internal node with exactly two non-empty children or (2) a leaf. A **complete** binary tree has a restricted shape obtained by starting at the root and filling the tree by levels from left to right. In the complete binary tree of height d, all levels except possibly level $d-1$ are completely full. The bottom level has its nodes filled in from the left side.

Figure 5.3 illustrates the differences between full and complete binary trees.[1] There is no particular relationship between these two tree shapes; that is, the tree of Figure 5.3(a) is full but not complete while the tree of Figure 5.3(b) is complete but

---

[1] While these definitions for full and complete binary tree are the ones most commonly used, they are not universal. Because the common meaning of the words "full" and "complete" are quite similar, there is little that you can do to distinguish between them other than to memorize the definitions. Here is a memory aid that you might find useful: "Complete" is a wider word than "full," and complete binary trees tend to be wider than full binary trees because each level of a complete binary tree is as wide as possible.

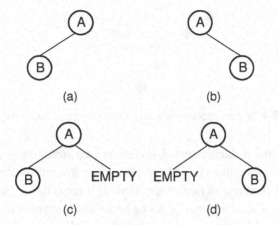

Figure 5.2 Two different binary trees. (a) A binary tree whose root has a non-empty left child. (b) A binary tree whose root has a non-empty right child. (c) The binary tree of (a) with the missing right child made explicit. (d) The binary tree of (b) with the missing left child made explicit.

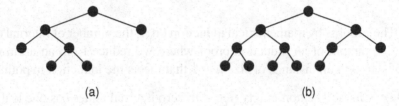

Figure 5.3 Examples of full and complete binary trees. (a) This tree is full (but not complete). (b) This tree is complete (but not full).

not full. The heap data structure (Section 5.5) is an example of a complete binary tree. The Huffman coding tree (Section 5.6) is an example of a full binary tree.

5.1.1 The Full Binary Tree Theorem

Some binary tree implementations store data only at the leaf nodes, using the internal nodes to provide structure to the tree. More generally, binary tree implementations might require some amount of space for internal nodes, and a different amount for leaf nodes. Thus, to analyze the space required by such implementations, it is useful to know the minimum and maximum fraction of the nodes that are leaves in a tree containing n internal nodes.

Unfortunately, this fraction is not fixed. A binary tree of n internal nodes might have only one leaf. This occurs when the internal nodes are arranged in a chain ending in a single leaf as shown in Figure 5.4. In this case, the number of leaves is low because each internal node has only one non-empty child. To find an upper bound on the number of leaves for a tree of n internal nodes, first note that the upper

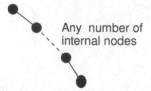

Figure 5.4 A tree containing many internal nodes and a single leaf.

bound will occur when each internal node has two non-empty children, that is, when the tree is full. However, this observation does not tell what shape of tree will yield the highest percentage of non-empty leaves. It turns out not to matter, because all full binary trees with n internal nodes have the same number of leaves. This fact allows us to compute the space requirements for a full binary tree implementation whose leaves require a different amount of space from its internal nodes.

Theorem 5.1 Full Binary Tree Theorem: *The number of leaves in a non-empty full binary tree is one more than the number of internal nodes.*

Proof: The proof is by mathematical induction on n, the number of internal nodes. This is an example of an induction proof where we reduce from an arbitrary instance of size n to an instance of size $n - 1$ that meets the induction hypothesis.

- **Base Cases**: The non-empty tree with zero internal nodes has one leaf node. A full binary tree with one internal node has two leaf nodes. Thus, the base cases for $n = 0$ and $n = 1$ conform to the theorem.

- **Induction Hypothesis**: Assume that any full binary tree **T** containing $n - 1$ internal nodes has n leaves.

- **Induction Step**: Given tree **T** with n internal nodes, select an internal node I whose children are both leaf nodes. Remove both of I's children, making I a leaf node. Call the new tree **T′**. **T′** has $n - 1$ internal nodes. From the induction hypothesis, **T′** has n leaves. Now, restore I's two children. We once again have tree **T** with n internal nodes. How many leaves does **T** have? Because **T′** has n leaves, adding the two children yields $n+2$. However, node I counted as one of the leaves in **T′** and has now become an internal node. Thus, tree **T** has $n + 1$ leaf nodes and n internal nodes.

By mathematical induction the theorem holds for all values of $n \geq 0$.   □

When analyzing the space requirements for a binary tree implementation, it is useful to know how many empty subtrees a tree contains. A simple extension of the Full Binary Tree Theorem tells us exactly how many empty subtrees there are in *any* binary tree, whether full or not. Here are two approaches to proving the following theorem, and each suggests a useful way of thinking about binary trees.

Theorem 5.2 *The number of empty subtrees in a non-empty binary tree is one more than the number of nodes in the tree.*

Proof 1: Take an arbitrary binary tree T and replace every empty subtree with a leaf node. Call the new tree T'. All nodes originally in T will be internal nodes in T' (because even the leaf nodes of T have children in T'). T' is a full binary tree, because every internal node of T now must have two children in T', and each leaf node in T must have two children in T' (the leaves just added). The Full Binary Tree Theorem tells us that the number of leaves in a full binary tree is one more than the number of internal nodes. Thus, the number of new leaves that were added to create T' is one more than the number of nodes in T. Each leaf node in T' corresponds to an empty subtree in T. Thus, the number of empty subtrees in T is one more than the number of nodes in T. □

Proof 2: By definition, every node in binary tree T has two children, for a total of $2n$ children in a tree of n nodes. Every node except the root node has one parent, for a total of $n - 1$ nodes with parents. In other words, there are $n - 1$ non-empty children. Because the total number of children is $2n$, the remaining $n + 1$ children must be empty. □

5.1.2 A Binary Tree Node ADT

Just as a linked list is comprised of a collection of link objects, a tree is comprised of a collection of node objects. Figure 5.5 shows an ADT for binary tree nodes, called **BinNode**. This class will be used by some of the binary tree structures presented later. Class **BinNode** is a template with parameter **E**, which is the type for the data record stored in the node. Member functions are provided that set or return the element value, set or return a pointer to the left child, set or return a pointer to the right child, or indicate whether the node is a leaf.

5.2 Binary Tree Traversals

Often we wish to process a binary tree by "visiting" each of its nodes, each time performing a specific action such as printing the contents of the node. Any process for visiting all of the nodes in some order is called a **traversal**. Any traversal that lists every node in the tree exactly once is called an **enumeration** of the tree's nodes. Some applications do not require that the nodes be visited in any particular order as long as each node is visited precisely once. For other applications, nodes must be visited in an order that preserves some relationship. For example, we might wish to make sure that we visit any given node *before* we visit its children. This is called a **preorder traversal**.

```
// Binary tree node abstract class
template <typename E> class BinNode {
public:
  virtual ~BinNode() {} // Base destructor

  // Return the node's value
  virtual E& element() = 0;

  // Set the node's value
  virtual void setElement(const E&) = 0;

  // Return the node's left child
  virtual BinNode* left() const = 0;

  // Set the node's left child
  virtual void setLeft(BinNode*) = 0;

  // Return the node's right child
  virtual BinNode* right() const = 0;

  // Set the node's right child
  virtual void setRight(BinNode*) = 0;

  // Return true if the node is a leaf, false otherwise
  virtual bool isLeaf() = 0;
};
```

Figure 5.5 A binary tree node ADT.

Example 5.1 The preorder enumeration for the tree of Figure 5.1 is

ABDCEGFHI.

The first node printed is the root. Then all nodes of the left subtree are printed (in preorder) before any node of the right subtree.

Alternatively, we might wish to visit each node only *after* we visit its children (and their subtrees). For example, this would be necessary if we wish to return all nodes in the tree to free store. We would like to delete the children of a node before deleting the node itself. But to do that requires that the children's children be deleted first, and so on. This is called a **postorder traversal**.

Example 5.2 The postorder enumeration for the tree of Figure 5.1 is

DBGEHIFCA.

An **inorder traversal** first visits the left child (including its entire subtree), then visits the node, and finally visits the right child (including its entire subtree). The binary search tree of Section 5.4 makes use of this traversal to print all nodes in ascending order of value.

Example 5.3 The inorder enumeration for the tree of Figure 5.1 is

BDAGECHFI.

A traversal routine is naturally written as a recursive function. Its input parameter is a pointer to a node which we will call **rt** because each node can be viewed as the root of a some subtree. The initial call to the traversal function passes in a pointer to the root node of the tree. The traversal function visits **rt** and its children (if any) in the desired order. For example, a preorder traversal specifies that **rt** be visited before its children. This can easily be implemented as follows.

```
template <typename E>
void preorder(BinNode<E>* root) {
  if (root == NULL) return; // Empty subtree, do nothing
  visit(root);              // Perform desired action
  preorder(root->left());
  preorder(root->right());
}
```

Function **preorder** first checks that the tree is not empty (if it is, then the traversal is done and **preorder** simply returns). Otherwise, **preorder** makes a call to **visit**, which processes the root node (i.e., prints the value or performs whatever computation as required by the application). Function **preorder** is then called recursively on the left subtree, which will visit all nodes in that subtree. Finally, **preorder** is called on the right subtree, visiting all nodes in the right subtree. Postorder and inorder traversals are similar. They simply change the order in which the node and its children are visited, as appropriate.

An important decision in the implementation of any recursive function on trees is when to check for an empty subtree. Function **preorder** first checks to see if the value for **root** is **NULL**. If not, it will recursively call itself on the left and right children of **root**. In other words, **preorder** makes no attempt to avoid calling itself on an empty child. Some programmers use an alternate design in which the left and right pointers of the current node are checked so that the recursive call is made only on non-empty children. Such a design typically looks as follows:

```
template <typename E>
void preorder2(BinNode<E>* root) {
  visit(root);  // Perform whatever action is desired
  if (root->left() != NULL) preorder2(root->left());
  if (root->right() != NULL) preorder2(root->right());
}
```

At first it might appear that **preorder2** is more efficient than **preorder**, because it makes only half as many recursive calls. (Why?) On the other hand,

preorder2 must access the left and right child pointers twice as often. The net result is little or no performance improvement.

In reality, the design of **preorder2** is inferior to that of **preorder** for two reasons. First, while it is not apparent in this simple example, for more complex traversals it can become awkward to place the check for the **NULL** pointer in the calling code. Even here we had to write two tests for **NULL**, rather than the one needed by **preorder**. The more important concern with **preorder2** is that it tends to be error prone. While **preorder2** insures that no recursive calls will be made on empty subtrees, it will fail if the initial call passes in a **NULL** pointer. This would occur if the original tree is empty. To avoid the bug, either **preorder2** needs an additional test for a **NULL** pointer at the beginning (making the subsequent tests redundant after all), or the caller of **preorder2** has a hidden obligation to pass in a non-empty tree, which is unreliable design. The net result is that many programmers forget to test for the possibility that the empty tree is being traversed. By using the first design, which explicitly supports processing of empty subtrees, the problem is avoided.

Another issue to consider when designing a traversal is how to define the visitor function that is to be executed on every node. One approach is simply to write a new version of the traversal for each such visitor function as needed. The disadvantage to this is that whatever function does the traversal must have access to the **BinNode** class. It is probably better design to permit only the tree class to have access to the **BinNode** class.

Another approach is for the tree class to supply a generic traversal function which takes the visitor either as a template parameter or as a function parameter. This is known as the **visitor design pattern**. A major constraint on this approach is that the **signature** for all visitor functions, that is, their return type and parameters, must be fixed in advance. Thus, the designer of the generic traversal function must be able to adequately judge what parameters and return type will likely be needed by potential visitor functions.

Handling information flow between parts of a program can be a significant design challenge, especially when dealing with recursive functions such as tree traversals. In general, we can run into trouble either with passing in the correct information needed by the function to do its work, or with returning information to the recursive function's caller. We will see many examples throughout the book that illustrate methods for passing information in and out of recursive functions as they traverse a tree structure. Here are a few simple examples.

First we consider the simple case where a computation requires that we communicate information back up the tree to the end user.

Example 5.4 We wish to count the number of nodes in a binary tree. The key insight is that the total count for any (non-empty) subtree is one for the

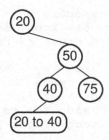

Figure 5.6 To be a binary search tree, the left child of the node with value 40 must have a value between 20 and 40.

root plus the counts for the left and right subtrees. Where do left and right subtree counts come from? Calls to function **count** on the subtrees will compute this for us. Thus, we can implement **count** as follows.

```
template <typename E>
int count(BinNode<E>* root) {
  if (root == NULL) return 0;  // Nothing to count
  return 1 + count(root->left())
           + count(root->right());
}
```

Another problem that occurs when recursively processing data collections is controlling which members of the collection will be visited. For example, some tree "traversals" might in fact visit only some tree nodes, while avoiding processing of others. Exercise 5.20 must solve exactly this problem in the context of a binary search tree. It must visit only those children of a given node that might possibly fall within a given range of values. Fortunately, it requires only a simple local calculation to determine which child(ren) to visit.

A more difficult situation is illustrated by the following problem. Given an arbitrary binary tree we wish to determine if, for every node *A*, are all nodes in *A*'s left subtree less than the value of *A*, and are all nodes in *A*'s right subtree greater than the value of *A*? (This happens to be the definition for a binary search tree, described in Section 5.4.) Unfortunately, to make this decision we need to know some context that is not available just by looking at the node's parent or children. As shown by Figure 5.6, it is not enough to verify that *A*'s left child has a value less than that of *A*, and that *A*'s right child has a greater value. Nor is it enough to verify that *A* has a value consistent with that of its parent. In fact, we need to know information about what range of values is legal for a given node. That information might come from any of the node's ancestors. Thus, relevant range information must be passed down the tree. We can implement this function as follows.

```
template <typename Key, typename E>
bool checkBST(BSTNode<Key,E>* root, Key low, Key high) {
  if (root == NULL) return true; // Empty subtree
  Key rootkey = root->key();
  if ((rootkey < low) || (rootkey > high))
    return false; // Out of range
  if (!checkBST<Key,E>(root->left(), low, rootkey))
    return false; // Left side failed
  return checkBST<Key,E>(root->right(), rootkey, high);
}
```

5.3   Binary Tree Node Implementations

In this section we examine ways to implement binary tree nodes. We begin with
some options for pointer-based binary tree node implementations. Then comes a
discussion on techniques for determining the space requirements for a given implementation. The section concludes with an introduction to the array-based implementation for complete binary trees.

5.3.1   Pointer-Based Node Implementations

By definition, all binary tree nodes have two children, though one or both children
can be empty. Binary tree nodes typically contain a value field, with the type of
the field depending on the application. The most common node implementation
includes a value field and pointers to the two children.

Figure 5.7 shows a simple implementation for the **BinNode** abstract class,
which we will name **BSTNode**. Class **BSTNode** includes a data member of type
E, (which is the second template parameter) for the element type. To support search
structures such as the Binary Search Tree, an additional field is included, with corresponding access methods, to store a key value (whose purpose is explained in
Section 4.4). Its type is determined by the first template parameter, named **Key**.
Every **BSTNode** object also has two pointers, one to its left child and another to
its right child. Overloaded **new** and **delete** operators could be added to support
a freelist, as described in Section 4.1.2.Figure 5.8 illustrates the **BSTNode** implementation.

Some programmers find it convenient to add a pointer to the node's parent,
allowing easy upward movement in the tree. Using a parent pointer is somewhat
analogous to adding a link to the previous node in a doubly linked list. In practice,
the parent pointer is almost always unnecessary and adds to the space overhead for
the tree implementation. It is not just a problem that parent pointers take space.
More importantly, many uses of the parent pointer are driven by improper understanding of recursion and so indicate poor programming. If you are inclined toward
using a parent pointer, consider if there is a more efficient implementation possible.

```
// Simple binary tree node implementation
template <typename Key, typename E>
class BSTNode : public BinNode<E> {
private:
  Key k;                    // The node's key
  E it;                     // The node's value
  BSTNode* lc;              // Pointer to left child
  BSTNode* rc;              // Pointer to right child

public:
  // Two constructors -- with and without initial values
  BSTNode() { lc = rc = NULL; }
  BSTNode(Key K, E e, BSTNode* l =NULL, BSTNode* r =NULL)
    { k = K; it = e; lc = l; rc = r; }
  ~BSTNode() {}                   // Destructor

  // Functions to set and return the value and key
  E& element() { return it; }
  void setElement(const E& e) { it = e; }
  Key& key() { return k; }
  void setKey(const Key& K) { k = K; }

  // Functions to set and return the children
  inline BSTNode* left() const { return lc; }
  void setLeft(BinNode<E>* b) { lc = (BSTNode*)b; }
  inline BSTNode* right() const { return rc; }
  void setRight(BinNode<E>* b) { rc = (BSTNode*)b; }

  // Return true if it is a leaf, false otherwise
  bool isLeaf() { return (lc == NULL) && (rc == NULL); }
};
```

Figure 5.7 A binary tree node class implementation.

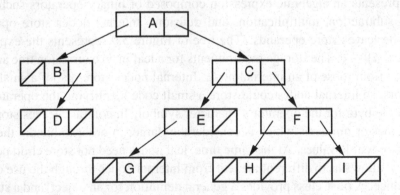

Figure 5.8 Illustration of a typical pointer-based binary tree implementation, where each node stores two child pointers and a value.

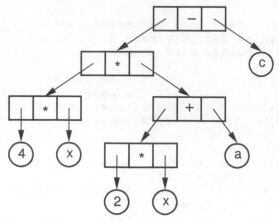

Figure 5.9 An expression tree for $4x(2x + a) - c$.

An important decision in the design of a pointer-based node implementation is whether the same class definition will be used for leaves and internal nodes. Using the same class for both will simplify the implementation, but might be an inefficient use of space. Some applications require data values only for the leaves. Other applications require one type of value for the leaves and another for the internal nodes. Examples include the binary trie of Section 13.1, the PR quadtree of Section 13.3, the Huffman coding tree of Section 5.6, and the expression tree illustrated by Figure 5.9. By definition, only internal nodes have non-empty children. If we use the same node implementation for both internal and leaf nodes, then both must store the child pointers. But it seems wasteful to store child pointers in the leaf nodes. Thus, there are many reasons why it can save space to have separate implementations for internal and leaf nodes.

As an example of a tree that stores different information at the leaf and internal nodes, consider the expression tree illustrated by Figure 5.9. The expression tree represents an algebraic expression composed of binary operators such as addition, subtraction, multiplication, and division. Internal nodes store operators, while the leaves store operands. The tree of Figure 5.9 represents the expression $4x(2x + a) - c$. The storage requirements for a leaf in an expression tree are quite different from those of an internal node. Internal nodes store one of a small set of operators, so internal nodes could store a small code identifying the operator such as a single byte for the operator's character symbol. In contrast, leaves store variable names or numbers, which is considerably larger in order to handle the wider range of possible values. At the same time, leaf nodes need not store child pointers.

C++ allows us to differentiate leaf from internal nodes through the use of class inheritance. A **base class** provides a general definition for an object, and a **subclass** modifies a base class to add more detail. A base class can be declared for binary tree nodes in general, with subclasses defined for the internal and leaf nodes. The base class of Figure 5.10 is named **VarBinNode**. It includes a virtual member function named **isLeaf**, which indicates the node type. Subclasses for the internal and leaf node types each implement **isLeaf**. Internal nodes store child pointers of the base class type; they do not distinguish their children's actual subclass. Whenever a node is examined, its version of **isLeaf** indicates the node's subclass.

Figure 5.10 includes two subclasses derived from class **VarBinNode**, named **LeafNode** and **IntlNode**. Class **IntlNode** can access its children through pointers of type **VarBinNode**. Function **traverse** illustrates the use of these classes. When **traverse** calls method **isLeaf**, C++'s runtime environment determines which subclass this particular instance of **rt** happens to be and calls that subclass's version of **isLeaf**. Method **isLeaf** then provides the actual node type to its caller. The other member functions for the derived subclasses are accessed by type-casting the base class pointer as appropriate, as shown in function **traverse**.

There is another approach that we can take to represent separate leaf and internal nodes, also using a virtual base class and separate node classes for the two types. This is to implement nodes using the **composite design pattern**. This approach is noticeably different from the one of Figure 5.10 in that the node classes themselves implement the functionality of **traverse**. Figure 5.11 shows the implementation. Here, base class **VarBinNode** declares a member function **traverse** that each subclass must implement. Each subclass then implements its own appropriate behavior for its role in a traversal. The whole traversal process is called by invoking **traverse** on the root node, which in turn invokes **traverse** on its children.

When comparing the implementations of Figures 5.10 and 5.11, each has advantages and disadvantages. The first does not require that the node classes know about the **traverse** function. With this approach, it is easy to add new methods to the tree class that do other traversals or other operations on nodes of the tree. However, we see that **traverse** in Figure 5.10 does need to be familiar with each node subclass. Adding a new node subclass would therefore require modifications to the **traverse** function. In contrast, the approach of Figure 5.11 requires that any new operation on the tree that requires a traversal also be implemented in the node subclasses. On the other hand, the approach of Figure 5.11 avoids the need for the **traverse** function to know anything about the distinct abilities of the node subclasses. Those subclasses handle the responsibility of performing a traversal on themselves. A secondary benefit is that there is no need for **traverse** to explicitly enumerate all of the different node subclasses, directing appropriate action for each. With only two node classes this is a minor point. But if there were many such subclasses, this could become a bigger problem. A disadvantage is that the traversal operation must not be called on a **NULL** pointer, because there is no object to catch the call. This problem could be avoided by using a flyweight (see Section 1.3.1) to implement empty nodes.

Typically, the version of Figure 5.10 would be preferred in this example if **traverse** is a member function of the tree class, and if the node subclasses are

```
// Node implementation with simple inheritance
class VarBinNode {    // Node abstract base class
public:
  virtual ~VarBinNode() {}
  virtual bool isLeaf() = 0;      // Subclasses must implement
};


class LeafNode : public VarBinNode { // Leaf node
private:
  Operand var;                             // Operand value

public:
  LeafNode(const Operand& val) { var = val; } // Constructor
  bool isLeaf() { return true; }      // Version for LeafNode
  Operand value() { return var; }     // Return node value
};


class IntlNode : public VarBinNode { // Internal node
private:
  VarBinNode* left;                   // Left child
  VarBinNode* right;                  // Right child
  Operator opx;                       // Operator value

public:
  IntlNode(const Operator& op, VarBinNode* l, VarBinNode* r)
    { opx = op; left = l; right = r; } // Constructor
  bool isLeaf() { return false; }     // Version for IntlNode
  VarBinNode* leftchild() { return left; }   // Left child
  VarBinNode* rightchild() { return right; } // Right child
  Operator value() { return opx; }           // Value
};


void traverse(VarBinNode *root) {     // Preorder traversal
  if (root == NULL) return;           // Nothing to visit
  if (root->isLeaf())                 // Do leaf node
    cout << "Leaf: " << ((LeafNode *)root)->value() << endl;
  else {                              // Do internal node
    cout << "Internal: "
         << ((IntlNode *)root)->value() << endl;
    traverse(((IntlNode *)root)->leftchild());
    traverse(((IntlNode *)root)->rightchild());
  }
}
```

Figure 5.10 An implementation for separate internal and leaf node representations using C++ class inheritance and virtual functions.

```
// Node implementation with the composite design pattern
class VarBinNode {    // Node abstract base class
public:
  virtual ~VarBinNode() {}        // Generic destructor
  virtual bool isLeaf() = 0;
  virtual void traverse() = 0;
};


class LeafNode : public VarBinNode { // Leaf node
private:
  Operand var;                         // Operand value

public:
  LeafNode(const Operand& val) { var = val; } // Constructor
  bool isLeaf() { return true; }       // isLeaf for Leafnode
  Operand value() { return var; }      // Return node value
  void traverse() { cout << "Leaf: " << value() << endl; }
};


class IntlNode : public VarBinNode { // Internal node
private:
  VarBinNode* lc;                      // Left child
  VarBinNode* rc;                      // Right child
  Operator opx;                        // Operator value

public:
  IntlNode(const Operator& op, VarBinNode* l, VarBinNode* r)
    { opx = op; lc = l; rc = r; }      // Constructor

  bool isLeaf() { return false; }      // isLeaf for IntlNode
  VarBinNode* left() { return lc; }    // Left child
  VarBinNode* right() { return rc; }   // Right child
  Operator value() { return opx; }     // Value

  void traverse() { // Traversal behavior for internal nodes
    cout << "Internal: " << value() << endl;
    if (left() != NULL) left()->traverse();
    if (right() != NULL) right()->traverse();
  }
};


// Do a preorder traversal
void traverse(VarBinNode *root) {
  if (root != NULL) root->traverse();
}
```

Figure 5.11 A second implementation for separate internal and leaf node representations using **C++** class inheritance and virtual functions using the composite design pattern. Here, the functionality of **traverse** is embedded into the node subclasses.

hidden from users of that tree class. On the other hand, if the nodes are objects that have meaning to users of the tree separate from their existence as nodes in the tree, then the version of Figure 5.11 might be preferred because hiding the internal behavior of the nodes becomes more important.

Another advantage of the composite design is that implementing each node type's functionality might be easier. This is because you can focus solely on the information passing and other behavior needed by this node type to do its job. This breaks down the complexity that many programmers feel overwhelmed by when dealing with complex information flows related to recursive processing.

5.3.2   Space Requirements

This section presents techniques for calculating the amount of overhead required by a binary tree implementation. Recall that overhead is the amount of space necessary to maintain the data structure. In other words, it is any space not used to store data records. The amount of overhead depends on several factors including which nodes store data values (all nodes, or just the leaves), whether the leaves store child pointers, and whether the tree is a full binary tree.

In a simple pointer-based implementation for the binary tree such as that of Figure 5.7, every node has two pointers to its children (even when the children are **NULL**). This implementation requires total space amounting to $n(2P + D)$ for a tree of n nodes. Here, P stands for the amount of space required by a pointer, and D stands for the amount of space required by a data value. The total overhead space will be $2Pn$ for the entire tree. Thus, the overhead fraction will be $2P/(2P + D)$. The actual value for this expression depends on the relative size of pointers versus data fields. If we arbitrarily assume that $P = D$, then a full tree has about two thirds of its total space taken up in overhead. Worse yet, Theorem 5.2 tells us that about half of the pointers are "wasted" **NULL** values that serve only to indicate tree structure, but which do not provide access to new data.

A commonimplementation is not to store any actual data in a node, but rather a pointer to the data record. In this case, each node will typically store three pointers, all of which are overhead, resulting in an overhead fraction of $3P/(3P + D)$.

If only leaves store data values, then the fraction of total space devoted to overhead depends on whether the tree is full. If the tree is not full, then conceivably there might only be one leaf node at the end of a series of internal nodes. Thus, the overhead can be an arbitrarily high percentage for non-full binary trees. The overhead fraction drops as the tree becomes closer to full, being lowest when the tree is truly full. In this case, about one half of the nodes are internal.

Great savings can be had by eliminating the pointers from leaf nodes in full binary trees. Because about half of the nodes are leaves and half internal nodes, and because only internal nodes now have overhead, the overhead fraction in this case will be approximately

$$\frac{\frac{n}{2}(2P)}{\frac{n}{2}(2P) + Dn} = \frac{P}{P + D}.$$

If $P = D$, the overhead drops to about one half of the total space. However, if only leaf nodes store useful information, the overhead fraction for this implementation is actually three quarters of the total space, because half of the "data" space is unused.

If a full binary tree needs to store data only at the leaf nodes, a better implementation would have the internal nodes store two pointers and no data field while the leaf nodes store only a data field. This implementation requires $2Pn + D(n + 1)$ units of space. If $P = D$, then the overhead is about $2P/(2P + D) = 2/3$. It might seem counter-intuitive that the overhead ratio has gone up while the total amount of space has gone down. The reason is because we have changed our definition of "data" to refer only to what is stored in the leaf nodes, so while the overhead fraction is higher, it is from a total storage requirement that is lower.

There is one serious flaw with this analysis. When using separate implementations for internal and leaf nodes, there must be a way to distinguish between the node types. When separate node types are implemented via **C++** subclasses, the runtime environment stores information with each object allowing it to determine, for example, the correct subclass to use when the **isLeaf** virtual function is called. Thus, each node requires additional space. Only one bit is truly necessary to distinguish the two possibilities. In rare applications where space is a critical resource, implementors can often find a spare bit within the node's value field in which to store the node type indicator. An alternative is to use a spare bit within a node pointer to indicate node type. For example, this is often possible when the compiler requires that structures and objects start on word boundaries, leaving the last bit of a pointer value always zero. Thus, this bit can be used to store the node-type flag and is reset to zero before the pointer is dereferenced. Another alternative when the leaf value field is smaller than a pointer is to replace the pointer to a leaf with that leaf's value. When space is limited, such techniques can make the difference between success and failure. In any other situation, such "bit packing" tricks should be avoided because they are difficult to debug and understand at best, and are often machine dependent at worst.[2]

---

[2]In the early to mid 1980s, I worked on a Geographic Information System that stored spatial data in quadtrees (see Section 13.3). At the time space was a critical resource, so we used a bit-packing approach where we stored the nodetype flag as the last bit in the parent node's pointer. This worked perfectly on various 32-bit workstations. Unfortunately, in those days IBM PC-compatibles used 16-bit pointers. We never did figure out how to port our code to the 16-bit machine.

5.3.3 Array Implementation for Complete Binary Trees

The previous section points out that a large fraction of the space in a typical binary tree node implementation is devoted to structural overhead, not to storing data. This section presents a simple, compact implementation for complete binary trees. Recall that complete binary trees have all levels except the bottom filled out completely, and the bottom level has all of its nodes filled in from left to right. Thus, a complete binary tree of n nodes has only one possible shape. You might think that a complete binary tree is such an unusual occurrence that there is no reason to develop a special implementation for it. However, the complete binary tree has practical uses, the most important being the heap data structure discussed in Section 5.5. Heaps are often used to implement priority queues (Section 5.5) and for external sorting algorithms (Section 8.5.2).

We begin by assigning numbers to the node positions in the complete binary tree, level by level, from left to right as shown in Figure 5.12(a). An array can store the tree's data values efficiently, placing each data value in the array position corresponding to that node's position within the tree. Figure 5.12(b) lists the array indices for the children, parent, and siblings of each node in Figure 5.12(a). From Figure 5.12(b), you should see a pattern regarding the positions of a node's relatives within the array. Simple formulas can be derived for calculating the array index for each relative of a node r from r's index. No explicit pointers are necessary to reach a node's left or right child. This means there is no overhead to the array implementation if the array is selected to be of size n for a tree of n nodes.

The formulae for calculating the array indices of the various relatives of a node are as follows. The total number of nodes in the tree is n. The index of the node in question is r, which must fall in the range 0 to $n-1$.

- Parent$(r) = \lfloor (r-1)/2 \rfloor$ if $r \neq 0$.
- Left child$(r) = 2r + 1$ if $2r + 1 < n$.
- Right child$(r) = 2r + 2$ if $2r + 2 < n$.
- Left sibling$(r) = r - 1$ if r is even.
- Right sibling$(r) = r + 1$ if r is odd and $r + 1 < n$.

5.4 Binary Search Trees

Section 4.4 presented the dictionary ADT, along with dictionary implementations based on sorted and unsorted lists. When implementing the dictionary with an unsorted list, inserting a new record into the dictionary can be performed quickly by putting it at the end of the list. However, searching an unsorted list for a particular record requires $\Theta(n)$ time in the average case. For a large database, this is probably much too slow. Alternatively, the records can be stored in a sorted list. If the list is implemented using a linked list, then no speedup to the search operation will

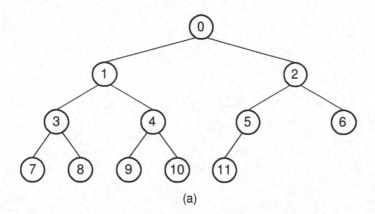

(a)

Position	0	1	2	3	4	5	6	7	8	9	10	11
Parent	–	0	0	1	1	2	2	3	3	4	4	5
Left Child	1	3	5	7	9	11	–	–	–	–	–	–
Right Child	2	4	6	8	10	–	–	–	–	–	–	–
Left Sibling	–	–	1	–	3	–	5	–	7	–	9	–
Right Sibling	–	2	–	4	–	6	–	8	–	10	–	–

(b)

Figure 5.12 A complete binary tree and its array implementation. (a) The complete binary tree with twelve nodes. Each node has been labeled with its position in the tree. (b) The positions for the relatives of each node. A dash indicates that the relative does not exist.

result from storing the records in sorted order. On the other hand, if we use a sorted array-based list to implement the dictionary, then binary search can be used to find a record in only $\Theta(\log n)$ time. However, insertion will now require $\Theta(n)$ time on average because, once the proper location for the new record in the sorted list has been found, many records might be shifted to make room for the new record.

Is there some way to organize a collection of records so that inserting records and searching for records can both be done quickly? This section presents the binary search tree (BST), which allows an improved solution to this problem.

A BST is a binary tree that conforms to the following condition, known as the **Binary Search Tree Property**: All nodes stored in the left subtree of a node whose key value is K have key values less than K. All nodes stored in the right subtree of a node whose key value is K have key values greater than or equal to K. Figure 5.13 shows two BSTs for a collection of values. One consequence of the Binary Search Tree Property is that if the BST nodes are printed using an inorder traversal (see Section 5.2), the resulting enumeration will be in sorted order from lowest to highest.

Figure 5.14 shows a class declaration for the BST that implements the dictionary ADT. The public member functions include those required by the dictionary

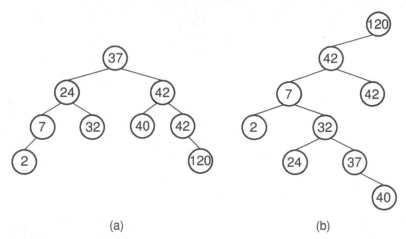

(a)   (b)

Figure 5.13 Two Binary Search Trees for a collection of values. Tree (a) results
if values are inserted in the order 37, 24, 42, 7, 2, 40, 42, 32, 120. Tree (b) results
if the same values are inserted in the order 120, 42, 42, 7, 2, 32, 37, 24, 40.

ADT, along with a constructor and destructor. Recall from the discussion in Section 4.4 that there are various ways to deal with keys and comparing records (three
approaches being key/value pairs, a special comparison method, and passing in a
comparator function). Our BST implementation will handle comparison by explicitly storing a key separate from the data value at each node of the tree.

To find a record with key value K in a BST, begin at the root. If the root stores
a record with key value K, then the search is over. If not, then we must search
deeper in the tree. What makes the BST efficient during search is that we need
search only one of the node's two subtrees. If K is less than the root node's key
value, we search only the left subtree. If K is greater than the root node's key
value, we search only the right subtree. This process continues until a record with
key value K is found, or we reach a leaf node. If we reach a leaf node without
encountering K, then no record exists in the BST whose key value is K.

Example 5.5 Consider searching for the node with key value 32 in the
tree of Figure 5.13(a). Because 32 is less than the root value of 37, the
search proceeds to the left subtree. Because 32 is greater than 24, we search
in 24's right subtree. At this point the node containing 32 is found. If
the search value were 35, the same path would be followed to the node
containing 32. Because this node has no children, we know that 35 is not
in the BST.

Notice that in Figure 5.14, public member function **find** calls private member
function **findhelp**. Method **find** takes the search key as an explicit parameter
and its BST as an implicit parameter, and returns the record that matches the key.

```cpp
// Binary Search Tree implementation for the Dictionary ADT
template <typename Key, typename E>
class BST : public Dictionary<Key,E> {
private:
  BSTNode<Key,E>* root;      // Root of the BST
  int nodecount;             // Number of nodes in the BST

  // Private "helper" functions
  void clearhelp(BSTNode<Key, E>*);
  BSTNode<Key,E>* inserthelp(BSTNode<Key, E>*,
                             const Key&, const E&);
  BSTNode<Key,E>* deletemin(BSTNode<Key, E>*);
  BSTNode<Key,E>* getmin(BSTNode<Key, E>*);
  BSTNode<Key,E>* removehelp(BSTNode<Key, E>*, const Key&);
  E findhelp(BSTNode<Key, E>*, const Key&) const;
  void printhelp(BSTNode<Key, E>*, int) const;

public:
  BST() { root = NULL; nodecount = 0; }  // Constructor
  ~BST() { clearhelp(root); }            // Destructor

  void clear()    // Reinitialize tree
    { clearhelp(root); root = NULL; nodecount = 0; }

  // Insert a record into the tree.
  // k Key value of the record.
  // e The record to insert.
  void insert(const Key& k, const E& e) {
    root = inserthelp(root, k, e);
    nodecount++;
  }

  // Remove a record from the tree.
  // k Key value of record to remove.
  // Return: The record removed, or NULL if there is none.
  E remove(const Key& k) {
    E temp = findhelp(root, k);    // First find it
    if (temp != NULL) {
      root = removehelp(root, k);
      nodecount--;
    }
    return temp;
  }
```

Figure 5.14 The binary search tree implementation.

```
// Remove and return the root node from the dictionary.
// Return: The record removed, null if tree is empty.
E removeAny() {   // Delete min value
  if (root != NULL) {
    E temp = root->element();
    root = removehelp(root, root->key());
    nodecount--;
    return temp;
  }
  else return NULL;
}

// Return Record with key value k, NULL if none exist.
// k: The key value to find. */
// Return some record matching "k".
// Return true if such exists, false otherwise. If
// multiple records match "k", return an arbitrary one.
E find(const Key& k) const { return findhelp(root, k); }

// Return the number of records in the dictionary.
int size() { return nodecount; }

void print() const { // Print the contents of the BST
  if (root == NULL) cout << "The BST is empty.\n";
  else printhelp(root, 0);
}
};
```

Figure 5.14 (continued)

However, the find operation is most easily implemented as a recursive function whose parameters are the root of a subtree and the search key. Member **findhelp** has the desired form for this recursive subroutine and is implemented as follows.

```
template <typename Key, typename E>
E BST<Key, E>::findhelp(BSTNode<Key, E>* root,
                                const Key& k) const {
  if (root == NULL) return NULL;              // Empty tree
  if (k < root->key())
    return findhelp(root->left(), k);    // Check left
  else if (k > root->key())
    return findhelp(root->right(), k);   // Check right
  else return root->element();   // Found it
}
```

Once the desired record is found, it is passed through return values up the chain of recursive calls. If a suitable record is not found, **null** is returned.

Inserting a record with key value k requires that we first find where that record would have been if it were in the tree. This takes us to either a leaf node, or to an

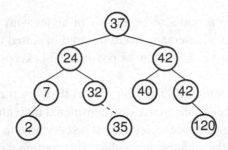

Figure 5.15 An example of BST insertion. A record with value 35 is inserted into the BST of Figure 5.13(a). The node with value 32 becomes the parent of the new node containing 35.

internal node with no child in the appropriate direction.[3] Call this node R'. We then add a new node containing the new record as a child of R'. Figure 5.15 illustrates this operation. The value 35 is added as the right child of the node with value 32. Here is the implementation for **inserthelp**:

```
template <typename Key, typename E>
BSTNode<Key, E>* BST<Key, E>::inserthelp(
    BSTNode<Key, E>* root, const Key& k, const E& it) {
  if (root == NULL)  // Empty tree: create node
    return new BSTNode<Key, E>(k, it, NULL, NULL);
  if (k < root->key())
    root->setLeft(inserthelp(root->left(), k, it));
  else root->setRight(inserthelp(root->right(), k, it));
  return root;          // Return tree with node inserted
}
```

You should pay careful attention to the implementation for **inserthelp**. Note that **inserthelp** returns a pointer to a **BSTNode**. What is being returned is a subtree identical to the old subtree, except that it has been modified to contain the new record being inserted. Each node along a path from the root to the parent of the new node added to the tree will have its appropriate child pointer assigned to it. Except for the last node in the path, none of these nodes will actually change their child's pointer value. In that sense, many of the assignments seem redundant. However, the cost of these additional assignments is worth paying to keep the insertion process simple. The alternative is to check if a given assignment is necessary, which is probably more expensive than the assignment!

The shape of a BST depends on the order in which elements are inserted. A new element is added to the BST as a new leaf node, potentially increasing the depth of the tree. Figure 5.13 illustrates two BSTs for a collection of values. It is possible

---

[3]This assumes that no node has a key value equal to the one being inserted. If we find a node that duplicates the key value to be inserted, we have two options. If the application does not allow nodes with equal keys, then this insertion should be treated as an error (or ignored). If duplicate keys are allowed, our convention will be to insert the duplicate in the right subtree.

for the BST containing n nodes to be a chain of nodes with height n. This would happen if, for example, all elements were inserted in sorted order. In general, it is preferable for a BST to be as shallow as possible. This keeps the average cost of a BST operation low.

Removing a node from a BST is a bit trickier than inserting a node, but it is not complicated if all of the possible cases are considered individually. Before tackling the general node removal process, let us first discuss how to remove from a given subtree the node with the smallest key value. This routine will be used later by the general node removal function. To remove the node with the minimum key value from a subtree, first find that node by continuously moving down the left link until there is no further left link to follow. Call this node S. To remove S, simply have the parent of S change its pointer to point to the right child of S. We know that S has no left child (because if S did have a left child, S would not be the node with minimum key value). Thus, changing the pointer as described will maintain a BST, with S removed. The code for this method, named **deletemin**, is as follows:

```
template <typename Key, typename E>
BSTNode<Key, E>* BST<Key, E>::
deletemin(BSTNode<Key, E>* rt) {
  if (rt->left() == NULL) // Found min
    return rt->right();
  else {                          // Continue left
    rt->setLeft(deletemin(rt->left()));
    return rt;
  }
}
```

Example 5.6 Figure 5.16 illustrates the **deletemin** process. Beginning at the root node with value 10, **deletemin** follows the left link until there is no further left link, in this case reaching the node with value 5. The node with value 10 is changed to point to the right child of the node containing the minimum value. This is indicated in Figure 5.16 by a dashed line.

A pointer to the node containing the minimum-valued element is stored in parameter **S**. The return value of the **deletemin** method is the subtree of the current node with the minimum-valued node in the subtree removed. As with method **inserthelp**, each node on the path back to the root has its left child pointer reassigned to the subtree resulting from its call to the **deletemin** method.

A useful companion method is **getmin** which returns a pointer to the node containing the minimum value in the subtree.

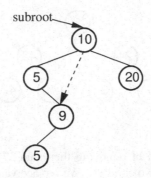

Figure 5.16 An example of deleting the node with minimum value. In this tree, the node with minimum value, 5, is the left child of the root. Thus, the root's **left** pointer is changed to point to 5's right child.

```
template <typename Key, typename E>
BSTNode<Key, E>* BST<Key, E>::
getmin(BSTNode<Key, E>* rt) {
  if (rt->left() == NULL)
    return rt;
  else return getmin(rt->left());
}
```

Removing a node with given key value R from the BST requires that we first find R and then remove it from the tree. So, the first part of the remove operation is a search to find R. Once R is found, there are several possibilities. If R has no children, then R's parent has its pointer set to **NULL**. If R has one child, then R's parent has its pointer set to R's child (similar to **deletemin**). The problem comes if R has two children. One simple approach, though expensive, is to set R's parent to point to one of R's subtrees, and then reinsert the remaining subtree's nodes one at a time. A better alternative is to find a value in one of the subtrees that can replace the value in R.

Thus, the question becomes: Which value can substitute for the one being removed? It cannot be any arbitrary value, because we must preserve the BST property without making major changes to the structure of the tree. Which value is most like the one being removed? The answer is the least key value greater than (or equal to) the one being removed, or else the greatest key value less than the one being removed. If either of these values replace the one being removed, then the BST property is maintained.

Example 5.7 Assume that we wish to remove the value 37 from the BST of Figure 5.13(a). Instead of removing the root node, we remove the node with the least value in the right subtree (using the **deletemin** operation). This value can then replace the value in the root. In this example we first remove the node with value 40, because it contains the least value in the

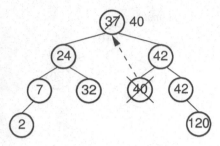

Figure 5.17 An example of removing the value 37 from the BST. The node containing this value has two children. We replace value 37 with the least value from the node's right subtree, in this case 40.

right subtree. We then substitute 40 as the new value for the root node. Figure 5.17 illustrates this process.

When duplicate node values do not appear in the tree, it makes no difference whether the replacement is the greatest value from the left subtree or the least value from the right subtree. If duplicates are stored, then we must select the replacement from the *right* subtree. To see why, call the greatest value in the left subtree G. If multiple nodes in the left subtree have value G, selecting G as the replacement value for the root of the subtree will result in a tree with equal values to the left of the node now containing G. Precisely this situation occurs if we replace value 120 with the greatest value in the left subtree of Figure 5.13(b). Selecting the least value from the right subtree does not have a similar problem, because it does not violate the Binary Search Tree Property if equal values appear in the right subtree.

From the above, we see that if we want to remove the record stored in a node with two children, then we simply call **deletemin** on the node's right subtree and substitute the record returned for the record being removed. Figure 5.18 shows an implementation for **removehelp**.

The cost for **findhelp** and **inserthelp** is the depth of the node found or inserted. The cost for **removehelp** is the depth of the node being removed, or in the case when this node has two children, the depth of the node with smallest value in its right subtree. Thus, in the worst case, the cost for any one of these operations is the depth of the deepest node in the tree. This is why it is desirable to keep BSTs **balanced**, that is, with least possible height. If a binary tree is balanced, then the height for a tree of n nodes is approximately $\log n$. However, if the tree is completely unbalanced, for example in the shape of a linked list, then the height for a tree with n nodes can be as great as n. Thus, a balanced BST will in the average case have operations costing $\Theta(\log n)$, while a badly unbalanced BST can have operations in the worst case costing $\Theta(n)$. Consider the situation where we construct a BST of n nodes by inserting records one at a time. If we are fortunate to have them arrive in an order that results in a balanced tree (a "random" order is

```
// Remove a node with key value k
// Return: The tree with the node removed
template <typename Key, typename E>
BSTNode<Key, E>* BST<Key, E>::
removehelp(BSTNode<Key, E>* rt, const Key& k) {
  if (rt == NULL) return NULL;       // k is not in tree
  else if (k < rt->key())
    rt->setLeft(removehelp(rt->left(), k));
  else if (k > rt->key())
    rt->setRight(removehelp(rt->right(), k));
  else {                             // Found: remove it
    BSTNode<Key, E>* temp = rt;
    if (rt->left() == NULL) {        // Only a right child
      rt = rt->right();              //  so point to right
      delete temp;
    }
    else if (rt->right() == NULL) { // Only a left child
      rt = rt->left();               //  so point to left
      delete temp;
    }
    else {                           // Both children are non-empty
      BSTNode<Key, E>* temp = getmin(rt->right());
      rt->setElement(temp->element());
      rt->setKey(temp->key());
      rt->setRight(deletemin(rt->right()));
      delete temp;
    }
  }
  return rt;
}
```

Figure 5.18 Implementation for the BST **removehelp** method.

likely to be good enough for this purpose), then each insertion will cost on average $\Theta(\log n)$, for a total cost of $\Theta(n \log n)$. However, if the records are inserted in order of increasing value, then the resulting tree will be a chain of height n. The cost of insertion in this case will be $\sum_{i=1}^{n} i = \Theta(n^2)$.

Traversing a BST costs $\Theta(n)$ regardless of the shape of the tree. Each node is visited exactly once, and each child pointer is followed exactly once.

Below are two example traversals. The first is member **clearhelp**, which returns the nodes of the BST to the freelist. Because the children of a node must be freed before the node itself, this is a postorder traversal.

```
template <typename Key, typename E>
void BST<Key, E>::
clearhelp(BSTNode<Key, E>* root) {
  if (root == NULL) return;
  clearhelp(root->left());
  clearhelp(root->right());
  delete root;
}
```

The next example is **printhelp**, which performs an inorder traversal on the BST to print the node values in ascending order. Note that **printhelp** indents each line to indicate the depth of the corresponding node in the tree. Thus we pass in the current level of the tree in **level**, and increment this value each time that we make a recursive call.

```
template <typename Key, typename E>
void BST<Key, E>::
printhelp(BSTNode<Key, E>* root, int level) const {
  if (root == NULL) return;            // Empty tree
  printhelp(root->left(), level+1);    // Do left subtree
  for (int i=0; i<level; i++)          // Indent to level
    cout << "   ";
  cout << root->key() << "\n";         // Print node value
  printhelp(root->right(), level+1);   // Do right subtree
}
```

While the BST is simple to implement and efficient when the tree is balanced, the possibility of its being unbalanced is a serious liability. There are techniques for organizing a BST to guarantee good performance. Two examples are the AVL tree and the splay tree of Section 13.2. Other search trees are guaranteed to remain balanced, such as the 2-3 tree of Section 10.4.

5.5   Heaps and Priority Queues

There are many situations, both in real life and in computing applications, where we wish to choose the next "most important" from a collection of people, tasks, or objects. For example, doctors in a hospital emergency room often choose to see next the "most critical" patient rather than the one who arrived first. When scheduling programs for execution in a multitasking operating system, at any given moment there might be several programs (usually called **jobs**) ready to run. The next job selected is the one with the highest **priority**. Priority is indicated by a particular value associated with the job (and might change while the job remains in the wait list).

When a collection of objects is organized by importance or priority, we call this a **priority queue**. A normal queue data structure will not implement a priority queue efficiently because search for the element with highest priority will take $\Theta(n)$ time. A list, whether sorted or not, will also require $\Theta(n)$ time for either insertion or removal. A BST that organizes records by priority could be used, with the total of n inserts and n remove operations requiring $\Theta(n \log n)$ time in the average case. However, there is always the possibility that the BST will become unbalanced, leading to bad performance. Instead, we would like to find a data structure that is guaranteed to have good performance for this special application.

This section presents the **heap**[4] data structure. A heap is defined by two properties. First, it is a complete binary tree, so heaps are nearly always implemented using the array representation for complete binary trees presented in Section 5.3.3. Second, the values stored in a heap are **partially ordered**. This means that there is a relationship between the value stored at any node and the values of its children. There are two variants of the heap, depending on the definition of this relationship.

A **max-heap** has the property that every node stores a value that is *greater* than or equal to the value of either of its children. Because the root has a value greater than or equal to its children, which in turn have values greater than or equal to their children, the root stores the maximum of all values in the tree.

A **min-heap** has the property that every node stores a value that is *less* than or equal to that of its children. Because the root has a value less than or equal to its children, which in turn have values less than or equal to their children, the root stores the minimum of all values in the tree.

Note that there is no necessary relationship between the value of a node and that of its sibling in either the min-heap or the max-heap. For example, it is possible that the values for all nodes in the left subtree of the root are greater than the values for every node of the right subtree. We can contrast BSTs and heaps by the strength of their ordering relationships. A BST defines a total order on its nodes in that, given the positions for any two nodes in the tree, the one to the "left" (equivalently, the one appearing earlier in an inorder traversal) has a smaller key value than the one to the "right." In contrast, a heap implements a partial order. Given their positions, we can determine the relative order for the key values of two nodes in the heap *only* if one is a descendant of the other.

Min-heaps and max-heaps both have their uses. For example, the Heapsort of Section 7.6 uses the max-heap, while the Replacement Selection algorithm of Section 8.5.2 uses a min-heap. The examples in the rest of this section will use a max-heap.

Be careful not to confuse the logical representation of a heap with its physical implementation by means of the array-based complete binary tree. The two are not synonymous because the logical view of the heap is actually a tree structure, while the typical physical implementation uses an array.

Figure 5.19 shows an implementation for heaps. The class is a template with two parameters. **E** defines the type for the data elements stored in the heap, while **Comp** is the comparison class for comparing two elements. This class can implement either a min-heap or a max-heap by changing the definition for **Comp**. **Comp** defines method **prior**, a binary Boolean function that returns true if the first parameter should come before the second in the heap.

This class definition makes two concessions to the fact that an array-based implementation is used. First, heap nodes are indicated by their logical position within

---

[4]The term "heap" is also sometimes used to refer to a memory pool. See Section 12.3.

```
// Heap class
template <typename E, typename Comp> class heap {
private:
  E* Heap;                 // Pointer to the heap array
  int maxsize;             // Maximum size of the heap
  int n;                   // Number of elements now in the heap

  // Helper function to put element in its correct place
  void siftdown(int pos) {
    while (!isLeaf(pos)) { // Stop if pos is a leaf
      int j = leftchild(pos);  int rc = rightchild(pos);
      if ((rc < n) && Comp::prior(Heap[rc], Heap[j]))
        j = rc;                 // Set j to greater child's value
      if (Comp::prior(Heap[pos], Heap[j])) return; // Done
      swap(Heap, pos, j);
      pos = j;                  // Move down
    }
  }

public:
  heap(E* h, int num, int max)      // Constructor
    { Heap = h;  n = num;  maxsize = max;  buildHeap(); }
  int size() const         // Return current heap size
    { return n; }
  bool isLeaf(int pos) const // True if pos is a leaf
    { return (pos >= n/2) && (pos < n); }
  int leftchild(int pos) const
    { return 2*pos + 1; }     // Return leftchild position
  int rightchild(int pos) const
    { return 2*pos + 2; }     // Return rightchild position
  int parent(int pos) const  // Return parent position
    { return (pos-1)/2; }
  void buildHeap()            // Heapify contents of Heap
    { for (int i=n/2-1; i>=0; i--) siftdown(i); }

  // Insert "it" into the heap
  void insert(const E& it) {
    Assert(n < maxsize, "Heap is full");
    int curr = n++;
    Heap[curr] = it;                // Start at end of heap
    // Now sift up until curr's parent > curr
    while ((curr!=0) &&
           (Comp::prior(Heap[curr], Heap[parent(curr)]))) {
      swap(Heap, curr, parent(curr));
      curr = parent(curr);
    }
  }
}
```

Figure 5.19 An implementation for the heap.

```
// Remove first value
E removefirst() {
  Assert (n > 0, "Heap is empty");
  swap(Heap, 0, --n);          // Swap first with last value
  if (n != 0) siftdown(0);     // Siftdown new root val
  return Heap[n];              // Return deleted value
}

// Remove and return element at specified position
E remove(int pos) {
  Assert((pos >= 0) && (pos < n), "Bad position");
  if (pos == (n-1)) n--; // Last element, no work to do
  else
  {
    swap(Heap, pos, --n);              // Swap with last value
    while ((pos != 0) &&
           (Comp::prior(Heap[pos], Heap[parent(pos)]))) {
      swap(Heap, pos, parent(pos)); // Push up large key
      pos = parent(pos);
    }
    if (n != 0) siftdown(pos);        // Push down small key
  }
  return Heap[n];
}
};
```

Figure 5.19 (continued)

the heap rather than by a pointer to the node. In practice, the logical heap position corresponds to the identically numbered physical position in the array. Second, the constructor takes as input a pointer to the array to be used. This approach provides the greatest flexibility for using the heap because all data values can be loaded into the array directly by the client. The advantage of this comes during the heap construction phase, as explained below. The constructor also takes an integer parameter indicating the initial size of the heap (based on the number of elements initially loaded into the array) and a second integer parameter indicating the maximum size allowed for the heap (the size of the array).

Method **heapsize** returns the current size of the heap. **H.isLeaf(pos)** returns **true** if position **pos** is a leaf in heap **H**, and **false** otherwise. Members **leftchild**, **rightchild**, and **parent** return the position (actually, the array index) for the left child, right child, and parent of the position passed, respectively.

One way to build a heap is to insert the elements one at a time. Method **insert** will insert a new element V into the heap. You might expect the heap insertion process to be similar to the insert function for a BST, starting at the root and working down through the heap. However, this approach is not likely to work because the heap must maintain the shape of a complete binary tree. Equivalently, if the heap takes up the first n positions of its array prior to the call to **insert**, it must take up the first $n + 1$ positions after. To accomplish this, **insert** first places V at position n of the array. Of course, V is unlikely to be in the correct position. To move V to the right place, it is compared to its parent's value. If the value of V is less than or equal to the value of its parent, then it is in the correct place and the insert routine is finished. If the value of V is greater than that of its parent, then the two elements swap positions. From here, the process of comparing V to its (current) parent continues until V reaches its correct position.

Since the heap is a complete binary tree, its height is guaranteed to be the minimum possible. In particular, a heap containing n nodes will have a height of $\Theta(n \log n)$. Intuitively, we can see that this must be true because each level that we add will slightly more than double the number of nodes in the tree (the ith level has 2^i nodes, and the sum of the first i levels is $2^{i+1} - 1$). Starting at 1, we can double only $\log n$ times to reach a value of n. To be precise, the height of a heap with n nodes is $\lceil \log(n + 1) \rceil$.

Each call to **insert** takes $\Theta(\log n)$ time in the worst case, because the value being inserted can move at most the distance from the bottom of the tree to the top of the tree. Thus, to insert n values into the heap, if we insert them one at a time, will take $\Theta(n \log n)$ time in the worst case.

If all n values are available at the beginning of the building process, we can build the heap faster than just inserting the values into the heap one by one. Consider Figure 5.20(a), which shows one series of exchanges that could be used to build the heap. All exchanges are between a node and one of its children. The heap is formed as a result of this exchange process. The array for the right-hand tree of Figure 5.20(a) would appear as follows:

7	4	6	1	2	3	5

Figure 5.20(b) shows an alternate series of exchanges that also forms a heap, but much more efficiently. The equivalent array representation would be

7	5	6	4	2	1	3

From this example, it is clear that the heap for any given set of numbers is not unique, and we see that some rearrangements of the input values require fewer exchanges than others to build the heap. So, how do we pick the best rearrangement?

One good algorithm stems from induction. Suppose that the left and right subtrees of the root are already heaps, and R is the name of the element at the root. This situation is illustrated by Figure 5.21. In this case there are two possibilities. (1) R has a value greater than or equal to its two children. In this case, construction is complete. (2) R has a value less than one or both of its children. In this case, R should be exchanged with the child that has greater value. The result will be a heap, except that R might still be less than one or both of its (new) children. In this case, we simply continue the process of "pushing down" R until it reaches a

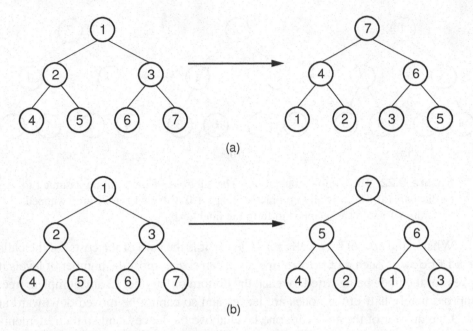

(a)

(b)

Figure 5.20 Two series of exchanges to build a max-heap. (a) This heap is built by a series of nine exchanges in the order (4-2), (4-1), (2-1), (5-2), (5-4), (6-3), (6-5), (7-5), (7-6). (b) This heap is built by a series of four exchanges in the order (5-2), (7-3), (7-1), (6-1).

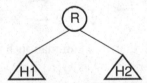

Figure 5.21 Final stage in the heap-building algorithm. Both subtrees of node R are heaps. All that remains is to push R down to its proper level in the heap.

level where it is greater than its children, or is a leaf node. This process is implemented by the private method **siftdown**. The siftdown operation is illustrated by Figure 5.22.

This approach assumes that the subtrees are already heaps, suggesting that a complete algorithm can be obtained by visiting the nodes in some order such that the children of a node are visited *before* the node itself. One simple way to do this is simply to work from the high index of the array to the low index. Actually, the build process need not visit the leaf nodes (they can never move down because they are already at the bottom), so the building algorithm can start in the middle of the array, with the first internal node. The exchanges shown in Figure 5.20(b) result from this process. Method **buildHeap** implements the building algorithm.

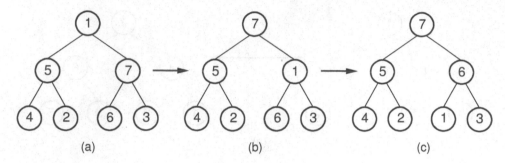

Figure 5.22 The siftdown operation. The subtrees of the root are assumed to be heaps. (a) The partially completed heap. (b) Values 1 and 7 are swapped. (c) Values 1 and 6 are swapped to form the final heap.

What is the cost of **buildHeap**? Clearly it is the sum of the costs for the calls to **siftdown**. Each **siftdown** operation can cost at most the number of levels it takes for the node being sifted to reach the bottom of the tree. In any complete tree, approximately half of the nodes are leaves and so cannot be moved downward at all. One quarter of the nodes are one level above the leaves, and so their elements can move down at most one level. At each step up the tree we get half the number of nodes as were at the previous level, and an additional height of one. The maximum sum of total distances that elements can go is therefore

$$\sum_{i=1}^{\log n}(i-1)\frac{n}{2^i} = \frac{n}{2}\sum_{i=1}^{\log n}\frac{i-1}{2^{i-1}}.$$

From Equation 2.9 we know that this summation has a closed-form solution of approximately 2, so this algorithm takes $\Theta(n)$ time in the worst case. This is far better than building the heap one element at a time, which would cost $\Theta(n \log n)$ in the worst case. It is also faster than the $\Theta(n \log n)$ average-case time and $\Theta(n^2)$ worst-case time required to build the BST.

Removing the maximum (root) value from a heap containing n elements requires that we maintain the complete binary tree shape, and that the remaining $n-1$ node values conform to the heap property. We can maintain the proper shape by moving the element in the last position in the heap (the current last element in the array) to the root position. We now consider the heap to be one element smaller. Unfortunately, the new root value is probably *not* the maximum value in the new heap. This problem is easily solved by using **siftdown** to reorder the heap. Because the heap is $\log n$ levels deep, the cost of deleting the maximum element is $\Theta(\log n)$ in the average and worst cases.

The heap is a natural implementation for the priority queue discussed at the beginning of this section. Jobs can be added to the heap (using their priority value as the ordering key) when needed. Method **removemax** can be called whenever a new job is to be executed.

Some applications of priority queues require the ability to change the priority of an object already stored in the queue. This might require that the object's position in the heap representation be updated. Unfortunately, a max-heap is not efficient when searching for an arbitrary value; it is only good for finding the maximum value. However, if we already know the index for an object within the heap, it is a simple matter to update its priority (including changing its position to maintain the heap property) or remove it. The **remove** method takes as input the position of the node to be removed from the heap. A typical implementation for priority queues requiring updating of priorities will need to use an auxiliary data structure that supports efficient search for objects (such as a BST). Records in the auxiliary data structure will store the object's heap index, so that the object can be deleted from the heap and reinserted with its new priority (see Project 5.5). Sections 11.4.1 and 11.5.1 present applications for a priority queue with priority updating.

5.6 Huffman Coding Trees

The space/time tradeoff principle from Section 3.9 states that one can often gain an improvement in space requirements in exchange for a penalty in running time. There are many situations where this is a desirable tradeoff. A typical example is storing files on disk. If the files are not actively used, the owner might wish to compress them to save space. Later, they can be uncompressed for use, which costs some time, but only once.

We often represent a set of items in a computer program by assigning a unique code to each item. For example, the standard ASCII coding scheme assigns a unique eight-bit value to each character. It takes a certain minimum number of bits to provide unique codes for each character. For example, it takes $\lceil \log 128 \rceil$ or seven bits to provide the 128 unique codes needed to represent the 128 symbols of the ASCII character set.[5]

The requirement for $\lceil \log n \rceil$ bits to represent n unique code values assumes that all codes will be the same length, as are ASCII codes. This is called a **fixed-length** coding scheme. If all characters were used equally often, then a fixed-length coding scheme is the most space efficient method. However, you are probably aware that not all characters are used equally often in many applications. For example, the various letters in an English language document have greatly different frequencies of use.

Figure 5.23 shows the relative frequencies of the letters of the alphabet. From this table we can see that the letter 'E' appears about 60 times more often than the letter 'Z.' In normal ASCII, the words "DEED" and "MUCK" require the same

---

[5]The ASCII standard is eight bits, not seven, even though there are only 128 characters represented. The eighth bit is used either to check for transmission errors, or to support "extended" ASCII codes with an additional 128 characters.

Letter	Frequency	Letter	Frequency
A	77	N	67
B	17	O	67
C	32	P	20
D	42	Q	5
E	120	R	59
F	24	S	67
G	17	T	85
H	50	U	37
I	76	V	12
J	4	W	22
K	7	X	4
L	42	Y	22
M	24	Z	2

Figure 5.23 Relative frequencies for the 26 letters of the alphabet as they appear in a selected set of English documents. "Frequency" represents the expected frequency of occurrence per 1000 letters, ignoring case.

amount of space (four bytes). It would seem that words such as "DEED," which are composed of relatively common letters, should be storable in less space than words such as "MUCK," which are composed of relatively uncommon letters.

If some characters are used more frequently than others, is it possible to take advantage of this fact and somehow assign them shorter codes? The price could be that other characters require longer codes, but this might be worthwhile if such characters appear rarely enough. This concept is at the heart of file compression techniques in common use today. The next section presents one such approach to assigning **variable-length** codes, called Huffman coding. While it is not commonly used in its simplest form for file compression (there are better methods), Huffman coding gives the flavor of such coding schemes. One motivation for studying Huffman coding is because it provides our first opportunity to see a type of tree structure referred to as a **search trie**.

5.6.1 Building Huffman Coding Trees

Huffman coding assigns codes to characters such that the length of the code depends on the relative frequency or **weight** of the corresponding character. Thus, it is a variable-length code. If the estimated frequencies for letters match the actual frequency found in an encoded message, then the length of that message will typically be less than if a fixed-length code had been used. The Huffman code for each letter is derived from a full binary tree called the **Huffman coding tree**, or simply the **Huffman tree**. Each leaf of the Huffman tree corresponds to a letter, and we define the weight of the leaf node to be the weight (frequency) of its associated

Letter	C	D	E	K	L	M	U	Z
Frequency	32	42	120	7	42	24	37	2

Figure 5.24 The relative frequencies for eight selected letters.

letter. The goal is to build a tree with the **minimum external path weight**. Define the **weighted path length** of a leaf to be its weight times its depth. The binary tree with minimum external path weight is the one with the minimum sum of weighted path lengths for the given set of leaves. A letter with high weight should have low depth, so that it will count the least against the total path length. As a result, another letter might be pushed deeper in the tree if it has less weight.

The process of building the Huffman tree for n letters is quite simple. First, create a collection of n initial Huffman trees, each of which is a single leaf node containing one of the letters. Put the n partial trees onto a priority queue organized by weight (frequency). Next, remove the first two trees (the ones with lowest weight) from the priority queue. Join these two trees together to create a new tree whose root has the two trees as children, and whose weight is the sum of the weights of the two trees. Put this new tree back into the priority queue. This process is repeated until all of the partial Huffman trees have been combined into one.

Example 5.8 Figure 5.25 illustrates part of the Huffman tree construction process for the eight letters of Figure 5.24. Ranking D and L arbitrarily by alphabetical order, the letters are ordered by frequency as

Letter	Z	K	M	C	U	D	L	E
Frequency	2	7	24	32	37	42	42	120

Because the first two letters on the list are Z and K, they are selected to be the first trees joined together.[6] They become the children of a root node with weight 9. Thus, a tree whose root has weight 9 is placed back on the list, where it takes up the first position. The next step is to take values 9 and 24 off the list (corresponding to the partial tree with two leaf nodes built in the last step, and the partial tree storing the letter M, respectively) and join them together. The resulting root node has weight 33, and so this tree is placed back into the list. Its priority will be between the trees with values 32 (for letter C) and 37 (for letter U). This process continues until a tree whose root has weight 306 is built. This tree is shown in Figure 5.26.

---

[6]For clarity, the examples for building Huffman trees show a sorted list to keep the letters ordered by frequency. But a real implementation would use a heap to implement the priority queue for efficiency.

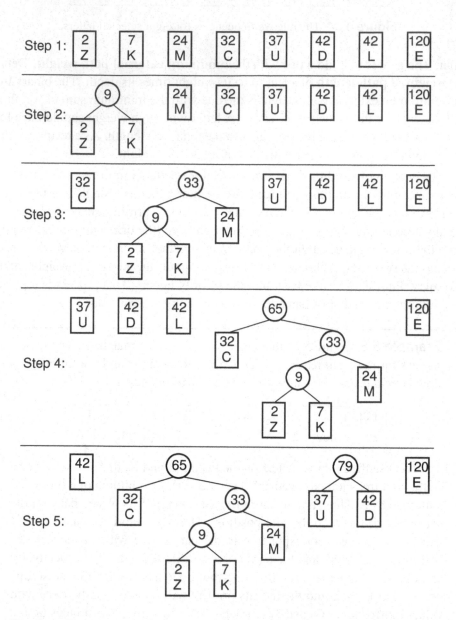

Figure 5.25 The first five steps of the building process for a sample Huffman tree.

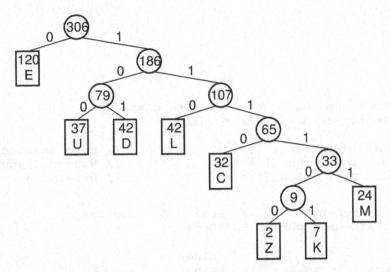

Figure 5.26 A Huffman tree for the letters of Figure 5.24.

Figure 5.27 shows an implementation for Huffman tree nodes. This implementation is similar to the **VarBinNode** implementation of Figure 5.10. There is an abstract base class, named **HuffNode**, and two subclasses, named **LeafNode** and **IntlNode**. This implementation reflects the fact that leaf and internal nodes contain distinctly different information.

Figure 5.28 shows the implementation for the Huffman tree. Figure 5.29 shows the C++ code for the tree-building process.

Huffman tree building is an example of a **greedy algorithm**. At each step, the algorithm makes a "greedy" decision to merge the two subtrees with least weight. This makes the algorithm simple, but does it give the desired result? This section concludes with a proof that the Huffman tree indeed gives the most efficient arrangement for the set of letters. The proof requires the following lemma.

Lemma 5.1 *For any Huffman tree built by function* **buildHuff** *containing at least two letters, the two letters with least frequency are stored in siblings nodes whose depth is at least as deep as any other leaf nodes in the tree.*

Proof: Call the two letters with least frequency l_1 and l_2. They must be siblings because **buildHuff** selects them in the first step of the construction process. Assume that l_1 and l_2 are not the deepest nodes in the tree. In this case, the Huffman tree must either look as shown in Figure 5.30, or in some sense be symmetrical to this. For this situation to occur, the parent of l_1 and l_2, labeled V, must have greater weight than the node labeled X. Otherwise, function **buildHuff** would have selected node V in place of node X as the child of node U. However, this is impossible because l_1 and l_2 are the letters with least frequency. □

```cpp
// Huffman tree node abstract base class
template <typename E> class HuffNode {
public:
  virtual ~HuffNode() {}                    // Base destructor
  virtual int weight() = 0;                 // Return frequency
  virtual bool isLeaf() = 0;                // Determine type
};

template <typename E>     // Leaf node subclass
class LeafNode : public HuffNode<E> {
private:
  E it;                    // Value
  int wgt;                 // Weight
public:
  LeafNode(const E& val, int freq)    // Constructor
    { it = val; wgt = freq; }
  int weight() { return wgt; }
  E val() { return it; }
  bool isLeaf() { return true; }
};

template <typename E>     // Internal node subclass
class IntlNode : public HuffNode<E> {
private:
  HuffNode<E>* lc;    // Left child
  HuffNode<E>* rc;    // Right child
  int wgt;                 // Subtree weight
public:
  IntlNode(HuffNode<E>* l, HuffNode<E>* r)
    { wgt = l->weight() + r->weight(); lc = l; rc = r; }
  int weight() { return wgt; }
  bool isLeaf() { return false; }
  HuffNode<E>* left() const { return lc; }
  void setLeft(HuffNode<E>* b)
    { lc = (HuffNode<E>*)b; }
  HuffNode<E>* right() const { return rc; }
  void setRight(HuffNode<E>* b)
    { rc = (HuffNode<E>*)b; }
};
```

Figure 5.27 Implementation for Huffman tree nodes. Internal nodes and leaf nodes are represented by separate classes, each derived from an abstract base class.

```
// HuffTree is a template of two parameters: the element
//  type being coded and a comparator for two such elements.
template <typename E>
class HuffTree {
private:
  HuffNode<E>* Root;            // Tree root
public:
  HuffTree(E& val, int freq) // Leaf constructor
    { Root = new LeafNode<E>(val, freq); }
  // Internal node constructor
  HuffTree(HuffTree<E>* l, HuffTree<E>* r)
    { Root = new IntlNode<E>(l->root(), r->root()); }
  ~HuffTree() {}                              // Destructor
  HuffNode<E>* root() { return Root; }     // Get root
  int weight() { return Root->weight(); } // Root weight
};
```

Figure 5.28 Class declarations for the Huffman tree.

```
// Build a Huffman tree from a collection of frequencies
template <typename E> HuffTree<E>*
buildHuff(HuffTree<E>** TreeArray, int count) {
  heap<HuffTree<E>*,minTreeComp>* forest =
    new heap<HuffTree<E>*, minTreeComp>(TreeArray,
                                        count, count);
  HuffTree<char> *temp1, *temp2, *temp3 = NULL;
  while (forest->size() > 1) {
    temp1 = forest->removefirst();   // Pull first two trees
    temp2 = forest->removefirst();   //    off the list
    temp3 = new HuffTree<E>(temp1, temp2);
    forest->insert(temp3);  // Put the new tree back on list
    delete temp1;          // Must delete the remnants
    delete temp2;          //    of the trees we created
  }
  return temp3;
}
```

Figure 5.29 Implementation for the Huffman tree construction function. **buildHuff** takes as input **fl**, the min-heap of partial Huffman trees, which initially are single leaf nodes as shown in Step 1 of Figure 5.25. The body of function **buildTree** consists mainly of a **for** loop. On each iteration of the **for** loop, the first two partial trees are taken off the heap and placed in variables **temp1** and **temp2**. A tree is created (**temp3**) such that the left and right subtrees are **temp1** and **temp2**, respectively. Finally, **temp3** is returned to **fl**.

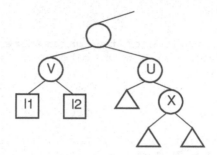

Figure 5.30 An impossible Huffman tree, showing the situation where the two nodes with least weight, l_1 and l_2, are not the deepest nodes in the tree. Triangles represent subtrees.

Theorem 5.3 *Function* **buildHuff** *builds the Huffman tree with the minimum external path weight for the given set of letters.*

Proof: The proof is by induction on n, the number of letters.

- **Base Case**: For $n = 2$, the Huffman tree must have the minimum external path weight because there are only two possible trees, each with identical weighted path lengths for the two leaves.
- **Induction Hypothesis**: Assume that any tree created by **buildHuff** that contains $n - 1$ leaves has minimum external path length.
- **Induction Step**: Given a Huffman tree **T** built by **buildHuff** with n leaves, $n \geq 2$, suppose that $w_1 \leq w_2 \leq \cdots \leq w_n$ where w_1 to w_n are the weights of the letters. Call V the parent of the letters with frequencies w_1 and w_2. From the lemma, we know that the leaf nodes containing the letters with frequencies w_1 and w_2 are as deep as any nodes in **T**. If any other leaf nodes in the tree were deeper, we could reduce their weighted path length by swapping them with w_1 or w_2. But the lemma tells us that no such deeper nodes exist. Call **T**$'$ the Huffman tree that is identical to **T** except that node V is replaced with a leaf node V' whose weight is $w_1 + w_2$. By the induction hypothesis, **T**$'$ has minimum external path length. Returning the children to V' restores tree **T**, which must also have minimum external path length.

Thus by mathematical induction, function **buildHuff** creates the Huffman tree with minimum external path length.   □

5.6.2   Assigning and Using Huffman Codes

Once the Huffman tree has been constructed, it is an easy matter to assign codes to individual letters. Beginning at the root, we assign either a '0' or a '1' to each edge in the tree. '0' is assigned to edges connecting a node with its left child, and '1' to edges connecting a node with its right child. This process is illustrated by

Letter	Freq	Code	Bits
C	32	1110	4
D	42	101	3
E	120	0	1
K	7	111101	6
L	42	110	3
M	24	11111	5
U	37	100	3
Z	2	111100	6

Figure 5.31 The Huffman codes for the letters of Figure 5.24.

Figure 5.26. The Huffman code for a letter is simply a binary number determined by the path from the root to the leaf corresponding to that letter. Thus, the code for E is '0' because the path from the root to the leaf node for E takes a single left branch. The code for K is '111101' because the path to the node for K takes four right branches, then a left, and finally one last right. Figure 5.31 lists the codes for all eight letters.

Given codes for the letters, it is a simple matter to use these codes to encode a text message. We simply replace each letter in the string with its binary code. A lookup table can be used for this purpose.

Example 5.9 Using the code generated by our example Huffman tree, the word "DEED" is represented by the bit string "10100101" and the word "MUCK" is represented by the bit string "111111001110111101."

Decoding the message is done by looking at the bits in the coded string from left to right until a letter is decoded. This can be done by using the Huffman tree in a reverse process from that used to generate the codes. Decoding a bit string begins at the root of the tree. We take branches depending on the bit value — left for '0' and right for '1' — until reaching a leaf node. This leaf contains the first character in the message. We then process the next bit in the code restarting at the root to begin the next character.

Example 5.10 To decode the bit string "1011001110111101" we begin at the root of the tree and take a right branch for the first bit which is '1.' Because the next bit is a '0' we take a left branch. We then take another right branch (for the third bit '1'), arriving at the leaf node corresponding to the letter D. Thus, the first letter of the coded word is D. We then begin again at the root of the tree to process the fourth bit, which is a '1.' Taking a right branch, then two left branches (for the next two bits which are '0'), we reach the leaf node corresponding to the letter U. Thus, the second letter is U. In similar manner we complete the decoding process to find that the last two letters are C and K, spelling the word "DUCK."

A set of codes is said to meet the **prefix property** if no code in the set is the prefix of another. The prefix property guarantees that there will be no ambiguity in how a bit string is decoded. In other words, once we reach the last bit of a code during the decoding process, we know which letter it is the code for. Huffman codes certainly have the prefix property because any prefix for a code would correspond to an internal node, while all codes correspond to leaf nodes. For example, the code for M is '11111.' Taking five right branches in the Huffman tree of Figure 5.26 brings us to the leaf node containing M. We can be sure that no letter can have code '111' because this corresponds to an internal node of the tree, and the tree-building process places letters only at the leaf nodes.

How efficient is Huffman coding? In theory, it is an optimal coding method whenever the true frequencies are known, and the frequency of a letter is independent of the context of that letter in the message. In practice, the frequencies of letters in an English text document do change depending on context. For example, while E is the most commonly used letter of the alphabet in English documents, T is more common as the first letter of a word. This is why most commercial compression utilities do not use Huffman coding as their primary coding method, but instead use techniques that take advantage of the context for the letters.

Another factor that affects the compression efficiency of Huffman coding is the relative frequencies of the letters. Some frequency patterns will save no space as compared to fixed-length codes; others can result in great compression. In general, Huffman coding does better when there is large variation in the frequencies of letters. In the particular case of the frequencies shown in Figure 5.31, we can determine the expected savings from Huffman coding if the actual frequencies of a coded message match the expected frequencies.

Example 5.11 Because the sum of the frequencies in Figure 5.31 is 306 and E has frequency 120, we expect it to appear 120 times in a message containing 306 letters. An actual message might or might not meet this expectation. Letters D, L, and U have code lengths of three, and together are expected to appear 121 times in 306 letters. Letter C has a code length of four, and is expected to appear 32 times in 306 letters. Letter M has a code length of five, and is expected to appear 24 times in 306 letters. Finally, letters K and Z have code lengths of six, and together are expected to appear only 9 times in 306 letters. The average expected cost per character is simply the sum of the cost for each character (c_i) times the probability of its occurring (p_i), or

$$c_1 p_1 + c_2 p_2 + \cdots + c_n p_n.$$

This can be reorganized as

$$\frac{c_1 f_1 + c_2 f_2 + \cdots + c_n f_n}{f_T}$$

where f_i is the (relative) frequency of letter i and f_T is the total for all letter frequencies. For this set of frequencies, the expected cost per letter is

$$[(1 \times 120) + (3 \times 121) + (4 \times 32) + (5 \times 24) + (6 \times 9)]/306 = 785/306 \approx 2.57$$

A fixed-length code for these eight characters would require $\log 8 = 3$ bits per letter as opposed to about 2.57 bits per letter for Huffman coding. Thus, Huffman coding is expected to save about 14% for this set of letters.

Huffman coding for all ASCII symbols should do better than this. The letters of Figure 5.31 are atypical in that there are too many common letters compared to the number of rare letters. Huffman coding for all 26 letters would yield an expected cost of 4.29 bits per letter. The equivalent fixed-length code would require about five bits. This is somewhat unfair to fixed-length coding because there is actually room for 32 codes in five bits, but only 26 letters. More generally, Huffman coding of a typical text file will save around 40% over ASCII coding if we charge ASCII coding at eight bits per character. Huffman coding for a binary file (such as a compiled executable) would have a very different set of distribution frequencies and so would have a different space savings. Most commercial compression programs use two or three coding schemes to adjust to different types of files.

In the preceding example, "DEED" was coded in 8 bits, a saving of 33% over the twelve bits required from a fixed-length coding. However, "MUCK" requires 18 bits, more space than required by the corresponding fixed-length coding. The problem is that "MUCK" is composed of letters that are not expected to occur often. If the message does not match the expected frequencies of the letters, than the length of the encoding will not be as expected either.

5.6.3 Search in Huffman Trees

When we decode a character using the Huffman coding tree, we follow a path through the tree dictated by the bits in the code string. Each '0' bit indicates a left branch while each '1' bit indicates a right branch. Now look at Figure 5.26 and consider this structure in terms of searching for a given letter (whose key value is its Huffman code). We see that all letters with codes beginning with '0' are stored in the left branch, while all letters with codes beginning with '1' are stored in the right branch. Contrast this with storing records in a BST. There, all records with key value less than the root value are stored in the left branch, while all records with key values greater than the root are stored in the right branch.

If we view all records stored in either of these structures as appearing at some point on a number line representing the key space, we can see that the splitting behavior of these two structures is very different. The BST splits the space based on the key values as they are encountered when going down the tree. But the splits in the key space are predetermined for the Huffman tree. Search tree structures whose splitting points in the key space are predetermined are given the special name **trie** to distinguish them from the type of search tree (like the BST) whose splitting points are determined by the data. Tries are discussed in more detail in Chapter 13.

5.7 Further Reading

See Shaffer and Brown [SB93] for an example of a tree implementation where an internal node pointer field stores the value of its child instead of a pointer to its child when the child is a leaf node.

Many techniques exist for maintaining reasonably balanced BSTs in the face of an unfriendly series of insert and delete operations. One example is the AVL tree of Adelson-Velskii and Landis, which is discussed by Knuth [Knu98]. The AVL tree (see Section 13.2) is actually a BST whose insert and delete routines reorganize the tree structure so as to guarantee that the subtrees rooted by the children of any node will differ in height by at most one. Another example is the splay tree [ST85], also discussed in Section 13.2.

See Bentley's Programming Pearl "Thanks, Heaps" [Ben85, Ben88] for a good discussion on the heap data structure and its uses.

The proof of Section 5.6.1 that the Huffman coding tree has minimum external path weight is from Knuth [Knu97]. For more information on data compression techniques, see *Managing Gigabytes* by Witten, Moffat, and Bell [WMB99], and *Codes and Cryptography* by Dominic Welsh [Wel88]. Tables 5.23 and 5.24 are derived from Welsh [Wel88].

5.8 Exercises

5.1 Section 5.1.1 claims that a full binary tree has the highest number of leaf nodes among all trees with n internal nodes. Prove that this is true.

5.2 Define the **degree** of a node as the number of its non-empty children. Prove by induction that the number of degree 2 nodes in any binary tree is one less than the number of leaves.

5.3 Define the **internal path length** for a tree as the sum of the depths of all internal nodes, while the **external path length** is the sum of the depths of all leaf nodes in the tree. Prove by induction that if tree **T** is a full binary tree with n internal nodes, I is **T**'s internal path length, and E is **T**'s external path length, then $E = I + 2n$ for $n \geq 0$.

5.4 Explain why function **preorder2** from Section 5.2 makes half as many recursive calls as function **preorder**. Explain why it makes twice as many accesses to left and right children.

5.5 **(a)** Modify the preorder traversal of Section 5.2 to perform an inorder traversal of a binary tree.

     (b) Modify the preorder traversal of Section 5.2 to perform a postorder traversal of a binary tree.

5.6 Write a recursive function named **search** that takes as input the pointer to the root of a binary tree (*not* a BST!) and a value K, and returns **true** if value K appears in the tree and **false** otherwise.

5.7 Write an algorithm that takes as input the pointer to the root of a binary tree and prints the node values of the tree in **level** order. Level order first prints the root, then all nodes of level 1, then all nodes of level 2, and so on. *Hint*: Preorder traversals make use of a stack through recursive calls. Consider making use of another data structure to help implement the level-order traversal.

5.8 Write a recursive function that returns the height of a binary tree.

5.9 Write a recursive function that returns a count of the number of leaf nodes in a binary tree.

5.10 Assume that a given BST stores integer values in its nodes. Write a recursive function that sums the values of all nodes in the tree.

5.11 Assume that a given BST stores integer values in its nodes. Write a recursive function that traverses a binary tree, and prints the value of every node who's grandparent has a value that is a multiple of five.

5.12 Write a recursive function that traverses a binary tree, and prints the value of every node which has at least four great-grandchildren.

5.13 Compute the overhead fraction for each of the following full binary tree implementations.

     (a) All nodes store data, two child pointers, and a parent pointer. The data field requires four bytes and each pointer requires four bytes.

     (b) All nodes store data and two child pointers. The data field requires sixteen bytes and each pointer requires four bytes.

     (c) All nodes store data and a parent pointer, and internal nodes store two child pointers. The data field requires eight bytes and each pointer requires four bytes.

     (d) Only leaf nodes store data; internal nodes store two child pointers. The data field requires eight bytes and each pointer requires four bytes.

5.14 Why is the BST Property defined so that nodes with values equal to the value of the root appear only in the right subtree, rather than allow equal-valued nodes to appear in either subtree?

5.15 **(a)** Show the BST that results from inserting the values 15, 20, 25, 18, 16, 5, and 7 (in that order).

(b) Show the enumerations for the tree of (a) that result from doing a pre-order traversal, an inorder traversal, and a postorder traversal.

5.16 Draw the BST that results from adding the value 5 to the BST shown in Figure 5.13(a).

5.17 Draw the BST that results from deleting the value 7 from the BST of Figure 5.13(b).

5.18 Write a function that prints out the node values for a BST in sorted order from highest to lowest.

5.19 Write a recursive function named **smallcount** that, given the pointer to the root of a BST and a key K, returns the number of nodes having key values less than or equal to K. Function **smallcount** should visit as few nodes in the BST as possible.

5.20 Write a recursive function named **printRange** that, given the pointer to the root of a BST, a low key value, and a high key value, prints in sorted order all records whose key values fall between the two given keys. Function **printRange** should visit as few nodes in the BST as possible.

5.21 Write a recursive function named **checkBST** that, given the pointer to the root of a binary tree, will return **true** if the tree is a BST, and **false** if it is not.

5.22 Describe a simple modification to the BST that will allow it to easily support finding the Kth smallest value in $\Theta(\log n)$ average case time. Then write a pseudo-code function for finding the Kth smallest value in your modified BST.

5.23 What are the minimum and maximum number of elements in a heap of height h?

5.24 Where in a max-heap might the smallest element reside?

5.25 Show the max-heap that results from running **buildHeap** on the following values stored in an array:

$$10 \quad 5 \quad 12 \quad 3 \quad 2 \quad 1 \quad 8 \quad 7 \quad 9 \quad 4$$

5.26 **(a)** Show the heap that results from deleting the maximum value from the max-heap of Figure 5.20b.

(b) Show the heap that results from deleting the element with value 5 from the max-heap of Figure 5.20b.

5.27 Revise the heap definition of Figure 5.19 to implement a min-heap. The member function **removemax** should be replaced by a new function called **removemin**.

5.28 Build the Huffman coding tree and determine the codes for the following set of letters and weights:

Letter	A	B	C	D	E	F	G	H	I	J	K	L
Frequency	2	3	5	7	11	13	17	19	23	31	37	41

What is the expected length in bits of a message containing n characters for this frequency distribution?

5.29 What will the Huffman coding tree look like for a set of sixteen characters all with equal weight? What is the average code length for a letter in this case? How does this differ from the smallest possible fixed length code for sixteen characters?

5.30 A set of characters with varying weights is assigned Huffman codes. If one of the characters is assigned code 001, then,

    (a) Describe all codes that *cannot* have been assigned.

    (b) Describe all codes that *must* have been assigned.

5.31 Assume that a sample alphabet has the following weights:

Letter	Q	Z	F	M	T	S	O	E
Frequency	2	3	10	10	10	15	20	30

    (a) For this alphabet, what is the worst-case number of bits required by the Huffman code for a string of n letters? What string(s) have the worst-case performance?

    (b) For this alphabet, what is the best-case number of bits required by the Huffman code for a string of n letters? What string(s) have the best-case performance?

    (c) What is the average number of bits required by a character using the Huffman code for this alphabet?

5.32 You must keep track of some data. Your options are:

    (1) A linked-list maintained in sorted order.

    (2) A linked-list of unsorted records.

    (3) A binary search tree.

    (4) An array-based list maintained in sorted order.

    (5) An array-based list of unsorted records.

For each of the following scenarios, which of these choices would be best? Explain your answer.

    (a) The records are guaranteed to arrive already sorted from lowest to highest (i.e., whenever a record is inserted, its key value will always be greater than that of the last record inserted). A total of 1000 inserts will be interspersed with 1000 searches.

    (b) The records arrive with values having a uniform random distribution (so the BST is likely to be well balanced). 1,000,000 insertions are performed, followed by 10 searches.

(c) The records arrive with values having a uniform random distribution (so the BST is likely to be well balanced). 1000 insertions are interspersed with 1000 searches.

(d) The records arrive with values having a uniform random distribution (so the BST is likely to be well balanced). 1000 insertions are performed, followed by 1,000,000 searches.

5.9 Projects

5.1 Re-implement the composite design for the binary tree node class of Figure 5.11 using a flyweight in place of **NULL** pointers to empty nodes.

5.2 One way to deal with the "problem" of **NULL** pointers in binary trees is to use that space for some other purpose. One example is the **threaded** binary tree. Extending the node implementation of Figure 5.7, the threaded binary tree stores with each node two additional bit fields that indicate if the child pointers **lc** and **rc** are regular pointers to child nodes or threads. If **lc** is not a pointer to a non-empty child (i.e., if it would be **NULL** in a regular binary tree), then it instead stores a pointer to the **inorder predecessor** of that node. The inorder predecessor is the node that would be printed immediately before the current node in an inorder traversal. If **rc** is not a pointer to a child, then it instead stores a pointer to the node's **inorder successor**. The inorder successor is the node that would be printed immediately after the current node in an inorder traversal. The main advantage of threaded binary trees is that operations such as inorder traversal can be implemented without using recursion or a stack.

Re-implement the BST as a threaded binary tree, and include a non-recursive version of the preorder traversal

5.3 Implement a city database using a BST to store the database records. Each database record contains the name of the city (a string of arbitrary length) and the coordinates of the city expressed as integer x- and y-coordinates. The BST should be organized by city name. Your database should allow records to be inserted, deleted by name or coordinate, and searched by name or coordinate. Another operation that should be supported is to print all records within a given distance of a specified point. Collect running-time statistics for each operation. Which operations can be implemented reasonably efficiently (i.e., in $\Theta(\log n)$ time in the average case) using a BST? Can the database system be made more efficient by using one or more additional BSTs to organize the records by location?

5.4 Create a binary tree ADT that includes generic traversal methods that take a visitor, as described in Section 5.2. Write functions **count** and **BSTcheck** of Section 5.2 as visitors to be used with the generic traversal method.

5.5 Implement a priority queue class based on the max-heap class implementation of Figure 5.19. The following methods should be supported for manipulating the priority queue:

```
void enqueue(int ObjectID, int priority);
int dequeue();
void changeweight(int ObjectID, int newPriority);
```

Method **enqueue** inserts a new object into the priority queue with ID number **ObjectID** and priority **priority**. Method **dequeue** removes the object with highest priority from the priority queue and returns its object ID. Method **changeweight** changes the priority of the object with ID number **ObjectID** to be **newPriority**. The type for **E** should be a class that stores the object ID and the priority for that object. You will need a mechanism for finding the position of the desired object within the heap. Use an array, storing the object with **ObjectID** i in position i. (Be sure in your testing to keep the **ObjectID**s within the array bounds.) You must also modify the heap implementation to store the object's position in the auxiliary array so that updates to objects in the heap can be updated as well in the array.

5.6 The Huffman coding tree function **buildHuff** of Figure 5.29 manipulates a sorted list. This could result in a $\Theta(n^2)$ algorithm, because placing an intermediate Huffman tree on the list could take $\Theta(n)$ time. Revise this algorithm to use a priority queue based on a min-heap instead of a list.

5.7 Complete the implementation of the Huffman coding tree, building on the code presented in Section 5.6. Include a function to compute and store in a table the codes for each letter, and functions to encode and decode messages. This project can be further extended to support file compression. To do so requires adding two steps: (1) Read through the input file to generate actual frequencies for all letters in the file; and (2) store a representation for the Huffman tree at the beginning of the encoded output file to be used by the decoding function. If you have trouble with devising such a representation, see Section 6.5.

6

Non-Binary Trees

Many organizations are hierarchical in nature, such as the military and most businesses. Consider a company with a president and some number of vice presidents who report to the president. Each vice president has some number of direct subordinates, and so on. If we wanted to model this company with a data structure, it would be natural to think of the president in the root node of a tree, the vice presidents at level 1, and their subordinates at lower levels in the tree as we go down the organizational hierarchy.

Because the number of vice presidents is likely to be more than two, this company's organization cannot easily be represented by a binary tree. We need instead to use a tree whose nodes have an arbitrary number of children. Unfortunately, when we permit trees to have nodes with an arbitrary number of children, they become much harder to implement than binary trees. We consider such trees in this chapter. To distinguish them from binary trees, we use the term **general tree**.

Section 6.1 presents general tree terminology. Section 6.2 presents a simple representation for solving the important problem of processing equivalence classes. Several pointer-based implementations for general trees are covered in Section 6.3. Aside from general trees and binary trees, there are also uses for trees whose internal nodes have a fixed number K of children where K is something other than two. Such trees are known as K-ary trees. Section 6.4 generalizes the properties of binary trees to K-ary trees. Sequential representations, useful for applications such as storing trees on disk, are covered in Section 6.5.

6.1 General Tree Definitions and Terminology

A **tree T** is a finite set of one or more nodes such that there is one designated node R, called the root of **T**. If the set $(\mathbf{T} - \{R\})$ is not empty, these nodes are partitioned into $n > 0$ disjoint subsets $\mathbf{T}_0$, $\mathbf{T}_1$, ..., $\mathbf{T}_{n-1}$, each of which is a tree, and whose roots R_1, R_2, ..., R_n, respectively, are children of R. The subsets $\mathbf{T}_i$ $(0 \leq i < n)$ are said to be **subtrees** of **T**. These subtrees are ordered in that $\mathbf{T}_i$ is said to come before

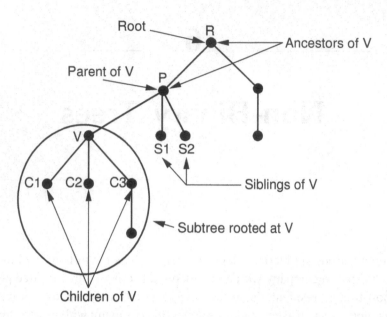

Figure 6.1 Notation for general trees. Node P is the parent of nodes V, $S1$, and $S2$. Thus, V, $S1$, and $S2$ are children of P. Nodes R and P are ancestors of V. Nodes V, $S1$, and $S2$ are called **siblings**. The oval surrounds the subtree having V as its root.

$\mathbf{T}_j$ if $i < j$. By convention, the subtrees are arranged from left to right with subtree $\mathbf{T}_0$ called the leftmost child of R. A node's **out degree** is the number of children for that node. A **forest** is a collection of one or more trees. Figure 6.1 presents further tree notation generalized from the notation for binary trees presented in Chapter 5.

Each node in a tree has precisely one parent, except for the root, which has no parent. From this observation, it immediately follows that a tree with n nodes must have $n - 1$ edges because each node, aside from the root, has one edge connecting that node to its parent.

6.1.1 An ADT for General Tree Nodes

Before discussing general tree implementations, we should first make precise what operations such implementations must support. Any implementation must be able to initialize a tree. Given a tree, we need access to the root of that tree. There must be some way to access the children of a node. In the case of the ADT for binary tree nodes, this was done by providing member functions that give explicit access to the left and right child pointers. Unfortunately, because we do not know in advance how many children a given node will have in the general tree, we cannot give explicit functions to access each child. An alternative must be found that works for an unknown number of children.

```
// General tree node ADT
template <typename E> class GTNode {
public:
  E value();                      // Return node's value
  bool isLeaf();                  // True if node is a leaf
  GTNode* parent();               // Return parent
  GTNode* leftmostChild();        // Return first child
  GTNode* rightSibling();         // Return right sibling
  void setValue(E&);              // Set node's value
  void insertFirst(GTNode<E>*);   // Insert first child
  void insertNext(GTNode<E>*);    // Insert next sibling
  void removeFirst();             // Remove first child
  void removeNext();              // Remove right sibling
};

// General tree ADT
template <typename E> class GenTree {
public:
  void clear();                   // Send all nodes to free store
  GTNode<E>* root();              // Return the root of the tree
  // Combine two subtrees
  void newroot(E&, GTNode<E>*, GTNode<E>*);
  void print();                   // Print a tree
};
```

Figure 6.2 Definitions for the general tree and general tree node

One choice would be to provide a function that takes as its parameter the index for the desired child. That combined with a function that returns the number of children for a given node would support the ability to access any node or process all children of a node. Unfortunately, this view of access tends to bias the choice for node implementations in favor of an array-based approach, because these functions favor random access to a list of children. In practice, an implementation based on a linked list is often preferred.

An alternative is to provide access to the first (or leftmost) child of a node, and to provide access to the next (or right) sibling of a node. Figure 6.2 shows class declarations for general trees and their nodes. Based on these two access functions, the children of a node can be traversed like a list. Trying to find the next sibling of the rightmost sibling would return **NULL**.

6.1.2 General Tree Traversals

In Section 5.2, three tree traversals were presented for binary trees: preorder, postorder, and inorder. For general trees, preorder and postorder traversals are defined with meanings similar to their binary tree counterparts. Preorder traversal of a general tree first visits the root of the tree, then performs a preorder traversal of each subtree from left to right. A postorder traversal of a general tree performs a postorder traversal of the root's subtrees from left to right, then visits the root. Inorder

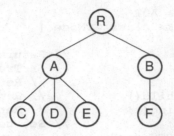

Figure 6.3 An example of a general tree.

traversal does not have a natural definition for the general tree, because there is no particular number of children for an internal node. An arbitrary definition — such as visit the leftmost subtree in inorder, then the root, then visit the remaining subtrees in inorder — can be invented. However, inorder traversals are generally not useful with general trees.

Example 6.1 A preorder traversal of the tree in Figure 6.3 visits the nodes in order $RACDEBF$.

A postorder traversal of this tree visits the nodes in order $CDEAFBR$.

To perform a preorder traversal, it is necessary to visit each of the children for a given node (say R) from left to right. This is accomplished by starting at R's leftmost child (call it T). From T, we can move to T's right sibling, and then to that node's right sibling, and so on.

Using the ADT of Figure 6.2, here is a **C++** implementation to print the nodes of a general tree in preorder. Note the **for** loop at the end, which processes the list of children by beginning with the leftmost child, then repeatedly moving to the next child until calling **next** returns **NULL**.

```
// Print using a preorder traversal
void printhelp(GTNode<E>* root) {
  if (root->isLeaf()) cout << "Leaf: ";
  else cout << "Internal: ";
  cout << root->value() << "\n";
  // Now process the children of "root"
  for (GTNode<E>* temp = root->leftmostChild();
      temp != NULL; temp = temp->rightSibling())
    printhelp(temp);
}
```

6.2   The Parent Pointer Implementation

Perhaps the simplest general tree implementation is to store for each node only a pointer to that node's parent. We will call this the **parent pointer** implementation. Clearly this implementation is not general purpose, because it is inadequate for such important operations as finding the leftmost child or the right sibling for a node. Thus, it may seem to be a poor idea to implement a general tree in this way. However, the parent pointer implementation stores precisely the information required to answer the following, useful question: "Given two nodes, are they in the same tree?" To answer the question, we need only follow the series of parent pointers from each node to its respective root. If both nodes reach the same root, then they must be in the same tree. If the roots are different, then the two nodes are not in the same tree. The process of finding the ultimate root for a given node we will call **FIND**.

The parent pointer representation is most often used to maintain a collection of disjoint sets. Two disjoint sets share no members in common (their intersection is empty). A collection of disjoint sets partitions some objects such that every object is in exactly one of the disjoint sets. There are two basic operations that we wish to support:

(1) determine if two objects are in the same set, and

(2) merge two sets together.

Because two merged sets are united, the merging operation is called UNION and the whole process of determining if two objects are in the same set and then merging the sets goes by the name "UNION/FIND."

To implement UNION/FIND, we represent each disjoint set with a separate general tree. Two objects are in the same disjoint set if they are in the same tree. Every node of the tree (except for the root) has precisely one parent. Thus, each node requires the same space to represent it. The collection of objects is typically stored in an array, where each element of the array corresponds to one object, and each element stores the object's value. The objects also correspond to nodes in the various disjoint trees (one tree for each disjoint set), so we also store the parent value with each object in the array. Those nodes that are the roots of their respective trees store an appropriate indicator. Note that this representation means that a single array is being used to implement a collection of trees. This makes it easy to merge trees together with UNION operations.

Figure 6.4 shows the parent pointer implementation for the general tree, called **ParPtrTree**. This class is greatly simplified from the declarations of Figure 6.2 because we need only a subset of the general tree operations. Instead of implementing a separate node class, **ParPtrTree** simply stores an array where each array element corresponds to a node of the tree. Each position i of the array stores the value for node i and the array position for the parent of node i. Class **ParPtrTree**

```
// General tree representation for UNION/FIND
class ParPtrTree {
private:
  int* array;                    // Node array
  int size;                      // Size of node array
  int FIND(int) const;           // Find root
public:
  ParPtrTree(int);                      // Constructor
  ~ParPtrTree() { delete [] array; } // Destructor
  void UNION(int, int);          // Merge equivalences
  bool differ(int, int);         // True if not in same tree
};

int ParPtrTree::FIND(int curr) const { // Find root
  while (array[curr] != ROOT) curr = array[curr];
  return curr;   // At root
}
```

Figure 6.4 General tree implementation using parent pointers for the UNION/ FIND algorithm.

is given two new methods, **differ** and **UNION**. Method **differ** checks if two objects are in different sets, and method **UNION** merges two sets together. A private method **FIND** is used to find the ultimate root for an object.

An application using the UNION/FIND operations should store a set of n objects, where each object is assigned a unique index in the range 0 to $n - 1$. The indices refer to the corresponding parent pointers in the array. Class **ParPtrTree** creates and initializes the UNION/FIND array, and methods **differ** and **UNION** take array indices as inputs.

Figure 6.5 illustrates the parent pointer implementation. Note that the nodes can appear in any order within the array, and the array can store up to n separate trees. For example, Figure 6.5 shows two trees stored in the same array. Thus, a single array can store a collection of items distributed among an arbitrary (and changing) number of disjoint subsets.

Consider the problem of assigning the members of a set to disjoint subsets called **equivalence classes**. Recall from Section 2.1 that an equivalence relation is reflexive, symmetric, and transitive. Thus, if objects A and B are equivalent, and objects B and C are equivalent, we must be able to recognize that objects A and C are also equivalent.

There are many practical uses for disjoint sets and representing equivalences. For example, consider Figure 6.6 which shows a graph of ten nodes labeled A through J. Notice that for nodes A through I, there is some series of edges that connects any pair of the nodes, but node J is disconnected from the rest of the nodes. Such a graph might be used to represent connections such as wires between components on a circuit board, or roads between cities. We can consider two nodes of the graph to be equivalent if there is a path between them. Thus,

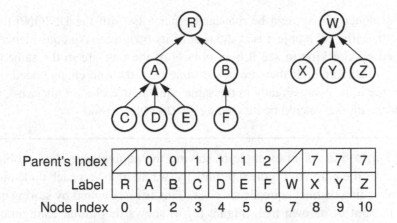

Parent's Index		0	0	1	1	1	2		7	7	7
Label	R	A	B	C	D	E	F	W	X	Y	Z
Node Index	0	1	2	3	4	5	6	7	8	9	10

Figure 6.5 The parent pointer array implementation. Each node corresponds to a position in the node array, which stores its value and a pointer to its parent. The parent pointers are represented by the position in the array of the parent. The root of any tree stores **ROOT**, represented graphically by a slash in the "Parent's Index" box. This figure shows two trees stored in the same parent pointer array, one rooted at R, and the other rooted at W.

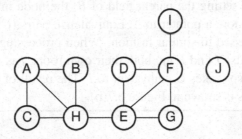

Figure 6.6 A graph with two connected components.

nodes A, H, and E would be equivalent in Figure 6.6, but J is not equivalent to any other. A subset of equivalent (connected) edges in a graph is called a **connected component**. The goal is to quickly classify the objects into disjoint sets that correspond to the connected components. Another application for UNION/FIND occurs in Kruskal's algorithm for computing the minimal cost spanning tree for a graph (Section 11.5.2).

The input to the UNION/FIND algorithm is typically a series of equivalence pairs. In the case of the connected components example, the equivalence pairs would simply be the set of edges in the graph. An equivalence pair might say that object C is equivalent to object A. If so, C and A are placed in the same subset. If a later equivalence relates A and B, then by implication C is also equivalent to B. Thus, an equivalence pair may cause two subsets to merge, each of which contains several objects.

Equivalence classes can be managed efficiently with the UNION/FIND algorithm. Initially, each object is at the root of its own tree. An equivalence pair is processed by checking to see if both objects of the pair are in the same tree using method **differ**. If they are in the same tree, then no change need be made because the objects are already in the same equivalence class. Otherwise, the two equivalence classes should be merged by the **UNION** method.

Example 6.2 As an example of solving the equivalence class problem, consider the graph of Figure 6.6. Initially, we assume that each node of the graph is in a distinct equivalence class. This is represented by storing each as the root of its own tree. Figure 6.7(a) shows this initial configuration using the parent pointer array representation. Now, consider what happens when equivalence relationship (A, B) is processed. The root of the tree containing A is A, and the root of the tree containing B is B. To make them equivalent, one of these two roots is set to be the parent of the other. In this case it is irrelevant which points to which, so we arbitrarily select the first in alphabetical order to be the root. This is represented in the parent pointer array by setting the parent field of B (the node in array position 1 of the array) to store a pointer to A. Equivalence pairs (C, H), (G, F), and (D, E) are processed in similar fashion. When processing the equivalence pair (I, F), because I and F are both their own roots, I is set to point to F. Note that this also makes G equivalent to I. The result of processing these five equivalences is shown in Figure 6.7(b).

The parent pointer representation places no limit on the number of nodes that can share a parent. To make equivalence processing as efficient as possible, the distance from each node to the root of its respective tree should be as small as possible. Thus, we would like to keep the height of the trees small when merging two equivalence classes together. Ideally, each tree would have all nodes pointing directly to the root. Achieving this goal all the time would require too much additional processing to be worth the effort, so we must settle for getting as close as possible.

A low-cost approach to reducing the height is to be smart about how two trees are joined together. One simple technique, called the **weighted union rule**, joins the tree with fewer nodes to the tree with more nodes by making the smaller tree's root point to the root of the bigger tree. This will limit the total depth of the tree to $O(\log n)$, because the depth of nodes only in the smaller tree will now increase by one, and the depth of the deepest node in the combined tree can only be at most one deeper than the deepest node before the trees were combined. The total number of nodes in the combined tree is therefore at least twice the number in the smaller

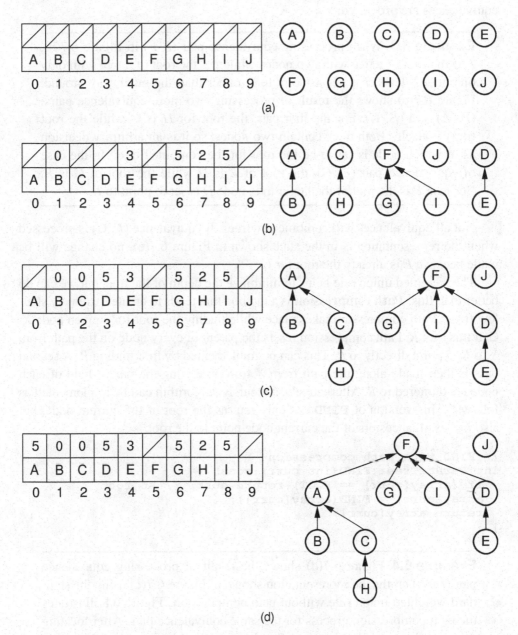

Figure 6.7 An example of equivalence processing. (a) Initial configuration for the ten nodes of the graph in Figure 6.6. The nodes are placed into ten independent equivalence classes. (b) The result of processing five edges: (A, B), (C, H), (G, F), (D, E), and (I, F). (c) The result of processing two more edges: (H, A) and (E, G). (d) The result of processing edge (H, E).

subtree. Thus, the depth of any node can be increased at most $\log n$ times when n equivalences are processed.

Example 6.3 When processing equivalence pair (I, F) in Figure 6.7(b), F is the root of a tree with two nodes while I is the root of a tree with only one node. Thus, I is set to point to F rather than the other way around. Figure 6.7(c) shows the result of processing two more equivalence pairs: (H, A) and (E, G). For the first pair, the root for H is C while the root for A is itself. Both trees contain two nodes, so it is an arbitrary decision as to which node is set to be the root for the combined tree. In the case of equivalence pair (E, G), the root of E is D while the root of G is F. Because F is the root of the larger tree, node D is set to point to F.

Not all equivalences will combine two trees. If equivalence (F, G) is processed when the representation is in the state shown in Figure 6.7(c), no change will be made because F is already the root for G.

The weighted union rule helps to minimize the depth of the tree, but we can do better than this. **Path compression** is a method that tends to create extremely shallow trees. Path compression takes place while finding the root for a given node X. Call this root R. Path compression resets the parent of every node on the path from X to R to point directly to R. This can be implemented by first finding R. A second pass is then made along the path from X to R, assigning the parent field of each node encountered to R. Alternatively, a recursive algorithm can be implemented as follows. This version of **FIND** not only returns the root of the current node, but also makes all ancestors of the current node point to the root.

```
// FIND with path compression
int ParPtrTree::FIND(int curr) const {
  if (array[curr] == ROOT) return curr; // At root
  array[curr] = FIND(array[curr]);
  return array[curr];
}
```

Example 6.4 Figure 6.7(d) shows the result of processing equivalence pair (H, E) on the the representation shown in Figure 6.7(c) using the standard weighted union rule without path compression. Figure 6.8 illustrates the path compression process for the same equivalence pair. After locating the root for node H, we can perform path compression to make H point directly to root object A. Likewise, E is set to point directly to its root, F. Finally, object A is set to point to root object F.

Note that path compression takes place during the FIND operation, *not* during the UNION operation. In Figure 6.8, this means that nodes B, C, and H have node A remain as their parent, rather than changing their parent to

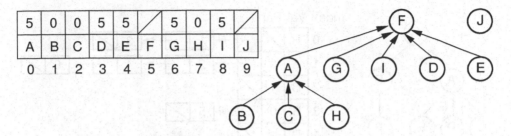

Figure 6.8 An example of path compression, showing the result of processing equivalence pair (H, E) on the representation of Figure 6.7(c).

be F. While we might prefer to have these nodes point to F, to accomplish this would require that additional information from the FIND operation be passed back to the UNION operation. This would not be practical.

Path compression keeps the cost of each FIND operation very close to constant. To be more precise about what is meant by "very close to constant," the cost of path compression for n FIND operations on n nodes (when combined with the weighted union rule for joining sets) is approximately[1] $\Theta(n \log^* n)$. The notation "$\log^* n$" means the number of times that the log of n must be taken before $n \leq 1$. For example, $\log^* 65536$ is 4 because $\log 65536 = 16$, $\log 16 = 4$, $\log 4 = 2$, and finally $\log 2 = 1$. Thus, $\log^* n$ grows *very* slowly, so the cost for a series of n FIND operations is very close to n.

Note that this does not mean that the tree resulting from processing n equivalence pairs necessarily has depth $\Theta(\log^* n)$. One can devise a series of equivalence operations that yields $\Theta(\log n)$ depth for the resulting tree. However, many of the equivalences in such a series will look only at the roots of the trees being merged, requiring little processing time. The *total* amount of processing time required for n operations will be $\Theta(n \log^* n)$, yielding nearly constant time for each equivalence operation. This is an example of amortized analysis, discussed further in Section 14.3.

6.3 General Tree Implementations

We now tackle the problem of devising an implementation for general trees that allows efficient processing for all member functions of the ADTs shown in Figure 6.2. This section presents several approaches to implementing general trees. Each implementation yields advantages and disadvantages in the amount of space required to store a node and the relative ease with which key operations can be performed. General tree implementations should place no restriction on how many

---

[1]To be more precise, this cost has been found to grow in time proportional to the inverse of Ackermann's function. See Section 6.6.

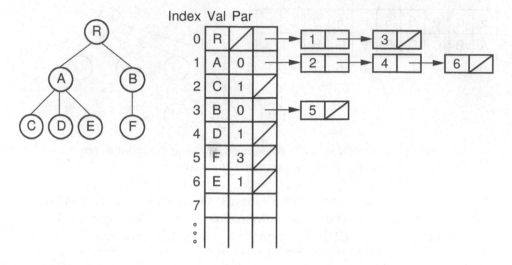

Figure 6.9 The "list of children" implementation for general trees. The column of numbers to the left of the node array labels the array indices. The column labeled "Val" stores node values. The column labeled "Par" stores indices (or pointers) to the parents. The last column stores pointers to the linked list of children for each internal node. Each element of the linked list stores a pointer to one of the node's children (shown as the array index of the target node).

children a node may have. In some applications, once a node is created the number of children never changes. In such cases, a fixed amount of space can be allocated for the node when it is created, based on the number of children for the node. Matters become more complicated if children can be added to or deleted from a node, requiring that the node's space allocation be adjusted accordingly.

6.3.1 List of Children

Our first attempt to create a general tree implementation is called the "list of children" implementation for general trees. It simply stores with each internal node a linked list of its children. This is illustrated by Figure 6.9.

The "list of children" implementation stores the tree nodes in an array. Each node contains a value, a pointer (or index) to its parent, and a pointer to a linked list of the node's children, stored in order from left to right. Each linked list element contains a pointer to one child. Thus, the leftmost child of a node can be found directly because it is the first element in the linked list. However, to find the right sibling for a node is more difficult. Consider the case of a node M and its parent P. To find M's right sibling, we must move down the child list of P until the linked list element storing the pointer to M has been found. Going one step further takes us to the linked list element that stores a pointer to M's right sibling. Thus, in the worst case, to find M's right sibling requires that all children of M's parent be searched.

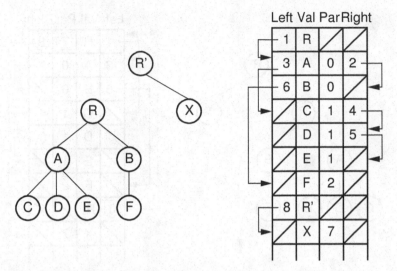

Figure 6.10 The "left-child/right-sibling" implementation.

Combining trees using this representation is difficult if each tree is stored in a separate node array. If the nodes of both trees are stored in a single node array, then adding tree **T** as a subtree of node *R* is done by simply adding the root of **T** to *R*'s list of children.

6.3.2 The Left-Child/Right-Sibling Implementation

With the "list of children" implementation, it is difficult to access a node's right sibling. Figure 6.10 presents an improvement. Here, each node stores its value and pointers to its parent, leftmost child, and right sibling. Thus, each of the basic ADT operations can be implemented by reading a value directly from the node. If two trees are stored within the same node array, then adding one as the subtree of the other simply requires setting three pointers. Combining trees in this way is illustrated by Figure 6.11. This implementation is more space efficient than the "list of children" implementation, and each node requires a fixed amount of space in the node array.

6.3.3 Dynamic Node Implementations

The two general tree implementations just described use an array to store the collection of nodes. In contrast, our standard implementation for binary trees stores each node as a separate dynamic object containing its value and pointers to its two children. Unfortunately, nodes of a general tree can have any number of children, and this number may change during the life of the node. A general tree node implementation must support these properties. One solution is simply to limit the number of children permitted for any node and allocate pointers for exactly that number of

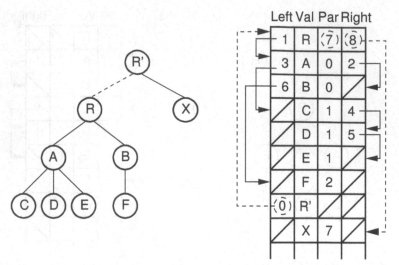

Figure 6.11 Combining two trees that use the "left-child/right-sibling" implementation. The subtree rooted at R in Figure 6.10 now becomes the first child of R'. Three pointers are adjusted in the node array: The left-child field of R' now points to node R, while the right-sibling field for R points to node X. The parent field of node R points to node R'.

children. There are two major objections to this. First, it places an undesirable limit on the number of children, which makes certain trees unrepresentable by this implementation. Second, this might be extremely wasteful of space because most nodes will have far fewer children and thus leave some pointer positions empty.

The alternative is to allocate variable space for each node. There are two basic approaches. One is to allocate an array of child pointers as part of the node. In essence, each node stores an array-based list of child pointers. Figure 6.12 illustrates the concept. This approach assumes that the number of children is known when the node is created, which is true for some applications but not for others. It also works best if the number of children does not change. If the number of children does change (especially if it increases), then some special recovery mechanism must be provided to support a change in the size of the child pointer array. One possibility is to allocate a new node of the correct size from free store and return the old copy of the node to free store for later reuse. This works especially well in a language with built-in garbage collection such as Java. For example, assume that a node M initially has two children, and that space for two child pointers is allocated when M is created. If a third child is added to M, space for a new node with three child pointers can be allocated, the contents of M is copied over to the new space, and the old space is then returned to free store. As an alternative to relying on the system's garbage collector, a memory manager for variable size storage units can be implemented, as described in Section 12.3. Another possibility is to use a collection of free lists, one for each array size, as described in Section 4.1.2. Note

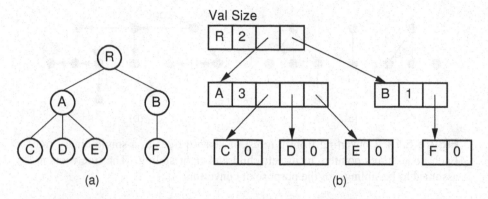

Figure 6.12 A dynamic general tree representation with fixed-size arrays for the child pointers. (a) The general tree. (b) The tree representation. For each node, the first field stores the node value while the second field stores the size of the child pointer array.

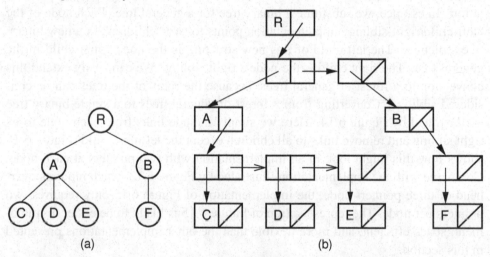

Figure 6.13 A dynamic general tree representation with linked lists of child pointers. (a) The general tree. (b) The tree representation.

in Figure 6.12 that the current number of children for each node is stored explicitly in a **size** field. The child pointers are stored in an array with **size** elements.

Another approach that is more flexible, but which requires more space, is to store a linked list of child pointers with each node as illustrated by Figure 6.13. This implementation is essentially the same as the "list of children" implementation of Section 6.3.1, but with dynamically allocated nodes rather than storing the nodes in an array.

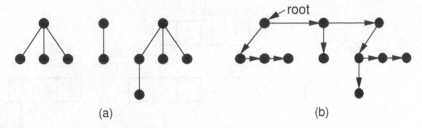

(a)   (b)

Figure 6.14 Converting from a forest of general trees to a single binary tree. Each node stores pointers to its left child and right sibling. The tree roots are assumed to be siblings for the purpose of converting.

6.3.4   Dynamic "Left-Child/Right-Sibling" Implementation

The "left-child/right-sibling" implementation of Section 6.3.2 stores a fixed number of pointers with each node. This can be readily adapted to a dynamic implementation. In essence, we substitute a binary tree for a general tree. Each node of the "left-child/right-sibling" implementation points to two "children" in a new binary tree structure. The left child of this new structure is the node's first child in the general tree. The right child is the node's right sibling. We can easily extend this conversion to a forest of general trees, because the roots of the trees can be considered siblings. Converting from a forest of general trees to a single binary tree is illustrated by Figure 6.14. Here we simply include links from each node to its right sibling and remove links to all children except the leftmost child. Figure 6.15 shows how this might look in an implementation with two pointers at each node. Compared with the implementation illustrated by Figure 6.13 which requires overhead of three pointers/node, the implementation of Figure 6.15 only requires two pointers per node. The representation of Figure 6.15 is likely to be easier to implement, space efficient, and more flexible than the other implementations presented in this section.

6.4 K-ary Trees

K-ary trees are trees whose internal nodes all have exactly K children. Thus, a full binary tree is a 2-ary tree. The PR quadtree discussed in Section 13.3 is an example of a 4-ary tree. Because K-ary tree nodes have a fixed number of children, unlike general trees, they are relatively easy to implement. In general, K-ary trees bear many similarities to binary trees, and similar implementations can be used for K-ary tree nodes. Note that as K becomes large, the potential number of **NULL** pointers grows, and the difference between the required sizes for internal nodes and leaf nodes increases. Thus, as K becomes larger, the need to choose separate implementations for the internal and leaf nodes becomes more pressing.

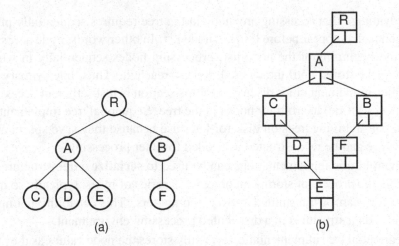

(a)   (b)

Figure 6.15 A general tree converted to the dynamic "left-child/right-sibling" representation. Compared to the representation of Figure 6.13, this representation requires less space.

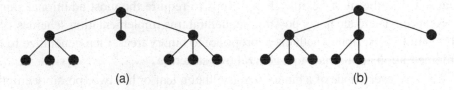

(a)   (b)

Figure 6.16 Full and complete 3-ary trees. (a) This tree is full (but not complete). (b) This tree is complete (but not full).

Full and **complete** K-ary trees are analogous to full and complete binary trees, respectively. Figure 6.16 shows full and complete K-ary trees for $K = 3$. In practice, most applications of K-ary trees limit them to be either full or complete.

Many of the properties of binary trees extend to K-ary trees. Equivalent theorems to those in Section 5.1.1 regarding the number of NULL pointers in a K-ary tree and the relationship between the number of leaves and the number of internal nodes in a K-ary tree can be derived. We can also store a complete K-ary tree in an array, using simple formulas to compute a node's relations in a manner similar to that used in Section 5.3.3.

6.5 Sequential Tree Implementations

Next we consider a fundamentally different approach to implementing trees. The goal is to store a series of node values with the minimum information needed to reconstruct the tree structure. This approach, known as a **sequential** tree implementation, has the advantage of saving space because no pointers are stored. It has the disadvantage that accessing any node in the tree requires sequentially process-ing all nodes that appear before it in the node list. In other words, node access must start at the beginning of the node list, processing nodes sequentially in whatever order they are stored until the desired node is reached. Thus, one primary virtue of the other implementations discussed in this section is lost: efficient access (typi-cally $\Theta(\log n)$ time) to arbitrary nodes in the tree. Sequential tree implementations are ideal for archiving trees on disk for later use because they save space, and the tree structure can be reconstructed as needed for later processing.

Sequential tree implementations can be used to **serialize** a tree structure. Seri-alization is the process of storing an object as a series of bytes, typically so that the data structure can be transmitted between computers. This capability is important when using data structures in a distributed processing environment.

A sequential tree implementation typically stores the node values as they would be enumerated by a preorder traversal, along with sufficient information to describe the tree's shape. If the tree has restricted form, for example if it is a full binary tree, then less information about structure typically needs to be stored. A general tree, because it has the most flexible shape, tends to require the most additional shape information. There are many possible sequential tree implementation schemes. We will begin by describing methods appropriate to binary trees, then generalize to an implementation appropriate to a general tree structure.

Because every node of a binary tree is either a leaf or has two (possibly empty) children, we can take advantage of this fact to implicitly represent the tree's struc-ture. The most straightforward sequential tree implementation lists every node value as it would be enumerated by a preorder traversal. Unfortunately, the node values alone do not provide enough information to recover the shape of the tree. In particular, as we read the series of node values, we do not know when a leaf node has been reached. However, we can treat all non-empty nodes as internal nodes with two (possibly empty) children. Only **NULL** values will be interpreted as leaf nodes, and these can be listed explicitly. Such an augmented node list provides enough information to recover the tree structure.

Example 6.5 For the binary tree of Figure 6.17, the corresponding se-quential representation would be as follows (assuming that '/' stands for **NULL**):

$$AB//D//CEG///FH//I// \hspace{2cm} (6.1)$$

To reconstruct the tree structure from this node list, we begin by setting node A to be the root. A's left child will be node B. Node B's left child is a **NULL** pointer, so node D must be B's right child. Node D has two **NULL** children, so node C must be the right child of node A.

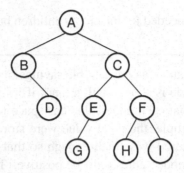

Figure 6.17 Sample binary tree for sequential tree implementation examples.

To illustrate the difficulty involved in using the sequential tree representation for processing, consider searching for the right child of the root node. We must first move sequentially through the node list of the left subtree. Only at this point do we reach the value of the root's right child. Clearly the sequential representation is space efficient, but not time efficient for descending through the tree along some arbitrary path.

Assume that each node value takes a constant amount of space. An example would be if the node value is a positive integer and **NULL** is indicated by the value zero. From the Full Binary Tree Theorem of Section 5.1.1, we know that the size of the node list will be about twice the number of nodes (i.e., the overhead fraction is 1/2). The extra space is required by the **NULL** pointers. We should be able to store the node list more compactly. However, any sequential implementation must recognize when a leaf node has been reached, that is, a leaf node indicates the end of a subtree. One way to do this is to explicitly list with each node whether it is an internal node or a leaf. If a node X is an internal node, then we know that its two children (which may be subtrees) immediately follow X in the node list. If X is a leaf node, then the next node in the list is the right child of some ancestor of X, not the right child of X. In particular, the next node will be the child of X's most recent ancestor that has not yet seen its right child. However, this assumes that each internal node does in fact have two children, in other words, that the tree is full. Empty children must be indicated in the node list explicitly. Assume that internal nodes are marked with a prime (′) and that leaf nodes show no mark. Empty children of internal nodes are indicated by '/', but the (empty) children of leaf nodes are not represented at all. Note that a full binary tree stores no **NULL** values with this implementation, and so requires less overhead.

Example 6.6 We can represent the tree of Figure 6.17 as follows:

$$A'B'/DC'E'G/F'HI \qquad (6.2)$$

Note that slashes are needed for the empty children because this is not a full binary tree.

Storing n extra bits can be a considerable savings over storing n **NULL** values. In Example 6.6, each node is shown with a mark if it is internal, or no mark if it is a leaf. This requires that each node value has space to store the mark bit. This might be true if, for example, the node value were stored as a 4-byte integer but the range of the values sored was small enough so that not all bits are used. An example would be if all node values must be positive. Then the high-order (sign) bit of the integer value could be used as the mark bit.

Another approach is to store a separate bit vector to represent the status of each node. In this case, each node of the tree corresponds to one bit in the bit vector. A value of '1' could indicate an internal node, and '0' could indicate a leaf node.

Example 6.7 The bit vector for the tree if Figure 6.17 (including positions for the null children of nodes B and E) would be

$$11001100100 \tag{6.3}$$

Storing general trees by means of a sequential implementation requires that more explicit structural information be included with the node list. Not only must the general tree implementation indicate whether a node is leaf or internal, it must also indicate how many children the node has. Alternatively, the implementation can indicate when a node's child list has come to an end. The next example dispenses with marks for internal or leaf nodes. Instead it includes a special mark (we will use the ")" symbol) to indicate the end of a child list. All leaf nodes are followed by a ")" symbol because they have no children. A leaf node that is also the last child for its parent would indicate this by two or more successive ")" symbols.

Example 6.8 For the general tree of Figure 6.3, we get the sequential representation

$$RAC)D)E))BF))) \tag{6.4}$$

Note that F is followed by three ")" marks, because it is a leaf, the last node of B's rightmost subtree, and the last node of R's rightmost subtree.

Note that this representation for serializing general trees cannot be used for binary trees. This is because a binary tree is not merely a restricted form of general tree with at most two children. Every binary tree node has a left and a right child, though either or both might be empty. For example, the representation of Example 6.8 cannot let us distinguish whether node D in Figure 6.17 is the left or right child of node B.

6.6   Further Reading

The expression $\log^* n$ cited in Section 6.2 is closely related to the inverse of Ackermann's function. For more information about Ackermann's function and the cost of path compression for UNION/FIND, see Robert E. Tarjan's paper "On the efficiency of a good but not linear set merging algorithm" [Tar75]. The article "Data Structures and Algorithms for Disjoint Set Union Problems" by Galil and Italiano [GI91] covers many aspects of the equivalence class problem.

Foundations of Multidimensional and Metric Data Structures by Hanan Samet [Sam06] treats various implementations of tree structures in detail within the context of K-ary trees. Samet covers sequential implementations as well as the linked and array implementations such as those described in this chapter and Chapter 5. While these books are ostensibly concerned with spatial data structures, many of the concepts treated are relevant to anyone who must implement tree structures.

6.7   Exercises

6.1 Write an algorithm to determine if two general trees are identical. Make the algorithm as efficient as you can. Analyze your algorithm's running time.

6.2 Write an algorithm to determine if two binary trees are identical when the ordering of the subtrees for a node is ignored. For example, if a tree has root node with value R, left child with value A and right child with value B, this would be considered identical to another tree with root node value R, left child value B, and right child value A. Make the algorithm as efficient as you can. Analyze your algorithm's running time. How much harder would it be to make this algorithm work on a general tree?

6.3 Write a postorder traversal function for general trees, similar to the preorder traversal function named **preorder** given in Section 6.1.2.

6.4 Write a function that takes as input a general tree and returns the number of nodes in that tree. Write your function to use the **GenTree** and **GTNode** ADTs of Figure 6.2.

6.5 Describe how to implement the weighted union rule efficiently. In particular, describe what information must be stored with each node and how this information is updated when two trees are merged. Modify the implementation of Figure 6.4 to support the weighted union rule.

6.6 A potential alternative to the weighted union rule for combining two trees is the height union rule. The height union rule requires that the root of the tree with greater height become the root of the union. Explain why the height union rule can lead to worse average time behavior than the weighted union rule.

6.7 Using the weighted union rule and path compression, show the array for the parent pointer implementation that results from the following series of equivalences on a set of objects indexed by the values 0 through 15. Initially, each element in the set should be in a separate equivalence class. When two trees to be merged are the same size, make the root with greater index value be the child of the root with lesser index value.

$(0, 2)\,(1, 2)\,(3, 4)\,(3, 1)\,(3, 5)\,(9, 11)\,(12, 14)\,(3, 9)\,(4, 14)\,(6, 7)\,(8, 10)\,(8, 7)$
$(7, 0)\,(10, 15)\,(10, 13)$

6.8 Using the weighted union rule and path compression, show the array for the parent pointer implementation that results from the following series of equivalences on a set of objects indexed by the values 0 through 15. Initially, each element in the set should be in a separate equivalence class. When two trees to be merged are the same size, make the root with greater index value be the child of the root with lesser index value.

$(2, 3)\,(4, 5)\,(6, 5)\,(3, 5)\,(1, 0)\,(7, 8)\,(1, 8)\,(3, 8)\,(9, 10)\,(11, 14)\,(11, 10)$
$(12, 13)\,(11, 13)\,(14, 1)$

6.9 Devise a series of equivalence statements for a collection of sixteen items that yields a tree of height 5 when both the weighted union rule and path compression are used. What is the total number of parent pointers followed to perform this series?

6.10 One alternative to path compression that gives similar performance gains is called **path halving**. In path halving, when the path is traversed from the node to the root, we make the grandparent of every other node i on the path the new parent of i. Write a version of **FIND** that implements path halving. Your **FIND** operation should work as you move up the tree, rather than require the two passes needed by path compression.

6.11 Analyze the fraction of overhead required by the "list of children" implementation, the "left-child/right-sibling" implementation, and the two linked implementations of Section 6.3.3. How do these implementations compare in space efficiency?

6.12 Using the general tree ADT of Figure 6.2, write a function that takes as input the root of a general tree and returns a binary tree generated by the conversion process illustrated by Figure 6.14.

6.13 Use mathematical induction to prove that the number of leaves in a non-empty full K-ary tree is $(K - 1)n + 1$, where n is the number of internal nodes.

6.14 Derive the formulas for computing the relatives of a non-empty complete K-ary tree node stored in the complete tree representation of Section 5.3.3.

6.15 Find the overhead fraction for a full K-ary tree implementation with space requirements as follows:

   (a) All nodes store data, K child pointers, and a parent pointer. The data field requires four bytes and each pointer requires four bytes.

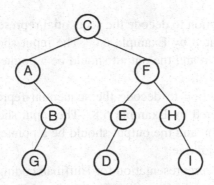

Figure 6.18 A sample tree for Exercise 6.16.

   (b) All nodes store data and K child pointers. The data field requires six-
        teen bytes and each pointer requires four bytes.
   (c) All nodes store data and a parent pointer, and internal nodes store K
        child pointers. The data field requires eight bytes and each pointer re-
        quires four bytes.
   (d) Only leaf nodes store data; only internal nodes store K child pointers.
        The data field requires four bytes and each pointer requires two bytes.

6.16 **(a)** Write out the sequential representation for Figure 6.18 using the coding
        illustrated by Example 6.5.
     (b) Write out the sequential representation for Figure 6.18 using the coding
        illustrated by Example 6.6.

6.17 Draw the binary tree representing the following sequential representation for
     binary trees illustrated by Example 6.5:

$$ABD//E//C/F//$$

6.18 Draw the binary tree representing the following sequential representation for
     binary trees illustrated by Example 6.6:

$$A'/B'/C'D'G/E$$

Show the bit vector for leaf and internal nodes (as illustrated by Example 6.7)
for this tree.

6.19 Draw the general tree represented by the following sequential representation
     for general trees illustrated by Example 6.8:

$$XPC)Q)RV)M))))$$

6.20 **(a)** Write a function to decode the sequential representation for binary trees
        illustrated by Example 6.5. The input should be the sequential repre-
        sentation and the output should be a pointer to the root of the resulting
        binary tree.

(b) Write a function to decode the sequential representation for full binary trees illustrated by Example 6.6. The input should be the sequential representation and the output should be a pointer to the root of the resulting binary tree.

(c) Write a function to decode the sequential representation for general trees illustrated by Example 6.8. The input should be the sequential representation and the output should be a pointer to the root of the resulting general tree.

6.21 Devise a sequential representation for Huffman coding trees suitable for use as part of a file compression utility (see Project 5.7).

6.8 Projects

6.1 Write classes that implement the general tree class declarations of Figure 6.2 using the dynamic "left-child/right-sibling" representation described in Section 6.3.4.

6.2 Write classes that implement the general tree class declarations of Figure 6.2 using the linked general tree implementation with child pointer arrays of Figure 6.12. Your implementation should support only fixed-size nodes that do not change their number of children once they are created. Then, re-implement these classes with the linked list of children representation of Figure 6.13. How do the two implementations compare in space and time efficiency and ease of implementation?

6.3 Write classes that implement the general tree class declarations of Figure 6.2 using the linked general tree implementation with child pointer arrays of Figure 6.12. Your implementation must be able to support changes in the number of children for a node. When created, a node should be allocated with only enough space to store its initial set of children. Whenever a new child is added to a node such that the array overflows, allocate a new array from free store that can store twice as many children.

6.4 Implement a BST file archiver. Your program should take a BST created in main memory using the implementation of Figure 5.14 and write it out to disk using one of the sequential representations of Section 6.5. It should also be able to read in disk files using your sequential representation and create the equivalent main memory representation.

6.5 Use the UNION/FIND algorithm to implement a solution to the following problem. Given a set of points represented by their xy-coordinates, assign the points to clusters. Any two points are defined to be in the same cluster if they are within a specified distance d of each other. For the purpose of this problem, clustering is an equivalence relationship. In other words, points A, B, and C are defined to be in the same cluster if the distance between A and B

is less than d and the distance between A and C is also less than d, even if the distance between B and C is greater than d. To solve the problem, compute the distance between each pair of points, using the equivalence processing algorithm to merge clusters whenever two points are within the specified distance. What is the asymptotic complexity of this algorithm? Where is the bottleneck in processing?

6.6 In this project, you will run some empirical tests to determine if some variations on path compression in the UNION/FIND algorithm will lead to improved performance. You should compare the following five implementations:

  (a) Standard UNION/FIND with path compression and weighted union.

  (b) Path compression and weighted union, except that path compression is done *after* the UNION, instead of during the FIND operation. That is, make all nodes along the paths traversed in both trees point directly to the root of the larger tree.

  (c) Weighted union and path halving as described in Exercise 6.10.

  (d) Weighted union and a simplified form of path compression. At the end of every FIND operation, make the node point to its tree's root (but don't change the pointers for other nodes along the path).

  (e) Weighted union and a simplified form of path compression. Both nodes in the equivalence will be set to point directly to the root of the larger tree after the UNION operation. For example, consider processing the equivalence (A, B) where A' is the root of A and B' is the root of B. Assume the tree with root A' is bigger than the tree with root B'. At the end of the UNION/FIND operation, nodes A, B, and B' will all point directly to A'.

PART III

Sorting and Searching

7

Internal Sorting

We sort many things in our everyday lives: A handful of cards when playing Bridge; bills and other piles of paper; jars of spices; and so on. And we have many intuitive strategies that we can use to do the sorting, depending on how many objects we have to sort and how hard they are to move around. Sorting is also one of the most frequently performed computing tasks. We might sort the records in a database so that we can search the collection efficiently. We might sort the records by zip code so that we can print and mail them more cheaply. We might use sorting as an intrinsic part of an algorithm to solve some other problem, such as when computing the minimum-cost spanning tree (see Section 11.5).

Because sorting is so important, naturally it has been studied intensively and many algorithms have been devised. Some of these algorithms are straightforward adaptations of schemes we use in everyday life. Others are totally alien to how humans do things, having been invented to sort thousands or even millions of records stored on the computer. After years of study, there are still unsolved problems related to sorting. New algorithms are still being developed and refined for special-purpose applications.

While introducing this central problem in computer science, this chapter has a secondary purpose of illustrating issues in algorithm design and analysis. For example, this collection of sorting algorithms shows multiple approaches to using divide-and-conquer. In particular, there are multiple ways to do the dividing: Mergesort divides a list in half; Quicksort divides a list into big values and small values; and Radix Sort divides the problem by working on one digit of the key at a time. Sorting algorithms can also illustrate a wide variety of analysis techniques. We'll find that it is possible for an algorithm to have an average case whose growth rate is significantly smaller than its worse case (Quicksort). We'll see how it is possible to speed up sorting algorithms (both Shellsort and Quicksort) by taking advantage of the best case behavior of another algorithm (Insertion sort). We'll see several examples of how we can tune an algorithm for better performance. We'll see that special case behavior by some algorithms makes them a good solution for special niche applications (Heapsort). Sorting provides an example of a significant technique for analyzing the lower bound for a problem. Sorting will also be used to motivate the introduction to file processing presented in Chapter 8.

The present chapter covers several standard algorithms appropriate for sorting a collection of records that fit in the computer's main memory. It begins with a discussion of three simple, but relatively slow, algorithms requiring $\Theta(n^2)$ time in the average and worst cases. Several algorithms with considerably better performance are then presented, some with $\Theta(n \log n)$ worst-case running time. The final sorting method presented requires only $\Theta(n)$ worst-case time under special conditions. The chapter concludes with a proof that sorting in general requires $\Omega(n \log n)$ time in the worst case.

7.1   Sorting Terminology and Notation

Except where noted otherwise, input to the sorting algorithms presented in this chapter is a collection of records stored in an array. Records are compared to one another by means of a comparator class, as introduced in Section 4.4. To simplify the discussion we will assume that each record has a key field whose value is extracted from the record by the comparator. The key method of the comparator class is **prior**, which returns true when its first argument should appear prior to its second argument in the sorted list. We also assume that for every record type there is a **swap** function that can interchange the contents of two records in the array(see the Appendix).

Given a set of records $r_1, r_2, ..., r_n$ with key values $k_1, k_2, ..., k_n$, the **Sorting Problem** is to arrange the records into any order s such that records $r_{s_1}, r_{s_2}, ..., r_{s_n}$ have keys obeying the property $k_{s_1} \leq k_{s_2} \leq ... \leq k_{s_n}$. In other words, the sorting problem is to arrange a set of records so that the values of their key fields are in non-decreasing order.

As defined, the Sorting Problem allows input with two or more records that have the same key value. Certain applications require that input not contain duplicate key values. The sorting algorithms presented in this chapter and in Chapter 8 can handle duplicate key values unless noted otherwise.

When duplicate key values are allowed, there might be an implicit ordering to the duplicates, typically based on their order of occurrence within the input. It might be desirable to maintain this initial ordering among duplicates. A sorting algorithm is said to be **stable** if it does not change the relative ordering of records with identical key values. Many, but not all, of the sorting algorithms presented in this chapter are stable, or can be made stable with minor changes.

When comparing two sorting algorithms, the most straightforward approach would seem to be simply program both and measure their running times. An example of such timings is presented in Figure 7.20. However, such a comparison can be misleading because the running time for many sorting algorithms depends on specifics of the input values. In particular, the number of records, the size of the keys and the records, the allowable range of the key values, and the amount by which the input records are "out of order" can all greatly affect the relative running times for sorting algorithms.

When analyzing sorting algorithms, it is traditional to measure the number of comparisons made between keys. This measure is usually closely related to the running time for the algorithm and has the advantage of being machine and data-type independent. However, in some cases records might be so large that their physical movement might take a significant fraction of the total running time. If so, it might be appropriate to measure the number of swap operations performed by the algorithm. In most applications we can assume that all records and keys are of fixed length, and that a single comparison or a single swap operation requires a constant amount of time regardless of which keys are involved. Some special situations "change the rules" for comparing sorting algorithms. For example, an application with records or keys having widely varying length (such as sorting a sequence of variable length strings) will benefit from a special-purpose sorting technique. Some applications require that a small number of records be sorted, but that the sort be performed frequently. An example would be an application that repeatedly sorts groups of five numbers. In such cases, the constants in the runtime equations that are usually ignored in an asymptotic analysis now become crucial. Finally, some situations require that a sorting algorithm use as little memory as possible. We will note which sorting algorithms require significant extra memory beyond the input array.

7.2 Three $\Theta(n^2)$ Sorting Algorithms

This section presents three simple sorting algorithms. While easy to understand and implement, we will soon see that they are unacceptably slow when there are many records to sort. Nonetheless, there are situations where one of these simple algorithms is the best tool for the job.

7.2.1 Insertion Sort

Imagine that you have a stack of phone bills from the past two years and that you wish to organize them by date. A fairly natural way to do this might be to look at the first two bills and put them in order. Then take the third bill and put it into the right order with respect to the first two, and so on. As you take each bill, you would add it to the sorted pile that you have already made. This naturally intuitive process is the inspiration for our first sorting algorithm, called **Insertion Sort**. Insertion Sort iterates through a list of records. Each record is inserted in turn at the correct position within a sorted list composed of those records already processed. The

i=1	2	3	4	5	6	7
42	20	17	13	13	13	13	13
20	42	20	17	17	14	14	14
17	17	42	20	20	17	17	15
13	13	13	42	28	20	20	17
28	28	28	28	42	28	23	20
14	14	14	14	14	42	28	23
23	23	23	23	23	23	42	28
15	15	15	15	15	15	15	42

Figure 7.1 An illustration of Insertion Sort. Each column shows the array after the iteration with the indicated value of **i** in the outer **for** loop. Values above the line in each column have been sorted. Arrows indicate the upward motions of records through the array.

following is a **C++** implementation. The input is an array of n records stored in array **A**.

```
template <typename E, typename Comp>
void inssort(E A[], int n) { // Insertion Sort
  for (int i=1; i<n; i++)        // Insert i'th record
    for (int j=i; (j>0) && (Comp::prior(A[j], A[j-1])); j--)
      swap(A, j, j-1);
}
```

Consider the case where **inssort** is processing the ith record, which has key value X. The record is moved upward in the array as long as X is less than the key value immediately above it. As soon as a key value less than or equal to X is encountered, **inssort** is done with that record because all records above it in the array must have smaller keys. Figure 7.1 illustrates how Insertion Sort works.

The body of **inssort** is made up of two nested **for** loops. The outer **for** loop is executed $n - 1$ times. The inner **for** loop is harder to analyze because the number of times it executes depends on how many keys in positions 1 to $i - 1$ have a value less than that of the key in position i. In the worst case, each record must make its way to the top of the array. This would occur if the keys are initially arranged from highest to lowest, in the reverse of sorted order. In this case, the number of comparisons will be one the first time through the **for** loop, two the second time, and so on. Thus, the total number of comparisons will be

$$\sum_{i=2}^{n} i \approx n^2/2 = \Theta(n^2).$$

In contrast, consider the best-case cost. This occurs when the keys begin in sorted order from lowest to highest. In this case, every pass through the inner **for** loop will fail immediately, and no values will be moved. The total number of comparisons will be $n - 1$, which is the number of times the outer **for** loop executes. Thus, the cost for Insertion Sort in the best case is $\Theta(n)$.

While the best case is significantly faster than the worst case, the worst case is usually a more reliable indication of the "typical" running time. However, there are situations where we can expect the input to be in sorted or nearly sorted order. One example is when an already sorted list is slightly disordered by a small number of additions to the list; restoring sorted order using Insertion Sort might be a good idea if we know that the disordering is slight. Examples of algorithms that take advantage of Insertion Sort's near-best-case running time are the Shellsort algorithm of Section 7.3 and the Quicksort algorithm of Section 7.5.

What is the average-case cost of Insertion Sort? When record i is processed, the number of times through the inner **for** loop depends on how far "out of order" the record is. In particular, the inner **for** loop is executed once for each key greater than the key of record i that appears in array positions 0 through $i - 1$. For example, in the leftmost column of Figure 7.1 the value 15 is preceded by five values greater than 15. Each such occurrence is called an **inversion**. The number of inversions (i.e., the number of values greater than a given value that occur prior to it in the array) will determine the number of comparisons and swaps that must take place. We need to determine what the average number of inversions will be for the record in position i. We expect on average that half of the keys in the first $i - 1$ array positions will have a value greater than that of the key at position i. Thus, the average case should be about half the cost of the worst case, or around $n^2/4$, which is still $\Theta(n^2)$. So, the average case is no better than the worst case in asymptotic complexity.

Counting comparisons or swaps yields similar results. Each time through the inner **for** loop yields both a comparison and a swap, except the last (i.e., the comparison that fails the inner **for** loop's test), which has no swap. Thus, the number of swaps for the entire sort operation is $n - 1$ less than the number of comparisons. This is 0 in the best case, and $\Theta(n^2)$ in the average and worst cases.

7.2.2 Bubble Sort

Our next sorting algorithm is called **Bubble Sort**. Bubble Sort is often taught to novice programmers in introductory computer science courses. This is unfortunate, because Bubble Sort has no redeeming features whatsoever. It is a relatively slow sort, it is no easier to understand than Insertion Sort, it does not correspond to any intuitive counterpart in "everyday" use, and it has a poor best-case running time. However, Bubble Sort can serve as the inspiration for a better sorting algorithm that will be presented in Section 7.2.3.

Bubble Sort consists of a simple double **for** loop. The first iteration of the inner **for** loop moves through the record array from bottom to top, comparing adjacent keys. If the lower-indexed key's value is greater than its higher-indexed

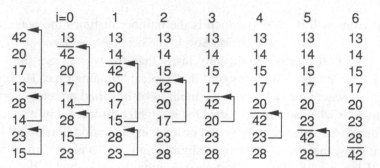

Figure 7.2 An illustration of Bubble Sort. Each column shows the array after the iteration with the indicated value of **i** in the outer **for** loop. Values above the line in each column have been sorted. Arrows indicate the swaps that take place during a given iteration.

neighbor, then the two values are swapped. Once the smallest value is encountered, this process will cause it to "bubble" up to the top of the array. The second pass through the array repeats this process. However, because we know that the smallest value reached the top of the array on the first pass, there is no need to compare the top two elements on the second pass. Likewise, each succeeding pass through the array compares adjacent elements, looking at one less value than the preceding pass. Figure 7.2 illustrates Bubble Sort. A **C++** implementation is as follows:

```
template <typename E, typename Comp>
void bubsort(E A[], int n) { // Bubble Sort
  for (int i=0; i<n-1; i++)      // Bubble up i'th record
    for (int j=n-1; j>i; j--)
      if (Comp::prior(A[j], A[j-1]))
        swap(A, j, j-1);
}
```

Determining Bubble Sort's number of comparisons is easy. Regardless of the arrangement of the values in the array, the number of comparisons made by the inner **for** loop is always i, leading to a total cost of

$$\sum_{i=1}^{n} i \approx n^2/2 = \Theta(n^2).$$

Bubble Sort's running time is roughly the same in the best, average, and worst cases.

The number of swaps required depends on how often a value is less than the one immediately preceding it in the array. We can expect this to occur for about half the comparisons in the average case, leading to $\Theta(n^2)$ for the expected number of swaps. The actual number of swaps performed by Bubble Sort will be identical to that performed by Insertion Sort.

	i=0	1	2	3	4	5	6
42	13	13	13	13	13	13	13
20	20	14	14	14	14	14	14
17	17	17	15	15	15	15	15
13	42	42	42	17	17	17	17
28	28	28	28	28	20	20	20
14	14	20	20	20	28	23	23
23	23	23	23	23	23	28	28
15	15	15	17	42	42	42	42

Figure 7.3 An example of Selection Sort. Each column shows the array after the iteration with the indicated value of **i** in the outer **for** loop. Numbers above the line in each column have been sorted and are in their final positions.

7.2.3 Selection Sort

Consider again the problem of sorting a pile of phone bills for the past year. Another intuitive approach might be to look through the pile until you find the bill for January, and pull that out. Then look through the remaining pile until you find the bill for February, and add that behind January. Proceed through the ever-shrinking pile of bills to select the next one in order until you are done. This is the inspiration for our last $\Theta(n^2)$ sort, called **Selection Sort**. The ith pass of Selection Sort "selects" the ith smallest key in the array, placing that record into position i. In other words, Selection Sort first finds the smallest key in an unsorted list, then the second smallest, and so on. Its unique feature is that there are few record swaps. To find the next smallest key value requires searching through the entire unsorted portion of the array, but only one swap is required to put the record in place. Thus, the total number of swaps required will be $n - 1$ (we get the last record in place "for free").

Figure 7.3 illustrates Selection Sort. Below is a **C++** implementation.

```
template <typename E, typename Comp>
void selsort(E A[], int n) { // Selection Sort
  for (int i=0; i<n-1; i++) {    // Select i'th record
    int lowindex = i;            // Remember its index
    for (int j=n-1; j>i; j--)    // Find the least value
      if (Comp::prior(A[j], A[lowindex]))
        lowindex = j;            // Put it in place
    swap(A, i, lowindex);
  }
}
```

Selection Sort (as written here) is essentially a Bubble Sort, except that rather than repeatedly swapping adjacent values to get the next smallest record into place, we instead remember the position of the element to be selected and do one swap at the end. Thus, the number of comparisons is still $\Theta(n^2)$, but the number of swaps is much less than that required by bubble sort. Selection Sort is particularly

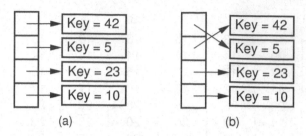

Figure 7.4 An example of swapping pointers to records. (a) A series of four records. The record with key value 42 comes before the record with key value 5. (b) The four records after the top two pointers have been swapped. Now the record with key value 5 comes before the record with key value 42.

advantageous when the cost to do a swap is high, for example, when the elements are long strings or other large records. Selection Sort is more efficient than Bubble Sort (by a constant factor) in most other situations as well.

There is another approach to keeping the cost of swapping records low that can be used by any sorting algorithm even when the records are large. This is to have each element of the array store a pointer to a record rather than store the record itself. In this implementation, a swap operation need only exchange the pointer values; the records themselves do not move. This technique is illustrated by Figure 7.4. Additional space is needed to store the pointers, but the return is a faster swap operation.

7.2.4   The Cost of Exchange Sorting

Figure 7.5 summarizes the cost of Insertion, Bubble, and Selection Sort in terms of their required number of comparisons and swaps[1] in the best, average, and worst cases. The running time for each of these sorts is $\Theta(n^2)$ in the average and worst cases.

The remaining sorting algorithms presented in this chapter are significantly better than these three under typical conditions. But before continuing on, it is instructive to investigate what makes these three sorts so slow. The crucial bottleneck is that only *adjacent* records are compared. Thus, comparisons and moves (in all but Selection Sort) are by single steps. Swapping adjacent records is called an **exchange**. Thus, these sorts are sometimes referred to as **exchange sorts**. The cost of any exchange sort can be at best the total number of steps that the records in the

---

[1]There is a slight anomaly with Selection Sort. The supposed advantage for Selection Sort is its low number of swaps required, yet Selection Sort's best-case number of swaps is worse than that for Insertion Sort or Bubble Sort. This is because the implementation given for Selection Sort does not avoid a swap in the case where record i is already in position i. One could put in a test to avoid swapping in this situation. But it usually takes more time to do the tests than would be saved by avoiding such swaps.

	Insertion	Bubble	Selection
Comparisons:			
Best Case	$\Theta(n)$	$\Theta(n^2)$	$\Theta(n^2)$
Average Case	$\Theta(n^2)$	$\Theta(n^2)$	$\Theta(n^2)$
Worst Case	$\Theta(n^2)$	$\Theta(n^2)$	$\Theta(n^2)$
Swaps:			
Best Case	0	0	$\Theta(n)$
Average Case	$\Theta(n^2)$	$\Theta(n^2)$	$\Theta(n)$
Worst Case	$\Theta(n^2)$	$\Theta(n^2)$	$\Theta(n)$

Figure 7.5 A comparison of the asymptotic complexities for three simple sorting algorithms.

array must move to reach their "correct" location (i.e., the number of inversions for each record).

What is the average number of inversions? Consider a list **L** containing n values. Define $\mathbf{L}_R$ to be **L** in reverse. **L** has $n(n-1)/2$ distinct pairs of values, each of which could potentially be an inversion. Each such pair must either be an inversion in **L** or in $\mathbf{L}_R$. Thus, the total number of inversions in **L** and $\mathbf{L}_R$ together is exactly $n(n-1)/2$ for an average of $n(n-1)/4$ per list. We therefore know with certainty that any sorting algorithm which limits comparisons to adjacent items will cost at least $n(n-1)/4 = \Omega(n^2)$ in the average case.

7.3 Shellsort

The next sorting algorithm that we consider is called **Shellsort**, named after its inventor, D.L. Shell. It is also sometimes called the **diminishing increment** sort. Unlike Insertion and Selection Sort, there is no real life intuitive equivalent to Shellsort. Unlike the exchange sorts, Shellsort makes comparisons and swaps between non-adjacent elements. Shellsort also exploits the best-case performance of Insertion Sort. Shellsort's strategy is to make the list "mostly sorted" so that a final Insertion Sort can finish the job. When properly implemented, Shellsort will give substantially better performance than $\Theta(n^2)$ in the worst case.

Shellsort uses a process that forms the basis for many of the sorts presented in the following sections: Break the list into sublists, sort them, then recombine the sublists. Shellsort breaks the array of elements into "virtual" sublists. Each sublist is sorted using an Insertion Sort. Another group of sublists is then chosen and sorted, and so on.

During each iteration, Shellsort breaks the list into disjoint sublists so that each element in a sublist is a fixed number of positions apart. For example, let us assume for convenience that n, the number of values to be sorted, is a power of two. One possible implementation of Shellsort will begin by breaking the list into $n/2$

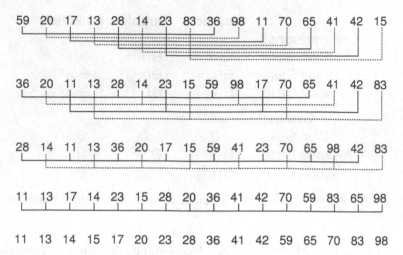

Figure 7.6 An example of Shellsort. Sixteen items are sorted in four passes. The first pass sorts 8 sublists of size 2 and increment 8. The second pass sorts 4 sublists of size 4 and increment 4. The third pass sorts 2 sublists of size 8 and increment 2. The fourth pass sorts 1 list of size 16 and increment 1 (a regular Insertion Sort).

sublists of 2 elements each, where the array index of the 2 elements in each sublist differs by $n/2$. If there are 16 elements in the array indexed from 0 to 15, there would initially be 8 sublists of 2 elements each. The first sublist would be the elements in positions 0 and 8, the second in positions 1 and 9, and so on. Each list of two elements is sorted using Insertion Sort.

The second pass of Shellsort looks at fewer, bigger lists. For our example the second pass would have $n/4$ lists of size 4, with the elements in the list being $n/4$ positions apart. Thus, the second pass would have as its first sublist the 4 elements in positions 0, 4, 8, and 12; the second sublist would have elements in positions 1, 5, 9, and 13; and so on. Each sublist of four elements would also be sorted using an Insertion Sort.

The third pass would be made on two lists, one consisting of the odd positions and the other consisting of the even positions.

The culminating pass in this example would be a "normal" Insertion Sort of all elements. Figure 7.6 illustrates the process for an array of 16 values where the sizes of the increments (the distances between elements on the successive passes) are 8, 4, 2, and 1. Figure 7.7 presents a **C++** implementation for Shellsort.

Shellsort will work correctly regardless of the size of the increments, *provided that the final pass has increment 1* (i.e., provided the final pass is a regular Insertion Sort). If Shellsort will aways conclude with a regular Insertion Sort, then how can it be any improvement on Insertion Sort? The expectation is that each of the (relatively cheap) sublist sorts will make the list "more sorted" than it was before.

```
// Modified version of Insertion Sort for varying increments
template <typename E, typename Comp>
void inssort2(E A[], int n, int incr) {
  for (int i=incr; i<n; i+=incr)
    for (int j=i; (j>=incr) &&
                    (Comp::prior(A[j], A[j-incr])); j-=incr)
      swap(A, j, j-incr);
}

template <typename E, typename Comp>
void shellsort(E A[], int n) { // Shellsort
  for (int i=n/2; i>2; i/=2)        // For each increment
    for (int j=0; j<i; j++)         // Sort each sublist
      inssort2<E,Comp>(&A[j], n-j, i);
  inssort2<E,Comp>(A, n, 1);
}
```

Figure 7.7 An implementation for Shell Sort.

It is not necessarily the case that this will be true, but it is almost always true in practice. When the final Insertion Sort is conducted, the list should be "almost sorted," yielding a relatively cheap final Insertion Sort pass.

Some choices for increments will make Shellsort run more efficiently than others. In particular, the choice of increments described above (2^k, 2^{k-1}, ..., 2, 1) turns out to be relatively inefficient. A better choice is the following series based on division by three: (..., 121, 40, 13, 4, 1).

The analysis of Shellsort is difficult, so we must accept without proof that the average-case performance of Shellsort (for "divisions by three" increments) is $O(n^{1.5})$. Other choices for the increment series can reduce this upper bound somewhat. Thus, Shellsort is substantially better than Insertion Sort, or any of the $\Theta(n^2)$ sorts presented in Section 7.2. In fact, Shellsort is not terrible when compared with the asymptotically better sorts to be presented whenever n is of medium size (thought is tends to be a little slower than these other algorithms when they are well implemented). Shellsort illustrates how we can sometimes exploit the special properties of an algorithm (in this case Insertion Sort) even if in general that algorithm is unacceptably slow.

7.4 Mergesort

A natural approach to problem solving is divide and conquer. In terms of sorting, we might consider breaking the list to be sorted into pieces, process the pieces, and then put them back together somehow. A simple way to do this would be to split the list in half, sort the halves, and then merge the sorted halves together. This is the idea behind **Mergesort**.

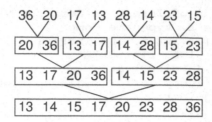

Figure 7.8 An illustration of Mergesort. The first row shows eight numbers that are to be sorted. Mergesort will recursively subdivide the list into sublists of one element each, then recombine the sublists. The second row shows the four sublists of size 2 created by the first merging pass. The third row shows the two sublists of size 4 created by the next merging pass on the sublists of row 2. The last row shows the final sorted list created by merging the two sublists of row 3.

Mergesort is one of the simplest sorting algorithms conceptually, and has good performance both in the asymptotic sense and in empirical running time. Surprisingly, even though it is based on a simple concept, it is relatively difficult to implement in practice. Figure 7.8 illustrates Mergesort. A pseudocode sketch of Mergesort is as follows:

```
List mergesort(List inlist) {
  if (inlist.length() <= 1) return inlist;;
  List L1 = half of the items from inlist;
  List L2 = other half of the items from inlist;
  return merge(mergesort(L1), mergesort(L2));
}
```

Before discussing how to implement Mergesort, we will first examine the merge function. Merging two sorted sublists is quite simple. Function **merge** examines the first element of each sublist and picks the smaller value as the smallest element overall. This smaller value is removed from its sublist and placed into the output list. Merging continues in this way, comparing the front elements of the sublists and continually appending the smaller to the output list until no more input elements remain.

Implementing Mergesort presents a number of technical difficulties. The first decision is how to represent the lists. Mergesort lends itself well to sorting a singly linked list because merging does not require random access to the list elements. Thus, Mergesort is the method of choice when the input is in the form of a linked list. Implementing **merge** for linked lists is straightforward, because we need only remove items from the front of the input lists and append items to the output list. Breaking the input list into two equal halves presents some difficulty. Ideally we would just break the lists into front and back halves. However, even if we know the length of the list in advance, it would still be necessary to traverse halfway down the linked list to reach the beginning of the second half. A simpler method, which does not rely on knowing the length of the list in advance, assigns elements of the

```
template <typename E, typename Comp>
void mergesort(E A[], E temp[], int left, int right) {
  if (left == right) return;              // List of one element
  int mid = (left+right)/2;
  mergesort<E,Comp>(A, temp, left, mid);
  mergesort<E,Comp>(A, temp, mid+1, right);
  for (int i=left; i<=right; i++)    // Copy subarray to temp
    temp[i] = A[i];
  // Do the merge operation back to A
  int i1 = left; int i2 = mid + 1;
  for (int curr=left; curr<=right; curr++) {
    if (i1 == mid+1)          // Left sublist exhausted
      A[curr] = temp[i2++];
    else if (i2 > right)  // Right sublist exhausted
      A[curr] = temp[i1++];
    else if (Comp::prior(temp[i1], temp[i2]))
      A[curr] = temp[i1++];
    else A[curr] = temp[i2++];
  }
}
```

Figure 7.9 Standard implementation for Mergesort.

input list alternating between the two sublists. The first element is assigned to the first sublist, the second element to the second sublist, the third to first sublist, the fourth to the second sublist, and so on. This requires one complete pass through the input list to build the sublists.

When the input to Mergesort is an array, splitting input into two subarrays is easy if we know the array bounds. Merging is also easy if we merge the subarrays into a second array. Note that this approach requires twice the amount of space as any of the sorting methods presented so far, which is a serious disadvantage for Mergesort. It is possible to merge the subarrays without using a second array, but this is extremely difficult to do efficiently and is not really practical. Merging the two subarrays into a second array, while simple to implement, presents another difficulty. The merge process ends with the sorted list in the auxiliary array. Consider how the recursive nature of Mergesort breaks the original array into subarrays, as shown in Figure 7.8. Mergesort is recursively called until subarrays of size 1 have been created, requiring $\log n$ levels of recursion. These subarrays are merged into subarrays of size 2, which are in turn merged into subarrays of size 4, and so on. We need to avoid having each merge operation require a new array. With some difficulty, an algorithm can be devised that alternates between two arrays. A much simpler approach is to copy the sorted sublists to the auxiliary array first, and then merge them back to the original array. Figure 7.9 shows a complete implementation for mergesort following this approach.

An optimized Mergesort implementation is shown in Figure 7.10. It reverses the order of the second subarray during the initial copy. Now the current positions of the two subarrays work inwards from the ends, allowing the end of each subarray

```
template <typename E, typename Comp>
void mergesort(E A[], E temp[], int left, int right) {
  if ((right-left) <= THRESHOLD) { // Small list
    inssort<E,Comp>(&A[left], right-left+1);
    return;
  }
  int i, j, k, mid = (left+right)/2;
  mergesort<E,Comp>(A, temp, left, mid);
  mergesort<E,Comp>(A, temp, mid+1, right);
  // Do the merge operation.  First, copy 2 halves to temp.
  for (i=mid; i>=left; i--) temp[i] = A[i];
  for (j=1; j<=right-mid; j++) temp[right-j+1] = A[j+mid];
  // Merge sublists back to A
  for (i=left,j=right,k=left; k<=right; k++)
    if (Comp::prior(temp[i], temp[j])) A[k] = temp[i++];
    else A[k] = temp[j--];
}
```

Figure 7.10 Optimized implementation for Mergesort.

to act as a sentinel for the other. Unlike the previous implementation, no test is needed to check for when one of the two subarrays becomes empty. This version also uses Insertion Sort to sort small subarrays.

Analysis of Mergesort is straightforward, despite the fact that it is a recursive algorithm. The merging part takes time $\Theta(i)$ where i is the total length of the two subarrays being merged. The array to be sorted is repeatedly split in half until subarrays of size 1 are reached, at which time they are merged to be of size 2, these merged to subarrays of size 4, and so on as shown in Figure 7.8. Thus, the depth of the recursion is $\log n$ for n elements (assume for simplicity that n is a power of two). The first level of recursion can be thought of as working on one array of size n, the next level working on two arrays of size $n/2$, the next on four arrays of size $n/4$, and so on. The bottom of the recursion has n arrays of size 1. Thus, n arrays of size 1 are merged (requiring $\Theta(n)$ total steps), $n/2$ arrays of size 2 (again requiring $\Theta(n)$ total steps), $n/4$ arrays of size 4, and so on. At each of the $\log n$ levels of recursion, $\Theta(n)$ work is done, for a total cost of $\Theta(n \log n)$. This cost is unaffected by the relative order of the values being sorted, thus this analysis holds for the best, average, and worst cases.

7.5 Quicksort

While Mergesort uses the most obvious form of divide and conquer (split the list in half then sort the halves), it is not the only way that we can break down the sorting problem. And we saw that doing the merge step for Mergesort when using an array implementation is not so easy. So perhaps a different divide and conquer strategy might turn out to be more efficient?

Quicksort is aptly named because, when properly implemented, it is the fastest known general-purpose in-memory sorting algorithm in the average case. It does not require the extra array needed by Mergesort, so it is space efficient as well. Quicksort is widely used, and is typically the algorithm implemented in a library sort routine such as the UNIX `qsort` function. Interestingly, Quicksort is hampered by exceedingly poor worst-case performance, thus making it inappropriate for certain applications.

Before we get to Quicksort, consider for a moment the practicality of using a Binary Search Tree for sorting. You could insert all of the values to be sorted into the BST one by one, then traverse the completed tree using an inorder traversal. The output would form a sorted list. This approach has a number of drawbacks, including the extra space required by BST pointers and the amount of time required to insert nodes into the tree. However, this method introduces some interesting ideas. First, the root of the BST (i.e., the first node inserted) splits the list into two sublists: The left subtree contains those values in the list less than the root value while the right subtree contains those values in the list greater than or equal to the root value. Thus, the BST implicitly implements a "divide and conquer" approach to sorting the left and right subtrees. Quicksort implements this concept in a much more efficient way.

Quicksort first selects a value called the **pivot**. (This is conceptually like the root node's value in the BST.) Assume that the input array contains k values less than the pivot. The records are then rearranged in such a way that the k values less than the pivot are placed in the first, or leftmost, k positions in the array, and the values greater than or equal to the pivot are placed in the last, or rightmost, $n - k$ positions. This is called a **partition** of the array. The values placed in a given partition need not (and typically will not) be sorted with respect to each other. All that is required is that all values end up in the correct partition. The pivot value itself is placed in position k. Quicksort then proceeds to sort the resulting subarrays now on either side of the pivot, one of size k and the other of size $n - k - 1$. How are these values sorted? Because Quicksort is such a good algorithm, using Quicksort on the subarrays would be appropriate.

Unlike some of the sorts that we have seen earlier in this chapter, Quicksort might not seem very "natural" in that it is not an approach that a person is likely to use to sort real objects. But it should not be too surprising that a really efficient sort for huge numbers of abstract objects on a computer would be rather different from our experiences with sorting a relatively few physical objects.

The C++ code for Quicksort is shown in Figure 7.11. Parameters `i` and `j` define the left and right indices, respectively, for the subarray being sorted. The initial call to Quicksort would be `qsort(array, 0, n-1)`.

Function `partition` will move records to the appropriate partition and then return `k`, the first position in the right partition. Note that the pivot value is initially

```
template <typename E, typename Comp>
void qsort(E A[], int i, int j) { // Quicksort
  if (j <= i) return; // Don't sort 0 or 1 element
  int pivotindex = findpivot(A, i, j);
  swap(A, pivotindex, j);      // Put pivot at end
  // k will be the first position in the right subarray
  int k = partition<E,Comp>(A, i-1, j, A[j]);
  swap(A, k, j);               // Put pivot in place
  qsort<E,Comp>(A, i, k-1);
  qsort<E,Comp>(A, k+1, j);
}
```

Figure 7.11 Implementation for Quicksort.

placed at the end of the array (position **j**). Thus, **partition** must not affect the value of array position **j**. After partitioning, the pivot value is placed in position **k**, which is its correct position in the final, sorted array. By doing so, we guarantee that at least one value (the pivot) will not be processed in the recursive calls to **qsort**. Even if a bad pivot is selected, yielding a completely empty partition to one side of the pivot, the larger partition will contain at most $n - 1$ elements.

Selecting a pivot can be done in many ways. The simplest is to use the first key. However, if the input is sorted or reverse sorted, this will produce a poor partitioning with all values to one side of the pivot. It is better to pick a value at random, thereby reducing the chance of a bad input order affecting the sort. Unfortunately, using a random number generator is relatively expensive, and we can do nearly as well by selecting the middle position in the array. Here is a simple **findpivot** function:

```
template <typename E>
inline int findpivot(E A[], int i, int j)
  { return (i+j)/2; }
```

We now turn to function **partition**. If we knew in advance how many keys are less than the pivot, **partition** could simply copy elements with key values less than the pivot to the low end of the array, and elements with larger keys to the high end. Because we do not know in advance how many keys are less than the pivot, we use a clever algorithm that moves indices inwards from the ends of the subarray, swapping values as necessary until the two indices meet. Figure 7.12 shows a **C++** implementation for the partition step.

Figure 7.13 illustrates **partition**. Initially, variables **l** and **r** are immediately outside the actual bounds of the subarray being partitioned. Each pass through the outer **do** loop moves the counters **l** and **r** inwards, until eventually they meet. Note that at each iteration of the inner **while** loops, the bounds are moved prior to checking against the pivot value. This ensures that progress is made by each **while** loop, even when the two values swapped on the last iteration of the **do** loop were equal to the pivot. Also note the check that **r > l** in the second **while**

```
template <typename E, typename Comp>
inline int partition(E A[], int l, int r, E& pivot) {
  do {                     // Move the bounds inward until they meet
    while (Comp::prior(A[++l], pivot));   // Move l right and
    while ((l < r) && Comp::prior(pivot, A[--r])); // r left
    swap(A, l, r);                    // Swap out-of-place values
  } while (l < r);                    // Stop when they cross
  return l;       // Return first position in right partition
}
```

Figure 7.12 The Quicksort partition implementation.

Initial	72	6	57	88	85	42	83	73	48	60
	l									r
Pass 1	72	6	57	88	85	42	83	73	48	60
	l								r	
Swap 1	48	6	57	88	85	42	83	73	72	60
	l								r	
Pass 2	48	6	57	88	85	42	83	73	72	60
				l		r				
Swap 2	48	6	57	42	85	88	83	73	72	60
				l		r				
Pass 3	48	6	57	42	85	88	83	73	72	60
				l,r						

Figure 7.13 The Quicksort partition step. The first row shows the initial positions for a collection of ten key values. The pivot value is 60, which has been swapped to the end of the array. The **do** loop makes three iterations, each time moving counters **l** and **r** inwards until they meet in the third pass. In the end, the left partition contains four values and the right partition contains six values. Function **qsort** will place the pivot value into position 4.

loop. This ensures that **r** does not run off the low end of the partition in the case where the pivot is the least value in that partition. Function **partition** returns the first index of the right partition so that the subarray bound for the recursive calls to **qsort** can be determined. Figure 7.14 illustrates the complete Quicksort algorithm.

To analyze Quicksort, we first analyze the **findpivot** and **partition** functions operating on a subarray of length k. Clearly, **findpivot** takes constant time. Function **partition** contains a **do** loop with two nested **while** loops. The total cost of the partition operation is constrained by how far **l** and **r** can move inwards. In particular, these two bounds variables together can move a

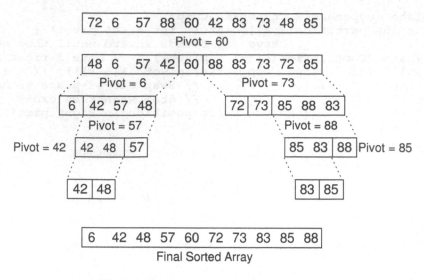

Figure 7.14 An illustration of Quicksort.

total of s steps for a subarray of length s. However, this does not directly tell us
how much work is done by the nested **while** loops. The **do** loop as a whole is
guaranteed to move both **l** and **r** inward at least one position on each first pass.
Each **while** loop moves its variable at least once (except in the special case where
r is at the left edge of the array, but this can happen only once). Thus, we see that
the **do** loop can be executed at most s times, the total amount of work done moving
l and **r** is s, and each **while** loop can fail its test at most s times. The total work
for the entire **partition** function is therefore $\Theta(s)$.

Knowing the cost of **findpivot** and **partition**, we can determine the
cost of Quicksort. We begin with a worst-case analysis. The worst case will occur
when the pivot does a poor job of breaking the array, that is, when there are no
elements in one partition, and $n - 1$ elements in the other. In this case, the divide
and conquer strategy has done a poor job of dividing, so the conquer phase will
work on a subproblem only one less than the size of the original problem. If this
happens at each partition step, then the total cost of the algorithm will be

$$\sum_{k=1}^{n} k = \Theta(n^2).$$

In the worst case, Quicksort is $\Theta(n^2)$. This is terrible, no better than Bubble
Sort.[2] When will this worst case occur? Only when each pivot yields a bad partitioning of the array. If the pivot values are selected at random, then this is extremely
unlikely to happen. When selecting the middle position of the current subarray, it

---

[2]The worst insult that I can think of for a sorting algorithm.

is still unlikely to happen. It does not take many good partitionings for Quicksort to work fairly well.

Quicksort's best case occurs when **findpivot** always breaks the array into two equal halves. Quicksort repeatedly splits the array into smaller partitions, as shown in Figure 7.14. In the best case, the result will be $\log n$ levels of partitions, with the top level having one array of size n, the second level two arrays of size $n/2$, the next with four arrays of size $n/4$, and so on. Thus, at each level, all partition steps for that level do a total of n work, for an overall cost of $n \log n$ work when Quicksort finds perfect pivots.

Quicksort's average-case behavior falls somewhere between the extremes of worst and best case. Average-case analysis considers the cost for all possible arrangements of input, summing the costs and dividing by the number of cases. We make one reasonable simplifying assumption: At each partition step, the pivot is equally likely to end in any position in the (sorted) array. In other words, the pivot is equally likely to break an array into partitions of sizes 0 and $n-1$, or 1 and $n-2$, and so on.

Given this assumption, the average-case cost is computed from the following equation:

$$\mathbf{T}(n) = cn + \frac{1}{n}\sum_{k=0}^{n-1}[\mathbf{T}(k) + \mathbf{T}(n-1-k)], \quad \mathbf{T}(0) = \mathbf{T}(1) = c.$$

This equation is in the form of a recurrence relation. Recurrence relations are discussed in Chapters 2 and 14, and this one is solved in Section 14.2.4. This equation says that there is one chance in n that the pivot breaks the array into subarrays of size 0 and $n-1$, one chance in n that the pivot breaks the array into subarrays of size 1 and $n-2$, and so on. The expression "$\mathbf{T}(k) + \mathbf{T}(n-1-k)$" is the cost for the two recursive calls to Quicksort on two arrays of size k and $n-1-k$. The initial cn term is the cost of doing the **findpivot** and **partition** steps, for some constant c. The closed-form solution to this recurrence relation is $\Theta(n \log n)$. Thus, Quicksort has average-case cost $\Theta(n \log n)$.

This is an unusual situation that the average case cost and the worst case cost have asymptotically different growth rates. Consider what "average case" actually means. We compute an average cost for inputs of size n by summing up for every possible input of size n the product of the running time cost of that input times the probability that that input will occur. To simplify things, we assumed that every permutation is equally likely to occur. Thus, finding the average means summing up the cost for every permutation and dividing by the number of inputs ($n!$). We know that some of these $n!$ inputs cost $O(n^2)$. But the sum of all the permutation costs has to be $(n!)(O(n \log n))$. Given the extremely high cost of the worst inputs, there must be very few of them. In fact, there cannot be a constant fraction of the inputs with cost $O(n^2)$. Even, say, 1% of the inputs with cost $O(n^2)$ would lead to an average cost of $O(n^2)$. Thus, as n grows, the fraction of inputs with high cost must be going toward a limit of zero. We can conclude that Quicksort will have good behavior if we can avoid those very few bad input permutations.

The running time for Quicksort can be improved (by a constant factor), and much study has gone into optimizing this algorithm. The most obvious place for improvement is the **findpivot** function. Quicksort's worst case arises when the pivot does a poor job of splitting the array into equal size subarrays. If we are willing to do more work searching for a better pivot, the effects of a bad pivot can be decreased or even eliminated. One good choice is to use the "median of three" algorithm, which uses as a pivot the middle of three randomly selected values. Using a random number generator to choose the positions is relatively expensive, so a common compromise is to look at the first, middle, and last positions of the current subarray. However, our simple **findpivot** function that takes the middle value as its pivot has the virtue of making it highly unlikely to get a bad input by chance, and it is quite cheap to implement. This is in sharp contrast to selecting the first or last element as the pivot, which would yield bad performance for many permutations that are nearly sorted or nearly reverse sorted.

A significant improvement can be gained by recognizing that Quicksort is relatively slow when n is small. This might not seem to be relevant if most of the time we sort large arrays, nor should it matter how long Quicksort takes in the rare instance when a small array is sorted because it will be fast anyway. But you should notice that Quicksort itself sorts many, many small arrays! This happens as a natural by-product of the divide and conquer approach.

A simple improvement might then be to replace Quicksort with a faster sort for small numbers, say Insertion Sort or Selection Sort. However, there is an even better — and still simpler — optimization. When Quicksort partitions are below a certain size, do nothing! The values within that partition will be out of order. However, we do know that all values in the array to the left of the partition are smaller than all values in the partition. All values in the array to the right of the partition are greater than all values in the partition. Thus, even if Quicksort only gets the values to "nearly" the right locations, the array will be close to sorted. This is an ideal situation in which to take advantage of the best-case performance of Insertion Sort. The final step is a single call to Insertion Sort to process the entire array, putting the elements into final sorted order. Empirical testing shows that the subarrays should be left unordered whenever they get down to nine or fewer elements.

The last speedup to be considered reduces the cost of making recursive calls. Quicksort is inherently recursive, because each Quicksort operation must sort two sublists. Thus, there is no simple way to turn Quicksort into an iterative algorithm. However, Quicksort can be implemented using a stack to imitate recursion, as the amount of information that must be stored is small. We need not store copies of a subarray, only the subarray bounds. Furthermore, the stack depth can be kept small if care is taken on the order in which Quicksort's recursive calls are executed. We can also place the code for **findpivot** and **partition** inline to eliminate the remaining function calls. Note however that by not processing sublists of size nine or less as suggested above, about three quarters of the function calls will already have been eliminated. Thus, eliminating the remaining function calls will yield only a modest speedup.

7.6   Heapsort

Our discussion of Quicksort began by considering the practicality of using a binary search tree for sorting. The BST requires more space than the other sorting methods and will be slower than Quicksort or Mergesort due to the relative expense of inserting values into the tree. There is also the possibility that the BST might be unbalanced, leading to a $\Theta(n^2)$ worst-case running time. Subtree balance in the BST is closely related to Quicksort's partition step. Quicksort's pivot serves roughly the same purpose as the BST root value in that the left partition (subtree) stores values less than the pivot (root) value, while the right partition (subtree) stores values greater than or equal to the pivot (root).

A good sorting algorithm can be devised based on a tree structure more suited to the purpose. In particular, we would like the tree to be balanced, space efficient, and fast. The algorithm should take advantage of the fact that sorting is a special-purpose application in that all of the values to be stored are available at the start. This means that we do not necessarily need to insert one value at a time into the tree structure.

Heapsort is based on the heap data structure presented in Section 5.5. Heapsort has all of the advantages just listed. The complete binary tree is balanced, its array representation is space efficient, and we can load all values into the tree at once, taking advantage of the efficient **buildheap** function. The asymptotic performance of Heapsort is $\Theta(n \log n)$ in the best, average, and worst cases. It is not as fast as Quicksort in the average case (by a constant factor), but Heapsort has special properties that will make it particularly useful when sorting data sets too large to fit in main memory, as discussed in Chapter 8.

A sorting algorithm based on max-heaps is quite straightforward. First we use the heap building algorithm of Section 5.5 to convert the array into max-heap order. Then we repeatedly remove the maximum value from the heap, restoring the heap property each time that we do so, until the heap is empty. Note that each time we remove the maximum element from the heap, it is placed at the end of the array. Assume the n elements are stored in array positions 0 through $n - 1$. After removing the maximum value from the heap and readjusting, the maximum value will now be placed in position $n - 1$ of the array. The heap is now considered to be of size $n - 1$. Removing the new maximum (root) value places the second largest value in position $n - 2$ of the array. After removing each of the remaining values in turn, the array will be properly sorted from least to greatest. This is why Heapsort uses a max-heap rather than a min-heap as might have been expected. Figure 7.15 illustrates Heapsort. The complete C++ implementation is as follows:

```
template <typename E, typename Comp>
void heapsort(E A[], int n) { // Heapsort
  E maxval;
  heap<E,Comp> H(A, n, n);     // Build the heap
  for (int i=0; i<n; i++)      // Now sort
    maxval = H.removefirst();  // Place maxval at end
}
```

Because building the heap takes $\Theta(n)$ time (see Section 5.5), and because n deletions of the maximum element each take $\Theta(\log n)$ time, we see that the entire Heapsort operation takes $\Theta(n \log n)$ time in the worst, average, and best cases. While typically slower than Quicksort by a constant factor, Heapsort has one special advantage over the other sorts studied so far. Building the heap is relatively cheap, requiring $\Theta(n)$ time. Removing the maximum element from the heap requires $\Theta(\log n)$ time. Thus, if we wish to find the k largest elements in an array, we can do so in time $\Theta(n + k \log n)$. If k is small, this is a substantial improvement over the time required to find the k largest elements using one of the other sorting methods described earlier (many of which would require sorting all of the array first). One situation where we are able to take advantage of this concept is in the implementation of Kruskal's minimum-cost spanning tree (MST) algorithm of Section 11.5.2. That algorithm requires that edges be visited in ascending order (so, use a min-heap), but this process stops as soon as the MST is complete. Thus, only a relatively small fraction of the edges need be sorted.

7.7 Binsort and Radix Sort

Imagine that for the past year, as you paid your various bills, you then simply piled all the paperwork onto the top of a table somewhere. Now the year has ended and its time to sort all of these papers by what the bill was for (phone, electricity, rent, etc.) and date. A pretty natural approach is to make some space on the floor, and as you go through the pile of papers, put the phone bills into one pile, the electric bills into another pile, and so on. Once this initial assignment of bills to piles is done (in one pass), you can sort each pile by date relatively quickly because they are each fairly small. This is the basic idea behind a Binsort.

Section 3.9 presented the following code fragment to sort a permutation of the numbers 0 through $n - 1$:

```
for (i=0; i<n; i++)
  B[A[i]] = A[i];
```

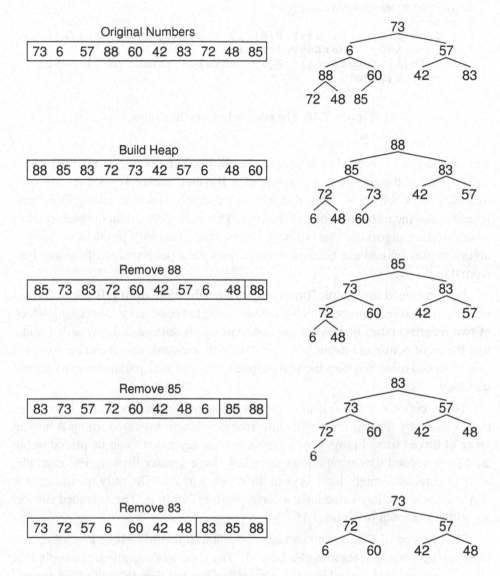

Figure 7.15 An illustration of Heapsort. The top row shows the values in their original order. The second row shows the values after building the heap. The third row shows the result of the first **removefirst** operation on key value 88. Note that 88 is now at the end of the array. The fourth row shows the result of the second **removefirst** operation on key value 85. The fifth row shows the result of the third **removefirst** operation on key value 83. At this point, the last three positions of the array hold the three greatest values in sorted order. Heapsort continues in this manner until the entire array is sorted.

```
template <typename E, class getKey>
void binsort(E A[], int n) {
  List<E> B[MaxKeyValue];
  E item;
  for (int i=0; i<n; i++) B[A[i]].append(getKey::key(A[i]));
  for (int i=0; i<MaxKeyValue; i++)
    for (B[i].setStart(); B[i].getValue(item); B[i].next())
      output(item);
}
```

Figure 7.16 The extended Binsort algorithm.

Here the key value is used to determine the position for a record in the final sorted array. This is the most basic example of a **Binsort**, where key values are used to assign records to **bins**. This algorithm is extremely efficient, taking $\Theta(n)$ time regardless of the initial ordering of the keys. This is far better than the performance of any sorting algorithm that we have seen so far. The only problem is that this algorithm has limited use because it works only for a permutation of the numbers from 0 to $n-1$.

We can extend this simple Binsort algorithm to be more useful. Because Binsort must perform direct computation on the key value (as opposed to just asking which of two records comes first as our previous sorting algorithms did), we will assume that the records use an integer key type. We further assume that it can be extracted from a record using the **key** method supplied by a template parameter class named **getKey**.

The simplest extension is to allow for duplicate values among the keys. This can be done by turning array slots into arbitrary-length bins by turning **B** into an array of linked lists. In this way, all records with key value i can be placed in bin **B[i]**. A second extension allows for a key range greater than n. For example, a set of n records might have keys in the range 1 to $2n$. The only requirement is that each possible key value have a corresponding bin in **B**. The extended Binsort algorithm is shown in Figure 7.16.

This version of Binsort can sort any collection of records whose key values fall in the range from 0 to **MaxKeyValue**-1. The total work required is simply that needed to place each record into the appropriate bin and then take all of the records out of the bins. Thus, we need to process each record twice, for $\Theta(n)$ work.

Unfortunately, there is a crucial oversight in this analysis. Binsort must also look at each of the bins to see if it contains a record. The algorithm must process **MaxKeyValue** bins, regardless of how many actually hold records. If **MaxKeyValue** is small compared to n, then this is not a great expense. Suppose that **MaxKeyValue** $= n^2$. In this case, the total amount of work done will be $\Theta(n + n^2) = \Theta(n^2)$. This results in a poor sorting algorithm, and the algorithm becomes even worse as the disparity between n and **MaxKeyValue** increases. In addition,

Initial List: 27 91 1 97 17 23 84 28 72 5 67 25

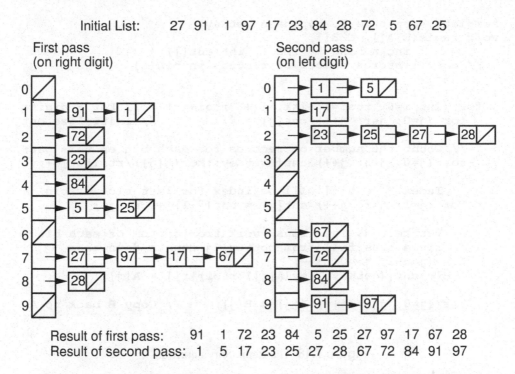

Result of first pass: 91 1 72 23 84 5 25 27 97 17 67 28
Result of second pass: 1 5 17 23 25 27 28 67 72 84 91 97

Figure 7.17 An example of Radix Sort for twelve two-digit numbers in base ten. Two passes are required to sort the list.

a large key range requires an unacceptably large array **B**. Thus, even the extended Binsort is useful only for a limited key range.

A further generalization to Binsort yields a **bucket sort**. Each bin is associated with not just one key, but rather a range of key values. A bucket sort assigns records to bins and then relies on some other sorting technique to sort the records within each bin. The hope is that the relatively inexpensive bucketing process will put only a small number of records in each bin, and that a "cleanup sort" within the bins will then be relatively cheap.

There is a way to keep the number of bins and the related processing small while allowing the cleanup sort to be based on Binsort. Consider a sequence of records with keys in the range 0 to 99. If we have ten bins available, we can first assign records to bins by taking their key value modulo 10. Thus, every key will be assigned to the bin matching its rightmost decimal digit. We can then take these records from the bins *in order* and reassign them to the bins on the basis of their leftmost (10's place) digit (define values in the range 0 to 9 to have a leftmost digit of 0). In other words, assign the ith record from array **A** to a bin using the formula **A[i]/10**. If we now gather the values from the bins in order, the result is a sorted list. Figure 7.17 illustrates this process.

```
template <typename E, typename getKey>
void radix(E A[], E B[],
           int n, int k, int r, int cnt[]) {
  // cnt[i] stores number of records in bin[i]
  int j;

  for (int i=0, rtoi=1; i<k; i++, rtoi*=r) { // For k digits
    for (j=0; j<r; j++) cnt[j] = 0;          // Initialize cnt

    // Count the number of records for each bin on this pass
    for (j=0; j<n; j++) cnt[(getKey::key(A[j])/rtoi)%r]++;

    // Index B: cnt[j] will be index for last slot of bin j.
    for (j=1; j<r; j++) cnt[j] = cnt[j-1] + cnt[j];

    // Put records into bins, work from bottom of each bin.
    // Since bins fill from bottom, j counts downwards
    for (j=n-1; j>=0; j--)
      B[--cnt[(getKey::key(A[j])/rtoi)%r]] = A[j];

    for (j=0; j<n; j++) A[j] = B[j];      // Copy B back to A
  }
}
```

Figure 7.18 The Radix Sort algorithm.

In this example, we have $r = 10$ bins and $n = 12$ keys in the range 0 to $r^2 - 1$. The total computation is $\Theta(n)$, because we look at each record and each bin a constant number of times. This is a great improvement over the simple Binsort where the number of bins must be as large as the key range. Note that the example uses $r = 10$ so as to make the bin computations easy to visualize: Records were placed into bins based on the value of first the rightmost and then the leftmost decimal digits. Any number of bins would have worked. This is an example of a **Radix Sort**, so called because the bin computations are based on the **radix** or the **base** of the key values. This sorting algorithm can be extended to any number of keys in any key range. We simply assign records to bins based on the keys' digit values working from the rightmost digit to the leftmost. If there are k digits, then this requires that we assign keys to bins k times.

As with Mergesort, an efficient implementation of Radix Sort is somewhat difficult to achieve. In particular, we would prefer to sort an array of values and avoid processing linked lists. If we know how many values will be in each bin, then an auxiliary array of size r can be used to hold the bins. For example, if during the first pass the 0 bin will receive three records and the 1 bin will receive five records, then we could simply reserve the first three array positions for the 0 bin and the next five array positions for the 1 bin. Exactly this approach is taken by the **C++** implementation of Figure 7.18. At the end of each pass, the records are copied back to the original array.

The first inner **for** loop initializes array **cnt**. The second loop counts the number of records to be assigned to each bin. The third loop sets the values in **cnt** to their proper indices within array **B**. Note that the index stored in **cnt[j]** is the *last* index for bin **j**; bins are filled from high index to low index. The fourth loop assigns the records to the bins (within array **B**). The final loop simply copies the records back to array **A** to be ready for the next pass. Variable **rtoi** stores r^i for use in bin computation on the i'th iteration. Figure 7.19 shows how this algorithm processes the input shown in Figure 7.17.

This algorithm requires k passes over the list of n numbers in base r, with $\Theta(n + r)$ work done at each pass. Thus the total work is $\Theta(nk + rk)$. What is this in terms of n? Because r is the size of the base, it might be rather small. One could use base 2 or 10. Base 26 would be appropriate for sorting character strings. For now, we will treat r as a constant value and ignore it for the purpose of determining asymptotic complexity. Variable k is related to the key range: It is the maximum number of digits that a key may have in base r. In some applications we can determine k to be of limited size and so might wish to consider it a constant. In this case, Radix Sort is $\Theta(n)$ in the best, average, and worst cases, making it the sort with best asymptotic complexity that we have studied.

Is it a reasonable assumption to treat k as a constant? Or is there some relationship between k and n? If the key range is limited and duplicate key values are common, there might be no relationship between k and n. To make this distinction clear, use N to denote the number of distinct key values used by the n records. Thus, $N \leq n$. Because it takes a minimum of $\log_r N$ base r digits to represent N distinct key values, we know that $k \geq \log_r N$.

Now, consider the situation in which no keys are duplicated. If there are n unique keys ($n = N$), then it requires n distinct code values to represent them. Thus, $k \geq \log_r n$. Because it requires *at least* $\Omega(\log n)$ digits (within a constant factor) to distinguish between the n distinct keys, k is in $\Omega(\log n)$. This yields an asymptotic complexity of $\Omega(n \log n)$ for Radix Sort to process n distinct key values.

It is possible that the key range is much larger; $\log_r n$ bits is merely the best case possible for n distinct values. Thus, the $\log_r n$ estimate for k could be overly optimistic. The moral of this analysis is that, for the general case of n distinct key values, Radix Sort is at best a $\Omega(n \log n)$ sorting algorithm.

Radix Sort can be much improved by making base r be as large as possible. Consider the case of an integer key value. Set $r = 2^i$ for some i. In other words, the value of r is related to the number of bits of the key processed on each pass. Each time the number of bits is doubled, the number of passes is cut in half. When processing an integer key value, setting $r = 256$ allows the key to be processed one byte at a time. Processing a 32-bit key requires only four passes. It is not unreasonable on most computers to use $r = 2^{16} = 64K$, resulting in only two passes for

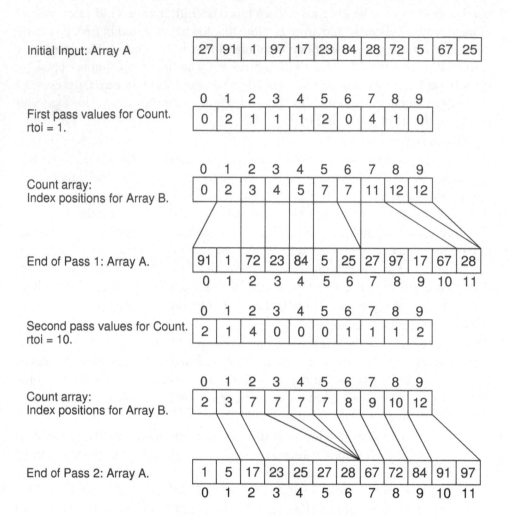

Figure 7.19 An example showing function **radix** applied to the input of Figure 7.17. Row 1 shows the initial values within the input array. Row 2 shows the values for array **cnt** after counting the number of records for each bin. Row 3 shows the index values stored in array **cnt**. For example, **cnt[0]** is 0, indicating no input values are in bin 0. **Cnt[1]** is 2, indicating that array **B** positions 0 and 1 will hold the values for bin 1. **Cnt[2]** is 3, indicating that array **B** position 2 will hold the (single) value for bin 2. **Cnt[7]** is 11, indicating that array **B** positions 7 through 10 will hold the four values for bin 7. Row 4 shows the results of the first pass of the Radix Sort. Rows 5 through 7 show the equivalent steps for the second pass.

a 32-bit key. Of course, this requires a `cnt` array of size 64K. Performance will be good only if the number of records is close to 64K or greater. In other words, the number of records must be large compared to the key size for Radix Sort to be efficient. In many sorting applications, Radix Sort can be tuned in this way to give good performance.

Radix Sort depends on the ability to make a fixed number of multiway choices based on a digit value, as well as random access to the bins. Thus, Radix Sort might be difficult to implement for certain key types. For example, if the keys are real numbers or arbitrary length strings, then some care will be necessary in implementation. In particular, Radix Sort will need to be careful about deciding when the "last digit" has been found to distinguish among real numbers, or the last character in variable length strings. Implementing the concept of Radix Sort with the trie data structure (Section 13.1) is most appropriate for these situations.

At this point, the perceptive reader might begin to question our earlier assumption that key comparison takes constant time. If the keys are "normal integer" values stored in, say, an integer variable, what is the size of this variable compared to n? In fact, it is almost certain that 32 (the number of bits in a standard `int` variable) is greater than $\log n$ for any practical computation. In this sense, comparison of two long integers requires $\Omega(\log n)$ work.

Computers normally do arithmetic in units of a particular size, such as a 32-bit word. Regardless of the size of the variables, comparisons use this native word size and require a constant amount of time since the comparison is implemented in hardware. In practice, comparisons of two 32-bit values take constant time, even though 32 is much greater than $\log n$. To some extent the truth of the proposition that there are constant time operations (such as integer comparison) is in the eye of the beholder. At the gate level of computer architecture, individual bits are compared. However, constant time comparison for integers is true in practice on most computers (they require a fixed number of machine instructions), and we rely on such assumptions as the basis for our analyses. In contrast, Radix Sort must do several arithmetic calculations on key values (each requiring constant time), where the number of such calculations is proportional to the key length. Thus, Radix Sort truly does $\Omega(n \log n)$ work to process n distinct key values.

7.8 An Empirical Comparison of Sorting Algorithms

Which sorting algorithm is fastest? Asymptotic complexity analysis lets us distinguish between $\Theta(n^2)$ and $\Theta(n \log n)$ algorithms, but it does not help distinguish between algorithms with the same asymptotic complexity. Nor does asymptotic analysis say anything about which algorithm is best for sorting small lists. For answers to these questions, we can turn to empirical testing.

Sort	10	100	1K	10K	100K	1M	Up	Down
Insertion	.00023	.007	0.66	64.98	7381.0	674420	0.04	129.05
Bubble	.00035	.020	2.25	277.94	27691.0	2820680	70.64	108.69
Selection	.00039	.012	0.69	72.47	7356.0	780000	69.76	69.58
Shell	.00034	.008	0.14	1.99	30.2	554	0.44	0.79
Shell/O	.00034	.008	0.12	1.91	29.0	530	0.36	0.64
Merge	.00050	.010	0.12	1.61	19.3	219	0.83	0.79
Merge/O	.00024	.007	0.10	1.31	17.2	197	0.47	0.66
Quick	.00048	.008	0.11	1.37	15.7	162	0.37	0.40
Quick/O	.00031	.006	0.09	1.14	13.6	143	0.32	0.36
Heap	.00050	.011	0.16	2.08	26.7	391	1.57	1.56
Heap/O	.00033	.007	0.11	1.61	20.8	334	1.01	1.04
Radix/4	.00838	.081	0.79	7.99	79.9	808	7.97	7.97
Radix/8	.00799	.044	0.40	3.99	40.0	404	4.00	3.99

Figure 7.20 Empirical comparison of sorting algorithms run on a 3.4-GHz Intel Pentium 4 CPU running Linux. Shellsort, Quicksort, Mergesort, and Heapsort each are shown with regular and optimized versions. Radix Sort is shown for 4- and 8-bit-per-pass versions. All times shown are milliseconds.

Figure 7.20 shows timing results for actual implementations of the sorting algorithms presented in this chapter. The algorithms compared include Insertion Sort, Bubble Sort, Selection Sort, Shellsort, Quicksort, Mergesort, Heapsort and Radix Sort. Shellsort shows both the basic version from Section 7.3 and another with increments based on division by three. Mergesort shows both the basic implementation from Section 7.4 and the optimized version (including calls to Insertion Sort for lists of length below nine). For Quicksort, two versions are compared: the basic implementation from Section 7.5 and an optimized version that does not partition sublists below length nine (with Insertion Sort performed at the end). The first Heapsort version uses the class definitions from Section 5.5. The second version removes all the class definitions and operates directly on the array using inlined code for all access functions.

Except for the rightmost columns, the input to each algorithm is a random array of integers. This affects the timing for some of the sorting algorithms. For example, Selection Sort is not being used to best advantage because the record size is small, so it does not get the best possible showing. The Radix Sort implementation certainly takes advantage of this key range in that it does not look at more digits than necessary. On the other hand, it was not optimized to use bit shifting instead of division, even though the bases used would permit this.

The various sorting algorithms are shown for lists of sizes 10, 100, 1000, 10,000, 100,000, and 1,000,000. The final two columns of each table show the performance for the algorithms on inputs of size 10,000 where the numbers are in ascending (sorted) and descending (reverse sorted) order, respectively. These columns demonstrate best-case performance for some algorithms and worst-case performance for others. They also show that for some algorithms, the order of input has little effect.

These figures show a number of interesting results. As expected, the $O(n^2)$ sorts are quite poor performers for large arrays. Insertion Sort is by far the best of this group, unless the array is already reverse sorted. Shellsort is clearly superior to any of these $O(n^2)$ sorts for lists of even 100 elements. Optimized Quicksort is clearly the best overall algorithm for all but lists of 10 elements. Even for small arrays, optimized Quicksort performs well because it does one partition step before calling Insertion Sort. Compared to the other $O(n \log n)$ sorts, unoptimized Heapsort is quite slow due to the overhead of the class structure. When all of this is stripped away and the algorithm is implemented to manipulate an array directly, it is still somewhat slower than mergesort. In general, optimizing the various algorithms makes a noticeable improvement for larger array sizes.

Overall, Radix Sort is a surprisingly poor performer. If the code had been tuned to use bit shifting of the key value, it would likely improve substantially; but this would seriously limit the range of element types that the sort could support.

7.9   Lower Bounds for Sorting

This book contains many analyses for algorithms. These analyses generally define the upper and lower bounds for algorithms in their worst and average cases. For many of the algorithms presented so far, analysis has been easy. This section considers a more difficult task — an analysis for the cost of a *problem* as opposed to an *algorithm*. The upper bound for a problem can be defined as the asymptotic cost of the fastest known algorithm. The lower bound defines the best possible efficiency for *any* algorithm that solves the problem, including algorithms not yet invented. Once the upper and lower bounds for the problem meet, we know that no future algorithm can possibly be (asymptotically) more efficient.

A simple estimate for a problem's lower bound can be obtained by measuring the size of the input that must be read and the output that must be written. Certainly no algorithm can be more efficient than the problem's I/O time. From this we see that the sorting problem cannot be solved by *any* algorithm in less than $\Omega(n)$ time because it takes at least n steps to read and write the n values to be sorted. Alternatively, any sorting algorithm must at least look at every input vale to recognize whether the input values are in sort order. So, based on our current knowledge of sorting algorithms and the size of the input, we know that the *problem* of sorting is bounded by $\Omega(n)$ and $O(n \log n)$.

Computer scientists have spent much time devising efficient general-purpose sorting algorithms, but no one has ever found one that is faster than $O(n \log n)$ in the worst or average cases. Should we keep searching for a faster sorting algorithm?

Or can we prove that there is no faster sorting algorithm by finding a tighter lower bound?

This section presents one of the most important and most useful proofs in computer science: No sorting algorithm based on key comparisons can possibly be faster than $\Omega(n \log n)$ in the worst case. This proof is important for three reasons. First, knowing that widely used sorting algorithms are asymptotically optimal is reassuring. In particular, it means that you need not bang your head against the wall searching for an $O(n)$ sorting algorithm (or at least not one in any way based on key comparisons). Second, this proof is one of the few non-trivial lower-bounds proofs that we have for any problem; that is, this proof provides one of the relatively few instances where our lower bound is tighter than simply measuring the size of the input and output. As such, it provides a useful model for proving lower bounds on other problems. Finally, knowing a lower bound for sorting gives us a lower bound in turn for other problems whose solution could be used as the basis for a sorting algorithm. The process of deriving asymptotic bounds for one problem from the asymptotic bounds of another is called a **reduction**, a concept further explored in Chapter 17.

Except for the Radix Sort and Binsort, all of the sorting algorithms presented in this chapter make decisions based on the direct comparison of two key values. For example, Insertion Sort sequentially compares the value to be inserted into the sorted list until a comparison against the next value in the list fails. In contrast, Radix Sort has no direct comparison of key values. All decisions are based on the value of specific digits in the key value, so it is possible to take approaches to sorting that do not involve key comparisons. Of course, Radix Sort in the end does not provide a more efficient sorting algorithm than comparison-based sorting. Thus, empirical evidence suggests that comparison-based sorting is a good approach.[3]

The proof that any comparison sort requires $\Omega(n \log n)$ comparisons in the worst case is structured as follows. First, comparison-based decisions can be modeled as the branches in a tree. This means that any sorting algorithm based on comparisons between records can be viewed as a binary tree whose nodes correspond to the comparisons, and whose branches correspond to the possible outcomes. Next, the minimum number of leaves in the resulting tree is shown to be the factorial of n. Finally, the minimum depth of a tree with $n!$ leaves is shown to be in $\Omega(n \log n)$.

Before presenting the proof of an $\Omega(n \log n)$ lower bound for sorting, we first must define the concept of a **decision tree**. A decision tree is a binary tree that can model the processing for any algorithm that makes binary decisions. Each (binary) decision is represented by a branch in the tree. For the purpose of modeling sorting algorithms, we count all comparisons of key values as decisions. If two keys are

---

[3]The truth is stronger than this statement implies. In reality, Radix Sort relies on comparisons as well and so can be modeled by the technique used in this section. The result is an $\Omega(n \log n)$ bound in the general case even for algorithms that look like Radix Sort.

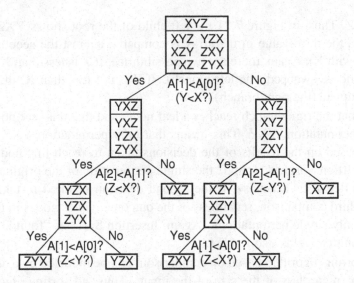

Figure 7.21 Decision tree for Insertion Sort when processing three values labeled X, Y, and Z, initially stored at positions 0, 1, and 2, respectively, in input array A.

compared and the first is less than the second, then this is modeled as a left branch in the decision tree. In the case where the first value is greater than the second, the algorithm takes the right branch.

Figure 7.21 shows the decision tree that models Insertion Sort on three input values. The first input value is labeled X, the second Y, and the third Z. They are initially stored in positions 0, 1, and 2, respectively, of input array **A**. Consider the possible outputs. Initially, we know nothing about the final positions of the three values in the sorted output array. The correct output could be any permutation of the input values. For three values, there are $n! = 6$ permutations. Thus, the root node of the decision tree lists all six permutations that might be the eventual result of the algorithm.

When $n = 3$, the first comparison made by Insertion Sort is between the second item in the input array (Y) and the first item in the array (X). There are two possibilities: Either the value of Y is less than that of X, or the value of Y is *not* less than that of X. This decision is modeled by the first branch in the tree. If Y is less than X, then the left branch should be taken and Y must appear before X in the final output. Only three of the original six permutations have this property, so the left child of the root lists the three permutations where Y appears before X: YXZ, YZX, and ZYX. Likewise, if Y were not less than X, then the right branch would be taken, and only the three permutations in which Y appears after X are possible outcomes: XYZ, XZY, and ZXY. These are listed in the right child of the root.

Let us assume for the moment that Y is less than X and so the left branch is taken. In this case, Insertion Sort swaps the two values. At this point the array stores YXZ. Thus, in Figure 7.21 the left child of the root shows YXZ above the line. Next, the third value in the array is compared against the second (i.e., Z is compared with X). Again, there are two possibilities. If Z is less than X, then these items should be swapped (the left branch). If Z is not less than X, then Insertion Sort is complete (the right branch).

Note that the right branch reaches a leaf node, and that this leaf node contains only one permutation: YXZ. This means that only permutation YXZ can be the outcome based on the results of the decisions taken to reach this node. In other words, Insertion Sort has "found" the single permutation of the original input that yields a sorted list. Likewise, if the second decision resulted in taking the left branch, a third comparison, regardless of the outcome, yields nodes in the decision tree with only single permutations. Again, Insertion Sort has "found" the correct permutation that yields a sorted list.

Any sorting algorithm based on comparisons can be modeled by a decision tree in this way, regardless of the size of the input. Thus, all sorting algorithms can be viewed as algorithms to "find" the correct permutation of the input that yields a sorted list. Each algorithm based on comparisons can be viewed as proceeding by making branches in the tree based on the results of key comparisons, and each algorithm can terminate once a node with a single permutation has been reached.

How is the worst-case cost of an algorithm expressed by the decision tree? The decision tree shows the decisions made by an algorithm for all possible inputs of a given size. Each path through the tree from the root to a leaf is one possible series of decisions taken by the algorithm. The depth of the deepest node represents the longest series of decisions required by the algorithm to reach an answer.

There are many comparison-based sorting algorithms, and each will be modeled by a different decision tree. Some decision trees might be well-balanced, others might be unbalanced. Some trees will have more nodes than others (those with more nodes might be making "unnecessary" comparisons). In fact, a poor sorting algorithm might have an arbitrarily large number of nodes in its decision tree, with leaves of arbitrary depth. There is no limit to how slow the "worst" possible sorting algorithm could be. However, we are interested here in knowing what the *best* sorting algorithm could have as its minimum cost in the worst case. In other words, we would like to know what is the *smallest* depth possible for the *deepest* node in the tree for any sorting algorithm.

The smallest depth of the deepest node will depend on the number of nodes in the tree. Clearly we would like to "push up" the nodes in the tree, but there is limited room at the top. A tree of height 1 can only store one node (the root); the tree of height 2 can store three nodes; the tree of height 3 can store seven nodes, and so on.

Here are some important facts worth remembering:

- A binary tree of height n can store at most $2^n - 1$ nodes.

- Equivalently, a tree with n nodes requires at least $\lceil \log(n+1) \rceil$ levels.

What is the minimum number of nodes that must be in the decision tree for any comparison-based sorting algorithm for n values? Because sorting algorithms are in the business of determining which unique permutation of the input corresponds to the sorted list, the decision tree for any sorting algorithm must contain at least one leaf node for each possible permutation. There are $n!$ permutations for a set of n numbers (see Section 2.2).

Because there are at least $n!$ nodes in the tree, we know that the tree must have $\Omega(\log n!)$ levels. From Stirling's approximation (Section 2.2), we know $\log n!$ is in $\Omega(n \log n)$. The decision tree for any comparison-based sorting algorithm must have nodes $\Omega(n \log n)$ levels deep. Thus, in the worst case, any such sorting algorithm must require $\Omega(n \log n)$ comparisons.

Any sorting algorithm requiring $\Omega(n \log n)$ comparisons in the worst case requires $\Omega(n \log n)$ running time in the worst case. Because any sorting algorithm requires $\Omega(n \log n)$ running time, the problem of sorting also requires $\Omega(n \log n)$ time. We already know of sorting algorithms with $O(n \log n)$ running time, so we can conclude that the problem of sorting requires $\Theta(n \log n)$ time. As a corollary, we know that no comparison-based sorting algorithm can improve on existing $\Theta(n \log n)$ time sorting algorithms by more than a constant factor.

7.10 Further Reading

The definitive reference on sorting is Donald E. Knuth's *Sorting and Searching* [Knu98]. A wealth of details is covered there, including optimal sorts for small size n and special purpose sorting networks. It is a thorough (although somewhat dated) treatment on sorting. For an analysis of Quicksort and a thorough survey on its optimizations, see Robert Sedgewick's *Quicksort* [Sed80]. Sedgewick's *Algorithms* [Sed11] discusses most of the sorting algorithms described here and pays special attention to efficient implementation. The optimized Mergesort version of Section 7.4 comes from Sedgewick.

While $\Omega(n \log n)$ is the theoretical lower bound in the worst case for sorting, many times the input is sufficiently well ordered that certain algorithms can take advantage of this fact to speed the sorting process. A simple example is Insertion Sort's best-case running time. Sorting algorithms whose running time is based on the amount of disorder in the input are called **adaptive**. For more information on adaptive sorting algorithms, see "A Survey of Adaptive Sorting Algorithms" by Estivill-Castro and Wood [ECW92].

7.11 Exercises

7.1 Using induction, prove that Insertion Sort will always produce a sorted array.

7.2 Write an Insertion Sort algorithm for integer key values. However, here's the catch: The input is a stack (*not* an array), and the only variables that your algorithm may use are a fixed number of integers and a fixed number of stacks. The algorithm should return a stack containing the records in sorted order (with the least value being at the top of the stack). Your algorithm should be $\Theta(n^2)$ in the worst case.

7.3 The Bubble Sort implementation has the following inner **for** loop:

```
for (int j=n-1; j>i; j--)
```

Consider the effect of replacing this with the following statement:

```
for (int j=n-1; j>0; j--)
```

Would the new implementation work correctly? Would the change affect the asymptotic complexity of the algorithm? How would the change affect the running time of the algorithm?

7.4 When implementing Insertion Sort, a binary search could be used to locate the position within the first $i - 1$ elements of the array into which element i should be inserted. How would this affect the number of comparisons required? How would using such a binary search affect the asymptotic running time for Insertion Sort?

7.5 Figure 7.5 shows the best-case number of swaps for Selection Sort as $\Theta(n)$. This is because the algorithm does not check to see if the ith record is already in the ith position; that is, it might perform unnecessary swaps.

  (a) Modify the algorithm so that it does not make unnecessary swaps.
  (b) What is your prediction regarding whether this modification actually improves the running time?
  (c) Write two programs to compare the actual running times of the original Selection Sort and the modified algorithm. Which one is actually faster?

7.6 Recall that a sorting algorithm is said to be stable if the original ordering for duplicate keys is preserved. Of the sorting algorithms Insertion Sort, Bubble Sort, Selection Sort, Shellsort, Mergesort, Quicksort, Heapsort, Binsort, and Radix Sort, which of these are stable, and which are not? For each one, describe either why it is or is not stable. If a minor change to the implementation would make it stable, describe the change.

7.7 Recall that a sorting algorithm is said to be stable if the original ordering for duplicate keys is preserved. We can make any algorithm stable if we alter the input keys so that (potentially) duplicate key values are made unique in a way that the first occurrence of the original duplicate value is less than the second occurrence, which in turn is less than the third, and so on. In the worst case, it is possible that all n input records have the same key value. Give an algorithm to modify the key values such that every modified key value is unique, the resulting key values give the same sort order as the original keys, the result is stable (in that the duplicate original key values remain in their original order), and the process of altering the keys is done in linear time using only a constant amount of additional space.

7.8 The discussion of Quicksort in Section 7.5 described using a stack instead of recursion to reduce the number of function calls made.

   (a) How deep can the stack get in the worst case?

   (b) Quicksort makes two recursive calls. The algorithm could be changed to make these two calls in a specific order. In what order should the two calls be made, and how does this affect how deep the stack can become?

7.9 Give a permutation for the values 0 through 7 that will cause Quicksort (as implemented in Section 7.5) to have its worst case behavior.

7.10 Assume **L** is an array, **length(L)** returns the number of records in the array, and **qsort(L, i, j)** sorts the records of **L** from **i** to **j** (leaving the records sorted in **L**) using the Quicksort algorithm. What is the average-case time complexity for each of the following code fragments?

   (a)
```
for (i=0; i<length(L); i++)
    qsort(L, 0, i);
```

   (b)
```
for (i=0; i<length(L); i++)
    qsort(L, 0, length(L)-1);
```

7.11 Modify Quicksort to find the smallest k values in an array of records. Your output should be the array modified so that the k smallest values are sorted in the first k positions of the array. Your algorithm should do the minimum amount of work necessary, that is, no more of the array than necessary should be sorted.

7.12 Modify Quicksort to sort a sequence of variable-length strings stored one after the other in a character array, with a second array (storing pointers to strings) used to index the strings. Your function should modify the index array so that the first pointer points to the beginning of the lowest valued string, and so on.

7.13 Graph $f_1(n) = n \log n$, $f_2(n) = n^{1.5}$, and $f_3(n) = n^2$ in the range $1 \le n \le 1000$ to visually compare their growth rates. Typically, the constant factor in the running-time expression for an implementation of Insertion Sort will be less than the constant factors for Shellsort or Quicksort. How many times greater can the constant factor be for Shellsort to be faster than Insertion Sort when $n = 1000$? How many times greater can the constant factor be for Quicksort to be faster than Insertion Sort when $n = 1000$?

7.14 Imagine that there exists an algorithm **SPLITk** that can split a list **L** of n elements into k sublists, each containing one or more elements, such that sublist i contains only elements whose values are less than all elements in sublist j for $i < j <= k$. If $n < k$, then $k - n$ sublists are empty, and the rest are of length 1. Assume that SPLITk has time complexity O(length of **L**). Furthermore, assume that the k lists can be concatenated again in constant time. Consider the following algorithm:

```
List SORTk(List L) {
  List sub[k]; // To hold the sublists
  if (L.length() > 1) {
    SPLITk(L, sub); // SPLITk places sublists into sub
    for (i=0; i<k; i++)
      sub[i] = SORTk(sub[i]); // Sort each sublist
    L = concatenation of k sublists in sub;
    return L;
  }
}
```

  (a) What is the worst-case asymptotic running time for SORTk? Why?
  (b) What is the average-case asymptotic running time of SORTk? Why?

7.15 Here is a variation on sorting. The problem is to sort a collection of n nuts and n bolts by size. It is assumed that for each bolt in the collection, there is a corresponding nut of the same size, but initially we do not know which nut goes with which bolt. The differences in size between two nuts or two bolts can be too small to see by eye, so you cannot rely on comparing the sizes of two nuts or two bolts directly. Instead, you can only compare the sizes of a nut and a bolt by attempting to screw one into the other (assume this comparison to be a constant time operation). This operation tells you that either the nut is bigger than the bolt, the bolt is bigger than the nut, or they are the same size. What is the minimum number of comparisons needed to sort the nuts and bolts in the worst case?

7.16 **(a)** Devise an algorithm to sort three numbers. It should make as few comparisons as possible. How many comparisons and swaps are required in the best, worst, and average cases?
  (b) Devise an algorithm to sort five numbers. It should make as few comparisons as possible. How many comparisons and swaps are required in the best, worst, and average cases?
  (c) Devise an algorithm to sort eight numbers. It should make as few comparisons as possible. How many comparisons and swaps are required in the best, worst, and average cases?

7.17 Devise an efficient algorithm to sort a set of numbers with values in the range 0 to 30,000. There are no duplicates. Keep memory requirements to a minimum.

7.18 Which of the following operations are best implemented by first sorting the list of numbers? For each operation, briefly describe an algorithm to implement it, and state the algorithm's asymptotic complexity.

   (a) Find the minimum value.
   (b) Find the maximum value.
   (c) Compute the arithmetic mean.
   (d) Find the median (i.e., the middle value).
   (e) Find the mode (i.e., the value that appears the most times).

7.19 Consider a recursive Mergesort implementation that calls Insertion Sort on sublists smaller than some threshold. If there are n calls to Mergesort, how many calls will there be to Insertion Sort? Why?

7.20 Implement Mergesort for the case where the input is a linked list.

7.21 Counting sort (assuming the input key values are integers in the range 0 to $m - 1$) works by counting the number of records with each key value in the first pass, and then uses this information to place the records in order in a second pass. Write an implementation of counting sort (see the implementation of radix sort for some ideas). What can we say about the relative values of m and n for this to be effective? If $m < n$, what is the running time of this algorithm?

7.22 Use an argument similar to that given in Section 7.9 to prove that $\log n$ is a worst-case lower bound for the problem of searching for a given value in a sorted array containing n elements.

7.12 Projects

7.1 One possible improvement for Bubble Sort would be to add a flag variable and a test that determines if an exchange was made during the current iteration. If no exchange was made, then the list is sorted and so the algorithm can stop early. This makes the best case performance become $O(n)$ (because if the list is already sorted, then no iterations will take place on the first pass, and the sort will stop right there).

Modify the Bubble Sort implementation to add this flag and test. Compare the modified implementation on a range of inputs to determine if it does or does not improve performance in practice.

7.2 Double Insertion Sort is a variation on Insertion Sort that works from the middle of the array out. At each iteration, some middle portion of the array is sorted. On the next iteration, take the two adjacent elements to the sorted portion of the array. If they are out of order with respect to each other, than swap them. Now, push the left element toward the right in the array so long as it is greater than the element to its right. And push the right element toward the left in the array so long as it is less than the element to its left.

The algorithm begins by processing the middle two elements of the array if the array is even. If the array is odd, then skip processing the middle item and begin with processing the elements to its immediate left and right.

First, explain what the cost of Double Insertion Sort will be in comparison to standard Insertion sort, and why. (Note that the two elements being processed in the current iteration, once initially swapped to be sorted with with respect to each other, cannot cross as they are pushed into sorted position.) Then, implement Double Insertion Sort, being careful to properly handle both when the array is odd and when it is even. Compare its running time in practice against standard Insertion Sort. Finally, explain how this speedup might affect the threshold level and running time for a Quicksort implementation.

7.3 Perform a study of Shellsort, using different increments. Compare the version shown in Section 7.3, where each increment is half the previous one, with others. In particular, try implementing "division by 3" where the increments on a list of length n will be $n/3$, $n/9$, etc. Do other increment schemes work as well?

7.4 The implementation for Mergesort given in Section 7.4 takes an array as input and sorts that array. At the beginning of Section 7.4 there is a simple pseudocode implementation for sorting a linked list using Mergesort. Implement both a linked list-based version of Mergesort and the array-based version of Mergesort, and compare their running times.

7.5 Starting with the **C++** code for Quicksort given in this chapter, write a series of Quicksort implementations to test the following optimizations on a wide range of input data sizes. Try these optimizations in various combinations to try and develop the fastest possible Quicksort implementation that you can.

   (a) Look at more values when selecting a pivot.

   (b) Do not make a recursive call to **qsort** when the list size falls below a given threshold, and use Insertion Sort to complete the sorting process. Test various values for the threshold size.

   (c) Eliminate recursion by using a stack and inline functions.

7.6 It has been proposed that Heapsort can be optimized by altering the heap's siftdown function. Call the value being sifted down X. Siftdown does two comparisons per level: First the children of X are compared, then the winner is compared to X. If X is too small, it is swapped with its larger child and the process repeated. The proposed optimization dispenses with the test against X. Instead, the larger child automatically replaces X, until X reaches the bottom level of the heap. At this point, X might be too large to remain in that position. This is corrected by repeatedly comparing X with its parent and swapping as necessary to "bubble" it up to its proper level. The claim is that this process will save a number of comparisons because most nodes when sifted down end up near the bottom of the tree anyway. Implement both versions of siftdown, and do an empirical study to compare their running times.

7.7 Radix Sort is typically implemented to support only a radix that is a power of two. This allows for a direct conversion from the radix to some number of bits in an integer key value. For example, if the radix is 16, then a 32-bit key will be processed in 8 steps of 4 bits each. This can lead to a more efficient implementation because bit shifting can replace the division operations shown in the implementation of Section 7.7. Re-implement the Radix Sort code given in Section 7.7 to use bit shifting in place of division. Compare the running time of the old and new Radix Sort implementations.

7.8 Write your own collection of sorting programs to implement the algorithms described in this chapter, and compare their running times. Be sure to implement optimized versions, trying to make each program as fast as possible. Do you get the same relative timings as shown in Figure 7.20? If not, why do you think this happened? How do your results compare with those of your classmates? What does this say about the difficulty of doing empirical timing studies?

8

File Processing and External Sorting

Earlier chapters presented basic data structures and algorithms that operate on data stored in main memory. Some applications require that large amounts of information be stored and processed — so much information that it cannot all fit into main memory. In that case, the information must reside on disk and be brought into main memory selectively for processing.

You probably already realize that main memory access is much faster than access to data stored on disk or other storage devices. The relative difference in access times is so great that efficient disk-based programs require a different approach to algorithm design than most programmers are used to. As a result, many programmers do a poor job when it comes to file processing applications.

This chapter presents the fundamental issues relating to the design of algorithms and data structures for disk-based applications.[1] We begin with a description of the significant differences between primary memory and secondary storage. Section 8.2 discusses the physical aspects of disk drives. Section 8.3 presents basic methods for managing buffer pools. Section 8.4 discusses the C++ model for random access to data stored on disk. Section 8.5 discusses the basic principles for sorting collections of records too large to fit in main memory.

8.1 Primary versus Secondary Storage

Computer storage devices are typically classified into **primary** or **main** memory and **secondary** or **peripheral** storage. Primary memory usually refers to **Random**

---

[1]Computer technology changes rapidly. I provide examples of disk drive specifications and other hardware performance numbers that are reasonably up to date as of the time when the book was written. When you read it, the numbers might seem out of date. However, the basic principles do not change. The approximate ratios for time, space, and cost between memory and disk have remained surprisingly steady for over 20 years.

Medium	1996	1997	2000	2004	2006	2008	2011
RAM	$45.00	7.00	1.500	0.3500	0.1500	0.0339	0.0138
Disk	0.25	0.10	0.010	0.0010	0.0005	0.0001	0.0001
USB drive	–	–	–	0.1000	0.0900	0.0029	0.0018
Floppy	0.50	0.36	0.250	0.2500	–	–	–
Tape	0.03	0.01	0.001	0.0003	–	–	–
Solid State	–	–	–	–	–	–	0.0021

Figure 8.1 Price comparison table for some writable electronic data storage media in common use. Prices are in US Dollars/MB.

Access Memory (RAM), while secondary storage refers to devices such as hard disk drives, solid state drives, removable "USB" drives, CDs, and DVDs. Primary memory also includes registers, cache, and video memories, but we will ignore them for this discussion because their existence does not affect the principal differences between primary and secondary memory.

Along with a faster CPU, every new model of computer seems to come with more main memory. As memory size continues to increase, is it possible that relatively slow disk storage will be unnecessary? Probably not, because the desire to store and process larger files grows at least as fast as main memory size. Prices for both main memory and peripheral storage devices have dropped dramatically in recent years, as demonstrated by Figure 8.1. However, the cost per unit of disk drive storage is about two orders of magnitude less than RAM and has been for many years.

There is now a wide range of removable media available for transferring data or storing data offline in relative safety. These include floppy disks (now largely obsolete), writable CDs and DVDs, "flash" drives, and magnetic tape. Optical storage such as CDs and DVDs costs roughly half the price of hard disk drive space per megabyte, and have become practical for use as backup storage within the past few years. Tape used to be much cheaper than other media, and was the preferred means of backup, but are not so popular now as other media have decreased in price. "Flash" drives cost the most per megabyte, but due to their storage capacity and flexibility, quickly replaced floppy disks as the primary storage device for transferring data between computer when direct network transfer is not available.

Secondary storage devices have at least two other advantages over RAM memory. Perhaps most importantly, disk, "flash," and optical media are **persistent**, meaning that they are not erased from the media when the power is turned off. In contrast, RAM used for main memory is usually **volatile** — all information is lost with the power. A second advantage is that CDs and "USB" drives can easily be transferred between computers. This provides a convenient way to take information from one computer to another.

In exchange for reduced storage costs, persistence, and portability, secondary storage devices pay a penalty in terms of increased access time. While not all accesses to disk take the same amount of time (more on this later), the typical time required to access a byte of storage from a disk drive in 2011 is around 9 ms (i.e., 9 *thousandths* of a second). This might not seem slow, but compared to the time required to access a byte from main memory, this is fantastically slow. Typical access time from standard personal computer RAM in 2011 is about 5-10 nanoseconds (i.e., 5-10 *billionths* of a second). Thus, the time to access a byte of data from a disk drive is about six orders of magnitude greater than that required to access a byte from main memory. While disk drive and RAM access times are both decreasing, they have done so at roughly the same rate. The relative speeds have remained the same for over several decades, in that the difference in access time between RAM and a disk drive has remained in the range between a factor of 100,000 and 1,000,000.

To gain some intuition for the significance of this speed difference, consider the time that it might take for you to look up the entry for disk drives in the index of this book, and then turn to the appropriate page. Call this your "primary memory" access time. If it takes you about 20 seconds to perform this access, then an access taking 500,000 times longer would require months.

It is interesting to note that while processing speeds have increased dramatically, and hardware prices have dropped dramatically, disk and memory access times have improved by less than an order of magnitude over the past 15 years. However, the situation is really much better than that modest speedup would suggest. During the same time period, the size of both disk and main memory has increased by over three orders of magnitude. Thus, the access times have actually decreased in the face of a massive increase in the density of these storage devices.

Due to the relatively slow access time for data on disk as compared to main memory, great care is required to create efficient applications that process disk-based information. The million-to-one ratio of disk access time versus main memory access time makes the following rule of paramount importance when designing disk-based applications:

Minimize the number of disk accesses!

There are generally two approaches to minimizing disk accesses. The first is to arrange information so that if you do access data from secondary memory, you will get what you need in as few accesses as possible, and preferably on the first access. **File structure** is the term used for a data structure that organizes data stored in secondary memory. File structures should be organized so as to minimize the required number of disk accesses. The other way to minimize disk accesses is to save information previously retrieved (or retrieve additional data with each access at little additional cost) that can be used to minimize the need for future accesses.

This requires the ability to guess accurately what information will be needed later and store it in primary memory now. This is referred to as **caching**.

8.2 Disk Drives

A **C++** programmer views a random access file stored on disk as a contiguous series of bytes, with those bytes possibly combining to form data records. This is called the **logical** file. The **physical** file actually stored on disk is usually not a contiguous series of bytes. It could well be in pieces spread all over the disk. The **file manager**, a part of the operating system, is responsible for taking requests for data from a logical file and mapping those requests to the physical location of the data on disk. Likewise, when writing to a particular logical byte position with respect to the beginning of the file, this position must be converted by the file manager into the corresponding physical location on the disk. To gain some appreciation for the the approximate time costs for these operations, you need to understand the physical structure and basic workings of a disk drive.

Disk drives are often referred to as **direct access** storage devices. This means that it takes roughly equal time to access any record in the file. This is in contrast to **sequential access** storage devices such as tape drives, which require the tape reader to process data from the beginning of the tape until the desired position has been reached. As you will see, the disk drive is only approximately direct access: At any given time, some records are more quickly accessible than others.

8.2.1 Disk Drive Architecture

A hard disk drive is composed of one or more round **platters**, stacked one on top of another and attached to a central **spindle**. Platters spin continuously at a constant rate. Each usable surface of each platter is assigned a **read/write head** or **I/O head** through which data are read or written, somewhat like the arrangement of a phonograph player's arm "reading" sound from a phonograph record. Unlike a phonograph needle, the disk read/write head does not actually touch the surface of a hard disk. Instead, it remains slightly above the surface, and any contact during normal operation would damage the disk. This distance is very small, much smaller than the height of a dust particle. It can be likened to a 5000-kilometer airplane trip across the United States, with the plane flying at a height of one meter!

A hard disk drive typically has several platters and several read/write heads, as shown in Figure 8.2(a). Each head is attached to an **arm**, which connects to the **boom**.[2] The boom moves all of the heads in or out together. When the heads are in some position over the platters, there are data on each platter directly accessible

---

[2]This arrangement, while typical, is not necessarily true for all disk drives. Nearly everything said here about the physical arrangement of disk drives represents a typical engineering compromise, not a fundamental design principle. There are many ways to design disk drives, and the engineering

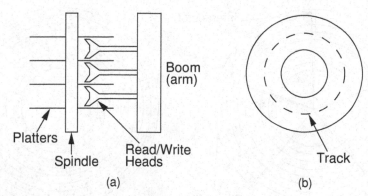

Platters

Spindle

Boom (arm)

Read/Write Heads

Track

(a)

(b)

Figure 8.2 (a) A typical disk drive arranged as a stack of platters. (b) One track on a disk drive platter.

to each head. The data on a single platter that are accessible to any one position of the head for that platter are collectively called a **track**, that is, all data on a platter that are a fixed distance from the spindle, as shown in Figure 8.2(b). The collection of all tracks that are a fixed distance from the spindle is called a **cylinder**. Thus, a cylinder is all of the data that can be read when the arms are in a particular position.

Each track is subdivided into **sectors**. Between each sector there are **inter-sector gaps** in which no data are stored. These gaps allow the read head to recognize the end of a sector. Note that each sector contains the same amount of data. Because the outer tracks have greater length, they contain fewer bits per inch than do the inner tracks. Thus, about half of the potential storage space is wasted, because only the innermost tracks are stored at the highest possible data density. This arrangement is illustrated by Figure 8.3a. Disk drives today actually group tracks into "zones" such that the tracks in the innermost zone adjust their data density going out to maintain the same radial data density, then the tracks of the next zone reset the data density to make better use of their storage ability, and so on. This arrangement is shown in Figure 8.3b.

In contrast to the physical layout of a hard disk, a CD-ROM consists of a single spiral track. Bits of information along the track are equally spaced, so the information density is the same at both the outer and inner portions of the track. To keep the information flow at a constant rate along the spiral, the drive must speed up the rate of disk spin as the I/O head moves toward the center of the disk. This makes for a more complicated and slower mechanism.

Three separate steps take place when reading a particular byte or series of bytes of data from a hard disk. First, the I/O head moves so that it is positioned over the track containing the data. This movement is called a **seek**. Second, the sector containing the data rotates to come under the head. When in use the disk is always

---

compromises change over time. In addition, most of the description given here for disk drives is a simplified version of the reality. But this is a useful working model to understand what is going on.

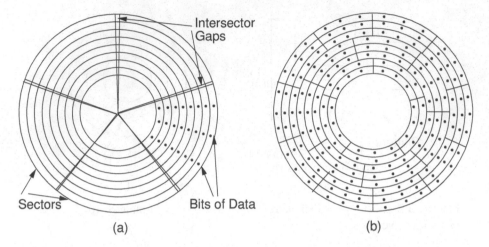

Figure 8.3 The organization of a disk platter. Dots indicate density of information. (a) Nominal arrangement of tracks showing decreasing data density when moving outward from the center of the disk. (b) A "zoned" arrangement with the sector size and density periodically reset in tracks further away from the center.

spinning. At the time of this writing, typical disk spin rates are 7200 rotations per minute (rpm). The time spent waiting for the desired sector to come under the I/O head is called **rotational delay** or **rotational latency**. The third step is the actual transfer (i.e., reading or writing) of data. It takes relatively little time to read information once the first byte is positioned under the I/O head, simply the amount of time required for it all to move under the head. In fact, disk drives are designed not to read one byte of data, but rather to read an entire sector of data at each request. Thus, a sector is the minimum amount of data that can be read or written at one time.

In general, it is desirable to keep all sectors for a file together on as few tracks as possible. This desire stems from two assumptions:

1. Seek time is slow (it is typically the most expensive part of an I/O operation), and
2. If one sector of the file is read, the next sector will probably soon be read.

Assumption (2) is called **locality of reference**, a concept that comes up frequently in computer applications.

Contiguous sectors are often grouped to form a **cluster**. A cluster is the smallest unit of allocation for a file, so all files are a multiple of the cluster size. The cluster size is determined by the operating system. The file manager keeps track of which clusters make up each file.

In Microsoft Windows systems, there is a designated portion of the disk called the **File Allocation Table**, which stores information about which sectors belong to which file. In contrast, UNIX does not use clusters. The smallest unit of file allocation and the smallest unit that can be read/written is a sector, which in UNIX terminology is called a **block**. UNIX maintains information about file organization in certain disk blocks called **i-nodes**.

A group of physically contiguous clusters from the same file is called an **extent**. Ideally, all clusters making up a file will be contiguous on the disk (i.e., the file will consist of one extent), so as to minimize seek time required to access different portions of the file. If the disk is nearly full when a file is created, there might not be an extent available that is large enough to hold the new file. Furthermore, if a file grows, there might not be free space physically adjacent. Thus, a file might consist of several extents widely spaced on the disk. The fuller the disk, and the more that files on the disk change, the worse this file fragmentation (and the resulting seek time) becomes. File fragmentation leads to a noticeable degradation in performance as additional seeks are required to access data.

Another type of problem arises when the file's logical record size does not match the sector size. If the sector size is not a multiple of the record size (or vice versa), records will not fit evenly within a sector. For example, a sector might be 2048 bytes long, and a logical record 100 bytes. This leaves room to store 20 records with 48 bytes left over. Either the extra space is wasted, or else records are allowed to cross sector boundaries. If a record crosses a sector boundary, two disk accesses might be required to read it. If the space is left empty instead, such wasted space is called **internal fragmentation**.

A second example of internal fragmentation occurs at cluster boundaries. Files whose size is not an even multiple of the cluster size must waste some space at the end of the last cluster. The worst case will occur when file size modulo cluster size is one (for example, a file of 4097 bytes and a cluster of 4096 bytes). Thus, cluster size is a tradeoff between large files processed sequentially (where a large cluster size is desirable to minimize seeks) and small files (where small clusters are desirable to minimize wasted storage).

Every disk drive organization requires that some disk space be used to organize the sectors, clusters, and so forth. The layout of sectors within a track is illustrated by Figure 8.4. Typical information that must be stored on the disk itself includes the File Allocation Table, **sector headers** that contain address marks and information about the condition (whether usable or not) for each sector, and gaps between sectors. The sector header also contains error detection codes to help verify that the data have not been corrupted. This is why most disk drives have a "nominal" size that is greater than the actual amount of user data that can be stored on the drive. The difference is the amount of space required to organize the information on the disk. Even more space will be lost due to fragmentation.

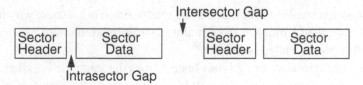

Figure 8.4 An illustration of sector gaps within a track. Each sector begins with a sector header containing the sector address and an error detection code for the contents of that sector. The sector header is followed by a small intra-sector gap, followed in turn by the sector data. Each sector is separated from the next sector by a larger inter-sector gap.

8.2.2 Disk Access Costs

When a seek is required, it is usually the primary cost when accessing information on disk. This assumes of course that a seek is necessary. When reading a file in sequential order (if the sectors comprising the file are contiguous on disk), little seeking is necessary. However, when accessing a random disk sector, seek time becomes the dominant cost for the data access. While the actual seek time is highly variable, depending on the distance between the track where the I/O head currently is and the track where the head is moving to, we will consider only two numbers. One is the track-to-track cost, or the minimum time necessary to move from a track to an adjacent track. This is appropriate when you want to analyze access times for files that are well placed on the disk. The second number is the average seek time for a random access. These two numbers are often provided by disk manufacturers. A typical example is the Western Digital Caviar serial ATA drive. The manufacturer's specifications indicate that the track-to-track time is 2.0 ms and the average seek time is 9.0 ms. In 2008 a typical drive in this line might be 120GB in size. In 2011, that same line of drives had sizes of up to 2 or 3TB. In both years, the advertised track-to-track and average seek times were identical.

For many years, typical rotation speed for disk drives was 3600 rpm, or one rotation every 16.7 ms. Most disk drives in 2011 had a rotation speed of 7200 rpm, or 8.3 ms per rotation. When reading a sector at random, you can expect that the disk will need to rotate halfway around to bring the desired sector under the I/O head, or 4.2 ms for a 7200-rpm disk drive.

Once under the I/O head, a sector of data can be transferred as fast as that sector rotates under the head. If an entire track is to be read, then it will require one rotation (8.3 ms at 7200 rpm) to move the full track under the head. If only part of the track is to be read, then proportionately less time will be required. For example, if there are 16,000 sectors on the track and one sector is to be read, this will require a trivial amount of time (1/16,000 of a rotation).

Example 8.1 Assume that an older disk drive has a total (nominal) capacity of 16.8GB spread among 10 platters, yielding 1.68GB/platter. Each platter contains 13,085 tracks and each track contains (after formatting) 256 sectors of 512 bytes/sector. Track-to-track seek time is 2.2 ms and average seek time for random access is 9.5 ms. Assume the operating system maintains a cluster size of 8 sectors per cluster (4KB), yielding 32 clusters per track. The disk rotation rate is 5400 rpm (11.1 ms per rotation). Based on this information we can estimate the cost for various file processing operations.

How much time is required to read the track? On average, it will require half a rotation to bring the first sector of the track under the I/O head, and then one complete rotation to read the track.

How long will it take to read a file of 1MB divided into 2048 sector-sized (512 byte) records? This file will be stored in 256 clusters, because each cluster holds 8 sectors. The answer to the question depends largely on how the file is stored on the disk, that is, whether it is all together or broken into multiple extents. We will calculate both cases to see how much difference this makes.

If the file is stored so as to fill all of the sectors of eight adjacent tracks, then the cost to read the first sector will be the time to seek to the first track (assuming this requires a random seek), then a wait for the initial rotational delay, and then the time to read (which is the same as the time to rotate the disk again). This requires

$$9.5 + 11.1 \times 1.5 = 26.2 \text{ ms}.$$

At this point, because we assume that the next seven tracks require only a track-to-track seek because they are adjacent. Each requires

$$2.2 + 11.1 \times 1.5 = 18.9 \text{ ms}.$$

The total time required is therefore

$$26.2\text{ms} + 7 \times 18.9\text{ms} = 158.5\text{ms}.$$

If the file's clusters are spread randomly across the disk, then we must perform a seek for each cluster, followed by the time for rotational delay. Once the first sector of the cluster comes under the I/O head, very little time is needed to read the cluster because only 8/256 of the track needs to rotate under the head, for a total time of about 5.9 ms for latency and read time. Thus, the total time required is about

$$256(9.5 + 5.9) \approx 3942\text{ms}$$

or close to 4 seconds. This is much longer than the time required when the file is all together on disk!

This example illustrates why it is important to keep disk files from becoming fragmented, and why so-called "disk defragmenters" can speed up file processing time. File fragmentation happens most commonly when the disk is nearly full and the file manager must search for free space whenever a file is created or changed.

8.3   Buffers and Buffer Pools

Given the specifications of the disk drive from Example 8.1, we find that it takes about $9.5 + 11.1 \times 1.5 = 26.2$ ms to read one track of data on average. It takes about $9.5 + 11.1/2 + (1/256) \times 11.1 = 15.1$ ms on average to read a single sector of data. This is a good savings (slightly over half the time), but less than 1% of the data on the track are read. If we want to read only a single byte, it would save us effectively no time over that required to read an entire sector. For this reason, nearly all disk drives automatically read or write an entire sector's worth of information whenever the disk is accessed, even when only one byte of information is requested.

Once a sector is read, its information is stored in main memory. This is known as **buffering** or **caching** the information. If the next disk request is to that same sector, then it is not necessary to read from disk again because the information is already stored in main memory. Buffering is an example of one method for minimizing disk accesses mentioned at the beginning of the chapter: Bring off additional information from disk to satisfy future requests. If information from files were accessed at random, then the chance that two consecutive disk requests are to the same sector would be low. However, in practice most disk requests are close to the location (in the logical file at least) of the previous request. This means that the probability of the next request "hitting the cache" is much higher than chance would indicate.

This principle explains one reason why average access times for new disk drives are lower than in the past. Not only is the hardware faster, but information is also now stored using better algorithms and larger caches that minimize the number of times information needs to be fetched from disk. This same concept is also used to store parts of programs in faster memory within the CPU, using the CPU cache that is prevalent in modern microprocessors.

Sector-level buffering is normally provided by the operating system and is often built directly into the disk drive controller hardware. Most operating systems maintain at least two buffers, one for input and one for output. Consider what would happen if there were only one buffer during a byte-by-byte copy operation. The sector containing the first byte would be read into the I/O buffer. The output operation would need to destroy the contents of the single I/O buffer to write this byte. Then the buffer would need to be filled again from disk for the second byte, only to be destroyed during output. The simple solution to this problem is to keep one buffer for input, and a second for output.

Most disk drive controllers operate independently from the CPU once an I/O request is received. This is useful because the CPU can typically execute millions of instructions during the time required for a single I/O operation. A technique that takes maximum advantage of this micro-parallelism is **double buffering**. Imagine that a file is being processed sequentially. While the first sector is being read, the CPU cannot process that information and so must wait or find something else to do in the meantime. Once the first sector is read, the CPU can start processing while the disk drive (in parallel) begins reading the second sector. If the time required for the CPU to process a sector is approximately the same as the time required by the disk controller to read a sector, it might be possible to keep the CPU continuously fed with data from the file. The same concept can also be applied to output, writing one sector to disk while the CPU is writing to a second output buffer in memory. Thus, in computers that support double buffering, it pays to have at least two input buffers and two output buffers available.

Caching information in memory is such a good idea that it is usually extended to multiple buffers. The operating system or an application program might store many buffers of information taken from some **backing storage** such as a disk file. This process of using buffers as an intermediary between a user and a disk file is called **buffering** the file. The information stored in a buffer is often called a **page**, and the collection of buffers is called a **buffer pool**. The goal of the buffer pool is to increase the amount of information stored in memory in hopes of increasing the likelihood that new information requests can be satisfied from the buffer pool rather than requiring new information to be read from disk.

As long as there is an unused buffer available in the buffer pool, new information can be read in from disk on demand. When an application continues to read new information from disk, eventually all of the buffers in the buffer pool will become full. Once this happens, some decision must be made about what information in the buffer pool will be sacrificed to make room for newly requested information.

When replacing information contained in the buffer pool, the goal is to select a buffer that has "unnecessary" information, that is, the information least likely to be requested again. Because the buffer pool cannot know for certain what the pattern of future requests will look like, a decision based on some **heuristic**, or best guess, must be used. There are several approaches to making this decision.

One heuristic is "first-in, first-out" (FIFO). This scheme simply orders the buffers in a queue. The buffer at the front of the queue is used next to store new information and then placed at the end of the queue. In this way, the buffer to be replaced is the one that has held its information the longest, in hopes that this information is no longer needed. This is a reasonable assumption when processing moves along the file at some steady pace in roughly sequential order. However, many programs work with certain key pieces of information over and over again, and the importance of information has little to do with how long ago the information was first accessed. Typically it is more important to know how many times the information has been accessed, or how recently the information was last accessed.

Another approach is called "least frequently used" (LFU). LFU tracks the number of accesses to each buffer in the buffer pool. When a buffer must be reused, the buffer that has been accessed the fewest number of times is considered to contain the "least important" information, and so it is used next. LFU, while it seems intuitively reasonable, has many drawbacks. First, it is necessary to store and update access counts for each buffer. Second, what was referenced many times in the past might now be irrelevant. Thus, some time mechanism where counts "expire" is often desirable. This also avoids the problem of buffers that slowly build up big counts because they get used just often enough to avoid being replaced. An alternative is to maintain counts for all sectors ever read, not just the sectors currently in the buffer pool. This avoids immediately replacing the buffer just read, which has not yet had time to build a high access count.

The third approach is called "least recently used" (LRU). LRU simply keeps the buffers in a list. Whenever information in a buffer is accessed, this buffer is brought to the front of the list. When new information must be read, the buffer at the back of the list (the one least recently used) is taken and its "old" information is either discarded or written to disk, as appropriate. This is an easily implemented approximation to LFU and is often the method of choice for managing buffer pools unless special knowledge about information access patterns for an application suggests a special-purpose buffer management scheme.

The main purpose of a buffer pool is to minimize disk I/O. When the contents of a block are modified, we could write the updated information to disk immediately. But what if the block is changed again? If we write the block's contents after every change, that might be a lot of disk write operations that can be avoided. It is more efficient to wait until either the file is to be closed, or the contents of the buffer containing that block is to be flushed from the buffer pool.

When a buffer's contents are to be replaced in the buffer pool, we only want to write the contents to disk if it is necessary. That would be necessary only if the contents have changed since the block was read in originally from the file. The way to insure that the block is written when necessary, but only when necessary, is to maintain a Boolean variable with the buffer (often referred to as the **dirty bit**) that is turned on when the buffer's contents are modified by the client. At the time when the block is flushed from the buffer pool, it is written to disk if and only if the dirty bit has been turned on.

Modern operating systems support **virtual memory**. Virtual memory is a technique that allows the programmer to write programs as though there is more of the faster main memory (such as RAM) than actually exists. Virtual memory makes use of a buffer pool to store data read from blocks on slower, secondary memory (such as on the disk drive). The disk stores the complete contents of the virtual memory. Blocks are read into main memory as demanded by memory accesses. Naturally, programs using virtual memory techniques are slower than programs whose data are stored completely in main memory. The advantage is reduced programmer effort because a good virtual memory system provides the appearance of larger main memory without modifying the program.

Example 8.2 Consider a virtual memory whose size is ten sectors, and which has a buffer pool of five buffers (each one sector in size) associated with it. We will use a LRU replacement scheme. The following series of memory requests occurs.

9017668135171

After the first five requests, the buffer pool will store the sectors in the order 6, 7, 1, 0, 9. Because Sector 6 is already at the front, the next request can be answered without reading new data from disk or reordering the buffers. The request to Sector 8 requires emptying the contents of the least recently used buffer, which contains Sector 9. The request to Sector 1 brings the buffer holding Sector 1's contents back to the front. Processing the remaining requests results in the buffer pool as shown in Figure 8.5.

Example 8.3 Figure 8.5 illustrates a buffer pool of five blocks mediating a virtual memory of ten blocks. At any given moment, up to five sectors of information can be in main memory. Assume that Sectors 1, 7, 5, 3, and 8 are currently in the buffer pool, stored in this order, and that we use the LRU buffer replacement strategy. If a request for Sector 9 is then received, then one sector currently in the buffer pool must be replaced. Because the buffer containing Sector 8 is the least recently used buffer, its contents will be copied back to disk at Sector 8. The contents of Sector 9 are then copied into this buffer, and it is moved to the front of the buffer pool (leaving the buffer containing Sector 3 as the new least-recently used buffer). If the next memory request were to Sector 5, no data would need to be read from disk. Instead, the buffer already containing Sector 5 would be moved to the front of the buffer pool.

When implementing buffer pools, there are two basic approaches that can be taken regarding the transfer of information between the user of the buffer pool and the buffer pool class itself. The first approach is to pass "messages" between the two. This approach is illustrated by the following abstract class:

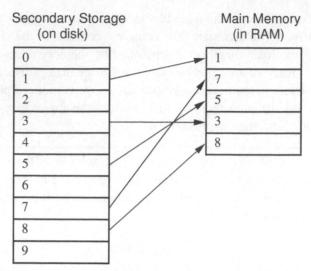

Figure 8.5 An illustration of virtual memory. The complete collection of information resides in the slower, secondary storage (on disk). Those sectors recently accessed are held in the fast main memory (in RAM). In this example, copies of Sectors 1, 7, 5, 3, and 8 from secondary storage are currently stored in the main memory. If a memory access to Sector 9 is received, one of the sectors currently in main memory must be replaced.

```
// ADT for buffer pools using the message-passing style
class BufferPool {
public:
  // Copy "sz" bytes from "space" to position "pos" in the
  //    buffered storage.
  virtual void insert(void* space, int sz, int pos) = 0;

  // Copy "sz" bytes from position "pos" of the buffered
  //    storage to "space".
  virtual void getbytes(void* space, int sz, int pos) = 0;
};
```

This simple class provides an interface with two member functions, **insert** and **getbytes**. The information is passed between the buffer pool user and the buffer pool through the **space** parameter. This is storage space, provided by the bufferpool client and at least **sz** bytes long, which the buffer pool can take information from (the **insert** function) or put information into (the **getbytes** function). Parameter **pos** indicates where the information will be placed in the buffer pool's logical storage space. Physically, it will actually be copied to the appropriate byte position in some buffer in the buffer pool. This ADT is similar to the **read** and **write** methods of the **RandomAccessFile** class discussed in Section 8.4.

Example 8.4 Assume each sector of the disk file (and thus each block in the buffer pool) stores 1024 bytes. Assume that the buffer pool is in the state shown in Figure 8.5. If the next request is to copy 40 bytes beginning at position 6000 of the file, these bytes should be placed into Sector 5 (whose bytes go from position 5120 to position 6143). Because Sector 5 is currently in the buffer pool, we simply copy the 40 bytes contained in **space** to byte positions 880-919. The buffer containing Sector 5 is then moved to the buffer pool ahead of the buffer containing Sector 1.

An alternative interface is to have the buffer pool provide to the user a direct pointer to a buffer that contains the requested information. Such an interface might look as follows:

```
// ADT for buffer pools using the buffer-passing style
class BufferPool {
public:
  // Return pointer to the requested block
  virtual void* getblock(int block) = 0;

  // Set the dirty bit for the buffer holding "block"
  virtual void dirtyblock(int block) = 0;

  // Tell the size of a buffer
  virtual int blocksize() = 0;
};
```

In this approach, the buffer pool user is made aware that the storage space is divided into blocks of a given size, where each block is the size of a buffer. The user requests specific blocks from the buffer pool, with a pointer to the buffer holding the requested block being returned to the user. The user might then read from or write to this space. If the user writes to the space, the buffer pool must be informed of this fact. The reason is that, when a given block is to be removed from the buffer pool, the contents of that block must be written to the backing storage if it has been modified. If the block has not been modified, then it is unnecessary to write it out.

Example 8.5 We wish to write 40 bytes beginning at logical position 6000 in the file. Assume that the buffer pool is in the state shown in Figure 8.5. Using the second ADT, the client would need to know that blocks (buffers) are of size 1024, and therefore would request access to Sector 5. A pointer to the buffer containing Sector 5 would be returned by the call to **getblock**. The client would then copy 40 bytes to positions 880-919 of the buffer, and call **dirtyblock** to warn the buffer pool that the contents of this block have been modified.

A variation on this approach is to have the **getblock** function take another parameter to indicate the "mode" of use for the information. If the mode is READ then the buffer pool assumes that no changes will be made to the buffer's contents (and so no write operation need be done when the buffer is reused to store another block). If the mode is WRITE then the buffer pool assumes that the client will not look at the contents of the buffer and so no read from the file is necessary. If the mode is READ AND WRITE then the buffer pool would read the existing contents of the block in from disk, and write the contents of the buffer to disk when the buffer is to be reused. Using the "mode" approach, the **dirtyblock** method is avoided.

One problem with the buffer-passing ADT is the risk of **stale pointers**. When the buffer pool user is given a pointer to some buffer space at time **T1**, that pointer does indeed refer to the desired data at that time. As further requests are made to the buffer pool, it is possible that the data in any given buffer will be removed and replaced with new data. If the buffer pool user at a later time **T2** then refers to the data referred to by the pointer given at time **T1**, it is possible that the data are no longer valid because the buffer contents have been replaced in the meantime. Thus the pointer into the buffer pool's memory has become "stale." To guarantee that a pointer is not stale, it should not be used if intervening requests to the buffer pool have taken place.

We can solve this problem by introducing the concept of a user (or possibly multiple users) gaining access to a buffer, and then releasing the buffer when done. We will add method **acquireBuffer** and **releaseBuffer** for this purpose. Method **acquireBuffer** takes a block ID as input and returns a pointer to the buffer that will be used to store this block. The buffer pool will keep a count of the number of requests currently active for this block. Method **releaseBuffer** will reduce the count of active users for the associated block. Buffers associated with active blocks will not be eligible for flushing from the buffer pool. This will lead to a problem if the client neglects to release active blocks when they are no longer needed. There would also be a problem if there were more total active blocks than buffers in the buffer pool. However, the buffer pool should always be initialized to include more buffers than should ever be active at one time.

An additional problem with both ADTs presented so far comes when the user intends to completely overwrite the contents of a block, and does not need to read in the old contents already on disk. However, the buffer pool cannot in general know whether the user wishes to use the old contents or not. This is especially true with the message-passing approach where a given message might overwrite only part of the block. In this case, the block will be read into memory even when not needed, and then its contents will be overwritten.

This inefficiency can be avoided (at least in the buffer-passing version) by separating the assignment of blocks to buffers from actually reading in data for the block. In particular, the following revised buffer-passing ADT does not actually read data in the **acquireBuffer** method. Users who wish to see the old contents must then issue a **readBlock** request to read the data from disk into the buffer, and then a **getDataPointer** request to gain direct access to the buffer's data contents.

```
// A single buffer in the buffer pool
class Buffer {
public:
  // Read the associated block from disk (if necessary) and
  // return a pointer to the data
  void *readBlock() = 0;

  // Return a pointer to the buffer's data array
  // (without reading from disk)
  void *getDataPointer() = 0;

  // Flag the buffer's contents as having changed, so that
  // flushing the block will write it back to disk
  void markDirty() = 0;

  // Release the block's access to this buffer. Further
  // accesses to this buffer are illegal.
  void releaseBuffer() = 0;
}

// The bufferpool
class BufferPool {
public:
  // Constructor: The bufferpool has "numbuff" buffers that
  // each contain "buffsize" bytes of data.
  BufferPool(int numbuff, int buffsize) = 0;

  // Relate a block to a buffer, returning a pointer to a
  // buffer object
  Buffer *acquireBuffer(int block) = 0;
}
```

Again, a mode parameter could be added to the **acquireBuffer** method, eliminating the need for the **readBlock** and **markDirty** methods.

Clearly, the buffer-passing approach places more obligations on the user of the buffer pool. These obligations include knowing the size of a block, not corrupting the buffer pool's storage space, and informing the buffer pool both when a block has been modified and when it is no longer needed. So many obligations make this approach prone to error. An advantage is that there is no need to do an extra copy step when getting information from the user to the buffer. If the size of the records stored is small, this is not an important consideration. If the size of the records is large (especially if the record size and the buffer size are the same, as typically is the case when implementing B-trees, see Section 10.5), then this efficiency issue might become important. Note however that the in-memory copy time will always be far less than the time required to write the contents of a buffer to disk. For applications where disk I/O is the bottleneck for the program, even the time to copy lots of information between the buffer pool user and the buffer might be inconsequential. Another advantage to buffer passing is the reduction in unnecessary read operations for data that will be overwritten anyway.

You should note that the implementations for class **BufferPool** above does not use templates. Instead, the **space** parameter and the buffer pointer are declared to be **void***.   When a class uses a template, that means that the record type is arbitrary, but that the class knows what the record type is.   In contrast, using a **void*** pointer for the space means that not only is the record type arbitrary, but also the buffer pool does not even know what the user's record type is. In fact, a given buffer pool might have many users who store many types of records.

In a buffer pool, the user decides where a given record will be stored but has no control over the precise mechanism by which data are transferred to the backing storage. This is in contrast to the memory manager described in Section 12.3 in which the user passes a record to the manager and has no control at all over where the record is stored.

8.4   The Programmer's View of Files

The **C**++ programmer's logical view of a random access file is a single stream of bytes. Interaction with a file can be viewed as a communications channel for issuing one of three instructions: read bytes from the current position in the file, write bytes to the current position in the file, and move the current position within the file. You do not normally see how the bytes are stored in sectors, clusters, and so forth. The mapping from logical to physical addresses is done by the file system, and sector-level buffering is done automatically by the disk controller.

When processing records in a disk file, the order of access can have a great effect on I/O time. A **random access** procedure processes records in an order independent of their logical order within the file. **Sequential access** processes records in order of their logical appearance within the file. Sequential processing requires less seek time if the physical layout of the disk file matches its logical layout, as would be expected if the file were created on a disk with a high percentage of free space.

C++ provides several mechanisms for manipulating disk files. One of the most commonly used is the **fstream** class. The following methods can be used to manipulate information in the file.

- **open(char *name, openmode flags)**: Open file name **name** for processing. **Flags** control various details such as whether the file permits reading, writing, or both; and whether its pre-existing contents should be deleted.

- **read(char *buff, int count)**: Read **count** bytes from the current position in the file. The current file position moves forward as the bytes are read. The bytes are read into array **buff**, which must be at least **count** bytes long.

- **write(char *buff, int count)**: Write **count** bytes at the current position in the file (overwriting the bytes already at that position). The current file position moves forward as these bytes are written. The bytes to be written come from array **buff**.

- **seekg(int pos)** and **seekp(int pos)**: Move the current position in the file to **pos**. This allows bytes at arbitrary places within the file to be read or written. There are actually two "current" positions: one for reading and one for writing. Function **seekg** changes the "get" or read position, while function **seekp** changes the "put" or write position.

- **close()**: Close a file at the end of processing.

Note that the spirit if this ADT is similar to the "message passing" version of the ADT for buffer pools described in Section 8.3.

8.5 External Sorting

We now consider the problem of sorting collections of records too large to fit in main memory. Because the records must reside in peripheral or external memory, such sorting methods are called **external sorts**. This is in contrast to the internal sorts discussed in Chapter 7 which assume that the records to be sorted are stored in main memory. Sorting large collections of records is central to many applications, such as processing payrolls and other large business databases. As a consequence, many external sorting algorithms have been devised. Years ago, sorting algorithm designers sought to optimize the use of specific hardware configurations, such as multiple tape or disk drives. Most computing today is done on personal computers and low-end workstations with relatively powerful CPUs, but only one or at most two disk drives. The techniques presented here are geared toward optimized processing on a single disk drive. This approach allows us to cover the most important issues in external sorting while skipping many less important machine-dependent details. Readers who have a need to implement efficient external sorting algorithms that take advantage of more sophisticated hardware configurations should consult the references in Section 8.6.

When a collection of records is too large to fit in main memory, the only practical way to sort it is to read some records from disk, do some rearranging, then write them back to disk. This process is repeated until the file is sorted, with each record read perhaps many times. Given the high cost of disk I/O, it should come as no surprise that the primary goal of an external sorting algorithm is to minimize the number of times information must be read from or written to disk. A certain amount of additional CPU processing can profitably be traded for reduced disk access.

Before discussing external sorting techniques, consider again the basic model for accessing information from disk. The file to be sorted is viewed by the programmer as a sequential series of fixed-size **blocks**. Assume (for simplicity) that each block contains the same number of fixed-size data records. Depending on the application, a record might be only a few bytes — composed of little or nothing more than the key — or might be hundreds of bytes with a relatively small key field. Records are assumed not to cross block boundaries. These assumptions can be relaxed for special-purpose sorting applications, but ignoring such complications makes the principles clearer.

As explained in Section 8.2, a sector is the basic unit of I/O. In other words, all disk reads and writes are for one or more complete sectors. Sector sizes are typically a power of two, in the range 512 to 16K bytes, depending on the operating system and the size and speed of the disk drive. The block size used for external sorting algorithms should be equal to or a multiple of the sector size.

Under this model, a sorting algorithm reads a block of data into a buffer in main memory, performs some processing on it, and at some future time writes it back to disk. From Section 8.1 we see that reading or writing a block from disk takes on the order of one million times longer than a memory access. Based on this fact, we can reasonably expect that the records contained in a single block can be sorted by an internal sorting algorithm such as Quicksort in less time than is required to read or write the block.

Under good conditions, reading from a file in sequential order is more efficient than reading blocks in random order. Given the significant impact of seek time on disk access, it might seem obvious that sequential processing is faster. However, it is important to understand precisely under what circumstances sequential file processing is actually faster than random access, because it affects our approach to designing an external sorting algorithm.

Efficient sequential access relies on seek time being kept to a minimum. The first requirement is that the blocks making up a file are in fact stored on disk in sequential order and close together, preferably filling a small number of contiguous tracks. At the very least, the number of extents making up the file should be small. Users typically do not have much control over the layout of their file on disk, but writing a file all at once in sequential order to a disk drive with a high percentage of free space increases the likelihood of such an arrangement.

The second requirement is that the disk drive's I/O head remain positioned over the file throughout sequential processing. This will not happen if there is competition of any kind for the I/O head. For example, on a multi-user time-shared computer the sorting process might compete for the I/O head with the processes of other users. Even when the sorting process has sole control of the I/O head, it is still likely that sequential processing will not be efficient. Imagine the situation where all processing is done on a single disk drive, with the typical arrangement of a single bank of read/write heads that move together over a stack of platters. If the sorting process involves reading from an input file, alternated with writing to an output file, then the I/O head will continuously seek between the input file and the output file. Similarly, if two input files are being processed simultaneously (such as during a merge process), then the I/O head will continuously seek between these two files.

The moral is that, with a single disk drive, there often is no such thing as efficient sequential processing of a data file. Thus, a sorting algorithm might be more efficient if it performs a smaller number of non-sequential disk operations rather than a larger number of logically sequential disk operations that require a large number of seeks in practice.

As mentioned previously, the record size might be quite large compared to the size of the key. For example, payroll entries for a large business might each store hundreds of bytes of information including the name, ID, address, and job title for each employee. The sort key might be the ID number, requiring only a few bytes. The simplest sorting algorithm might be to process such records as a whole, reading the entire record whenever it is processed. However, this will greatly increase the amount of I/O required, because only a relatively few records will fit into a single disk block. Another alternative is to do a **key sort**. Under this method, the keys are all read and stored together in an **index file**, where each key is stored along with a pointer indicating the position of the corresponding record in the original data file. The key and pointer combination should be substantially smaller than the size of the original record; thus, the index file will be much smaller than the complete data file. The index file will then be sorted, requiring much less I/O because the index records are smaller than the complete records.

Once the index file is sorted, it is possible to reorder the records in the original database file. This is typically not done for two reasons. First, reading the records in sorted order from the record file requires a random access for each record. This can take a substantial amount of time and is only of value if the complete collection of records needs to be viewed or processed in sorted order (as opposed to a search for selected records). Second, database systems typically allow searches to be done on multiple keys. For example, today's processing might be done in order of ID numbers. Tomorrow, the boss might want information sorted by salary. Thus, there might be no single "sorted" order for the full record. Instead, multiple index files are often maintained, one for each sort key. These ideas are explored further in Chapter 10.

8.5.1   Simple Approaches to External Sorting

If your operating system supports virtual memory, the simplest "external" sort is
to read the entire file into virtual memory and run an internal sorting method such
as Quicksort. This approach allows the virtual memory manager to use its normal
buffer pool mechanism to control disk accesses. Unfortunately, this might not always be a viable option. One potential drawback is that the size of virtual memory
is usually limited to something much smaller than the disk space available. Thus,
your input file might not fit into virtual memory. Limited virtual memory can be
overcome by adapting an internal sorting method to make use of your own buffer
pool.

A more general problem with adapting an internal sorting algorithm to external sorting is that it is not likely to be as efficient as designing a new algorithm
with the specific goal of minimizing disk I/O. Consider the simple adaptation of
Quicksort to use a buffer pool. Quicksort begins by processing the entire array of
records, with the first partition step moving indices inward from the two ends. This
can be implemented efficiently using a buffer pool. However, the next step is to
process each of the subarrays, followed by processing of sub-subarrays, and so on.
As the subarrays get smaller, processing quickly approaches random access to the
disk drive. Even with maximum use of the buffer pool, Quicksort still must read
and write each record $\log n$ times on average. We can do much better. Finally,
even if the virtual memory manager can give good performance using a standard
Quicksort, this will come at the cost of using a lot of the system's working memory, which will mean that the system cannot use this space for other work. Better
methods can save time while also using less memory.

Our approach to external sorting is derived from the Mergesort algorithm. The
simplest form of external Mergesort performs a series of sequential passes over
the records, merging larger and larger sublists on each pass. The first pass merges
sublists of size 1 into sublists of size 2; the second pass merges the sublists of size
2 into sublists of size 4; and so on. A sorted sublist is called a **run**. Thus, each pass
is merging pairs of runs to form longer runs. Each pass copies the contents of the
file to another file. Here is a sketch of the algorithm, as illustrated by Figure 8.6.

1. Split the original file into two equal-sized **run files**.
2. Read one block from each run file into input buffers.
3. Take the first record from each input buffer, and write a run of length two to
   an output buffer in sorted order.
4. Take the next record from each input buffer, and write a run of length two to
   a second output buffer in sorted order.
5. Repeat until finished, alternating output between the two output run buffers.
   Whenever the end of an input block is reached, read the next block from the
   appropriate input file. When an output buffer is full, write it to the appropriate
   output file.

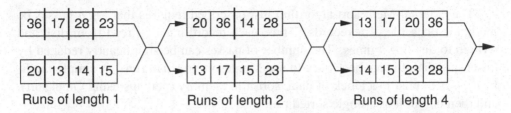

Runs of length 1   Runs of length 2   Runs of length 4

Figure 8.6 A simple external Mergesort algorithm. Input records are divided equally between two input files. The first runs from each input file are merged and placed into the first output file. The second runs from each input file are merged and placed in the second output file. Merging alternates between the two output files until the input files are empty. The roles of input and output files are then reversed, allowing the runlength to be doubled with each pass.

6. Repeat steps 2 through 5, using the original output files as input files. On the second pass, the first two records of each input run file are already in sorted order. Thus, these two runs may be merged and output as a single run of four elements.

7. Each pass through the run files provides larger and larger runs until only one run remains.

Example 8.6 Using the input of Figure 8.6, we first create runs of length one split between two input files. We then process these two input files sequentially, making runs of length two. The first run has the values 20 and 36, which are output to the first output file. The next run has 13 and 17, which is output to the second file. The run 14, 28 is sent to the first file, then run 15, 23 is sent to the second file, and so on. Once this pass has completed, the roles of the input files and output files are reversed. The next pass will merge runs of length two into runs of length four. Runs 20, 36 and 13, 17 are merged to send 13, 17, 20, 36 to the first output file. Then runs 14, 28 and 15, 23 are merged to send run 14, 15, 23, 28 to the second output file. In the final pass, these runs are merged to form the final run 13, 14, 15, 17, 20, 23, 28, 36.

This algorithm can easily take advantage of the double buffering techniques described in Section 8.3. Note that the various passes read the input run files sequentially and write the output run files sequentially. For sequential processing and double buffering to be effective, however, it is necessary that there be a separate I/O head available for each file. This typically means that each of the input and output files must be on separate disk drives, requiring a total of four disk drives for maximum efficiency.

The external Mergesort algorithm just described requires that $\log n$ passes be made to sort a file of n records. Thus, each record must be read from disk and written to disk $\log n$ times. The number of passes can be significantly reduced by observing that it is not necessary to use Mergesort on small runs. A simple modification is to read in a block of data, sort it in memory (perhaps using Quicksort), and then output it as a single sorted run.

Example 8.7 Assume that we have blocks of size 4KB, and records are eight bytes with four bytes of data and a 4-byte key. Thus, each block contains 512 records. Standard Mergesort would require nine passes to generate runs of 512 records, whereas processing each block as a unit can be done in one pass with an internal sort. These runs can then be merged by Mergesort. Standard Mergesort requires eighteen passes to process 256K records. Using an internal sort to create initial runs of 512 records reduces this to one initial pass to create the runs and nine merge passes to put them all together, approximately half as many passes.

We can extend this concept to improve performance even further. Available main memory is usually much more than one block in size. If we process larger initial runs, then the number of passes required by Mergesort is further reduced. For example, most modern computers can provide tens or even hundreds of megabytes of RAM to the sorting program. If all of this memory (excepting a small amount for buffers and local variables) is devoted to building initial runs as large as possible, then quite large files can be processed in few passes. The next section presents a technique for producing large runs, typically twice as large as could fit directly into main memory.

Another way to reduce the number of passes required is to increase the number of runs that are merged together during each pass. While the standard Mergesort algorithm merges two runs at a time, there is no reason why merging needs to be limited in this way. Section 8.5.3 discusses the technique of multiway merging.

Over the years, many variants on external sorting have been presented, but all are based on the following two steps:

1. Break the file into large initial runs.
2. Merge the runs together to form a single sorted file.

8.5.2 Replacement Selection

This section treats the problem of creating initial runs as large as possible from a disk file, assuming a fixed amount of RAM is available for processing. As mentioned previously, a simple approach is to allocate as much RAM as possible to a large array, fill this array from disk, and sort the array using Quicksort. Thus, if

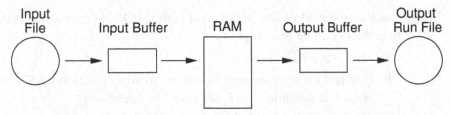

Figure 8.7 Overview of replacement selection. Input records are processed sequentially. Initially RAM is filled with M records. As records are processed, they are written to an output buffer. When this buffer becomes full, it is written to disk. Meanwhile, as replacement selection needs records, it reads them from the input buffer. Whenever this buffer becomes empty, the next block of records is read from disk.

the size of memory available for the array is M records, then the input file can be broken into initial runs of length M. A better approach is to use an algorithm called **replacement selection** that, on average, creates runs of $2M$ records in length. Replacement selection is actually a slight variation on the Heapsort algorithm. The fact that Heapsort is slower than Quicksort is irrelevant in this context because I/O time will dominate the total running time of any reasonable external sorting algorithm. Building longer initial runs will reduce the total I/O time required.

Replacement selection views RAM as consisting of an array of size M in addition to an input buffer and an output buffer. (Additional I/O buffers might be desirable if the operating system supports double buffering, because replacement selection does sequential processing on both its input and its output.) Imagine that the input and output files are streams of records. Replacement selection takes the next record in sequential order from the input stream when needed, and outputs runs one record at a time to the output stream. Buffering is used so that disk I/O is performed one block at a time. A block of records is initially read and held in the input buffer. Replacement selection removes records from the input buffer one at a time until the buffer is empty. At this point the next block of records is read in. Output to a buffer is similar: Once the buffer fills up it is written to disk as a unit. This process is illustrated by Figure 8.7.

Replacement selection works as follows. Assume that the main processing is done in an array of size M records.

1. Fill the array from disk. Set LAST $= M - 1$.

2. Build a min-heap. (Recall that a min-heap is defined such that the record at each node has a key value *less* than the key values of its children.)

3. Repeat until the array is empty:

    (a) Send the record with the minimum key value (the root) to the output buffer.

(b) Let R be the next record in the input buffer. If R's key value is greater than the key value just output ...

    i. Then place R at the root.

    ii. Else replace the root with the record in array position LAST, and place R at position LAST. Set LAST = LAST − 1.

(c) Sift down the root to reorder the heap.

When the test at step 3(b) is successful, a new record is added to the heap, eventually to be output as part of the run. As long as records coming from the input file have key values greater than the last key value output to the run, they can be safely added to the heap. Records with smaller key values cannot be output as part of the current run because they would not be in sorted order. Such values must be stored somewhere for future processing as part of another run. However, because the heap will shrink by one element in this case, there is now a free space where the last element of the heap used to be! Thus, replacement selection will slowly shrink the heap and at the same time use the discarded heap space to store records for the next run. Once the first run is complete (i.e., the heap becomes empty), the array will be filled with records ready to be processed for the second run. Figure 8.8 illustrates part of a run being created by replacement selection.

It should be clear that the minimum length of a run will be M records if the size of the heap is M, because at least those records originally in the heap will be part of the run. Under good conditions (e.g., if the input is sorted), then an arbitrarily long run is possible. In fact, the entire file could be processed as one run. If conditions are bad (e.g., if the input is reverse sorted), then runs of only size M result.

What is the expected length of a run generated by replacement selection? It can be deduced from an analogy called the **snowplow argument**. Imagine that a snowplow is going around a circular track during a heavy, but steady, snowstorm. After the plow has been around at least once, snow on the track must be as follows. Immediately behind the plow, the track is empty because it was just plowed. The greatest level of snow on the track is immediately in front of the plow, because this is the place least recently plowed. At any instant, there is a certain amount of snow S on the track. Snow is constantly falling throughout the track at a steady rate, with some snow falling "in front" of the plow and some "behind" the plow. (On a circular track, everything is actually "in front" of the plow, but Figure 8.9 illustrates the idea.) During the next revolution of the plow, all snow S on the track is removed, plus half of what falls. Because everything is assumed to be in steady state, after one revolution S snow is still on the track, so $2S$ snow must fall during a revolution, and $2S$ snow is removed during a revolution (leaving S snow behind).

At the beginning of replacement selection, nearly all values coming from the input file are greater (i.e., "in front of the plow") than the latest key value output for this run, because the run's initial key values should be small. As the run progresses,

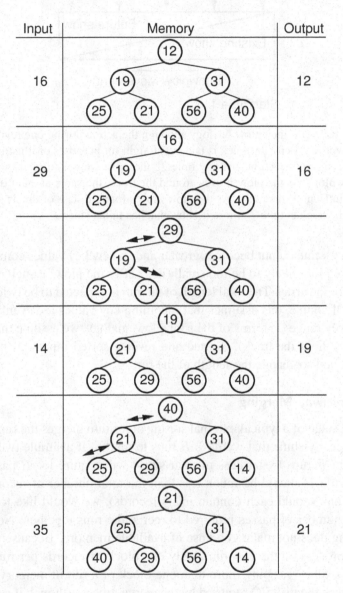

Figure 8.8 Replacement selection example. After building the heap, root value 12 is output and incoming value 16 replaces it. Value 16 is output next, replaced with incoming value 29. The heap is reordered, with 19 rising to the root. Value 19 is output next. Incoming value 14 is too small for this run and is placed at end of the array, moving value 40 to the root. Reordering the heap results in 21 rising to the root, which is output next.

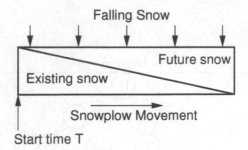

Figure 8.9 The snowplow analogy showing the action during one revolution of
the snowplow. A circular track is laid out straight for purposes of illustration, and
is shown in cross section. At any time T, the most snow is directly in front of
the snowplow. As the plow moves around the track, the same amount of snow is
always in front of the plow. As the plow moves forward, less of this is snow that
was in the track at time T; more is snow that has fallen since.

the latest key value output becomes greater and so new key values coming from the
input file are more likely to be too small (i.e., "after the plow"); such records go to
the bottom of the array. The total length of the run is expected to be twice the size of
the array. Of course, this assumes that incoming key values are evenly distributed
within the key range (in terms of the snowplow analogy, we assume that snow falls
evenly throughout the track). Sorted and reverse sorted inputs do not meet this
expectation and so change the length of the run.

8.5.3 Multiway Merging

The second stage of a typical external sorting algorithm merges the runs created by
the first stage. Assume that we have R runs to merge. If a simple two-way merge
is used, then R runs (regardless of their sizes) will require $\log R$ passes through
the file. While R should be much less than the total number of records (because
the initial runs should each contain many records), we would like to reduce still
further the number of passes required to merge the runs together. Note that two-
way merging does not make good use of available memory. Because merging is a
sequential process on the two runs, only one block of records per run need be in
memory at a time. Keeping more than one block of a run in memory at any time
will not reduce the disk I/O required by the merge process (though if several blocks
are read from a file at once time, at least they take advantage of sequential access).
Thus, most of the space just used by the heap for replacement selection (typically
many blocks in length) is not being used by the merge process.

We can make better use of this space and at the same time greatly reduce the
number of passes needed to merge the runs if we merge several runs at a time.
Multiway merging is similar to two-way merging. If we have B runs to merge,
with a block from each run available in memory, then the B-way merge algorithm

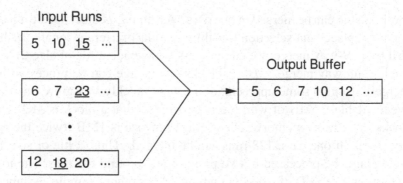

Figure 8.10 Illustration of multiway merge. The first value in each input run is examined and the smallest sent to the output. This value is removed from the input and the process repeated. In this example, values 5, 6, and 12 are compared first. Value 5 is removed from the first run and sent to the output. Values 10, 6, and 12 will be compared next. After the first five values have been output, the "current" value of each block is the one underlined.

simply looks at B values (the front-most value for each input run) and selects the smallest one to output. This value is removed from its run, and the process is repeated. When the current block for any run is exhausted, the next block from that run is read from disk. Figure 8.10 illustrates a multiway merge.

Conceptually, multiway merge assumes that each run is stored in a separate file. However, this is not necessary in practice. We only need to know the position of each run within a single file, and use **seekg** to move to the appropriate block whenever we need new data from a particular run. Naturally, this approach destroys the ability to do sequential processing on the input file. However, if all runs were stored on a single disk drive, then processing would not be truly sequential anyway because the I/O head would be alternating between the runs. Thus, multiway merging replaces several (potentially) sequential passes with a single random access pass. If the processing would not be sequential anyway (such as when all processing is on a single disk drive), no time is lost by doing so.

Multiway merging can greatly reduce the number of passes required. If there is room in memory to store one block for each run, then all runs can be merged in a single pass. Thus, replacement selection can build initial runs in one pass, and multiway merging can merge all runs in one pass, yielding a total cost of two passes. However, for truly large files, there might be too many runs for each to get a block in memory. If there is room to allocate B blocks for a B-way merge, and the number of runs R is greater than B, then it will be necessary to do multiple merge passes. In other words, the first B runs are merged, then the next B, and so on. These super-runs are then merged by subsequent passes, B super-runs at a time.

How big a file can be merged in one pass? Assuming B blocks were allocated to the heap for replacement selection (resulting in runs of average length $2B$ blocks), followed by a B-way merge, we can process on average a file of size $2B^2$ blocks in a single multiway merge. $2B^{k+1}$ blocks on average can be processed in k B-way merges. To gain some appreciation for how quickly this grows, assume that we have available 0.5MB of working memory, and that a block is 4KB, yielding 128 blocks in working memory. The average run size is 1MB (twice the working memory size). In one pass, 128 runs can be merged. Thus, a file of size 128MB can, on average, be processed in two passes (one to build the runs, one to do the merge) with only 0.5MB of working memory. As another example, assume blocks are 1KB long and working memory is 1MB = 1024 blocks. Then 1024 runs of average length 2MB (which is about 2GB) can be combined in a single merge pass. A larger block size would reduce the size of the file that can be processed in one merge pass for a fixed-size working memory; a smaller block size or larger working memory would increase the file size that can be processed in one merge pass. Two merge passes allow much bigger files to be processed. With 0.5MB of working memory and 4KB blocks, a file of size 16 gigabytes could be processed in two merge passes, which is big enough for most applications. Thus, this is a very effective algorithm for single disk drive external sorting.

Figure 8.11 shows a comparison of the running time to sort various-sized files for the following implementations: (1) standard Mergesort with two input runs and two output runs, (2) two-way Mergesort with large initial runs (limited by the size of available memory), and (3) R-way Mergesort performed after generating large initial runs. In each case, the file was composed of a series of four-byte records (a two-byte key and a two-byte data value), or 256K records per megabyte of file size. We can see from this table that using even a modest memory size (two blocks) to create initial runs results in a tremendous savings in time. Doing 4-way merges of the runs provides another considerable speedup, however large-scale multi-way merges for R beyond about 4 or 8 runs does not help much because a lot of time is spent determining which is the next smallest element among the R runs.

We see from this experiment that building large initial runs reduces the running time to slightly more than one third that of standard Mergesort, depending on file and memory sizes. Using a multiway merge further cuts the time nearly in half.

In summary, a good external sorting algorithm will seek to do the following:

- Make the initial runs as long as possible.
- At all stages, overlap input, processing, and output as much as possible.
- Use as much working memory as possible. Applying more memory usually speeds processing. In fact, more memory will have a greater effect than a faster disk. A faster CPU is unlikely to yield much improvement in running time for external sorting, because disk I/O speed is the limiting factor.

File Size (Mb)	Sort 1	Sort 2 Memory size (in blocks)				Sort 3 Memory size (in blocks)		
		2	4	16	256	2	4	16
1	0.61	0.27	0.24	0.19	0.10	0.21	0.15	0.13
	4,864	2,048	1,792	1,280	256	2,048	1,024	512
4	2.56	1.30	1.19	0.96	0.61	1.15	0.68	0.66*
	21,504	10,240	9,216	7,168	3,072	10,240	5,120	2,048
16	11.28	6.12	5.63	4.78	3.36	5.42	3.19	3.10
	94,208	49,152	45,056	36,864	20,480	49,152	24,516	12,288
256	220.39	132.47	123.68	110.01	86.66	115.73	69.31	68.71
	1,769K	1,048K	983K	852K	589K	1,049K	524K	262K

Figure 8.11 A comparison of three external sorts on a collection of small records for files of various sizes. Each entry in the table shows time in seconds and total number of blocks read and written by the program. File sizes are in Megabytes. For the third sorting algorithm, on a file size of 4MB, the time and blocks shown in the last column are for a 32-way merge (marked with an asterisk). 32 is used instead of 16 because 32 is a root of the number of blocks in the file (while 16 is not), thus allowing the same number of runs to be merged at every pass.

- If possible, use additional disk drives for more overlapping of processing with I/O, and to allow for sequential file processing.

8.6 Further Reading

A good general text on file processing is Folk and Zoellick's *File Structures: A Conceptual Toolkit* [FZ98]. A somewhat more advanced discussion on key issues in file processing is Betty Salzberg's *File Structures: An Analytical Approach* [Sal88]. A great discussion on external sorting methods can be found in Salzberg's book. The presentation in this chapter is similar in spirit to Salzberg's.

For details on disk drive modeling and measurement, see the article by Ruemmler and Wilkes, "An Introduction to Disk Drive Modeling" [RW94]. See Andrew S. Tanenbaum's *Structured Computer Organization* [Tan06] for an introduction to computer hardware and organization. An excellent, detailed description of memory and hard disk drives can be found online at "The PC Guide," by Charles M. Kozierok [Koz05] (www.pcguide.com). The PC Guide also gives detailed descriptions of the Microsoft Windows and UNIX (Linux) file systems.

See "Outperforming LRU with an Adaptive Replacement Cache Algorithm" by Megiddo and Modha [MM04] for an example of a more sophisticated algorithm than LRU for managing buffer pools.

The snowplow argument comes from Donald E. Knuth's *Sorting and Searching* [Knu98], which also contains a wide variety of external sorting algorithms.

8.7   Exercises

8.1 Computer memory and storage prices change rapidly. Find out what the current prices are for the media listed in Figure 8.1. Does your information change any of the basic conclusions regarding disk processing?

8.2 Assume a disk drive from the late 1990s is configured as follows. The total storage is approximately 675MB divided among 15 surfaces. Each surface has 612 tracks; there are 144 sectors/track, 512 bytes/sector, and 8 sectors/cluster. The disk turns at 3600 rpm. The track-to-track seek time is 20 ms, and the average seek time is 80 ms. Now assume that there is a 360KB file on the disk. On average, how long does it take to read all of the data in the file? Assume that the first track of the file is randomly placed on the disk, that the entire file lies on adjacent tracks, and that the file completely fills each track on which it is found. A seek must be performed each time the I/O head moves to a new track. Show your calculations.

8.3 Using the specifications for the disk drive given in Exercise 8.2, calculate the expected time to read one entire track, one sector, and one byte. Show your calculations.

8.4 Using the disk drive specifications given in Exercise 8.2, calculate the time required to read a 10MB file assuming

   (a) The file is stored on a series of contiguous tracks, as few tracks as possible.
   (b) The file is spread randomly across the disk in 4KB clusters.

Show your calculations.

8.5 Assume that a disk drive is configured as follows. The total storage is approximately 1033MB divided among 15 surfaces. Each surface has 2100 tracks, there are 64 sectors/track, 512 bytes/sector, and 8 sectors/cluster. The disk turns at 7200 rpm. The track-to-track seek time is 3 ms, and the average seek time is 20 ms. Now assume that there is a 512KB file on the disk. On average, how long does it take to read all of the data on the file? Assume that the first track of the file is randomly placed on the disk, that the entire file lies on contiguous tracks, and that the file completely fills each track on which it is found. Show your calculations.

8.6 Using the specifications for the disk drive given in Exercise 8.5, calculate the expected time to read one entire track, one sector, and one byte. Show your calculations.

8.7 Using the disk drive specifications given in Exercise 8.5, calculate the time required to read a 10MB file assuming

   (a) The file is stored on a series of contiguous tracks, as few tracks as possible.
   (b) The file is spread randomly across the disk in 4KB clusters.

Show your calculations.

8.8 A typical disk drive from 2004 has the following specifications.[3] The total storage is approximately 120GB on 6 platter surfaces or 20GB/platter. Each platter has 16K tracks with 2560 sectors/track (a sector holds 512 bytes) and 16 sectors/cluster. The disk turns at 7200 rpm. The track-to-track seek time is 2.0 ms, and the average seek time is 10.0 ms. Now assume that there is a 6MB file on the disk. On average, how long does it take to read all of the data on the file? Assume that the first track of the file is randomly placed on the disk, that the entire file lies on contiguous tracks, and that the file completely fills each track on which it is found. Show your calculations.

8.9 Using the specifications for the disk drive given in Exercise 8.8, calculate the expected time to read one entire track, one sector, and one byte. Show your calculations.

8.10 Using the disk drive specifications given in Exercise 8.8, calculate the time required to read a 10MB file assuming

(a) The file is stored on a series of contiguous tracks, as few tracks as possible.

(b) The file is spread randomly across the disk in 8KB clusters.

Show your calculations.

8.11 At the end of 2004, the fastest disk drive I could find specifications for was the Maxtor Atlas. This drive had a nominal capacity of 73.4GB using 4 platters (8 surfaces) or 9.175GB/surface. Assume there are 16,384 tracks with an average of 1170 sectors/track and 512 bytes/sector.[4] The disk turns at 15,000 rpm. The track-to-track seek time is 0.4 ms and the average seek time is 3.6 ms. How long will it take on average to read a 6MB file, assuming that the first track of the file is randomly placed on the disk, that the entire file lies on contiguous tracks, and that the file completely fills each track on which it is found. Show your calculations.

8.12 Using the specifications for the disk drive given in Exercise 8.11, calculate the expected time to read one entire track, one sector, and one byte. Show your calculations.

8.13 Using the disk drive specifications given in Exercise 8.11, calculate the time required to read a 10MB file assuming

(a) The file is stored on a series of contiguous tracks, as few tracks as possible.

---

[3]To make the exercise doable, this specification is completely fictitious with respect to the track and sector layout. While sectors do have 512 bytes, and while the number of platters and amount of data per track is plausible, the reality is that all modern drives use a zoned organization to keep the data density from inside to outside of the disk reasonably high. The rest of the numbers are typical for a drive from 2004.

[4]Again, this track layout does does not account for the zoned arrangement on modern disk drives.

(b) The file is spread randomly across the disk in 8KB clusters.

Show your calculations.

8.14 Prove that two tracks selected at random from a disk are separated on average by one third the number of tracks on the disk.

8.15 Assume that a file contains one million records sorted by key value. A query to the file returns a single record containing the requested key value. Files are stored on disk in sectors each containing 100 records. Assume that the average time to read a sector selected at random is 10.0 ms. In contrast, it takes only 2.0 ms to read the sector adjacent to the current position of the I/O head. The "batch" algorithm for processing queries is to first sort the queries by order of appearance in the file, and then read the entire file sequentially, processing all queries in sequential order as the file is read. This algorithm implies that the queries must all be available before processing begins. The "interactive" algorithm is to process each query in order of its arrival, searching for the requested sector each time (unless by chance two queries in a row are to the same sector). Carefully define under what conditions the batch method is more efficient than the interactive method.

8.16 Assume that a virtual memory is managed using a buffer pool. The buffer pool contains five buffers and each buffer stores one block of data. Memory accesses are by block ID. Assume the following series of memory accesses takes place:

5 2 5 12 3 6 5 9 3 2 4 1 5 9 8 15 3 7 2 5 9 10 4 6 8 5

For each of the following buffer pool replacement strategies, show the contents of the buffer pool at the end of the series, and indicate how many times a block was found in the buffer pool (instead of being read into memory). Assume that the buffer pool is initially empty.

(a) First-in, first out.

(b) Least frequently used (with counts kept only for blocks currently in memory, counts for a page are lost when that page is removed, and the oldest item with the smallest count is removed when there is a tie).

(c) Least frequently used (with counts kept for all blocks, and the oldest item with the smallest count is removed when there is a tie).

(d) Least recently used.

(e) Most recently used (replace the block that was most recently accessed).

8.17 Suppose that a record is 32 bytes, a block is 1024 bytes (thus, there are 32 records per block), and that working memory is 1MB (there is also additional space available for I/O buffers, program variables, etc.). What is the *expected* size for the largest file that can be merged using replacement selection followed by a *single* pass of multiway merge? Explain how you got your answer.

8.18 Assume that working memory size is 256KB broken into blocks of 8192 bytes (there is also additional space available for I/O buffers, program variables, etc.). What is the *expected* size for the largest file that can be merged using replacement selection followed by *two* passes of multiway merge? Explain how you got your answer.

8.19 Prove or disprove the following proposition: Given space in memory for a heap of M records, replacement selection will completely sort a file if no record in the file is preceded by M or more keys of greater value.

8.20 Imagine a database containing ten million records, with each record being 100 bytes long. Provide an estimate of the time it would take (in seconds) to sort the database on a typical desktop or laptop computer.

8.21 Assume that a company has a computer configuration satisfactory for processing their monthly payroll. Further assume that the bottleneck in payroll processing is a sorting operation on all of the employee records, and that an external sorting algorithm is used. The company's payroll program is so good that it plans to hire out its services to do payroll processing for other companies. The president has an offer from a second company with 100 times as many employees. She realizes that her computer is not up to the job of sorting 100 times as many records in an acceptable amount of time. Describe what impact each of the following modifications to the computing system is likely to have in terms of reducing the time required to process the larger payroll database.

   (a) A factor of two speedup to the CPU.
   (b) A factor of two speedup to disk I/O time.
   (c) A factor of two speedup to main memory access time.
   (d) A factor of two increase to main memory size.

8.22 How can the external sorting algorithm described in this chapter be extended to handle variable-length records?

8.8 Projects

8.1 For a database application, assume it takes 10 ms to read a block from disk, 1 ms to search for a record in a block stored in memory, and that there is room in memory for a buffer pool of 5 blocks. Requests come in for records, with the request specifying which block contains the record. If a block is accessed, there is a 10% probability for each of the next ten requests that the request will be to the same block. What will be the expected performance improvement for each of the following modifications to the system?

   (a) Get a CPU that is twice as fast.
   (b) Get a disk drive that is twice as fast.

(c) Get enough memory to double the buffer pool size.

Write a simulation to analyze this problem.

8.2 Pictures are typically stored as an array, row by row, on disk. Consider the case where the picture has 16 colors. Thus, each pixel can be represented using 4 bits. If you allow 8 bits per pixel, no processing is required to unpack the pixels (because a pixel corresponds to a byte, the lowest level of addressing on most machines). If you pack two pixels per byte, space is saved but the pixels must be unpacked. Which takes more time to read from disk and access every pixel of the image: 8 bits per pixel, or 4 bits per pixel with 2 pixels per byte? Program both and compare the times.

8.3 Implement a disk-based buffer pool class based on the LRU buffer pool replacement strategy. Disk blocks are numbered consecutively from the beginning of the file with the first block numbered as 0. Assume that blocks are 4096 bytes in size, with the first 4 bytes used to store the block ID corresponding to that buffer. Use the first **BufferPool** abstract class given in Section 8.3 as the basis for your implementation.

8.4 Implement an external sort based on replacement selection and multiway merging as described in this chapter. Test your program both on files with small records and on files with large records. For what size record do you find that key sorting would be worthwhile?

8.5 Implement a Quicksort for large files on disk by replacing all array access in the normal Quicksort application with access to a virtual array implemented using a buffer pool. That is, whenever a record in the array would be read or written by Quicksort, use a call to a buffer pool function instead. Compare the running time of this implementation with implementations for external sorting based on mergesort as described in this chapter.

8.6 Section 8.5.1 suggests that an easy modification to the basic 2-way mergesort is to read in a large chunk of data into main memory, sort it with Quicksort, and write it out for initial runs. Then, a standard 2-way merge is used in a series of passes to merge the runs together. However, this makes use of only two blocks of working memory at a time. Each block read is essentially random access, because the various files are read in an unknown order, even though each of the input and output files is processed sequentially on each pass. A possible improvement would be, on the merge passes, to divide working memory into four equal sections. One section is allocated to each of the two input files and two output files. All reads during merge passes would be in full sections, rather than single blocks. While the total number of blocks read and written would be the same as a regular 2-way Mergesort, it is possible that this would speed processing because a series of blocks that are logically adjacent in the various input and output files would be read/written each time. Implement this variation, and compare its running time against a standard series of 2-way merge passes that read/write only a single block at a time. Before beginning implementation, write down your hypothesis on how the running time will be affected by this change. After implementing, did you find that this change has any meaningful effect on performance?

9

Searching

Organizing and retrieving information is at the heart of most computer applications, and searching is surely the most frequently performed of all computing tasks. Search can be viewed abstractly as a process to determine if an element with a particular value is a member of a particular set. The more common view of searching is an attempt to find the record within a collection of records that has a particular key value, or those records in a collection whose key values meet some criterion such as falling within a range of values.

We can define searching formally as follows. Suppose that we have a collection **L** of n records of the form

$$(k_1, I_1), (k_2, I_2), ..., (k_n, I_n)$$

where I_j is information associated with key k_j from record j for $1 \leq j \leq n$. Given a particular key value K, the **search problem** is to locate a record (k_j, I_j) in **L** such that $k_j = K$ (if one exists). **Searching** is a systematic method for locating the record (or records) with key value $k_j = K$.

A **successful** search is one in which a record with key $k_j = K$ is found. An **unsuccessful** search is one in which no record with $k_j = K$ is found (and no such record exists).

An **exact-match query** is a search for the record whose key value matches a specified key value. A **range query** is a search for all records whose key value falls within a specified range of key values.

We can categorize search algorithms into three general approaches:

1. Sequential and list methods.
2. Direct access by key value (hashing).
3. Tree indexing methods.

This and the following chapter treat these three approaches in turn. Any of these approaches are potentially suitable for implementing the Dictionary ADT introduced in Section 4.4. However, each has different performance characteristics that make it the method of choice in particular circumstances.

The current chapter considers methods for searching data stored in lists. List in this context means any list implementation including a linked list or an array. Most of these methods are appropriate for sequences (i.e., duplicate key values are allowed), although special techniques applicable to sets are discussed in Section 9.3. The techniques from the first three sections of this chapter are most appropriate for searching a collection of records stored in RAM. Section 9.4 discusses hashing, a technique for organizing data in an array such that the location of each record within the array is a function of its key value. Hashing is appropriate when records are stored either in RAM or on disk.

Chapter 10 discusses tree-based methods for organizing information on disk, including a commonly used file structure called the B-tree. Nearly all programs that must organize large collections of records stored on disk use some variant of either hashing or the B-tree. Hashing is practical for only certain access functions (exact-match queries) and is generally appropriate only when duplicate key values are not allowed. B-trees are the method of choice for dynamic disk-based applications anytime hashing is not appropriate.

9.1 Searching Unsorted and Sorted Arrays

The simplest form of search has already been presented in Example 3.1: the sequential search algorithm. Sequential search on an unsorted list requires $\Theta(n)$ time in the worst case.

How many comparisons does linear search do on average? A major consideration is whether K is in list $\mathbf{L}$ at all. We can simplify our analysis by ignoring everything about the input except the position of K if it is found in $\mathbf{L}$. Thus, we have $n + 1$ distinct possible events: That K is in one of positions 0 to $n - 1$ in $\mathbf{L}$ (each position having its own probability), or that it is not in $\mathbf{L}$ at all. We can express the probability that K is not in $\mathbf{L}$ as

$$\mathbf{P}(K \notin \mathbf{L}) = 1 - \sum_{i=1}^{n} \mathbf{P}(K = \mathbf{L}[i])$$

where $\mathbf{P}(x)$ is the probability of event x.

Let p_i be the probability that K is in position i of $\mathbf{L}$ (indexed from 0 to $n - 1$. For any position i in the list, we must look at $i + 1$ records to reach it. So we say that the cost when K is in position i is $i + 1$. When K is not in $\mathbf{L}$, sequential search will require n comparisons. Let p_n be the probability that K is not in $\mathbf{L}$. Then the average cost $\mathbf{T}(n)$ will be

$$\mathbf{T}(n) = np_n + \sum_{i=0}^{n-1}(i+1)p_i.$$

What happens to the equation if we assume all the p_i's are equal (except p_0)?

$$
\begin{aligned}
\mathbf{T}(n) &= p_n n + \sum_{i=0}^{n-1}(i+1)p \\
&= p_n n + p\sum_{i=1}^{n} i \\
&= p_n n + p\frac{n(n+1)}{2} \\
&= p_n n + \frac{1-p_n}{n}\frac{n(n+1)}{2} \\
&= \frac{n+1+p_n(n-1)}{2}
\end{aligned}
$$

Depending on the value of p_n, $\frac{n+1}{2} \leq \mathbf{T}(n) \leq n$.

For large collections of records that are searched repeatedly, sequential search is unacceptably slow. One way to reduce search time is to preprocess the records by sorting them. Given a sorted array, an obvious improvement over simple linear search is to test if the current element in **L** is greater than K. If it is, then we know that K cannot appear later in the array, and we can quit the search early. But this still does not improve the worst-case cost of the algorithm.

We can also observe that if we look first at position 1 in sorted array **L** and find that K is bigger, then we rule out position 0 as well as position 1. Because more is often better, what if we look at position 2 in **L** and find that K is bigger yet? This rules out positions 0, 1, and 2 with one comparison. What if we carry this to the extreme and look first at the last position in **L** and find that K is bigger? Then we know in one comparison that K is not in **L**. This is very useful to know, but what is wrong with the conclusion that we should always start by looking at the last position? The problem is that, while we learn a lot sometimes (in one comparison we might learn that K is not in the list), usually we learn only a little bit (that the last element is not K).

The question then becomes: What is the right amount to jump? This leads us to an algorithm known as **Jump Search**. For some value j, we check every j'th element in **L**, that is, we check elements $\mathbf{L}[j]$, $\mathbf{L}[2j]$, and so on. So long as K is greater than the values we are checking, we continue on. But when we reach a value in **L** greater than K, we do a linear search on the piece of length $j - 1$ that we know brackets K if it is in the list.

If we define m such that $mj \leq n < (m + 1)j$, then the total cost of this algorithm is at most $m + j - 1$ 3-way comparisons. (They are 3-way because at each comparison of K with some **L**$[i]$ we need to know if K is less than, equal to, or greater than **L**$[i]$.) Therefore, the cost to run the algorithm on n items with a jump of size j is

$$\mathbf{T}(n, j) = m + j - 1 = \left\lfloor \frac{n}{j} \right\rfloor + j - 1.$$

What is the best value that we can pick for j? We want to minimize the cost:

$$\min_{1 \leq j \leq n} \left\{ \left\lfloor \frac{n}{j} \right\rfloor + j - 1 \right\}$$

Take the derivative and solve for $f'(j) = 0$ to find the minimum, which is $j = \sqrt{n}$. In this case, the worst case cost will be roughly $2\sqrt{n}$.

This example invokes a basic principle of algorithm design. We want to balance the work done while selecting a sublist with the work done while searching a sublist. In general, it is a good strategy to make subproblems of equal effort. This is an example of a **divide and conquer** algorithm.

What if we extend this idea to three levels? We would first make jumps of some size j to find a sublist of size $j - 1$ whose end values bracket value K. We would then work through this sublist by making jumps of some smaller size, say j_1. Finally, once we find a bracketed sublist of size $j_1 - 1$, we would do sequential search to complete the process.

This probably sounds convoluted to do two levels of jumping to be followed by a sequential search. While it might make sense to do a two-level algorithm (that is, jump search jumps to find a sublist and then does sequential search on the sublist), it almost never seems to make sense to do a three-level algorithm. Instead, when we go beyond two levels, we nearly always generalize by using recursion. This leads us to the most commonly used search algorithm for sorted arrays, the binary search described in Section 3.5.

If we know nothing about the distribution of key values, then binary search is the best algorithm available for searching a sorted array (see Exercise 9.22). However, sometimes we do know something about the expected key distribution. Consider the typical behavior of a person looking up a word in a large dictionary. Most people certainly do not use sequential search! Typically, people use a modified form of binary search, at least until they get close to the word that they are looking for. The search generally does not start at the middle of the dictionary. A person looking for a word starting with 'S' generally assumes that entries beginning with 'S' start about three quarters of the way through the dictionary. Thus, he or she will first open the dictionary about three quarters of the way through and then make a decision based on what is found as to where to look next. In other words, people typically use some knowledge about the expected distribution of key values to "compute" where to look next. This form of "computed" binary search is called a **dictionary search** or **interpolation search**. In a dictionary search, we search $\mathbf{L}$ at a position p that is appropriate to the value of K as follows.

$$p = \frac{K - \mathbf{L}[1]}{\mathbf{L}[n] - \mathbf{L}[1]}$$

This equation is computing the position of K as a fraction of the distance between the smallest and largest key values. This will next be translated into that position which is the same fraction of the way through the array, and this position is checked first. As with binary search, the value of the key found eliminates all records either above or below that position. The actual value of the key found can then be used to compute a new position within the remaining range of the array. The next check is made based on the new computation. This proceeds until either the desired record is found, or the array is narrowed until no records are left.

A variation on dictionary search is known as **Quadratic Binary Search** (QBS), and we will analyze this in detail because its analysis is easier than that of the general dictionary search. QBS will first compute p and then examine $\mathbf{L}[\lceil pn \rceil]$. If $K < \mathbf{L}[\lceil pn \rceil]$ then QBS will sequentially probe to the left by steps of size $\sqrt{n}$, that is, we step through

$$\mathbf{L}[\lceil pn - i\sqrt{n} \rceil], i = 1, 2, 3, \ldots$$

until we reach a value less than or equal to K. Similarly for $K > \mathbf{L}[\lceil pn \rceil]$ we will step to the right by $\sqrt{n}$ until we reach a value in $\mathbf{L}$ that is greater than K. We are now within $\sqrt{n}$ positions of K. Assume (for now) that it takes a constant number of comparisons to bracket K within a sublist of size $\sqrt{n}$. We then take this sublist and repeat the process recursively. That is, at the next level we compute an interpolation to start somewhere in the subarray. We then step to the left or right (as appropriate) by steps of size $\sqrt{\sqrt{n}}$.

What is the cost for QBS? Note that $\sqrt{c^n} = c^{n/2}$, and we will be repeatedly taking square roots of the current sublist size until we find the item that we are looking for. Because $n = 2^{\log n}$ and we can cut $\log n$ in half only $\log \log n$ times, the cost is $\Theta(\log \log n)$ *if* the number of probes on jump search is constant.

Say that the number of comparisons needed is i, in which case the cost is i (since we have to do i comparisons). If $\mathbf{P}_i$ is the probability of needing exactly i probes, then

$$\sum_{i=1}^{\sqrt{n}} i\mathbf{P}(\text{need exactly } i \text{ probes})$$

$$= 1\mathbf{P}_1 + 2\mathbf{P}_2 + 3\mathbf{P}_3 + \cdots + \sqrt{n}\mathbf{P}_{\sqrt{n}}$$

We now show that this is the same as

$$\sum_{i=1}^{\sqrt{n}} \mathbf{P}(\text{need at least } i \text{ probes})$$

$$
\begin{aligned}
&= 1 + (1 - \mathbf{P}_1) + (1 - \mathbf{P}_1 - \mathbf{P}_2) + \cdots + \mathbf{P}_{\sqrt{n}} \\
&= (\mathbf{P}_1 + \dots + \mathbf{P}_{\sqrt{n}}) + (\mathbf{P}_2 + \dots + \mathbf{P}_{\sqrt{n}}) + \\
&\quad (\mathbf{P}_3 + \dots + \mathbf{P}_{\sqrt{n}}) + \cdots \\
&= 1\mathbf{P}_1 + 2\mathbf{P}_2 + 3\mathbf{P}_3 + \cdots + \sqrt{n}\mathbf{P}_{\sqrt{n}}
\end{aligned}
$$

We require at least two probes to set the bounds, so the cost is

$$2 + \sum_{i=3}^{\sqrt{n}} \mathbf{P}(\text{need at least } i \text{ probes}).$$

We now make take advantage of a useful fact known as Čebyšev's Inequality. Čebyšev's inequality states that $\mathbf{P}(\text{need exactly } i \text{ probes})$, or $\mathbf{P}_i$, is

$$\mathbf{P}_i \le \frac{p(1-p)n}{(i-2)^2 n} \le \frac{1}{4(i-2)^2}$$

because $p(1-p) \le 1/4$ for any probability p. This assumes uniformly distributed data. Thus, the expected number of probes is

$$2 + \sum_{i=3}^{\sqrt{n}} \frac{1}{4(i-2)^2} < 2 + \frac{1}{4} \sum_{i=1}^{\infty} \frac{1}{i^2} = 2 + \frac{1}{4}\frac{\pi}{6} \approx 2.4112$$

Is QBS better than binary search? Theoretically yes, because $O(\log\log n)$ grows slower than $O(\log n)$. However, we have a situation here which illustrates the limits to the model of asymptotic complexity in some practical situations. Yes, $c_1 \log n$ does grow faster than $c_2 \log\log n$. In fact, it is exponentially faster! But even so, for practical input sizes, the absolute cost difference is fairly small. Thus, the constant factors might play a role. First we compare $\lg\lg n$ to $\lg n$.

n	$\lg n$	$\lg\lg n$	Factor Difference
16	4	2	2
256	8	3	2.7
2^{16}	16	4	4
2^{32}	32	5	6.4

It is not always practical to reduce an algorithm's growth rate. There is a "practicality window" for every problem, in that we have a practical limit to how big an input we wish to solve for. If our problem size never grows too big, it might not matter if we can reduce the cost by an extra log factor, because the constant factors in the two algorithms might differ by more than the log of the log of the input size.

For our two algorithms, let us look further and check the actual number of comparisons used. For binary search, we need about $\lg n - 1$ total comparisons. Quadratic binary search requires about $2.4 \lg \lg n$ comparisons. If we incorporate this observation into our table, we get a different picture about the relative differences.

n	$\lg n - 1$	$2.4 \lg \lg n$	Factor Difference
16	3	4.8	worse
256	7	7.2	$\approx$ same
64K	15	9.6	1.6
2^{32}	31	12	2.6

But we still are not done. This is only a count of raw comparisons. Binary search is inherently much simpler than QBS, because binary search only needs to calculate the midpoint position of the array before each comparison, while quadratic binary search must calculate an interpolation point which is more expensive. So the constant factors for QBS are even higher.

Not only are the constant factors worse on average, but QBS is far more dependent than binary search on good data distribution to perform well. For example, imagine that you are searching a telephone directory for the name "Young." Normally you would look near the back of the book. If you found a name beginning with 'Z,' you might look just a little ways toward the front. If the next name you find also begins with 'Z,' you would look a little further toward the front. If this particular telephone directory were unusual in that half of the entries begin with 'Z,' then you would need to move toward the front many times, each time eliminating relatively few records from the search. In the extreme, the performance of interpolation search might not be much better than sequential search if the distribution of key values is badly calculated.

While it turns out that QBS is not a practical algorithm, this is not a typical situation. Fortunately, algorithm growth rates are usually well behaved, so that asymptotic algorithm analysis nearly always gives us a practical indication for which of two algorithms is better.

9.2 Self-Organizing Lists

While ordering of lists is most commonly done by key value, this is not the only viable option. Another approach to organizing lists to speed search is to order the records by expected frequency of access. While the benefits might not be as great as when organized by key value, the cost to organize (at least approximately) by frequency of access can be much cheaper, and thus can speed up sequential search in some situations.

Assume that we know, for each key k_i, the probability p_i that the record with key k_i will be requested. Assume also that the list is ordered so that the most frequently requested record is first, then the next most frequently requested record, and so on. Search in the list will be done sequentially, beginning with the first position. Over the course of many searches, the expected number of comparisons required for one search is

$$\overline{C}_n = 1p_0 + 2p_1 + \dots + np_{n-1}.$$

In other words, the cost to access the record in **L**[0] is 1 (because one key value is looked at), and the probability of this occurring is p_0. The cost to access the record in **L**[1] is 2 (because we must look at the first and the second records' key values), with probability p_1, and so on. For n records, assuming that all searches are for records that actually exist, the probabilities p_0 through p_{n-1} must sum to one.

Certain probability distributions give easily computed results.

Example 9.1 Calculate the expected cost to search a list when each record has equal chance of being accessed (the classic sequential search through an unsorted list). Setting $p_i = 1/n$ yields

$$\overline{C}_n = \sum_{i=1}^{n} i/n = (n+1)/2.$$

This result matches our expectation that half the records will be accessed on average by normal sequential search. If the records truly have equal access probabilities, then ordering records by frequency yields no benefit. We saw in Section 9.1 the more general case where we must consider the probability (labeled p_n) that the search key does not match that for any record in the array. In that case, in accordance with our general formula, we get

$$(1-p_n)\frac{n+1}{2} + p_n n = \frac{n+1-np_n n - p_n + 2p_n}{2} = \frac{n+1+p_0(n-1)}{2}.$$

Thus, $\frac{n+1}{2} \leq \overline{C}_n \leq n$, depending on the value of p_0.

A geometric probability distribution can yield quite different results.

Example 9.2 Calculate the expected cost for searching a list ordered by frequency when the probabilities are defined as

$$p_i = \begin{cases} 1/2^i & \text{if } 0 \leq i \leq n-2 \\ 1/2^n & \text{if } i = n-1. \end{cases}$$

Then,

$$\overline{C}_n \approx \sum_{i=0}^{n-1} (i+1)/2^{i+1} = \sum_{i=1}^{n} (i/2^i) \approx 2.$$

For this example, the expected number of accesses is a constant. This is because the probability for accessing the first record is high (one half), the second is much lower (one quarter) but still much higher than for the third record, and so on. This shows that for some probability distributions, ordering the list by frequency can yield an efficient search technique.

In many search applications, real access patterns follow a rule of thumb called the **80/20 rule**. The 80/20 rule says that 80% of the record accesses are to 20% of the records. The values of 80 and 20 are only estimates; every data access pattern has its own values. However, behavior of this nature occurs surprisingly often in practice (which explains the success of caching techniques widely used by web browsers for speeding access to web pages, and by disk drive and CPU manufacturers for speeding access to data stored in slower memory; see the discussion on buffer pools in Section 8.3). When the 80/20 rule applies, we can expect considerable improvements to search performance from a list ordered by frequency of access over standard sequential search in an unordered list.

Example 9.3 The 80/20 rule is an example of a **Zipf distribution**. Naturally occurring distributions often follow a Zipf distribution. Examples include the observed frequency for the use of words in a natural language such as English, and the size of the population for cities (i.e., view the relative proportions for the populations as equivalent to the "frequency of use"). Zipf distributions are related to the Harmonic Series defined in Equation 2.10. Define the Zipf frequency for item i in the distribution for n records as $1/(i\mathcal{H}_n)$ (see Exercise 9.4). The expected cost for the series whose members follow this Zipf distribution will be

$$\overline{C}_n = \sum_{i=1}^{n} i/i\mathcal{H}_n = n/\mathcal{H}_n \approx n/\log_e n.$$

When a frequency distribution follows the 80/20 rule, the average search looks at about 10-15% of the records in a list ordered by frequency.

This is potentially a useful observation that typical "real-life" distributions of record accesses, if the records were ordered by frequency, would require that we visit on average only 10-15% of the list when doing sequential search. This means that if we had an application that used sequential search, and we wanted to make it go a bit faster (by a constant amount), we could do so without a major rewrite to the system to implement something like a search tree. But that is only true if there is an easy way to (at least approximately) order the records by frequency.

In most applications, we have no means of knowing in advance the frequencies of access for the data records. To complicate matters further, certain records might be accessed frequently for a brief period of time, and then rarely thereafter. Thus, the probability of access for records might change over time (in most database systems, this is to be expected). **Self-organizing lists** seek to solve both of these problems.

Self-organizing lists modify the order of records within the list based on the actual pattern of record access. Self-organizing lists use a heuristic for deciding how to to reorder the list. These heuristics are similar to the rules for managing buffer pools (see Section 8.3). In fact, a buffer pool is a form of self-organizing list. Ordering the buffer pool by expected frequency of access is a good strategy, because typically we must search the contents of the buffers to determine if the desired information is already in main memory. When ordered by frequency of access, the buffer at the end of the list will be the one most appropriate for reuse when a new page of information must be read. Below are three traditional heuristics for managing self-organizing lists:

1. The most obvious way to keep a list ordered by frequency would be to store a count of accesses to each record and always maintain records in this order. This method will be referred to as **count**. Count is similar to the least frequently used buffer replacement strategy. Whenever a record is accessed, it might move toward the front of the list if its number of accesses becomes greater than a record preceding it. Thus, count will store the records in the order of frequency that has actually occurred so far. Besides requiring space for the access counts, count does not react well to changing frequency of access over time. Once a record has been accessed a large number of times under the frequency count system, it will remain near the front of the list regardless of further access history.

2. Bring a record to the front of the list when it is found, pushing all the other records back one position. This is analogous to the least recently used buffer replacement strategy and is called **move-to-front**. This heuristic is easy to implement if the records are stored using a linked list. When records are stored in an array, bringing a record forward from near the end of the array will result in a large number of records (slightly) changing position. Move-to-front's cost is bounded in the sense that it requires at most twice the num-

ber of accesses required by the **optimal static ordering** for n records when at least n searches are performed. In other words, if we had known the series of (at least n) searches in advance and had stored the records in order of frequency so as to minimize the total cost for these accesses, this cost would be at least half the cost required by the move-to-front heuristic. (This will be proved using amortized analysis in Section 14.3.) Finally, move-to-front responds well to local changes in frequency of access, in that if a record is frequently accessed for a brief period of time it will be near the front of the list during that period of access. Move-to-front does poorly when the records are processed in sequential order, especially if that sequential order is then repeated multiple times.

3. Swap any record found with the record immediately preceding it in the list. This heuristic is called **transpose**. Transpose is good for list implementations based on either linked lists or arrays. Frequently used records will, over time, move to the front of the list. Records that were once frequently accessed but are no longer used will slowly drift toward the back. Thus, it appears to have good properties with respect to changing frequency of access. Unfortunately, there are some pathological sequences of access that can make transpose perform poorly. Consider the case where the last record of the list (call it X) is accessed. This record is then swapped with the next-to-last record (call it Y), making Y the last record. If Y is now accessed, it swaps with X. A repeated series of accesses alternating between X and Y will continually search to the end of the list, because neither record will ever make progress toward the front. However, such pathological cases are unusual in practice. A variation on transpose would be to move the accessed record forward in the list by some fixed number of steps.

Example 9.4 Assume that we have eight records, with key values A to H, and that they are initially placed in alphabetical order. Now, consider the result of applying the following access pattern:

$$F D F G E G F A D F G E.$$

Assume that when a record's frequency count goes up, it moves forward in the list to become the last record with that value for its frequency count. After the first two accesses, F will be the first record and D will be the second. The final list resulting from these accesses will be

$$F G D E A B C H,$$

and the total cost for the twelve accesses will be 45 comparisons.

If the list is organized by the move-to-front heuristic, then the final list will be

$$E G F D A B C H,$$

and the total number of comparisons required is 54.

Finally, if the list is organized by the transpose heuristic, then the final list will be

$$A\ B\ F\ D\ G\ E\ C\ H,$$

and the total number of comparisons required is 62.

While self-organizing lists do not generally perform as well as search trees or a sorted list, both of which require $O(\log n)$ search time, there are many situations in which self-organizing lists prove a valuable tool. Obviously they have an advantage over sorted lists in that they need not be sorted. This means that the cost to insert a new record is low, which could more than make up for the higher search cost when insertions are frequent. Self-organizing lists are simpler to implement than search trees and are likely to be more efficient for small lists. Nor do they require additional space. Finally, in the case of an application where sequential search is "almost" fast enough, changing an unsorted list to a self-organizing list might speed the application enough at a minor cost in additional code.

As an example of applying self-organizing lists, consider an algorithm for compressing and transmitting messages. The list is self-organized by the move-to-front rule. Transmission is in the form of words and numbers, by the following rules:

1. If the word has been seen before, transmit the current position of the word in the list. Move the word to the front of the list.
2. If the word is seen for the first time, transmit the word. Place the word at the front of the list.

Both the sender and the receiver keep track of the position of words in the list in the same way (using the move-to-front rule), so they agree on the meaning of the numbers that encode repeated occurrences of words. Consider the following example message to be transmitted (for simplicity, ignore case in letters).

The car on the left hit the car I left.

The first three words have not been seen before, so they must be sent as full words. The fourth word is the second appearance of "the," which at this point is the third word in the list. Thus, we only need to transmit the position value "3." The next two words have not yet been seen, so must be sent as full words. The seventh word is the third appearance of "the," which coincidentally is again in the third position. The eighth word is the second appearance of "car," which is now in the fifth position of the list. "I" is a new word, and the last word "left" is now in the fifth position. Thus the entire transmission would be

The car on 3 left hit 3 5 I 5.

0	1	2	3	4	5	6	7	8	9	10	11	12	13	14	15
0	0	1	1	0	1	0	1	0	0	0	1	0	1	0	0

Figure 9.1 The bit array for the set of primes in the range 0 to 15. The bit at position i is set to 1 if and only if i is prime.

This approach to compression is similar in spirit to Ziv-Lempel coding, which is a class of coding algorithms commonly used in file compression utilities. Ziv-Lempel coding replaces repeated occurrences of strings with a pointer to the location in the file of the first occurrence of the string. The codes are stored in a self-organizing list in order to speed up the time required to search for a string that has previously been seen.

9.3   Bit Vectors for Representing Sets

Determining whether a value is a member of a particular set is a special case of searching for keys in a sequence of records. Thus, any of the search methods discussed in this book can be used to check for set membership. However, we can also take advantage of the restricted circumstances imposed by this problem to develop another representation.

In the case where the set values fall within a limited range, we can represent the set using a bit array with a bit position allocated for each potential member. Those members actually in the set store a value of 1 in their corresponding bit; those members not in the set store a value of 0 in their corresponding bit. For example, consider the set of primes between 0 and 15. Figure 9.1 shows the corresponding bit array. To determine if a particular value is prime, we simply check the corresponding bit. This representation scheme is called a **bit vector** or a **bitmap**. The mark array used in several of the graph algorithms of Chapter 11 is an example of such a set representation.

If the set fits within a single computer word, then set union, intersection, and difference can be performed by logical bit-wise operations. The union of sets A and B is the bit-wise OR function (whose symbol is | in C++). The intersection of sets A and B is the bit-wise AND function (whose symbol is & in C++). For example, if we would like to compute the set of numbers between 0 and 15 that are both prime and odd numbers, we need only compute the expression

$$0011010100010100 \ \& \ 0101010101010101.$$

The set difference $A - B$ can be implemented in C++ using the expression **A&˜B** (˜ is the symbol for bit-wise negation). For larger sets that do not fit into a single computer word, the equivalent operations can be performed in turn on the series of words making up the entire bit vector.

This method of computing sets from bit vectors is sometimes applied to document retrieval. Consider the problem of picking from a collection of documents those few which contain selected keywords. For each keyword, the document retrieval system stores a bit vector with one bit for each document. If the user wants to know which documents contain a certain three keywords, the corresponding three bit vectors are AND'ed together. Those bit positions resulting in a value of 1 correspond to the desired documents. Alternatively, a bit vector can be stored for each document to indicate those keywords appearing in the document. Such an organization is called a **signature file**. The signatures can be manipulated to find documents with desired combinations of keywords.

9.4 Hashing

This section presents a completely different approach to searching arrays: by direct access based on key value. The process of finding a record using some computation to map its key value to a position in the array is called **hashing**. Most hashing schemes place records in the array in whatever order satisfies the needs of the address calculation, thus the records are not ordered by value or frequency. The function that maps key values to positions is called a **hash function** and will be denoted by **h**. The array that holds the records is called the **hash table** and will be denoted by **HT**. A position in the hash table is also known as a **slot**. The number of slots in hash table **HT** will be denoted by the variable M, with slots numbered from 0 to $M - 1$. The goal for a hashing system is to arrange things such that, for any key value K and some hash function **h**, $i = \mathbf{h}(K)$ is a slot in the table such that $0 \leq \mathbf{h}(K) < M$, and we have the key of the record stored at **HT**$[i]$ equal to K.

Hashing is not good for applications where multiple records with the same key value are permitted. Hashing is not a good method for answering range searches. In other words, we cannot easily find all records (if any) whose key values fall within a certain range. Nor can we easily find the record with the minimum or maximum key value, or visit the records in key order. Hashing is most appropriate for answering the question, "What record, if any, has key value K?" For applications where access involves only exact-match queries, hashing is usually the search method of choice because it is extremely efficient when implemented correctly. As you will see in this section, however, there are many approaches to hashing and it is easy to devise an inefficient implementation. Hashing is suitable for both in-memory and disk-based searching and is one of the two most widely used methods for organizing large databases stored on disk (the other is the B-tree, which is covered in Chapter 10).

As a simple (though unrealistic) example of hashing, consider storing n records each with a unique key value in the range 0 to $n - 1$. In this simple case, a record with key k can be stored in **HT**$[k]$, and the hash function is simply $\mathbf{h}(k) = k$. To find the record with key value k, simply look in **HT**$[k]$.

Typically, there are many more values in the key range than there are slots in the hash table. For a more realistic example, suppose that the key can take any value in the range 0 to 65,535 (i.e., the key is a two-byte unsigned integer), and that we expect to store approximately 1000 records at any given time. It is impractical in this situation to use a hash table with 65,536 slots, because most of the slots will be left empty. Instead, we must devise a hash function that allows us to store the records in a much smaller table. Because the possible key range is larger than the size of the table, at least some of the slots must be mapped to from multiple key values. Given a hash function **h** and two keys k_1 and k_2, if $\mathbf{h}(k_1) = \beta = \mathbf{h}(k_2)$ where β is a slot in the table, then we say that k_1 and k_2 have a **collision** at slot β under hash function **h**.

Finding a record with key value K in a database organized by hashing follows a two-step procedure:

1. Compute the table location $\mathbf{h}(K)$.
2. Starting with slot $\mathbf{h}(K)$, locate the record containing key K using (if necessary) a **collision resolution policy**.

9.4.1 Hash Functions

Hashing generally takes records whose key values come from a large range and stores those records in a table with a relatively small number of slots. Collisions occur when two records hash to the same slot in the table. If we are careful—or lucky—when selecting a hash function, then the actual number of collisions will be few. Unfortunately, even under the best of circumstances, collisions are nearly unavoidable.[1] For example, consider a classroom full of students. What is the probability that some pair of students shares the same birthday (i.e., the same day of the year, not necessarily the same year)? If there are 23 students, then the odds are about even that two will share a birthday. This is despite the fact that there are 365 days in which students can have birthdays (ignoring leap years), on most of which no student in the class has a birthday. With more students, the probability of a shared birthday increases. The mapping of students to days based on their

---

[1] The exception to this is **perfect hashing**. Perfect hashing is a system in which records are hashed such that there are no collisions. A hash function is selected for the specific set of records being hashed, which requires that the entire collection of records be available before selecting the hash function. Perfect hashing is efficient because it always finds the record that we are looking for exactly where the hash function computes it to be, so only one access is required. Selecting a perfect hash function can be expensive, but might be worthwhile when extremely efficient search performance is required. An example is searching for data on a read-only CD. Here the database will never change, the time for each access is expensive, and the database designer can build the hash table before issuing the CD.

birthday is similar to assigning records to slots in a table (of size 365) using the birthday as a hash function. Note that this observation tells us nothing about *which* students share a birthday, or on *which* days of the year shared birthdays fall.

To be practical, a database organized by hashing must store records in a hash table that is not so large that it wastes space. Typically, this means that the hash table will be around half full. Because collisions are extremely likely to occur under these conditions (by chance, any record inserted into a table that is half full will have a collision half of the time), does this mean that we need not worry about the ability of a hash function to avoid collisions? Absolutely not. The difference between a good hash function and a bad hash function makes a big difference in practice. Technically, any function that maps all possible key values to a slot in the hash table is a hash function. In the extreme case, even a function that maps all records to the same slot is a hash function, but it does nothing to help us find records during a search operation.

We would like to pick a hash function that stores the actual records in the collection such that each slot in the hash table has equal probability of being filled. Unfortunately, we normally have no control over the key values of the actual records, so how well any particular hash function does this depends on the distribution of the keys within the allowable key range. In some cases, incoming data are well distributed across their key range. For example, if the input is a set of random numbers selected uniformly from the key range, any hash function that assigns the key range so that each slot in the hash table receives an equal share of the range will likely also distribute the input records uniformly within the table. However, in many applications the incoming records are highly clustered or otherwise poorly distributed. When input records are not well distributed throughout the key range it can be difficult to devise a hash function that does a good job of distributing the records throughout the table, especially if the input distribution is not known in advance.

There are many reasons why data values might be poorly distributed.

1. Natural frequency distributions tend to follow a common pattern where a few of the entities occur frequently while most entities occur relatively rarely. For example, consider the populations of the 100 largest cities in the United States. If you plot these populations on a number line, most of them will be clustered toward the low side, with a few outliers on the high side. This is an example of a Zipf distribution (see Section 9.2). Viewed the other way, the home town for a given person is far more likely to be a particular large city than a particular small town.

2. Collected data are likely to be skewed in some way. Field samples might be rounded to, say, the nearest 5 (i.e., all numbers end in 5 or 0).

3. If the input is a collection of common English words, the beginning letter will be poorly distributed.

Note that in examples 2 and 3, either high- or low-order bits of the key are poorly distributed.

When designing hash functions, we are generally faced with one of two situations.

1. We know nothing about the distribution of the incoming keys. In this case, we wish to select a hash function that evenly distributes the key range across the hash table, while avoiding obvious opportunities for clustering such as hash functions that are sensitive to the high- or low-order bits of the key value.
2. We know something about the distribution of the incoming keys. In this case, we should use a distribution-dependent hash function that avoids assigning clusters of related key values to the same hash table slot. For example, if hashing English words, we should *not* hash on the value of the first character because this is likely to be unevenly distributed.

Below are several examples of hash functions that illustrate these points.

Example 9.5 Consider the following hash function used to hash integers to a table of sixteen slots:

```
int h(int x) {
  return x % 16;
}
```

The value returned by this hash function depends solely on the least significant four bits of the key. Because these bits are likely to be poorly distributed (as an example, a high percentage of the keys might be even numbers, which means that the low order bit is zero), the result will also be poorly distributed. This example shows that the size of the table M can have a big effect on the performance of a hash system because this value is typically used as the modulus to ensure that the hash function produces a number in the range 0 to $M - 1$.

Example 9.6 A good hash function for numerical values comes from the **mid-square** method. The mid-square method squares the key value, and then takes the middle r bits of the result, giving a value in the range 0 to $2^r - 1$. This works well because most or all bits of the key value contribute to the result. For example, consider records whose keys are 4-digit numbers in base 10. The goal is to hash these key values to a table of size 100 (i.e., a range of 0 to 99). This range is equivalent to two digits in base 10. That is, $r = 2$. If the input is the number 4567, squaring yields an 8-digit number, 20857489. The middle two digits of this result are 57. All digits

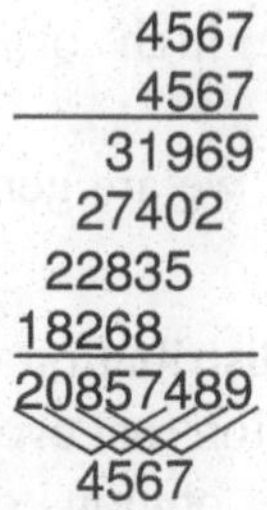

$$
\begin{array}{r}
4567 \\
4567 \\
\hline
31969 \\
27402 \\
22835 \\
18268 \\
\hline
20857489 \\
\end{array}
$$

4567

Figure 9.2 An illustration of the mid-square method, showing the details of long multiplication in the process of squaring the value 4567. The bottom of the figure indicates which digits of the answer are most influenced by each digit of the operands.

(equivalently, all bits when the number is viewed in binary) contribute to the middle two digits of the squared value. Figure 9.2 illustrates the concept. Thus, the result is not dominated by the distribution of the bottom digit or the top digit of the original key value.

Example 9.7 Here is a hash function for strings of characters:

```
int h(char* x) {
  int i, sum;
  for (sum=0, i=0; x[i] != '\0'; i++)
    sum += (int) x[i];
  return sum % M;
}
```

This function sums the ASCII values of the letters in a string. If the hash table size M is small, this hash function should do a good job of distributing strings evenly among the hash table slots, because it gives equal weight to all characters. This is an example of the **folding** approach to designing a hash function. Note that the order of the characters in the string has no effect on the result. A similar method for integers would add the digits of the key value, assuming that there are enough digits to (1) keep any one or two digits with bad distribution from skewing the results of the process and (2) generate a sum much larger than M. As with many other hash functions, the final step is to apply the modulus operator to the result, using table size M to generate a value within the table range. If the sum is not sufficiently large, then the modulus operator will yield a poor distribution. For example, because the ASCII value for "A" is 65 and "Z" is 90, **sum** will always be in the range 650 to 900 for a string of ten upper case letters. For a hash table of size 100 or less, a reasonable distribution results. For a hash table of size 1000, the distribution is terrible because only slots 650 to 900 can possibly be the home slot for some key value, and the values are not evenly distributed even within those slots.

Example 9.8 Here is a much better hash function for strings.

```
// Use folding on a string, summed 4 bytes at a time
int sfold(char* key) {
  unsigned int *lkey = (unsigned int *)key;
  int intlength = strlen(key)/4;
  unsigned int sum = 0;
  for(int i=0; i<intlength; i++)
    sum += lkey[i];

  // Now deal with the extra chars at the end
  int extra = strlen(key) - intlength*4;
  char temp[4];
  lkey = (unsigned int *)temp;
  lkey[0] = 0;
  for(int i=0; i<extra; i++)
    temp[i] = key[intlength*4+i];
  sum += lkey[0];

  return sum % M;
}
```

This function takes a string as input. It processes the string four bytes at a time, and interprets each of the four-byte chunks as a single (unsigned) long integer value. The integer values for the four-byte chunks are added together. In the end, the resulting sum is converted to the range 0 to $M-1$ using the modulus operator.[2]

For example, if the string "aaaabbbb" is passed to **sfold**, then the first four bytes ("aaaa") will be interpreted as the integer value 1,633,771,873 and the next four bytes ("bbbb") will be interpreted as the integer value 1,650,614,882. Their sum is 3,284,386,755 (when viewed as an unsigned integer). If the table size is 101 then the modulus function will cause this key to hash to slot 75 in the table. Note that for any sufficiently long string, the sum for the integer quantities will typically cause a 32-bit integer to overflow (thus losing some of the high-order bits) because the resulting values are so large. But this causes no problems when the goal is to compute a hash function.

[2]Recall from Section 2.2 that the implementation for $n \bmod m$ on many **C++** and Java compilers will yield a negative number if n is negative. Implementors for hash functions need to be careful that their hash function does not generate a negative number. This can be avoided either by insuring that n is positive when computing $n \bmod m$, or adding m to the result if $n \bmod m$ is negative. All computation in **sfold** is done using unsigned long values in part to protect against taking the modulus of an negative number.

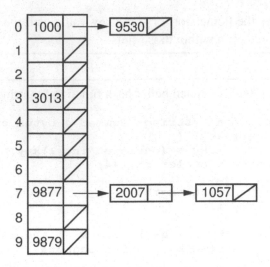

Figure 9.3 An illustration of open hashing for seven numbers stored in a ten-slot hash table using the hash function $h(K) = K \bmod 10$. The numbers are inserted in the order 9877, 2007, 1000, 9530, 3013, 9879, and 1057. Two of the values hash to slot 0, one value hashes to slot 2, three of the values hash to slot 7, and one value hashes to slot 9.

9.4.2   Open Hashing

While the goal of a hash function is to minimize collisions, some collisions are unavoidable in practice. Thus, hashing implementations must include some form of collision resolution policy. Collision resolution techniques can be broken into two classes: **open hashing** (also called **separate chaining**) and **closed hashing** (also called **open addressing**).[3] The difference between the two has to do with whether collisions are stored outside the table (open hashing), or whether collisions result in storing one of the records at another slot in the table (closed hashing). Open hashing is treated in this section, and closed hashing in Section 9.4.3.

The simplest form of open hashing defines each slot in the hash table to be the head of a linked list. All records that hash to a particular slot are placed on that slot's linked list. Figure 9.3 illustrates a hash table where each slot stores one record and a link pointer to the rest of the list.

Records within a slot's list can be ordered in several ways: by insertion order, by key value order, or by frequency-of-access order. Ordering the list by key value provides an advantage in the case of an unsuccessful search, because we know to stop searching the list once we encounter a key that is greater than the one being

---

[3]Yes, it is confusing when "open hashing" means the opposite of "open addressing," but unfortunately, that is the way it is.

searched for. If records on the list are unordered or ordered by frequency, then an unsuccessful search will need to visit every record on the list.

Given a table of size M storing N records, the hash function will (ideally) spread the records evenly among the M positions in the table, yielding on average N/M records for each list. Assuming that the table has more slots than there are records to be stored, we can hope that few slots will contain more than one record. In the case where a list is empty or has only one record, a search requires only one access to the list. Thus, the average cost for hashing should be $\Theta(1)$. However, if clustering causes many records to hash to only a few of the slots, then the cost to access a record will be much higher because many elements on the linked list must be searched.

Open hashing is most appropriate when the hash table is kept in main memory, with the lists implemented by a standard in-memory linked list. Storing an open hash table on disk in an efficient way is difficult, because members of a given linked list might be stored on different disk blocks. This would result in multiple disk accesses when searching for a particular key value, which defeats the purpose of using hashing.

There are similarities between open hashing and Binsort. One way to view open hashing is that each record is simply placed in a bin. While multiple records may hash to the same bin, this initial binning should still greatly reduce the number of records accessed by a search operation. In a similar fashion, a simple Binsort reduces the number of records in each bin to a small number that can be sorted in some other way.

9.4.3 Closed Hashing

Closed hashing stores all records directly in the hash table. Each record R with key value k_R has a **home position** that is $h(k_R)$, the slot computed by the hash function. If R is to be inserted and another record already occupies R's home position, then R will be stored at some other slot in the table. It is the business of the collision resolution policy to determine which slot that will be. Naturally, the same policy must be followed during search as during insertion, so that any record not found in its home position can be recovered by repeating the collision resolution process.

Bucket Hashing

One implementation for closed hashing groups hash table slots into **buckets**. The M slots of the hash table are divided into B buckets, with each bucket consisting of M/B slots. The hash function assigns each record to the first slot within one of the buckets. If this slot is already occupied, then the bucket slots are searched sequentially until an open slot is found. If a bucket is entirely full, then the record is stored in an **overflow bucket** of infinite capacity at the end of the table. All

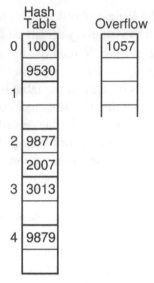

Figure 9.4 An illustration of bucket hashing for seven numbers stored in a five-bucket hash table using the hash function $\mathbf{h}(K) = K \bmod 5$. Each bucket contains two slots. The numbers are inserted in the order 9877, 2007, 1000, 9530, 3013, 9879, and 1057. Two of the values hash to bucket 0, three values hash to bucket 2, one value hashes to bucket 3, and one value hashes to bucket 4. Because bucket 2 cannot hold three values, the third one ends up in the overflow bucket.

buckets share the same overflow bucket. A good implementation will use a hash function that distributes the records evenly among the buckets so that as few records as possible go into the overflow bucket. Figure 9.4 illustrates bucket hashing.

When searching for a record, the first step is to hash the key to determine which bucket should contain the record. The records in this bucket are then searched. If the desired key value is not found and the bucket still has free slots, then the search is complete. If the bucket is full, then it is possible that the desired record is stored in the overflow bucket. In this case, the overflow bucket must be searched until the record is found or all records in the overflow bucket have been checked. If many records are in the overflow bucket, this will be an expensive process.

A simple variation on bucket hashing is to hash a key value to some slot in the hash table as though bucketing were not being used. If the home position is full, then the collision resolution process is to move down through the table toward the end of the bucket while searching for a free slot in which to store the record. If the bottom of the bucket is reached, then the collision resolution routine wraps around to the top of the bucket to continue the search for an open slot. For example, assume that buckets contain eight records, with the first bucket consisting of slots 0 through 7. If a record is hashed to slot 5, the collision resolution process will attempt to insert the record into the table in the order 5, 6, 7, 0, 1, 2, 3, and finally 4. If all slots in this bucket are full, then the record is assigned to the overflow bucket.

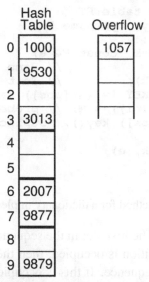

Figure 9.5 An variant of bucket hashing for seven numbers stored in a 10-slot hash table using the hash function $\mathbf{h}(K) = K \bmod 10$. Each bucket contains two slots. The numbers are inserted in the order 9877, 2007, 1000, 9530, 3013, 9879, and 1057. Value 9877 first hashes to slot 7, so when value 2007 attempts to do likewise, it is placed in the other slot associated with that bucket which is slot 6. When value 1057 is inserted, there is no longer room in the bucket and it is placed into overflow. The other collision occurs after value 1000 is inserted to slot 0, causing 9530 to be moved to slot 1.

The advantage of this approach is that initial collisions are reduced, Because any slot can be a home position rather than just the first slot in the bucket. Figure 9.5 shows another example for this form of bucket hashing.

Bucket methods are good for implementing hash tables stored on disk, because the bucket size can be set to the size of a disk block. Whenever search or insertion occurs, the entire bucket is read into memory. Because the entire bucket is then in memory, processing an insert or search operation requires only one disk access, unless the bucket is full. If the bucket is full, then the overflow bucket must be retrieved from disk as well. Naturally, overflow should be kept small to minimize unnecessary disk accesses.

Linear Probing

We now turn to the most commonly used form of hashing: closed hashing with no bucketing, and a collision resolution policy that can potentially use any slot in the hash table.

During insertion, the goal of collision resolution is to find a free slot in the hash table when the home position for the record is already occupied. We can view any collision resolution method as generating a sequence of hash table slots that can

```
// Insert e into hash table HT
template <typename Key, typename E>
void hashdict<Key, E>::
hashInsert(const Key& k, const E& e) {
  int home;                          // Home position for e
  int pos = home = h(k);             // Init probe sequence
  for (int i=1; EMPTYKEY != (HT[pos]).key(); i++) {
    pos = (home + p(k, i)) % M; // probe
    Assert(k != (HT[pos]).key(), "Duplicates not allowed");
  }
  KVpair<Key,E> temp(k, e);
  HT[pos] = temp;
}
```

Figure 9.6 Insertion method for a dictionary implemented by a hash table.

potentially hold the record. The first slot in the sequence will be the home position for the key. If the home position is occupied, then the collision resolution policy goes to the next slot in the sequence. If this is occupied as well, then another slot must be found, and so on. This sequence of slots is known as the **probe sequence**, and it is generated by some **probe function** that we will call **p**. The insert function is shown in Figure 9.6.

Method **hashInsert** first checks to see if the home slot for the key is empty. If the home slot is occupied, then we use the probe function, $p(k, i)$ to locate a free slot in the table. Function **p** has two parameters, the key k and a count i for where in the probe sequence we wish to be. That is, to get the first position in the probe sequence after the home slot for key K, we call $p(K, 1)$. For the next slot in the probe sequence, call $p(K, 2)$. Note that the probe function returns an offset from the original home position, rather than a slot in the hash table. Thus, the **for** loop in **hashInsert** is computing positions in the table at each iteration by adding the value returned from the probe function to the home position. The ith call to **p** returns the ith offset to be used.

Searching in a hash table follows the same probe sequence that was followed when inserting records. In this way, a record not in its home position can be recovered. A **C++** implementation for the search procedure is shown in Figure 9.7.

The insert and search routines assume that at least one slot on the probe sequence of every key will be empty. Otherwise, they will continue in an infinite loop on unsuccessful searches. Thus, the dictionary should keep a count of the number of records stored, and refuse to insert into a table that has only one free slot.

The discussion on bucket hashing presented a simple method of collision resolution. If the home position for the record is occupied, then move down the bucket until a free slot is found. This is an example of a technique for collision resolution known as **linear probing**. The probe function for simple linear probing is

$$p(K, i) = i.$$

```
// Search for the record with Key K
template <typename Key, typename E>
E hashdict<Key, E>::
hashSearch(const Key& k) const {
  int home;                 // Home position for k
  int pos = home = h(k);    // Initial position is home slot
  for (int i = 1; (k != (HT[pos]).key()) &&
                  (EMPTYKEY != (HT[pos]).key()); i++)
    pos = (home + p(k, i)) % M; // Next on probe sequence
  if (k == (HT[pos]).key())     // Found it
    return (HT[pos]).value();
  else return NULL;             // k not in hash table
}
```

Figure 9.7 Search method for a dictionary implemented by a hash table.

That is, the ith offset on the probe sequence is just i, meaning that the ith step is simply to move down i slots in the table.

Once the bottom of the table is reached, the probe sequence wraps around to the beginning of the table. Linear probing has the virtue that all slots in the table will be candidates for inserting a new record before the probe sequence returns to the home position.

While linear probing is probably the first idea that comes to mind when considering collision resolution policies, it is not the only one possible. Probe function **p** allows us many options for how to do collision resolution. In fact, linear probing is one of the worst collision resolution methods. The main problem is illustrated by Figure 9.8. Here, we see a hash table of ten slots used to store four-digit numbers, with hash function $h(K) = K \bmod 10$. In Figure 9.8(a), five numbers have been placed in the table, leaving five slots remaining.

The ideal behavior for a collision resolution mechanism is that each empty slot in the table will have equal probability of receiving the next record inserted (assuming that every slot in the table has equal probability of being hashed to initially). In this example, assume that the hash function gives each slot (roughly) equal probability of being the home position for the next key. However, consider what happens to the next record if its key has its home position at slot 0. Linear probing will send the record to slot 2. The same will happen to records whose home position is at slot 1. A record with home position at slot 2 will remain in slot 2. Thus, the probability is 3/10 that the next record inserted will end up in slot 2. In a similar manner, records hashing to slots 7 or 8 will end up in slot 9. However, only records hashing to slot 3 will be stored in slot 3, yielding one chance in ten of this happening. Likewise, there is only one chance in ten that the next record will be stored in slot 4, one chance in ten for slot 5, and one chance in ten for slot 6. Thus, the resulting probabilities are not equal.

To make matters worse, if the next record ends up in slot 9 (which already has a higher than normal chance of happening), then the following record will end up

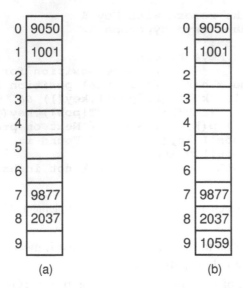

Figure 9.8 Example of problems with linear probing. (a) Four values are inserted
in the order 1001, 9050, 9877, and 2037 using hash function $\mathbf{h}(K) = K \bmod 10$.
(b) The value 1059 is added to the hash table.

in slot 2 with probability 6/10. This is illustrated by Figure 9.8(b). This tendency
of linear probing to cluster items together is known as **primary clustering**. Small
clusters tend to merge into big clusters, making the problem worse. The objection
to primary clustering is that it leads to long probe sequences.

Improved Collision Resolution Methods

How can we avoid primary clustering? One possible improvement might be to use
linear probing, but to skip slots by a constant c other than 1. This would make the
probe function

$$\mathbf{p}(K, i) = ci,$$

and so the ith slot in the probe sequence will be $(\mathbf{h}(K) + ic) \bmod M$. In this way,
records with adjacent home positions will not follow the same probe sequence. For
example, if we were to skip by twos, then our offsets from the home slot would
be 2, then 4, then 6, and so on.

   One quality of a good probe sequence is that it will cycle through all slots in
the hash table before returning to the home position. Clearly linear probing (which
"skips" slots by one each time) does this. Unfortunately, not all values for c will
make this happen. For example, if $c = 2$ and the table contains an even number
of slots, then any key whose home position is in an even slot will have a probe
sequence that cycles through only the even slots. Likewise, the probe sequence
for a key whose home position is in an odd slot will cycle through the odd slots.
Thus, this combination of table size and linear probing constant effectively divides

the records into two sets stored in two disjoint sections of the hash table. So long as both sections of the table contain the same number of records, this is not really important. However, just from chance it is likely that one section will become fuller than the other, leading to more collisions and poorer performance for those records. The other section would have fewer records, and thus better performance. But the overall system performance will be degraded, as the additional cost to the side that is more full outweighs the improved performance of the less-full side.

Constant c must be relatively prime to M to generate a linear probing sequence that visits all slots in the table (that is, c and M must share no factors). For a hash table of size $M = 10$, if c is any one of 1, 3, 7, or 9, then the probe sequence will visit all slots for any key. When $M = 11$, any value for c between 1 and 10 generates a probe sequence that visits all slots for every key.

Consider the situation where $c = 2$ and we wish to insert a record with key k_1 such that $\mathbf{h}(k_1) = 3$. The probe sequence for k_1 is 3, 5, 7, 9, and so on. If another key k_2 has home position at slot 5, then its probe sequence will be 5, 7, 9, and so on. The probe sequences of k_1 and k_2 are linked together in a manner that contributes to clustering. In other words, linear probing with a value of $c > 1$ does not solve the problem of primary clustering. We would like to find a probe function that does not link keys together in this way. We would prefer that the probe sequence for k_1 after the first step on the sequence should not be identical to the probe sequence of k_2. Instead, their probe sequences should diverge.

The ideal probe function would select the next position on the probe sequence at random from among the unvisited slots; that is, the probe sequence should be a random permutation of the hash table positions. Unfortunately, we cannot actually select the next position in the probe sequence at random, because then we would not be able to duplicate this same probe sequence when searching for the key. However, we can do something similar called **pseudo-random probing**. In pseudo-random probing, the ith slot in the probe sequence is $(\mathbf{h}(K) + r_i) \bmod M$ where r_i is the ith value in a random permutation of the numbers from 1 to $M - 1$. All insertion and search operations use the same random permutation. The probe function is

$$\mathbf{p}(K, i) = \texttt{Perm}[i - 1],$$

where **Perm** is an array of length $M - 1$ containing a random permutation of the values from 1 to $M - 1$.

Example 9.9 Consider a table of size $M = 101$, with $\texttt{Perm}[1] = 5$, $\texttt{Perm}[2] = 2$, and $\texttt{Perm}[3] = 32$. Assume that we have two keys k_1 and k_2 where $\mathbf{h}(k_1) = 30$ and $\mathbf{h}(k_2) = 35$. The probe sequence for k_1 is 30, then 35, then 32, then 62. The probe sequence for k_2 is 35, then 40, then 37, then 67. Thus, while k_2 will probe to k_1's home position as its second choice, the two keys' probe sequences diverge immediately thereafter.

Another probe function that eliminates primary clustering is called **quadratic probing**. Here the probe function is some quadratic function

$$\mathbf{p}(K, i) = c_1 i^2 + c_2 i + c_3$$

for some choice of constants c_1, c_2, and c_3. The simplest variation is $\mathbf{p}(K, i) = i^2$ (i.e., $c_1 = 1$, $c_2 = 0$, and $c_3 = 0$. Then the ith value in the probe sequence would be $(\mathbf{h}(K) + i^2) \bmod M$. Under quadratic probing, two keys with different home positions will have diverging probe sequences.

Example 9.10 Given a hash table of size $M = 101$, assume for keys k_1 and k_2 that $\mathbf{h}(k_1) = 30$ and $\mathbf{h}(k_2) = 29$. The probe sequence for k_1 is 30, then 31, then 34, then 39. The probe sequence for k_2 is 29, then 30, then 33, then 38. Thus, while k_2 will probe to k_1's home position as its second choice, the two keys' probe sequences diverge immediately thereafter.

Unfortunately, quadratic probing has the disadvantage that typically not all hash table slots will be on the probe sequence. Using $\mathbf{p}(K, i) = i^2$ gives particularly inconsistent results. For many hash table sizes, this probe function will cycle through a relatively small number of slots. If all slots on that cycle happen to be full, then the record cannot be inserted at all! For example, if our hash table has three slots, then records that hash to slot 0 can probe only to slots 0 and 1 (that is, the probe sequence will never visit slot 2 in the table). Thus, if slots 0 and 1 are full, then the record cannot be inserted even though the table is not full. A more realistic example is a table with 105 slots. The probe sequence starting from any given slot will only visit 23 other slots in the table. If all 24 of these slots should happen to be full, even if other slots in the table are empty, then the record cannot be inserted because the probe sequence will continually hit only those same 24 slots.

Fortunately, it is possible to get good results from quadratic probing at low cost. The right combination of probe function and table size will visit many slots in the table. In particular, if the hash table size is a prime number and the probe function is $\mathbf{p}(K, i) = i^2$, then at least half the slots in the table will be visited. Thus, if the table is less than half full, we can be certain that a free slot will be found. Alternatively, if the hash table size is a power of two and the probe function is $\mathbf{p}(K, i) = (i^2 + i)/2$, then every slot in the table will be visited by the probe function.

Both pseudo-random probing and quadratic probing eliminate primary clustering, which is the problem of keys sharing substantial segments of a probe sequence. If two keys hash to the same home position, however, then they will always follow the same probe sequence for every collision resolution method that we have seen so far. The probe sequences generated by pseudo-random and quadratic probing (for example) are entirely a function of the home position, not the original key value.

This is because function **p** ignores its input parameter K for these collision resolution methods. If the hash function generates a cluster at a particular home position, then the cluster remains under pseudo-random and quadratic probing. This problem is called **secondary clustering**.

To avoid secondary clustering, we need to have the probe sequence make use of the original key value in its decision-making process. A simple technique for doing this is to return to linear probing by a constant step size for the probe function, but to have that constant be determined by a second hash function, $\mathbf{h_2}$. Thus, the probe sequence would be of the form $\mathbf{p}(K, i) = i * \mathbf{h_2}(K)$. This method is called **double hashing**.

Example 9.11 Assume a hash table has size $M = 101$, and that there are three keys k_1, k_2, and k_3 with $\mathbf{h}(k_1) = 30$, $\mathbf{h}(k_2) = 28$, $\mathbf{h}(k_3) = 30$, $\mathbf{h_2}(k_1) = 2$, $\mathbf{h_2}(k_2) = 5$, and $\mathbf{h_2}(k_3) = 5$. Then, the probe sequence for k_1 will be 30, 32, 34, 36, and so on. The probe sequence for k_2 will be 28, 33, 38, 43, and so on. The probe sequence for k_3 will be 30, 35, 40, 45, and so on. Thus, none of the keys share substantial portions of the same probe sequence. Of course, if a fourth key k_4 has $\mathbf{h}(k_4) = 28$ and $\mathbf{h_2}(k_4) = 2$, then it will follow the same probe sequence as k_1. Pseudo-random or quadratic probing can be combined with double hashing to solve this problem.

A good implementation of double hashing should ensure that all of the probe sequence constants are relatively prime to the table size M. This can be achieved easily. One way is to select M to be a prime number, and have $\mathbf{h_2}$ return a value in the range $1 \le \mathbf{h_2}(K) \le M - 1$. Another way is to set $M = 2^m$ for some value m and have $\mathbf{h_2}$ return an odd value between 1 and 2^m.

Figure 9.9 shows an implementation of the dictionary ADT by means of a hash table. The simplest hash function is used, with collision resolution by linear probing, as the basis for the structure of a hash table implementation. A suggested project at the end of this chapter asks you to improve the implementation with other hash functions and collision resolution policies.

9.4.4 Analysis of Closed Hashing

How efficient is hashing? We can measure hashing performance in terms of the number of record accesses required when performing an operation. The primary operations of concern are insertion, deletion, and search. It is useful to distinguish between successful and unsuccessful searches. Before a record can be deleted, it must be found. Thus, the number of accesses required to delete a record is equivalent to the number required to successfully search for it. To insert a record, an empty slot along the record's probe sequence must be found. This is equivalent to

```
// Dictionary implemented with a hash table
template <typename Key, typename E>
class hashdict : public Dictionary<Key,E> {
private:
  KVpair<Key,E>* HT;   // The hash table
  int M;          // Size of HT
  int currcnt;    // The current number of elements in HT
  Key EMPTYKEY;   // User-supplied key value for an empty slot

  int p(Key K, int i) const // Probe using linear probing
    { return i; }

  int h(int x) const { return x % M; } // Poor hash function
  int h(char* x) const { // Hash function for character keys
    int i, sum;
    for (sum=0, i=0; x[i] != '\0'; i++) sum += (int) x[i];
    return sum % M;
  }

  void hashInsert(const Key&, const E&);
  E hashSearch(const Key&) const;

public:
  hashdict(int sz, Key k){ // "k" defines an empty slot
    M = sz;
    EMPTYKEY = k;
    currcnt = 0;
    HT = new KVpair<Key,E>[sz]; // Make HT of size sz
    for (int i=0; i<M; i++)
      (HT[i]).setKey(EMPTYKEY); // Initialize HT
  }

  ~hashdict() { delete HT; }

  // Find some record with key value "K"
  E find(const Key& k) const
    { return hashSearch(k); }
  int size() { return currcnt; } // Number stored in table

  // Insert element "it" with Key "k" into the dictionary.
  void insert(const Key& k, const E& it) {
    Assert(currcnt < M, "Hash table is full");
    hashInsert(k, it);
    currcnt++;
  }
```

Figure 9.9 A partial implementation for the dictionary ADT using a hash table. This uses a poor hash function and a poor collision resolution policy (linear probing), which can easily be replaced. Member functions **hashInsert** and **hashSearch** appear in Figures 9.6 and 9.7, respectively.

an unsuccessful search for the record (recall that a successful search for the record during insertion should generate an error because two records with the same key are not allowed to be stored in the table).

When the hash table is empty, the first record inserted will always find its home position free. Thus, it will require only one record access to find a free slot. If all records are stored in their home positions, then successful searches will also require only one record access. As the table begins to fill up, the probability that a record can be inserted into its home position decreases. If a record hashes to an occupied slot, then the collision resolution policy must locate another slot in which to store it. Finding records not stored in their home position also requires additional record accesses as the record is searched for along its probe sequence. As the table fills up, more and more records are likely to be located ever further from their home positions.

From this discussion, we see that the expected cost of hashing is a function of how full the table is. Define the **load factor** for the table as $\alpha = N/M$, where N is the number of records currently in the table.

An estimate of the expected cost for an insertion (or an unsuccessful search) can be derived analytically as a function of α in the case where we assume that the probe sequence follows a random permutation of the slots in the hash table. Assuming that every slot in the table has equal probability of being the home slot for the next record, the probability of finding the home position occupied is α. The probability of finding both the home position occupied and the next slot on the probe sequence occupied is $\frac{N(N-1)}{M(M-1)}$. The probability of i collisions is

$$\frac{N(N-1)\cdots(N-i+1)}{M(M-1)\cdots(M-i+1)}.$$

If N and M are large, then this is approximately $(N/M)^i$. The expected number of probes is one plus the sum over $i \geq 1$ of the probability of i collisions, which is approximately

$$1 + \sum_{i=1}^{\infty}(N/M)^i = 1/(1-\alpha).$$

The cost for a successful search (or a deletion) has the same cost as originally inserting that record. However, the expected value for the insertion cost depends on the value of α not at the time of deletion, but rather at the time of the original insertion. We can derive an estimate of this cost (essentially an average over all the insertion costs) by integrating from 0 to the current value of α, yielding a result of

$$\frac{1}{\alpha}\int_0^{\alpha}\frac{1}{1-x}dx = \frac{1}{\alpha}\log_e\frac{1}{1-\alpha}.$$

Chap. 9 Searching

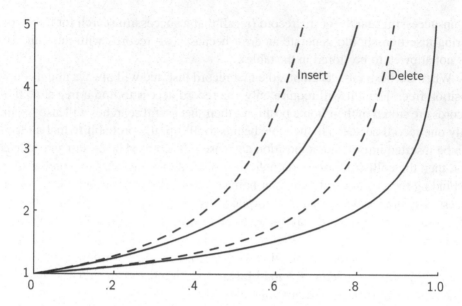

Figure 9.10 Growth of expected record accesses with α. The horizontal axis is the value for α, the vertical axis is the expected number of accesses to the hash table. Solid lines show the cost for "random" probing (a theoretical lower bound on the cost), while dashed lines show the cost for linear probing (a relatively poor collision resolution strategy). The two leftmost lines show the cost for insertion (equivalently, unsuccessful search); the two rightmost lines show the cost for deletion (equivalently, successful search).

It is important to realize that these equations represent the expected cost for operations using the unrealistic assumption that the probe sequence is based on a random permutation of the slots in the hash table (thus avoiding all expense resulting from clustering). Thus, these costs are lower-bound estimates in the average case. The true average cost under linear probing is $\frac{1}{2}(1 + 1/(1 - \alpha)^2)$ for insertions or unsuccessful searches and $\frac{1}{2}(1 + 1/(1 - \alpha))$ for deletions or successful searches. Proofs for these results can be found in the references cited in Section 9.5.

Figure 9.10 shows the graphs of these four equations to help you visualize the expected performance of hashing based on the load factor. The two solid lines show the costs in the case of a "random" probe sequence for (1) insertion or unsuccessful search and (2) deletion or successful search. As expected, the cost for insertion or unsuccessful search grows faster, because these operations typically search further down the probe sequence. The two dashed lines show equivalent costs for linear probing. As expected, the cost of linear probing grows faster than the cost for "random" probing.

From Figure 9.10 we see that the cost for hashing when the table is not too full is typically close to one record access. This is extraordinarily efficient, much better than binary search which requires $\log n$ record accesses. As α increases, so does the expected cost. For small values of α, the expected cost is low. It remains below two until the hash table is about half full. When the table is nearly empty, adding a new record to the table does not increase the cost of future search operations by much. However, the additional search cost caused by each additional insertion increases rapidly once the table becomes half full. Based on this analysis, the rule of thumb is to design a hashing system so that the hash table never gets above half full. Beyond that point performance will degrade rapidly. This requires that the implementor have some idea of how many records are likely to be in the table at maximum loading, and select the table size accordingly.

You might notice that a recommendation to never let a hash table become more than half full contradicts the disk-based space/time tradeoff principle, which strives to minimize disk space to increase information density. Hashing represents an unusual situation in that there is no benefit to be expected from locality of reference. In a sense, the hashing system implementor does everything possible to eliminate the effects of locality of reference! Given the disk block containing the last record accessed, the chance of the next record access coming to the same disk block is no better than random chance in a well-designed hash system. This is because a good hashing implementation breaks up relationships between search keys. Instead of improving performance by taking advantage of locality of reference, hashing trades increased hash table space for an improved chance that the record will be in its home position. Thus, the more space available for the hash table, the more efficient hashing should be.

Depending on the pattern of record accesses, it might be possible to reduce the expected cost of access even in the face of collisions. Recall the 80/20 rule: 80% of the accesses will come to 20% of the data. In other words, some records are accessed more frequently. If two records hash to the same home position, which would be better placed in the home position, and which in a slot further down the probe sequence? The answer is that the record with higher frequency of access should be placed in the home position, because this will reduce the total number of record accesses. Ideally, records along a probe sequence will be ordered by their frequency of access.

One approach to approximating this goal is to modify the order of records along the probe sequence whenever a record is accessed. If a search is made to a record that is not in its home position, a self-organizing list heuristic can be used. For example, if the linear probing collision resolution policy is used, then whenever a record is located that is not in its home position, it can be swapped with the record preceding it in the probe sequence. That other record will now be further from its home position, but hopefully it will be accessed less frequently. Note that this approach will not work for the other collision resolution policies presented in this section, because swapping a pair of records to improve access to one might remove the other from its probe sequence.

Another approach is to keep access counts for records and periodically rehash the entire table. The records should be inserted into the hash table in frequency order, ensuring that records that were frequently accessed during the last series of requests have the best chance of being near their home positions.

9.4.5 Deletion

When deleting records from a hash table, there are two important considerations.

1. Deleting a record must not hinder later searches. In other words, the search process must still pass through the newly emptied slot to reach records whose probe sequence passed through this slot. Thus, the delete process cannot simply mark the slot as empty, because this will isolate records further down the probe sequence. For example, in Figure 9.8(a), keys 9877 and 2037 both hash to slot 7. Key 2037 is placed in slot 8 by the collision resolution policy. If 9877 is deleted from the table, a search for 2037 must still pass through Slot 7 as it probes to slot 8.

2. We do not want to make positions in the hash table unusable because of deletion. The freed slot should be available to a future insertion.

Both of these problems can be resolved by placing a special mark in place of the deleted record, called a **tombstone**. The tombstone indicates that a record once occupied the slot but does so no longer. If a tombstone is encountered when searching along a probe sequence, the search procedure continues with the search. When a tombstone is encountered during insertion, that slot can be used to store the new record. However, to avoid inserting duplicate keys, it will still be necessary for the search procedure to follow the probe sequence until a truly empty position has been found, simply to verify that a duplicate is not in the table. However, the new record would actually be inserted into the slot of the first tombstone encountered.

The use of tombstones allows searches to work correctly and allows reuse of deleted slots. However, after a series of intermixed insertion and deletion operations, some slots will contain tombstones. This will tend to lengthen the average distance from a record's home position to the record itself, beyond where it could be if the tombstones did not exist. A typical database application will first load a collection of records into the hash table and then progress to a phase of intermixed insertions and deletions. After the table is loaded with the initial collection of records, the first few deletions will lengthen the average probe sequence distance for records (it will add tombstones). Over time, the average distance will reach an equilibrium point because insertions will tend to decrease the average distance by filling in tombstone slots. For example, after initially loading records into the database, the average path distance might be 1.2 (i.e., an average of 0.2 accesses per search beyond the home position will be required). After a series of insertions and deletions, this average distance might increase to 1.6 due to tombstones. This seems like a small increase, but it is three times longer on average beyond the home position than before deletions.

Two possible solutions to this problem are

1. Do a local reorganization upon deletion to try to shorten the average path length. For example, after deleting a key, continue to follow the probe sequence of that key and swap records further down the probe sequence into the slot of the recently deleted record (being careful not to remove any key from its probe sequence). This will not work for all collision resolution policies.

2. Periodically rehash the table by reinserting all records into a new hash table. Not only will this remove the tombstones, but it also provides an opportunity to place the most frequently accessed records into their home positions.

9.5   Further Reading

For a comparison of the efficiencies for various self-organizing techniques, see Bentley and McGeoch, "Amortized Analysis of Self-Organizing Sequential Search Heuristics" [BM85]. The text compression example of Section 9.2 comes from Bentley et al., "A Locally Adaptive Data Compression Scheme" [BSTW86]. For more on Ziv-Lempel coding, see *Data Compression: Methods and Theory* by James A. Storer [Sto88]. Knuth covers self-organizing lists and Zipf distributions in Volume 3 of *The Art of Computer Programming*[Knu98].

Introduction to Modern Information Retrieval by Salton and McGill [SM83] is an excellent source for more information about document retrieval techniques.

See the paper "Practical Minimal Perfect Hash Functions for Large Databases" by Fox et al. [FHCD92] for an introduction and a good algorithm for perfect hashing.

For further details on the analysis for various collision resolution policies, see Knuth, Volume 3 [Knu98] and *Concrete Mathematics: A Foundation for Computer Science* by Graham, Knuth, and Patashnik [GKP94].

The model of hashing presented in this chapter has been of a fixed-size hash table. A problem not addressed is what to do when the hash table gets half full and more records must be inserted. This is the domain of dynamic hashing methods. A good introduction to this topic is "Dynamic Hashing Schemes" by R.J. Enbody and H.C. Du [ED88].

9.6   Exercises

9.1 Create a graph showing expected cost versus the probability of an unsuccessful search when performing sequential search (see Section 9.1). What can you say qualitatively about the rate of increase in expected cost as the probability of unsuccessful search grows?

9.2 Modify the binary search routine of Section 3.5 to implement interpolation search. Assume that keys are in the range 1 to 10,000, and that all key values within the range are equally likely to occur.

9.3 Write an algorithm to find the Kth smallest value in an unsorted array of n numbers ($K <= n$). Your algorithm should require $\Theta(n)$ time in the average case. Hint: Your algorithm should look similar to Quicksort.

9.4 Example 9.9.3 discusses a distribution where the relative frequencies of the records match the harmonic series. That is, for every occurrence of the first record, the second record will appear half as often, the third will appear one third as often, the fourth one quarter as often, and so on. The actual probability for the ith record was defined to be $1/(i\mathcal{H}_n)$. Explain why this is correct.

9.5 Graph the equations $\mathbf{T}(n) = \log_2 n$ and $\mathbf{T}(n) = n/\log_e n$. Which gives the better performance, binary search on a sorted list, or sequential search on a list ordered by frequency where the frequency conforms to a Zipf distribution? Characterize the difference in running times.

9.6 Assume that the values A through H are stored in a self-organizing list, initially in ascending order. Consider the three self-organizing list heuristics: count, move-to-front, and transpose. For count, assume that the record is moved ahead in the list passing over any other record that its count is now greater than. For each, show the resulting list and the total number of comparisons required resulting from the following series of accesses:

$$D\ H\ H\ G\ H\ E\ G\ H\ G\ H\ E\ C\ E\ H\ G.$$

9.7 For each of the three self-organizing list heuristics (count, move-to-front, and transpose), describe a series of record accesses for which it would require the greatest number of comparisons of the three.

9.8 Write an algorithm to implement the frequency count self-organizing list heuristic, assuming that the list is implemented using an array. In particular, write a function **FreqCount** that takes as input a value to be searched for and which adjusts the list appropriately. If the value is not already in the list, add it to the end of the list with a frequency count of one.

9.9 Write an algorithm to implement the move-to-front self-organizing list heuristic, assuming that the list is implemented using an array. In particular, write a function **MoveToFront** that takes as input a value to be searched for and which adjusts the list appropriately. If the value is not already in the list, add it to the beginning of the list.

9.10 Write an algorithm to implement the transpose self-organizing list heuristic, assuming that the list is implemented using an array. In particular, write a function **Transpose** that takes as input a value to be searched for and which adjusts the list appropriately. If the value is not already in the list, add it to the end of the list.

9.11 Write functions for computing union, intersection, and set difference on arbitrarily long bit vectors used to represent set membership as described in Section 9.3. Assume that for each operation both vectors are of equal length.

9.12 Compute the probabilities for the following situations. These probabilities can be computed analytically, or you may write a computer program to generate the probabilities by simulation.

  (a) Out of a group of 23 students, what is the probability that 2 students share the same birthday?
  (b) Out of a group of 100 students, what is the probability that 3 students share the same birthday?
  (c) How many students must be in the class for the probability to be at least 50% that there are 2 who share a birthday in the same month?

9.13 Assume that you are hashing key K to a hash table of n slots (indexed from 0 to $n - 1$). For each of the following functions $h(K)$, is the function acceptable as a hash function (i.e., would the hash program work correctly for both insertions and searches), and if so, is it a good hash function? Function **Random(n)** returns a random integer between 0 and $n - 1$, inclusive.

  (a) $h(k) = k/n$ where k and n are integers.
  (b) $h(k) = 1$.
  (c) $h(k) = (k + \text{Random}(n)) \bmod n$.
  (d) $h(k) = k \bmod n$ where n is a prime number.

9.14 Assume that you have a seven-slot closed hash table (the slots are numbered 0 through 6). Show the final hash table that would result if you used the hash function $h(\mathbf{k}) = \mathbf{k} \bmod 7$ and linear probing on this list of numbers: 3, 12, 9, 2. After inserting the record with key value 2, list for each empty slot the probability that it will be the next one filled.

9.15 Assume that you have a ten-slot closed hash table (the slots are numbered 0 through 9). Show the final hash table that would result if you used the hash function $h(\mathbf{k}) = \mathbf{k} \bmod 10$ and quadratic probing on this list of numbers: 3, 12, 9, 2, 79, 46. After inserting the record with key value 46, list for each empty slot the probability that it will be the next one filled.

9.16 Assume that you have a ten-slot closed hash table (the slots are numbered 0 through 9). Show the final hash table that would result if you used the hash function $h(\mathbf{k}) = \mathbf{k} \bmod 10$ and pseudo-random probing on this list of numbers: 3, 12, 9, 2, 79, 44. The permutation of offsets to be used by the pseudo-random probing will be: 5, 9, 2, 1, 4, 8, 6, 3, 7. After inserting the record with key value 44, list for each empty slot the probability that it will be the next one filled.

9.17 What is the result of running **sfold** from Section 9.4.1 on the following strings? Assume a hash table size of 101 slots.

    (a) HELLO WORLD
    (b) NOW HEAR THIS
    (c) HEAR THIS NOW

9.18 Using closed hashing, with double hashing to resolve collisions, insert the following keys into a hash table of thirteen slots (the slots are numbered 0 through 12). The hash functions to be used are H1 and H2, defined below. You should show the hash table after all eight keys have been inserted. Be sure to indicate how you are using H1 and H2 to do the hashing. Function $Rev(k)$ reverses the decimal digits of k, for example, $Rev(37) = 73$; $Rev(7) = 7$.

$H1(k) = k \bmod 13$.
$H2(k) = (Rev(k + 1) \bmod 11)$.

Keys: 2, 8, 31, 20, 19, 18, 53, 27.

9.19 Write an algorithm for a deletion function for hash tables that replaces the record with a special value indicating a tombstone. Modify the functions **hashInsert** and **hashSearch** to work correctly with tombstones.

9.20 Consider the following permutation for the numbers 1 to 6:

$$2, 4, 6, 1, 3, 5.$$

Analyze what will happen if this permutation is used by an implementation of pseudo-random probing on a hash table of size seven. Will this permutation solve the problem of primary clustering? What does this say about selecting a permutation for use when implementing pseudo-random probing?

9.7 Projects

9.1 Implement a binary search and the quadratic binary search of Section 9.1. Run your implementations over a large range of problem sizes, timing the results for each algorithm. Graph and compare these timing results.

9.2 Implement the three self-organizing list heuristics count, move-to-front, and transpose. Compare the cost for running the three heuristics on various input data. The cost metric should be the total number of comparisons required when searching the list. It is important to compare the heuristics using input data for which self-organizing lists are reasonable, that is, on frequency distributions that are uneven. One good approach is to read text files. The list should store individual words in the text file. Begin with an empty list, as was done for the text compression example of Section 9.2. Each time a word is encountered in the text file, search for it in the self-organizing list. If the word is found, reorder the list as appropriate. If the word is not in the list, add it to the end of the list and then reorder as appropriate.

9.3 Implement the text compression system described in Section 9.2.

9.4 Implement a system for managing document retrieval. Your system should have the ability to insert (abstract references to) documents into the system, associate keywords with a given document, and to search for documents with specified keywords.

9.5 Implement a database stored on disk using bucket hashing. Define records to be 128 bytes long with a 4-byte key and 120 bytes of data. The remaining 4 bytes are available for you to store necessary information to support the hash table. A bucket in the hash table will be 1024 bytes long, so each bucket has space for 8 records. The hash table should consist of 27 buckets (total space for 216 records with slots indexed by positions 0 to 215) followed by the overflow bucket at record position 216 in the file. The hash function for key value K should be $K \bmod 213$. (Note that this means the last three slots in the table will not be home positions for any record.) The collision resolution function should be linear probing with wrap-around within the bucket. For example, if a record is hashed to slot 5, the collision resolution process will attempt to insert the record into the table in the order 5, 6, 7, 0, 1, 2, 3, and finally 4. If a bucket is full, the record should be placed in the overflow section at the end of the file.

Your hash table should implement the dictionary ADT of Section 4.4. When you do your testing, assume that the system is meant to store about 100 or so records at a time.

9.6 Implement the dictionary ADT of Section 4.4 by means of a hash table with linear probing as the collision resolution policy. You might wish to begin with the code of Figure 9.9. Using empirical simulation, determine the cost of insert and delete as α grows (i.e., reconstruct the dashed lines of Figure 9.10). Then, repeat the experiment using quadratic probing and pseudo-random probing. What can you say about the relative performance of these three collision resolution policies?

10

Indexing

Many large-scale computing applications are centered around data sets that are too large to fit into main memory. The classic example is a large database of records with multiple search keys, requiring the ability to insert, delete, and search for records. Hashing provides outstanding performance for such situations, but only in the limited case in which all searches are of the form "find the record with key value K." Many applications require more general search capabilities. One example is a range query search for all records whose key lies within some range. Other queries might involve visiting all records in order of their key value, or finding the record with the greatest key value. Hash tables are not organized to support any of these queries efficiently.

This chapter introduces file structures used to organize a large collection of records stored on disk. Such file structures support efficient insertion, deletion, and search operations, for exact-match queries, range queries, and largest/smallest key value searches.

Before discussing such file structures, we must become familiar with some basic file-processing terminology. An **entry-sequenced file** stores records in the order that they were added to the file. Entry-sequenced files are the disk-based equivalent to an unsorted list and so do not support efficient search. The natural solution is to sort the records by order of the search key. However, a typical database, such as a collection of employee or customer records maintained by a business, might contain multiple search keys. To answer a question about a particular customer might require a search on the name of the customer. Businesses often wish to sort and output the records by zip code order for a bulk mailing. Government paperwork might require the ability to search by Social Security number. Thus, there might not be a single "correct" order in which to store the records.

Indexing is the process of associating a key with the location of a corresponding data record. Section 8.5 discussed the concept of a key sort, in which an **index file** is created whose records consist of key/pointer pairs. Here, each key is associated with a pointer to a complete record in the main database file. The index file could be sorted or organized using a tree structure, thereby imposing a logical order on the records without physically rearranging them. One database might have several associated index files, each supporting efficient access through a different key field.

Each record of a database normally has a unique identifier, called the **primary key**. For example, the primary key for a set of personnel records might be the Social Security number or ID number for the individual. Unfortunately, the ID number is generally an inconvenient value on which to perform a search because the searcher is unlikely to know it. Instead, the searcher might know the desired employee's name. Alternatively, the searcher might be interested in finding all employees whose salary is in a certain range. If these are typical search requests to the database, then the name and salary fields deserve separate indices. However, key values in the name and salary indices are not likely to be unique.

A key field such as salary, where a particular key value might be duplicated in multiple records, is called a **secondary key**. Most searches are performed using a secondary key. The secondary key index (or more simply, **secondary index**) will associate a secondary key value with the primary key of each record having that secondary key value. At this point, the full database might be searched directly for the record with that primary key, or there might be a primary key index (or **primary index**) that relates each primary key value with a pointer to the actual record on disk. In the latter case, only the primary index provides the location of the actual record on disk, while the secondary indices refer to the primary index.

Indexing is an important technique for organizing large databases, and many indexing methods have been developed. Direct access through hashing is discussed in Section 9.4. A simple list sorted by key value can also serve as an index to the record file. Indexing disk files by sorted lists are discussed in the following section. Unfortunately, a sorted list does not perform well for insert and delete operations.

A third approach to indexing is the tree index. Trees are typically used to organize large databases that must support record insertion, deletion, and key range searches. Section 10.2 briefly describes ISAM, a tentative step toward solving the problem of storing a large database that must support insertion and deletion of records. Its shortcomings help to illustrate the value of tree indexing techniques. Section 10.3 introduces the basic issues related to tree indexing. Section 10.4 introduces the 2-3 tree, a balanced tree structure that is a simple form of the B-tree covered in Section 10.5. B-trees are the most widely used indexing method for large disk-based databases, and for implementing file systems. Since they have such great practical importance, many variations have been invented. Section 10.5 begins with a discussion of the variant normally referred to simply as a "B-tree." Section 10.5.1 presents the most widely implemented variant, the B^+-tree.

Linear Index

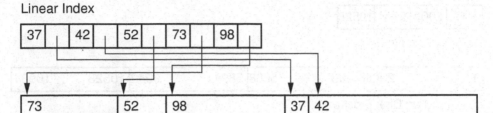

Database Records

Figure 10.1 Linear indexing for variable-length records. Each record in the index file is of fixed length and contains a pointer to the beginning of the corresponding record in the database file.

10.1   Linear Indexing

A **linear index** is an index file organized as a sequence of key/pointer pairs where the keys are in sorted order and the pointers either (1) point to the position of the complete record on disk, (2) point to the position of the primary key in the primary index, or (3) are actually the value of the primary key. Depending on its size, a linear index might be stored in main memory or on disk. A linear index provides a number of advantages. It provides convenient access to variable-length database records, because each entry in the index file contains a fixed-length key field and a fixed-length pointer to the beginning of a (variable-length) record as shown in Figure 10.1. A linear index also allows for efficient search and random access to database records, because it is amenable to binary search.

If the database contains enough records, the linear index might be too large to store in main memory. This makes binary search of the index more expensive because many disk accesses would typically be required by the search process. One solution to this problem is to store a second-level linear index in main memory that indicates which disk block in the index file stores a desired key. For example, the linear index on disk might reside in a series of 1024-byte blocks. If each key/pointer pair in the linear index requires 8 bytes (a 4-byte key and a 4-byte pointer), then 128 key/pointer pairs are stored per block. The second-level index, stored in main memory, consists of a simple table storing the value of the key in the first position of each block in the linear index file. This arrangement is shown in Figure 10.2. If the linear index requires 1024 disk blocks (1MB), the second-level index contains only 1024 entries, one per disk block. To find which disk block contains a desired search key value, first search through the 1024-entry table to find the greatest value less than or equal to the search key. This directs the search to the proper block in the index file, which is then read into memory. At this point, a binary search within this block will produce a pointer to the actual record in the database. Because the

1	2003	5894	10528

Second Level Index

1	2001	2003	5688	5894	9942	10528	10984

Linear Index: Disk Blocks

Figure 10.2 A simple two-level linear index. The linear index is stored on disk. The smaller, second-level index is stored in main memory. Each element in the second-level index stores the first key value in the corresponding disk block of the index file. In this example, the first disk block of the linear index stores keys in the range 1 to 2001, and the second disk block stores keys in the range 2003 to 5688. Thus, the first entry of the second-level index is key value 1 (the first key in the first block of the linear index), while the second entry of the second-level index is key value 2003.

second-level index is stored in main memory, accessing a record by this method requires two disk reads: one from the index file and one from the database file for the actual record.

Every time a record is inserted to or deleted from the database, all associated secondary indices must be updated. Updates to a linear index are expensive, because the entire contents of the array might be shifted. Another problem is that multiple records with the same secondary key each duplicate that key value within the index. When the secondary key field has many duplicates, such as when it has a limited range (e.g., a field to indicate job category from among a small number of possible job categories), this duplication might waste considerable space.

One improvement on the simple sorted array is a two-dimensional array where each row corresponds to a secondary key value. A row contains the primary keys whose records have the indicated secondary key value. Figure 10.3 illustrates this approach. Now there is no duplication of secondary key values, possibly yielding a considerable space savings. The cost of insertion and deletion is reduced, because only one row of the table need be adjusted. Note that a new row is added to the array when a new secondary key value is added. This might lead to moving many records, but this will happen infrequently in applications suited to using this arrangement.

A drawback to this approach is that the array must be of fixed size, which imposes an upper limit on the number of primary keys that might be associated with a particular secondary key. Furthermore, those secondary keys with fewer records than the width of the array will waste the remainder of their row. A better approach is to have a one-dimensional array of secondary key values, where each secondary key is associated with a linked list. This works well if the index is stored in main memory, but not so well when it is stored on disk because the linked list for a given key might be scattered across several disk blocks.

Jones	AA10	AB12	AB39	FF37
Smith	AX33	AX35	ZX45	
Zukowski	ZQ99			

Figure 10.3 A two-dimensional linear index. Each row lists the primary keys associated with a particular secondary key value. In this example, the secondary key is a name. The primary key is a unique four-character code.

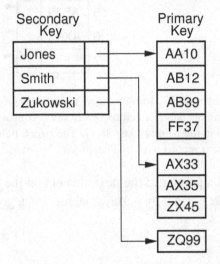

Figure 10.4 Illustration of an inverted list. Each secondary key value is stored in the secondary key list. Each secondary key value on the list has a pointer to a list of the primary keys whose associated records have that secondary key value.

Consider a large database of employee records. If the primary key is the employee's ID number and the secondary key is the employee's name, then each record in the name index associates a name with one or more ID numbers. The ID number index in turn associates an ID number with a unique pointer to the full record on disk. The secondary key index in such an organization is also known as an **inverted list** or **inverted file**. It is inverted in that searches work backwards from the secondary key to the primary key to the actual data record. It is called a list because each secondary key value has (conceptually) a list of primary keys associated with it. Figure 10.4 illustrates this arrangement. Here, we have last names as the secondary key. The primary key is a four-character unique identifier.

Figure 10.5 shows a better approach to storing inverted lists. An array of secondary key values is shown as before. Associated with each secondary key is a pointer to an array of primary keys. The primary key array uses a linked-list implementation. This approach combines the storage for all of the secondary key lists into a single array, probably saving space. Each record in this array consists of a

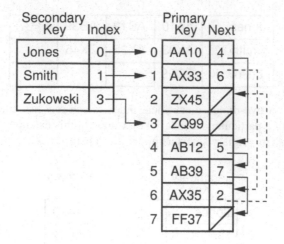

Figure 10.5 An inverted list implemented as an array of secondary keys and combined lists of primary keys. Each record in the secondary key array contains a pointer to a record in the primary key array. The **next** field of the primary key array indicates the next record with that secondary key value.

primary key value and a pointer to the next element on the list. It is easy to insert and delete secondary keys from this array, making this a good implementation for disk-based inverted files.

10.2   ISAM

How do we handle large databases that require frequent update? The main problem with the linear index is that it is a single, large array that does not adjust well to updates because a single update can require changing the position of every key in the index. Inverted lists reduce this problem, but they are only suitable for secondary key indices with many fewer secondary key values than records. The linear index would perform well as a primary key index if it could somehow be broken into pieces such that individual updates affect only a part of the index. This concept will be pursued throughout the rest of this chapter, eventually culminating in the B^+-tree, the most widely used indexing method today. But first, we begin by studying ISAM, an early attempt to solve the problem of large databases requiring frequent update. Its weaknesses help to illustrate why the B^+-tree works so well.

   Before the invention of effective tree indexing schemes, a variety of disk-based indexing methods were in use. All were rather cumbersome, largely because no adequate method for handling updates was known. Typically, updates would cause the index to degrade in performance. ISAM is one example of such an index and was widely used by IBM prior to adoption of the B-tree.

   ISAM is based on a modified form of the linear index, as illustrated by Figure 10.6. Records are stored in sorted order by primary key. The disk file is divided

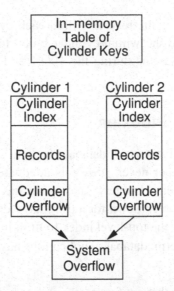

Figure 10.6 Illustration of the ISAM indexing system.

among a number of cylinders on disk.[1] Each cylinder holds a section of the list in sorted order. Initially, each cylinder is not filled to capacity, and the extra space is set aside in the **cylinder overflow**. In memory is a table listing the lowest key value stored in each cylinder of the file. Each cylinder contains a table listing the lowest key value for each block in that cylinder, called the **cylinder index**. When new records are inserted, they are placed in the correct cylinder's overflow area (in effect, a cylinder acts as a bucket). If a cylinder's overflow area fills completely, then a system-wide overflow area is used. Search proceeds by determining the proper cylinder from the system-wide table kept in main memory. The cylinder's block table is brought in from disk and consulted to determine the correct block. If the record is found in that block, then the search is complete. Otherwise, the cylinder's overflow area is searched. If that is full, and the record is not found, then the system-wide overflow is searched.

After initial construction of the database, so long as no new records are inserted or deleted, access is efficient because it requires only two disk fetches. The first disk fetch recovers the block table for the desired cylinder. The second disk fetch recovers the block that, under good conditions, contains the record. After many inserts, the overflow list becomes too long, resulting in significant search time as the cylinder overflow area fills up. Under extreme conditions, many searches might eventually lead to the system overflow area. The "solution" to this problem is to periodically reorganize the entire database. This means re-balancing the records

---

[1]Recall from Section 8.2.1 that a cylinder is all of the tracks readable from a particular placement of the heads on the multiple platters of a disk drive.

among the cylinders, sorting the records within each cylinder, and updating both the system index table and the within-cylinder block table. Such reorganization was typical of database systems during the 1960s and would normally be done each night or weekly.

10.3   Tree-based Indexing

Linear indexing is efficient when the database is static, that is, when records are inserted and deleted rarely or never. ISAM is adequate for a limited number of updates, but not for frequent changes. Because it has essentially two levels of indexing, ISAM will also break down for a truly large database where the number of cylinders is too great for the top-level index to fit in main memory.

In their most general form, database applications have the following characteristics:

1. Large sets of records that are frequently updated.
2. Search is by one or a combination of several keys.
3. Key range queries or min/max queries are used.

For such databases, a better organization must be found. One approach would be to use the binary search tree (BST) to store primary and secondary key indices. BSTs can store duplicate key values, they provide efficient insertion and deletion as well as efficient search, and they can perform efficient range queries. When there is enough main memory, the BST is a viable option for implementing both primary and secondary key indices.

Unfortunately, the BST can become unbalanced. Even under relatively good conditions, the depth of leaf nodes can easily vary by a factor of two. This might not be a significant concern when the tree is stored in main memory because the time required is still $\Theta(\log n)$ for search and update. When the tree is stored on disk, however, the depth of nodes in the tree becomes crucial. Every time a BST node B is visited, it is necessary to visit all nodes along the path from the root to B. Each node on this path must be retrieved from disk. Each disk access returns a block of information. If a node is on the same block as its parent, then the cost to find that node is trivial once its parent is in main memory. Thus, it is desirable to keep subtrees together on the same block. Unfortunately, many times a node is not on the same block as its parent. Thus, each access to a BST node could potentially require that another block to be read from disk. Using a buffer pool to store multiple blocks in memory can mitigate disk access problems if BST accesses display good locality of reference. But a buffer pool cannot eliminate disk I/O entirely. The problem becomes greater if the BST is unbalanced, because nodes deep in the tree have the potential of causing many disk blocks to be read. Thus, there are two significant issues that must be addressed to have efficient search from a disk-based

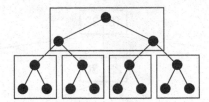

Figure 10.7 Breaking the BST into blocks. The BST is divided among disk blocks, each with space for three nodes. The path from the root to any leaf is contained on two blocks.

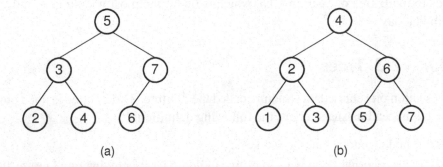

Figure 10.8 An attempt to re-balance a BST after insertion can be expensive. (a) A BST with six nodes in the shape of a complete binary tree. (b) A node with value 1 is inserted into the BST of (a). To maintain both the complete binary tree shape and the BST property, a major reorganization of the tree is required.

BST. The first is how to keep the tree balanced. The second is how to arrange the nodes on blocks so as to keep the number of blocks encountered on any path from the root to the leaves at a minimum.

We could select a scheme for balancing the BST and allocating BST nodes to blocks in a way that minimizes disk I/O, as illustrated by Figure 10.7. However, maintaining such a scheme in the face of insertions and deletions is difficult. In particular, the tree should remain balanced when an update takes place, but doing so might require much reorganization. Each update should affect only a few blocks, or its cost will be too high. As you can see from Figure 10.8, adopting a rule such as requiring the BST to be complete can cause a great deal of rearranging of data within the tree.

We can solve these problems by selecting another tree structure that automatically remains balanced after updates, and which is amenable to storing in blocks. There are a number of balanced tree data structures, and there are also techniques for keeping BSTs balanced. Examples are the AVL and splay trees discussed in Section 13.2. As an alternative, Section 10.4 presents the **2-3 tree**, which has the property that its leaves are always at the same level. The main reason for discussing the 2-3 tree here in preference to the other balanced search trees is that it naturally

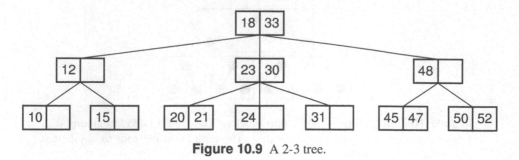

Figure 10.9 A 2-3 tree.

leads to the B-tree of Section 10.5, which is by far the most widely used indexing method today.

10.4 2-3 Trees

This section presents a data structure called the 2-3 tree. The 2-3 tree is not a binary tree, but instead its shape obeys the following definition:

1. A node contains one or two keys.
2. Every internal node has either two children (if it contains one key) or three children (if it contains two keys). Hence the name.
3. All leaves are at the same level in the tree, so the tree is always height balanced.

In addition to these shape properties, the 2-3 tree has a search tree property analogous to that of a BST. For every node, the values of all descendants in the left subtree are less than the value of the first key, while values in the center subtree are greater than or equal to the value of the first key. If there is a right subtree (equivalently, if the node stores two keys), then the values of all descendants in the center subtree are less than the value of the second key, while values in the right subtree are greater than or equal to the value of the second key. To maintain these shape and search properties requires that special action be taken when nodes are inserted and deleted. The 2-3 tree has the advantage over the BST in that the 2-3 tree can be kept height balanced at relatively low cost.

Figure 10.9 illustrates the 2-3 tree. Nodes are shown as rectangular boxes with two key fields. (These nodes actually would contain complete records or pointers to complete records, but the figures will show only the keys.) Internal nodes with only two children have an empty right key field. Leaf nodes might contain either one or two keys. Figure 10.10 is an implementation for the 2-3 tree node. Class **TTNode** is assumed to be a private class of the the 2-3 tree class **TTTree**, and thus the data members of **TTNode** will be made public to simplify the presentation.

Note that this sample declaration does not distinguish between leaf and internal nodes and so is space inefficient, because leaf nodes store three pointers each. The

```
template <typename Key, typename E>
class TTNode {          // 2-3 tree node structure
public:
  E lval;               // The node's left record
  Key lkey;             // Left record's key
  E rval;               // The node's right record
  Key rkey;             // Right record's key
  TTNode* left;         // Pointer to left child
  TTNode* center;       // Pointer to middle child
  TTNode* right;        // Pointer to right child
  TTNode() {
    center = left = right = NULL;
    lkey = rkey = EMPTYKEY;
  }
  TTNode(Key lk, E lv, Key rk, E rv, TTNode<Key,E>* p1,
              TTNode<Key,E>* p2, TTNode<Key,E>* p3) {
    lkey = lk; rkey = rk;
    lval = lv; rval = rv;
    left = p1; center = p2; right = p3;
  }
  ~TTNode() { }
  bool isLeaf() { return left == NULL; }
  TTNode<Key,E>* add(TTNode<Key,E>* it);
};
```

Figure 10.10 The 2-3 tree node implementation.

techniques of Section 5.3.1 can be applied here to implement separate internal and leaf node types.

From the defining rules for 2-3 trees we can derive relationships between the number of nodes in the tree and the depth of the tree. A 2-3 tree of height k has at least 2^{k-1} leaves, because if every internal node has two children it degenerates to the shape of a complete binary tree. A 2-3 tree of height k has at most 3^{k-1} leaves, because each internal node can have at most three children.

Searching for a value in a 2-3 tree is similar to searching in a BST. Search begins at the root. If the root does not contain the search key K, then the search progresses to the only subtree that can possibly contain K. The value(s) stored in the root node determine which is the correct subtree. For example, if searching for the value 30 in the tree of Figure 10.9, we begin with the root node. Because 30 is between 18 and 33, it can only be in the middle subtree. Searching the middle child of the root node yields the desired record. If searching for 15, then the first step is again to search the root node. Because 15 is less than 18, the first (left) branch is taken. At the next level, we take the second branch to the leaf node containing 15. If the search key were 16, then upon encountering the leaf containing 15 we would find that the search key is not in the tree. Figure 10.11 is an implementation for the 2-3 tree search method.

```
// Find the record that matches a given key value
template <typename Key, typename E>
E TTTree<Key, E>::
findhelp(TTNode<Key,E>* root, Key k) const {
  if (root == NULL) return NULL;             // value not found
  if (k == root->lkey) return root->lval;
  if (k == root->rkey) return root->rval;
  if (k < root->lkey)                        // Go left
    return findhelp(root->left, k);
  else if (root->rkey == EMPTYKEY)           // 2 child node
    return findhelp(root->center, k);        // Go center
  else if (k < root->rkey)
    return findhelp(root->center, k);        // Go center
  else return findhelp(root->right, k);      // Go right
}
```

Figure 10.11 Implementation for the 2-3 tree search method.

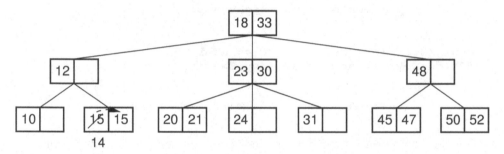

Figure 10.12 Simple insert into the 2-3 tree of Figure 10.9. The value 14 is inserted into the tree at the leaf node containing 15. Because there is room in the node for a second key, it is simply added to the left position with 15 moved to the right position.

Insertion into a 2-3 tree is similar to insertion into a BST to the extent that the new record is placed in the appropriate leaf node. Unlike BST insertion, a new child is not created to hold the record being inserted, that is, the 2-3 tree does not grow downward. The first step is to find the leaf node that would contain the record if it were in the tree. If this leaf node contains only one value, then the new record can be added to that node with no further modification to the tree, as illustrated in Figure 10.12. In this example, a record with key value 14 is inserted. Searching from the root, we come to the leaf node that stores 15. We add 14 as the left value (pushing the record with key 15 to the rightmost position).

If we insert the new record into a leaf node L that already contains two records, then more space must be created. Consider the two records of node L and the record to be inserted without further concern for which two were already in L and which is the new record. The first step is to split L into two nodes. Thus, a new node — call it L' — must be created from free store. L receives the record with the least of the three key values. L' receives the greatest of the three. The record

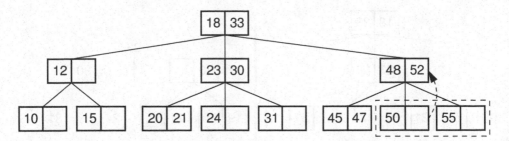

Figure 10.13 A simple node-splitting insert for a 2-3 tree. The value 55 is added to the 2-3 tree of Figure 10.9. This makes the node containing values 50 and 52 split, promoting value 52 to the parent node.

with the middle of the three key value is passed up to the parent node along with a pointer to L'. This is called a **promotion**. The promoted key is then inserted into the parent. If the parent currently contains only one record (and thus has only two children), then the promoted record and the pointer to L' are simply added to the parent node. If the parent is full, then the split-and-promote process is repeated. Figure 10.13 illustrates a simple promotion. Figure 10.14 illustrates what happens when promotions require the root to split, adding a new level to the tree. In either case, all leaf nodes continue to have equal depth. Figures 10.15 and 10.16 present an implementation for the insertion process.

Note that `inserthelp` of Figure 10.15 takes three parameters. The first is a pointer to the root of the current subtree, named `rt`. The second is the key for the record to be inserted, and the third is the record itself. The return value for `inserthelp` is a pointer to a 2-3 tree node. If `rt` is unchanged, then a pointer to `rt` is returned. If `rt` is changed (due to the insertion causing the node to split), then a pointer to the new subtree root is returned, with the key value and record value in the leftmost fields, and a pointer to the (single) subtree in the center pointer field. This revised node will then be added to the parent, as illustrated in Figure 10.14.

When deleting a record from the 2-3 tree, there are three cases to consider. The simplest occurs when the record is to be removed from a leaf node containing two records. In this case, the record is simply removed, and no other nodes are affected. The second case occurs when the only record in a leaf node is to be removed. The third case occurs when a record is to be removed from an internal node. In both the second and the third cases, the deleted record is replaced with another that can take its place while maintaining the correct order, similar to removing a node from a BST. If the tree is sparse enough, there is no such record available that will allow all nodes to still maintain at least one record. In this situation, sibling nodes are merged together. The delete operation for the 2-3 tree is excessively complex and will not be described further. Instead, a complete discussion of deletion will be postponed until the next section, where it can be generalized for a particular variant of the B-tree.

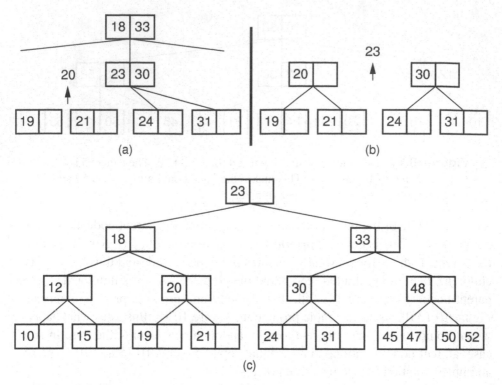

Figure 10.14 Example of inserting a record that causes the 2-3 tree root to split. (a) The value 19 is added to the 2-3 tree of Figure 10.9. This causes the node containing 20 and 21 to split, promoting 20. (b) This in turn causes the internal node containing 23 and 30 to split, promoting 23. (c) Finally, the root node splits, promoting 23 to become the left record in the new root. The result is that the tree becomes one level higher.

The 2-3 tree insert and delete routines do not add new nodes at the bottom of the tree. Instead they cause leaf nodes to split or merge, possibly causing a ripple effect moving up the tree to the root. If necessary the root will split, causing a new root node to be created and making the tree one level deeper. On deletion, if the last two children of the root merge, then the root node is removed and the tree will lose a level. In either case, all leaf nodes are always at the same level. When all leaf nodes are at the same level, we say that a tree is **height balanced**. Because the 2-3 tree is height balanced, and every internal node has at least two children, we know that the maximum depth of the tree is $\log n$. Thus, all 2-3 tree insert, find, and delete operations require $\Theta(\log n)$ time.

10.5   B-Trees

This section presents the B-tree. B-trees are usually attributed to R. Bayer and E. McCreight who described the B-tree in a 1972 paper. By 1979, B-trees had re-

```
template <typename Key, typename E>
TTNode<Key,E>* TTTree<Key, E>::
inserthelp(TTNode<Key,E>* rt, const Key k, const E e) {
  TTNode<Key,E>* retval;
  if (rt == NULL) // Empty tree: create a leaf node for root
    return new TTNode<Key,E>(k, e, EMPTYKEY, NULL,
                             NULL, NULL, NULL);
  if (rt->isLeaf()) // At leaf node: insert here
    return rt->add(new TTNode<Key,E>(k, e, EMPTYKEY, NULL,
                                     NULL, NULL, NULL));
  // Add to internal node
  if (k < rt->lkey) {
    retval = inserthelp(rt->left, k, e);
    if (retval == rt->left) return rt;
    else return rt->add(retval);
  }
  else if((rt->rkey == EMPTYKEY) || (k < rt->rkey)) {
    retval = inserthelp(rt->center, k, e);
    if (retval == rt->center) return rt;
    else return rt->add(retval);
  }
  else { // Insert right
    retval = inserthelp(rt->right, k, e);
    if (retval == rt->right) return rt;
    else return rt->add(retval);
  }
}
```

Figure 10.15 The 2-3 tree insert routine.

placed virtually all large-file access methods other than hashing. B-trees, or some variant of B-trees, are *the* standard file organization for applications requiring insertion, deletion, and key range searches. They are used to implement most modern file systems. B-trees address effectively all of the major problems encountered when implementing disk-based search trees:

1. B-trees are always height balanced, with all leaf nodes at the same level.
2. Update and search operations affect only a few disk blocks. The fewer the number of disk blocks affected, the less disk I/O is required.
3. B-trees keep related records (that is, records with similar key values) on the same disk block, which helps to minimize disk I/O on searches due to locality of reference.
4. B-trees guarantee that every node in the tree will be full at least to a certain minimum percentage. This improves space efficiency while reducing the typical number of disk fetches necessary during a search or update operation.

A B-tree of order m is defined to have the following shape properties:

- The root is either a leaf or has at least two children.
- Each internal node, except for the root, has between $\lceil m/2 \rceil$ and m children.

```
// Add a new key/value pair to the node. There might be a
// subtree associated with the record being added. This
// information comes in the form of a 2-3 tree node with
// one key and a (possibly NULL) subtree through the
// center pointer field.
template <typename Key, typename E>
TTNode<Key,E>* TTNode<Key, E>::add(TTNode<Key,E>* it) {
  if (rkey == EMPTYKEY) { // Only one key, add here
    if (lkey < it->lkey) {
      rkey = it->lkey; rval = it->lval;
      right = center; center = it->center;
    }
    else {
      rkey = lkey; rval = lval; right = center;
      lkey = it->lkey; lval = it->lval;
      center = it->center;
    }
    return this;
  }
  else if (lkey >= it->lkey) { // Add left
    center = new TTNode<Key,E>(rkey, rval, EMPTYKEY, NULL,
                               center, right, NULL);
    rkey = EMPTYKEY; rval = NULL; right = NULL;
    it->left = left; left = it;
    return this;
  }
  else if (rkey < it->lkey) { // Add center
    it->center = new TTNode<Key,E>(rkey, rval, EMPTYKEY,
                          NULL, it->center, right, NULL);
    it->left = this;
    rkey = EMPTYKEY; rval = NULL; right = NULL;
    return it;
  }
  else { // Add right
    TTNode<Key,E>* N1 = new TTNode<Key,E>(rkey, rval,
                          EMPTYKEY, NULL, this, it, NULL);
    it->left = right;
    right = NULL; rkey = EMPTYKEY; rval = NULL;
    return N1;
  }
}
```

Figure 10.16 The 2-3 tree node **add** method.

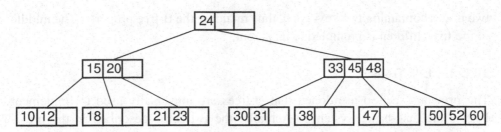

Figure 10.17 A B-tree of order four.

- All leaves are at the same level in the tree, so the tree is always height balanced.

The B-tree is a generalization of the 2-3 tree. Put another way, a 2-3 tree is a B-tree of order three. Normally, the size of a node in the B-tree is chosen to fill a disk block. A B-tree node implementation typically allows 100 or more children. Thus, a B-tree node is equivalent to a disk block, and a "pointer" value stored in the tree is actually the number of the block containing the child node (usually interpreted as an offset from the beginning of the corresponding disk file). In a typical application, the B-tree's access to the disk file will be managed using a buffer pool and a block-replacement scheme such as LRU (see Section 8.3).

Figure 10.17 shows a B-tree of order four. Each node contains up to three keys, and internal nodes have up to four children.

Search in a B-tree is a generalization of search in a 2-3 tree. It is an alternating two-step process, beginning with the root node of the B-tree.

1. Perform a binary search on the records in the current node. If a record with the search key is found, then return that record. If the current node is a leaf node and the key is not found, then report an unsuccessful search.
2. Otherwise, follow the proper branch and repeat the process.

For example, consider a search for the record with key value 47 in the tree of Figure 10.17. The root node is examined and the second (right) branch taken. After examining the node at level 1, the third branch is taken to the next level to arrive at the leaf node containing a record with key value 47.

B-tree insertion is a generalization of 2-3 tree insertion. The first step is to find the leaf node that should contain the key to be inserted, space permitting. If there is room in this node, then insert the key. If there is not, then split the node into two and promote the middle key to the parent. If the parent becomes full, then it is split in turn, and its middle key promoted.

Note that this insertion process is guaranteed to keep all nodes at least half full. For example, when we attempt to insert into a full internal node of a B-tree of order four, there will now be five children that must be dealt with. The node is split into two nodes containing two keys each, thus retaining the B-tree property. The middle of the five children is promoted to its parent.

10.5.1 B^+-Trees

The previous section mentioned that B-trees are universally used to implement large-scale disk-based systems. Actually, the B-tree as described in the previous section is almost never implemented, nor is the 2-3 tree as described in Section 10.4. What is most commonly implemented is a variant of the B-tree, called the B^+-tree. When greater efficiency is required, a more complicated variant known as the B^*-tree is used.

When data are static, a linear index provides an extremely efficient way to search. The problem is how to handle those pesky inserts and deletes. We could try to keep the core idea of storing a sorted array-based list, but make it more flexible by breaking the list into manageable chunks that are more easily updated. How might we do that? First, we need to decide how big the chunks should be. Since the data are on disk, it seems reasonable to store a chunk that is the size of a disk block, or a small multiple of the disk block size. If the next record to be inserted belongs to a chunk that hasn't filled its block then we can just insert it there. The fact that this might cause other records in that chunk to move a little bit in the array is not important, since this does not cause any extra disk accesses so long as we move data within that chunk. But what if the chunk fills up the entire block that contains it? We could just split it in half. What if we want to delete a record? We could just take the deleted record out of the chunk, but we might not want a lot of near-empty chunks. So we could put adjacent chunks together if they have only a small amount of data between them. Or we could shuffle data between adjacent chunks that together contain more data. The big problem would be how to find the desired chunk when processing a record with a given key. Perhaps some sort of tree-like structure could be used to locate the appropriate chunk. These ideas are exactly what motivate the B^+-tree. The B^+-tree is essentially a mechanism for managing a sorted array-based list, where the list is broken into chunks.

The most significant difference between the B^+-tree and the BST or the standard B-tree is that the B^+-tree stores records only at the leaf nodes. Internal nodes store key values, but these are used solely as placeholders to guide the search. This means that internal nodes are significantly different in structure from leaf nodes. Internal nodes store keys to guide the search, associating each key with a pointer to a child B^+-tree node. Leaf nodes store actual records, or else keys and pointers to actual records in a separate disk file if the B^+-tree is being used purely as an index. Depending on the size of a record as compared to the size of a key, a leaf node in a B^+-tree of order m might have enough room to store more or less than m records. The requirement is simply that the leaf nodes store enough records to remain at least half full. The leaf nodes of a B^+-tree are normally linked together

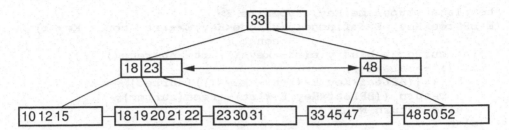

Figure 10.18 Example of a B^+-tree of order four. Internal nodes must store between two and four children. For this example, the record size is assumed to be such that leaf nodes store between three and five records.

to form a doubly linked list. Thus, the entire collection of records can be traversed in sorted order by visiting all the leaf nodes on the linked list. Here is a C++-like pseudocode representation for the B^+-tree node class. Leaf node and internal node subclasses would implement this base class.

```
// Abstract class definition for B+-trees
template <typename Key, typename E>class BPNode {
public:
  BPNode* lftptr;  BPNode* rghtptr; // Links to siblings
  virtual ~BPNode() {} // Base destructor
  virtual bool isLeaf() const =0;  // True if node is a leaf
  virtual bool isFull() const =0;  // True if node is full
  virtual int numrecs() const =0;  // Current num of records
  virtual Key* keys() const=0;     // Return array of keys
};
```

An important implementation detail to note is that while Figure 10.17 shows internal nodes containing three keys and four pointers, class **BPNode** is slightly different in that it stores key/pointer pairs. Figure 10.17 shows the B^+-tree as it is traditionally drawn. To simplify implementation in practice, nodes really do associate a key with each pointer. Each internal node should be assumed to hold in the leftmost position an additional key that is less than or equal to any possible key value in the node's leftmost subtree. B^+-tree implementations typically store an additional dummy record in the leftmost leaf node whose key value is less than any legal key value.

B^+-trees are exceptionally good for range queries. Once the first record in the range has been found, the rest of the records with keys in the range can be accessed by sequential processing of the remaining records in the first node, and then continuing down the linked list of leaf nodes as far as necessary. Figure 10.18 illustrates the B^+-tree.

Search in a B^+-tree is nearly identical to search in a regular B-tree, except that the search must always continue to the proper leaf node. Even if the search-key value is found in an internal node, this is only a placeholder and does not provide

```
template <typename Key, typename E>
E BPTree<Key, E>::findhelp(BPNode<Key,E>* rt, const Key k)
                              const {
  int currec = binaryle(rt->keys(), rt->numrecs(), k);
  if (rt->isLeaf())
    if ((((BPLeaf<Key,E>*)rt)->keys())[currec] == k)
      return ((BPLeaf<Key,E>*)rt)->recs(currec);
    else return NULL;
  else
    return findhelp(((BPInternal<Key,E>*)rt)->
                              pointers(currec), k);
}
```

Figure 10.19 Implementation for the B$^+$-tree search method.

access to the actual record. To find a record with key value 33 in the B$^+$-tree of
Figure 10.18, search begins at the root. The value 33 stored in the root merely
serves as a placeholder, indicating that keys with values greater than or equal to 33
are found in the second subtree. From the second child of the root, the first branch
is taken to reach the leaf node containing the actual record (or a pointer to the actual
record) with key value 33. Figure 10.19 shows a pseudocode sketch of the B$^+$-tree
search algorithm.

B$^+$-tree insertion is similar to B-tree insertion. First, the leaf L that should
contain the record is found. If L is not full, then the new record is added, and no
other B$^+$-tree nodes are affected. If L is already full, split it in two (dividing the
records evenly among the two nodes) and promote a copy of the least-valued key
in the newly formed right node. As with the 2-3 tree, promotion might cause the
parent to split in turn, perhaps eventually leading to splitting the root and causing
the B$^+$-tree to gain a new level. B$^+$-tree insertion keeps all leaf nodes at equal
depth. Figure 10.20 illustrates the insertion process through several examples. Figure 10.21 shows a C++-like pseudocode sketch of the B$^+$-tree insert algorithm.

To delete record R from the B$^+$-tree, first locate the leaf L that contains R. If L
is more than half full, then we need only remove R, leaving L still at least half full.
This is demonstrated by Figure 10.22.

If deleting a record reduces the number of records in the node below the minimum threshold (called an **underflow**), then we must do something to keep the
node sufficiently full. The first choice is to look at the node's adjacent siblings to
determine if they have a spare record that can be used to fill the gap. If so, then
enough records are transferred from the sibling so that both nodes have about the
same number of records. This is done so as to delay as long as possible the next
time when a delete causes this node to underflow again. This process might require
that the parent node has its placeholder key value revised to reflect the true first key
value in each node. Figure 10.23 illustrates the process.

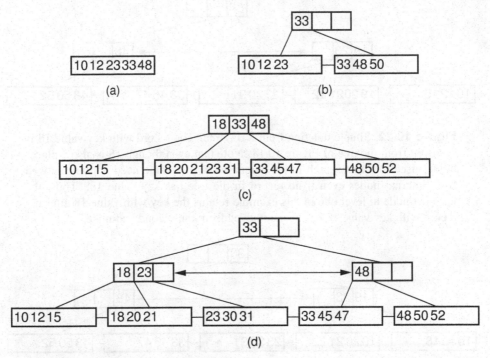

Figure 10.20 Examples of B$^+$-tree insertion. (a) A B$^+$-tree containing five records. (b) The result of inserting a record with key value 50 into the tree of (a). The leaf node splits, causing creation of the first internal node. (c) The B$^+$-tree of (b) after further insertions. (d) The result of inserting a record with key value 30 into the tree of (c). The second leaf node splits, which causes the internal node to split in turn, creating a new root.

```
template <typename Key, typename E>
BPNode<Key,E>* BPTree<Key, E>::inserthelp(BPNode<Key,E>* rt,
                      const Key& k, const E& e) {
  if (rt->isLeaf()) // At leaf node: insert here
    return ((BPLeaf<Key,E>*)rt)->add(k, e);
  // Add to internal node
  int currec = binaryle(rt->keys(), rt->numrecs(), k);
  BPNode<Key,E>* temp = inserthelp(
        ((BPInternal<Key,E>*)root)->pointers(currec), k, e);
  if (temp != ((BPInternal<Key,E>*)rt)->pointers(currec))
    return ((BPInternal<Key,E>*)rt)->
                  add(k, (BPInternal<Key,E>*)temp);
  else
    return rt;
}
```

Figure 10.21 A C++-like pseudocode sketch of the B$^+$-tree insert algorithm.

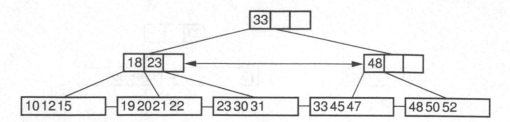

Figure 10.22 Simple deletion from a B⁺-tree. The record with key value 18 is removed from the tree of Figure 10.18. Note that even though 18 is also a place-holder used to direct search in the parent node, that value need not be removed from internal nodes even if no record in the tree has key value 18. Thus, the leftmost node at level one in this example retains the key with value 18 after the record with key value 18 has been removed from the second leaf node.

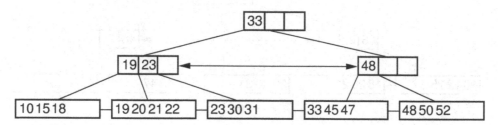

Figure 10.23 Deletion from the B⁺-tree of Figure 10.18 via borrowing from a sibling. The key with value 12 is deleted from the leftmost leaf, causing the record with key value 18 to shift to the leftmost leaf to take its place. Note that the parent must be updated to properly indicate the key range within the subtrees. In this example, the parent node has its leftmost key value changed to 19.

If neither sibling can lend a record to the under-full node (call it N), then N must give its records to a sibling and be removed from the tree. There is certainly room to do this, because the sibling is at most half full (remember that it had no records to contribute to the current node), and N has become less than half full because it is under-flowing. This merge process combines two subtrees of the parent, which might cause it to underflow in turn. If the last two children of the root merge together, then the tree loses a level. Figure 10.24 illustrates the node-merge deletion process. Figure 10.25 shows C++-like pseudocode for the B⁺-tree delete algorithm.

The B⁺-tree requires that all nodes be at least half full (except for the root). Thus, the storage utilization must be at least 50%. This is satisfactory for many implementations, but note that keeping nodes fuller will result both in less space required (because there is less empty space in the disk file) and in more efficient processing (fewer blocks on average will be read into memory because the amount of information in each block is greater). Because B-trees have become so popular, many algorithm designers have tried to improve B-tree performance. One method

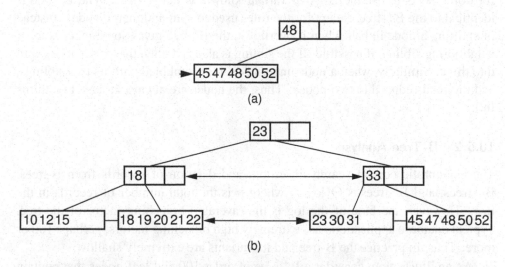

Figure 10.24 Deleting the record with key value 33 from the B+-tree of Figure 10.18 via collapsing siblings. (a) The two leftmost leaf nodes merge together to form a single leaf. Unfortunately, the parent node now has only one child. (b) Because the left subtree has a spare leaf node, that node is passed to the right subtree. The placeholder values of the root and the right internal node are updated to reflect the changes. Value 23 moves to the root, and old root value 33 moves to the rightmost internal node.

```
/** Delete a record with the given key value, and
      return true if the root underflows */
template <typename Key, typename E>
bool BPTree<Key, E>::removehelp(BPNode<Key,E>* rt,
                                    const Key& k) {
  int currec = binaryle(rt->keys(), rt->numrecs(), k);
  if (rt->isLeaf())
    if (((BPLeaf<Key,E>*)rt)->keys()[currec] == k)
      return ((BPLeaf<Key,E>*)rt)->del(currec);
    else return false;
  else // Process internal node
    if (removehelp(((BPInternal<Key,E>*)rt)->
                              pointers(currec), k))
      // Child will merge if necessary
      return ((BPInternal<Key,E>*)rt)->underflow(currec);
    else return false;
}
```

Figure 10.25 C++-like pseudocode for the B+-tree delete algorithm.

for doing so is to use the B^+-tree variant known as the B^*-tree. The B^*-tree is identical to the B^+-tree, except for the rules used to split and merge nodes. Instead of splitting a node in half when it overflows, the B^*-tree gives some records to its neighboring sibling, if possible. If the sibling is also full, then these two nodes split into three. Similarly, when a node underflows, it is combined with its two siblings, and the total reduced to two nodes. Thus, the nodes are always at least two thirds full.[2]

10.5.2   B-Tree Analysis

The asymptotic cost of search, insertion, and deletion of records from B-trees, B^+-trees, and B^*-trees is $\Theta(\log n)$ where n is the total number of records in the tree. However, the base of the log is the (average) branching factor of the tree. Typical database applications use extremely high branching factors, perhaps 100 or more. Thus, in practice the B-tree and its variants are extremely shallow.

As an illustration, consider a B^+-tree of order 100 and leaf nodes that contain up to 100 records. A B^+-tree with height one (that is, just a single leaf node) can have at most 100 records. A B^+-tree with height two (a root internal node whose children are leaves) must have at least 100 records (2 leaves with 50 records each). It has at most 10,000 records (100 leaves with 100 records each). A B^+-tree with height three must have at least 5000 records (two second-level nodes with 50 children containing 50 records each) and at most one million records (100 second-level nodes with 100 full children each). A B^+-tree with height four must have at least 250,000 records and at most 100 million records. Thus, it would require an *extremely* large database to generate a B^+-tree of more than height four.

The B^+-tree split and insert rules guarantee that every node (except perhaps the root) is at least half full. So they are on average about $3/4$ full. But the internal nodes are purely overhead, since the keys stored there are used only by the tree to direct search, rather than store actual data. Does this overhead amount to a significant use of space? No, because once again the high fan-out rate of the tree structure means that the vast majority of nodes are leaf nodes. Recall (from Section 6.4) that a full K-ary tree has approximately $1/K$ of its nodes as internal nodes. This means that while half of a full binary tree's nodes are internal nodes, in a B^+-tree of order 100 probably only about $1/75$ of its nodes are internal nodes. This means that the overhead associated with internal nodes is very low.

We can reduce the number of disk fetches required for the B-tree even more by using the following methods. First, the upper levels of the tree can be stored in

---

[2]This concept can be extended further if higher space utilization is required. However, the update routines become much more complicated. I once worked on a project where we implemented 3-for-4 node split and merge routines. This gave better performance than the 2-for-3 node split and merge routines of the B^*-tree. However, the spitting and merging routines were so complicated that even their author could no longer understand them once they were completed!

main memory at all times. Because the tree branches so quickly, the top two levels (levels 0 and 1) require relatively little space. If the B-tree is only height four, then at most two disk fetches (internal nodes at level two and leaves at level three) are required to reach the pointer to any given record.

A buffer pool could be used to manage nodes of the B-tree. Several nodes of the tree would typically be in main memory at one time. The most straightforward approach is to use a standard method such as LRU to do node replacement. However, sometimes it might be desirable to "lock" certain nodes such as the root into the buffer pool. In general, if the buffer pool is even of modest size (say at least twice the depth of the tree), no special techniques for node replacement will be required because the upper-level nodes will naturally be accessed frequently.

10.6 Further Reading

For an expanded discussion of the issues touched on in this chapter, see a general file processing text such as *File Structures: A Conceptual Toolkit* by Folk and Zoellick [FZ98]. In particular, Folk and Zoellick provide a good discussion of the relationship between primary and secondary indices. The most thorough discussion on various implementations for the B-tree is the survey article by Comer [Com79]. Also see [Sal88] for further details on implementing B-trees. See Shaffer and Brown [SB93] for a discussion of buffer pool management strategies for B^+-tree-like data structures.

10.7 Exercises

10.1 Assume that a computer system has disk blocks of 1024 bytes, and that you are storing records that have 4-byte keys and 4-byte data fields. The records are sorted and packed sequentially into the disk file.

  (a) Assume that a linear index uses 4 bytes to store the key and 4 bytes to store the block ID for the associated records. What is the greatest number of records that can be stored in the file if a linear index of size 256KB is used?

  (b) What is the greatest number of records that can be stored in the file if the linear index is also stored on disk (and thus its size is limited only by the second-level index) when using a second-level index of 1024 bytes (i.e., 256 key values) as illustrated by Figure 10.2? Each element of the second-level index references the smallest key value for a disk block of the linear index.

10.2 Assume that a computer system has disk blocks of 4096 bytes, and that you are storing records that have 4-byte keys and 64-byte data fields. The records are sorted and packed sequentially into the disk file.

(a) Assume that a linear index uses 4 bytes to store the key and 4 bytes to store the block ID for the associated records. What is the greatest number of records that can be stored in the file if a linear index of size 2MB is used?

(b) What is the greatest number of records that can be stored in the file if the linear index is also stored on disk (and thus its size is limited only by the second-level index) when using a second-level index of 4096 bytes (i.e., 1024 key values) as illustrated by Figure 10.2? Each element of the second-level index references the smallest key value for a disk block of the linear index.

10.3 Modify the function **binary** of Section 3.5 so as to support variable-length records with fixed-length keys indexed by a simple linear index as illustrated by Figure 10.1.

10.4 Assume that a database stores records consisting of a 2-byte integer key and a variable-length data field consisting of a string. Show the linear index (as illustrated by Figure 10.1) for the following collection of records:

397	Hello world!
82	XYZ
1038	This string is rather long
1037	This is shorter
42	ABC
2222	Hello new world!

10.5 Each of the following series of records consists of a four-digit primary key (with no duplicates) and a four-character secondary key (with many duplicates).

3456	DEER
2398	DEER
2926	DUCK
9737	DEER
7739	GOAT
9279	DUCK
1111	FROG
8133	DEER
7183	DUCK
7186	FROG

(a) Show the inverted list (as illustrated by Figure 10.4) for this collection of records.

(b) Show the improved inverted list (as illustrated by Figure 10.5) for this collection of records.

10.6 Under what conditions will ISAM be more efficient than a B^+-tree implementation?

10.7 Prove that the number of leaf nodes in a 2-3 tree with height k is between 2^{k-1} and 3^{k-1}.

10.8 Show the result of inserting the values 55 and 46 into the 2-3 tree of Figure 10.9.

10.9 You are given a series of records whose keys are letters. The records arrive in the following order: C, S, D, T, A, M, P, I, B, W, N, G, U, R, K, E, H, O, L, J. Show the 2-3 tree that results from inserting these records.

10.10 You are given a series of records whose keys are letters. The records are inserted in the following order: C, S, D, T, A, M, P, I, B, W, N, G, U, R, K, E, H, O, L, J. Show the tree that results from inserting these records when the 2-3 tree is modified to be a $2\text{-}3^+$ tree, that is, the internal nodes act only as placeholders. Assume that the leaf nodes are capable of holding up to two records.

10.11 Show the result of inserting the value 55 into the B-tree of Figure 10.17.

10.12 Show the result of inserting the values 1, 2, 3, 4, 5, and 6 (in that order) into the B^+-tree of Figure 10.18.

10.13 Show the result of deleting the values 18, 19, and 20 (in that order) from the B^+-tree of Figure 10.24b.

10.14 You are given a series of records whose keys are letters. The records are inserted in the following order: C, S, D, T, A, M, P, I, B, W, N, G, U, R, K, E, H, O, L, J. Show the B^+-tree of order four that results from inserting these records. Assume that the leaf nodes are capable of storing up to three records.

10.15 Assume that you have a B^+-tree whose internal nodes can store up to 100 children and whose leaf nodes can store up to 15 records. What are the minimum and maximum number of records that can be stored by the B^+-tree with heights 1, 2, 3, 4, and 5?

10.16 Assume that you have a B^+-tree whose internal nodes can store up to 50 children and whose leaf nodes can store up to 50 records. What are the minimum and maximum number of records that can be stored by the B^+-tree with heights 1, 2, 3, 4, and 5?

10.8 Projects

10.1 Implement a two-level linear index for variable-length records as illustrated by Figures 10.1 and 10.2. Assume that disk blocks are 1024 bytes in length. Records in the database file should typically range between 20 and 200 bytes, including a 4-byte key value. Each record of the index file should store a key value and the byte offset in the database file for the first byte of the corresponding record. The top-level index (stored in memory) should be a simple array storing the lowest key value on the corresponding block in the index file.

10.2 Implement the 2-3$^+$ tree, that is, a 2-3 tree where the internal nodes act only as placeholders. Your 2-3$^+$ tree should implement the dictionary interface of Section 4.4.

10.3 Implement the dictionary ADT of Section 4.4 for a large file stored on disk by means of the B$^+$-tree of Section 10.5. Assume that disk blocks are 1024 bytes, and thus both leaf nodes and internal nodes are also 1024 bytes. Records should store a 4-byte (`int`) key value and a 60-byte data field. Internal nodes should store key value/pointer pairs where the "pointer" is actually the block number on disk for the child node. Both internal nodes and leaf nodes will need room to store various information such as a count of the records stored on that node, and a pointer to the next node on that level. Thus, leaf nodes will store 15 records, and internal nodes will have room to store about 120 to 125 children depending on how you implement them. Use a buffer pool (Section 8.3) to manage access to the nodes stored on disk.

PART IV

Advanced Data Structures

11

Graphs

Graphs provide the ultimate in data structure flexibility. Graphs can model both real-world systems and abstract problems, so they are used in hundreds of applications. Here is a small sampling of the range of problems that graphs are routinely applied to.

1. Modeling connectivity in computer and communications networks.
2. Representing a map as a set of locations with distances between locations; used to compute shortest routes between locations.
3. Modeling flow capacities in transportation networks.
4. Finding a path from a starting condition to a goal condition; for example, in artificial intelligence problem solving.
5. Modeling computer algorithms, showing transitions from one program state to another.
6. Finding an acceptable order for finishing subtasks in a complex activity, such as constructing large buildings.
7. Modeling relationships such as family trees, business or military organizations, and scientific taxonomies.

We begin in Section 11.1 with some basic graph terminology and then define two fundamental representations for graphs, the adjacency matrix and adjacency list. Section 11.2 presents a graph ADT and simple implementations based on the adjacency matrix and adjacency list. Section 11.3 presents the two most commonly used graph traversal algorithms, called depth-first and breadth-first search, with application to topological sorting. Section 11.4 presents algorithms for solving some problems related to finding shortest routes in a graph. Finally, Section 11.5 presents algorithms for finding the minimum-cost spanning tree, useful for determining lowest-cost connectivity in a network. Besides being useful and interesting in their own right, these algorithms illustrate the use of some data structures presented in earlier chapters.

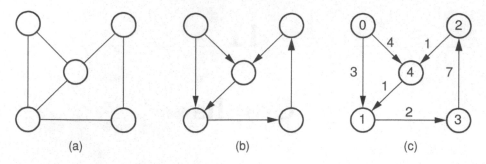

Figure 11.1 Examples of graphs and terminology. (a) A graph. (b) A directed graph (digraph). (c) A labeled (directed) graph with weights associated with the edges. In this example, there is a simple path from Vertex 0 to Vertex 3 containing Vertices 0, 1, and 3. Vertices 0, 1, 3, 2, 4, and 1 also form a path, but not a simple path because Vertex 1 appears twice. Vertices 1, 3, 2, 4, and 1 form a simple cycle.

11.1   Terminology and Representations

A graph $\mathbf{G} = (\mathbf{V}, \mathbf{E})$ consists of a set of vertices $\mathbf{V}$ and a set of edges $\mathbf{E}$, such that each edge in $\mathbf{E}$ is a connection between a pair of vertices in $\mathbf{V}$.[1] The number of vertices is written $|\mathbf{V}|$, and the number of edges is written $|\mathbf{E}|$. $|\mathbf{E}|$ can range from zero to a maximum of $|\mathbf{V}|^2 - |\mathbf{V}|$. A graph with relatively few edges is called **sparse**, while a graph with many edges is called **dense**. A graph containing all possible edges is said to be **complete**.

A graph with edges directed from one vertex to another (as in Figure 11.1(b)) is called a **directed graph** or **digraph**. A graph whose edges are not directed is called an **undirected graph** (as illustrated by Figure 11.1(a)). A graph with labels associated with its vertices (as in Figure 11.1(c)) is called a **labeled graph**. Two vertices are **adjacent** if they are joined by an edge. Such vertices are also called **neighbors**. An edge connecting Vertices U and V is written (U, V). Such an edge is said to be **incident** on Vertices U and V. Associated with each edge may be a cost or **weight**. Graphs whose edges have weights (as in Figure 11.1(c)) are said to be **weighted**.

A sequence of vertices $v_1, v_2, ..., v_n$ forms a **path** of length $n - 1$ if there exist edges from v_i to v_{i+1} for $1 \leq i < n$. A path is **simple** if all vertices on the path are distinct. The **length** of a path is the number of edges it contains. A **cycle** is a path of length three or more that connects some vertex v_1 to itself. A cycle is **simple** if the path is simple, except for the first and last vertices being the same.

---

[1]Some graph applications require that a given pair of vertices can have multiple or parallel edges connecting them, or that a vertex can have an edge to itself. However, the applications discussed in this book do not require either of these special cases, so for simplicity we will assume that they cannot occur.

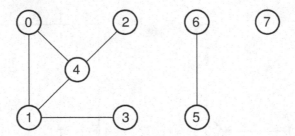

Figure 11.2 An undirected graph with three connected components. Vertices 0, 1, 2, 3, and 4 form one connected component. Vertices 5 and 6 form a second connected component. Vertex 7 by itself forms a third connected component.

A **subgraph S** is formed from graph **G** by selecting a subset $\mathbf{V}_s$ of **G**'s vertices and a subset $\mathbf{E}_s$ of **G**'s edges such that for every edge E in $\mathbf{E}_s$, both of E's vertices are in $\mathbf{V}_s$.

An undirected graph is **connected** if there is at least one path from any vertex to any other. The maximally connected subgraphs of an undirected graph are called **connected components**. For example, Figure 11.2 shows an undirected graph with three connected components.

A graph without cycles is called **acyclic**. Thus, a directed graph without cycles is called a **directed acyclic graph** or DAG.

A **free tree** is a connected, undirected graph with no simple cycles. An equivalent definition is that a free tree is connected and has $|\mathbf{V}| - 1$ edges.

There are two commonly used methods for representing graphs. The **adjacency matrix** is illustrated by Figure 11.3(b). The adjacency matrix for a graph is a $|\mathbf{V}| \times |\mathbf{V}|$ array. Assume that $|\mathbf{V}| = n$ and that the vertices are labeled from v_0 through v_{n-1}. Row i of the adjacency matrix contains entries for Vertex v_i. Column j in row i is marked if there is an edge from v_i to v_j and is not marked otherwise. Thus, the adjacency matrix requires one bit at each position. Alternatively, if we wish to associate a number with each edge, such as the weight or distance between two vertices, then each matrix position must store that number. In either case, the space requirements for the adjacency matrix are $\Theta(|\mathbf{V}|^2)$.

The second common representation for graphs is the **adjacency list**, illustrated by Figure 11.3(c). The adjacency list is an array of linked lists. The array is $|\mathbf{V}|$ items long, with position i storing a pointer to the linked list of edges for Vertex v_i. This linked list represents the edges by the vertices that are adjacent to Vertex v_i. The adjacency list is therefore a generalization of the "list of children" representation for trees described in Section 6.3.1.

Example 11.1 The entry for Vertex 0 in Figure 11.3(c) stores 1 and 4 because there are two edges in the graph leaving Vertex 0, with one going

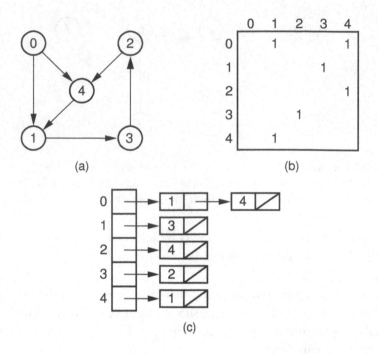

Figure 11.3 Two graph representations. (a) A directed graph. (b) The adjacency matrix for the graph of (a). (c) The adjacency list for the graph of (a).

to Vertex 1 and one going to Vertex 4. The list for Vertex 2 stores an entry for Vertex 4 because there is an edge from Vertex 2 to Vertex 4, but no entry for Vertex 3 because this edge comes into Vertex 2 rather than going out.

The storage requirements for the adjacency list depend on both the number of edges and the number of vertices in the graph. There must be an array entry for each vertex (even if the vertex is not adjacent to any other vertex and thus has no elements on its linked list), and each edge must appear on one of the lists. Thus, the cost is $\Theta(|\mathbf{V}| + |\mathbf{E}|)$.

Both the adjacency matrix and the adjacency list can be used to store directed or undirected graphs. Each edge of an undirected graph connecting Vertices U and V is represented by two directed edges: one from U to V and one from V to U. Figure 11.4 illustrates the use of the adjacency matrix and the adjacency list for undirected graphs.

Which graph representation is more space efficient depends on the number of edges in the graph. The adjacency list stores information only for those edges that actually appear in the graph, while the adjacency matrix requires space for each potential edge, whether it exists or not. However, the adjacency matrix requires no overhead for pointers, which can be a substantial cost, especially if the only

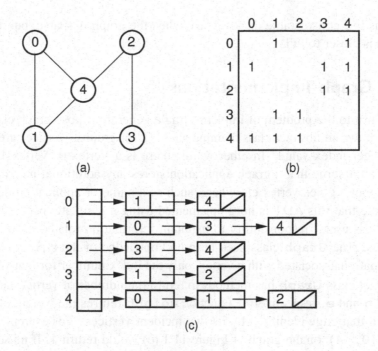

Figure 11.4 Using the graph representations for undirected graphs. (a) An undirected graph. (b) The adjacency matrix for the graph of (a). (c) The adjacency list for the graph of (a).

information stored for an edge is one bit to indicate its existence. As the graph becomes denser, the adjacency matrix becomes relatively more space efficient. Sparse graphs are likely to have their adjacency list representation be more space efficient.

Example 11.2 Assume that a vertex index requires two bytes, a pointer requires four bytes, and an edge weight requires two bytes. Then the adjacency matrix for the graph of Figure 11.3 requires $2|V^2| = 50$ bytes while the adjacency list requires $4|V| + 6|E| = 56$ bytes. For the graph of Figure 11.4, the adjacency matrix requires the same space as before, while the adjacency list requires $4|V| + 6|E| = 92$ bytes (because there are now 12 edges instead of 6).

The adjacency matrix often requires a higher asymptotic cost for an algorithm than would result if the adjacency list were used. The reason is that it is common for a graph algorithm to visit each neighbor of each vertex. Using the adjacency list, only the actual edges connecting a vertex to its neighbors are examined. However, the adjacency matrix must look at each of its $|V|$ potential edges, yielding a total cost of $\Theta(|V^2|)$ time when the algorithm might otherwise require only $\Theta(|V|+|E|)$

time. This is a considerable disadvantage when the graph is sparse, but not when the graph is closer to full.

11.2 Graph Implementations

We next turn to the problem of implementing a general-purpose graph class. Figure 11.5 shows an abstract class defining an ADT for graphs. Vertices are defined by an integer index value. In other words, there is a Vertex 0, Vertex 1, and so on. We can assume that a graph application stores any additional information of interest about a given vertex elsewhere, such as a name or application-dependent value. Note that this ADT is not implemented using a template, because it is the **Graph** class users' responsibility to maintain information related to the vertices themselves. The **Graph** class need have no knowledge of the type or content of the information associated with a vertex, only the index number for that vertex.

Abstract class **Graph** has methods to return the number of vertices and edges (methods **n** and **e**, respectively). Function **weight** returns the weight of a given edge, with that edge identified by its two incident vertices. For example, calling **weight(0, 4)** on the graph of Figure 11.1 (c) would return 4. If no such edge exists, the weight is defined to be 0. So calling **weight(0, 2)** on the graph of Figure 11.1 (c) would return 0.

Functions **setEdge** and **delEdge** set the weight of an edge and remove an edge from the graph, respectively. Again, an edge is identified by its two incident vertices. **setEdge** does not permit the user to set the weight to be 0, because this value is used to indicate a non-existent edge, nor are negative edge weights permitted. Functions **getMark** and **setMark** get and set, respectively, a requested value in the **Mark** array (described below) for Vertex V.

Nearly every graph algorithm presented in this chapter will require visits to all neighbors of a given vertex. Two methods are provided to support this. They work in a manner similar to linked list access functions. Function **first** takes as input a vertex V, and returns the edge to the first neighbor for V (we assume the neighbor list is sorted by vertex number). Function **next** takes as input Vertices $V1$ and $V2$ and returns the index for the vertex forming the next edge with $V1$ after $V2$ on $V1$'s edge list. Function **next** will return a value of $n = |V|$ once the end of the edge list for $V1$ has been reached. The following line appears in many graph algorithms:

```
for (w = G=>first(v); w < G->n(); w = G->next(v,w))
```

This **for** loop gets the first neighbor of **v**, then works through the remaining neighbors of **v** until a value equal to **G->n()** is returned, signaling that all neighbors of **v** have been visited. For example, **first(1)** in Figure 11.4 would return 0. **next(1, 0)** would return 3. **next(0, 3)** would return 4. **next(1, 4)** would return 5, which is not a vertex in the graph.

```
// Graph abstract class. This ADT assumes that the number
// of vertices is fixed when the graph is created.
class Graph {
private:
  void operator =(const Graph&) {}      // Protect assignment
  Graph(const Graph&) {}                // Protect copy constructor

public:
  Graph() {}               // Default constructor
  virtual ~Graph() {} // Base destructor

  // Initialize a graph of n vertices
  virtual void Init(int n) =0;

  // Return: the number of vertices and edges
  virtual int n() =0;
  virtual int e() =0;

  // Return v's first neighbor
  virtual int first(int v) =0;

 // Return v's next neighbor
  virtual int next(int v, int w) =0;

  // Set the weight for an edge
  // i, j: The vertices
  // wgt: Edge weight
  virtual void setEdge(int v1, int v2, int wght) =0;

  // Delete an edge
  // i, j: The vertices
  virtual void delEdge(int v1, int v2) =0;

  // Determine if an edge is in the graph
  // i, j: The vertices
  // Return: true if edge i,j has non-zero weight
  virtual bool isEdge(int i, int j) =0;

  // Return an edge's weight
  // i, j: The vertices
  // Return: The weight of edge i,j, or zero
  virtual int weight(int v1, int v2) =0;

  // Get and Set the mark value for a vertex
  // v: The vertex
  // val: The value to set
  virtual int getMark(int v) =0;
  virtual void setMark(int v, int val) =0;
};
```

Figure 11.5 A graph ADT. This ADT assumes that the number of vertices is fixed when the graph is created, but that edges can be added and removed. It also supports a mark array to aid graph traversal algorithms.

It is reasonably straightforward to implement our graph and edge ADTs using either the adjacency list or adjacency matrix. The sample implementations presented here do not address the issue of how the graph is actually created. The user of these implementations must add functionality for this purpose, perhaps reading the graph description from a file. The graph can be built up by using the **setEdge** function provided by the ADT.

Figure 11.6 shows an implementation for the adjacency matrix. Array **Mark** stores the information manipulated by the **setMark** and **getMark** functions. The edge matrix is implemented as an integer array of size $n \times n$ for a graph of n vertices. Position (i, j) in the matrix stores the weight for edge (i, j) if it exists. A weight of zero for edge (i, j) is used to indicate that no edge connects Vertices i and j.

Given a vertex V, function **first** locates the position in **matrix** of the first edge (if any) of V by beginning with edge $(V, 0)$ and scanning through row V until an edge is found. If no edge is incident on V, then **first** returns n.

Function **next** locates the edge following edge (i, j) (if any) by continuing down the row of Vertex i starting at position $j + 1$, looking for an edge. If no such edge exists, **next** returns n. Functions **setEdge** and **delEdge** adjust the appropriate value in the array. Function **weight** returns the value stored in the appropriate position in the array.

Figure 11.7 presents an implementation of the adjacency list representation for graphs. Its main data structure is an array of linked lists, one linked list for each vertex. These linked lists store objects of type **Edge**, which merely stores the index for the vertex pointed to by the edge, along with the weight of the edge. Because the **Edge** class is assumed to be private to the **Graphl** class, its data members have been made public for convenience.

```
// Edge class for Adjacency List graph representation
class Edge {
  int vert, wt;
public:
  Edge() { vert = -1; wt = -1; }
  Edge(int v, int w) { vert = v; wt = w; }
  int vertex() { return vert; }
  int weight() { return wt; }
};
```

Implementation for **Graphl** member functions is straightforward in principle, with the key functions being **setEdge**, **delEdge**, and **weight**. They simply start at the beginning of the adjacency list and move along it until the desired vertex has been found. Note that **isEdge** checks to see if j is already the current neighbor in i's adjacency list, since this will often be true when processing the neighbors of each vertex in turn.

```
// Implementation for the adjacency matrix representation
class Graphm : public Graph {
private:
  int numVertex, numEdge;  // Store number of vertices, edges
  int **matrix;            // Pointer to adjacency matrix
  int *mark;               // Pointer to mark array
public:
  Graphm(int numVert)      // Constructor
    { Init(numVert); }

  ~Graphm() {              // Destructor
    delete [] mark;  // Return dynamically allocated memory
    for (int i=0; i<numVertex; i++)
      delete [] matrix[i];
    delete [] matrix;
  }

  void Init(int n) { // Initialize the graph
    int i;
    numVertex = n;
    numEdge = 0;
    mark = new int[n];       // Initialize mark array
    for (i=0; i<numVertex; i++)
      mark[i] = UNVISITED;
    matrix = (int**) new int*[numVertex]; // Make matrix
    for (i=0; i<numVertex; i++)
      matrix[i] = new int[numVertex];
    for (i=0; i< numVertex; i++) // Initialize to 0 weights
      for (int j=0; j<numVertex; j++)
        matrix[i][j] = 0;
  }

  int n() { return numVertex; } // Number of vertices
  int e() { return numEdge; }   // Number of edges

  // Return first neighbor of "v"
  int first(int v) {
    for (int i=0; i<numVertex; i++)
      if (matrix[v][i] != 0) return i;
    return numVertex;              // Return n if none
  }

  // Return v's next neighbor after w
  int next(int v, int w) {
    for(int i=w+1; i<numVertex; i++)
      if (matrix[v][i] != 0)
        return i;
    return numVertex;              // Return n if none
  }
```

Figure 11.6 An implementation for the adjacency matrix implementation.

```
// Set edge (v1, v2) to "wt"
void setEdge(int v1, int v2, int wt) {
  Assert(wt>0, "Illegal weight value");
  if (matrix[v1][v2] == 0) numEdge++;
  matrix[v1][v2] = wt;
}

void delEdge(int v1, int v2) { // Delete edge (v1, v2)
  if (matrix[v1][v2] != 0) numEdge--;
  matrix[v1][v2] = 0;
}

bool isEdge(int i, int j) // Is (i, j) an edge?
{ return matrix[i][j] != 0; }

int weight(int v1, int v2) { return matrix[v1][v2]; }
int getMark(int v) { return mark[v]; }
void setMark(int v, int val) { mark[v] = val; }
};
```

Figure 11.6 (continued)

11.3 Graph Traversals

Often it is useful to visit the vertices of a graph in some specific order based on the graph's topology. This is known as a **graph traversal** and is similar in concept to a tree traversal. Recall that tree traversals visit every node exactly once, in some specified order such as preorder, inorder, or postorder. Multiple tree traversals exist because various applications require the nodes to be visited in a particular order. For example, to print a BST's nodes in ascending order requires an inorder traversal as opposed to some other traversal. Standard graph traversal orders also exist. Each is appropriate for solving certain problems. For example, many problems in artificial intelligence programming are modeled using graphs. The problem domain may consist of a large collection of states, with connections between various pairs of states. Solving the problem may require getting from a specified start state to a specified goal state by moving between states only through the connections. Typically, the start and goal states are not directly connected. To solve this problem, the vertices of the graph must be searched in some organized manner.

Graph traversal algorithms typically begin with a start vertex and attempt to visit the remaining vertices from there. Graph traversals must deal with a number of troublesome cases. First, it may not be possible to reach all vertices from the start vertex. This occurs when the graph is not connected. Second, the graph may contain cycles, and we must make sure that cycles do not cause the algorithm to go into an infinite loop.

```cpp
class Graphl : public Graph {
private:
  List<Edge>** vertex;         // List headers
  int numVertex, numEdge;      // Number of vertices, edges
  int *mark;                   // Pointer to mark array
public:
  Graphl(int numVert)
    { Init(numVert); }

  ~Graphl() {            // Destructor
    delete [] mark; // Return dynamically allocated memory
    for (int i=0; i<numVertex; i++) delete [] vertex[i];
    delete [] vertex;
  }

  void Init(int n) {
    int i;
    numVertex = n;
    numEdge = 0;
    mark = new int[n];  // Initialize mark array
    for (i=0; i<numVertex; i++) mark[i] = UNVISITED;
    // Create and initialize adjacency lists
    vertex = (List<Edge>**) new List<Edge>*[numVertex];
    for (i=0; i<numVertex; i++)
      vertex[i] = new LList<Edge>();
  }

  int n() { return numVertex; } // Number of vertices
  int e() { return numEdge; }   // Number of edges

  int first(int v) { // Return first neighbor of "v"
    if (vertex[v]->length() == 0)
      return numVertex;        // No neighbor
    vertex[v]->moveToStart();
    Edge it = vertex[v]->getValue();
    return it.vertex();
  }

  // Get v's next neighbor after w
  int next(int v, int w) {
    Edge it;
    if (isEdge(v, w)) {
      if ((vertex[v]->currPos()+1) < vertex[v]->length()) {
        vertex[v]->next();
        it = vertex[v]->getValue();
        return it.vertex();
      }
    }
    return n(); // No neighbor
  }
```

Figure 11.7 An implementation for the adjacency list.

```
  // Set edge (i, j) to "weight"
  void setEdge(int i, int j, int weight) {
    Assert(weight>0, "May not set weight to 0");
    Edge currEdge(j, weight);
    if (isEdge(i, j)) { // Edge already exists in graph
      vertex[i]->remove();
      vertex[i]->insert(currEdge);
    }
    else { // Keep neighbors sorted by vertex index
      numEdge++;
      for (vertex[i]->moveToStart();
           vertex[i]->currPos() < vertex[i]->length();
           vertex[i]->next()) {
        Edge temp = vertex[i]->getValue();
        if (temp.vertex() > j) break;
      }
      vertex[i]->insert(currEdge);
    }
  }

  void delEdge(int i, int j) {  // Delete edge (i, j)
    if (isEdge(i,j)) {
      vertex[i]->remove();
      numEdge--;
    }
  }

  bool isEdge(int i, int j) { // Is (i,j) an edge?
    Edge it;
    for (vertex[i]->moveToStart();
         vertex[i]->currPos() < vertex[i]->length();
         vertex[i]->next()) {             // Check whole list
      Edge temp = vertex[i]->getValue();
      if (temp.vertex() == j) return true;
    }
    return false;
  }

  int weight(int i, int j) { // Return weight of (i, j)
    Edge curr;
    if (isEdge(i, j)) {
      curr = vertex[i]->getValue();
      return curr.weight();
    }
    else return 0;
  }

  int getMark(int v) { return mark[v]; }
  void setMark(int v, int val) { mark[v] = val; }
};
```

Figure 11.7 (continued)

Graph traversal algorithms can solve both of these problems by maintaining a
mark bit for each vertex on the graph. At the beginning of the algorithm, the mark
bit for all vertices is cleared. The mark bit for a vertex is set when the vertex is first
visited during the traversal. If a marked vertex is encountered during traversal, it is
not visited a second time. This keeps the program from going into an infinite loop
when it encounters a cycle.

Once the traversal algorithm completes, we can check to see if all vertices have
been processed by checking the mark bit array. If not all vertices are marked, we
can continue the traversal from another unmarked vertex. Note that this process
works regardless of whether the graph is directed or undirected. To ensure visiting
all vertices, `graphTraverse` could be called as follows on a graph **G**:

```
void graphTraverse(Graph* G) {
  int v;
  for (v=0; v<G->n(); v++)
    G->setMark(v, UNVISITED);  // Initialize mark bits
  for (v=0; v<G->n(); v++)
    if (G->getMark(v) == UNVISITED)
      doTraverse(G, v);
}
```

Function "`doTraverse`" might be implemented by using one of the graph traversals described in this section.

11.3.1 Depth-First Search

The first method of organized graph traversal is called **depth-first search** (DFS).
Whenever a vertex V is visited during the search, DFS will recursively visit all
of V's unvisited neighbors. Equivalently, DFS will add all edges leading out of v
to a stack. The next vertex to be visited is determined by popping the stack and
following that edge. The effect is to follow one branch through the graph to its
conclusion, then it will back up and follow another branch, and so on. The DFS
process can be used to define a **depth-first search tree**. This tree is composed of
the edges that were followed to any new (unvisited) vertex during the traversal, and
leaves out the edges that lead to already visited vertices. DFS can be applied to
directed or undirected graphs. Here is an implementation for the DFS algorithm:

```
void DFS(Graph* G, int v) { // Depth first search
  PreVisit(G, v);                // Take appropriate action
  G->setMark(v, VISITED);
  for (int w=G->first(v); w<G->n(); w = G->next(v,w))
    if (G->getMark(w) == UNVISITED)
      DFS(G, w);
  PostVisit(G, v);              // Take appropriate action
}
```

This implementation contains calls to functions `PreVisit` and `PostVisit`.
These functions specify what activity should take place during the search. Just

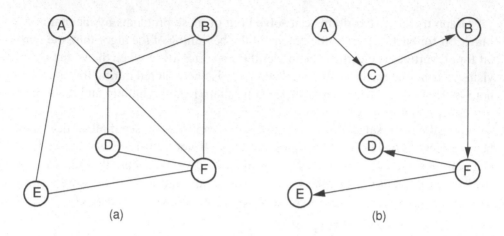

Figure 11.8 (a) A graph. (b) The depth-first search tree for the graph when starting at Vertex *A*.

as a preorder tree traversal requires action before the subtrees are visited, some graph traversals require that a vertex be processed before ones further along in the DFS. Alternatively, some applications require activity *after* the remaining vertices are processed; hence the call to function **PostVisit**. This would be a natural opportunity to make use of the visitor design pattern described in Section 1.3.2.

Figure 11.8 shows a graph and its corresponding depth-first search tree. Figure 11.9 illustrates the DFS process for the graph of Figure 11.8(a).

DFS processes each edge once in a directed graph. In an undirected graph, DFS processes each edge from both directions. Each vertex must be visited, but only once, so the total cost is $\Theta(|\mathbf{V}| + |\mathbf{E}|)$.

11.3.2 Breadth-First Search

Our second graph traversal algorithm is known as a **breadth-first search** (BFS). BFS examines all vertices connected to the start vertex before visiting vertices further away. BFS is implemented similarly to DFS, except that a queue replaces the recursion stack. Note that if the graph is a tree and the start vertex is at the root, BFS is equivalent to visiting vertices level by level from top to bottom. Figure 11.10 provides an implementation for the BFS algorithm. Figure 11.11 shows a graph and the corresponding breadth-first search tree. Figure 11.12 illustrates the BFS process for the graph of Figure 11.11(a).

11.3.3 Topological Sort

Assume that we need to schedule a series of tasks, such as classes or construction jobs, where we cannot start one task until after its prerequisites are completed. We wish to organize the tasks into a linear order that allows us to complete them one

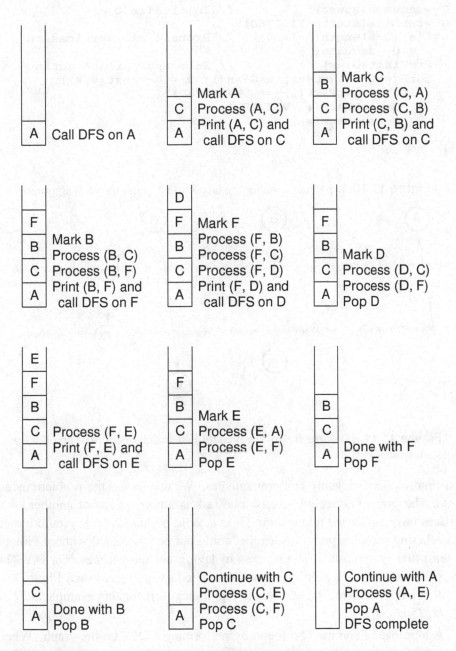

Figure 11.9 A detailed illustration of the DFS process for the graph of Figure 11.8(a) starting at Vertex A. The steps leading to each change in the recursion stack are described.

```
void BFS(Graph* G, int start, Queue<int>* Q) {
  int v, w;
  Q->enqueue(start);              // Initialize Q
  G->setMark(start, VISITED);
  while (Q->length() != 0) { // Process all vertices on Q
    v = Q->dequeue();
    PreVisit(G, v);               // Take appropriate action
    for (w=G->first(v); w<G->n(); w = G->next(v,w))
      if (G->getMark(w) == UNVISITED) {
        G->setMark(w, VISITED);
        Q->enqueue(w);
      }
  }
}
```

Figure 11.10 Implementation for the breadth-first graph traversal algorithm

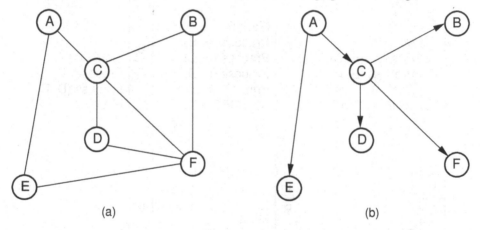

(a)   (b)

Figure 11.11 (a) A graph. (b) The breadth-first search tree for the graph when starting at Vertex *A*.

at a time without violating any prerequisites. We can model the problem using a DAG. The graph is directed because one task is a prerequisite of another — the vertices have a directed relationship. It is acyclic because a cycle would indicate a conflicting series of prerequisites that could not be completed without violating at least one prerequisite. The process of laying out the vertices of a DAG in a linear order to meet the prerequisite rules is called a **topological sort**. Figure 11.14 illustrates the problem. An acceptable topological sort for this example is *J1, J2, J3, J4, J5, J6, J7*.

A topological sort may be found by performing a DFS on the graph. When a vertex is visited, no action is taken (i.e., function **PreVisit** does nothing). When the recursion pops back to that vertex, function **PostVisit** prints the vertex. This yields a topological sort in reverse order. It does not matter where the sort starts, as long as all vertices are visited in the end. Figure 11.13 shows an implementation for the DFS-based algorithm.

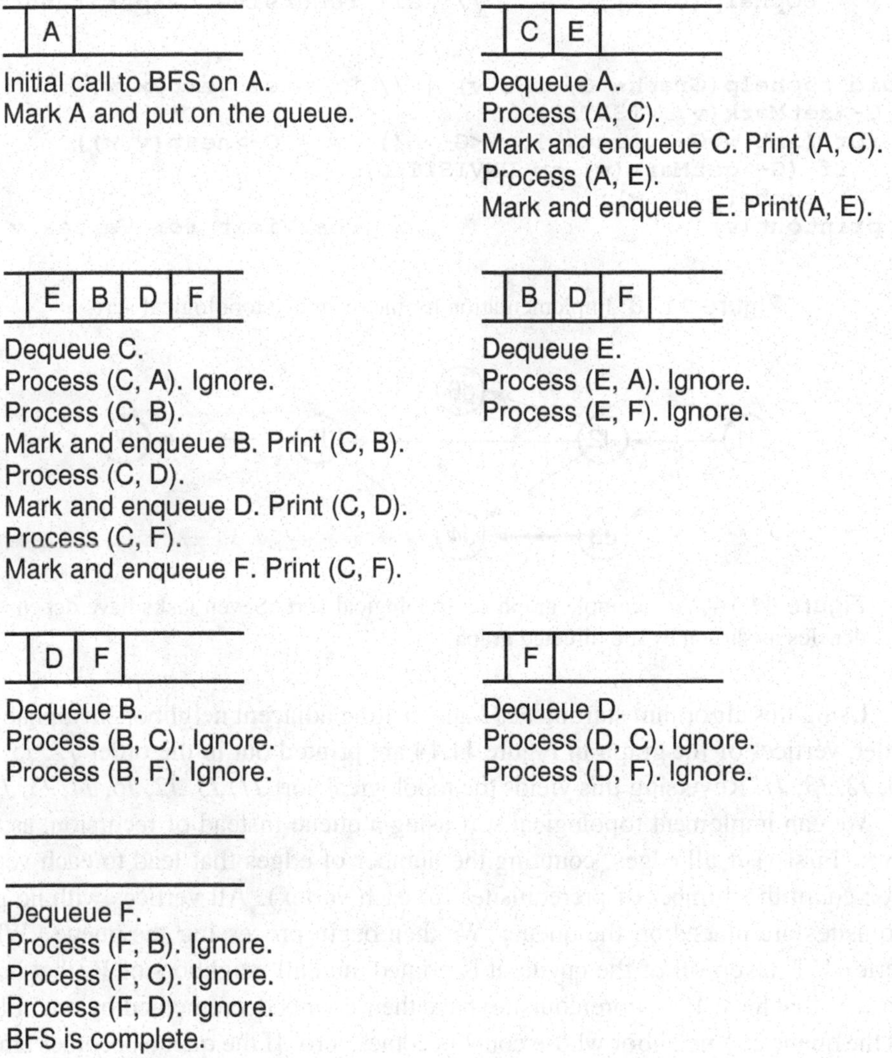

A			

Initial call to BFS on A.
Mark A and put on the queue.

C	E		

Dequeue A.
Process (A, C).
Mark and enqueue C. Print (A, C).
Process (A, E).
Mark and enqueue E. Print(A, E).

E	B	D	F

Dequeue C.
Process (C, A). Ignore.
Process (C, B).
Mark and enqueue B. Print (C, B).
Process (C, D).
Mark and enqueue D. Print (C, D).
Process (C, F).
Mark and enqueue F. Print (C, F).

B	D	F	

Dequeue E.
Process (E, A). Ignore.
Process (E, F). Ignore.

D	F		

Dequeue B.
Process (B, C). Ignore.
Process (B, F). Ignore.

F			

Dequeue D.
Process (D, C). Ignore.
Process (D, F). Ignore.

Dequeue F.
Process (F, B). Ignore.
Process (F, C). Ignore.
Process (F, D). Ignore.
BFS is complete.

Figure 11.12 A detailed illustration of the BFS process for the graph of Figure 11.11(a) starting at Vertex A. The steps leading to each change in the queue are described.

```
void topsort(Graph* G) {    // Topological sort: recursive
  int i;
  for (i=0; i<G->n(); i++) // Initialize Mark array
    G->setMark(i, UNVISITED);
  for (i=0; i<G->n(); i++) // Process all vertices
    if (G->getMark(i) == UNVISITED)
      tophelp(G, i);        // Call recursive helper function
}

void tophelp(Graph* G, int v) { // Process vertex v
  G->setMark(v, VISITED);
  for (int w=G->first(v); w<G->n(); w = G->next(v,w))
    if (G->getMark(w) == UNVISITED)
      tophelp(G, w);
  printout(v);                    // PostVisit for Vertex v
}
```

Figure 11.13 Implementation for the recursive topological sort.

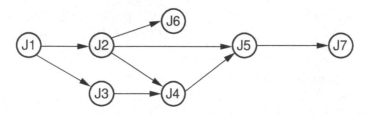

Figure 11.14 An example graph for topological sort. Seven tasks have dependencies as shown by the directed graph.

Using this algorithm starting at *J1* and visiting adjacent neighbors in alphabetic order, vertices of the graph in Figure 11.14 are printed out in the order *J7, J5, J4, J6, J2, J3, J1*. Reversing this yields the topological sort *J1, J3, J2, J6, J4, J5, J7*.

We can implement topological sort using a queue instead of recursion, as follows. First visit all edges, counting the number of edges that lead to each vertex (i.e., count the number of prerequisites for each vertex). All vertices with no prerequisites are placed on the queue. We then begin processing the queue. When Vertex *V* is taken off of the queue, it is printed, and all neighbors of *V* (that is, all vertices that have *V* as a prerequisite) have their counts decremented by one. Place on the queue any neighbor whose count becomes zero. If the queue becomes empty without printing all of the vertices, then the graph contains a cycle (i.e., there is no possible ordering for the tasks that does not violate some prerequisite). The printed order for the vertices of the graph in Figure 11.14 using the queue version of topological sort is **J1, J2, J3, J6, J4, J5, J7**. Figure 11.15 shows an implementation for the algorithm.

```
// Topological sort: Queue
void topsort(Graph* G, Queue<int>* Q) {
  int Count[G->n()];
  int v, w;
  for (v=0; v<G->n(); v++) Count[v] = 0; // Initialize
  for (v=0; v<G->n(); v++)     // Process every edge
    for (w=G->first(v); w<G->n(); w = G->next(v,w))
      Count[w]++;              // Add to v2's prereq count
  for (v=0; v<G->n(); v++)     // Initialize queue
    if (Count[v] == 0)         // Vertex has no prerequisites
      Q->enqueue(v);
  while (Q->length() != 0) {   // Process the vertices
    v = Q->dequeue();
    printout(v);               // PreVisit for "v"
    for (w=G->first(v); w<G->n(); w = G->next(v,w)) {
      Count[w]--;              // One less prerequisite
      if (Count[w] == 0)       // This vertex is now free
        Q->enqueue(w);
    }
  }
}
```

Figure 11.15 A queue-based topological sort algorithm.

11.4   Shortest-Paths Problems

On a road map, a road connecting two towns is typically labeled with its distance. We can model a road network as a directed graph whose edges are labeled with real numbers. These numbers represent the distance (or other cost metric, such as travel time) between two vertices. These labels may be called **weights**, **costs**, or **distances**, depending on the application. Given such a graph, a typical problem is to find the total length of the shortest path between two specified vertices. This is not a trivial problem, because the shortest path may not be along the edge (if any) connecting two vertices, but rather may be along a path involving one or more intermediate vertices. For example, in Figure 11.16, the cost of the path from A to B to D is 15. The cost of the edge directly from A to D is 20. The cost of the path from A to C to B to D is 10. Thus, the shortest path from A to D is 10 (not along the edge connecting A to D). We use the notation $d(A, D) = 10$ to indicate that the shortest distance from A to D is 10. In Figure 11.16, there is no path from E to B, so we set $d(E, B) = \infty$. We define $w(A, D) = 20$ to be the weight of edge (A, D), that is, the weight of the direct connection from A to D. Because there is no edge from E to B, $w(E, B) = \infty$. Note that $w(D, A) = \infty$ because the graph of Figure 11.16 is directed. We assume that all weights are positive.

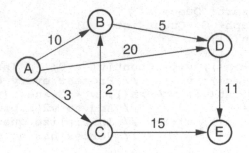

Figure 11.16 Example graph for shortest-path definitions.

11.4.1 Single-Source Shortest Paths

This section presents an algorithm to solve the **single-source shortest-paths** problem. Given Vertex S in Graph **G**, find a shortest path from S to every other vertex in **G**. We might want only the shortest path between two vertices, S and T. However in the worst case, while finding the shortest path from S to T, we might find the shortest paths from S to every other vertex as well. So there is no better algorithm (in the worst case) for finding the shortest path to a single vertex than to find shortest paths to all vertices. The algorithm described here will only compute the distance to every such vertex, rather than recording the actual path. Recording the path requires modifications to the algorithm that are left as an exercise.

Computer networks provide an application for the single-source shortest-paths problem. The goal is to find the cheapest way for one computer to broadcast a message to all other computers on the network. The network can be modeled by a graph with edge weights indicating time or cost to send a message to a neighboring computer.

For unweighted graphs (or whenever all edges have the same cost), the single-source shortest paths can be found using a simple breadth-first search. When weights are added, BFS will not give the correct answer.

One approach to solving this problem when the edges have differing weights might be to process the vertices in a fixed order. Label the vertices v_0 to v_{n-1}, with $S = v_0$. When processing Vertex v_1, we take the edge connecting v_0 and v_1. When processing v_2, we consider the shortest distance from v_0 to v_2 and compare that to the shortest distance from v_0 to v_1 to v_2. When processing Vertex v_i, we consider the shortest path for Vertices v_0 through v_{i-1} that have already been processed. Unfortunately, the true shortest path to v_i might go through Vertex v_j for $j > i$. Such a path will not be considered by this algorithm. However, the problem would not occur if we process the vertices in order of distance from S. Assume that we have processed in order of distance from S to the first $i - 1$ vertices that are closest to S; call this set of vertices **S**. We are now about to process the ith closest vertex;

```
// Compute shortest path distances from "s".
// Return these distances in "D".
void Dijkstra(Graph* G, int* D, int s) {
  int i, v, w;
  for (i=0; i<G->n(); i++) {        // Process the vertices
    v = minVertex(G, D);
    if (D[v] == INFINITY) return; // Unreachable vertices
    G->setMark(v, VISITED);
    for (w=G->first(v); w<G->n(); w = G->next(v,w))
      if (D[w] > (D[v] + G->weight(v, w)))
        D[w] = D[v] + G->weight(v, w);
  }
}
```

Figure 11.17 An implementation for Dijkstra's algorithm.

call it X. A shortest path from S to X must have its next-to-last vertex in **S**. Thus,

$$d(S,X) = \min_{U \in \mathbf{S}}(d(S,U) + w(U,X)).$$

In other words, the shortest path from S to X is the minimum over all paths that go from S to U, then have an edge from U to X, where U is some vertex in **S**.

This solution is usually referred to as Dijkstra's algorithm. It works by maintaining a distance estimate $\mathbf{D}(X)$ for all vertices X in **V**. The elements of **D** are initialized to the value **INFINITE**. Vertices are processed in order of distance from S. Whenever a vertex V is processed, $\mathbf{D}(X)$ is updated for every neighbor X of V. Figure 11.17 shows an implementation for Dijkstra's algorithm. At the end, array D will contain the shortest distance values.

There are two reasonable solutions to the key issue of finding the unvisited vertex with minimum distance value during each pass through the main **for** loop. The first method is simply to scan through the list of $|\mathbf{V}|$ vertices searching for the minimum value, as follows:

```
int minVertex(Graph* G, int* D) { // Find min cost vertex
  int i, v = -1;
  // Initialize v to some unvisited vertex
  for (i=0; i<G->n(); i++)
    if (G->getMark(i) == UNVISITED) { v = i; break; }
  for (i++; i<G->n(); i++)   // Now find smallest D value
    if ((G->getMark(i) == UNVISITED) && (D[i] < D[v]))
      v = i;
  return v;
}
```

Because this scan is done $|\mathbf{V}|$ times, and because each edge requires a constant-time update to D, the total cost for this approach is $\Theta(|\mathbf{V}|^2 + |\mathbf{E}|) = \Theta(|\mathbf{V}|^2)$, because $|\mathbf{E}|$ is in $O(|\mathbf{V}|^2)$.

The second method is to store unprocessed vertices in a min-heap ordered by distance values. The next-closest vertex can be found in the heap in $\Theta(\log |\mathbf{V}|)$

time. Every time we modify **D**(X), we could reorder X in the heap by deleting and reinserting it. This is an example of a priority queue with priority update, as described in Section 5.5. To implement true priority updating, we would need to store with each vertex its array index within the heap. A simpler approach is to add the new (smaller) distance value for a given vertex as a new record in the heap. The smallest value for a given vertex currently in the heap will be found first, and greater distance values found later will be ignored because the vertex will already be marked as **VISITED**. The only disadvantage to repeatedly inserting distance values is that it will raise the number of elements in the heap from $\Theta(|\mathbf{V}|)$ to $\Theta(|\mathbf{E}|)$ in the worst case. The time complexity is $\Theta((|\mathbf{V}| + |\mathbf{E}|) \log |\mathbf{E}|)$, because for each edge we must reorder the heap. Because the objects stored on the heap need to know both their vertex number and their distance, we create a simple class for the purpose called **DijkElem**, as follows. **DijkElem** is quite similar to the **Edge** class used by the adjacency list representation.

```
class DijkElem {
public:
  int vertex, distance;
  DijkElem() { vertex = -1; distance = -1; }
  DijkElem(int v, int d) { vertex = v; distance = d; }
};
```

Figure 11.18 shows an implementation for Dijkstra's algorithm using the priority queue.

Using **MinVertex** to scan the vertex list for the minimum value is more efficient when the graph is dense, that is, when $|\mathbf{E}|$ approaches $|\mathbf{V}|^2$. Using a priority queue is more efficient when the graph is sparse because its cost is $\Theta((|\mathbf{V}| + |\mathbf{E}|) \log |\mathbf{E}|)$. However, when the graph is dense, this cost can become as great as $\Theta(|\mathbf{V}|^2 \log |\mathbf{E}|) = \Theta(|V|^2 \log |V|)$.

Figure 11.19 illustrates Dijkstra's algorithm. The start vertex is A. All vertices except A have an initial value of ∞. After processing Vertex A, its neighbors have their D estimates updated to be the direct distance from A. After processing C (the closest vertex to A), Vertices B and E are updated to reflect the shortest path through C. The remaining vertices are processed in order B, D, and E.

11.5 Minimum-Cost Spanning Trees

The **minimum-cost spanning tree** (MST) problem takes as input a connected, undirected graph **G**, where each edge has a distance or weight measure attached. The MST is the graph containing the vertices of **G** along with the subset of **G**'s edges that (1) has minimum total cost as measured by summing the values for all of the edges in the subset, and (2) keeps the vertices connected. Applications where a solution to this problem is useful include soldering the shortest set of wires needed

```
// Dijkstra's shortest paths algorithm with priority queue
void Dijkstra(Graph* G, int* D, int s) {
  int i, v, w;                  // v is current vertex
  DijkElem temp;
  DijkElem E[G->e()];           // Heap array with lots of space
  temp.distance = 0; temp.vertex = s;
  E[0] = temp;                  // Initialize heap array
  heap<DijkElem, DDComp> H(E, 1, G->e()); // Create heap
  for (i=0; i<G->n(); i++) {              // Now, get distances
    do {
      if (H.size() == 0) return; // Nothing to remove
      temp = H.removefirst();
      v = temp.vertex;
    } while (G->getMark(v) == VISITED);
    G->setMark(v, VISITED);
    if (D[v] == INFINITY) return;    // Unreachable vertices
    for (w=G->first(v); w<G->n(); w = G->next(v,w))
      if (D[w] > (D[v] + G->weight(v, w))) { // Update D
        D[w] = D[v] + G->weight(v, w);
        temp.distance = D[w]; temp.vertex = w;
        H.insert(temp);     // Insert new distance in heap
      }
  }
}
```

Figure 11.18 An implementation for Dijkstra's algorithm using a priority queue.

	A	B	C	D	E
Initial	0	∞	∞	∞	∞
Process A	0	10	3	20	∞
Process C	0	5	3	20	18
Process B	0	5	3	10	18
Process D	0	5	3	10	18
Process E	0	5	3	10	18

Figure 11.19 A listing for the progress of Dijkstra's algorithm operating on the graph of Figure 11.16. The start vertex is A.

to connect a set of terminals on a circuit board, and connecting a set of cities by telephone lines in such a way as to require the least amount of cable.

The MST contains no cycles. If a proposed MST did have a cycle, a cheaper MST could be had by removing any one of the edges in the cycle. Thus, the MST is a free tree with $|\mathbf{V}| - 1$ edges. The name "minimum-cost spanning tree" comes from the fact that the required set of edges forms a tree, it spans the vertices (i.e., it connects them together), and it has minimum cost. Figure 11.20 shows the MST for an example graph.

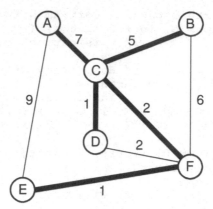

Figure 11.20 A graph and its MST. All edges appear in the original graph. Those edges drawn with heavy lines indicate the subset making up the MST. Note that edge (C, F) could be replaced with edge (D, F) to form a different MST with equal cost.

11.5.1 Prim's Algorithm

The first of our two algorithms for finding MSTs is commonly referred to as Prim's algorithm. Prim's algorithm is very simple. Start with any Vertex N in the graph, setting the MST to be N initially. Pick the least-cost edge connected to N. This edge connects N to another vertex; call this M. Add Vertex M and Edge (N, M) to the MST. Next, pick the least-cost edge coming from either N or M to any other vertex in the graph. Add this edge and the new vertex it reaches to the MST. This process continues, at each step expanding the MST by selecting the least-cost edge from a vertex currently in the MST to a vertex not currently in the MST.

Prim's algorithm is quite similar to Dijkstra's algorithm for finding the single-source shortest paths. The primary difference is that we are seeking not the next closest vertex to the start vertex, but rather the next closest vertex to any vertex currently in the MST. Thus we replace the lines

```
if (D[w] > (D[v] + G->weight(v, w)))
  D[w] = D[v] + G->weight(v, w);
```

in Djikstra's algorithm with the lines

```
if (D[w] > G->weight(v, w))
  D[w] = G->weight(v, w);
```

in Prim's algorithm.

Figure 11.21 shows an implementation for Prim's algorithm that searches the distance matrix for the next closest vertex. For each vertex I, when I is processed by Prim's algorithm, an edge going to I is added to the MST that we are building. Array **V[I]** stores the previously visited vertex that is closest to Vertex I. This information lets us know which edge goes into the MST when Vertex I is processed.

```
void Prim(Graph* G, int* D, int s) { // Prim's MST algorithm
  int V[G->n()];                      // Store closest vertex
  int i, w;
  for (i=0; i<G->n(); i++) {          // Process the vertices
    int v = minVertex(G, D);
    G->setMark(v, VISITED);
    if (v != s)
      AddEdgetoMST(V[v], v);          // Add edge to MST
    if (D[v] == INFINITY) return;     // Unreachable vertices
    for (w=G->first(v); w<G->n(); w = G->next(v,w))
      if (D[w] > G->weight(v,w)) {
        D[w] = G->weight(v,w);        // Update distance
        V[w] = v;                     // Where it came from
      }
  }
}
```

Figure 11.21 An implementation for Prim's algorithm.

The implementation of Figure 11.21 also contains calls to **AddEdgetoMST** to indicate which edges are actually added to the MST.

Alternatively, we can implement Prim's algorithm using a priority queue to find the next closest vertex, as shown in Figure 11.22. As with the priority queue version of Dijkstra's algorithm, the heap's **Elem** type stores a **DijkElem** object.

Prim's algorithm is an example of a greedy algorithm. At each step in the **for** loop, we select the least-cost edge that connects some marked vertex to some unmarked vertex. The algorithm does not otherwise check that the MST really should include this least-cost edge. This leads to an important question: Does Prim's algorithm work correctly? Clearly it generates a spanning tree (because each pass through the **for** loop adds one edge and one unmarked vertex to the spanning tree until all vertices have been added), but does this tree have minimum cost?

Theorem 11.1 *Prim's algorithm produces a minimum-cost spanning tree.*

Proof: We will use a proof by contradiction. Let $G = (V, E)$ be a graph for which Prim's algorithm does *not* generate an MST. Define an ordering on the vertices according to the order in which they were added by Prim's algorithm to the MST: $v_0, v_1, ..., v_{n-1}$. Let edge e_i connect (v_x, v_i) for some $x < i$ and $i \geq 1$. Let e_j be the lowest numbered (first) edge added by Prim's algorithm such that the set of edges selected so far *cannot* be extended to form an MST for G. In other words, e_j is the first edge where Prim's algorithm "went wrong." Let T be the "true" MST. Call v_p $(p < j)$ the vertex connected by edge e_j, that is, $e_j = (v_p, v_j)$.

Because T is a tree, there exists some path in T connecting v_p and v_j. There must be some edge e' in this path connecting vertices v_u and v_w, with $u < j$ and $w \geq j$. Because e_j is not part of T, adding edge e_j to T forms a cycle. Edge e' must

```
// Prim's MST algorithm: priority queue version
void Prim(Graph* G, int* D, int s) {
  int i, v, w;              // "v" is current vertex
  int V[G->n()];            // V[I] stores I's closest neighbor
  DijkElem temp;
  DijkElem E[G->e()];       // Heap array with lots of space
  temp.distance = 0; temp.vertex = s;
  E[0] = temp;              // Initialize heap array
  heap<DijkElem, DDComp> H(E, 1, G->e()); // Create heap
  for (i=0; i<G->n(); i++) {                // Now build MST
    do {
      if(H.size() == 0) return; // Nothing to remove
      temp = H.removefirst();
      v = temp.vertex;
    } while (G->getMark(v) == VISITED);
    G->setMark(v, VISITED);
    if (v != s) AddEdgetoMST(V[v], v); // Add edge to MST
    if (D[v] == INFINITY) return;      // Ureachable vertex
    for (w=G->first(v); w<G->n(); w = G->next(v,w))
      if (D[w] > G->weight(v, w)) {    // Update D
        D[w] = G->weight(v, w);
        V[w] = v;            // Update who it came from
        temp.distance = D[w]; temp.vertex = w;
        H.insert(temp);      // Insert new distance in heap
      }
  }
}
```

Figure 11.22 An implementation of Prim's algorithm using a priority queue.

be of lower cost than edge e_j, because Prim's algorithm did not generate an MST. This situation is illustrated in Figure 11.23. However, Prim's algorithm would have selected the least-cost edge available. It would have selected e', not e_j. Thus, it is a contradiction that Prim's algorithm would have selected the wrong edge, and thus, Prim's algorithm must be correct.   □

Example 11.3 For the graph of Figure 11.20, assume that we begin by marking Vertex A. From A, the least-cost edge leads to Vertex C. Vertex C and edge (A, C) are added to the MST. At this point, our candidate edges connecting the MST (Vertices A and C) with the rest of the graph are (A, E), (C, B), (C, D), and (C, F). From these choices, the least-cost edge from the MST is (C, D). So we add Vertex D to the MST. For the next iteration, our edge choices are (A, E), (C, B), (C, F), and (D, F). Because edges (C, F) and (D, F) happen to have equal cost, it is an arbitrary decision as to which gets selected. Say we pick (C, F). The next step marks Vertex E and adds edge (F, E) to the MST. Following in this manner, Vertex B (through edge (C, B)) is marked. At this point, the algorithm terminates.

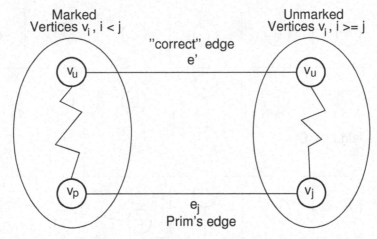

Figure 11.23 Prim's MST algorithm proof. The left oval contains that portion of the graph where Prim's MST and the "true" MST **T** agree. The right oval contains the rest of the graph. The two portions of the graph are connected by (at least) edges e_j (selected by Prim's algorithm to be in the MST) and e' (the "correct" edge to be placed in the MST). Note that the path from v_w to v_j cannot include any marked vertex v_i, $i \leq j$, because to do so would form a cycle.

11.5.2 Kruskal's Algorithm

Our next MST algorithm is commonly referred to as Kruskal's algorithm. Kruskal's algorithm is also a simple, greedy algorithm. First partition the set of vertices into $|\mathbf{V}|$ equivalence classes (see Section 6.2), each consisting of one vertex. Then process the edges in order of weight. An edge is added to the MST, and two equivalence classes combined, if the edge connects two vertices in different equivalence classes. This process is repeated until only one equivalence class remains.

Example 11.4 Figure 11.24 shows the first three steps of Kruskal's Algorithm for the graph of Figure 11.20. Edge (C, D) has the least cost, and because C and D are currently in separate MSTs, they are combined. We next select edge (E, F) to process, and combine these vertices into a single MST. The third edge we process is (C, F), which causes the MST containing Vertices C and D to merge with MST containing Vertices E and F. The next edge to process is (D, F). But because Vertices D and F are currently in the same MST, this edge is rejected. The algorithm will continue on to accept edges (B, C) and (A, C) into the MST.

The edges can be processed in order of weight by using a min-heap. This is generally faster than sorting the edges first, because in practice we need only visit a small fraction of the edges before completing the MST. This is an example of finding only a few smallest elements in a list, as discussed in Section 7.6.

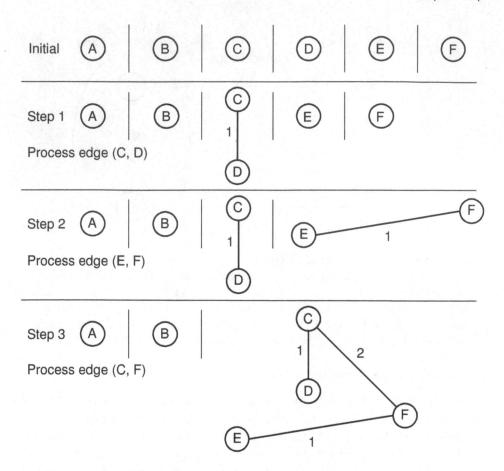

Figure 11.24 Illustration of the first three steps of Kruskal's MST algorithm as applied to the graph of Figure 11.20.

The only tricky part to this algorithm is determining if two vertices belong to the same equivalence class. Fortunately, the ideal algorithm is available for the purpose — the UNION/FIND algorithm based on the parent pointer representation for trees described in Section 6.2. Figure 11.25 shows an implementation for the algorithm. Class **KruskalElem** is used to store the edges on the min-heap.

Kruskal's algorithm is dominated by the time required to process the edges. The **differ** and **UNION** functions are nearly constant in time if path compression and weighted union is used. Thus, the total cost of the algorithm is $\Theta(|E| \log |E|)$ in the worst case, when nearly all edges must be processed before all the edges of the spanning tree are found and the algorithm can stop. More often the edges of the spanning tree are the shorter ones,and only about $|V|$ edges must be processed. If so, the cost is often close to $\Theta(|V| \log |E|)$ in the average case.

```
class KruskElem {              // An element for the heap
public:
  int from, to, distance; // The edge being stored
  KruskElem() { from = -1;  to = -1; distance = -1; }
  KruskElem(int f, int t, int d)
    { from = f; to = t; distance = d; }
};

void Kruskel(Graph* G) {    // Kruskal's MST algorithm
  ParPtrTree A(G->n());     // Equivalence class array
  KruskElem E[G->e()];      // Array of edges for min-heap
  int i;
  int edgecnt = 0;
  for (i=0; i<G->n(); i++) // Put the edges on the array
    for (int w=G->first(i); w<G->n(); w = G->next(i,w)) {
      E[edgecnt].distance = G->weight(i, w);
      E[edgecnt].from = i;
      E[edgecnt++].to = w;
    }
  // Heapify the edges
  heap<KruskElem, Comp> H(E, edgecnt, edgecnt);
  int numMST = G->n();        // Initially n equiv classes
  for (i=0; numMST>1; i++) { // Combine equiv classes
    KruskElem temp;
    temp = H.removefirst(); // Get next cheapest edge
    int v = temp.from;  int u = temp.to;
    if (A.differ(v, u)) {  // If in different equiv classes
      A.UNION(v, u);         // Combine equiv classes
      AddEdgetoMST(temp.from, temp.to);  // Add edge to MST
      numMST--;              // One less MST
    }
  }
}
```

Figure 11.25 An implementation for Kruskal's algorithm.

11.6   Further Reading

Many interesting properties of graphs can be investigated by playing with the programs in the Stanford Graphbase. This is a collection of benchmark databases and
graph processing programs. The Stanford Graphbase is documented in [Knu94].

11.7   Exercises

11.1 Prove by induction that a graph with n vertices has at most $n(n-1)/2$ edges.
11.2 Prove the following implications regarding free trees.

    (a) IF an undirected graph is connected and has no simple cycles, THEN
        the graph has $|\mathbf{V}| - 1$ edges.
    (b) IF an undirected graph has $|\mathbf{V}| - 1$ edges and no cycles, THEN the
        graph is connected.

11.3 (a) Draw the adjacency matrix representation for the graph of Figure 11.26.
  (b) Draw the adjacency list representation for the same graph.
  (c) If a pointer requires four bytes, a vertex label requires two bytes, and an edge weight requires two bytes, which representation requires more space for this graph?
  (d) If a pointer requires four bytes, a vertex label requires one byte, and an edge weight requires two bytes, which representation requires more space for this graph?

11.4 Show the DFS tree for the graph of Figure 11.26, starting at Vertex 1.

11.5 Write a pseudocode algorithm to create a DFS tree for an undirected, connected graph starting at a specified vertex V.

11.6 Show the BFS tree for the graph of Figure 11.26, starting at Vertex 1.

11.7 Write a pseudocode algorithm to create a BFS tree for an undirected, connected graph starting at a specified vertex V.

11.8 The BFS topological sort algorithm can report the existence of a cycle if one is encountered. Modify this algorithm to print the vertices possibly appearing in cycles (if there are any cycles).

11.9 Explain why, in the worst case, Dijkstra's algorithm is (asymptotically) as efficient as any algorithm for finding the shortest path from some vertex I to another vertex J.

11.10 Show the shortest paths generated by running Dijkstra's shortest-paths algorithm on the graph of Figure 11.26, beginning at Vertex 4. Show the D values as each vertex is processed, as in Figure 11.19.

11.11 Modify the algorithm for single-source shortest paths to actually store and return the shortest paths rather than just compute the distances.

11.12 The root of a DAG is a vertex R such that every vertex of the DAG can be reached by a directed path from R. Write an algorithm that takes a directed graph as input and determines the root (if there is one) for the graph. The running time of your algorithm should be $\Theta(|\mathbf{V}| + |\mathbf{E}|)$.

11.13 Write an algorithm to find the longest path in a DAG, where the length of the path is measured by the number of edges that it contains. What is the asymptotic complexity of your algorithm?

11.14 Write an algorithm to determine whether a directed graph of $|\mathbf{V}|$ vertices contains a cycle. Your algorithm should run in $\Theta(|\mathbf{V}| + |\mathbf{E}|)$ time.

11.15 Write an algorithm to determine whether an undirected graph of $|\mathbf{V}|$ vertices contains a cycle. Your algorithm should run in $\Theta(|\mathbf{V}|)$ time.

11.16 The **single-destination shortest-paths** problem for a directed graph is to find the shortest path *from* every vertex to a specified vertex V. Write an algorithm to solve the single-destination shortest-paths problem.

11.17 List the order in which the edges of the graph in Figure 11.26 are visited when running Prim's MST algorithm starting at Vertex 3. Show the final MST.

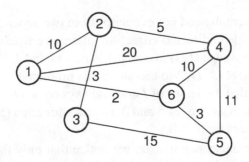

Figure 11.26 Example graph for Chapter 11 exercises.

11.18 List the order in which the edges of the graph in Figure 11.26 are visited
when running Kruskal's MST algorithm. Each time an edge is added to the
MST, show the result on the equivalence array, (e.g., show the array as in
Figure 6.7).

11.19 Write an algorithm to find a **maximum** cost spanning tree, that is, the spanning tree with highest possible cost.

11.20 When can Prim's and Kruskal's algorithms yield different MSTs?

11.21 Prove that, if the costs for the edges of Graph **G** are distinct, then only one
MST exists for **G**.

11.22 Does either Prim's or Kruskal's algorithm work if there are negative edge
weights?

11.23 Consider the collection of edges selected by Dijkstra's algorithm as the shortest paths to the graph's vertices from the start vertex. Do these edges form
a spanning tree (not necessarily of minimum cost)? Do these edges form an
MST? Explain why or why not.

11.24 Prove that a tree is a bipartite graph.

11.25 Prove that any tree (i.e., a connected, undirected graph with no cycles) can
be two-colored. (A graph can be two colored if every vertex can be assigned
one of two colors such that no adjacent vertices have the same color.)

11.26 Write an algorithm that determines if an arbitrary undirected graph is a bipartite graph. If the graph is bipartite, then your algorithm should also identify
the vertices as to which of the two partitions each belongs to.

11.8 Projects

11.1 Design a format for storing graphs in files. Then implement two functions:
one to read a graph from a file and the other to write a graph to a file. Test
your functions by implementing a complete MST program that reads an undirected graph in from a file, constructs the MST, and then writes to a second
file the graph representing the MST.

11.2 An undirected graph need not explicitly store two separate directed edges to represent a single undirected edge. An alternative would be to store only a single undirected edge (I, J) to connect Vertices I and J. However, what if the user asks for edge (J, I)? We can solve this problem by consistently storing the edge such that the lesser of I and J always comes first. Thus, if we have an edge connecting Vertices 5 and 3, requests for edge (5, 3) and (3, 5) both map to (3, 5) because $3 < 5$.

Looking at the adjacency matrix, we notice that only the lower triangle of the array is used. Thus we could cut the space required by the adjacency matrix from $|\mathbf{V}|^2$ positions to $|\mathbf{V}|(|\mathbf{V}| - 1)/2$ positions. Read Section 12.2 on triangular matrices. The re-implement the adjacency matrix representation of Figure 11.6 to implement undirected graphs using a triangular array.

11.3 While the underlying implementation (whether adjacency matrix or adjacency list) is hidden behind the graph ADT, these two implementations can have an impact on the efficiency of the resulting program. For Dijkstra's shortest paths algorithm, two different implementations were given in Section 11.4.1 that provide different ways for determining the next closest vertex at each iteration of the algorithm. The relative costs of these two variants depend on who sparse or dense the graph is. They might also depend on whether the graph is implemented using an adjacency list or adjacency matrix.

Design and implement a study to compare the effects on performance for three variables: (i) the two graph representations (adjacency list and adjacency matrix); (ii) the two implementations for Djikstra's shortest paths algorithm (searching the table of vertex distances or using a priority queue to track the distances), and (iii) sparse versus dense graphs. Be sure to test your implementations on a variety of graphs that are sufficiently large to generate meaningful times.

11.4 The example implementations for DFS and BFS show calls to functions **PreVisit** and **PostVisit**. Re-implement the BFS and DFS functions to make use of the visitor design pattern to handle the pre/post visit functionality.

11.5 Write a program to label the connected components for an undirected graph. In other words, all vertices of the first component are given the first component's label, all vertices of the second component are given the second component's label, and so on. Your algorithm should work by defining any two vertices connected by an edge to be members of the same equivalence class. Once all of the edges have been processed, all vertices in a given equivalence class will be connected. Use the UNION/FIND implementation from Section 6.2 to implement equivalence classes.

12

Lists and Arrays Revisited

Simple lists and arrays are the right tools for the many applications. Other situations require support for operations that cannot be implemented efficiently by the standard list representations of Chapter 4. This chapter presents a range of topics, whose unifying thread is that the data structures included are all list- or array-like. These structures overcome some of the problems of simple linked list and contiguous array representations. This chapter also seeks to reinforce the concept of logical representation versus physical implementation, as some of the "list" implementations have quite different organizations internally.

Section 12.1 describes a series of representations for multilists, which are lists that may contain sublists. Section 12.2 discusses representations for implementing sparse matrices, large matrices where most of the elements have zero values. Section 12.3 discusses memory management techniques, which are essentially a way of allocating variable-length sections from a large array.

12.1 Multilists

Recall from Chapter 4 that a list is a finite, ordered sequence of items of the form $\langle x_0, x_1, ..., x_{n-1} \rangle$ where $n \geq 0$. We can represent the empty list by **NULL** or $\langle \rangle$. In Chapter 4 we assumed that all list elements had the same data type. In this section, we extend the definition of lists to allow elements to be arbitrary in nature. In general, list elements are one of two types.

1. An **atom**, which is a data record of some type such as a number, symbol, or string.
2. Another list, which is called a **sublist**.

A list containing sublists will be written as

$$\langle x1, \langle y1, \langle a1, a2 \rangle, y3 \rangle, \langle z1, z2 \rangle, x4 \rangle.$$

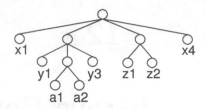

Figure 12.1 Example of a multilist represented by a tree.

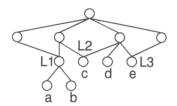

Figure 12.2 Example of a reentrant multilist. The shape of the structure is a DAG (all edges point downward).

In this example, the list has four elements. The second element is the sublist $\langle y1, \langle a1, a2 \rangle, y3 \rangle$ and the third is the sublist $\langle z1, z2 \rangle$. The sublist $\langle y1, \langle a1, a2 \rangle, y3 \rangle$ itself contains a sublist. If a list **L** has one or more sublists, we call **L** a **multi-list**. Lists with no sublists are often referred to as **linear lists** or **chains**. Note that this definition for multilist fits well with our definition of sets from Definition 2.1, where a set's members can be either primitive elements or sets.

We can restrict the sublists of a multilist in various ways, depending on whether the multilist should have the form of a tree, a DAG, or a generic graph. A **pure list** is a list structure whose graph corresponds to a tree, such as in Figure 12.1. In other words, there is exactly one path from the root to any node, which is equivalent to saying that no object may appear more than once in the list. In the pure list, each pair of angle brackets corresponds to an internal node of the tree. The members of the list correspond to the children for the node. Atoms on the list correspond to leaf nodes.

A **reentrant list** is a list structure whose graph corresponds to a DAG. Nodes might be accessible from the root by more than one path, which is equivalent to saying that objects (including sublists) may appear multiple times in the list as long as no cycles are formed. All edges point downward, from the node representing a list or sublist to its elements. Figure 12.2 illustrates a reentrant list. To write out this list in bracket notation, we can duplicate nodes as necessary. Thus, the bracket notation for the list of Figure 12.2 could be written

$$\langle \langle \langle a, b \rangle \rangle, \langle \langle a, b \rangle, c \rangle, \langle c, d, e \rangle, \langle e \rangle \rangle.$$

For convenience, we will adopt a convention of allowing sublists and atoms to be labeled, such as "*L1*:". Whenever a label is repeated, the element corresponding to

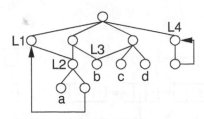

Figure 12.3 Example of a cyclic list. The shape of the structure is a directed graph.

that label will be substituted when we write out the list. Thus, the bracket notation for the list of Figure 12.2 could be written

$$\langle\langle L1 : \langle a, b\rangle\rangle, \langle L1, L2 : c\rangle, \langle L2, d, L3 : e\rangle, \langle L3\rangle\rangle.$$

A **cyclic list** is a list structure whose graph corresponds to any directed graph, possibly containing cycles. Figure 12.3 illustrates such a list. Labels are required to write this in bracket notation. Here is the bracket notation for the list of Figure 12.3.

$$\langle L1 : \langle L2 : \langle a, L1\rangle\rangle, \langle L2, L3 : b\rangle, \langle L3, c, d\rangle, L4 : \langle L4\rangle\rangle.$$

Multilists can be implemented in a number of ways. Most of these should be familiar from implementations suggested earlier in the book for list, tree, and graph data structures.

One simple approach is to use a simple array to represent the list. This works well for chains with fixed-length elements, equivalent to the simple array-based list of Chapter 4. We can view nested sublists as variable-length elements. To use this approach, we require some indication of the beginning and end of each sublist. In essence, we are using a sequential tree implementation as discussed in Section 6.5. This should be no surprise, because the pure list is equivalent to a general tree structure. Unfortunately, as with any sequential representation, access to the nth sublist must be done sequentially from the beginning of the list.

Because pure lists are equivalent to trees, we can also use linked allocation methods to support direct access to the list of children. Simple linear lists are represented by linked lists. Pure lists can be represented as linked lists with an additional tag field to indicate whether the node is an atom or a sublist. If it is a sublist, the data field points to the first element on the sublist. This is illustrated by Figure 12.4.

Another approach is to represent all list elements with link nodes storing two pointer fields, except for atoms. Atoms just contain data. This is the system used by the programming language LISP. Figure 12.5 illustrates this representation. Either the pointer contains a tag bit to identify what it points to, or the object being pointed to stores a tag bit to identify itself. Tags distinguish atoms from list nodes. This

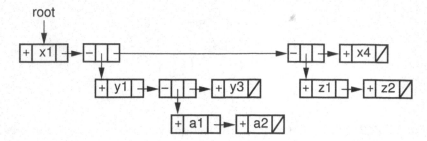

Figure 12.4 Linked representation for the pure list of Figure 12.1. The first field in each link node stores a tag bit. If the tag bit stores "$+$," then the data field stores an atom. If the tag bit stores "$-$," then the data field stores a pointer to a sublist.

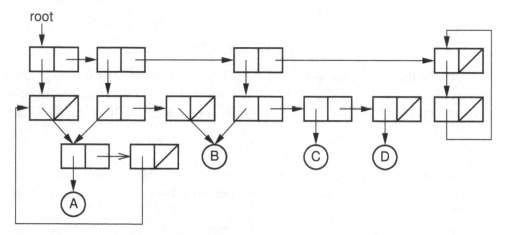

Figure 12.5 LISP-like linked representation for the cyclic multilist of Figure 12.3. Each link node stores two pointers. A pointer either points to an atom, or to another link node. Link nodes are represented by two boxes, and atoms by circles.

implementation can easily support reentrant and cyclic lists, because non-atoms can point to any other node.

12.2   Matrix Representations

Sometimes we need to represent a large, two-dimensional matrix where many of the elements have a value of zero. One example is the lower triangular matrix that results from solving systems of simultaneous equations. A lower triangular matrix stores zero values at all positions $[r, c]$ such that $r < c$, as shown in Figure 12.6(a). Thus, the upper-right triangle of the matrix is always zero. Another example is representing undirected graphs in an adjacency matrix (see Project 11.2). Because all edges between Vertices i and j go in both directions, there is no need to store both. Instead we can just store one edge going from the higher-indexed vertex to

a_{00}	0	0	0
a_{10}	a_{11}	0	0
a_{20}	a_{21}	a_{22}	0
a_{30}	a_{31}	a_{32}	a_{33}

a_{00}	a_{01}	a_{02}	a_{03}
0	a_{11}	a_{12}	a_{13}
0	0	a_{22}	a_{23}
0	0	0	a_{33}

(a)   (b)

Figure 12.6 Triangular matrices. (a) A lower triangular matrix. (b) An upper triangular matrix.

the lower-indexed vertex. In this case, only the lower triangle of the matrix can have non-zero values.

We can take advantage of this fact to save space. Instead of storing $n(n+1)/2$ pieces of information in an $n \times n$ array, it would save space to use a list of length $n(n+1)/2$. This is only practical if some means can be found to locate within the list the element that would correspond to position $[r, c]$ in the original matrix.

We will derive an equation to convert position $[r, c]$ to a position in a one-dimensional list to store the lower triangular matrix. Note that row 0 of the matrix has one non-zero value, row 1 has two non-zero values, and so on. Thus, row r is preceded by r rows with a total of $\sum_{k=1}^{r} k = (r^2 + r)/2$ non-zero elements. Adding c to reach the cth position in the rth row yields the following equation to convert position $[r, c]$ in the original matrix to the correct position in the list.

$$\text{matrix}[r, c] = \text{list}[(r^2 + r)/2 + c].$$

A similar equation can be used to convert coordinates in an upper triangular matrix, that is, a matrix with zero values at positions $[r, c]$ such that $r > c$, as shown in Figure 12.6(b). For an $n \times n$ upper triangular matrix, the equation to convert from matrix coordinates to list positions would be

$$\text{matrix}[r, c] = \text{list}[rn - (r^2 + r)/2 + c].$$

A more difficult situation arises when the vast majority of values stored in an $n \times m$ matrix are zero, but there is no restriction on which positions are zero and which are non-zero. This is known as a **sparse matrix**.

One approach to representing a sparse matrix is to concatenate (or otherwise combine) the row and column coordinates into a single value and use this as a key in a hash table. Thus, if we want to know the value of a particular position in the matrix, we search the hash table for the appropriate key. If a value for this position is not found, it is assumed to be zero. This is an ideal approach when all queries to the matrix are in terms of access by specified position. However, if we wish to find the first non-zero element in a given row, or the next non-zero element below the current one in a given column, then the hash table requires us to check sequentially through all possible positions in some row or column.

Another approach is to implement the matrix as an **orthogonal list**. Consider the following sparse matrix:

$$
\begin{array}{ccccccc}
10 & 23 & 0 & 0 & 0 & 0 & 19 \\
45 & 5 & 0 & 93 & 0 & 0 & 0 \\
0 & 0 & 0 & 0 & 0 & 0 & 0 \\
0 & 0 & 0 & 0 & 0 & 0 & 0 \\
40 & 0 & 0 & 0 & 0 & 0 & 0 \\
0 & 0 & 0 & 0 & 0 & 0 & 0 \\
0 & 0 & 0 & 0 & 0 & 0 & 0 \\
0 & 32 & 0 & 12 & 0 & 0 & 7 \\
\end{array}
$$

The corresponding orthogonal array is shown in Figure 12.7. Here we have a list of row headers, each of which contains a pointer to a list of matrix records. A second list of column headers also contains pointers to matrix records. Each non-zero matrix element stores pointers to its non-zero neighbors in the row, both following and preceding it. Each non-zero element also stores pointers to its non-zero neighbors following and preceding it in the column. Thus, each non-zero element stores its own value, its position within the matrix, and four pointers. Non-zero elements are found by traversing a row or column list. Note that the first non-zero element in a given row could be in any column; likewise, the neighboring non-zero element in any row or column list could be at any (higher) row or column in the array. Thus, each non-zero element must also store its row and column position explicitly.

To find if a particular position in the matrix contains a non-zero element, we traverse the appropriate row or column list. For example, when looking for the element at Row 7 and Column 1, we can traverse the list either for Row 7 or for Column 1. When traversing a row or column list, if we come to an element with the correct position, then its value is non-zero. If we encounter an element with a higher position, then the element we are looking for is not in the sparse matrix. In this case, the element's value is zero. For example, when traversing the list for Row 7 in the matrix of Figure 12.7, we first reach the element at Row 7 and Column 1. If this is what we are looking for, then the search can stop. If we are looking for the element at Row 7 and Column 2, then the search proceeds along the Row 7 list to next reach the element at Column 3. At this point we know that no element at Row 7 and Column 2 is stored in the sparse matrix.

Insertion and deletion can be performed by working in a similar way to insert or delete elements within the appropriate row and column lists.

Each non-zero element stored in the sparse matrix representation takes much more space than an element stored in a simple $n \times n$ matrix. When is the sparse matrix more space efficient than the standard representation? To calculate this, we need to determine how much space the standard matrix requires, and how much

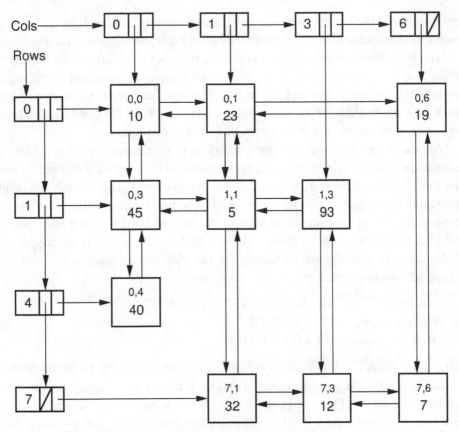

Figure 12.7 The orthogonal list sparse matrix representation.

the sparse matrix requires. The size of the sparse matrix depends on the number of non-zero elements (we will refer to this value as *NNZ*), while the size of the standard matrix representation does not vary. We need to know the (relative) sizes of a pointer and a data value. For simplicity, our calculation will ignore the space taken up by the row and column header (which is not much affected by the number of elements in the sparse array).

As an example, assume that a data value, a row or column index, and a pointer each require four bytes. An $n \times m$ matrix requires $4nm$ bytes. The sparse matrix requires 28 bytes per non-zero element (four pointers, two array indices, and one data value). If we set X to be the percentage of non-zero elements, we can solve for the value of X below which the sparse matrix representation is more space efficient. Using the equation

$$28X = 4mn$$

and solving for X, we find that the sparse matrix using this implementation is more space efficient when $X < 1/7$, that is, when less than about 14% of the elements are non-zero. Different values for the relative sizes of data values, pointers, or matrix indices can lead to a different break-even point for the two implementations.

The time required to process a sparse matrix should ideally depend on NNZ. When searching for an element, the cost is the number of elements preceding the desired element on its row or column list. The cost for operations such as adding two matrices should be $\Theta(n + m)$ in the worst case when the one matrix stores n non-zero elements and the other stores m non-zero elements.

Another representation for sparse matrices is sometimes called the Yale representation. Matlab uses a similar representation, with a primary difference being that the Matlab representation uses column-major order.[1] The Matlab representation stores the sparse matrix using three lists. The first is simply all of the non-zero element values, in column-major order. The second list stores the start position within the first list for each column. The third list stores the row positions for each of the corresponding non-zero values. In the Yale representation, the matrix of Figure 12.7 would appear as:

Values:	10 45 40 23 5 32 93 12 19 7
Column starts:	0 3 5 5 7 7 7 7
Row positions:	0 1 4 0 1 7 1 7 0 7

If the matrix has c columns, then the total space required will be proportional to $c + 2NNZ$. This is good in terms of space. It allows fairly quick access to any column, and allows for easy processing of the non-zero values along a column. However, it does not do a good job of providing access to the values along a row, and is terrible when values need to be added or removed from the representation. Fortunately, when doing computations such as adding or multiplying two sparse matrices, the processing of the input matrices and construction of the output matrix can be done reasonably efficiently.

12.3 Memory Management

Most data structures are designed to store and access objects of uniform size. A typical example would be an integer stored in a list or a queue. Some applications require the ability to store variable-length records, such as a string of arbitrary length. One solution is to store in the list or queue fixed-length pointers to the variable-length strings. This is fine for data structures stored in main memory. But if the collection of strings is meant to be stored on disk, then we might need to worry about where exactly these strings are stored. And even when stored in main memory, something has to figure out where there are available bytes to hold the string. We could easily store variable-size records in a queue or stack, where

---

[1]Scientific packages tend to prefer column-oriented representations for matrices since this the dominant access need for the operations to be performed.

```
// Memory Manager abstract class
class MemManager {
public:
  virtual ~MemManager() {} // Base destructor

  // Store a record and return a handle to it
  virtual MemHandle insert(void* info, int length) =0;

  // Get back a copy of a stored record
  virtual int get(void* info, MemHandle h) =0;

  // Release the space associated with a record
  virtual void release(MemHandle h) =0;
};
```

Figure 12.8 A simple ADT for a memory manager.

the restricted order of insertions and deletions makes this easy to deal with. But in a language like **C**++ or Java, programmers can allocate and deallocate space in complex ways through use of **new**. Where does this space come from? This section discusses memory management techniques for the general problem of handling space requests of variable size.

The basic model for memory management is that we have a (large) block of contiguous memory locations, which we will call the **memory pool**. Periodically, memory requests are issued for some amount of space in the pool. The **memory manager** has the job of finding a contiguous block of locations of at least the requested size from somewhere within the memory pool. Honoring such a request is called a **memory allocation**. The memory manager will typically return some piece of information that the requester can hold on to so that later it can recover the record that was just stored by the memory manager. This piece of information is called a **handle**. At some point, space that has been requested might no longer be needed, and this space can be returned to the memory manager so that it can be reused. This is called a **memory deallocation**. The memory manager should then be able to reuse this space to satisfy later memory requests. We can define an ADT for the memory manager as shown in Figure 12.8.

The user of the **MemManager** ADT provides a pointer (in parameter **info**) to space that holds some record or message to be stored or retrieved. This is similar to the **C**++ basic file read/write methods presented in Section 8.4. The fundamental idea is that the client gives messages to the memory manager for safe keeping. The memory manager returns a "receipt" for the message in the form of a **MemHandle** object. Of course to be practical, a **MemHandle** must be much smaller than the typical message to be stored. The client holds the **MemHandle** object until it wishes to get the message back.

Method **insert** lets the client tell the memory manager the length and contents of the message to be stored. This ADT assumes that the memory manager will

Figure 12.9 Dynamic storage allocation model. Memory is made up of a series
of variable-size blocks, some allocated and some free. In this example, shaded
areas represent memory currently allocated and unshaded areas represent unused
memory available for future allocation.

remember the length of the message associated with a given handle (perhaps in the
handle itself), thus method **get** does not include a length parameter but instead
returns the length of the message actually stored. Method **release** allows the
client to tell the memory manager to release the space that stores a given message.

When all inserts and releases follow a simple pattern, such as last requested,
first released (stack order), or first requested, first released (queue order), memory
management is fairly easy. We are concerned here with the general case where
blocks of any size might be requested and released in any order. This is known
as **dynamic storage allocation**. One example of dynamic storage allocation is
managing free store for a compiler's runtime environment, such as the system-level
new and **delete** operations in C++. Another example is managing main memory
in a multitasking operating system. Here, a program might require a certain amount
of space, and the memory manager must keep track of which programs are using
which parts of the main memory. Yet another example is the file manager for a
disk drive. When a disk file is created, expanded, or deleted, the file manager must
allocate or deallocate disk space.

A block of memory or disk space managed in this way is sometimes referred to
as a **heap**. The term "heap" is being used here in a different way than the heap data
structure discussed in Section 5.5. Here "heap" refers to the memory controlled by
a dynamic memory management scheme.

In the rest of this section, we first study techniques for dynamic memory management. We then tackle the issue of what to do when no single block of memory
in the memory pool is large enough to honor a given request.

12.3.1 Dynamic Storage Allocation

For the purpose of dynamic storage allocation, we view memory as a single array
which, after a series of memory requests and releases tends to become broken into
a series of variable-size blocks, where some of the blocks are **free** and some are
reserved or already allocated to store messages. The memory manager typically
uses a linked list to keep track of the free blocks, called the **freelist**, which is used
for servicing future memory requests. Figure 12.9 illustrates the situation that can
arise after a series of memory allocations and deallocations.

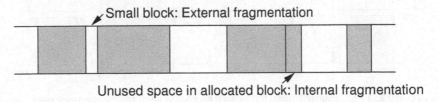

Figure 12.10 An illustration of internal and external fragmentation. The small white block labeled "External fragmentation" is too small to satisfy typical memory requests. The small grey block labeled "Internal fragmentation" was allocated as part of the grey block to its left, but it does not actually store information.

When a memory request is received by the memory manager, some block on the freelist must be found that is large enough to service the request. If no such block is found, then the memory manager must resort to a **failure policy** such as discussed in Section 12.3.2.

If there is a request for m words, and no block exists of exactly size m, then a larger block must be used instead. One possibility in this case is that the entire block is given away to the memory allocation request. This might be desirable when the size of the block is only slightly larger than the request. This is because saving a tiny block that is too small to be useful for a future memory request might not be worthwhile. Alternatively, for a free block of size k, with $k > m$, up to $k - m$ space may be retained by the memory manager to form a new free block, while the rest is used to service the request.

Memory managers can suffer from two types of **fragmentation**, which refers to unused space that is too small to be useful. **External fragmentation** occurs when a series of memory requests and releases results in small free blocks. **Internal fragmentation** occurs when more than m words are allocated to a request for m words, wasting free storage. This is equivalent to the internal fragmentation that occurs when files are allocated in multiples of the cluster size. The difference between internal and external fragmentation is illustrated by Figure 12.10.

Some memory management schemes sacrifice space to internal fragmentation to make memory management easier (and perhaps reduce external fragmentation). For example, external fragmentation does not happen in file management systems that allocate file space in clusters. Another example of sacrificing space to internal fragmentation so as to simplify memory management is the **buddy method** described later in this section.

The process of searching the memory pool for a block large enough to service the request, possibly reserving the remaining space as a free block, is referred to as a **sequential fit** method.

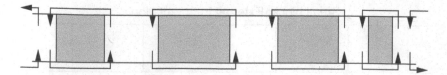

Figure 12.11 A doubly linked list of free blocks as seen by the memory manager. Shaded areas represent allocated memory. Unshaded areas are part of the freelist.

Sequential Fit Methods

Sequential-fit methods attempt to find a "good" block to service a storage request. The three sequential-fit methods described here assume that the free blocks are organized into a doubly linked list, as illustrated by Figure 12.11.

There are two basic approaches to implementing the freelist. The simpler approach is to store the freelist separately from the memory pool. In other words, a simple linked-list implementation such as described in Chapter 4 can be used, where each node of the linked list contains a pointer to a single free block in the memory pool. This is fine if there is space available for the linked list itself, separate from the memory pool.

The second approach to storing the freelist is more complicated but saves space. Because the free space is free, it can be used by the memory manager to help it do its job. That is, the memory manager can temporarily "borrow" space within the free blocks to maintain its doubly linked list. To do so, each unallocated block must be large enough to hold these pointers. In addition, it is usually worthwhile to let the memory manager add a few bytes of space to each reserved block for its own purposes. In other words, a request for m bytes of space might result in slightly more than m bytes being allocated by the memory manager, with the extra bytes used by the memory manager itself rather than the requester. We will assume that all memory blocks are organized as shown in Figure 12.12, with space for tags and linked list pointers. Here, free and reserved blocks are distinguished by a tag bit at both the beginning and the end of the block, for reasons that will be explained. In addition, both free and reserved blocks have a size indicator immediately after the tag bit at the beginning of the block to indicate how large the block is. Free blocks have a second size indicator immediately preceding the tag bit at the end of the block. Finally, free blocks have left and right pointers to their neighbors in the free block list.

The information fields associated with each block permit the memory manager to allocate and deallocate blocks as needed. When a request comes in for m words of storage, the memory manager searches the linked list of free blocks until it finds a "suitable" block for allocation. How it determines which block is suitable will be discussed below. If the block contains exactly m words (plus space for the tag and size fields), then it is removed from the freelist. If the block (of size k) is large

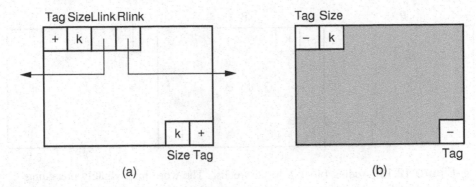

Figure 12.12 Blocks as seen by the memory manager. Each block includes additional information such as freelist link pointers, start and end tags, and a size field. (a) The layout for a free block. The beginning of the block contains the tag bit field, the block size field, and two pointers for the freelist. The end of the block contains a second tag field and a second block size field. (b) A reserved block of k bytes. The memory manager adds to these k bytes an additional tag bit field and block size field at the beginning of the block, and a second tag field at the end of the block.

enough, then the remaining $k - m$ words are reserved as a block on the freelist, in the current location.

When a block F is freed, it must be merged into the freelist. If we do not care about merging adjacent free blocks, then this is a simple insertion into the doubly linked list of free blocks. However, we would like to merge adjacent blocks, because this allows the memory manager to serve requests of the largest possible size. Merging is easily done due to the tag and size fields stored at the ends of each block, as illustrated by Figure 12.13. Here, the memory manager first checks the unit of memory immediately preceding block F to see if the preceding block (call it P) is also free. If it is, then the memory unit before P's tag bit stores the size of P, thus indicating the position for the beginning of the block in memory. P can then simply have its size extended to include block F. If block P is not free, then we just add block F to the freelist. Finally, we also check the bit following the end of block F. If this bit indicates that the following block (call it S) is free, then S is removed from the freelist and the size of F is extended appropriately.

We now consider how a "suitable" free block is selected to service a memory request. To illustrate the process, assume that we have a memory pool with 200 units of storage. After some series of allocation requests and releases, we have reached a point where there are four free blocks on the freelist of sizes 25, 35, 32, and 45 (in that order). Assume that a request is made for 30 units of storage. For our examples, we ignore the overhead imposed for the tag, link, and size fields discussed above.

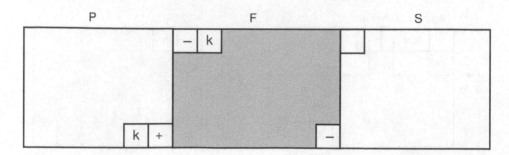

Figure 12.13 Adding block F to the freelist. The word immediately preceding the start of F in the memory pool stores the tag bit of the preceding block P. If P is free, merge F into P. We find the end of F by using F's size field. The word following the end of F is the tag field for block S. If S is free, merge it into F.

The simplest method for selecting a block would be to move down the free block list until a block of size at least 30 is found. Any remaining space in this block is left on the freelist. If we begin at the beginning of the list and work down to the first free block at least as large as 30, we select the block of size 35. 30 units of storage will be allocated, leaving a free block with 5 units of space. Because this approach selects the first block with enough space, it is called **first fit**. A simple variation that will improve performance is, instead of always beginning at the head of the freelist, remember the last position reached in the previous search and start from there. When the end of the freelist is reached, search begins again at the head of the freelist. This modification reduces the number of unnecessary searches through small blocks that were passed over by previous requests.

There is a potential disadvantage to first fit: It might "waste" larger blocks by breaking them up, and so they will not be available for large requests later. A strategy that avoids using large blocks unnecessarily is called **best fit**. Best fit looks at the entire list and picks the smallest block that is at least as large as the request (i.e., the "best" or closest fit to the request). Continuing with the preceding example, the best fit for a request of 30 units is the block of size 32, leaving a remainder of size 2. Best fit has the disadvantage that it requires that the entire list be searched. Another problem is that the remaining portion of the best-fit block is likely to be small, and thus useless for future requests. In other words, best fit tends to maximize problems of external fragmentation while it minimizes the chance of not being able to service an occasional large request.

A strategy contrary to best fit might make sense because it tends to minimize the effects of external fragmentation. This is called **worst fit**, which always allocates the largest block on the list hoping that the remainder of the block will be useful for servicing a future request. In our example, the worst fit is the block of size 45, leaving a remainder of size 15. If there are a few unusually large requests, this approach will have less chance of servicing them. If requests generally tend to be of the same size, then this might be an effective strategy. Like best fit, worst fit requires searching the entire freelist at each memory request to find the largest block. Alternatively, the freelist can be ordered from largest to smallest free block, possibly by using a priority queue implementation.

Which strategy is best? It depends on the expected types of memory requests. If the requests are of widely ranging size, best fit might work well. If the requests tend to be of similar size, with rare large and small requests, first or worst fit might work well. Unfortunately, there are always request patterns that one of the three sequential fit methods will service, but which the other two will not be able to service. For example, if the series of requests 600, 650, 900, 500, 100 is made to a freelist containing blocks 500, 700, 650, 900 (in that order), the requests can all be serviced by first fit, but not by best fit. Alternatively, the series of requests 600, 500, 700, 900 can be serviced by best fit but not by first fit on this same freelist.

Buddy Methods

Sequential-fit methods rely on a linked list of free blocks, which must be searched for a suitable block at each memory request. Thus, the time to find a suitable free block would be $\Theta(n)$ in the worst case for a freelist containing n blocks. Merging adjacent free blocks is somewhat complicated. Finally, we must either use additional space for the linked list, or use space within the memory pool to support the memory manager operations. In the second option, both free and reserved blocks require tag and size fields. Fields in free blocks do not cost any space (because they are stored in memory that is not otherwise being used), but fields in reserved blocks create additional overhead.

The buddy system solves most of these problems. Searching for a block of the proper size is efficient, merging adjacent free blocks is simple, and no tag or other information fields need be stored within reserved blocks. The buddy system assumes that memory is of size 2^N for some integer N. Both free and reserved blocks will always be of size 2^k for $k \leq N$. At any given time, there might be both free and reserved blocks of various sizes. The buddy system keeps a separate list for free blocks of each size. There can be at most N such lists, because there can only be N distinct block sizes.

When a request comes in for m words, we first determine the smallest value of k such that $2^k \geq m$. A block of size 2^k is selected from the free list for that block size if one exists. The buddy system does not worry about internal fragmentation: The entire block of size 2^k is allocated.

If no block of size 2^k exists, the next larger block is located. This block is split in half (repeatedly if necessary) until the desired block of size 2^k is created. Any other blocks generated as a by-product of this splitting process are placed on the appropriate freelists.

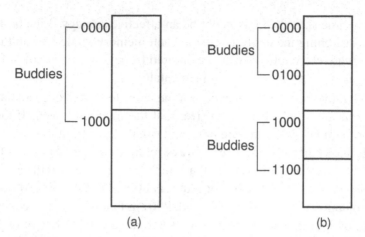

Figure 12.14 Example of the buddy system. (a) Blocks of size 8. (b) Blocks of size 4.

The disadvantage of the buddy system is that it allows internal fragmentation. For example, a request for 257 words will require a block of size 512. The primary advantages of the buddy system are (1) there is less external fragmentation; (2) search for a block of the right size is cheaper than, say, best fit because we need only find the first available block on the block list for blocks of size 2^k; and (3) merging adjacent free blocks is easy.

The reason why this method is called the buddy system is because of the way that merging takes place. The **buddy** for any block of size 2^k is another block of the same size, and with the same address (i.e., the byte position in memory, read as a binary value) except that the kth bit is reversed. For example, the block of size 8 with beginning address 0000 in Figure 12.14(a) has buddy with address 1000. Likewise, in Figure 12.14(b), the block of size 4 with address 0000 has buddy 0100. If free blocks are sorted by address value, the buddy can be found by searching the correct block-size list. Merging simply requires that the address for the combined buddies be moved to the freelist for the next larger block size.

Other Memory Allocation Methods

In addition to sequential-fit and buddy methods, there are many ad hoc approaches to memory management. If the application is sufficiently complex, it might be desirable to break available memory into several memory **zones**, each with a different memory management scheme. For example, some zones might have a simple memory access pattern of first-in, first-out. This zone can therefore be managed efficiently by using a simple stack. Another zone might allocate only records of fixed size, and so can be managed with a simple freelist as described in Section 4.1.2. Other zones might need one of the general-purpose memory allocation methods discussed in this section. The advantage of zones is that some portions of memory can be managed more efficiently. The disadvantage is that one zone might fill up while other zones have excess free memory if the zone sizes are chosen poorly.

Another approach to memory management is to impose a standard size on all memory requests. We have seen an example of this concept already in disk file management, where all files are allocated in multiples of the cluster size. This approach leads to internal fragmentation, but managing files composed of clusters is easier than managing arbitrarily sized files. The cluster scheme also allows us to relax the restriction that the memory request be serviced by a contiguous block of memory. Most disk file managers and operating system main memory managers work on a cluster or page system. Block management is usually done with a buffer pool to allocate available blocks in main memory efficiently.

12.3.2   Failure Policies and Garbage Collection

At some point when processing a series of requests, a memory manager could encounter a request for memory that it cannot satisfy. In some situations, there might be nothing that can be done: There simply might not be enough free memory to service the request, and the application may require that the request be serviced immediately. In this case, the memory manager has no option but to return an error, which could in turn lead to a failure of the application program. However, in many cases there are alternatives to simply returning an error. The possible options are referred to collectively as **failure policies**.

In some cases, there might be sufficient free memory to satisfy the request, but it is scattered among small blocks. This can happen when using a sequential-fit memory allocation method, where external fragmentation has led to a series of small blocks that collectively could service the request. In this case, it might be possible to **compact** memory by moving the reserved blocks around so that the free space is collected into a single block. A problem with this approach is that the application must somehow be able to deal with the fact that its data have now been moved to different locations. If the application program relies on the absolute positions of the data in any way, this would be disastrous. One approach for dealing with this problem involves the handles returned by the memory manager. A handle works as a second level of indirection to a memory location. The memory allocation routine does not return a pointer to the block of storage, but rather a pointer to a the handle that in turn gives access to the storage. The handle never moves its position, but the position of the block might be moved and the value of the handle updated. Of course, this requires that the memory manager keep track of the handles and how they associate with the stored messages. Figure 12.15 illustrates the concept.

Another failure policy that might work in some applications is to defer the memory request until sufficient memory becomes available. For example, a multitasking operating system could adopt the strategy of not allowing a process to run until there is sufficient memory available. While such a delay might be annoying

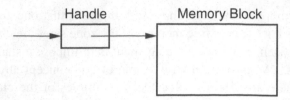

Figure 12.15 Using handles for dynamic memory management. The memory manager returns the address of the handle in response to a memory request. The handle stores the address of the actual memory block. In this way, the memory block might be moved (with its address updated in the handle) without disrupting the application program.

to the user, it is better than halting the entire system. The assumption here is that other processes will eventually terminate, freeing memory.

Another option might be to allocate more memory to the memory manager. In a zoned memory allocation system where the memory manager is part of a larger system, this might be a viable option. In a C++ program that implements its own memory manager, it might be possible to get more memory from the system-level **new** operator, such as is done by the freelist of Section 4.1.2.

The last failure policy that we will consider is **garbage collection**. Consider the following series of statements.

```
int* p = new int[5];
int* q = new int[10];
p = q;
```

While in Java this would be no problem (due to automatic garbage collection), in languages such as C++, this would be considered bad form because the original space allocated to **p** is lost as a result of the third assignment. This space cannot be used again by the program. Such lost memory is referred to as **garbage**, also known as a **memory leak**. When no program variable points to a block of space, no future access to that space is possible. Of course, if another variable had first been assigned to point to **p**'s space, then reassigning **p** would not create garbage.

Some programming languages take a different view towards garbage. In particular, the LISP programming language uses the multilist representation of Figure 12.5, and all storage is in the form either of internal nodes with two pointers or atoms. Figure 12.16 shows a typical collection of LISP structures, headed by variables named *A*, *B*, and *C*, along with a freelist.

In LISP, list objects are constantly being put together in various ways as temporary variables, and then all reference to them is lost when the object is no longer needed. Thus, garbage is normal in LISP, and in fact cannot be avoided during routine program behavior. When LISP runs out of memory, it resorts to a garbage collection process to recover the space tied up in garbage. Garbage collection consists of examining the managed memory pool to determine which parts are still

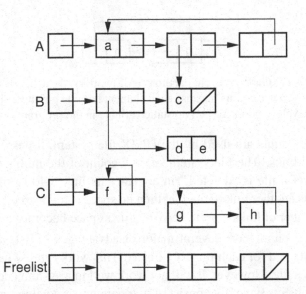

Figure 12.16 Example of LISP list variables, including the system freelist.

being used and which parts are garbage. In particular, a list is kept of all program variables, and any memory locations not reachable from one of these variables are considered to be garbage. When the garbage collector executes, all unused memory locations are placed in free store for future access. This approach has the advantage that it allows for easy collection of garbage. It has the disadvantage, from a user's point of view, that every so often the system must halt while it performs garbage collection. For example, garbage collection is noticeable in the Emacs text editor, which is normally implemented in LISP. Occasionally the user must wait for a moment while the memory management system performs garbage collection.

The Java programming language also makes use of garbage collection. As in LISP, it is common practice in Java to allocate dynamic memory as needed, and to later drop all references to that memory. The garbage collector is responsible for reclaiming such unused space as necessary. This might require extra time when running the program, but it makes life considerably easier for the programmer. In contrast, many large applications written in C++ (even commonly used commercial software) contain memory leaks that will in time cause the program to fail.

Several algorithms have been used for garbage collection. One is the **reference count** algorithm. Here, every dynamically allocated memory block includes space for a count field. Whenever a pointer is directed to a memory block, the reference count is increased. Whenever a pointer is directed away from a memory block, the reference count is decreased. If the count ever becomes zero, then the memory block is considered garbage and is immediately placed in free store. This approach has the advantage that it does not require an explicit garbage collection phase, because information is put in free store immediately when it becomes garbage.

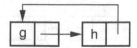

Figure 12.17 Garbage cycle example. All memory elements in the cycle have non-zero reference counts because each element has one pointer to it, even though the entire cycle is garbage (i.e., no static variable in the program points to it).

Reference counts are used by the UNIX file system. Files can have multiple names, called links. The file system keeps a count of the number of links to each file. Whenever a file is "deleted," in actuality its link field is simply reduced by one. If there is another link to the file, then no space is recovered by the file system. When the number of links goes to zero, the file's space becomes available for reuse.

Reference counts have several major disadvantages. First, a reference count must be maintained for each memory object. This works well when the objects are large, such as a file. However, it will not work well in a system such as LISP where the memory objects typically consist of two pointers or a value (an atom). Another major problem occurs when garbage contains cycles. Consider Figure 12.17. Here each memory object is pointed to once, but the collection of objects is still garbage because no pointer points to the collection. Thus, reference counts only work when the memory objects are linked together without cycles, such as the UNIX file system where files can only be organized as a DAG.

Another approach to garbage collection is the **mark/sweep** strategy. Here, each memory object needs only a single mark bit rather than a reference counter field. When free store is exhausted, a separate garbage collection phase takes place as follows.

1. Clear all mark bits.
2. Perform depth-first search (DFS) following pointers beginning with each variable on the system's list of static variables. Each memory element encountered during the DFS has its mark bit turned on.
3. A "sweep" is made through the memory pool, visiting all elements. Unmarked elements are considered garbage and placed in free store.

The advantages of the mark/sweep approach are that it needs less space than is necessary for reference counts, and it works for cycles. However, there is a major disadvantage. This is a "hidden" space requirement needed to do the processing. DFS is a recursive algorithm: Either it must be implemented recursively, in which case the compiler's runtime system maintains a stack, or else the memory manager can maintain its own stack. What happens if all memory is contained in a single linked list? Then the depth of the recursion (or the size of the stack) is the number of memory cells! Unfortunately, the space for the DFS stack must be available at the worst conceivable time, that is, when free memory has been exhausted.

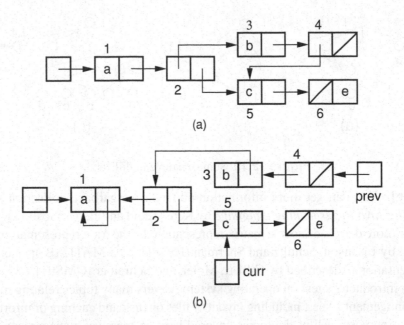

Figure 12.18 Example of the Deutsch-Schorr-Waite garbage collection algorithm. (a) The initial multilist structure. (b) The multilist structure of (a) at the instant when link node 5 is being processed by the garbage collection algorithm. A chain of pointers stretching from variable **prev** to the head node of the structure has been (temporarily) created by the garbage collection algorithm.

Fortunately, a clever technique allows DFS to be performed without requiring additional space for a stack. Instead, the structure being traversed is used to hold the stack. At each step deeper into the traversal, instead of storing a pointer on the stack, we "borrow" the pointer being followed. This pointer is set to point back to the node we just came from in the previous step, as illustrated by Figure 12.18. Each borrowed pointer stores an additional bit to tell us whether we came down the left branch or the right branch of the link node being pointed to. At any given instant we have passed down only one path from the root, and we can follow the trail of pointers back up. As we return (equivalent to popping the recursion stack), we set the pointer back to its original position so as to return the structure to its original condition. This is known as the Deutsch-Schorr-Waite garbage collection algorithm.

12.4 Further Reading

For information on LISP, see *The Little LISPer* by Friedman and Felleisen [FF89]. Another good LISP reference is *Common LISP: The Language* by Guy L. Steele [Ste90]. For information on Emacs, which is both an excellent text editor and a programming environment, see the *GNU Emacs Manual* by Richard Stallman

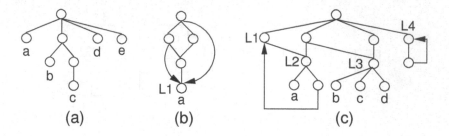

Figure 12.19 Some example multilists.

[Sta11b]. You can get more information about Java's garbage collection system from *The Java Programming Language* by Ken Arnold and James Gosling [AG06].

For more details on sparse matrix representations, the Yale representation is described by Eisenstat, Schultz and Sherman [ESS81]. The MATLAB sparse matrix representation is described by Gilbert, Moler, and Schreiber [GMS91].

An introductory text on operating systems covers many topics relating to memory management issues, including layout of files on disk and caching of information in main memory. All of the topics covered here on memory management, buffer pools, and paging are relevant to operating system implementation. For example, see *Operating Systems* by William Stallings[Sta11a].

12.5 Exercises

12.1 For each of the following bracket notation descriptions, draw the equivalent multilist in graphical form such as shown in Figure 12.2.

    (a) $\langle a, b, \langle c, d, e\rangle, \langle f, \langle g\rangle, h\rangle\rangle$
    (b) $\langle a, b, \langle c, d, L1\!:\!e\rangle, L1\rangle$
    (c) $\langle L1\!:\!a, L1, \langle L2\!:\!b\rangle, L2, \langle L1\rangle\rangle$

12.2 **(a)** Show the bracket notation for the list of Figure 12.19(a).
    (b) Show the bracket notation for the list of Figure 12.19(b).
    (c) Show the bracket notation for the list of Figure 12.19(c).

12.3 Given the linked representation of a pure list such as

$$\langle x_1, \langle y_1, y_2, \langle z_1, z_2\rangle, y_4\rangle, \langle w_1, w_2\rangle, x_4\rangle,$$

write an in-place reversal algorithm to reverse the sublists at all levels including the topmost level. For this example, the result would be a linked representation corresponding to

$$\langle x_4, \langle w_2, w_1\rangle, \langle y_4, \langle z_2, z_1\rangle, y_2, y_1\rangle, x_1\rangle.$$

12.4 What fraction of the values in a matrix must be zero for the sparse matrix representation of Section 12.2 to be more space efficient than the standard two-dimensional matrix representation when data values require eight bytes, array indices require two bytes, and pointers require four bytes?

12.5 Write a function to add an element at a given position to the sparse matrix representation of Section 12.2.

12.6 Write a function to delete an element from a given position in the sparse matrix representation of Section 12.2.

12.7 Write a function to transpose a sparse matrix as represented in Section 12.2.

12.8 Write a function to add two sparse matrices as represented in Section 12.2.

12.9 Write memory manager allocation and deallocation routines for the situation where all requests and releases follow a last-requested, first-released (stack) order.

12.10 Write memory manager allocation and deallocation routines for the situation where all requests and releases follow a last-requested, last-released (queue) order.

12.11 Show the result of allocating the following blocks from a memory pool of size 1000 using first fit for each series of block requests. State if a given request cannot be satisfied.

   (a) Take 300 (call this block A), take 500, release A, take 200, take 300.

   (b) Take 200 (call this block A), take 500, release A, take 200, take 300.

   (c) Take 500 (call this block A), take 300, release A, take 300, take 200.

12.12 Show the result of allocating the following blocks from a memory pool of size 1000 using best fit for each series of block requests. State if a given request cannot be satisfied.

   (a) Take 300 (call this block A), take 500, release A, take 200, take 300.

   (b) Take 200 (call this block A), take 500, release A, take 200, take 300.

   (c) Take 500 (call this block A), take 300, release A, take 300, take 200.

12.13 Show the result of allocating the following blocks from a memory pool of size 1000 using worst fit for each series of block requests. State if a given request cannot be satisfied.

   (a) Take 300 (call this block A), take 500, release A, take 200, take 300.

   (b) Take 200 (call this block A), take 500, release A, take 200, take 300.

   (c) Take 500 (call this block A), take 300, release A, take 300, take 200.

12.14 Assume that the memory pool contains three blocks of free storage. Their sizes are 1300, 2000, and 1000. Give examples of storage requests for which

   (a) first-fit allocation will work, but not best fit or worst fit.

   (b) best-fit allocation will work, but not first fit or worst fit.

   (c) worst-fit allocation will work, but not first fit or best fit.

12.6 Projects

12.1 Implement the orthogonal list sparse matrix representation of Section 12.2. Your implementation should support the following operations on the matrix:

- insert an element at a given position,
- delete an element from a given position,
- return the value of the element at a given position,
- take the transpose of a matrix,
- add two matrices, and
- multiply two matrices.

12.2 Implement the Yale model for sparse matrices described at the end of Section 12.2. Your implementation should support the following operations on the matrix:

- insert an element at a given position,
- delete an element from a given position,
- return the value of the element at a given position,
- take the transpose of a matrix,
- add two matrices, and
- multiply two matrices.

12.3 Implement the **MemManager** ADT shown at the beginning of Section 12.3. Use a separate linked list to implement the freelist. Your implementation should work for any of the three sequential-fit methods: first fit, best fit, and worst fit. Test your system empirically to determine under what conditions each method performs well.

12.4 Implement the **MemManager** ADT shown at the beginning of Section 12.3. Do not use separate memory for the free list, but instead embed the free list into the memory pool as shown in Figure 12.12. Your implementation should work for any of the three sequential-fit methods: first fit, best fit, and worst fit. Test your system empirically to determine under what conditions each method performs well.

12.5 Implement the **MemManager** ADT shown at the beginning of Section 12.3 using the buddy method of Section 12.3.1. Your system should support requests for blocks of a specified size and release of previously requested blocks.

12.6 Implement the Deutsch-Schorr-Waite garbage collection algorithm that is illustrated by Figure 12.18.

13

Advanced Tree Structures

This chapter introduces several tree structures designed for use in specialized applications. The trie of Section 13.1 is commonly used to store and retrieve strings. It also serves to illustrate the concept of a key space decomposition. The AVL tree and splay tree of Section 13.2 are variants on the BST. They are examples of self-balancing search trees and have guaranteed good performance regardless of the insertion order for records. An introduction to several spatial data structures used to organize point data by xy-coordinates is presented in Section 13.3.

Descriptions of the fundamental operations are given for each data structure. One purpose for this chapter is to provide opportunities for class programming projects, so detailed implementations are left to the reader.

13.1 Tries

Recall that the shape of a BST is determined by the order in which its data records are inserted. One permutation of the records might yield a balanced tree while another might yield an unbalanced tree, with the extreme case becoming the shape of a linked list. The reason is that the value of the key stored in the root node splits the key range into two parts: those key values less than the root's key value, and those key values greater than the root's key value. Depending on the relationship between the root node's key value and the distribution of the key values for the other records in the the tree, the resulting BST might be balanced or unbalanced. Thus, the BST is an example of a data structure whose organization is based on an **object space decomposition**, so called because the decomposition of the key range is driven by the objects (i.e., the key values of the data records) stored in the tree.

The alternative to object space decomposition is to predefine the splitting position within the key range for each node in the tree. In other words, the root could be predefined to split the key range into two equal halves, regardless of the particular values or order of insertion for the data records. Those records with keys in the lower half of the key range will be stored in the left subtree, while those records with keys in the upper half of the key range will be stored in the right subtree. While such a decomposition rule will not necessarily result in a balanced tree (the tree will be unbalanced if the records are not well distributed within the key range), at least the shape of the tree will not depend on the order of key insertion. Furthermore, the depth of the tree will be limited by the resolution of the key range; that is, the depth of the tree can never be greater than the number of bits required to store a key value. For example, if the keys are integers in the range 0 to 1023, then the resolution for the key is ten bits. Thus, two keys can be identical only until the tenth bit. In the worst case, two keys will follow the same path in the tree only until the tenth branch. As a result, the tree will never be more than ten levels deep. In contrast, a BST containing n records could be as much as n levels deep.

Splitting based on predetermined subdivisions of the key range is called **key space decomposition**. In computer graphics, the technique is known as **image space** decomposition, and this term is sometimes used to describe the process for data structures as well. A data structure based on key space decomposition is called a **trie**. Folklore has it that "trie" comes from "retrieval." Unfortunately, that would imply that the word is pronounced "tree," which would lead to confusion with regular use of the word "tree." "Trie" is actually pronounced as "try."

Like the B^+-tree, a trie stores data records only in leaf nodes. Internal nodes serve as placeholders to direct the search process. but since the split points are predetermined, internal nodes need not store "traffic-directing" key values. Figure 13.1 illustrates the trie concept. Upper and lower bounds must be imposed on the key values so that we can compute the middle of the key range. Because the largest value inserted in this example is 120, a range from 0 to 127 is assumed, as 128 is the smallest power of two greater than 120. The binary value of the key determines whether to select the left or right branch at any given point during the search. The most significant bit determines the branch direction at the root. Figure 13.1 shows a **binary trie**, so called because in this example the trie structure is based on the value of the key interpreted as a binary number, which results in a binary tree.

The Huffman coding tree of Section 5.6 is another example of a binary trie. All data values in the Huffman tree are at the leaves, and each branch splits the range of possible letter codes in half. The Huffman codes are actually reconstructed from the letter positions within the trie.

These are examples of binary tries, but tries can be built with any branching factor. Normally the branching factor is determined by the alphabet used. For binary numbers, the alphabet is {0, 1} and a binary trie results. Other alphabets lead to other branching factors.

One application for tries is to store a dictionary of words. Such a trie will be referred to as an **alphabet trie**. For simplicity, our examples will ignore case in letters. We add a special character ($) to the 26 standard English letters. The $ character is used to represent the end of a string. Thus, the branching factor for

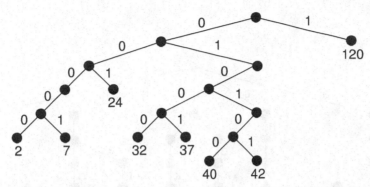

Figure 13.1 The binary trie for the collection of values 2, 7, 24, 31, 37, 40, 42, 120. All data values are stored in the leaf nodes. Edges are labeled with the value of the bit used to determine the branching direction of each node. The binary form of the key value determines the path to the record, assuming that each key is represented as a 7-bit value representing a number in the range 0 to 127.

each node is (up to) 27. Once constructed, the alphabet trie is used to determine if a given word is in the dictionary. Consider searching for a word in the alphabet trie of Figure 13.2. The first letter of the search word determines which branch to take from the root, the second letter determines which branch to take at the next level, and so on. Only the letters that lead to a word are shown as branches. In Figure 13.2(b) the leaf nodes of the trie store a copy of the actual words, while in Figure 13.2(a) the word is built up from the letters associated with each branch.

One way to implement a node of the alphabet trie is as an array of 27 pointers indexed by letter. Because most nodes have branches to only a small fraction of the possible letters in the alphabet, an alternate implementation is to use a linked list of pointers to the child nodes, as in Figure 6.9.

The depth of a leaf node in the alphabet trie of Figure 13.2(b) has little to do with the number of nodes in the trie, or even with the length of the corresponding string. Rather, a node's depth depends on the number of characters required to distinguish this node's word from any other. For example, if the words "anteater" and "antelope" are both stored in the trie, it is not until the fifth letter that the two words can be distinguished. Thus, these words must be stored at least as deep as level five. In general, the limiting factor on the depth of nodes in the alphabet trie is the length of the words stored.

Poor balance and clumping can result when certain prefixes are heavily used. For example, an alphabet trie storing the common words in the English language would have many words in the "th" branch of the tree, but none in the "zq" branch.

Any multiway branching trie can be replaced with a binary trie by replacing the original trie's alphabet with an equivalent binary code. Alternatively, we can use the techniques of Section 6.3.4 for converting a general tree to a binary tree without modifying the alphabet.

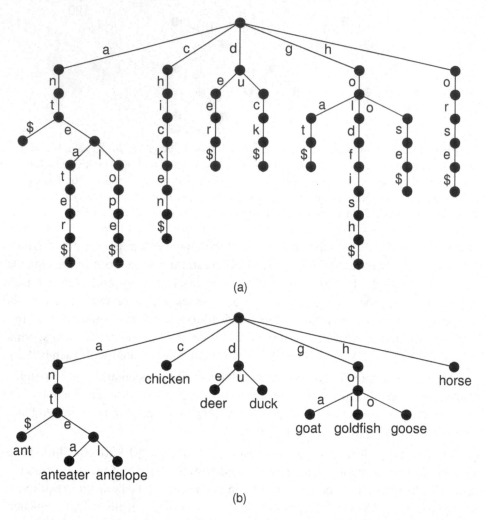

(a)

(b)

Figure 13.2 Two variations on the alphabet trie representation for a set of ten words. (a) Each node contains a set of links corresponding to single letters, and each letter in the set of words has a corresponding link. "$" is used to indicate the end of a word. Internal nodes direct the search and also spell out the word one letter per link. The word need not be stored explicitly. "$" is needed to recognize the existence of words that are prefixes to other words, such as 'ant' in this example. (b) Here the trie extends only far enough to discriminate between the words. Leaf nodes of the trie each store a complete word; internal nodes merely direct the search.

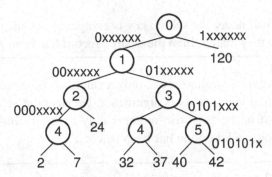

Figure 13.3 The PAT trie for the collection of values 2, 7, 24, 32, 37, 40, 42, 120. Contrast this with the binary trie of Figure 13.1. In the PAT trie, all data values are stored in the leaf nodes, while internal nodes store the bit position used to determine the branching decision, assuming that each key is represented as a 7-bit value representing a number in the range 0 to 127. Some of the branches in this PAT trie have been labeled to indicate the binary representation for all values in that subtree. For example, all values in the left subtree of the node labeled 0 must have value 0xxxxxx (where x means that bit can be either a 0 or a 1). All nodes in the right subtree of the node labeled 3 must have value 0101xxx. However, we can skip branching on bit 2 for this subtree because all values currently stored have a value of 0 for that bit.

The trie implementations illustrated by Figures 13.1 and 13.2 are potentially quite inefficient as certain key sets might lead to a large number of nodes with only a single child. A variant on trie implementation is known as PATRICIA, which stands for "Practical Algorithm To Retrieve Information Coded In Alphanumeric." In the case of a binary alphabet, a PATRICIA trie (referred to hereafter as a PAT trie) is a full binary tree that stores data records in the leaf nodes. Internal nodes store only the position within the key's bit pattern that is used to decide on the next branching point. In this way, internal nodes with single children (equivalently, bit positions within the key that do not distinguish any of the keys within the current subtree) are eliminated. A PAT trie corresponding to the values of Figure 13.1 is shown in Figure 13.3.

Example 13.1 When searching for the value 7 (0000111 in binary) in the PAT trie of Figure 13.3, the root node indicates that bit position 0 (the leftmost bit) is checked first. Because the 0th bit for value 7 is 0, take the left branch. At level 1, branch depending on the value of bit 1, which again is 0. At level 2, branch depending on the value of bit 2, which again is 0. At level 3, the index stored in the node is 4. This means that bit 4 of the key is checked next. (The value of bit 3 is irrelevant, because all values stored in that subtree have the same value at bit position 3.) Thus, the single branch that extends from the equivalent node in Figure 13.1 is just skipped. For key value 7, bit 4 has value 1, so the rightmost branch is taken. Because this leads to a leaf node, the search key is compared against the key stored in that node. If they match, then the desired record has been found.

Note that during the search process, only a single bit of the search key is compared at each internal node. This is significant, because the search key could be quite large. Search in the PAT trie requires only a single full-key comparison, which takes place once a leaf node has been reached.

Example 13.2 Consider the situation where we need to store a library of DNA sequences. A DNA sequence is a series of letters, usually many thousands of characters long, with the string coming from an alphabet of only four letters that stand for the four amino acids making up a DNA strand. Similar DNA sequences might have long sections of their string that are identical. The PAT trie would avoid making multiple full key comparisons when searching for a specific sequence.

13.2 Balanced Trees

We have noted several times that the BST has a high risk of becoming unbalanced, resulting in excessively expensive search and update operations. One solution to this problem is to adopt another search tree structure such as the 2-3 tree or the binary trie. An alternative is to modify the BST access functions in some way to guarantee that the tree performs well. This is an appealing concept, and it works well for heaps, whose access functions maintain the heap in the shape of a complete binary tree. Unfortunately, requiring that the BST always be in the shape of a complete binary tree requires excessive modification to the tree during update, as discussed in Section 10.3.

If we are willing to weaken the balance requirements, we can come up with alternative update routines that perform well both in terms of cost for the update and in balance for the resulting tree structure. The AVL tree works in this way, using insertion and deletion routines altered from those of the BST to ensure that, for every node, the depths of the left and right subtrees differ by at most one. The AVL tree is described in Section 13.2.1.

A different approach to improving the performance of the BST is to not require that the tree always be balanced, but rather to expend some effort toward making the BST more balanced every time it is accessed. This is a little like the idea of path compression used by the UNION/FIND algorithm presented in Section 6.2. One example of such a compromise is called the **splay tree**. The splay tree is described in Section 13.2.2.

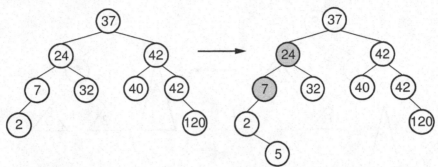

Figure 13.4 Example of an insert operation that violates the AVL tree balance property. Prior to the insert operation, all nodes of the tree are balanced (i.e., the depths of the left and right subtrees for every node differ by at most one). After inserting the node with value 5, the nodes with values 7 and 24 are no longer balanced.

13.2.1 The AVL Tree

The AVL tree (named for its inventors Adelson-Velskii and Landis) should be viewed as a BST with the following additional property: For every node, the heights of its left and right subtrees differ by at most 1. As long as the tree maintains this property, if the tree contains n nodes, then it has a depth of at most $O(\log n)$. As a result, search for any node will cost $O(\log n)$, and if the updates can be done in time proportional to the depth of the node inserted or deleted, then updates will also cost $O(\log n)$, even in the worst case.

The key to making the AVL tree work is to alter the insert and delete routines so as to maintain the balance property. Of course, to be practical, we must be able to implement the revised update routines in $\Theta(\log n)$ time.

Consider what happens when we insert a node with key value 5, as shown in Figure 13.4. The tree on the left meets the AVL tree balance requirements. After the insertion, two nodes no longer meet the requirements. Because the original tree met the balance requirement, nodes in the new tree can only be unbalanced by a difference of at most 2 in the subtrees. For the bottommost unbalanced node, call it S, there are 4 cases:

1. The extra node is in the left child of the left child of S.
2. The extra node is in the right child of the left child of S.
3. The extra node is in the left child of the right child of S.
4. The extra node is in the right child of the right child of S.

Cases 1 and 4 are symmetrical, as are cases 2 and 3. Note also that the unbalanced nodes must be on the path from the root to the newly inserted node.

Our problem now is how to balance the tree in $O(\log n)$ time. It turns out that we can do this using a series of local operations known as **rotations**. Cases 1 and

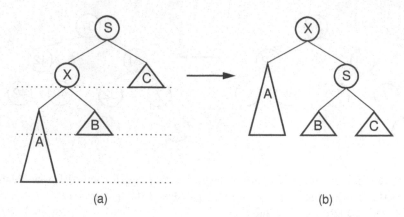

(a)   (b)

Figure 13.5 A single rotation in an AVL tree. This operation occurs when the excess node (in subtree A) is in the left child of the left child of the unbalanced node labeled S. By rearranging the nodes as shown, we preserve the BST property, as well as re-balance the tree to preserve the AVL tree balance property. The case where the excess node is in the right child of the right child of the unbalanced node is handled in the same way.

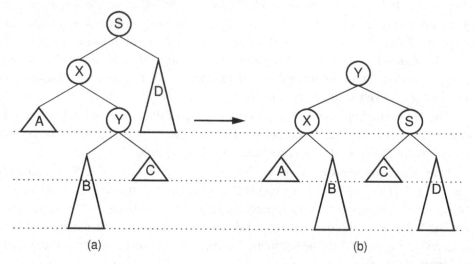

(a)   (b)

Figure 13.6 A double rotation in an AVL tree. This operation occurs when the excess node (in subtree B) is in the right child of the left child of the unbalanced node labeled S. By rearranging the nodes as shown, we preserve the BST property, as well as re-balance the tree to preserve the AVL tree balance property. The case where the excess node is in the left child of the right child of S is handled in the same way.

4 can be fixed using a **single rotation**, as shown in Figure 13.5. Cases 2 and 3 can be fixed using a **double rotation**, as shown in Figure 13.6.

The AVL tree insert algorithm begins with a normal BST insert. Then as the recursion unwinds up the tree, we perform the appropriate rotation on any node that is found to be unbalanced. Deletion is similar; however, consideration for unbalanced nodes must begin at the level of the **deletemin** operation.

Example 13.3 In Figure 13.4 (b), the bottom-most unbalanced node has value 7. The excess node (with value 5) is in the right subtree of the left child of 7, so we have an example of Case 2. This requires a double rotation to fix. After the rotation, 5 becomes the left child of 24, 2 becomes the left child of 5, and 7 becomes the right child of 5.

13.2.2   The Splay Tree

Like the AVL tree, the splay tree is not actually a distinct data structure, but rather reimplements the BST insert, delete, and search methods to improve the performance of a BST. The goal of these revised methods is to provide guarantees on the time required by a series of operations, thereby avoiding the worst-case linear time behavior of standard BST operations. No single operation in the splay tree is guaranteed to be efficient. Instead, the splay tree access rules guarantee that a series of m operations will take $O(m \log n)$ time for a tree of n nodes whenever $m \geq n$. Thus, a single insert or search operation could take $O(n)$ time. However, m such operations are guaranteed to require a total of $O(m \log n)$ time, for an average cost of $O(\log n)$ per access operation. This is a desirable performance guarantee for any search-tree structure.

Unlike the AVL tree, the splay tree is not guaranteed to be height balanced. What is guaranteed is that the total cost of the entire series of accesses will be cheap. Ultimately, it is the cost of the series of operations that matters, not whether the tree is balanced. Maintaining balance is really done only for the sake of reaching this time efficiency goal.

The splay tree access functions operate in a manner reminiscent of the move-to-front rule for self-organizing lists from Section 9.2, and of the path compression technique for managing parent-pointer trees from Section 6.2. These access functions tend to make the tree more balanced, but an individual access will not necessarily result in a more balanced tree.

Whenever a node S is accessed (e.g., when S is inserted, deleted, or is the goal of a search), the splay tree performs a process called **splaying**. Splaying moves S to the root of the BST. When S is being deleted, splaying moves the parent of S to the root. As in the AVL tree, a splay of node S consists of a series of **rotations**. A rotation moves S higher in the tree by adjusting its position with respect to its parent and grandparent. A side effect of the rotations is a tendency to balance the tree. There are three types of rotation.

A **single rotation** is performed only if S is a child of the root node. The single rotation is illustrated by Figure 13.7. It basically switches S with its parent in a

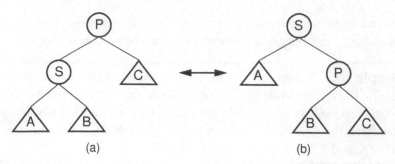

Figure 13.7 Splay tree single rotation. This rotation takes place only when the node being splayed is a child of the root. Here, node S is promoted to the root, rotating with node P. Because the value of S is less than the value of P, P must become S's right child. The positions of subtrees A, B, and C are altered as appropriate to maintain the BST property, but the contents of these subtrees remains unchanged. (a) The original tree with P as the parent. (b) The tree after a rotation takes place. Performing a single rotation a second time will return the tree to its original shape. Equivalently, if (b) is the initial configuration of the tree (i.e., S is at the root and P is its right child), then (a) shows the result of a single rotation to splay P to the root.

way that retains the BST property. While Figure 13.7 is slightly different from Figure 13.5, in fact the splay tree single rotation is identical to the AVL tree single rotation.

Unlike the AVL tree, the splay tree requires two types of double rotation. Double rotations involve S, its parent (call it P), and S's grandparent (call it G). The effect of a double rotation is to move S up two levels in the tree.

The first double rotation is called a **zigzag rotation**. It takes place when either of the following two conditions are met:

1. S is the left child of P, and P is the right child of G.
2. S is the right child of P, and P is the left child of G.

In other words, a zigzag rotation is used when G, P, and S form a zigzag. The zigzag rotation is illustrated by Figure 13.8.

The other double rotation is known as a **zigzig** rotation. A zigzig rotation takes place when either of the following two conditions are met:

1. S is the left child of P, which is in turn the left child of G.
2. S is the right child of P, which is in turn the right child of G.

Thus, a zigzig rotation takes place in those situations where a zigzag rotation is not appropriate. The zigzig rotation is illustrated by Figure 13.9. While Figure 13.9 appears somewhat different from Figure 13.6, in fact the zigzig rotation is identical to the AVL tree double rotation.

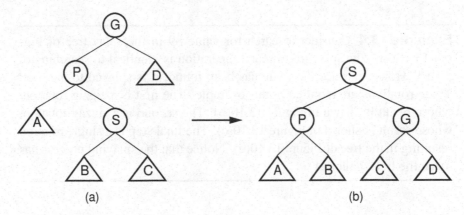

Figure 13.8 Splay tree zigzag rotation. (a) The original tree with *S*, *P*, and *G* in zigzag formation. (b) The tree after the rotation takes place. The positions of subtrees *A*, *B*, *C*, and *D* are altered as appropriate to maintain the BST property.

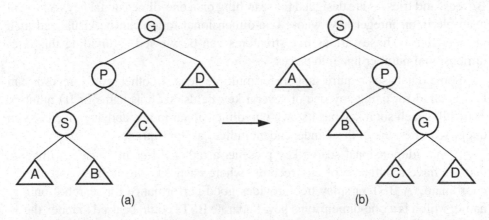

Figure 13.9 Splay tree zigzig rotation. (a) The original tree with *S*, *P*, and *G* in zigzig formation. (b) The tree after the rotation takes place. The positions of subtrees *A*, *B*, *C*, and *D* are altered as appropriate to maintain the BST property.

Note that zigzag rotations tend to make the tree more balanced, because they bring subtrees *B* and *C* up one level while moving subtree *D* down one level. The result is often a reduction of the tree's height by one. Zigzig promotions and single rotations do not typically reduce the height of the tree; they merely bring the newly accessed record toward the root.

Splaying node *S* involves a series of double rotations until *S* reaches either the root or the child of the root. Then, if necessary, a single rotation makes *S* the root. This process tends to re-balance the tree. Regardless of balance, splaying will make frequently accessed nodes stay near the top of the tree, resulting in reduced access cost. Proof that the splay tree meets the guarantee of $O(m \log n)$ is beyond the scope of this book. Such a proof can be found in the references in Section 13.4.

Example 13.4 Consider a search for value 89 in the splay tree of Figure 13.10(a). The splay tree's search operation is identical to searching in a BST. However, once the value has been found, it is splayed to the root. Three rotations are required in this example. The first is a zigzig rotation, whose result is shown in Figure 13.10(b). The second is a zigzag rotation, whose result is shown in Figure 13.10(c). The final step is a single rotation resulting in the tree of Figure 13.10(d). Notice that the splaying process has made the tree shallower.

13.3   Spatial Data Structures

All of the search trees discussed so far — BSTs, AVL trees, splay trees, 2-3 trees, B-trees, and tries — are designed for searching on a one-dimensional key. A typical example is an integer key, whose one-dimensional range can be visualized as a number line. These various tree structures can be viewed as dividing this one-dimensional number line into pieces.

Some databases require support for multiple keys. In other words, records can be searched for using any one of several key fields, such as name or ID number. Typically, each such key has its own one-dimensional index, and any given search query searches one of these independent indices as appropriate.

A multidimensional search key presents a rather different concept. Imagine that we have a database of city records, where each city has a name and an xy-coordinate. A BST or splay tree provides good performance for searches on city name, which is a one-dimensional key. Separate BSTs could be used to index the x- and y-coordinates. This would allow us to insert and delete cities, and locate them by name or by one coordinate. However, search on one of the two coordinates is not a natural way to view search in a two-dimensional space. Another option is to combine the xy-coordinates into a single key, say by concatenating the two coordinates, and index cities by the resulting key in a BST. That would allow search by coordinate, but would not allow for efficient two-dimensional **range queries** such as searching for all cities within a given distance of a specified point. The problem is that the BST only works well for one-dimensional keys, while a coordinate is a two-dimensional key where neither dimension is more important than the other.

Multidimensional range queries are the defining feature of a **spatial application**. Because a coordinate gives a position in space, it is called a **spatial attribute**. To implement spatial applications efficiently requires the use of **spatial data structures**. Spatial data structures store data objects organized by position and are an important class of data structures used in geographic information systems, computer graphics, robotics, and many other fields.

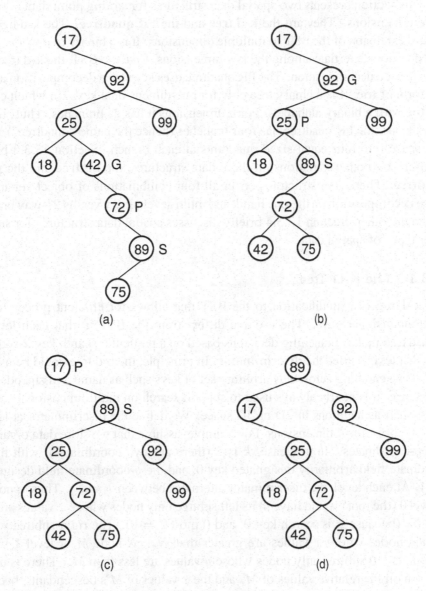

Figure 13.10 Example of splaying after performing a search in a splay tree. After finding the node with key value 89, that node is splayed to the root by performing three rotations. (a) The original splay tree. (b) The result of performing a zigzig rotation on the node with key value 89 in the tree of (a). (c) The result of performing a zigzag rotation on the node with key value 89 in the tree of (b). (d) The result of performing a single rotation on the node with key value 89 in the tree of (c). If the search had been for 91, the search would have been unsuccessful with the node storing key value 89 being that last one visited. In that case, the same splay operations would take place.

This section presents two spatial data structures for storing point data in two or more dimensions. They are the **k-d tree** and the **PR quadtree**. The k-d tree is a natural extension of the BST to multiple dimensions. It is a binary tree whose splitting decisions alternate among the key dimensions. Like the BST, the k-d tree uses object space decomposition. The PR quadtree uses key space decomposition and so is a form of trie. It is a binary tree only for one-dimensional keys (in which case it is a trie with a binary alphabet). For d dimensions it has 2^d branches. Thus, in two dimensions, the PR quadtree has four branches (hence the name "quadtree"), splitting space into four equal-sized quadrants at each branch. Section 13.3.3 briefly mentions two other variations on these data structures, the **bintree** and the **point quadtree**. These four structures cover all four combinations of object versus key space decomposition on the one hand, and multi-level binary versus 2^d-way branching on the other. Section 13.3.4 briefly discusses spatial data structures for storing other types of spatial data.

13.3.1   The K-D Tree

The k-d tree is a modification to the BST that allows for efficient processing of multidimensional keys. The k-d tree differs from the BST in that each level of the k-d tree makes branching decisions based on a particular search key associated with that level, called the **discriminator**. In principle, the k-d tree could be used to unify key searching across any arbitrary set of keys such as name and zipcode. But in practice, it is nearly always used to support search on multidimensional coordinates, such as locations in 2D or 3D space. We define the discriminator at level i to be $i \bmod k$ for k dimensions. For example, assume that we store data organized by xy-coordinates. In this case, k is 2 (there are two coordinates), with the x-coordinate field arbitrarily designated key 0, and the y-coordinate field designated key 1. At each level, the discriminator alternates between x and y. Thus, a node N at level 0 (the root) would have in its left subtree only nodes whose x values are less than N_x (because x is search key 0, and $0 \bmod 2 = 0$). The right subtree would contain nodes whose x values are greater than N_x. A node M at level 1 would have in its left subtree only nodes whose y values are less than M_y. There is no restriction on the relative values of M_x and the x values of M's descendants, because branching decisions made at M are based solely on the y coordinate. Figure 13.11 shows an example of how a collection of two-dimensional points would be stored in a k-d tree.

In Figure 13.11 the region containing the points is (arbitrarily) restricted to a 128×128 square, and each internal node splits the search space. Each split is shown by a line, vertical for nodes with x discriminators and horizontal for nodes with y discriminators. The root node splits the space into two parts; its children further subdivide the space into smaller parts. The children's split lines do not cross the root's split line. Thus, each node in the k-d tree helps to decompose the

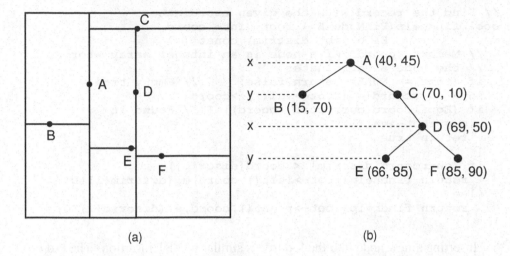

Figure 13.11 Example of a k-d tree. (a) The k-d tree decomposition for a 128×128-unit region containing seven data points. (b) The k-d tree for the region of (a).

space into rectangles that show the extent of where nodes can fall in the various subtrees.

Searching a k-d tree for the record with a specified xy-coordinate is like searching a BST, except that each level of the k-d tree is associated with a particular discriminator.

Example 13.5 Consider searching the k-d tree for a record located at $P = (69, 50)$. First compare P with the point stored at the root (record A in Figure 13.11). If P matches the location of A, then the search is successful. In this example the positions do not match (A's location $(40, 45)$ is not the same as $(69, 50)$), so the search must continue. The x value of A is compared with that of P to determine in which direction to branch. Because A_x's value of 40 is less than P's x value of 69, we branch to the right subtree (all cities with x value greater than or equal to 40 are in the right subtree). A_y does not affect the decision on which way to branch at this level. At the second level, P does not match record C's position, so another branch must be taken. However, at this level we branch based on the relative y values of point P and record C (because $1 \bmod 2 = 1$, which corresponds to the y-coordinate). Because C_y's value of 10 is less than P_y's value of 50, we branch to the right. At this point, P is compared against the position of D. A match is made and the search is successful.

If the search process reaches a **NULL** pointer, then that point is not contained in the tree. Here is a k-d tree search implementation, equivalent to the **findhelp** function of the BST class. **KD** class private member **D** stores the key's dimension.

```
// Find the record with the given coordinates
bool findhelp(BinNode<E>* root, int* coord,
              E& e, int discrim) const {
  // Member "coord" of a node is an integer array storing
  // the node's coordinates.
  if (root == NULL) return false;       // Empty tree
  int* currcoord = (root->val())->coord();
  if (EqualCoord(currcoord, coord)) { // Found it
    e = root->val();
    return true;
  }
  if (currcoord[discrim] < coord[discrim])
    return findhelp(root->left(),coord,e,(discrim+1)%D);
  else
    return findhelp(root->right(),coord,e,(discrim+1)%D);
}
```

Inserting a new node into the k-d tree is similar to BST insertion. The k-d tree search procedure is followed until a **NULL** pointer is found, indicating the proper place to insert the new node.

Example 13.6 Inserting a record at location (10, 50) in the k-d tree of Figure 13.11 first requires a search to the node containing record B. At this point, the new record is inserted into B's left subtree.

Deleting a node from a k-d tree is similar to deleting from a BST, but slightly harder. As with deleting from a BST, the first step is to find the node (call it N) to be deleted. It is then necessary to find a descendant of N which can be used to replace N in the tree. If N has no children, then N is replaced with a **NULL** pointer. Note that if N has one child that in turn has children, we cannot simply assign N's parent to point to N's child as would be done in the BST. To do so would change the level of all nodes in the subtree, and thus the discriminator used for a search would also change. The result is that the subtree would no longer be a k-d tree because a node's children might now violate the BST property for that discriminator.

Similar to BST deletion, the record stored in N should be replaced either by the record in N's right subtree with the least value of N's discriminator, or by the record in N's left subtree with the greatest value for this discriminator. Assume that N was at an odd level and therefore y is the discriminator. N could then be replaced by the record in its right subtree with the least y value (call it Y_{min}). The problem is that Y_{min} is not necessarily the leftmost node, as it would be in the BST. A modified search procedure to find the least y value in the left subtree must be used to find it instead. The implementation for **findmin** is shown in Figure 13.12. A recursive call to the delete routine will then remove Y_{min} from the tree. Finally, Y_{min}'s record is substituted for the record in node N.

Note that we can replace the node to be deleted with the least-valued node from the right subtree only if the right subtree exists. If it does not, then a suitable

```
// Return a pointer to the node with the least value in root
// for the selected descriminator
BinNode<E>* findmin(BinNode<E>* root,
                        int discrim, int currdis) const {
  // discrim: discriminator key used for minimum search;
  // currdis: current level (mod D);
  if (root == NULL) return NULL;
  BinNode<E> *minnode = findmin(root->left(), discrim,
                                   (currdis+1)%D);
  if (discrim != currdis) { // If not at descrim's level,
                              // we must search both subtrees
    BinNode<E> *rightmin =
        findmin(root->right(), discrim, (currdis+1)%D);
    // Check if right side has smaller key value
    minnode = min(minnode, rightmin, discrim);
  } // Now, minnode has the smallest value in children
  return min(minnode, root, discrim);
}
```

Figure 13.12 The k-d tree **findmin** method. On levels using the minimum value's discriminator, branching is to the left. On other levels, both children's subtrees must be visited. Helper function **min** takes two nodes and a discriminator as input, and returns the node with the smaller value in that discriminator.

replacement must be found in the left subtree. Unfortunately, it is not satisfactory to replace N's record with the record having the greatest value for the discriminator in the left subtree, because this new value might be duplicated. If so, then we would have equal values for the discriminator in N's left subtree, which violates the ordering rules for the k-d tree. Fortunately, there is a simple solution to the problem. We first move the left subtree of node N to become the right subtree (i.e., we simply swap the values of N's left and right child pointers). At this point, we proceed with the normal deletion process, replacing the record of N to be deleted with the record containing the *least* value of the discriminator from what is now N's right subtree.

Assume that we want to print out a list of all records that are within a certain distance d of a given point P. We will use Euclidean distance, that is, point P is defined to be within distance d of point N if[1]

$$\sqrt{(P_x - N_x)^2 + (P_y - N_y)^2} \leq d.$$

If the search process reaches a node whose key value for the discriminator is more than d above the corresponding value in the search key, then it is not possible that any record in the right subtree can be within distance d of the search key because all key values in that dimension are always too great. Similarly, if the current node's key value in the discriminator is d less than that for the search key value,

---

[1]A more efficient computation is $(P_x - N_x)^2 + (P_y - N_y)^2 \leq d^2$. This avoids performing a square root function.

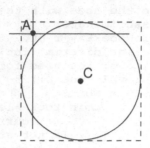

Figure 13.13 Function `InCircle` must check the Euclidean distance between a record and the query point. It is possible for a record A to have x- and y-coordinates each within the query distance of the query point C, yet have A itself lie outside the query circle.

then no record in the left subtree can be within the radius. In such cases, the subtree in question need not be searched, potentially saving much time. In the average case, the number of nodes that must be visited during a range query is linear on the number of data records that fall within the query circle.

Example 13.7 We will now find all cities in the k-d tree of Figure 13.14 within 25 units of the point (25, 65). The search begins with the root node, which contains record A. Because (40, 45) is exactly 25 units from the search point, it will be reported. The search procedure then determines which branches of the tree to take. The search circle extends to both the left and the right of A's (vertical) dividing line, so both branches of the tree must be searched. The left subtree is processed first. Here, record B is checked and found to fall within the search circle. Because the node storing B has no children, processing of the left subtree is complete. Processing of A's right subtree now begins. The coordinates of record C are checked and found not to fall within the circle. Thus, it should not be reported. However, it is possible that cities within C's subtrees could fall within the search circle even if C does not. As C is at level 1, the discriminator at this level is the y-coordinate. Because $65 - 25 > 10$, no record in C's left subtree (i.e., records above C) could possibly be in the search circle. Thus, C's left subtree (if it had one) need not be searched. However, cities in C's right subtree could fall within the circle. Thus, search proceeds to the node containing record D. Again, D is outside the search circle. Because $25 + 25 < 69$, no record in D's right subtree could be within the search circle. Thus, only D's left subtree need be searched. This leads to comparing record E's coordinates against the search circle. Record E falls outside the search circle, and processing is complete. So we see that we only search subtrees whose rectangles fall within the search circle.

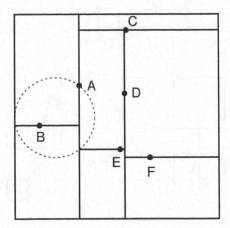

Figure 13.14 Searching in the k-d tree of Figure 13.11. (a) The k-d tree decomposition for a 128×128-unit region containing seven data points. (b) The k-d tree for the region of (a).

```
// Print all points within distance "rad" of "coord"
void regionhelp(BinNode<E>* root, int* coord,
                int rad, int discrim) const {
  if (root == NULL) return;        // Empty tree
  // Check if record at root is in circle
  if (InCircle((root->val())->coord(), coord, rad))
    cout << root->val() << endl;   // Do what is appropriate
  int* currcoord = (root->val())->coord();
  if (currcoord[discrim] > (coord[discrim] - rad))
    regionhelp(root->left(), coord, rad, (discrim+1)%D);
  if (currcoord[discrim] < (coord[discrim] + rad))
    regionhelp(root->right(), coord, rad, (discrim+1)%D);
}
```

Figure 13.15 The k-d tree region search method.

Figure 13.15 shows an implementation for the region search method. When a node is visited, function **InCircle** is used to check the Euclidean distance between the node's record and the query point. It is not enough to simply check that the differences between the x- and y-coordinates are each less than the query distances because the the record could still be outside the search circle, as illustrated by Figure 13.13.

13.3.2   The PR quadtree

In the Point-Region Quadtree (hereafter referred to as the PR quadtree) each node either has exactly four children or is a leaf. That is, the PR quadtree is a full four-way branching (4-ary) tree in shape. The PR quadtree represents a collection of data points in two dimensions by decomposing the region containing the data points into four equal quadrants, subquadrants, and so on, until no leaf node contains more

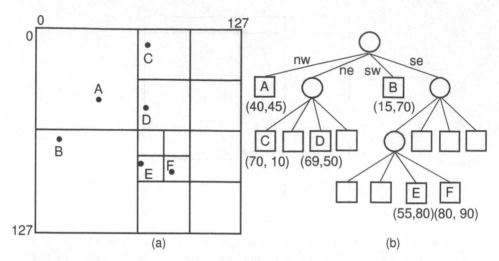

Figure 13.16 Example of a PR quadtree. (a) A map of data points. We define the region to be square with origin at the upper-left-hand corner and sides of length 128. (b) The PR quadtree for the points in (a). (a) also shows the block decomposition imposed by the PR quadtree for this region.

than a single point. In other words, if a region contains zero or one data points, then it is represented by a PR quadtree consisting of a single leaf node. If the region contains more than a single data point, then the region is split into four equal quadrants. The corresponding PR quadtree then contains an internal node and four subtrees, each subtree representing a single quadrant of the region, which might in turn be split into subquadrants. Each internal node of a PR quadtree represents a single split of the two-dimensional region. The four quadrants of the region (or equivalently, the corresponding subtrees) are designated (in order) NW, NE, SW, and SE. Each quadrant containing more than a single point would in turn be recursively divided into subquadrants until each leaf of the corresponding PR quadtree contains at most one point.

For example, consider the region of Figure 13.16(a) and the corresponding PR quadtree in Figure 13.16(b). The decomposition process demands a fixed key range. In this example, the region is assumed to be of size 128×128. Note that the internal nodes of the PR quadtree are used solely to indicate decomposition of the region; internal nodes do not store data records. Because the decomposition lines are predetermined (i.e, key-space decomposition is used), the PR quadtree is a trie.

Search for a record matching point Q in the PR quadtree is straightforward. Beginning at the root, we continuously branch to the quadrant that contains Q until our search reaches a leaf node. If the root is a leaf, then just check to see if the node's data record matches point Q. If the root is an internal node, proceed to the child that contains the search coordinate. For example, the NW quadrant of Figure 13.16 contains points whose x and y values each fall in the range 0 to 63.

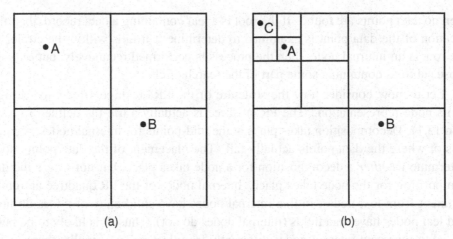

Figure 13.17 PR quadtree insertion example. (a) The initial PR quadtree containing two data points. (b) The result of inserting point *C*. The block containing *A* must be decomposed into four sub-blocks. Points *A* and *C* would still be in the same block if only one subdivision takes place, so a second decomposition is required to separate them.

The NE quadrant contains points whose x value falls in the range 64 to 127, and whose y value falls in the range 0 to 63. If the root's child is a leaf node, then that child is checked to see if Q has been found. If the child is another internal node, the search process continues through the tree until a leaf node is found. If this leaf node stores a record whose position matches Q then the query is successful; otherwise Q is not in the tree.

Inserting record P into the PR quadtree is performed by first locating the leaf node that contains the location of P. If this leaf node is empty, then P is stored at this leaf. If the leaf already contains P (or a record with P's coordinates), then a duplicate record should be reported. If the leaf node already contains another record, then the node must be repeatedly decomposed until the existing record and P fall into different leaf nodes. Figure 13.17 shows an example of such an insertion.

Deleting a record P is performed by first locating the node N of the PR quadtree that contains P. Node N is then changed to be empty. The next step is to look at N's three siblings. N and its siblings must be merged together to form a single node N' if only one point is contained among them. This merging process continues until some level is reached at which at least two points are contained in the subtrees represented by node N' and its siblings. For example, if point C is to be deleted from the PR quadtree representing Figure 13.17(b), the resulting node must be merged with its siblings, and that larger node again merged with its siblings to restore the PR quadtree to the decomposition of Figure 13.17(a).

Region search is easily performed with the PR quadtree. To locate all points within radius r of query point Q, begin at the root. If the root is an empty leaf node, then no data points are found. If the root is a leaf containing a data record, then the location of the data point is examined to determine if it falls within the circle. If the root is an internal node, then the process is performed recursively, but *only* on those subtrees containing some part of the search circle.

Let us now consider how the structure of the PR quadtree affects the design of its node representation. The PR quadtree is actually a trie (as defined in Section 13.1). Decomposition takes place at the mid-points for internal nodes, regardless of where the data points actually fall. The placement of the data points does determine *whether* a decomposition for a node takes place, but not *where* the decomposition for the node takes place. Internal nodes of the PR quadtree are quite different from leaf nodes, in that internal nodes have children (leaf nodes do not) and leaf nodes have data fields (internal nodes do not). Thus, it is likely to be beneficial to represent internal nodes differently from leaf nodes. Finally, there is the fact that approximately half of the leaf nodes will contain no data field.

Another issue to consider is: How does a routine traversing the PR quadtree get the coordinates for the square represented by the current PR quadtree node? One possibility is to store with each node its spatial description (such as upper-left corner and width). However, this will take a lot of space — perhaps as much as the space needed for the data records, depending on what information is being stored.

Another possibility is to pass in the coordinates when the recursive call is made. For example, consider the search process. Initially, the search visits the root node of the tree, which has origin at (0, 0), and whose width is the full size of the space being covered. When the appropriate child is visited, it is a simple matter for the search routine to determine the origin for the child, and the width of the square is simply half that of the parent. Not only does passing in the size and position information for a node save considerable space, but avoiding storing such information in the nodes enables a good design choice for empty leaf nodes, as discussed next.

How should we represent empty leaf nodes? On average, half of the leaf nodes in a PR quadtree are empty (i.e., do not store a data point). One implementation option is to use a **NULL** pointer in internal nodes to represent empty nodes. This will solve the problem of excessive space requirements. There is an unfortunate side effect that using a **NULL** pointer requires the PR quadtree processing methods to understand this convention. In other words, you are breaking encapsulation on the node representation because the tree now must know things about how the nodes are implemented. This is not too horrible for this particular application, because the node class can be considered private to the tree class, in which case the node implementation is completely invisible to the outside world. However, it is undesirable if there is another reasonable alternative.

Fortunately, there is a good alternative. It is called the Flyweight design pattern. In the PR quadtree, a flyweight is a single empty leaf node that is reused in all places where an empty leaf node is needed. You simply have *all* of the internal nodes with empty leaf children point to the same node object. This node object is created once at the beginning of the program, and is never removed. The node class recognizes from the pointer value that the flyweight is being accessed, and acts accordingly.

Note that when using the Flyweight design pattern, you *cannot* store coordinates for the node in the node. This is an example of the concept of intrinsic versus extrinsic state. Intrinsic state for an object is state information stored in the object. If you stored the coordinates for a node in the node object, those coordinates would be intrinsic state. Extrinsic state is state information about an object stored elsewhere in the environment, such as in global variables or passed to the method. If your recursive calls that process the tree pass in the coordinates for the current node, then the coordinates will be extrinsic state. A flyweight can have in its intrinsic state *only* information that is accurate for *all* instances of the flyweight. Clearly coordinates do not qualify, because each empty leaf node has its own location. So, if you want to use a flyweight, you must pass in coordinates.

Another design choice is: Who controls the work, the node class or the tree class? For example, on an insert operation, you could have the tree class control the flow down the tree, looking at (querying) the nodes to see their type and reacting accordingly. This is the approach used by the BST implementation in Section 5.4. An alternate approach is to have the node class do the work. That is, you have an insert method for the nodes. If the node is internal, it passes the city record to the appropriate child (recursively). If the node is a flyweight, it replaces itself with a new leaf node. If the node is a full node, it replaces itself with a subtree. This is an example of the Composite design pattern, discussed in Section 5.3.1. Use of the composite design would be difficult if **NULL** pointers are used to represent empty leaf nodes. It turns out that the PR quadtree insert and delete methods are easier to implement when using the composite design.

13.3.3   Other Point Data Structures

The differences between the k-d tree and the PR quadtree illustrate many of the design choices encountered when creating spatial data structures. The k-d tree provides an object space decomposition of the region, while the PR quadtree provides a key space decomposition (thus, it is a trie). The k-d tree stores records at all nodes, while the PR quadtree stores records only at the leaf nodes. Finally, the two trees have different structures. The k-d tree is a binary tree (and need not be full), while the PR quadtree is a full tree with 2^d branches (in the two-dimensional case, $2^2 = 4$). Consider the extension of this concept to three dimensions. A k-d tree for three dimensions would alternate the discriminator through the x, y, and z dimensions. The three-dimensional equivalent of the PR quadtree would be a tree with 2^3 or eight branches. Such a tree is called an **octree**.

We can also devise a binary trie based on a key space decomposition in each dimension, or a quadtree that uses the two-dimensional equivalent to an object

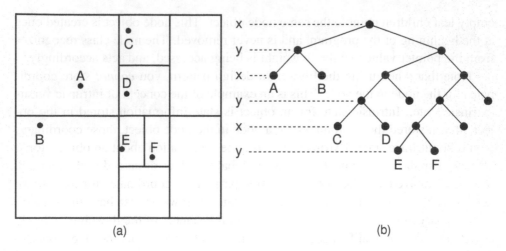

(a)   (b)

Figure 13.18 An example of the bintree, a binary tree using key space decomposition and discriminators rotating among the dimensions. Compare this with the k-d tree of Figure 13.11 and the PR quadtree of Figure 13.16.

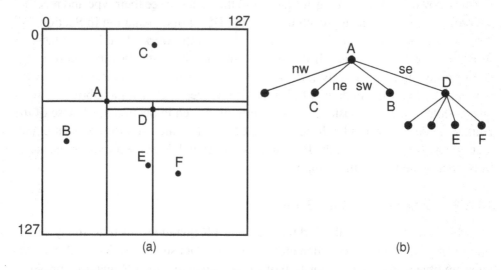

(a)   (b)

Figure 13.19 An example of the point quadtree, a 4-ary tree using object space decomposition. Compare this with the PR quadtree of Figure 13.11.

space decomposition. The **bintree** is a binary trie that uses keyspace decomposition and alternates discriminators at each level in a manner similar to the k-d tree. The bintree for the points of Figure 13.11 is shown in Figure 13.18. Alternatively, we can use a four-way decomposition of space centered on the data points. The tree resulting from such a decomposition is called a **point quadtree**. The point quadtree for the data points of Figure 13.11 is shown in Figure 13.19.

13.3.4   Other Spatial Data Structures

This section has barely scratched the surface of the field of spatial data structures. Dozens of distinct spatial data structures have been invented, many with variations and alternate implementations. Spatial data structures exist for storing many forms of spatial data other than points. The most important distinctions between are the tree structure (binary or not, regular decompositions or not) and the decomposition rule used to decide when the data contained within a region is so complex that the region must be subdivided.

One such spatial data structure is the Region Quadtree for storing images where the pixel values tend to be blocky, such as a map of the countries of the world. The region quadtree uses a four-way regular decomposition scheme similar to the PR quadtree. The decomposition rule is simply to divide any node containing pixels of more than one color or value.

Spatial data structures can also be used to store line object, rectangle object, or objects of arbitrary shape (such as polygons in two dimensions or polyhedra in three dimensions). A simple, yet effective, data structure for storing rectangles or arbitrary polygonal shapes can be derived from the PR quadtree. Pick a threshold value c, and subdivide any region into four quadrants if it contains more than c objects. A special case must be dealt with when more than c object intersect.

Some of the most interesting developments in spatial data structures have to do with adapting them for disk-based applications. However, all such disk-based implementations boil down to storing the spatial data structure within some variant on either B-trees or hashing.

13.4   Further Reading

PATRICIA tries and other trie implementations are discussed in *Information Retrieval: Data Structures & Algorithms*, Frakes and Baeza-Yates, eds. [FBY92].

See Knuth [Knu97] for a discussion of the AVL tree. For further reading on splay trees, see "Self-adjusting Binary Search" by Sleator and Tarjan [ST85].

The world of spatial data structures is rich and rapidly evolving. For a good introduction, see *Foundations of Multidimensional and Metric Data Structures* by Hanan Samet [Sam06]. This is also the best reference for more information on the PR quadtree. The k-d tree was invented by John Louis Bentley. For further information on the k-d tree, in addition to [Sam06], see [Ben75]. For information on using a quadtree to store arbitrary polygonal objects, see [SH92].

For a discussion on the relative space requirements for two-way versus multi-way branching, see "A Generalized Comparison of Quadtree and Bintree Storage Requirements" by Shaffer, Juvvadi, and Heath [SJH93].

Closely related to spatial data structures are data structures for storing multi-dimensional data (which might not necessarily be spatial in nature). A popular data structure for storing such data is the R-tree, which was originally proposed by Guttman [Gut84].

13.5 Exercises

13.1 Show the binary trie (as illustrated by Figure 13.1) for the following collection of values: 42, 12, 100, 10, 50, 31, 7, 11, 99.

13.2 Show the PAT trie (as illustrated by Figure 13.3) for the following collection of values: 42, 12, 100, 10, 50, 31, 7, 11, 99.

13.3 Write the insertion routine for a binary trie as shown in Figure 13.1.

13.4 Write the deletion routine for a binary trie as shown in Figure 13.1.

13.5 **(a)** Show the result (including appropriate rotations) of inserting the value 39 into the AVL tree on the left in Figure 13.4.
    (b) Show the result (including appropriate rotations) of inserting the value 300 into the AVL tree on the left in Figure 13.4.
    (c) Show the result (including appropriate rotations) of inserting the value 50 into the AVL tree on the left in Figure 13.4.
    (d) Show the result (including appropriate rotations) of inserting the value 1 into the AVL tree on the left in Figure 13.4.

13.6 Show the splay tree that results from searching for value 75 in the splay tree of Figure 13.10(d).

13.7 Show the splay tree that results from searching for value 18 in the splay tree of Figure 13.10(d).

13.8 Some applications do not permit storing two records with duplicate key values. In such a case, an attempt to insert a duplicate-keyed record into a tree structure such as a splay tree should result in a failure on insert. What is the appropriate action to take in a splay tree implementation when the insert routine is called with a duplicate-keyed record?

13.9 Show the result of deleting point A from the k-d tree of Figure 13.11.

13.10 **(a)** Show the result of building a k-d tree from the following points (inserted in the order given). A (20, 20), B (10, 30), C (25, 50), D (35, 25), E (30, 45), F (30, 35), G (55, 40), H (45, 35), I (50, 30).
    (b) Show the result of deleting point A from the tree you built in part (a).

13.11 **(a)** Show the result of deleting F from the PR quadtree of Figure 13.16.
    (b) Show the result of deleting records E and F from the PR quadtree of Figure 13.16.

13.12 **(a)** Show the result of building a PR quadtree from the following points (inserted in the order given). Assume the tree is representing a space of 64 by 64 units. A (20, 20), B (10, 30), C (25, 50), D (35, 25), E (30, 45), F (30, 35), G (45, 25), H (45, 30), I (50, 30).
    (b) Show the result of deleting point C from the tree you built in part (a).

    (c) Show the result of deleting point F from the resulting tree in part (b).

13.13 On average, how many leaf nodes of a PR quadtree will typically be empty? Explain why.

13.14 When performing a region search on a PR quadtree, we need only search those subtrees of an internal node whose corresponding square falls within the query circle. This is most easily computed by comparing the x and y ranges of the query circle against the x and y ranges of the square corresponding to the subtree. However, as illustrated by Figure 13.13, the x and y ranges might overlap without the circle actually intersecting the square. Write a function that accurately determines if a circle and a square intersect.

13.15   **(a)** Show the result of building a bintree from the following points (inserted in the order given). Assume the tree is representing a space of 64 by 64 units. A (20, 20), B (10, 30), C (25, 50), D (35, 25), E (30, 45), F (30, 35), G (45, 25), H (45, 30), I (50, 30).

    (b) Show the result of deleting point C from the tree you built in part (a).

    (c) Show the result of deleting point F from the resulting tree in part (b).

13.16 Compare the trees constructed for Exercises 12 and 15 in terms of the number of internal nodes, full leaf nodes, empty leaf nodes, and total depths of the two trees.

13.17 Show the result of building a point quadtree from the following points (inserted in the order given). Assume the tree is representing a space of 64 by 64 units. A (20, 20), B (10, 30), C (25, 50), D (35, 25), E (30, 45), F (31, 35), G (45, 26), H (44, 30), I (50, 30).

13.6   Projects

13.1 Use the trie data structure to devise a program to sort variable-length strings. The program's running time should be proportional to the total number of letters in all of the strings. Note that some strings might be very long while most are short.

13.2 Define the set of **suffix strings** for a string S to be S, S without its first character, S without its first two characters, and so on. For example, the complete set of suffix strings for "HELLO" would be

$$\{HELLO, ELLO, LLO, LO, O\}.$$

A **suffix tree** is a PAT trie that contains all of the suffix strings for a given string, and associates each suffix with the complete string. The advantage of a suffix tree is that it allows a search for strings using "wildcards." For example, the search key "TH*" means to find all strings with "TH" as the first two characters. This can easily be done with a regular trie. Searching for "*TH" is not efficient in a regular trie, but it is efficient in a suffix tree.

Implement the suffix tree for a dictionary of words or phrases, with support for wildcard search.

13.3 Revise the BST class of Section 5.4 to use the AVL tree rotations. Your new implementation should not modify the original BST class ADT. Compare your AVL tree against an implementation of the standard BST over a wide variety of input data. Under what conditions does the splay tree actually save time?

13.4 Revise the BST class of Section 5.4 to use the splay tree rotations. Your new implementation should not modify the original BST class ADT. Compare your splay tree against an implementation of the standard BST over a wide variety of input data. Under what conditions does the splay tree actually save time?

13.5 Implement a city database using the k-d tree. Each database record contains the name of the city (a string of arbitrary length) and the coordinates of the city expressed as integer x- and y-coordinates. Your database should allow records to be inserted, deleted by name or coordinate, and searched by name or coordinate. You should also support region queries, that is, a request to print all records within a given distance of a specified point.

13.6 Implement a city database using the PR quadtree. Each database record contains the name of the city (a string of arbitrary length) and the coordinates of the city expressed as integer x- and y-coordinates. Your database should allow records to be inserted, deleted by name or coordinate, and searched by name or coordinate. You should also support region queries, that is, a request to print all records within a given distance of a specified point.

13.7 Implement and test the PR quadtree, using the composite design to implement the insert, search, and delete operations.

13.8 Implement a city database using the bintree. Each database record contains the name of the city (a string of arbitrary length) and the coordinates of the city expressed as integer x- and y-coordinates. Your database should allow records to be inserted, deleted by name or coordinate, and searched by name or coordinate. You should also support region queries, that is, a request to print all records within a given distance of a specified point.

13.9 Implement a city database using the point quadtree. Each database record contains the name of the city (a string of arbitrary length) and the coordinates of the city expressed as integer x- and y-coordinates. Your database should allow records to be inserted, deleted by name or coordinate, and searched by name or coordinate. You should also support region queries, that is, a request to print all records within a given distance of a specified point.

13.10 Use the PR quadtree to implement an efficient solution to Problem 6.5. That is, store the set of points in a PR quadtree. For each point, the PR quadtree is used to find those points within distance D that should be equivalenced. What is the asymptotic complexity of this solution?

13.11 Select any two of the point representations described in this chapter (i.e., the k-d tree, the PR quadtree, the bintree, and the point quadtree). Implement your two choices and compare them over a wide range of data sets. Describe which is easier to implement, which appears to be more space efficient, and which appears to be more time efficient.

13.12 Implement a representation for a collection of (two dimensional) rectangles using a quadtree based on regular decomposition. Assume that the space being represented is a square whose width and height are some power of two. Rectangles are assumed to have integer coordinates and integer width and height. Pick some value c, and use as a decomposition rule that a region is subdivided into four equal-sized regions whenever it contains more that c rectangles. A special case occurs if all of these rectangles intersect at some point within the current region (because decomposing such a node would never reach termination). In this situation, the node simply stores pointers to more than c rectangles. Try your representation on data sets of rectangles with varying values of c.

PART V

Theory of Algorithms

14

Analysis Techniques

Often it is easy to invent an equation to model the behavior of an algorithm or data structure. Often it is easy to derive a closed-form solution for the equation should it contain a recurrence or summation. But sometimes analysis proves more difficult. It may take a clever insight to derive the right model, such as the snowplow argument for analyzing the average run length resulting from Replacement Selection (Section 8.5.2). In this example, once the snowplow argument is understood, the resulting equations follow naturally. Sometimes, developing the model is straightforward but analyzing the resulting equations is not. An example is the average-case analysis for Quicksort. The equation given in Section 7.5 simply enumerates all possible cases for the pivot position, summing corresponding costs for the recursive calls to Quicksort. However, deriving a closed-form solution for the resulting recurrence relation is not as easy.

Many analyses of iterative algorithms use a summation to model the cost of a loop. Techniques for finding closed-form solutions to summations are presented in Section 14.1. The cost for many algorithms based on recursion are best modeled by recurrence relations. A discussion of techniques for solving recurrences is provided in Section 14.2. These sections build on the introduction to summations and recurrences provided in Section 2.4, so the reader should already be familiar with that material.

Section 14.3 provides an introduction to the topic of **amortized analysis**. Amortized analysis deals with the cost of a series of operations. Perhaps a single operation in the series has high cost, but as a result the cost of the remaining operations is limited. Amortized analysis has been used successfully to analyze several of the algorithms presented in previous sections, including the cost of a series of UNION/FIND operations (Section 6.2), the cost of partition in Quicksort (Section 7.5), the cost of a series of splay tree operations (Section 13.2), and the cost of a series of operations on self-organizing lists (Section 9.2). Section 14.3 discusses the topic in more detail.

14.1 Summation Techniques

Consider the following simple summation.

$$\sum_{i=1}^{n} i.$$

In Section 2.6.3 it was proved by induction that this summation has the well-known closed form $n(n+1)/2$. But while induction is a good technique for proving that a proposed closed-form expression is correct, how do we find a candidate closed-form expression to test in the first place? Let us try to think through this problem from first principles, as though we had never seen it before.

A good place to begin analyzing a summation it is to give an estimate of its value for a given n. Observe that the biggest term for this summation is n, and there are n terms being summed up. So the total must be less than n^2. Actually, most terms are much less than n, and the sizes of the terms grows linearly. If we were to draw a picture with bars for the size of the terms, their heights would form a line, and we could enclose them in a box n units wide and n units high. It is easy to see from this that a closer estimate for the summation is about $(n^2)/2$. Having this estimate in hand helps us when trying to determine an exact closed-form solution, because we will hopefully recognize if our proposed solution is badly wrong.

Let us now consider some ways that we might hit upon an exact equation for the closed form solution to this summation. One particularly clever approach we can take is to observe that we can "pair up" the first and last terms, the second and $(n-1)$th terms, and so on. Each pair sums to $n+1$. The number of pairs is $n/2$. Thus, the solution is $n(n+1)/2$. This is pretty, and there is no doubt about it being correct. The problem is that it is not a useful technique for solving many other summations.

Now let us try to do something a bit more general. We already recognized that, because the largest term is n and there are n terms, the summation is less than n^2. If we are lucky, the closed form solution is a polynomial. Using that as a working assumption, we can invoke a technique called **guess-and-test**. We will guess that the closed-form solution for this summation is a polynomial of the form $c_1 n^2 + c_2 n + c_3$ for some constants c_1, c_2, and c_3. If this is true, then we can plug in the answers to small cases of the summation to solve for the coefficients. For this example, substituting 0, 1, and 2 for n leads to three simultaneous equations. Because the summation when $n=0$ is just 0, c_3 must be 0. For $n=1$ and $n=2$ we get the two equations

$$c_1 + c_2 = 1$$
$$4c_1 + 2c_2 = 3,$$

which in turn yield $c_1 = 1/2$ and $c_2 = 1/2$. Thus, if the closed-form solution for the summation is a polynomial, it can only be

$$1/2n^2 + 1/2n + 0$$

which is more commonly written

$$\frac{n(n+1)}{2}.$$

At this point, we still must do the "test" part of the guess-and-test approach. We can use an induction proof to verify whether our candidate closed-form solution is correct. In this case it is indeed correct, as shown by Example 2.11. The induction proof is necessary because our initial assumption that the solution is a simple polynomial could be wrong. For example, it might have been that the true solution includes a logarithmic term, such as $c_1 n^2 + c_2 n \log n$. The process shown here is essentially fitting a curve to a fixed number of points. Because there is always an n-degree polynomial that fits $n + 1$ points, we have not done enough work to be sure that we to know the true equation without the induction proof.

Guess-and-test is useful whenever the solution is a polynomial expression. In particular, similar reasoning can be used to solve for $\sum_{i=1}^{n} i^2$, or more generally $\sum_{i=1}^{n} i^c$ for c any positive integer. Why is this not a universal approach to solving summations? Because many summations do not have a polynomial as their closed form solution.

A more general approach is based on the **subtract-and-guess** or **divide-and-guess** strategies. One form of subtract-and-guess is known as the **shifting method**. The shifting method subtracts the summation from a variation on the summation. The variation selected for the subtraction should be one that makes most of the terms cancel out. To solve sum f, we pick a known function g and find a pattern in terms of $f(n) - g(n)$ or $f(n)/g(n)$.

Example 14.1 Find the closed form solution for $\sum_{i=1}^{n} i$ using the divide-and-guess approach. We will try two example functions to illustrate the divide-and-guess method: dividing by n and dividing by $f(n-1)$. Our goal is to find patterns that we can use to guess a closed-form expression as our candidate for testing with an induction proof. To aid us in finding such patterns, we can construct a table showing the first few numbers of each function, and the result of dividing one by the other, as follows.

n	1	2	3	4	5	6	7	8	9	10
$f(n)$	1	3	6	10	15	21	28	36	46	57
n	1	2	3	4	5	6	7	8	9	10
$f(n)/n$	2/2	3/2	4/2	5/2	6/2	7/2	8/2	9/2	10/2	11/2
$f(n-1)$	0	1	3	6	10	15	21	28	36	46
$f(n)/f(n-1)$		3/1	4/2	5/3	6/4	7/5	8/6	9/7	10/8	11/9

Dividing by both n and $f(n-1)$ happen to give us useful patterns to work with. $\frac{f(n)}{n} = \frac{n+1}{2}$, and $\frac{f(n)}{f(n-1)} = \frac{n+1}{n-1}$. Of course, lots of other guesses for function g do not work. For example, $f(n) - n = f(n - 1)$. Knowing that $f(n) = f(n-1) + n$ is not useful for determining the closed form solution to this summation. Or consider $f(n) - f(n-1) = n$. Again, knowing that $f(n) = f(n-1) + n$ is not useful. Finding the right combination of equations can be like finding a needle in a haystack.

In our first example, we can see directly what the closed-form solution should be. Since $\frac{f(n)}{n} = \frac{n+1}{2}$, obviously $f(n) = n(n+1)/2$.

Dividing $f(n)$ by $f(n - 1)$ does not give so obvious a result, but it provides another useful illustration.

$$
\begin{aligned}
\frac{f(n)}{f(n-1)} &= \frac{n+1}{n-1} \\
f(n)(n-1) &= (n+1)f(n-1) \\
f(n)(n-1) &= (n+1)(f(n) - n) \\
nf(n) - f(n) &= nf(n) + f(n) - n^2 - n \\
2f(n) &= n^2 + n = n(n+1) \\
f(n) &= \frac{n(n+1)}{2}
\end{aligned}
$$

Once again, we still do not have a proof that $f(n) = n(n+1)/2$. Why? Because we did not prove that $f(n)/n = (n + 1)/2$ nor that $f(n)/f(n-1) = (n + 1)(n - 1)$. We merely hypothesized patterns from looking at a few terms. Fortunately, it is easy to check our hypothesis with induction.

Example 14.2 Solve the summation

$$
\sum_{i=1}^{n} 1/2^i.
$$

We will begin by writing out a table listing the first few values of the summation, to see if we can detect a pattern.

n	1	2	3	4	5	6
$f(n)$	$\frac{1}{2}$	$\frac{3}{4}$	$\frac{7}{8}$	$\frac{15}{16}$	$\frac{31}{32}$	$\frac{63}{64}$
$1 - f(n)$	$\frac{1}{2}$	$\frac{1}{4}$	$\frac{1}{8}$	$\frac{1}{16}$	$\frac{1}{32}$	$\frac{1}{64}$

By direct inspection of the second line of the table, we might recognize the pattern $f(n) = \frac{2^n-1}{2^n}$. A simple induction proof can then prove that this always holds true. Alternatively, consider if we hadn't noticed the pattern for the form of $f(n)$. We might observe that $f(n)$ appears to be reaching an asymptote at one. In which case, we might consider looking at the difference between $f(n)$ and the expected asymptote. This result is shown in the last line of the table, which has a clear pattern since the ith entry is of $1/2^i$. From this we can easily deduce a guess that $f(n) = 1 - \frac{1}{2^n}$. Again, a simple induction proof will verify the guess.

Example 14.3 Solve the summation

$$f(n) = \sum_{i=0}^{n} ar^i = a + ar + ar^2 + \cdots + ar^n.$$

This is called a geometric series. Our goal is to find some function $g(n)$ such that the difference between $f(n)$ and $g(n)$ one from the other leaves us with an easily manipulated equation. Because the difference between consecutive terms of the summation is a factor of r, we can shift terms if we multiply the entire expression by r:

$$rf(n) = r\sum_{i=0}^{n} ar^i = ar + ar^2 + ar^3 + \cdots + ar^{n+1}.$$

We can now subtract the one equation from the other, as follows:

$$
\begin{aligned}
f(n) - rf(n) = a \quad + \quad & ar + ar^2 + ar^3 + \cdots + ar^n \\
- \quad & (ar + ar^2 + ar^3 + \cdots + ar^n) - ar^{n+1}.
\end{aligned}
$$

The result leaves only the end terms:

$$
\begin{aligned}
f(n) - rf(n) &= \sum_{i=0}^{n} ar^i - r\sum_{i=0}^{n} ar^i. \\
(1-r)f(n) &= a - ar^{n+1}.
\end{aligned}
$$

Thus, we get the result

$$f(n) = \frac{a - ar^{n+1}}{1 - r}$$

where $r \neq 1$.

Example 14.4 For our second example of the shifting method, we solve

$$f(n) = \sum_{i=1}^{n} i2^i = 1 \cdot 2^1 + 2 \cdot 2^2 + 3 \cdot 2^3 + \cdots + n \cdot 2^n.$$

We can achieve our goal if we multiply by two:

$$2f(n) = 2\sum_{i=1}^{n} i2^i = 1 \cdot 2^2 + 2 \cdot 2^3 + 3 \cdot 2^4 + \cdots + (n-1) \cdot 2^n + n \cdot 2^{n+1}.$$

The ith term of $2f(n)$ is $i \cdot 2^{i+1}$, while the $(i+1)$th term of $f(n)$ is $(i+1) \cdot 2^{i+1}$. Subtracting one expression from the other yields the summation of 2^i and a few non-canceled terms:

$$2f(n) - f(n) = 2\sum_{i=1}^{n} i2^i - \sum_{i=1}^{n} i2^i$$

$$= \sum_{i=1}^{n} i2^{i+1} - \sum_{i=1}^{n} i2^i.$$

Shift i's value in the second summation, substituting $(i+1)$ for i:

$$= n2^{n+1} + \sum_{i=0}^{n-1} i2^{i+1} - \sum_{i=0}^{n-1} (i+1)2^{i+1}.$$

Break the second summation into two parts:

$$= n2^{n+1} + \sum_{i=0}^{n-1} i2^{i+1} - \sum_{i=0}^{n-1} i2^{i+1} - \sum_{i=0}^{n-1} 2^{i+1}.$$

Cancel like terms:

$$= n2^{n+1} - \sum_{i=0}^{n-1} 2^{i+1}.$$

Again shift i's value in the summation, substituting i for $(i+1)$:

$$= n2^{n+1} - \sum_{i=1}^{n} 2^i.$$

Replace the new summation with a solution that we already know:

$$= n2^{n+1} - \left(2^{n+1} - 2\right).$$

Finally, reorganize the equation:

$$= (n-1)2^{n+1} + 2.$$

14.2 Recurrence Relations

Recurrence relations are often used to model the cost of recursive functions. For example, the standard Mergesort (Section 7.4) takes a list of size n, splits it in half, performs Mergesort on each half, and finally merges the two sublists in n steps. The cost for this can be modeled as

$$\mathbf{T}(n) = 2\mathbf{T}(n/2) + n.$$

In other words, the cost of the algorithm on input of size n is two times the cost for input of size $n/2$ (due to the two recursive calls to Mergesort) plus n (the time to merge the sublists together again).

There are many approaches to solving recurrence relations, and we briefly consider three here. The first is an estimation technique: Guess the upper and lower bounds for the recurrence, use induction to prove the bounds, and tighten as required. The second approach is to expand the recurrence to convert it to a summation and then use summation techniques. The third approach is to take advantage of already proven theorems when the recurrence is of a suitable form. In particular, typical divide and conquer algorithms such as Mergesort yield recurrences of a form that fits a pattern for which we have a ready solution.

14.2.1 Estimating Upper and Lower Bounds

The first approach to solving recurrences is to guess the answer and then attempt to prove it correct. If a correct upper or lower bound estimate is given, an easy induction proof will verify this fact. If the proof is successful, then try to tighten the bound. If the induction proof fails, then loosen the bound and try again. Once the upper and lower bounds match, you are finished. This is a useful technique when you are only looking for asymptotic complexities. When seeking a precise closed-form solution (i.e., you seek the constants for the expression), this method will probably be too much work.

Example 14.5 Use the guessing technique to find the asymptotic bounds for Mergesort, whose running time is described by the equation

$$\mathbf{T}(n) = 2\mathbf{T}(n/2) + n; \quad \mathbf{T}(2) = 1.$$

We begin by guessing that this recurrence has an upper bound in $O(n^2)$. To be more precise, assume that

$$\mathbf{T}(n) \leq n^2.$$

We prove this guess is correct by induction. In this proof, we assume that n is a power of two, to make the calculations easy. For the base case,

$T(2) = 1 \leq 2^2$. For the induction step, we need to show that $T(n) \leq n^2$ implies that $T(2n) \leq (2n)^2$ for $n = 2^N, N \geq 1$. The induction hypothesis is

$$T(i) \leq i^2, \text{for all } i \leq n.$$

It follows that

$$T(2n) = 2T(n) + 2n \leq 2n^2 + 2n \leq 4n^2 \leq (2n)^2$$

which is what we wanted to prove. Thus, $T(n)$ is in $O(n^2)$.

Is $O(n^2)$ a good estimate? In the next-to-last step we went from $n^2 + 2n$ to the much larger $4n^2$. This suggests that $O(n^2)$ is a high estimate. If we guess something smaller, such as $T(n) \leq cn$ for some constant c, it should be clear that this cannot work because $c2n = 2cn$ and there is no room for the extra n cost to join the two pieces together. Thus, the true cost must be somewhere between cn and n^2.

Let us now try $T(n) \leq n \log n$. For the base case, the definition of the recurrence sets $T(2) = 1 \leq (2 \cdot \log 2) = 2$. Assume (induction hypothesis) that $T(n) \leq n \log n$. Then,

$$T(2n) = 2T(n) + 2n \leq 2n \log n + 2n \leq 2n(\log n + 1) \leq 2n \log 2n$$

which is what we seek to prove. In similar fashion, we can prove that $T(n)$ is in $\Omega(n \log n)$. Thus, $T(n)$ is also $\Theta(n \log n)$.

Example 14.6 We know that the factorial function grows exponentially. How does it compare to 2^n? To n^n? Do they all grow "equally fast" (in an asymptotic sense)? We can begin by looking at a few initial terms.

n	1	2	3	4	5	6	7	8	9
$n!$	1	2	6	24	120	720	5040	40320	362880
2^n	2	4	8	16	32	64	128	256	512
n^n	1	4	9	256	3125	46656	823543	16777216	387420489

We can also look at these functions in terms of their recurrences.

$$n! = \begin{cases} 1 & n = 1 \\ n(n-1)! & n > 1 \end{cases}$$

$$2^n = \begin{cases} 2 & n = 1 \\ 2(2^{n-1}) & n > 1 \end{cases}$$

$$n^n = \begin{cases} n & n = 1 \\ n(n^{n-1}) & n > 1 \end{cases}$$

At this point, our intuition should be telling us pretty clearly the relative growth rates of these three functions. But how do we prove formally which grows the fastest? And how do we decide if the differences are significant in an asymptotic sense, or just constant factor differences?

We can use logarithms to help us get an idea about the relative growth rates of these functions. Clearly, $\log 2^n = n$. Equally clearly, $\log n^n = n \log n$. We can easily see from this that 2^n is $o(n^n)$, that is, n^n grows asymptotically faster than 2^n.

How does $n!$ fit into this? We can again take advantage of logarithms. Obviously $n! \leq n^n$, so we know that $\log n!$ is $O(n \log n)$. But what about a lower bound for the factorial function? Consider the following.

$$\begin{aligned} n! &= n \times (n-1) \times \cdots \times \frac{n}{2} \times (\frac{n}{2} - 1) \times \cdots \times 2 \times 1 \\ &\geq \frac{n}{2} \times \frac{n}{2} \times \cdots \times \frac{n}{2} \times 1 \times \cdots \times 1 \times 1 \\ &= (\frac{n}{2})^{n/2} \end{aligned}$$

Therefore

$$\log n! \geq \log(\frac{n}{2})^{n/2} = (\frac{n}{2}) \log(\frac{n}{2}).$$

In other words, $\log n!$ is in $\Omega(n \log n)$. Thus, $\log n! = \Theta(n \log n)$.

Note that this does **not** mean that $n! = \Theta(n^n)$. Because $\log n^2 = 2 \log n$, it follows that $\log n = \Theta(\log n^2)$ but $n \neq \Theta(n^2)$. The log function often works as a "flattener" when dealing with asymptotics. That is, whenever $\log f(n)$ is in $O(\log g(n))$ we know that $f(n)$ is in $O(g(n))$. But knowing that $\log f(n) = \Theta(\log g(n))$ does not necessarily mean that $f(n) = \Theta(g(n))$.

Example 14.7 What is the growth rate of the Fibonacci sequence? We define the Fibonacci sequence as $f(n) = f(n-1) + f(n-2)$ for $n \geq 2$; $f(0) = f(1) = 1$.

In this case it is useful to compare the ratio of $f(n)$ to $f(n-1)$. The following table shows the first few values.

n	1	2	3	4	5	6	7
$f(n)$	1	2	3	5	8	13	21
$f(n)/f(n-1)$	1	2	1.5	1.666	1.625	1.615	1.619

If we continue for more terms, the ratio appears to converge on a value slightly greater then 1.618. Assuming $f(n)/f(n-1)$ really does converge to a fixed value as n grows, we can determine what that value must be.

$$\frac{f(n)}{f(n-2)} = \frac{f(n-1)}{f(n-2)} + \frac{f(n-2)}{f(n-2)} \to x+1$$

For some value x. This follows from the fact that $f(n) = f(n-1) + f(n-2)$. We divide by $f(n-2)$ to make the second term go away, and we also get something useful in the first term. Remember that the goal of such manipulations is to give us an equation that relates $f(n)$ to something without recursive calls.

For large n, we also observe that:

$$\frac{f(n)}{f(n-2)} = \frac{f(n)}{f(n-1)}\frac{f(n-1)}{f(n-2)} \to x^2$$

as n gets big. This comes from multiplying $f(n)/f(n-2)$ by $f(n-1)/f(n-1)$ and rearranging.

If x exists, then $x^2 - x - 1 \to 0$. Using the quadratic equation, the only solution greater than one is

$$x = \frac{1+\sqrt 5}{2} \approx 1.618.$$

This expression also has the name ϕ. What does this say about the growth rate of the Fibonacci sequence? It is exponential, with $f(n) = \Theta(\phi^n)$. More precisely, $f(n)$ converges to

$$\frac{\phi^n - (1-\phi)^n}{\sqrt 5}.$$

14.2.2 Expanding Recurrences

Estimating bounds is effective if you only need an approximation to the answer. More precise techniques are required to find an exact solution. One approach is called **expanding** the recurrence. In this method, the smaller terms on the right side of the equation are in turn replaced by their definition. This is the expanding step. These terms are again expanded, and so on, until a full series with no recurrence results. This yields a summation, and techniques for solving summations can then be used. A couple of simple expansions were shown in Section 2.4. A more complex example is given below.

Example 14.8 Find the solution for

$$\mathbf{T}(n) = 2\mathbf{T}(n/2) + 5n^2; \quad \mathbf{T}(1) = 7.$$

For simplicity we assume that n is a power of two, so we will rewrite it as $n = 2^k$. This recurrence can be expanded as follows:

$$
\begin{aligned}
\mathbf{T}(n) &= 2\mathbf{T}(n/2) + 5n^2 \\
&= 2(2\mathbf{T}(n/4) + 5(n/2)^2) + 5n^2 \\
&= 2(2(2\mathbf{T}(n/8) + 5(n/4)^2) + 5(n/2)^2) + 5n^2 \\
&= 2^k\mathbf{T}(1) + 2^{k-1} \cdot 5 \left(\frac{n}{2^{k-1}}\right)^2 + \cdots + 2 \cdot 5 \left(\frac{n}{2}\right)^2 + 5n^2.
\end{aligned}
$$

This last expression can best be represented by a summation as follows:

$$
7n + 5 \sum_{i=0}^{k-1} n^2/2^i
$$

$$
= 7n + 5n^2 \sum_{i=0}^{k-1} 1/2^i.
$$

From Equation 2.6, we have:

$$
\begin{aligned}
&= 7n + 5n^2 \left(2 - 1/2^{k-1}\right) \\
&= 7n + 5n^2(2 - 2/n) \\
&= 7n + 10n^2 - 10n \\
&= 10n^2 - 3n.
\end{aligned}
$$

This is the *exact* solution to the recurrence for n a power of two. At this point, we should use a simple induction proof to verify that our solution is indeed correct.

Example 14.9 Our next example models the cost of the algorithm to build a heap. Recall from Section 5.5 that to build a heap, we first heapify the two subheaps, then push down the root to its proper position. The cost is:

$$f(n) \leq 2f(n/2) + 2\log n.$$

Let us find a closed form solution for this recurrence. We can expand the recurrence a few times to see that

$$
\begin{aligned}
f(n) &\le 2f(n/2) + 2\log n \\
&\le 2[2f(n/4) + 2\log n/2] + 2\log n \\
&\le 2[2(2f(n/8) + 2\log n/4) + 2\log n/2] + 2\log n
\end{aligned}
$$

We can deduce from this expansion that this recurrence is equivalent to following summation and its derivation:

$$
\begin{aligned}
f(n) &\le \sum_{i=0}^{\log n-1} 2^{i+1} \log(n/2^i) \\
&= 2 \sum_{i=0}^{\log n-1} 2^i(\log n - i) \\
&= 2\log n \sum_{i=0}^{\log n-1} 2^i - 4 \sum_{i=0}^{\log n-1} i2^{i-1} \\
&= 2n\log n - 2\log n - 2n\log n + 4n - 4 \\
&= 4n - 2\log n - 4.
\end{aligned}
$$

14.2.3 Divide and Conquer Recurrences

The third approach to solving recurrences is to take advantage of known theorems that provide the solution for classes of recurrences. Of particular practical use is a theorem that gives the answer for a class known as **divide and conquer** recurrences. These have the form

$$
\mathbf{T}(n) = a\mathbf{T}(n/b) + cn^k; \quad \mathbf{T}(1) = c
$$

where a, b, c, and k are constants. In general, this recurrence describes a problem of size n divided into a subproblems of size n/b, while cn^k is the amount of work necessary to combine the partial solutions. Mergesort is an example of a divide and conquer algorithm, and its recurrence fits this form. So does binary search. We use the method of expanding recurrences to derive the general solution for any divide and conquer recurrence, assuming that $n = b^m$.

$$
\begin{aligned}
\mathbf{T}(n) &= a\mathbf{T}(n/b) + cn^k \\
&= a(a\mathbf{T}(n/b^2) + c(n/b)^k) + cn^k \\
&= a(a[a\mathbf{T}(n/b^3) + c(n/b^2)^k] + c(n/b)^k) + cn^k
\end{aligned}
$$

$$
\begin{aligned}
&= a^m \mathbf{T}(1) + a^{m-1} c(n/b^{m-1})^k + \cdots + ac(n/b)^k + cn^k \\
&= a^m c + a^{m-1} c(n/b^{m-1})^k + \cdots + ac(n/b)^k + cn^k \\
&= c \sum_{i=0}^{m} a^{m-i} b^{ik} \\
&= ca^m \sum_{i=0}^{m} (b^k/a)^i.
\end{aligned}
$$

Note that

$$ a^m = a^{\log_b n} = n^{\log_b a}. \tag{14.1} $$

The summation is a geometric series whose sum depends on the ratio $r = b^k/a$. There are three cases.

1. $r < 1$. From Equation 2.4,

$$ \sum_{i=0}^{m} r^i < 1/(1-r), \text{a constant.} $$

Thus,

$$ \mathbf{T}(n) = \Theta(a^m) = \Theta(n^{log_b a}). $$

2. $r = 1$. Because $r = b^k/a$, we know that $a = b^k$. From the definition of logarithms it follows immediately that $k = \log_b a$. We also note from Equation 14.1 that $m = \log_b n$. Thus,

$$ \sum_{i=0}^{m} r = m + 1 = \log_b n + 1. $$

Because $a^m = n \log_b a = n^k$, we have

$$ \mathbf{T}(n) = \Theta(n^{\log_b a} \log n) = \Theta(n^k \log n). $$

3. $r > 1$. From Equation 2.5,

$$ \sum_{i=0}^{m} r = \frac{r^{m+1} - 1}{r - 1} = \Theta(r^m). $$

Thus,

$$ \mathbf{T}(n) = \Theta(a^m r^m) = \Theta(a^m (b^k/a)^m) = \Theta(b^{km}) = \Theta(n^k). $$

We can summarize the above derivation as the following theorem, sometimes referred to as the **Master Theorem**.

Theorem 14.1 *(The Master Theorem) For any recurrence relation of the form* $\mathbf{T}(n) = a\mathbf{T}(n/b) + cn^k, \mathbf{T}(1) = c$, *the following relationships hold.*

$$\mathbf{T}(n) = \begin{cases} \Theta(n^{\log_b a}) & if\, a > b^k \\ \Theta(n^k \log n) & if\, a = b^k \\ \Theta(n^k) & if\, a < b^k. \end{cases}$$

This theorem may be applied whenever appropriate, rather than re-deriving the solution for the recurrence.

Example 14.10 Apply the Master Theorem to solve

$$\mathbf{T}(n) = 3\mathbf{T}(n/5) + 8n^2.$$

Because $a = 3$, $b = 5$, $c = 8$, and $k = 2$, we find that $3 < 5^2$. Applying case (3) of the theorem, $\mathbf{T}(n) = \Theta(n^2)$.

Example 14.11 Use the Master Theorem to solve the recurrence relation for Mergesort:

$$\mathbf{T}(n) = 2\mathbf{T}(n/2) + n; \quad \mathbf{T}(1) = 1.$$

Because $a = 2$, $b = 2$, $c = 1$, and $k = 1$, we find that $2 = 2^1$. Applying case (2) of the theorem, $\mathbf{T}(n) = \Theta(n \log n)$.

14.2.4 Average-Case Analysis of Quicksort

In Section 7.5, we determined that the average-case analysis of Quicksort had the following recurrence:

$$\mathbf{T}(n) = cn + \frac{1}{n}\sum_{k=0}^{n-1}[\mathbf{T}(k) + \mathbf{T}(n-1-k)], \qquad \mathbf{T}(0) = \mathbf{T}(1) = c.$$

The cn term is an upper bound on the **findpivot** and **partition** steps. This equation comes from assuming that the partitioning element is equally likely to occur in any position k. It can be simplified by observing that the two recurrence terms $\mathbf{T}(k)$ and $\mathbf{T}(n-1-k)$ are equivalent, because one simply counts up from $T(0)$ to $T(n-1)$ while the other counts down from $T(n-1)$ to $T(0)$. This yields

$$\mathbf{T}(n) = cn + \frac{2}{n}\sum_{k=0}^{n-1}\mathbf{T}(k).$$

This form is known as a recurrence with **full history**. The key to solving such a recurrence is to cancel out the summation terms. The shifting method for summations provides a way to do this. Multiply both sides by n and subtract the result from the formula for $n\mathbf{T}(n+1)$:

$$n\mathbf{T}(n) = cn^2 + 2\sum_{k=1}^{n-1}\mathbf{T}(k)$$

$$(n+1)\mathbf{T}(n+1) = c(n+1)^2 + 2\sum_{k=1}^{n}\mathbf{T}(k).$$

Subtracting $n\mathbf{T}(n)$ from both sides yields:

$$(n+1)\mathbf{T}(n+1) - n\mathbf{T}(n) = c(n+1)^2 - cn^2 + 2\mathbf{T}(n)$$
$$(n+1)\mathbf{T}(n+1) - n\mathbf{T}(n) = c(2n+1) + 2\mathbf{T}(n)$$
$$(n+1)\mathbf{T}(n+1) = c(2n+1) + (n+2)\mathbf{T}(n)$$
$$\mathbf{T}(n+1) = \frac{c(2n+1)}{n+1} + \frac{n+2}{n+1}\mathbf{T}(n).$$

At this point, we have eliminated the summation and can now use our normal methods for solving recurrences to get a closed-form solution. Note that $\frac{c(2n+1)}{n+1} < 2c$, so we can simplify the result. Expanding the recurrence, we get

$$
\begin{aligned}
\mathbf{T}(n+1) &\leq 2c + \frac{n+2}{n+1}\mathbf{T}(n) \\
&= 2c + \frac{n+2}{n+1}\left(2c + \frac{n+1}{n}\mathbf{T}(n-1)\right) \\
&= 2c + \frac{n+2}{n+1}\left(2c + \frac{n+1}{n}\left(2c + \frac{n}{n-1}\mathbf{T}(n-2)\right)\right) \\
&= 2c + \frac{n+2}{n+1}\left(2c + \cdots + \frac{4}{3}(2c + \frac{3}{2}\mathbf{T}(1))\right) \\
&= 2c\left(1 + \frac{n+2}{n+1} + \frac{n+2}{n+1}\frac{n+1}{n} + \cdots + \frac{n+2}{n+1}\frac{n+1}{n}\cdots\frac{3}{2}\right) \\
&= 2c\left(1 + (n+2)\left(\frac{1}{n+1} + \frac{1}{n} + \cdots + \frac{1}{2}\right)\right) \\
&= 2c + 2c(n+2)\left(\mathcal{H}_{n+1} - 1\right)
\end{aligned}
$$

for $\mathcal{H}_{n+1}$, the Harmonic Series. From Equation 2.10, $\mathcal{H}_{n+1} = \Theta(\log n)$, so the final solution is $\Theta(n \log n)$.

14.3 Amortized Analysis

This section presents the concept of **amortized analysis**, which is the analysis for a series of operations taken as a whole. In particular, amortized analysis allows us to deal with the situation where the worst-case cost for n operations is less than n times the worst-case cost of any one operation. Rather than focusing on the individual cost of each operation independently and summing them, amortized analysis looks at the cost of the entire series and "charges" each individual operation with a share of the total cost.

We can apply the technique of amortized analysis in the case of a series of sequential searches in an unsorted array. For n random searches, the average-case cost for each search is $n/2$, and so the *expected* total cost for the series is $n^2/2$. Unfortunately, in the worst case all of the searches would be to the last item in the array. In this case, each search costs n for a total worst-case cost of n^2. Compare this to the cost for a series of n searches such that each item in the array is searched for precisely once. In this situation, some of the searches *must* be expensive, but also some searches *must* be cheap. The total number of searches, in the best, average, and worst case, for this problem must be $\sum_{i=i}^{n} i \approx n^2/2$. This is a factor of two better than the more pessimistic analysis that charges each operation in the series with its worst-case cost.

As another example of amortized analysis, consider the process of incrementing a binary counter. The algorithm is to move from the lower-order (rightmost) bit toward the high-order (leftmost) bit, changing 1s to 0s until the first 0 is encountered. This 0 is changed to a 1, and the increment operation is done. Below is **C++** code to implement the increment operation, assuming that a binary number of length n is stored in array **A** of length n.

```
for (i=0; ((i<n) && (A[i] == 1)); i++)
  A[i] = 0;
if (i < n)
  A[i] = 1;
```

If we count from 0 through $2^n - 1$, (requiring a counter with at least n bits), what is the average cost for an increment operation in terms of the number of bits processed? Naive worst-case analysis says that if all n bits are 1 (except for the high-order bit), then n bits need to be processed. Thus, if there are 2^n increments, then the cost is $n2^n$. However, this is much too high, because it is rare for so many bits to be processed. In fact, half of the time the low-order bit is 0, and so only that bit is processed. One quarter of the time, the low-order two bits are 01, and so only the low-order two bits are processed. Another way to view this is that the low-order bit is always flipped, the bit to its left is flipped half the time, the next bit one quarter of the time, and so on. We can capture this with the summation

(charging costs to bits going from right to left)

$$\sum_{i=0}^{n-1} \frac{1}{2^i} < 2.$$

In other words, the average number of bits flipped on each increment is 2, leading to a total cost of only $2 \cdot 2^n$ for a series of 2^n increments.

A useful concept for amortized analysis is illustrated by a simple variation on the stack data structure, where the **pop** function is slightly modified to take a second parameter k indicating that k pop operations are to be performed. This revised pop function, called **multipop**, might look as follows:

```
// pop k elements from stack
void multipop(int k);
```

The "local" worst-case analysis for **multipop** is $\Theta(n)$ for n elements in the stack. Thus, if there are m_1 calls to **push** and m_2 calls to **multipop**, then the naive worst-case cost for the series of operation is $m_1 + m_2 \cdot n = m_1 + m_2 \cdot m_1$. This analysis is unreasonably pessimistic. Clearly it is not really possible to pop m_1 elements each time **multipop** is called. Analysis that focuses on single operations cannot deal with this global limit, and so we turn to amortized analysis to model the entire series of operations.

The key to an amortized analysis of this problem lies in the concept of **potential**. At any given time, a certain number of items may be on the stack. The cost for **multipop** can be no more than this number of items. Each call to **push** places another item on the stack, which can be removed by only a single **multipop** operation. Thus, each call to **push** raises the potential of the stack by one item. The sum of costs for all calls to **multipop** can never be more than the total potential of the stack (aside from a constant time cost associated with each call to **multipop** itself).

The amortized cost for any series of **push** and **multipop** operations is the sum of three costs. First, each of the **push** operations takes constant time. Second, each **multipop** operation takes a constant time in overhead, regardless of the number of items popped on that call. Finally, we count the sum of the potentials expended by all **multipop** operations, which is at most m_1, the number of **push** operations. This total cost can therefore be expressed as

$$m_1 + (m_2 + m_1) = \Theta(m_1 + m_2).$$

A similar argument was used in our analysis for the partition function in the Quicksort algorithm (Section 7.5). While on any given pass through the while loop the left or right pointers might move all the way through the remainder of the partition, doing so would reduce the number of times that the while loop can be further executed.

Our final example uses amortized analysis to prove a relationship between the cost of the move-to-front self-organizing list heuristic from Section 9.2 and the cost for the optimal static ordering of the list.

Recall that, for a series of search operations, the minimum cost for a static list results when the list is sorted by frequency of access to its records. This is the optimal ordering for the records if we never allow the positions of records to change, because the most-frequently accessed record is first (and thus has least cost), followed by the next most frequently accessed record, and so on.

Theorem 14.2 *The total number of comparisons required by any series S of n or more searches on a self-organizing list of length n using the move-to-front heuristic is never more than twice the total number of comparisons required when series S is applied to the list stored in its optimal static order.*

Proof: Each comparison of the search key with a record in the list is either successful or unsuccessful. For m searches, there must be exactly m successful comparisons for both the self-organizing list and the static list. The total number of unsuccessful comparisons in the self-organizing list is the sum, over all pairs of distinct keys, of the number of unsuccessful comparisons made between that pair.

Consider a particular pair of keys A and B. For any sequence of searches S, the total number of (unsuccessful) comparisons between A and B is identical to the number of comparisons between A and B required for the subsequence of S made up only of searches for A or B. Call this subsequence S_{AB}. In other words, including searches for other keys does not affect the relative position of A and B and so does not affect the relative contribution to the total cost of the unsuccessful comparisons between A and B.

The number of unsuccessful comparisons between A and B made by the move-to-front heuristic on subsequence S_{AB} is at most twice the number of unsuccessful comparisons between A and B required when S_{AB} is applied to the optimal static ordering for the list. To see this, assume that S_{AB} contains i As and j Bs, with $i \leq j$. Under the optimal static ordering, i unsuccessful comparisons are required because B must appear before A in the list (because its access frequency is higher). Move-to-front will yield an unsuccessful comparison whenever the request sequence changes from A to B or from B to A. The total number of such changes possible is $2i$ because each change involves an A and each A can be part of at most two changes.

Because the total number of unsuccessful comparisons required by move-to-front for any given pair of keys is at most twice that required by the optimal static ordering, the total number of unsuccessful comparisons required by move-to-front for all pairs of keys is also at most twice as high. Because the number of successful comparisons is the same for both methods, the total number of comparisons required by move-to-front is less than twice the number of comparisons required by the optimal static ordering. □

14.4   Further Reading

A good introduction to solving recurrence relations appears in *Applied Combinatorics* by Fred S. Roberts [Rob84]. For a more advanced treatment, see *Concrete Mathematics* by Graham, Knuth, and Patashnik [GKP94].

Cormen, Leiserson, and Rivest provide a good discussion on various methods for performing amortized analysis in *Introduction to Algorithms* [CLRS09]. For an amortized analysis that the splay tree requires $m \log n$ time to perform a series of m operations on n nodes when $m > n$, see "Self-Adjusting Binary Search Trees" by Sleator and Tarjan [ST85]. The proof for Theorem 14.2 comes from "Amortized Analysis of Self-Organizing Sequential Search Heuristics" by Bentley and McGeoch [BM85].

14.5   Exercises

14.1 Use the technique of guessing a polynomial and deriving the coefficients to solve the summation

$$\sum_{i=1}^{n} i^2.$$

14.2 Use the technique of guessing a polynomial and deriving the coefficients to solve the summation

$$\sum_{i=1}^{n} i^3.$$

14.3 Find, and prove correct, a closed-form solution for

$$\sum_{i=a}^{b} i^2.$$

14.4 Use subtract-and-guess or divide-and-guess to find the closed form solution for the following summation. You must first find a pattern from which to deduce a potential closed form solution, and then prove that the proposed solution is correct.

$$\sum_{i=1}^{n} i/2^i$$

14.5 Use the shifting method to solve the summation

$$\sum_{i=1}^{n} i^2.$$

14.6 Use the shifting method to solve the summation

$$\sum_{i=1}^{n} 2^i.$$

14.7 Use the shifting method to solve the summation

$$\sum_{i=1}^{n} i2^{n-i}.$$

14.8 Consider the following code fragment.

```
sum = 0; inc = 0;
for (i=1; i<=n; i++)
  for (j=1; j<=i; j++) {
    sum = sum + inc;
    inc++;
  }
```

(a) Determine a summation that defines the final value for variable sum as a function of n.

(b) Determine a closed-form solution for your summation.

14.9 A chocolate company decides to promote its chocolate bars by including a coupon with each bar. A bar costs a dollar, and with c coupons you get a free bar. So depending on the value of c, you get more than one bar of chocolate for a dollar when considering the value of the coupons. How much chocolate is a dollar worth (as a function of c)?

14.10 Write and solve a recurrence relation to compute the number of times Fibr is called in the Fibr function of Exercise 2.11.

14.11 Give and prove the closed-form solution for the recurrence relation $\mathbf{T}(n) = \mathbf{T}(n-1) + 1, \mathbf{T}(1) = 1$.

14.12 Give and prove the closed-form solution for the recurrence relation $\mathbf{T}(n) = \mathbf{T}(n-1) + c, \mathbf{T}(1) = c$.

14.13 Prove by induction that the closed-form solution for the recurrence relation

$$\mathbf{T}(n) = 2\mathbf{T}(n/2) + n; \quad \mathbf{T}(2) = 1$$

is in $\Omega(n \log n)$.

14.14 For the following recurrence, give a closed-form solution. You should not give an exact solution, but only an asymptotic solution (i.e., using Θ notation). You may assume that n is a power of 2. Prove that your answer is correct.

$$\mathbf{T}(n) = \mathbf{T}(n/2) + \sqrt{n} \text{ for } n > 1; \quad \mathbf{T}(1) = 1.$$

14.15 Using the technique of expanding the recurrence, find the exact closed-form solution for the recurrence relation

$$\mathbf{T}(n) = 2\mathbf{T}(n/2) + n; \quad \mathbf{T}(2) = 2.$$

You may assume that n is a power of 2.

14.16 Section 5.5 provides an asymptotic analysis for the worst-case cost of function **buildHeap**. Give an exact worst-case analysis for **buildHeap**.

14.17 For each of the following recurrences, find and then prove (using induction) an exact closed-form solution. When convenient, you may assume that n is a power of 2.

    (a) $\mathbf{T}(n) = \mathbf{T}(n-1) + n/2$ for $n > 1$; $\mathbf{T}(1) = 1$.
    (b) $\mathbf{T}(n) = 2\mathbf{T}(n/2) + n$ for $n > 2$; $\mathbf{T}(2) = 2$.

14.18 Use Theorem 14.1 to prove that binary search requires $\Theta(\log n)$ time.

14.19 Recall that when a hash table gets to be more than about one half full, its performance quickly degrades. One solution to this problem is to reinsert all elements of the hash table into a new hash table that is twice as large. Assuming that the (expected) average case cost to insert into a hash table is $\Theta(1)$, prove that the average cost to insert is still $\Theta(1)$ when this re-insertion policy is used.

14.20 Given a 2-3 tree with N nodes, prove that inserting M additional nodes requires $O(M + N)$ node splits.

14.21 One approach to implementing an array-based list where the list size is unknown is to let the array grow and shrink. This is known as a **dynamic array**. When necessary, we can grow or shrink the array by copying the array's contents to a new array. If we are careful about the size of the new array, this copy operation can be done rarely enough so as not to affect the amortized cost of the operations.

    (a) What is the amortized cost of inserting elements into the list if the array is initially of size 1 and we double the array size whenever the number of elements that we wish to store exceeds the size of the array? Assume that the insert itself cost $O(1)$ time per operation and so we are just concerned with minimizing the copy time to the new array.

(b) Consider an underflow strategy that cuts the array size in half whenever the array falls below half full. Give an example where this strategy leads to a bad amortized cost. Again, we are only interested in measuring the time of the array copy operations.

(c) Give a better underflow strategy than that suggested in part (b). Your goal is to find a strategy whose amortized analysis shows that array copy requires $O(n)$ time for a series of n operations.

14.22 Recall that two vertices in an undirected graph are in the same connected component if there is a path connecting them. A good algorithm to find the connected components of an undirected graph begins by calling a DFS on the first vertex. All vertices reached by the DFS are in the same connected component and are so marked. We then look through the vertex **mark** array until an unmarked vertex i is found. Again calling the DFS on i, all vertices reachable from i are in a second connected component. We continue working through the **mark** array until all vertices have been assigned to some connected component. A sketch of the algorithm is as follows:

```
void DFS_component(Graph* G, int v, int component) {
  G->setMark(v, component);
  for (int w=G->first(v); w<G->n(); w = G->next(v,w))
    if (G->getMark(w) == 0)
      DFS_component(G, w, component);
}

void concom(Graph* G) {
  int i;
  int component = 1;    // Counter for current component
  for (i=0; i<G->n(); i++) // For n vertices in graph
    G->setMark(i, 0); // Vertices start in no component
  for (i=0; i<G->n(); i++)
    if (G->getMark(i) == 0) // Start a new component
      DFS_component(G, i, component++);
}
```

Use the concept of potential from amortized analysis to explain why the total cost of this algorithm is $\Theta(|V| + |E|)$. (Note that this will not be a true amortized analysis because this algorithm does not allow an arbitrary series of DFS operations but rather is fixed to do a single call to DFS from each vertex.)

14.23 Give a proof similar to that used for Theorem 14.2 to show that the total number of comparisons required by any series of n or more searches S on a self-organizing list of length n using the count heuristic is never more than twice the total number of comparisons required when series S is applied to the list stored in its optimal static order.

14.24 Use mathematical induction to prove that

$$\sum_{i=1}^{n} Fib(i) = Fib(n-2) - 1, \text{for } n \geq 1.$$

14.25 Use mathematical induction to prove that Fib(i) is even if and only if n is divisible by 3.

14.26 Use mathematical induction to prove that for $n \geq 6$, $fib(n) > (3/2)^{n-1}$.

14.27 Find closed forms for each of the following recurrences.

    (a) $F(n) = F(n-1) + 3; F(1) = 2.$
    (b) $F(n) = 2F(n-1); F(0) = 1.$
    (c) $F(n) = 2F(n-1) + 1; F(1) = 1.$
    (d) $F(n) = 2nF(n-1); F(0) = 1.$
    (e) $F(n) = 2^n F(n-1); F(0) = 1.$
    (f) $F(n) = 2 + \sum_{i=1}^{n-1} F(i); F(1) = 1.$

14.28 Find Θ for each of the following recurrence relations.
    (a) $T(n) = 2T(n/2) + n^2.$
    (b) $T(n) = 2T(n/2) + 5.$
    (c) $T(n) = 4T(n/2) + n.$
    (d) $T(n) = 2T(n/2) + n^2.$
    (e) $T(n) = 4T(n/2) + n^3.$
    (f) $T(n) = 4T(n/3) + n.$
    (g) $T(n) = 4T(n/3) + n^2.$
    (h) $T(n) = 2T(n/2) + \log n.$
    (i) $T(n) = 2T(n/2) + n \log n.$

14.6 Projects

14.1 Implement the UNION/FIND algorithm of Section 6.2 using both path compression and the weighted union rule. Count the total number of node accesses required for various series of equivalences to determine if the actual performance of the algorithm matches the expected cost of $\Theta(n \log^* n)$.

15

Lower Bounds

How do I know if I have a good algorithm to solve a problem? If my algorithm runs in $\Theta(n \log n)$ time, is that good? It would be if I were sorting the records stored in an array. But it would be terrible if I were searching the array for the largest element. The value of an algorithm must be determined in relation to the inherent complexity of the problem at hand.

In Section 3.6 we defined the upper bound for a problem to be the upper bound of the best algorithm we know for that problem, and the lower bound to be the tightest lower bound that we can prove over all algorithms for that problem. While we usually can recognize the upper bound for a given algorithm, finding the tightest lower bound for all possible algorithms is often difficult, especially if that lower bound is more than the "trivial" lower bound determined by measuring the amount of input that must be processed.

The benefits of being able to discover a strong lower bound are significant. In particular, when we can make the upper and lower bounds for a problem meet, this means that we truly understand our problem in a theoretical sense. It also saves us the effort of attempting to discover more (asymptotically) efficient algorithms when no such algorithm can exist.

Often the most effective way to determine the lower bound for a problem is to find a reduction to another problem whose lower bound is already known. This is the subject of Chapter 17. However, this approach does not help us when we cannot find a suitable "similar problem." Our focus in this chapter is discovering and proving lower bounds from first principles. Our most significant example of a lower bounds argument so far is the proof from Section 7.9 that the problem of sorting is $O(n \log n)$ in the worst case.

Section 15.1 reviews the concept of a lower bound for a problem and presents the basic "algorithm" for finding a good algorithm. Section 15.2 discusses lower bounds on searching in lists, both those that are unordered and those that are ordered. Section 15.3 deals with finding the maximum value in a list, and presents a model for selection based on building a partially ordered set. Section 15.4 presents the concept of an adversarial lower bounds proof. Section 15.5 illustrates the concept of a state space lower bound. Section 15.6 presents a linear time worst-case algorithm for finding the ith biggest element on a list. Section 15.7 continues our discussion of sorting with a quest for the algorithm that requires the absolute fewest number of comparisons needed to sort a list.

15.1   Introduction to Lower Bounds Proofs

The lower bound for the problem is the tightest (highest) lower bound that we can prove *for all possible algorithms* that solve the problem.[1] This can be a difficult bar, given that we cannot possibly know all algorithms for any problem, because there are theoretically an infinite number. However, we can often recognize a simple lower bound based on the amount of input that must be examined. For example, we can argue that the lower bound for any algorithm to find the maximum-valued element in an unsorted list must be $\Omega(n)$ because any algorithm must examine all of the inputs to be sure that it actually finds the maximum value.

In the case of maximum finding, the fact that we know of a simple algorithm that runs in $O(n)$ time, combined with the fact that any algorithm needs $\Omega(n)$ time, is significant. Because our upper and lower bounds meet (within a constant factor), we know that we do have a "good" algorithm for solving the problem. It is possible that someone can develop an implementation that is a "little" faster than an existing one, by a constant factor. But we know that its not possible to develop one that is asymptotically better.

We must be careful about how we interpret this last statement, however. The world is certainly better off for the invention of Quicksort, even though Mergesort was available at the time. Quicksort is not asymptotically faster than Mergesort, yet is not merely a "tuning" of Mergesort either. Quicksort is a substantially different approach to sorting. So even when our upper and lower bounds for a problem meet, there are still benefits to be gained from a new, clever algorithm.

So now we have an answer to the question "How do I know if I have a good algorithm to solve a problem?" An algorithm is good (asymptotically speaking) if its upper bound matches the problem's lower bound. If they match, we know to stop trying to find an (asymptotically) faster algorithm. What if the (known) upper bound for our algorithm does not match the (known) lower bound for the problem? In this case, we might not know what to do. Is our upper bound flawed, and the algorithm is really faster than we can prove? Is our lower bound weak, and the true lower bound for the problem is greater? Or is our algorithm simply not the best?

---

[1]Throughout this discussion, it should be understood that any mention of bounds must specify what class of inputs are being considered. Do we mean the bound for the worst case input? The average cost over all inputs? Regardless of which class of inputs we consider, all of the issues raised apply equally.

Now we know precisely what we are aiming for when designing an algorithm: We want to find an algorithm who's upper bound matches the lower bound of the problem. Putting together all that we know so far about algorithms, we can organize our thinking into the following "algorithm for designing algorithms."[2]

> **If** the upper and lower bounds match,
> **then** stop,
> **else if** the bounds are close or the problem isn't important,
>> **then** stop,
>> **else if** the problem definition focuses on the wrong thing,
>>> **then** restate it,
>>> **else if** the algorithm is too slow,
>>>> **then** find a faster algorithm,
>>>> **else if** lower bound is too weak,
>>>>> **then** generate a stronger bound.

We can repeat this process until we are satisfied or exhausted.

This brings us smack up against one of the toughest tasks in analysis. Lower bounds proofs are notoriously difficult to construct. The problem is coming up with arguments that truly cover all of the things that *any* algorithm possibly *could* do. The most common fallacy is to argue from the point of view of what some good algorithm actually *does* do, and claim that any algorithm must do the same. This simply is not true, and any lower bounds proof that refers to specific behavior that must take place should be viewed with some suspicion.

Let us consider the Towers of Hanoi problem again. Recall from Section 2.5 that our basic algorithm is to move $n - 1$ disks (recursively) to the middle pole, move the bottom disk to the third pole, and then move $n-1$ disks (again recursively) from the middle to the third pole. This algorithm generates the recurrence $\mathbf{T}(n) = 2\mathbf{T}(n - 1) + 1 = 2^n - 1$. So, the upper bound for our algorithm is $2^n - 1$. But is this the best algorithm for the problem? What is the lower bound for the problem?

For our first try at a lower bounds proof, the "trivial" lower bound is that we must move every disk at least once, for a minimum cost of n. Slightly better is to observe that to get the bottom disk to the third pole, we must move every other disk at least twice (once to get them off the bottom disk, and once to get them over to the third pole). This yields a cost of $2n - 1$, which still is not a good match for our algorithm. Is the problem in the algorithm or in the lower bound?

We can get to the correct lower bound by the following reasoning: To move the biggest disk from first to the last pole, we must first have all of the other $n-1$ disks out of the way, and the only way to do that is to move them all to the middle pole (for a cost of at least $\mathbf{T}(n - 1)$). We then must move the bottom disk (for a cost of

---

[2]This is a minor reformulation of the "algorithm" given by Gregory J.E. Rawlins in his book "Compared to What?"

at least one). After that, we must move the $n - 1$ remaining disks from the middle pole to the third pole (for a cost of at least $\mathbf{T}(n - 1)$). Thus, no possible algorithm can solve the problem in less than $2^n - 1$ steps. Thus, our algorithm is optimal.[3]

Of course, there are variations to a given problem. Changes in the problem definition might or might not lead to changes in the lower bound. Two possible changes to the standard Towers of Hanoi problem are:

- Not all disks need to start on the first pole.
- Multiple disks can be moved at one time.

The first variation does not change the lower bound (at least not asymptotically). The second one does.

15.2   Lower Bounds on Searching Lists

In Section 7.9 we presented an important lower bounds proof to show that the problem of sorting is $\Theta(n \log n)$ in the worst case. In Chapter 9 we discussed a number of algorithms to search in sorted and unsorted lists, but we did not provide any lower bounds proofs to this important problem. We will extend our pool of techniques for lower bounds proofs in this section by studying lower bounds for searching unsorted and sorted lists.

15.2.1   Searching in Unsorted Lists

Given an (unsorted) list $\mathbf{L}$ of n elements and a search key K, we seek to identify one element in $\mathbf{L}$ which has key value K, if any exists. For the rest of this discussion, we will assume that the key values for the elements in $\mathbf{L}$ are unique, that the set of all possible keys is totally ordered (that is, the operations $<$, $=$, and $>$ are defined for all pairs of key values), and that comparison is our only way to find the relative ordering of two keys. Our goal is to solve the problem using the minimum number of comparisons.

Given this definition for searching, we can easily come up with the standard sequential search algorithm, and we can also see that the lower bound for this problem is "obviously" n comparisons. (Keep in mind that the key K might not actually appear in the list.) However, lower bounds proofs are a bit slippery, and it is instructive to see how they can go wrong.

Theorem 15.1 *The lower bound for the problem of searching in an unsorted list is n comparisons.*

---

[3]Recalling the advice to be suspicious of any lower bounds proof that argues a given behavior "must" happen, this proof should be raising red flags. However, in this particular case the problem is so constrained that there really is no (better) alternative to this particular sequence of events.

Here is our first attempt at proving the theorem.

Proof 1: We will try a proof by contradiction. Assume an algorithm A exists that requires only $n - 1$ (or less) comparisons of K with elements of **L**. Because there are n elements of **L**, A must have avoided comparing K with **L[i]** for some value i. We can feed the algorithm an input with K in position i. Such an input is legal in our model, so the algorithm is incorrect. □

Is this proof correct? Unfortunately no. First of all, any given algorithm need not necessarily consistently skip any given position i in its $n - 1$ searches. For example, it is not necessary that all algorithms search the list from left to right. It is not even necessary that all algorithms search the same $n - 1$ positions first each time through the list.

We can try to dress up the proof as follows: **Proof 2:** On any given run of the algorithm, if $n - 1$ elements are compared against K, then *some* element position (call it position i) gets skipped. It is possible that K is in position i at that time, and will not be found. Therefore, n comparisons are required. □

Unfortunately, there is another error that needs to be fixed. It is not true that all algorithms for solving the problem must work by comparing elements of **L** against K. An algorithm might make useful progress by comparing elements of **L** against each other. For example, if we compare two elements of **L**, then compare the greater against K and find that this element is less than K, we know that the other element is also less than K. It seems intuitively obvious that such comparisons won't actually lead to a faster algorithm, but how do we know for sure? We somehow need to generalize the proof to account for this approach.

We will now present a useful abstraction for expressing the state of knowledge for the value relationships among a set of objects. A **total order** defines relationships within a collection of objects such that for every pair of objects, one is greater than the other. A **partially ordered set** or **poset** is a set on which only a partial order is defined. That is, there can be pairs of elements for which we cannot decide which is "greater". For our purpose here, the partial order is the state of our current knowledge about the objects, such that zero or more of the order relations between pairs of elements are known. We can represent this knowledge by drawing directed acyclic graphs (DAGs) showing the known relationships, as illustrated by Figure 15.1.

Proof 3: Initially, we know nothing about the relative order of the elements in **L**, or their relationship to K. So initially, we can view the n elements in **L** as being in n separate partial orders. Any comparison between two elements in **L** can affect the structure of the partial orders. This is somewhat similar to the UNION/FIND algorithm implemented using parent pointer trees, described in Section 6.2.

Now, every comparison between elements in **L** can at best combine two of the partial orders together. Any comparison between K and an element, say A, in **L** can at best eliminate the partial order that contains A. Thus, if we spend m comparisons

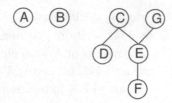

Figure 15.1 Illustration of using a poset to model our current knowledge of the relationships among a collection of objects. A directed acyclic graph (DAG) is used to draw the poset (assume all edges are directed downward). In this example, our knowledge is such that we don't know how A or B relate to any of the other objects. However, we know that both C and G are greater than E and F. Further, we know that C is greater than D, and that E is greater than F.

comparing elements in **L** we have at least $n - m$ partial orders. Every such partial order needs at least one comparison against K to make sure that K is not somewhere in that partial order. Thus, any algorithm must make at least n comparisons in the worst case.   □

15.2.2 Searching in Sorted Lists

We will now assume that list **L** is sorted. In this case, is linear search still optimal? Clearly no, but why not? Because we have additional information to work with that we do not have when the list is unsorted. We know that the standard binary search algorithm has a worst case cost of $O(\log n)$. Can we do better than this? We can prove that this is the best possible in the worst case with a proof similar to that used to show the lower bound on sorting.

Again we use the decision tree to model our algorithm. Unlike when searching an unsorted list, comparisons between elements of **L** tell us nothing new about their relative order, so we consider only comparisons between K and an element in **L**. At the root of the decision tree, our knowledge rules out no positions in **L**, so all are potential candidates. As we take branches in the decision tree based on the result of comparing K to an element in **L**, we gradually rule out potential candidates. Eventually we reach a leaf node in the tree representing the single position in **L** that can contain K. There must be at least $n + 1$ nodes in the tree because we have $n + 1$ distinct positions that K can be in (any position in **L**, plus not in **L** at all). Some path in the tree must be at least $\log n$ levels deep, and the deepest node in the tree represents the worst case for that algorithm. Thus, any algorithm on a sorted array requires at least $\Omega(\log n)$ comparisons in the worst case.

We can modify this proof to find the average cost lower bound. Again, we model algorithms using decision trees. Except now we are interested not in the depth of the deepest node (the worst case) and therefore the tree with the least-deepest node. Instead, we are interested in knowing what the minimum possible is for the "average depth" of the leaf nodes. Define the **total path length** as the sum of the levels for each node. The cost of an outcome is the level of the corresponding node plus 1. The average cost of the algorithm is the average cost of the outcomes (total path length/n). What is the tree with the least average depth? This is equivalent to the tree that corresponds to binary search. Thus, binary search is optimal in the average case.

While binary search is indeed an optimal algorithm for a sorted list in the worst and average cases when searching a sorted array, there are a number of circumstances that might lead us to select another algorithm instead. One possibility is that we know something about the distribution of the data in the array. We saw in Section 9.1 that if each position in **L** is equally likely to hold X (equivalently, the data are well distributed along the full key range), then an interpolation search is $\Theta(\log \log n)$ in the average case. If the data are not sorted, then using binary search requires us to pay the cost of sorting the list in advance, which is only worthwhile if many (at least $O(\log n)$) searches will be performed on the list. Binary search also requires that the list (even if sorted) be implemented using an array or some other structure that supports random access to all elements with equal cost. Finally, if we know all search requests in advance, we might prefer to sort the list by frequency and do linear search in extreme search distributions, as discussed in Section 9.2.

15.3 Finding the Maximum Value

How can we find the ith largest value in a sorted list? Obviously we just go to the ith position. But what if we have an unsorted list? Can we do better than to sort it? If we are looking for the minimum or maximum value, certainly we can do better than sorting the list. Is this true for the second biggest value? For the median value? In later sections we will examine those questions. For this section, we will continue our examination of lower bounds proofs by reconsidering the simple problem of finding the maximum value in an unsorted list.

Here is a simple algorithm for finding the largest value.

```
// Return position of largest value in "A" of size "n"
int largest(int A[], int n) {
  int currlarge = 0; // Holds largest element position
  for (int i=1; i<n; i++)    // For each array element
    if (A[currlarge] < A[i]) // if A[i] is larger
      currlarge = i;         //    remember its position
  return currlarge;          // Return largest position
}
```

Obviously this algorithm requires n comparisons. Is this optimal? It should be intuitively obvious that it is, but let us try to prove it. (Before reading further you might try writing down your own proof.)

Proof 1: The winner must compare against all other elements, so there must be $n - 1$ comparisons. □

This proof is clearly wrong, because the winner does not need to explicitly compare against all other elements to be recognized. For example, a standard single-elimination playoff sports tournament requires only $n - 1$ comparisons, and the winner does not play every opponent. So let's try again.

Proof 2: Only the winner does not lose. There are $n - 1$ losers. A single comparison generates (at most) one (new) loser. Therefore, there must be $n - 1$ comparisons. □

This proof is sound. However, it will be useful later to abstract this by introducing the concept of posets as we did in Section 15.2.1. We can view the maximum-finding problem as starting with a poset where there are no known relationships, so every member of the collection is in its own separate DAG of one element.

Proof 2a: To find the largest value, we start with a poset of n DAGs each with a single element, and we must build a poset having all elements in one DAG such that there is one maximum value (and by implication, $n - 1$ losers). We wish to connect the elements of the poset into a single DAG with the minimum number of links. This requires at least $n - 1$ links. A comparison provides at most one new link. Thus, a minimum of $n - 1$ comparisons must be made. □

What is the average cost of **largest**? Because it always does the same number of comparisons, clearly it must cost $n - 1$ comparisons. We can also consider the number of assignments that **largest** must do. Function **largest** might do an assignment on any iteration of the **for** loop.

Because this event does happen, or does not happen, if we are given no information about distribution we could guess that an assignment is made after each comparison with a probability of one half. But this is clearly wrong. In fact, **largest** does an assignment on the ith iteration if and only if $A[i]$ is the biggest of the the first i elements. Assuming all permutations are equally likely, the probability of this being true is $1/i$. Thus, the average number of assignments done is

$$1 + \sum_{i=2}^{n} \frac{1}{i} = \sum_{i=1}^{n} \frac{1}{i}$$

which is the Harmonic Series $\mathcal{H}_n$. $\mathcal{H}_n = \Theta(\log n)$. More exactly, $\mathcal{H}_n$ is close to $\log_e n$.

How "reliable" is this average? That is, how much will a given run of the program deviate from the mean cost? According to Čebyšev's Inequality, an observation will fall within two standard deviations of the mean at least 75% of the time. For **Largest**, the variance is

$$\mathcal{H}_n - \frac{\pi^2}{6} = \log_e n - \frac{\pi^2}{6}.$$

The standard deviation is thus about $\sqrt{\log_e n}$. So, 75% of the observations are between $\log_e n - 2\sqrt{\log_e n}$ and $\log_e n + 2\sqrt{\log_e n}$. Is this a narrow spread or a wide spread? Compared to the mean value, this spread is pretty wide, meaning that the number of assignments varies widely from run to run of the program.

15.4   Adversarial Lower Bounds Proofs

Our next problem will be finding the second largest in a collection of objects. Consider what happens in a standard single-elimination tournament. Even if we assume that the "best" team wins in every game, is the second best the one that loses in the finals? Not necessarily. We might expect that the second best must lose to the best, but they might meet at any time.

Let us go through our standard "algorithm for finding algorithms" by first proposing an algorithm, then a lower bound, and seeing if they match. Unlike our analysis for most problems, this time we are going to count the exact number of comparisons involved and attempt to minimize this count. A simple algorithm for finding the second largest is to first find the maximum (in $n - 1$ comparisons), discard it, and then find the maximum of the remaining elements (in $n - 2$ comparisons) for a total cost of $2n - 3$ comparisons. Is this optimal? That seems doubtful, but let us now proceed to the step of attempting to prove a lower bound.

Theorem 15.2 *The lower bound for finding the second largest value is* $2n - 3$.

Proof: Any element that loses to anything other than the maximum cannot be second. So, the only candidates for second place are those that lost to the maximum. Function **largest** might compare the maximum element to $n - 1$ others. Thus, we might need $n - 2$ additional comparisons to find the second largest.   □

This proof is wrong. It exhibits the **necessity fallacy**: "Our algorithm does something, therefore all algorithms solving the problem must do the same."

This leaves us with our best lower bounds argument at the moment being that finding the second largest must cost at least as much as finding the largest, or $n - 1$. Let us take another try at finding a better algorithm by adopting a strategy of divide and conquer. What if we break the list into halves, and run **largest** on each half? We can then compare the two winners (we have now used a total of $n - 1$ comparisons), and remove the winner from its half. Another call to **largest** on the winner's half yields its second best. A final comparison against the winner of the other half gives us the true second place winner. The total cost is $\lceil 3n/2 \rceil - 2$. Is this optimal? What if we break the list into four pieces? The best would be $\lceil 5n/4 \rceil$. What if we break the list into eight pieces? Then the cost would be about $\lceil 9n/8 \rceil$. Notice that as we break the list into more parts, comparisons among the winners of the parts becomes a larger concern.

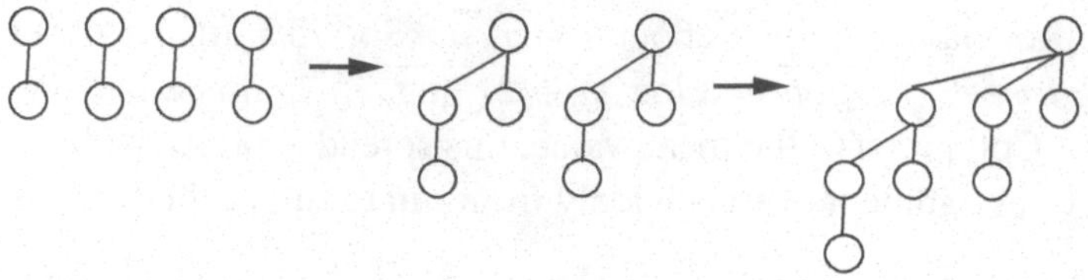

Figure 15.2 An example of building a binomial tree. Pairs of elements are combined by choosing one of the parents to be the root of the entire tree. Given two trees of size four, one of the roots is chosen to be the root for the combined tree of eight nodes.

Looking at this another way, the only candidates for second place are losers to the eventual winner, and our goal is to have as few of these as possible. So we need to keep track of the set of elements that have lost in direct comparison to the (eventual) winner. We also observe that we learn the most from a comparison when both competitors are known to be larger than the same number of other values. So we would like to arrange our comparisons to be against "equally strong" competitors. We can do all of this with a **binomial tree**. A binomial tree of height m has 2^m nodes. Either it is a single node (if $m = 0$), or else it is two height $m - 1$ binomial trees with one tree's root becoming a child of the other. Figure 15.2 illustrates how a binomial tree with eight nodes would be constructed.

The resulting algorithm is simple in principle: Build the binomial tree for all n elements, and then compare the $\lceil \log n \rceil$ children of the root to find second place. We could store the binomial tree as an explicit tree structure, and easily build it in time linear on the number of comparisons as each comparison requires one link be added. Because the shape of a binomial tree is heavily constrained, we can also store the binomial tree implicitly in an array, much as we do for a heap. Assume that two trees, each with 2^k nodes, are in the array. The first tree is in positions 1 to 2^k. The second tree is in positions $2^k + 1$ to 2^{k+1}. The root of each subtree is in the final array position for that subtree.

To join two trees, we simply compare the roots of the subtrees. If necessary, swap the subtrees so that tree with the the larger root element becomes the second subtree. This trades space (we only need space for the data values, no node pointers) for time (in the worst case, all of the data swapping might cost $O(n \log n)$, though this does not affect the number of comparisons required). Note that for some applications, this is an important observation that the array's data swapping requires no comparisons. If a comparison is simply a check between two integers, then of course moving half the values within the array is too expensive. But if a comparison requires that a competition be held between two sports teams, then the cost of a little bit (or even a lot) of book keeping becomes irrelevent.

Because the binomial tree's root has $\log n$ children, and building the tree requires $n - 1$ comparisons, the number of comparisons required by this algorithm is $n + \lceil \log n \rceil - 2$. This is clearly better than our previous algorithm. Is it optimal?

We now go back to trying to improve the lower bounds proof. To do this, we introduce the concept of an **adversary**. The adversary's job is to make an algorithm's cost as high as possible. Imagine that the adversary keeps a list of all possible inputs. We view the algorithm as asking the adversary for information about the algorithm's input. The adversary may never lie, in that its answer must be consistent with the previous answers. But it is permitted to "rearrange" the input as it sees fit in order to drive the total cost for the algorithm as high as possible. In particular, when the algorithm asks a question, the adversary must answer in a way that is consistent with at least one remaining input. The adversary then crosses out all remaining inputs inconsistent with that answer. Keep in mind that there is not really an entity within the computer program that is the adversary, and we don't actually modify the program. The adversary operates merely as an analysis device, to help us reason about the program.

As an example of the adversary concept, consider the standard game of Hangman. Player A picks a word and tells player B how many letters the word has. Player B guesses various letters. If B guesses a letter in the word, then A will indicate which position(s) in the word have the letter. Player B is permitted to make only so many guesses of letters not in the word before losing.

In the Hangman game example, the adversary is imagined to hold a dictionary of words of some selected length. Each time the player guesses a letter, the adversary consults the dictionary and decides if more words will be eliminated by accepting the letter (and indicating which positions it holds) or saying that its not in the word. The adversary can make any decision it chooses, so long as at least one word in the dictionary is consistent with all of the decisions. In this way, the adversary can hope to make the player guess as many letters as possible.

Before explaining how the adversary plays a role in our lower bounds proof, first observe that at least $n - 1$ values must lose at least once. This requires at least $n - 1$ compares. In addition, at least $k - 1$ values must lose to the second largest value. That is, k direct losers to the winner must be compared. There must be at least $n + k - 2$ comparisons. The question is: How low can we make k?

Call the **strength** of element $A[i]$ the number of elements that $A[i]$ is (known to be) bigger than. If $A[i]$ has strength a, and $A[j]$ has strength b, then the winner has strength $a + b + 1$. The algorithm gets to know the (current) strengths for each element, and it gets to pick which two elements are compared next. The adversary gets to decide who wins any given comparison. What strategy by the adversary would cause the algorithm to learn the least from any given comparison? It should minimize the rate at which any element improves it strength. It can do this by making the element with the greater strength win at every comparison. This is a "fair" use of an adversary in that it represents the results of providing a worst-case input for that given algorithm.

To minimize the effects of worst-case behavior, the algorithm's best strategy is to maximize the minimum improvement in strength by balancing the strengths of any two competitors. From the algorithm's point of view, the best outcome is that an element doubles in strength. This happens whenever $a = b$, where a and b are the strengths of the two elements being compared. All strengths begin at zero, so the winner must make at least k comparisons when $2^{k-1} < n \le 2^k$. Thus, there must be at least $n + \lceil \log n \rceil - 2$ comparisons. So our algorithm is optimal.

15.5   State Space Lower Bounds Proofs

We now consider the problem of finding both the minimum and the maximum from an (unsorted) list of values. This might be useful if we want to know the range of a collection of values to be plotted, for the purpose of drawing the plot's scales. Of course we could find them independently in $2n - 2$ comparisons. A slight modification is to find the maximum in $n - 1$ comparisons, remove it from the list, and then find the minimum in $n - 2$ further comparisons for a total of $2n - 3$ comparisons. Can we do better than this?

Before continuing, think a moment about how this problem of finding the minimum and the maximum compares to the problem of the last section, that of finding the second biggest value (and by implication, the maximum). Which of these two problems do you think is harder? It is probably not at all obvious to you that one problem is harder or easier than the other. There is intuition that argues for either case. On the one hand intuition might argue that the process of finding the maximum should tell you something about the second biggest value, more than that process should tell you about the minimum value. On the other hand, any given comparison tells you something about which of two can be a candidate for maximum value, and which can be a candidate for minimum value, thus making progress in both directions.

We will start by considering a simple divide-and-conquer approach to finding the minimum and maximum. Split the list into two parts and find the minimum and maximum elements in each part. Then compare the two minimums and maximums to each other with a further two comparisons to get the final result. The algorithm is shown in Figure 15.3.

The cost of this algorithm can be modeled by the following recurrence.

$$\mathbf{T}(n) = \begin{cases} 0 & n = 1 \\ 1 & n = 2 \\ \mathbf{T}(\lfloor n/2 \rfloor) + \mathbf{T}(\lceil n/2 \rceil) + 2 & n > 2 \end{cases}$$

This is a rather interesting recurrence, and its solution ranges between $3n/2 - 2$ (when $n = 2^i$ or $n = 2^1 \pm 1$) and $5n/3 - 2$ (when $n = 3 \times 2^i$). We can infer from this behavior that how we divide the list affects the performance of the algorithm.

```
// Return the minimum and maximum values in A
// between positions l and r
template <typename E>
void MinMax(E A[], int l, int r, E& Min, E& Max) {
  if (l == r) {        // n=1
    Min = A[r];
    Max = A[r];
  }
  else if (l+1 == r) { // n=2
    Min = min(A[l], A[r]);
    Max = max(A[l], A[r]);
  }
  else {               // n>2
    int Min1, Min2, Max1, Max2;
    int mid = (l + r)/2;
    MinMax(A, l, mid, Min1, Max1);
    MinMax(A, mid+1, r, Min2, Max2);
    Min = min(Min1, Min2);
    Max = max(Max1, Max2);
  }
}
```

Figure 15.3 Recursive algorithm for finding the minimum and maximum values in an array.

For example, what if we have six items in the list? If we break the list into two sublists of three elements, the cost would be 8. If we break the list into a sublist of size two and another of size four, then the cost would only be 7.

With divide and conquer, the best algorithm is the one that minimizes the work, not necessarily the one that balances the input sizes. One lesson to learn from this example is that it can be important to pay attention to what happens for small sizes of n, because any division of the list will eventually produce many small lists.

We can model all possible divide-and-conquer strategies for this problem with the following recurrence.

$$\mathbf{T}(n) = \begin{cases} 0 & n = 1 \\ 1 & n = 2 \\ \min_{1 \le k \le n-1}\{\mathbf{T}(k) + \mathbf{T}(n - k)\} + 2 & n > 2 \end{cases}$$

That is, we want to find a way to break up the list that will minimize the total work. If we examine various ways of breaking up small lists, we will eventually recognize that breaking the list into a sublist of size 2 and a sublist of size $n - 2$ will always produce results as good as any other division. This strategy yields the following recurrence.

$$\mathbf{T}(n) = \begin{cases} 0 & n = 1 \\ 1 & n = 2 \\ \mathbf{T}(n - 2) + 3 & n > 2 \end{cases}$$

This recurrence (and the corresponding algorithm) yields $\mathbf{T}(n) = \lceil 3n/2 \rceil - 2$ comparisons. Is this optimal? We now introduce yet another tool to our collection of lower bounds proof techniques: The state space proof.

We will model our algorithm by defining a **state** that the algorithm must be in at any given instant. We can then define the start state, the end state, and the transitions between states that any algorithm can support. From this, we will reason about the minimum number of states that the algorithm must go through to get from the start to the end, to reach a state space lower bound.

At any given instant, we can track the following four categories of elements:

- Untested: Elements that have not been tested.
- Winners: Elements that have won at least once, and never lost.
- Losers: Elements that have lost at least once, and never won.
- Middle: Elements that have both won and lost at least once.

We define the current state to be a vector of four values, (U, W, L, M) for untested, winners, losers, and middles, respectively. For a set of n elements, the initial state of the algorithm is $(n, 0, 0, 0)$ and the end state is $(0, 1, 1, n-2)$. Thus, every run for any algorithm must go from state $(n, 0, 0, 0)$ to state $(0, 1, 1, n-2)$. We also observe that once an element is identified to be a middle, it can then be ignored because it can neither be the minimum nor the maximum.

Given that there are four types of elements, there are 10 types of comparison. Comparing with a middle cannot be more efficient than other comparisons, so we should ignore those, leaving six comparisons of interest. We can enumerate the effects of each comparison type as follows. If we are in state (i, j, k, l) and we have a comparison, then the state changes are as follows.

$$
\begin{array}{llllll}
U:U & (i-2, & j+1, & k+1, & l) \\
W:W & (i, & j-1, & k, & l+1) \\
L:L & (i, & j, & k-1, & l+1) \\
L:U & (i-1, & j+1, & k, & l) \\
\quad or & (i-1, & j, & k, & l+1) \\
W:U & (i-1, & j, & k+1, & l) \\
\quad or & (i-1, & j, & k, & l+1) \\
W:L & (i, & j, & k, & l) \\
\quad or & (i, & j-1, & k-1, & l+2) \\
\end{array}
$$

Now, let us consider what an adversary will do for the various comparisons. The adversary will make sure that each comparison does the least possible amount of work in taking the algorithm toward the goal state. For example, comparing a winner to a loser is of no value because the worst case result is always to learn nothing new (the winner remains a winner and the loser remains a loser). Thus, only the following five transitions are of interest:

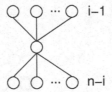

Figure 15.4 The poset that represents the minimum information necessary to determine the ith element in a list. We need to know which element has $i - 1$ values less and $n - i$ values more, but we do not need to know the relationships among the elements with values less or greater than the ith element.

$$
\begin{array}{llllll}
U : U & (i - 2, & j + 1, & k + 1, & l) \\
L : U & (i - 1, & j + 1, & k, & l) \\
W : U & (i - 1, & j, & k + 1, & l) \\
\hline
W : W & (i, & j - 1, & k, & l + 1) \\
L : L & (i, & j, & k - 1, & l + 1)
\end{array}
$$

Only the last two transition types increase the number of middles, so there must be $n - 2$ of these. The number of untested elements must go to 0, and the first transition is the most efficient way to do this. Thus, $\lceil n/2 \rceil$ of these are required. Our conclusion is that the minimum possible number of transitions (comparisons) is $n + \lceil n/2 \rceil - 2$. Thus, our algorithm is optimal.

15.6 Finding the ith Best Element

We now tackle the problem of finding the ith best element in a list. As observed earlier, one solution is to sort the list and simply look in the ith position. However, this process provides considerably more information than we need to solve the problem. The minimum amount of information that we actually need to know can be visualized as shown in Figure 15.4. That is, all we need to know is the $i - 1$ items less than our desired value, and the $n - i$ items greater. We do not care about the relative order within the upper and lower groups. So can we find the required information faster than by first sorting? Looking at the lower bound, can we tighten that beyond the trivial lower bound of n comparisons? We will focus on the specific question of finding the median element (i.e., the element with rank $n/2$), because the resulting algorithm can easily be modified to find the ith largest value for any i.

Looking at the Quicksort algorithm might give us some insight into solving the median problem. Recall that Quicksort works by selecting a pivot value, partitioning the array into those elements less than the pivot and those greater than the pivot, and moving the pivot to its proper location in the array. If the pivot is in position i, then we are done. If not, we can solve the subproblem recursively by only considering one of the sublists. That is, if the pivot ends up in position $k > i$, then we

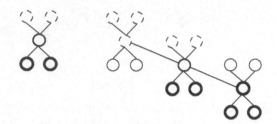

Figure 15.5 A method for finding a pivot for partitioning a list that guarantees at least a fixed fraction of the list will be in each partition. We divide the list into groups of five elements, and find the median for each group. We then recursively find the median of these $n/5$ medians. The median of five elements is guaranteed to have at least two in each partition. The median of three medians from a collection of 15 elements is guaranteed to have at least five elements in each partition.

simply solve by finding the ith best element in the left partition. If the pivot is at position $k < i$, then we wish to find the $i - k$th element in the right partition.

What is the worst case cost of this algorithm? As with Quicksort, we get bad performance if the pivot is the first or last element in the array. This would lead to possibly $O(n^2)$ performance. However, if the pivot were to always cut the array in half, then our cost would be modeled by the recurrence $\mathbf{T}(n) = \mathbf{T}(n/2) + n = 2n$ or $O(n)$ cost.

Finding the average cost requires us to use a recurrence with full history, similar to the one we used to model the cost of Quicksort. If we do this, we will find that $\mathbf{T}(n)$ is in $O(n)$ in the average case.

Is it possible to modify our algorithm to get worst-case linear time? To do this, we need to pick a pivot that is guaranteed to discard a fixed fraction of the elements. We cannot just choose a pivot at random, because doing so will not meet this guarantee. The ideal situation would be if we could pick the median value for the pivot each time. But that is essentially the same problem that we are trying to solve to begin with.

Notice, however, that if we choose any constant c, and then if we pick the median from a sample of size n/c, then we can guarantee that we will discard at least $n/2c$ elements. Actually, we can do better than this by selecting small subsets of a constant size (so we can find the median of each in constant time), and then taking the median of these medians. Figure 15.5 illustrates this idea. This observation leads directly to the following algorithm.

- Choose the $n/5$ medians for groups of five elements from the list. Choosing the median of five items can be done in constant time.
- Recursively, select M, the median of the $n/5$ medians-of-fives.
- Partition the list into those elements larger and smaller than M.

While selecting the median in this way is guaranteed to eliminate a fraction of the elements (leaving at most $\lceil (7n-5)/10 \rceil$ elements left), we still need to be sure that our recursion yields a linear-time algorithm. We model the algorithm by the following recurrence.

$$\mathbf{T}(n) \le \mathbf{T}(\lceil n/5 \rceil) + \mathbf{T}(\lceil (7n-5)/10 \rceil) + 6\lceil n/5 \rceil + n - 1.$$

The $\mathbf{T}(\lceil n/5 \rceil)$ term comes from computing the median of the medians-of-fives, the $6\lceil n/5 \rceil$ term comes from the cost to calculate the median-of-fives (exactly six comparisons for each group of five element), and the $\mathbf{T}(\lceil (7n-5)/10 \rceil)$ term comes from the recursive call of the remaining (up to) 70% of the elements that might be left.

We will prove that this recurrence is linear by assuming that it is true for some constant r, and then show that $\mathbf{T}(n) \le rn$ for all n greater than some bound.

$$
\begin{aligned}
\mathbf{T}(n) &\le \mathbf{T}(\lceil \tfrac{n}{5} \rceil) + \mathbf{T}(\lceil \tfrac{7n-5}{10} \rceil) + 6\lceil \tfrac{n}{5} \rceil + n - 1 \\
&\le r(\tfrac{n}{5} + 1) + r(\tfrac{7n-5}{10} + 1) + 6(\tfrac{n}{5} + 1) + n - 1 \\
&\le (\tfrac{r}{5} + \tfrac{7r}{10} + \tfrac{11}{5})n + \tfrac{3r}{2} + 5 \\
&\le \tfrac{9r+22}{10} n + \tfrac{3r+10}{2}.
\end{aligned}
$$

This is true for $r \ge 23$ and $n \ge 380$. This provides a base case that allows us to use induction to prove that $\forall n \ge 380, \mathbf{T}(n) \le 23n$.

In reality, this algorithm is not practical because its constant factor costs are so high. So much work is being done to guarantee linear time performance that it is more efficient on average to rely on chance to select the pivot, perhaps by picking it at random or picking the middle value out of the current subarray.

15.7 Optimal Sorting

We conclude this section with an effort to find the sorting algorithm with the absolute fewest possible comparisons. It might well be that the result will not be practical for a general-purpose sorting algorithm. But recall our analogy earlier to sports tournaments. In sports, a "comparison" between two teams or individuals means doing a competition between the two. This is fairly expensive (at least compared to some minor book keeping in a computer), and it might be worth trading a fair amount of book keeping to cut down on the number of games that need to be played. What if we want to figure out how to hold a tournament that will give us the exact ordering for all teams in the fewest number of total games? Of course, we are assuming that the results of each game will be "accurate" in that we assume not only that the outcome of A playing B would always be the same (at least over the time period of the tournament), but that transitivity in the results also holds. In practice these are unrealistic assumptions, but such assumptions are implicitly part of many tournament organizations. Like most tournament organizers, we can simply accept these assumptions and come up with an algorithm for playing the games that gives us some rank ordering based on the results we obtain.

Recall Insertion Sort, where we put element i into a sorted sublist of the first $i-1$ elements. What if we modify the standard Insertion Sort algorithm to use binary search to locate where the ith element goes in the sorted sublist? This algorithm is called **binary insert sort**. As a general-purpose sorting algorithm, this is not practical because we then have to (on average) move about $i/2$ elements to make room for the newly inserted element in the sorted sublist. But if we count *only* comparisons, binary insert sort is pretty good. And we can use some ideas from binary insert sort to get closer to an algorithm that uses the absolute minimum number of comparisons needed to sort.

Consider what happens when we run binary insert sort on five elements. How many comparisons do we need to do? We can insert the second element with one comparison, the third with two comparisons, and the fourth with 2 comparisons. When we insert the fifth element into the sorted list of four elements, we need to do three comparisons in the worst case. Notice exactly what happens when we attempt to do this insertion. We compare the fifth element against the second. If the fifth is bigger, we have to compare it against the third, and if it is bigger we have to compare it against the fourth. In general, when is binary search most efficient? When we have $2^i - 1$ elements in the list. It is least efficient when we have 2^i elements in the list. So, we can do a bit better if we arrange our insertions to avoid inserting an element into a list of size 2^i if possible.

Figure 15.6 illustrates a different organization for the comparisons that we might do. First we compare the first and second element, and the third and fourth elements. The two winners are then compared, yielding a binomial tree. We can view this as a (sorted) chain of three elements, with element A hanging off from the root. If we then insert element B into the sorted chain of three elements, we will end up with one of the two posets shown on the right side of Figure 15.6, at a cost of 2 comparisons. We can then merge A into the chain, for a cost of two comparisons (because we already know that it is smaller then either one or two elements, we are actually merging it into a list of two or three elements). Thus, the total number of comparisons needed to sort the five elements is at most seven instead of eight.

If we have ten elements to sort, we can first make five pairs of elements (using five compares) and then sort the five winners using the algorithm just described (using seven more compares). Now all we need to do is to deal with the original losers. We can generalize this process for any number of elements as:

- Pair up all the nodes with $\lfloor \frac{n}{2} \rfloor$ comparisons.

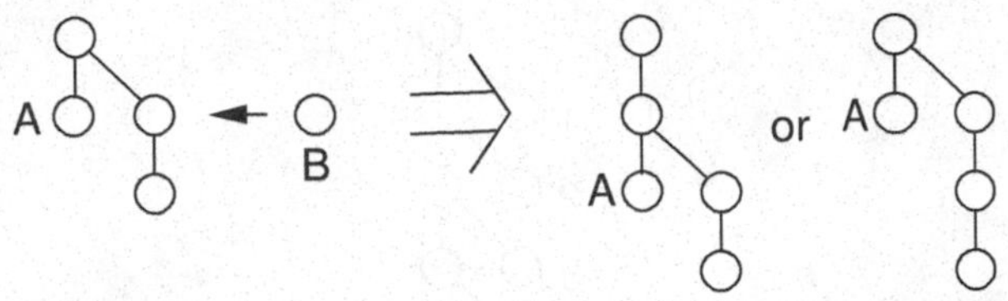

Figure 15.6 Organizing comparisons for sorting five elements. First we order two pairs of elements, and then compare the two winners to form a binomial tree of four elements. The original loser to the root is labeled A, and the remaining three elements form a sorted chain. We then insert element B into the sorted chain. Finally, we put A into the resulting chain to yield a final sorted list.

- Recursively sort the winners.
- Fold in the losers.

We use binary insert to place the losers. However, we are free to choose the best ordering for inserting, keeping in mind the fact that binary search has the same cost for 2^i through $2^{i+1} - 1$ items. For example, binary search requires three comparisons in the worst case for lists of size 4, 5, 6, or 7. So we pick the order of inserts to optimize the binary searches, which means picking an order that avoids growing a sublist size such that it crosses the boundary on list size to require an additional comparison. This sort is called **merge insert sort**, and also known as the Ford and Johnson sort.

For ten elements, given the poset shown in Figure 15.7 we fold in the last four elements (labeled 1 to 4) in the order Element 3, Element 4, Element 1, and finally Element 2. Element 3 will be inserted into a list of size three, costing two comparisons. Depending on where Element 3 then ends up in the list, Element 4 will now be inserted into a list of size 2 or 3, costing two comparisons in either case. Depending on where Elements 3 and 4 are in the list, Element 1 will now be inserted into a list of size 5, 6, or 7, all of which requires three comparisons to place in sort order. Finally, Element 2 will be inserted into a list of size 5, 6, or 7.

Merge insert sort is pretty good, but is it optimal? Recall from Section 7.9 that no sorting algorithm can be faster than $\Omega(n \log n)$. To be precise, the **information theoretic lower bound** for sorting can be proved to be $\lceil \log n! \rceil$. That is, we can prove a lower bound of exactly $\lceil \log n! \rceil$ comparisons. Merge insert sort gives us a number of comparisons equal to this information theoretic lower bound for all values up to $n = 12$. At $n = 12$, merge insert sort requires 30 comparisons while the information theoretic lower bound is only 29 comparisons. However, for such a small number of elements, it is possible to do an exhaustive study of every possible arrangement of comparisons. It turns out that there is in fact no possible arrangement of comparisons that makes the lower bound less than 30 comparisons when $n = 12$. Thus, the information theoretic lower bound is an underestimate in this case, because 30 really is the best that can be done.

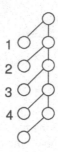

Figure 15.7 Merge insert sort for ten elements. First five pairs of elements are compared. The five winners are then sorted. This leaves the elements labeled 1-4 to be sorted into the chain made by the remaining six elements.

Call the optimal worst cost for n elements $S(n)$. We know that $S(n + 1) \leq S(n) + \lceil \log(n+1) \rceil$ because we could sort n elements and use binary insert for the last one. For all n and m, $S(n + m) \leq S(n) + S(m) + M(m, n)$ where $M(m, n)$ is the best time to merge two sorted lists. For $n = 47$, it turns out that we can do better by splitting the list into pieces of size 5 and 42, and then merging. Thus, merge sort is not quite optimal. But it is extremely good, and nearly optimal for smallish numbers of elements.

15.8 Further Reading

Much of the material in this book is also covered in many other textbooks on data structures and algorithms. The biggest exception is that not many other textbooks cover lower bounds proofs in any significant detail, as is done in this chapter. Those that do focus on the same example problems (search and selection) because it tells such a tight and compelling story regarding related topics, while showing off the major techniques for lower bounds proofs. Two examples of such textbooks are "Computer Algorithms" by Baase and Van Gelder [BG00], and "Compared to What?" by Gregory J.E. Rawlins [Raw92]. "Fundamentals of Algorithmics" by Brassard and Bratley [BB96] also covers lower bounds proofs.

15.9 Exercises

15.1 Consider the so-called "algorithm for algorithms" in Section 15.1. Is this really an algorithm? Review the definition of an algorithm from Section 1.4. Which parts of the definition apply, and which do not? Is the "algorithm for algorithms" a heuristic for finding a good algorithm? Why or why not?

15.2 Single-elimination tournaments are notorious for their scheduling difficulties. Imagine that you are organizing a tournament for n basketball teams (you may assume that $n = 2^i$ for some integer i). We will further simplify things by assuming that each game takes less than an hour, and that each team can be scheduled for a game every hour if necessary. (Note that everything said here about basketball courts is also true about processors in a parallel algorithm to solve the maximum-finding problem).

    (a) How many basketball courts do we need to insure that every team can play whenever we want to minimize the total tournament time?

    (b) How long will the tournament be in this case?

    (c) What is the total number of "court-hours" available? How many total hours are courts being used? How many total court-hours are unused?

    (d) Modify the algorithm in such a way as to reduce the total number of courts needed, by perhaps not letting every team play whenever possible. This will increase the total hours of the tournament, but try to keep the increase as low as possible. For your new algorithm, how long is the tournament, how many courts are needed, how many total court-hours are available, how many court-hours are used, and how many unused?

15.3 Explain why the cost of splitting a list of six into two lists of three to find the minimum and maximum elements requires eight comparisons, while splitting the list into a list of two and a list of four costs only seven comparisons.

15.4 Write out a table showing the number of comparisons required to find the minimum and maximum for all divisions for all values of $n \leq 13$.

15.5 Present an adversary argument as a lower bounds proof to show that $n - 1$ comparisons are necessary to find the maximum of n values in the worst case.

15.6 Present an adversary argument as a lower bounds proof to show that n comparisons are necessary in the worst case when searching for an element with value X (if one exists) from among n elements.

15.7 Section 15.6 claims that by picking a pivot that always discards at least a fixed fraction c of the remaining array, the resulting algorithm will be linear. Explain why this is true. Hint: The Master Theorem (Theorem 14.1) might help you.

15.8 Show that any comparison-based algorithm for finding the median must use at least $n - 1$ comparisons.

15.9 Show that any comparison-based algorithm for finding the second-smallest of n values can be extended to find the smallest value also, without requiring any more comparisons to be performed.

15.10 Show that any comparison-based algorithm for sorting can be modified to remove all duplicates without requiring any more comparisons to be performed.

15.11 Show that any comparison-based algorithm for removing duplicates from a list of values must use $\Omega(n \log n)$ comparisons.

15.12 Given a list of n elements, an element of the list is a *majority* if it appears more than $n/2$ times.

    (a) Assume that the input is a list of integers. Design an algorithm that is linear in the number of integer-integer comparisons in the worst case that will find and report the majority if one exists, and report that there is no majority if no such integer exists in the list.

    (b) Assume that the input is a list of elements that have no relative ordering, such as colors or fruit. So all that you can do when you compare two elements is ask if they are the same or not. Design an algorithm that is linear in the number of element-element comparisons in the worst case that will find a majority if one exists, and report that there is no majority if no such element exists in the list.

15.13 Given an undirected graph G, the problem is to determine whether or not G is connected. Use an adversary argument to prove that it is necessary to look at all $(n^2 - n)/2$ potential edges in the worst case.

15.14 **(a)** Write an equation that describes the average cost for finding the median.

      (b) Solve your equation from part (a).

15.15 **(a)** Write an equation that describes the average cost for finding the ith-smallest value in an array. This will be a function of both n and i, $\mathbf{T}(n, i)$.

      (b) Solve your equation from part (a).

15.16 Suppose that you have n objects that have identical weight, except for one that is a bit heavier than the others. You have a balance scale. You can place objects on each side of the scale and see which collection is heavier. Your goal is to find the heavier object, with the minimum number of weighings. Find and prove matching upper and lower bounds for this problem.

15.17 Imagine that you are organizing a basketball tournament for 10 teams. You know that the merge insert sort will give you a full ranking of the 10 teams with the minimum number of games played. Assume that each game can be played in less than an hour, and that any team can play as many games in a row as necessary. Show a schedule for this tournament that also attempts to minimize the number of total hours for the tournament and the number of courts used. If you have to make a tradeoff between the two, then attempt to minimize the total number of hours that basketball courts are idle.

15.18 Write the complete algorithm for the merge insert sort sketched out in Section 15.7.

15.19 Here is a suggestion for what might be a truly optimal sorting algorithm. Pick the best set of comparisons for input lists of size 2. Then pick the best set of comparisons for size 3, size 4, size 5, and so on. Combine them together into one program with a big case statement. Is this an algorithm?

15.10   Projects

15.1 Implement the median-finding algorithm of Section 15.6. Then, modify this algorithm to allow finding the ith element for any value $i < n$.

16

Patterns of Algorithms

This chapter presents several fundamental topics related to the theory of algorithms. Included are dynamic programming (Section 16.1), randomized algorithms (Section 16.2), and the concept of a transform (Section 16.3.5). Each of these can be viewed as an example of an "algorithmic pattern" that is commonly used for a wide variety of applications. In addition, Section 16.3 presents a number of numerical algorithms. Section 16.2 on randomized algorithms includes the Skip List (Section 16.2.2). The Skip List is a probabilistic data structure that can be used to implement the dictionary ADT. The Skip List is no more complicated than the BST. Yet it often outperforms the BST because the Skip List's efficiency is not tied to the values or insertion order of the dataset being stored.

16.1 Dynamic Programming

Consider again the recursive function for computing the nth Fibonacci number.

```
long fibr(int n) { // Recursive Fibonacci generator
  // fibr(46) is largest value that fits in a long
  Assert((n > 0) && (n < 47), "Input out of range");
  if ((n == 1) || (n == 2)) return 1; // Base cases
  return fibr(n-1) + fibr(n-2);        // Recursion
}
```

The cost of this algorithm (in terms of function calls) is the size of the nth Fibonacci number itself, which our analysis of Section 14.2 showed to be exponential (approximately $n^{1.62}$). Why is this so expensive? Primarily because two recursive calls are made by the function, and the work that they do is largely redundant. That is, each of the two calls is recomputing most of the series, as is each sub-call, and so on. Thus, the smaller values of the function are being recomputed a huge number of times. If we could eliminate this redundancy, the cost would be greatly reduced. The approach that we will use can also improve any algorithm that spends most of its time recomputing common subproblems.

One way to accomplish this goal is to keep a table of values, and first check the table to see if the computation can be avoided. Here is a straightforward example of doing so.

```
int Fibrt(int n, int* Values) {
  // Assume Values has at least n slots, and all
  // slots are initialized to 0
  if (n <= 1) return 1;                 // Base case
  if (Values[n] != 0)
    Values[n] = Fibr(n-1, Values) + Fibr(n-2, Values);
  return Values[n];
}
```

This version of the algorithm will not compute a value more than once, so its cost should be linear. Of course, we didn't actually need to use a table storing all of the values, since future computations do not need access to all prior subproblems. Instead, we could build the value by working from 0 and 1 up to n rather than backwards from n down to 0 and 1. Going up from the bottom we only need to store the previous two values of the function, as is done by our iterative version.

```
long fibi(int n) { // Iterative Fibonacci generator
  // fibi(46) is largest value that fits in a long
  Assert((n > 0) && (n < 47), "Input out of range");
  long past, prev, curr;   // Store temporary values
  past = prev = curr = 1;      // initialize
  for (int i=3; i<=n; i++) { // Compute next value
    past = prev;               // past holds fibi(i-2)
    prev = curr;               // prev holds fibi(i-1)
    curr = past + prev;        // curr now holds fibi(i)
  }
  return curr;
}
```

Recomputing of subproblems comes up in many algorithms. It is not so common that we can store only a few prior results as we did for **Fibi**. Thus, there are many times where storing a complete table of subresults will be useful.

This approach to designing an algorithm that works by storing a table of results for subproblems is called dynamic programming. The name is somewhat arcane, because it doesn't bear much obvious similarity to the process that is taking place when storing subproblems in a table. However, it comes originally from the field of dynamic control systems, which got its start before what we think of as computer programming. The act of storing precomputed values in a table for later reuse is referred to as "programming" in that field.

Dynamic programming is a powerful alternative to the standard principle of divide and conquer. In divide and conquer, a problem is split into subproblems, the subproblems are solved (independently), and then recombined into a solution for the problem being solved. Dynamic programming is appropriate whenever (1) subproblems are solved repeatedly, and (2) we can find a suitable way of doing the necessary bookkeeping. Dynamic programming algorithms are usually not implemented by simply using a table to store subproblems for recursive calls (i.e., going backwards as is done by `Fibrt`). Instead, such algorithms are typically implemented by building the table of subproblems from the bottom up. Thus, `Fibi` better represents the most common form of dynamic programming than does `Fibrt`, even though it doesn't use the complete table.

16.1.1 The Knapsack Problem

We will next consider a problem that appears with many variations in a variety of commercial settings. Many businesses need to package items with the greatest efficiency. One way to describe this basic idea is in terms of packing items into a knapsack, and so we will refer to this as the Knapsack Problem. We will first define a particular formulation of the knapsack problem, and then we will discuss an algorithm to solve it based on dynamic programming. We will see other versions of the knapsack problem in the exercises and in Chapter 17.

Assume that we have a knapsack with a certain amount of space that we will define using integer value K. We also have n items each with a certain size such that that item i has integer size k_i. The problem is to find a subset of the n items whose sizes exactly sum to K, if one exists. For example, if our knapsack has capacity $K = 5$ and the two items are of size $k_1 = 2$ and $k_2 = 4$, then no such subset exists. But if we add a third item of size $k_3 = 1$, then we can fill the knapsack exactly with the first and third items. We can define the problem more formally as: Find $S \subset \{1, 2, ..., n\}$ such that

$$\sum_{i \in S} k_i = K.$$

Example 16.1 Assume that we are given a knapsack of size $K = 163$ and 10 items of sizes 4, 9, 15, 19, 27, 44, 54, 68, 73, 101. Can we find a subset of the items that exactly fills the knapsack? You should take a few minutes and try to do this before reading on and looking at the answer.

One solution to the problem is: 19, 27, 44, 73.

Example 16.2 Having solved the previous example for knapsack of size 163, how hard is it now to solve for a knapsack of size 164?

Unfortunately, knowing the answer for 163 is of almost no use at all when solving for 164. One solution is: 9, 54, 101.

If you tried solving these examples, you probably found yourself doing a lot of trial-and-error and a lot of backtracking. To come up with an algorithm, we want an organized way to go through the possible subsets. Is there a way to make the problem smaller, so that we can apply divide and conquer? We essentially have two parts to the input: The knapsack size K and the n items. It probably will not do us much good to try and break the knapsack into pieces and solve the sub-pieces (since we already saw that knowing the answer for a knapsack of size 163 did nothing to help us solve the problem for a knapsack of size 164).

So, what can we say about solving the problem with or without the nth item? This seems to lead to a way to break down the problem. If the nth item is not needed for a solution (that is, if we can solve the problem with the first $n-1$ items) then we can also solve the problem when the nth item is available (we just ignore it). On the other hand, if we do include the nth item as a member of the solution subset, then we now would need to solve the problem with the first $n-1$ items and a knapsack of size $K - k_n$ (since the nth item is taking up k_n space in the knapsack).

To organize this process, we can define the problem in terms of two parameters: the knapsack size K and the number of items n. Denote a given instance of the problem as $P(n, K)$. Now we can say that $P(n, K)$ has a solution if and only if there exists a solution for either $P(n-1, K)$ or $P(n-1, K-k_n)$. That is, we can solve $P(n, K)$ only if we can solve one of the sub problems where we use or do not use the nth item. Of course, the ordering of the items is arbitrary. We just need to give them some order to keep things straight.

Continuing this idea, to solve any subproblem of size $n-1$, we need only to solve two subproblems of size $n-2$. And so on, until we are down to only one item that either fills the knapsack or not. This naturally leads to a cost expressed by the recurrence relation $T(n) = 2T(n-1) + c = \Theta(2^n)$. That can be pretty expensive!

But... we should quickly realize that there are only $n(K+1)$ subproblems to solve! Clearly, there is the possibility that many subproblems are being solved repeatedly. This is a natural opportunity to apply dynamic programming. We simply build an array of size $n \times K + 1$ to contain the solutions for all subproblems $P(i, k), 1 \le i \le n, 0 \le k \le K$.

There are two approaches to actually solving the problem. One is to start with our problem of size $P(n, K)$ and make recursive calls to solve the subproblems, each time checking the array to see if a subproblem has been solved, and filling in the corresponding cell in the array whenever we get a new subproblem solution. The other is to start filling the array for row 1 (which indicates a successful solution only for a knapsack of size k_1). We then fill in the succeeding rows from $i = 2$ to n, left to right, as follows.

if $P(n-1, K)$ has a solution,

then $P(n, K)$ has a solution
else if $P(n - 1, K - k_n)$ has a solution
   then $P(n, K)$ has a solution
   else $P(n, K)$ has no solution.

In other words, a new slot in the array gets its solution by looking at two slots in the preceding row. Since filling each slot in the array takes constant time, the total cost of the algorithm is $\Theta(nK)$.

Example 16.3 Solve the Knapsack Problem for $K = 10$ and five items with sizes 9, 2, 7, 4, 1. We do this by building the following array.

	0	1	2	3	4	5	6	7	8	9	10
$k_1 = 9$	O	–	–	–	–	–	–	–	–	I	–
$k_2 = 2$	O	–	I	–	–	–	–	–	–	O	–
$k_3 = 7$	O	–	O	–	–	–	–	I	–	I/O	–
$k_4 = 4$	O	–	O	–	I	–	I	O	–	O	–
$k_5 = 1$	O	I	O	I	O	I	O	I/O	I	O	I

Key:
  -: No solution for $P(i, k)$.
  O: Solution(s) for $P(i, k)$ with i omitted.
  I: Solution(s) for $P(i, k)$ with i included.
  I/O: Solutions for $P(i, k)$ with i included AND omitted.

For example, $P(3, 9)$ stores value I/O. It contains O because $P(2, 9)$ has a solution. It contains I because $P(2, 2) = P(2, 9 - 7)$ has a solution. Since $P(5, 10)$ is marked with an I, it has a solution. We can determine what that solution actually is by recognizing that it includes the 5th item (of size 1), which then leads us to look at the solution for $P(4, 9)$. This in turn has a solution that omits the 4th item, leading us to $P(3, 9)$. At this point, we can either use the third item or not. We can find a solution by taking one branch. We can find all solutions by following all branches when there is a choice.

16.1.2   All-Pairs Shortest Paths

We next consider the problem of finding the shortest distance between all pairs of vertices in the graph, called the **all-pairs shortest-paths** problem. To be precise, for every $u, v \in \mathbf{V}$, calculate d(u, v).

One solution is to run Dijkstra's algorithm for finding the single-source shortest path (see Section 11.4.1) $|\mathbf{V}|$ times, each time computing the shortest path from a different start vertex. If $\mathbf{G}$ is sparse (that is, $|\mathbf{E}| = \Theta(|\mathbf{V}|)$) then this is a good

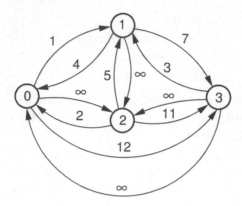

Figure 16.1 An example of k-paths in Floyd's algorithm. Path 1, 3 is a 0-path by definition. Path 3, 0, 2 is not a 0-path, but it is a 1-path (as well as a 2-path, a 3-path, and a 4-path) because the largest intermediate vertex is 0. Path 1, 3, 2 is a 4-path, but not a 3-path because the intermediate vertex is 3. All paths in this graph are 4-paths.

solution, because the total cost will be $\Theta(|\mathbf{V}|^2 + |\mathbf{V}||\mathbf{E}|\log|\mathbf{V}|) = \Theta(|\mathbf{V}|^2\log|\mathbf{V}|)$ for the version of Dijkstra's algorithm based on priority queues. For a dense graph, the priority queue version of Dijkstra's algorithm yields a cost of $\Theta(|\mathbf{V}|^3\log|\mathbf{V}|)$, but the version using **MinVertex** yields a cost of $\Theta(|\mathbf{V}|^3)$.

Another solution that limits processing time to $\Theta(|\mathbf{V}|^3)$ regardless of the number of edges is known as Floyd's algorithm. It is an example of dynamic programming. The chief problem with solving this problem is organizing the search process so that we do not repeatedly solve the same subproblems. We will do this organization through the use of the k-path. Define a **k-path** from vertex v to vertex u to be any path whose intermediate vertices (aside from v and u) all have indices less than k. A 0-path is defined to be a direct edge from v to u. Figure 16.1 illustrates the concept of k-paths.

Define $\mathrm{D}_k(v, u)$ to be the length of the shortest k-path from vertex v to vertex u. Assume that we already know the shortest k-path from v to u. The shortest $(k+1)$-path either goes through vertex k or it does not. If it does go through k, then the best path is the best k-path from v to k followed by the best k-path from k to u. Otherwise, we should keep the best k-path seen before. Floyd's algorithm simply checks all of the possibilities in a triple loop. Here is the implementation for Floyd's algorithm. At the end of the algorithm, array **D** stores the all-pairs shortest distances.

```
// Floyd's all-pairs shortest paths algorithm
// Store the pair-wise distances in "D"
void Floyd(Graph* G) {
  for (int i=0; i<G->n(); i++) // Initialize D with weights
    for (int j=0; j<G->n(); j++)
      if (G->weight(i, j) != 0) D[i][j] = G->weight(i, j);
  for (int k=0; k<G->n(); k++) // Compute all k paths
    for (int i=0; i<G->n(); i++)
      for (int j=0; j<G->n(); j++)
        if (D[i][j] > (D[i][k] + D[k][j]))
          D[i][j] = D[i][k] + D[k][j];
}
```

Clearly this algorithm requires $\Theta(|\mathbf{V}|^3)$ running time, and it is the best choice for dense graphs because it is (relatively) fast and easy to implement.

16.2 Randomized Algorithms

In this section, we will consider how introducing randomness into our algorithms might speed things up, although perhaps at the expense of accuracy. But often we can reduce the possibility for error to be as low as we like, while still speeding up the algorithm.

16.2.1 Randomized algorithms for finding large values

In Section 15.1 we determined that the lower bound cost of finding the maximum value in an unsorted list is $\Omega(n)$. This is the least time needed to be certain that we have found the maximum value. But what if we are willing to relax our requirement for certainty? The first question is: What do we mean by this? There are many aspects to "certainty" and we might relax the requirement in various ways.

There are several possible guarantees that we might require from an algorithm that produces X as the maximum value, when the true maximum is Y. So far we have assumed that we require X to equal Y. This is known as an exact or deterministic algorithm to solve the problem. We could relax this and require only that X's rank is "close to" Y's rank (perhaps within a fixed distance or percentage). This is known as an approximation algorithm. We could require that X is "usually" Y. This is known as a probabilistic algorithm. Finally, we could require only that X's rank is "usually" "close" to Y's rank. This is known as a heuristic algorithm.

There are also different ways that we might choose to sacrifice reliability for speed. These types of algorithms also have names.

1. **Las Vegas Algorithms**: We always find the maximum value, and "usually" we find it fast. Such algorithms have a guaranteed result, but do not guarantee fast running time.

2. **Monte Carlo Algorithms**: We find the maximum value fast, or we don't get an answer at all (but fast). While such algorithms have good running time, their result is not guaranteed.

Here is an example of an algorithm for finding a large value that gives up its guarantee of getting the best value in exchange for an improved running time. This is an example of a **probabilistic** algorithm, since it includes steps that are affected by **random** events. Choose m elements at random, and pick the best one of those as the answer. For large n, if $m \approx \log n$, the answer is pretty good. The cost is $m - 1$ compares (since we must find the maximum of m values). But we don't know for sure what we will get. However, we can estimate that the rank will be about $\frac{mn}{m+1}$. For example, if $n = 1,000,000$ and $m = \log n = 20$, then we expect that the largest of the 20 randomly selected values be among the top 5% of the n values.

Next, consider a slightly different problem where the goal is to pick a number in the upper half of n values. We would pick the maximum from among the first $\frac{n+1}{2}$ values for a cost of $n/2$ comparisons. Can we do better than this? Not if we want to guarantee getting the correct answer. But if we are willing to accept near certainty instead of absolute certainty, we can gain a lot in terms of speed.

As an alternative, consider this probabilistic algorithm. Pick 2 numbers and choose the greater. This will be in the upper half with probability 3/4 (since it is not in the upper half only when both numbers we choose happen to be in the lower half). Is a probability of 3/4 not good enough? Then we simply pick more numbers! For k numbers, the greatest is in upper half with probability $1 - \frac{1}{2^k}$, regardless of the number n that we pick from, so long as n is much larger than k (otherwise the chances might become even better). If we pick ten numbers, then the chance of failure is only one in $2^{10} = 1024$. What if we really want to be sure, because lives depend on drawing a number from the upper half? If we pick 30 numbers, we can fail only one time in a billion. If we pick enough numbers, then the chance of picking a small number is less than the chance of the power failing during the computation. Picking 100 numbers means that we can fail only one time in 10^{100} which is less chance than any disaster that you can imagine disrupting the process.

16.2.2 Skip Lists

This section presents a probabilistic search structure called the Skip List. Like BSTs, Skip Lists are designed to overcome a basic limitation of array-based and linked lists: Either search or update operations require linear time. The Skip List is an example of a **probabilistic data structure**, because it makes some of its decisions at random.

Skip Lists provide an alternative to the BST and related tree structures. The primary problem with the BST is that it may easily become unbalanced. The 2-3 tree of Chapter 10 is guaranteed to remain balanced regardless of the order in which data values are inserted, but it is rather complicated to implement. Chapter 13 presents the AVL tree and the splay tree, which are also guaranteed to provide good performance, but at the cost of added complexity as compared to the BST. The Skip List is easier to implement than known balanced tree structures. The Skip List is not guaranteed to provide good performance (where good performance is defined as $\Theta(\log n)$ search, insertion, and deletion time), but it will provide good performance with extremely high probability (unlike the BST which has a good chance of performing poorly). As such it represents a good compromise between difficulty of implementation and performance.

Figure 16.2 illustrates the concept behind the Skip List. Figure 16.2(a) shows a simple linked list whose nodes are ordered by key value. To search a sorted linked list requires that we move down the list one node at a time, visiting $\Theta(n)$ nodes in the average case. What if we add a pointer to every other node that lets us skip alternating nodes, as shown in Figure 16.2(b)? Define nodes with a single pointer as level 0 Skip List nodes, and nodes with two pointers as level 1 Skip List nodes.

To search, follow the level 1 pointers until a value greater than the search key has been found, go back to the previous level 1 node, then revert to a level 0 pointer to travel one more node if necessary. This effectively cuts the work in half. We can continue adding pointers to selected nodes in this way — give a third pointer to every fourth node, give a fourth pointer to every eighth node, and so on — until we reach the ultimate of $\log n$ pointers in the first and middle nodes for a list of n nodes as illustrated in Figure 16.2(c). To search, start with the bottom row of pointers, going as far as possible and skipping many nodes at a time. Then, shift up to shorter and shorter steps as required. With this arrangement, the worst-case number of accesses is $\Theta(\log n)$.

We will store with each Skip List node an array named **forward** that stores the pointers as shown in Figure 16.2(c). Position **forward[0]** stores a level 0 pointer, **forward[1]** stores a level 1 pointer, and so on. The Skip List object includes data member **level** that stores the highest level for any node currently in the Skip List. The Skip List stores a header node named **head** with **level** pointers. The **find** function is shown in Figure 16.3.

Searching for a node with value 62 in the Skip List of Figure 16.2(c) begins at the header node. Follow the header node's pointer at **level**, which in this example is level 2. This points to the node with value 31. Because 31 is less than 62, we next try the pointer from **forward[2]** of 31's node to reach 69. Because 69 is greater than 62, we cannot go forward but must instead decrement the current level counter to 1. We next try to follow **forward[1]** of 31 to reach the node with value 58. Because 58 is smaller than 62, we follow 58's **forward[1]** pointer to 69. Because 69 is too big, follow 58's level 0 pointer to 62. Because 62 is not less than 62, we fall out of the **while** loop and move one step forward to the node with value 62.

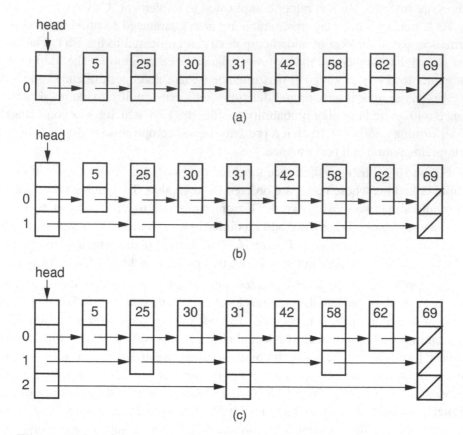

Figure 16.2 Illustration of the Skip List concept. (a) A simple linked list. (b) Augmenting the linked list with additional pointers at every other node. To find the node with key value 62, we visit the nodes with values 25, 31, 58, and 69, then we move from the node with key value 58 to the one with value 62. (c) The ideal Skip List, guaranteeing $O(\log n)$ search time. To find the node with key value 62, we visit nodes in the order 31, 69, 58, then 69 again, and finally, 62.

```
E find(const Key& k) const {
  SkipNode<Key,E> *x = head;               // Dummy header node
  for (int i=level; i>=0; i--)
    while ((x->forward[i] != NULL) &&
           (k > x->forward[i]->k))
      x = x->forward[i];
  x = x->forward[0];   // Move to actual record, if it exists
  if ((x != NULL) && (k == x->k)) return x->it;
  return NULL;
}
```

Figure 16.3 Implementation for the Skip List **find** function.

```
void insert(const Key& k, const E& it) {
  int i;
  SkipNode<Key,E> *x = head;    // Start at header node
  int newLevel = randomLevel(); // Select level for new node
  if (newLevel > level) {       // New node is deepest in list
    AdjustHead(newLevel);       // Add null pointers to header
    level = newLevel;
  }
  SkipNode<Key,E>* update[level+1]; // Track level ends
  for(i=level; i>=0; i--) {    // Search for insert position
    while((x->forward[i] != NULL) && (x->forward[i]->k < k))
      x = x->forward[i];
    update[i] = x;              // Keep track of end at level i
  }
  x = new SkipNode<Key,E>(k, it, newLevel);    // New node
  for (i=0; i<=newLevel; i++) {              // Splice into list
    x->forward[i] = update[i]->forward[i]; // Where x points
    update[i]->forward[i] = x;                // What points to x
  }
  reccount++;
}
```

Figure 16.4 Implementation for the Skip List **Insert** function.

The ideal Skip List of Figure 16.2(c) has been organized so that (if the first and last nodes are not counted) half of the nodes have only one pointer, one quarter have two, one eighth have three, and so on. The distances are equally spaced; in effect this is a "perfectly balanced" Skip List. Maintaining such balance would be expensive during the normal process of insertions and deletions. The key to Skip Lists is that we do not worry about any of this. Whenever inserting a node, we assign it a level (i.e., some number of pointers). The assignment is random, using a geometric distribution yielding a 50% probability that the node will have one pointer, a 25% probability that it will have two, and so on. The following function determines the level based on such a distribution:

```
// Pick a level using an exponential distribution
int randomLevel(void) {
  int level = 0;
  while (Random(2) == 0) level++;
  return level;
}
```

Once the proper level for the node has been determined, the next step is to find where the node should be inserted and link it in as appropriate at all of its levels. Figure 16.4 shows an implementation for inserting a new value into the Skip List.

Figure 16.5 illustrates the Skip List insertion process. In this example, we begin by inserting a node with value 10 into an empty Skip List. Assume that **randomLevel** returns a value of 1 (i.e., the node is at level 1, with 2 pointers). Because the empty Skip List has no nodes, the level of the list (and thus the level

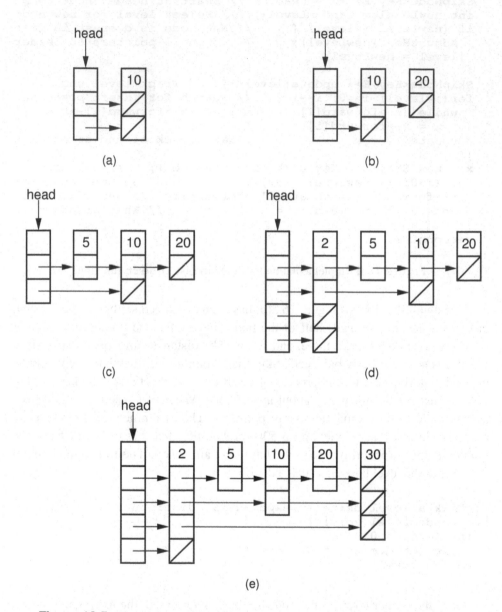

Figure 16.5 Illustration of Skip List insertion. (a) The Skip List after inserting initial value 10 at level 1. (b) The Skip List after inserting value 20 at level 0. (c) The Skip List after inserting value 5 at level 0. (d) The Skip List after inserting value 2 at level 3. (e) The final Skip List after inserting value 30 at level 2.

of the header node) must be set to 1. The new node is inserted, yielding the Skip List of Figure 16.5(a).

Next, insert the value 20. Assume this time that **randomLevel** returns 0. The search process goes to the node with value 10, and the new node is inserted after, as shown in Figure 16.5(b). The third node inserted has value 5, and again assume that **randomLevel** returns 0. This yields the Skip List of Figure 16.5.c.

The fourth node inserted has value 2, and assume that **randomLevel** returns 3. This means that the level of the Skip List must rise, causing the header node to gain an additional two (**NULL**) pointers. At this point, the new node is added to the front of the list, as shown in Figure 16.5(d).

Finally, insert a node with value 30 at level 2. This time, let us take a close look at what array **update** is used for. It stores the farthest node reached at each level during the search for the proper location of the new node. The search process begins in the header node at level 3 and proceeds to the node storing value 2. Because **forward[3]** for this node is **NULL**, we cannot go further at this level. Thus, **update[3]** stores a pointer to the node with value 2. Likewise, we cannot proceed at level 2, so **update[2]** also stores a pointer to the node with value 2. At level 1, we proceed to the node storing value 10. This is as far as we can go at level 1, so **update[1]** stores a pointer to the node with value 10. Finally, at level 0 we end up at the node with value 20. At this point, we can add in the new node with value 30. For each value **i**, the new node's **forward[i]** pointer is set to be **update[i]->forward[i]**, and the nodes stored in **update[i]** for indices 0 through 2 have their **forward[i]** pointers changed to point to the new node. This "splices" the new node into the Skip List at all levels.

The **remove** function is left as an exercise. It is similar to insertion in that the **update** array is built as part of searching for the record to be deleted. Then those nodes specified by the update array have their forward pointers adjusted to point around the node being deleted.

A newly inserted node could have a high level generated by **randomLevel**, or a low level. It is possible that many nodes in the Skip List could have many pointers, leading to unnecessary insert cost and yielding poor (i.e., $\Theta(n)$) performance during search, because not many nodes will be skipped. Conversely, too many nodes could have a low level. In the worst case, all nodes could be at level 0, equivalent to a regular linked list. If so, search will again require $\Theta(n)$ time. However, the probability that performance will be poor is quite low. There is only one chance in 1024 that ten nodes in a row will be at level 0. The motto of probabilistic data structures such as the Skip List is "Don't worry, be happy." We simply accept the results of **randomLevel** and expect that probability will eventually work in our favor. The advantage of this approach is that the algorithms are simple, while requiring only $\Theta(\log n)$ time for all operations in the average case.

In practice, the Skip List will probably have better performance than a BST. The BST can have bad performance caused by the order in which data are inserted. For example, if n nodes are inserted into a BST in ascending order of their key value, then the BST will look like a linked list with the deepest node at depth $n - 1$. The Skip List's performance does not depend on the order in which values are inserted into the list. As the number of nodes in the Skip List increases, the probability of encountering the worst case decreases geometrically. Thus, the Skip List illustrates a tension between the theoretical worst case (in this case, $\Theta(n)$ for a Skip List operation), and a rapidly increasing probability of average-case performance of $\Theta(\log n)$, that characterizes probabilistic data structures.

16.3   Numerical Algorithms

This section presents a variety of algorithms related to mathematical computations on numbers. Examples are activities like multiplying two numbers or raising a number to a given power. In particular, we are concerned with situations where built-in integer or floating-point operations cannot be used because the values being operated on are too large. Similar concerns arise for operations on polynomials or matrices.

Since we cannot rely on the hardware to process the inputs in a single constant-time operation, we are concerned with how to most effectively implement the operation to minimize the time cost. This begs a question as to how we should apply our normal measures of asymptotic cost in terms of growth rates on input size. First, what is an instance of addition or multiplication? Each value of the operands yields a different problem instance. And what is the input size when multiplying two numbers? If we view the input size as two (since two numbers are input), then any non-constant-time algorithm has a growth rate that is infinitely high compared to the growth of the input. This makes no sense, especially in light of the fact that we know from grade school arithmetic that adding or multiplying numbers does seem to get more difficult as the value of the numbers involved increases. In fact, we know from standard grade school algorithms that the cost of standard addition is linear on the number of digits being added, and multiplication has cost $n \times m$ when multiplying an m-digit number by an n-digit number.

The number of digits for the operands does appear to be a key consideration when we are performing a numeric algorithm that is sensitive to input size. The number of digits is simply the log of the value, for a suitable base of the log. Thus, for the purpose of calculating asymptotic growth rates of algorithms, we will consider the "size" of an input value to be the log of that value. Given this view, there are a number of features that seem to relate such operations.

- Arithmetic operations on large values are not cheap.
- There is only one instance of value n.

- There are 2^k instances of length k or less.
- The size (length) of value n is $\log n$.
- The cost of a particular algorithm can decrease when n increases in value (say when going from a value of $2^k - 1$ to 2^k to $2^k + 1$), but generally increases when n increases in length.

16.3.1 Exponentiation

We will start our examination of standard numerical algorithms by considering how to perform exponentiation. That is, how do we compute m^n? We could multiply by m a total of $n - 1$ times. Can we do better? Yes, there is a simple divide and conquer approach that we can use. We can recognize that, when n is even, $m^n = m^{n/2}m^{n/2}$. If n is odd, then $m^n = m^{\lfloor n/2 \rfloor}m^{\lfloor n/2 \rfloor}m$. This leads to the following recursive algorithm

```
int Power(base, exp) {
  if exp = 0 return 1;
  int half = Power(base, exp/2); // integer division of exp
  half = half * half;
  if (odd(exp)) then half = half * base;
  return half;
}
```

Function **Power** has recurrence relation

$$f(n) = \begin{cases} 0 & n = 1 \\ f(\lfloor n/2 \rfloor) + 1 + n \bmod 2 & n > 1 \end{cases}$$

whose solution is

$$f(n) = \lfloor \log n \rfloor + \beta(n) - 1$$

where β is the number of 1's in the binary representation of n.

How does this cost compare with the problem size? The original problem size is $\log m + \log n$, and the number of multiplications required is $\log n$. This is far better (in fact, exponentially better) than performing $n - 1$ multiplications.

16.3.2 Largest Common Factor

We will next present Euclid's algorithm for finding the largest common factor (LCF) for two integers. The LCF is the largest integer that divides both inputs evenly.

First we make this observation: If k divides n and m, then k divides $n - m$. We know this is true because if k divides n then $n = ak$ for some integer a, and if k divides m then $m = bk$ for some integer b. So, $LCF(n, m) = LCF(n - m, n) = LCF(m, n - m) = LCF(m, n)$.

Now, for any value n there exists k and l such that

$$n = km + l \text{ where } m > l \geq 0.$$

From the definition of the mod function, we can derive the fact that

$$n = \lfloor n/m \rfloor m + n \bmod m.$$

Since the LCF is a factor of both n and m, and since $n = km + l$, the LCF must therefore be a factor of both km and l, and also the largest common factor of each of these terms. As a consequence, $LCF(n, m) = LCF(m, l) = LCF(m, n \bmod m)$.

This observation leads to a simple algorithm. We will assume that $n \geq m$. At each iteration we replace n with m and m with $n \bmod m$ until we have driven m to zero.

```
int LCF(int n, int m) {
  if (m == 0) return n;
  return LCF(m, n % m);
}
```

To determine how expensive this algorithm is, we need to know how much progress we are making at each step. Note that after two iterations, we have replaced n with $n \bmod m$. So the key question becomes: How big is $n \bmod m$ relative to n?

$$
\begin{aligned}
n \geq m \;\Rightarrow\;& n/m \geq 1 \\
\Rightarrow\;& 2\lfloor n/m \rfloor > n/m \\
\Rightarrow\;& m\lfloor n/m \rfloor > n/2 \\
\Rightarrow\;& n - n/2 > n - m\lfloor n/m \rfloor = n \bmod m \\
\Rightarrow\;& n/2 > n \bmod m
\end{aligned}
$$

Thus, function LCF will halve its first parameter in no more than 2 iterations. The total cost is then $O(\log n)$.

16.3.3 Matrix Multiplication

The standard algorithm for multiplying two $n \times n$ matrices requires $\Theta(n^3)$ time. It is possible to do better than this by rearranging and grouping the multiplications in various ways. One example of this is known as Strassen's matrix multiplication algorithm.

For simplicity, we will assume that n is a power of two. In the following, A and B are $n \times n$ arrays, while A_{ij} and B_{ij} refer to arrays of size $n/2 \times n/2$. Using this notation, we can think of matrix multiplication using divide and conquer in the following way:

$$\begin{bmatrix} A_{11} & A_{12} \\ A_{21} & A_{22} \end{bmatrix} \begin{bmatrix} B_{11} & B_{12} \\ B_{21} & B_{22} \end{bmatrix} = \begin{bmatrix} A_{11}B_{11} + A_{12}B_{21} & A_{11}B_{12} + A_{12}B_{22} \\ A_{21}B_{11} + A_{22}B_{21} & A_{21}B_{12} + A_{22}B_{22} \end{bmatrix}.$$

Of course, each of the multiplications and additions on the right side of this equation are recursive calls on arrays of half size, and additions of arrays of half size, respectively. The recurrence relation for this algorithm is

$$T(n) = 8T(n/2) + 4(n/2)^2 = \Theta(n^3).$$

This closed form solution can easily be obtained by applying the Master Theorem 14.1.

Strassen's algorithm carefully rearranges the way that the various terms are multiplied and added together. It does so in a particular order, as expressed by the following equation:

$$\begin{bmatrix} A_{11} & A_{12} \\ A_{21} & A_{22} \end{bmatrix} \begin{bmatrix} B_{11} & B_{12} \\ B_{21} & B_{22} \end{bmatrix} = \begin{bmatrix} s_1 + s_2 - s_4 + s_6 & s_4 + s_5 \\ s_6 + s_7 & s_2 - s_3 + s_5 - s_7 \end{bmatrix}.$$

In other words, the result of the multiplication for an $n \times n$ array is obtained by a different series of matrix multiplications and additions for $n/2 \times n/2$ arrays. Multiplications between subarrays also use Strassen's algorithm, and the addition of two subarrays requires $\Theta(n^2)$ time. The subfactors are defined as follows:

$$
\begin{aligned}
s_1 &= (A_{12} - A_{22}) \cdot (B_{21} + B_{22}) \\
s_2 &= (A_{11} + A_{22}) \cdot (B_{11} + B_{22}) \\
s_3 &= (A_{11} - A_{21}) \cdot (B_{11} + B_{12}) \\
s_4 &= (A_{11} + A_{12}) \cdot B_{22} \\
s_5 &= A_{11} \cdot (B_{12} - B_{22}) \\
s_6 &= A_{22} \cdot (B_{21} - B_{11}) \\
s_7 &= (A_{21} + A_{22}) \cdot B_{11}
\end{aligned}
$$

With a little effort, you should be able to verify that this peculiar combination of operations does in fact produce the correct answer!

Now, looking at the list of operations to compute the s factors, and then counting the additions/subtractions needed to put them together to get the final answers, we see that we need a total of seven (array) multiplications and 18 (array) additions/subtractions to do the job. This leads to the recurrence

$$
\begin{aligned}
T(n) &= 7T(n/2) + 18(n/2)^2 \\
T(n) &= \Theta(n^{\log_2 7}) = \Theta(n^{2.81}).
\end{aligned}
$$

We obtained this closed form solution again by applying the Master Theorem.

Unfortunately, while Strassen's algorithm does in fact reduce the asymptotic complexity over the standard algorithm, the cost of the large number of addition and subtraction operations raises the constant factor involved considerably. This means that an extremely large array size is required to make Strassen's algorithm practical in real applications.

16.3.4 Random Numbers

The success of randomized algorithms such as were presented in Section 16.2 depend on having access to a good random number generator. While modern compilers are likely to include a random number generator that is good enough for most purposes, it is helpful to understand how they work, and to even be able to construct your own in case you don't trust the one provided. This is easy to do.

First, let us consider what a random sequence. From the following list, which appears to be a sequence of "random" numbers?

- 1, 1, 1, 1, 1, 1, 1, 1, 1, ...
- 1, 2, 3, 4, 5, 6, 7, 8, 9, ...
- 2, 7, 1, 8, 2, 8, 1, 8, 2, ...

In fact, all three happen to be the beginning of a some sequence in which one could continue the pattern to generate more values (in case you do not recognize it, the third one is the initial digits of the irrational constant e). Viewed as a series of digits, ideally every possible sequence has equal probability of being generated (even the three sequences above). In fact, definitions of randomness generally have features such as:

- One cannot predict the next item. The series is **unpredictable**.
- The series cannot be described more briefly than simply listing it out. This is the **equidistribution** property.

There is no such thing as a random number sequence, only "random enough" sequences. A sequence is **pseudorandom** if no future term can be predicted in polynomial time, given all past terms.

Most computer systems use a deterministic algorithm to select pseudorandom numbers.[1] The most commonly used approach historically is known as the **Linear Congruential Method** (LCM). The LCM method is quite simple. We begin by picking a **seed** that we will call $r(1)$. Then, we can compute successive terms as follows.

$$r(i) = (r(i-1) \times b) \bmod t$$

where b and t are constants.

---

[1] Another approach is based on using a computer chip that generates random numbers resulting from "thermal noise" in the system. Time will tell if this approach replaces deterministic approaches.

By definition of the mod function, all generated numbers must be in the range 0 to $t - 1$. Now, consider what happens when $r(i) = r(j)$ for values i and j. Of course then $r(i + 1) = r(j + 1)$ which means that we have a repeating cycle.

Since the values coming out of the random number generator are between 0 and $t - 1$, the longest cycle that we can hope for has length t. In fact, since $r(0) = 0$, it cannot even be quite this long. It turns out that to get a good result, it is crucial to pick good values for both b and t. To see why, consider the following example.

Example 16.4 Given a t value of 13, we can get very different results depending on the b value that we pick, in ways that are hard to predict.
$$r(i) = 6r(i - 1) \bmod 13 =$$
..., 1, 6, 10, 8, 9, 2, 12, 7, 3, 5, 4, 11, 1, ...
$$r(i) = 7r(i - 1) \bmod 13 =$$
..., 1, 7, 10, 5, 9, 11, 12, 6, 3, 8, 4, 2, 1, ...
$$r(i) = 5r(i - 1) \bmod 13 =$$
..., 1, 5, 12, 8, 1, ...
..., 2, 10, 11, 3, 2, ...
..., 4, 7, 9, 6, 4, ...
..., 0, 0, ...
Clearly, a b value of 5 is far inferior to b values of 6 or 7 in this example.

If you would like to write a simple LCM random number generator of your own, an effective one can be made with the following formula.

$$r(i) = 16807r(i - 1) \bmod 2^{31} - 1.$$

16.3.5 The Fast Fourier Transform

As noted at the beginning of this section, multiplication is considerably more difficult than addition. The cost to multiply two n-bit numbers directly is $O(n^2)$, while addition of two n-bit numbers is $O(n)$.

Recall from Section 2.3 that one property of logarithms is

$$\log nm = \log n + \log m.$$

Thus, if taking logarithms and anti-logarithms were cheap, then we could reduce multiplication to addition by taking the log of the two operands, adding, and then taking the anti-log of the sum.

Under normal circumstances, taking logarithms and anti-logarithms is expensive, and so this reduction would not be considered practical. However, this reduction is precisely the basis for the slide rule. The slide rule uses a logarithmic scale to measure the lengths of two numbers, in effect doing the conversion to logarithms automatically. These two lengths are then added together, and the inverse logarithm of the sum is read off another logarithmic scale. The part normally considered expensive (taking logarithms and anti-logarithms) is cheap because it is a physical part of the slide rule. Thus, the entire multiplication process can be done cheaply via a reduction to addition. In the days before electronic calculators, slide rules were routinely used by scientists and engineers to do basic calculations of this nature.

Now consider the problem of multiplying polynomials. A vector **a** of n values can uniquely represent a polynomial of degree $n - 1$, expressed as

$$P_{\mathbf{a}}(x) = \sum_{i=0}^{n-1} \mathbf{a}_i x^i.$$

Alternatively, a polynomial can be uniquely represented by a list of its values at n distinct points. Finding the value for a polynomial at a given point is called **evaluation**. Finding the coefficients for the polynomial given the values at n points is called **interpolation**.

To multiply two $n - 1$-degree polynomials A and B normally takes $\Theta(n^2)$ coefficient multiplications. However, if we evaluate both polynomials (at the same points), we can simply multiply the corresponding pairs of values to get the corresponding values for polynomial AB.

Example 16.5 Polynomial A: $x^2 + 1$.
    Polynomial B: $2x^2 - x + 1$.
    Polynomial AB: $2x^4 - x^3 + 3x^2 - x + 1$.
    When we multiply the evaluations of A and B at points 0, 1, and -1, we get the following results.

$$AB(-1) = (2)(4) = 8$$
$$AB(0) = (1)(1) = 1$$
$$AB(1) = (2)(2) = 4$$

These results are the same as when we evaluate polynomial AB at these points.

Note that evaluating any polynomial at 0 is easy. If we evaluate at 1 and -1, we can share a lot of the work between the two evaluations. But we would need five points to nail down polynomial AB, since it is a degree-4 polynomial. Fortunately, we can speed processing for any pair of values c and $-c$. This seems to indicate some promising ways to speed up the process of evaluating polynomials. But, evaluating two points in roughly the same time as evaluating one point only speeds the process by a constant factor. Is there some way to generalized these observations to speed things up further? And even if we do find a way to evaluate many points quickly, we will also need to interpolate the five values to get the coefficients of AB back.

So we see that we could multiply two polynomials in less than $\Theta(n^2)$ operations *if* a fast way could be found to do evaluation/interpolation of $2n - 1$ points. Before considering further how this might be done, first observe again the relationship between evaluating a polynomial at values c and $-c$. In general, we can write $P_a(x) = E_a(x) + O_a(x)$ where E_a is the even powers and O_a is the odd powers. So,

$$P_a(x) = \sum_{i=0}^{n/2-1} a_{2i}x^{2i} + \sum_{i=0}^{n/2-1} a_{2i+1}x^{2i+1}$$

The significance is that when evaluating the pair of values c and $-c$, we get

$$E_a(c) + O_a(c) = E_a(c) - O_a(-c)$$
$$O_a(c) = -O_a(-c)$$

Thus, we only need to compute the Es and Os once instead of twice to get both evaluations.

The key to fast polynomial multiplication is finding the right points to use for evaluation/interpolation to make the process efficient. In particular, we want to take advantage of symmetries, such as the one we see for evaluating x and $-x$. But we need to find even more symmetries between points if we want to do more than cut the work in half. We have to find symmetries not just between pairs of values, but also further symmetries between pairs of pairs, and then pairs of pairs of pairs, and so on.

Recall that a **complex** number z has a real component and an imaginary component. We can consider the position of z on a number line if we use the y dimension for the imaginary component. Now, we will define a **primitive nth root of unity** if

1. $z^n = 1$ and
2. $z^k \neq 1$ for $0 < k < n$.

$z^0, z^1, ..., z^{n-1}$ are called the **nth roots of unity**. For example, when $n = 4$, then $z = i$ or $z = -i$. In general, we have the identities $e^{i\pi} = -1$, and $z^j = e^{2\pi ij/n} = -1^{2j/n}$. The significance is that we can find as many points on a unit circle as we would need (see Figure 16.6). But these points are special in that they will allow us to do just the right computation necessary to get the needed symmetries to speed up the overall process of evaluating many points at once.

The next step is to define how the computation is done. Define an $n \times n$ matrix A_z with row i and column j as

$$A_z = (z^{ij}).$$

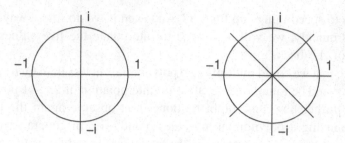

Figure 16.6 Examples of the 4th and 8th roots of unity.

The idea is that there is a row for each root (row i for z^i) while the columns correspond to the power of the exponent of the x value in the polynomial. For example, when $n = 4$ we have $z = i$. Thus, the A_z array appears as follows.

$$A_z = \begin{matrix} 1 & 1 & 1 & 1 \\ 1 & i & -1 & -i \\ 1 & -1 & 1 & -1 \\ 1 & -i & -1 & i \end{matrix}$$

Let $a = [a_0, a_1, ..., a_{n-1}]^T$ be a vector that stores the coefficients for the polynomial being evaluated. We can then do the calculations to evaluate the polynomial at the nth roots of unity by multiplying the A_z matrix by the coefficient vector. The resulting vector F_z is called the Discrete Fourier Transform for the polynomial.

$$F_z = A_z a = b.$$

$$b_i = \sum_{k=0}^{n-1} a_k z^{ik}.$$

When $n = 8$, then $z = \sqrt{i}$, since $\sqrt{i}^8 = 1$. So, the corresponding matrix is as follows.

$$A_z = \begin{matrix} 1 & 1 & 1 & 1 & 1 & 1 & 1 & 1 \\ 1 & \sqrt{i} & i & i\sqrt{i} & -1 & -\sqrt{i} & -i & -i\sqrt{i} \\ 1 & i & -1 & -i & 1 & i & -1 & -i \\ 1 & i\sqrt{i} & -i & \sqrt{i} & -1 & -i\sqrt{i} & i & -\sqrt{i} \\ 1 & -1 & 1 & -1 & 1 & -1 & 1 & -1 \\ 1 & -\sqrt{i} & i & -i\sqrt{i} & -1 & \sqrt{i} & -i & i\sqrt{i} \\ 1 & -i & -1 & i & 1 & -i & -1 & i \\ 1 & -i\sqrt{i} & -i & -\sqrt{i} & -1 & i\sqrt{i} & i & \sqrt{i} \end{matrix}$$

We still have two problems. We need to be able to multiply this matrix and the vector faster than just by performing a standard matrix-vector multiplication, otherwise the cost is still n^2 multiplies to do the evaluation. Even if we can multiply the matrix and vector cheaply, we still need to be able to reverse the process. That is, after transforming the two input polynomials by evaluating them, and then pair-wise multiplying the evaluated points, we must interpolate those points to get the resulting polynomial back that corresponds to multiplying the original input polynomials.

The interpolation step is nearly identical to the evaluation step.

$$F_z^{-1} = A_z^{-1} b' = a'.$$

We need to find A_z^{-1}. This turns out to be simple to compute, and is defined as follows.

$$A_z^{-1} = \frac{1}{n} A_{1/z}.$$

In other words, interpolation (the inverse transformation) requires the same computation as evaluation, except that we substitute $1/z$ for z (and multiply by $1/n$ at the end). So, if we can do one fast, we can do the other fast.

If you examine the example A_z matrix for $n = 8$, you should see that there are symmetries within the matrix. For example, the top half is identical to the bottom half with suitable sign changes on some rows and columns. Likewise for the left and right halves. An efficient divide and conquer algorithm exists to perform both the evaluation and the interpolation in $\Theta(n \log n)$ time. This is called the **Discrete Fourier Transform** (DFT). It is a recursive function that decomposes the matrix multiplications, taking advantage of the symmetries made available by doing evaluation at the nth roots of unity. The algorithm is as follows.

```
Fourier_Transform(double *Polynomial, int n) {
  // Compute the Fourier transform of Polynomial
  // with degree n. Polynomial is a list of
  // coefficients indexed from 0 to n-1. n is
  // assumed to be a power of 2.
  double Even[n/2], Odd[n/2], List1[n/2], List2[n/2];

  if (n==1) return Polynomial[0];

  for (j=0; j<=n/2-1; j++) {
    Even[j] = Polynomial[2j];
    Odd[j] = Polynomial[2j+1];
  }
  List1 = Fourier_Transform(Even, n/2);
  List2 = Fourier_Transform(Odd, n/2);
  for (j=0; j<=n-1, J++) {
    Imaginary z = pow(E, 2*i*PI*j/n);
    k = j % (n/2);
    Polynomial[j] = List1[k] + z*List2[k];
  }
  return Polynomial;
}
```

Thus, the full process for multiplying polynomials A and B using the Fourier transform is as follows.

1. Represent an $n - 1$-degree polynomial as $2n - 1$ coefficients:

$$[a_0, a_1, ..., a_{n-1}, 0, ..., 0]$$

2. Perform **Fourier_Transform** on the representations for A and B
3. Pairwise multiply the results to get $2n - 1$ values.
4. Perform the inverse **Fourier_Transform** to get the $2n - 1$ degree polynomial AB.

16.4 Further Reading

For further information on Skip Lists, see "Skip Lists: A Probabilistic Alternative to Balanced Trees" by William Pugh [Pug90].

16.5 Exercises

16.1 Solve Towers of Hanoi using a dynamic programming algorithm.

16.2 There are six possible permutations of the lines

```
for (int k=0; k<G.n(); k++)
  for (int i=0; i<G.n(); i++)
    for (int j=0; j<G.n(); j++)
```

in Floyd's algorithm. Which ones give a correct algorithm?

16.3 Show the result of running Floyd's all-pairs shortest-paths algorithm on the graph of Figure 11.26.

16.4 The implementation for Floyd's algorithm given in Section 16.1.2 is inefficient for adjacency lists because the edges are visited in a bad order when initializing array **D**. What is the cost of of this initialization step for the adjacency list? How can this initialization step be revised so that it costs $\Theta(|\mathbf{V}|^2)$ in the worst case?

16.5 State the greatest possible lower bound that you can prove for the all-pairs shortest-paths problem, and justify your answer.

16.6 Show the Skip List that results from inserting the following values. Draw the Skip List after each insert. With each value, assume the depth of its corresponding node is as given in the list.

value	depth
5	2
20	0
30	0
2	0
25	1
26	3
31	0

16.7 If we had a linked list that would never be modified, we can use a simpler approach than the Skip List to speed access. The concept would remain the same in that we add additional pointers to list nodes for efficient access to the ith element. How can we add a second pointer to each element of a singly linked list to allow access to an arbitrary element in $O(\log n)$ time?

16.8 What is the expected (average) number of pointers for a Skip List node?

16.9 Write a function to remove a node with given value from a Skip List.

16.10 Write a function to find the ith node on a Skip List.

16.6 Projects

16.1 Complete the implementation of the Skip List-based dictionary begun in Section 16.2.2.

16.2 Implement both a standard $\Theta(n^3)$ matrix multiplication algorithm and Strassen's matrix multiplication algorithm (see Exercise 14.16.3.3). Using empirical testing, try to estimate the constant factors for the runtime equations of the two algorithms. How big must n be before Strassen's algorithm becomes more efficient than the standard algorithm?

17

Limits to Computation

This book describes data structures that can be used in a wide variety of problems, and many examples of efficient algorithms. In general, our search algorithms strive to be at worst in $O(\log n)$ to find a record, and our sorting algorithms strive to be in $O(n \log n)$. A few algorithms have higher asymptotic complexity. Both Floyd's all-pairs shortest-paths algorithm and standard matrix multiply have running times of $\Theta(n^3)$ (though for both, the amount of data being processed is $\Theta(n^2)$).

We can solve many problems efficiently because we have available (and choose to use) efficient algorithms. Given any problem for which you know *some* algorithm, it is always possible to write an inefficient algorithm to "solve" the problem. For example, consider a sorting algorithm that tests every possible permutation of its input until it finds the correct permutation that provides a sorted list. The running time for this algorithm would be unacceptably high, because it is proportional to the number of permutations which is $n!$ for n inputs. When solving the minimum-cost spanning tree problem, if we were to test every possible subset of edges to see which forms the shortest minimum spanning tree, the amount of work would be proportional to $2^{|E|}$ for a graph with $|E|$ edges. Fortunately, for both of these problems we have more clever algorithms that allow us to find answers (relatively) quickly without explicitly testing every possible solution.

Unfortunately, there are many computing problems for which the best possible algorithm takes a long time to run. A simple example is the Towers of Hanoi problem, which requires 2^n moves to "solve" a tower with n disks. It is not possible for any computer program that solves the Towers of Hanoi problem to run in less than $\Omega(2^n)$ time, because that many moves must be printed out.

Besides those problems whose solutions *must* take a long time to run, there are also many problems for which we simply do not know if there are efficient algorithms or not. The best algorithms that we know for such problems are very slow, but perhaps there are better ones waiting to be discovered. Of course, while having a problem with high running time is bad, it is even worse to have a problem that cannot be solved at all! Such problems do exist, and are discussed in Section 17.3.

This chapter presents a brief introduction to the theory of expensive and impossible problems. Section 17.1 presents the concept of a reduction, which is the central tool used for analyzing the difficulty of a problem (as opposed to analyzing the cost of an algorithm). Reductions allow us to relate the difficulty of various problems, which is often much easier than doing the analysis for a problem from first principles. Section 17.2 discusses "hard" problems, by which we mean problems that require, or at least appear to require, time exponential on the input size. Finally, Section 17.3 considers various problems that, while often simple to define and comprehend, are in fact impossible to solve using a computer program. The classic example of such a problem is deciding whether an arbitrary computer program will go into an infinite loop when processing a specified input. This is known as the **halting problem**.

17.1 Reductions

We begin with an important concept for understanding the relationships between problems, called **reduction**. Reduction allows us to solve one problem in terms of another. Equally importantly, when we wish to understand the difficulty of a problem, reduction allows us to make relative statements about upper and lower bounds on the cost of a problem (as opposed to an algorithm or program).

Because the concept of a problem is discussed extensively in this chapter, we want notation to simplify problem descriptions. Throughout this chapter, a problem will be defined in terms of a mapping between inputs and outputs, and the name of the problem will be given in all capital letters. Thus, a complete definition of the sorting problem could appear as follows:

SORTING:
    Input: A sequence of integers $x_0, x_1, x_2, ..., x_{n-1}$.
    Output: A permutation $y_0, y_1, y_2, ..., y_{n-1}$ of the sequence such that $y_i \leq y_j$ whenever $i < j$.

When you buy or write a program to solve one problem, such as sorting, you might be able to use it to help solve a different problem. This is known in software engineering as **software reuse**. To illustrate this, let us consider another problem.

PAIRING:
    Input: Two sequences of integers $X = (x_0, x_1, ..., x_{n-1})$ and $Y = (y_0, y_1, ..., y_{n-1})$.
    Output: A pairing of the elements in the two sequences such that the least value in X is paired with the least value in Y, the next least value in X is paired with the next least value in Y, and so on.

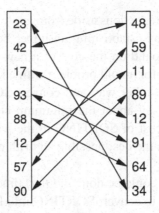

Figure 17.1 An illustration of PAIRING. The two lists of numbers are paired up so that the least values from each list make a pair, the next smallest values from each list make a pair, and so on.

Figure 17.1 illustrates PAIRING. One way to solve PAIRING is to use an existing sorting program to sort each of the two sequences, and then pair off items based on their position in sorted order. Technically we say that in this solution, PAIRING is **reduced** to SORTING, because SORTING is used to solve PAIRING.

Notice that reduction is a three-step process. The first step is to convert an instance of PAIRING into two instances of SORTING. The conversion step in this example is not very interesting; it simply takes each sequence and assigns it to an array to be passed to SORTING. The second step is to sort the two arrays (i.e., apply SORTING to each array). The third step is to convert the output of SORTING to the output for PAIRING. This is done by pairing the first elements in the sorted arrays, the second elements, and so on.

A reduction of PAIRING to SORTING helps to establish an upper bound on the cost of PAIRING. In terms of asymptotic notation, assuming that we can find one method to convert the inputs to PAIRING into inputs to SORTING "fast enough," and a second method to convert the result of SORTING back to the correct result for PAIRING "fast enough," then the asymptotic cost of PAIRING cannot be more than the cost of SORTING. In this case, there is little work to be done to convert from PAIRING to SORTING, or to convert the answer from SORTING back to the answer for PAIRING, so the dominant cost of this solution is performing the sort operation. Thus, an upper bound for PAIRING is in $O(n \log n)$.

It is important to note that the pairing problem does *not* require that elements of the two sequences be sorted. This is merely one possible way to solve the problem. PAIRING only requires that the elements of the sequences be paired correctly. Perhaps there is another way to do it? Certainly if we use sorting to solve PAIRING, the algorithms will require $\Omega(n \log n)$ time. But, another approach might conceivably be faster.

There is another use of reductions aside from applying an old algorithm to solve a new problem (and thereby establishing an upper bound for the new problem). That is to prove a lower bound on the cost of a new problem by showing that it could be used as a solution for an old problem with a known lower bound.

Assume we can go the other way and convert SORTING to PAIRING "fast enough." What does this say about the minimum cost of PAIRING? We know from Section 7.9 that the cost of SORTING in the worst and average cases is in $\Omega(n \log n)$. In other words, the best possible algorithm for sorting requires at least $n \log n$ time.

Assume that PAIRING could be done in $O(n)$ time. Then, one way to create a sorting algorithm would be to convert SORTING into PAIRING, run the algorithm for PAIRING, and finally convert the answer back to the answer for SORTING. Provided that we can convert SORTING to/from PAIRING "fast enough," this process would yield an $O(n)$ algorithm for sorting! Because this contradicts what we know about the lower bound for SORTING, and the only flaw in the reasoning is the initial assumption that PAIRING can be done in $O(n)$ time, we can conclude that there is no $O(n)$ time algorithm for PAIRING. This reduction process tells us that PAIRING must be at least as expensive as SORTING and so must itself have a lower bound in $\Omega(n \log n)$.

To complete this proof regarding the lower bound for PAIRING, we need now to find a way to reduce SORTING to PAIRING. This is easily done. Take an instance of SORTING (i.e., an array A of n elements). A second array B is generated that simply stores i in position i for $0 \leq i < n$. Pass the two arrays to PAIRING. Take the resulting set of pairs, and use the value from the B half of the pair to tell which position in the sorted array the A half should take; that is, we can now reorder the records in the A array using the corresponding value in the B array as the sort key and running a simple $\Theta(n)$ Binsort. The conversion of SORTING to PAIRING can be done in $O(n)$ time, and likewise the conversion of the output of PAIRING can be converted to the correct output for SORTING in $O(n)$ time. Thus, the cost of this "sorting algorithm" is dominated by the cost for PAIRING.

Consider any two problems for which a suitable reduction from one to the other can be found. The first problem takes an arbitrary instance of its input, which we will call I, and transforms I to a solution, which we will call SLN. The second problem takes an arbitrary instance of its input, which we will call I', and transforms I' to a solution, which we will call SLN'. We can define reduction more formally as a three-step process:

1. Transform an arbitrary instance of the first problem to an instance of the second problem. In other words, there must be a transformation from any instance I of the first problem to an instance I' of the second problem.

2. Apply an algorithm for the second problem to the instance I', yielding a solution SLN'.

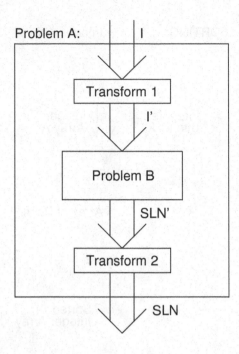

Figure 17.2 The general process for reduction shown as a "blackbox" diagram.

3. Transform *SLN'* to the solution of *I*, known as *SLN*. Note that *SLN* must in fact be the correct solution for *I* for the reduction to be acceptable.

Figure 17.2 shows a graphical representation of the general reduction process, showing the role of the two problems, and the two transformations. Figure 17.3 shows a similar diagram for the reduction of SORTING to PAIRING.

It is important to note that the reduction process does not give us an algorithm for solving either problem by itself. It merely gives us a method for solving the first problem given that we already have a solution to the second. More importantly for the topics to be discussed in the remainder of this chapter, reduction gives us a way to understand the bounds of one problem in terms of another. Specifically, given efficient transformations, the upper bound of the first problem is at most the upper bound of the second. Conversely, the lower bound of the second problem is at least the lower bound of the first.

As a second example of reduction, consider the simple problem of multiplying two *n*-digit numbers. The standard long-hand method for multiplication is to multiply the last digit of the first number by the second number (taking $\Theta(n)$ time), multiply the second digit of the first number by the second number (again taking $\Theta(n)$ time), and so on for each of the *n* digits of the first number. Finally, the intermediate results are added together. Note that adding two numbers of length *M* and *N* can easily be done in $\Theta(M+N)$ time. Because each digit of the first number

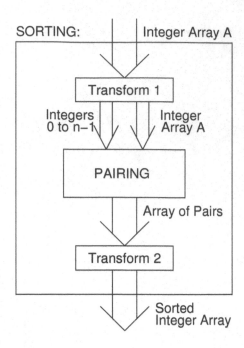

Figure 17.3 A reduction of SORTING to PAIRING shown as a "blackbox" diagram.

is multiplied against each digit of the second, this algorithm requires $\Theta(n^2)$ time. Asymptotically faster (but more complicated) algorithms are known, but none is so fast as to be in $O(n)$.

Next we ask the question: Is squaring an n-digit number as difficult as multiplying two n-digit numbers? We might hope that something about this special case will allow for a faster algorithm than is required by the more general multiplication problem. However, a simple reduction proof serves to show that squaring is "as hard" as multiplying.

The key to the reduction is the following formula:

$$X \times Y = \frac{(X + Y)^2 - (X - Y)^2}{4}.$$

The significance of this formula is that it allows us to convert an arbitrary instance of multiplication to a series of operations involving three addition/subtractions (each of which can be done in linear time), two squarings, and a division by 4. Note that the division by 4 can be done in linear time (simply convert to binary, shift right by two digits, and convert back).

This reduction shows that if a linear time algorithm for squaring can be found, it can be used to construct a linear time algorithm for multiplication.

Our next example of reduction concerns the multiplication of two $n \times n$ matrices. For this problem, we will assume that the values stored in the matrices are simple integers and that multiplying two simple integers takes constant time (because multiplication of two `int` variables takes a fixed number of machine instructions). The standard algorithm for multiplying two matrices is to multiply each element of the first matrix's first row by the corresponding element of the second matrix's first column, then adding the numbers. This takes $\Theta(n)$ time. Each of the n^2 elements of the solution are computed in similar fashion, requiring a total of $\Theta(n^3)$ time. Faster algorithms are known (see the discussion of Strassen's Algorithm in Section 16.3.3), but none are so fast as to be in $O(n^2)$.

Now, consider the case of multiplying two **symmetric** matrices. A symmetric matrix is one in which entry ij is equal to entry ji; that is, the upper-right triangle of the matrix is a mirror image of the lower-left triangle. Is there something about this restricted case that allows us to multiply two symmetric matrices faster than in the general case? The answer is no, as can be seen by the following reduction. Assume that we have been given two $n \times n$ matrices A and B. We can construct a $2n \times 2n$ symmetric matrix from an arbitrary matrix A as follows:

$$\begin{bmatrix} 0 & A \\ A^{\mathrm{T}} & 0 \end{bmatrix}.$$

Here 0 stands for an $n \times n$ matrix composed of zero values, A is the original matrix, and A^{T} stands for the transpose of matrix A.[1] Note that the resulting matrix is now symmetric. We can convert matrix B to a symmetric matrix in a similar manner. If symmetric matrices could be multiplied "quickly" (in particular, if they could be multiplied together in $\Theta(n^2)$ time), then we could find the result of multiplying two arbitrary $n \times n$ matrices in $\Theta(n^2)$ time by taking advantage of the following observation:

$$\begin{bmatrix} 0 & A \\ A^{\mathrm{T}} & 0 \end{bmatrix} \begin{bmatrix} 0 & B^{\mathrm{T}} \\ B & 0 \end{bmatrix} = \begin{bmatrix} AB & 0 \\ 0 & A^{\mathrm{T}}B^{\mathrm{T}} \end{bmatrix}.$$

In the above formula, AB is the result of multiplying matrices A and B together.

17.2 Hard Problems

There are several ways that a problem could be considered hard. For example, we might have trouble understanding the definition of the problem itself. At the beginning of a large data collection and analysis project, developers and their clients might have only a hazy notion of what their goals actually are, and need to work that out over time. For other types of problems, we might have trouble finding or understanding an algorithm to solve the problem. Understanding spoken English

---

[1] The transpose operation takes position ij of the original matrix and places it in position ji of the transpose matrix. This can easily be done in n^2 time for an $n \times n$ matrix.

and translating it to written text is an example of a problem whose goals are easy to define, but whose solution is not easy to discover. But even though a natural language processing algorithm might be difficult to write, the program's running time might be fairly fast. There are many practical systems today that solve aspects of this problem in reasonable time.

None of these is what is commonly meant when a computer theoretician uses the word "hard." Throughout this section, "hard" means that the best-known algorithm for the problem is expensive in its running time. One example of a hard problem is Towers of Hanoi. It is easy to understand this problem and its solution. It is also easy to write a program to solve this problem. But, it takes an extremely long time to run for any "reasonably" large value of n. Try running a program to solve Towers of Hanoi for only 30 disks!

The Towers of Hanoi problem takes exponential time, that is, its running time is $\Theta(2^n)$. This is radically different from an algorithm that takes $\Theta(n \log n)$ time or $\Theta(n^2)$ time. It is even radically different from a problem that takes $\Theta(n^4)$ time. These are all examples of polynomial running time, because the exponents for all terms of these equations are constants. Recall from Chapter 3 that if we buy a new computer that runs twice as fast, the size of problem with complexity $\Theta(n^4)$ that we can solve in a certain amount of time is increased by the fourth root of two. In other words, there is a multiplicative factor increase, even if it is a rather small one. This is true for any algorithm whose running time can be represented by a polynomial.

Consider what happens if you buy a computer that is twice as fast and try to solve a bigger Towers of Hanoi problem in a given amount of time. Because its complexity is $\Theta(2^n)$, we can solve a problem only one disk bigger! There is no multiplicative factor, and this is true for any exponential algorithm: A constant factor increase in processing power results in only a fixed addition in problem-solving power.

There are a number of other fundamental differences between polynomial running times and exponential running times that argues for treating them as qualitatively different. Polynomials are closed under composition and addition. Thus, running polynomial-time programs in sequence, or having one program with polynomial running time call another a polynomial number of times yields polynomial time. Also, all computers known are polynomially related. That is, any program that runs in polynomial time on any computer today, when transferred to any other computer, will still run in polynomial time.

There is a practical reason for recognizing a distinction. In practice, most polynomial time algorithms are "feasible" in that they can run reasonably large inputs in reasonable time. In contrast, most algorithms requiring exponential time are not practical to run even for fairly modest sizes of input. One could argue that a program with high polynomial degree (such as n^{100}) is not practical, while an exponential-time program with cost 1.001^n is practical. But the reality is that we know of almost no problems where the best polynomial-time algorithm has high degree (they nearly all have degree four or less), while almost no exponential-time algorithms (whose cost is $(O(c^n))$ have their constant c close to one. So there is not much gray area between polynomial and exponential time algorithms in practice.

For the rest of this chapter, we define a **hard algorithm** to be one that runs in exponential time, that is, in $\Omega(c^n)$ for some constant $c > 1$. A definition for a hard *problem* will be presented in the next section.

17.2.1   The Theory of $\mathcal{NP}$-Completeness

Imagine a magical computer that works by guessing the correct solution from among all of the possible solutions to a problem. Another way to look at this is to imagine a super parallel computer that could test all possible solutions simultaneously. Certainly this magical (or highly parallel) computer can do anything a normal computer can do. It might also solve some problems more quickly than a normal computer can. Consider some problem where, given a guess for a solution, checking the solution to see if it is correct can be done in polynomial time. Even if the number of possible solutions is exponential, any given guess can be checked in polynomial time (equivalently, all possible solutions are checked simultaneously in polynomial time), and thus the problem can be solved in polynomial time by our hypothetical magical computer. Another view of this concept is this: If you cannot get the answer to a problem in polynomial time by guessing the right answer and then checking it, then you cannot do it in polynomial time in any other way.

The idea of "guessing" the right answer to a problem — or checking all possible solutions in parallel to determine which is correct — is called **non-determinism**. An algorithm that works in this manner is called a **non-deterministic algorithm**, and any problem with an algorithm that runs on a non-deterministic machine in polynomial time is given a special name: It is said to be a problem in $\mathcal{NP}$. Thus, problems in $\mathcal{NP}$ are those problems that can be solved in polynomial time on a non-deterministic machine.

Not all problems requiring exponential time on a regular computer are in $\mathcal{NP}$. For example, Towers of Hanoi is *not* in $\mathcal{NP}$, because it must print out $O(2^n)$ moves for n disks. A non-deterministic machine cannot "guess" and print the correct answer in less time.

On the other hand, consider the TRAVELING SALESMAN problem.

TRAVELING SALESMAN (1)

   Input: A complete, directed graph **G** with positive distances assigned to each edge in the graph.

   Output: The shortest simple cycle that includes every vertex.

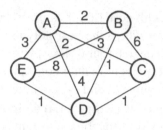

Figure 17.4 An illustration of the TRAVELING SALESMAN problem. Five vertices are shown, with edges between each pair of cities. The problem is to visit all of the cities exactly once, returning to the start city, with the least total cost.

Figure 17.4 illustrates this problem. Five vertices are shown, with edges and associated costs between each pair of edges. (For simplicity Figure 17.4 shows an undirected graph, assuming that the cost is the same in both directions, though this need not be the case.) If the salesman visits the cities in the order ABCDEA, he will travel a total distance of 13. A better route would be ABDCEA, with cost 11. The best route for this particular graph would be ABEDCA, with cost 9.

We cannot solve this problem in polynomial time with a guess-and-test non-deterministic computer. The problem is that, given a candidate cycle, while we can quickly check that the answer is indeed a cycle of the appropriate form, and while we can quickly calculate the length of the cycle, we have no easy way of knowing if it is in fact the *shortest* such cycle. However, we can solve a variant of this problem cast in the form of a **decision problem**. A decision problem is simply one whose answer is either YES or NO. The decision problem form of TRAVELING SALESMAN is as follows:

TRAVELING SALESMAN (2)

Input: A complete, directed graph **G** with positive distances assigned to each edge in the graph, and an integer k.

Output: YES if there is a simple cycle with total distance $\leq k$ containing every vertex in **G**, and NO otherwise.

We can solve this version of the problem in polynomial time with a non-deterministic computer. The non-deterministic algorithm simply checks all of the possible subsets of edges in the graph, in parallel. If any subset of the edges is an appropriate cycle of total length less than or equal to k, the answer is YES; otherwise the answer is NO. Note that it is only necessary that *some* subset meet the requirement; it does not matter how many subsets fail. Checking a particular subset is done in polynomial time by adding the distances of the edges and verifying that the edges form a cycle that visits each vertex exactly once. Thus, the checking algorithm runs in polynomial time. Unfortunately, there are $2^{|E|}$ subsets to check, so this algorithm cannot be converted to a polynomial time algorithm on a regular computer. Nor does anybody in the world know of any other polynomial time algorithm to solve TRAVELING SALESMAN on a regular computer, despite the fact that the problem has been studied extensively by many computer scientists for many years.

It turns out that there is a large collection of problems with this property: We know efficient non-deterministic algorithms, but we do not know if there are efficient deterministic algorithms. At the same time, we have not been able to prove that any of these problems do *not* have efficient deterministic algorithms. This class of problems is called $\mathcal{NP}$-**complete**. What is truly strange and fascinating about $\mathcal{NP}$-complete problems is that if anybody ever finds the solution to any one of them that runs in polynomial time on a regular computer, then by a series of reductions, every other problem that is in $\mathcal{NP}$ can also be solved in polynomial time on a regular computer!

Define a problem to be $\mathcal{NP}$-**hard** if *any* problem in $\mathcal{NP}$ can be reduced to X in polynomial time. Thus, X is *as hard as* any problem in $\mathcal{NP}$. A problem X is defined to be $\mathcal{NP}$-complete if

1. X is in $\mathcal{NP}$, and
2. X is $\mathcal{NP}$-hard.

The requirement that a problem be $\mathcal{NP}$-hard might seem to be impossible, but in fact there are hundreds of such problems, including TRAVELING SALESMAN. Another such problem is called K-CLIQUE.

K-CLIQUE
  Input: An arbitrary undirected graph **G** and an integer k.
  Output: YES if there is a complete subgraph of at least k vertices, and NO otherwise.

Nobody knows whether there is a polynomial time solution for K-CLIQUE, but if such an algorithm is found for K-CLIQUE *or* for TRAVELING SALESMAN, then that solution can be modified to solve the other, or any other problem in $\mathcal{NP}$, in polynomial time.

The primary theoretical advantage of knowing that a problem P1 is $\mathcal{NP}$-complete is that it can be used to show that another problem P2 is $\mathcal{NP}$-complete. This is done by finding a polynomial time reduction of P1 to P2. Because we already know that all problems in $\mathcal{NP}$ can be reduced to P1 in polynomial time (by the definition of $\mathcal{NP}$-complete), we now know that all problems can be reduced to P2 as well by the simple algorithm of reducing to P1 and then from there reducing to P2.

There is a practical advantage to knowing that a problem is $\mathcal{NP}$-complete. It relates to knowing that if a polynomial time solution can be found for *any* prob-

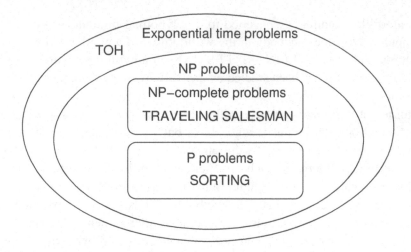

Figure 17.5 Our knowledge regarding the world of problems requiring exponential time or less. Some of these problems are solvable in polynomial time by a non-deterministic computer. Of these, some are known to be $\mathcal{NP}$-complete, and some are known to be solvable in polynomial time on a regular computer.

lem that is $\mathcal{NP}$-complete, then a polynomial solution can be found for *all* such problems. The implication is that,

1. Because no one has yet found such a solution, it must be difficult or impossible to do; and
2. Effort to find a polynomial time solution for one $\mathcal{NP}$-complete problem can be considered to have been expended for all $\mathcal{NP}$-complete problems.

How is $\mathcal{NP}$-completeness of practical significance for typical programmers? Well, if your boss demands that you provide a fast algorithm to solve a problem, she will not be happy if you come back saying that the best you could do was an exponential time algorithm. But, if you can prove that the problem is $\mathcal{NP}$-complete, while she still won't be happy, at least she should not be mad at you! By showing that her problem is $\mathcal{NP}$-complete, you are in effect saying that the most brilliant computer scientists for the last 50 years have been trying and failing to find a polynomial time algorithm for her problem.

Problems that are solvable in polynomial time on a regular computer are said to be in class $\mathcal{P}$. Clearly, all problems in $\mathcal{P}$ are solvable in polynomial time on a non-deterministic computer simply by neglecting to use the non-deterministic capability. Some problems in $\mathcal{NP}$ are $\mathcal{NP}$-complete. We can consider all problems solvable in exponential time or better as an even bigger class of problems because all problems solvable in polynomial time are solvable in exponential time. Thus, we can view the world of exponential-time-or-better problems in terms of Figure 17.5.

The most important unanswered question in theoretical computer science is whether $\mathcal{P} = \mathcal{NP}$. If they are equal, then there is a polynomial time algorithm for TRAVELING SALESMAN and all related problems. Because TRAVELING SALESMAN is known to be $\mathcal{NP}$-complete, if a polynomial time algorithm were to be found for this problem, then *all* problems in $\mathcal{NP}$ would also be solvable in polynomial time. Conversely, if we were able to prove that TRAVELING SALESMAN has an exponential time lower bound, then we would know that $\mathcal{P} \neq \mathcal{NP}$.

17.2.2 $\mathcal{NP}$-Completeness Proofs

To start the process of being able to prove problems are $\mathcal{NP}$-complete, we need to prove just one problem H is $\mathcal{NP}$-complete. After that, to show that any problem X is $\mathcal{NP}$-hard, we just need to reduce H to X. When doing $\mathcal{NP}$-completeness proofs, it is very important not to get this reduction backwards! If we reduce candidate problem X to known hard problem H, this means that we use H as a step to solving X. All that means is that we have found a (known) hard way to solve X. However, when we reduce known hard problem H to candidate problem X, that means we are using X as a step to solve H. And if we know that H is hard, that means X must also be hard (because if X were not hard, then neither would H be hard).

So a crucial first step to getting this whole theory off the ground is finding one problem that is $\mathcal{NP}$-hard. The first proof that a problem is $\mathcal{NP}$-hard (and because it is in $\mathcal{NP}$, therefore $\mathcal{NP}$-complete) was done by Stephen Cook. For this feat, Cook won the first Turing award, which is the closest Computer Science equivalent to the Nobel Prize. The "grand-daddy" $\mathcal{NP}$-complete problem that Cook used is call SATISFIABILITY (or SAT for short).

A **Boolean expression** includes Boolean variables combined using the operators AND ($\cdot$), OR ($+$), and NOT (to negate Boolean variable x we write $\overline{x}$). A **literal** is a Boolean variable or its negation. A **clause** is one or more literals OR'ed together. Let E be a Boolean expression over variables $x_1, x_2, ..., x_n$. Then we define **Conjunctive Normal Form** (CNF) to be a Boolean expression written as a series of clauses that are AND'ed together. For example,

$$E = (x_5 + x_7 + \overline{x_8} + x_{10}) \cdot (\overline{x_2} + x_3) \cdot (x_1 + \overline{x_3} + x_6)$$

is in CNF, and has three clauses. Now we can define the problem SAT.

SATISFIABILITY (SAT)

Input: A Boolean expression E over variables $x_1, x_2, ...$ in Conjunctive Normal Form.

Output: YES if there is an assignment to the variables that makes E true, NO otherwise.

Cook proved that SAT is $\mathcal{NP}$-hard. Explaining Cook's proof is beyond the scope of this book. But we can briefly summarize it as follows. Any decision problem F can be recast as some language acceptance problem L:

$$F(I) = \text{YES} \Leftrightarrow L(I') = \text{ACCEPT}.$$

That is, if a decision problem F yields YES on input I, then there is a language L containing string I' where I' is some suitable transformation of input I. Conversely, if F would give answer NO for input I, then I's transformed version I' is not in the language L.

Turing machines are a simple model of computation for writing programs that are language acceptors. There is a "universal" Turing machine that can take as input a description for a Turing machine, and an input string, and return the execution of that machine on that string. This Turing machine in turn can be cast as a Boolean expression such that the expression is satisfiable if and only if the Turing machine yields ACCEPT for that string. Cook used Turing machines in his proof because they are simple enough that he could develop this transformation of Turing machines to Boolean expressions, but rich enough to be able to compute any function that a regular computer can compute. The significance of this transformation is that *any* decision problem that is performable by the Turing machine is transformable to SAT. Thus, SAT is $\mathcal{NP}$-hard.

As explained above, to show that a decision problem X is $\mathcal{NP}$-complete, we prove that X is in $\mathcal{NP}$ (normally easy, and normally done by giving a suitable polynomial-time, nondeterministic algorithm) and then prove that X is $\mathcal{NP}$-hard. To prove that X is $\mathcal{NP}$-hard, we choose a known $\mathcal{NP}$-complete problem, say A. We describe a polynomial-time transformation that takes an *arbitrary* instance I of A to an instance I' of X. We then describe a polynomial-time transformation from SLN' to SLN such that SLN is the solution for I. The following example provides a model for how an $\mathcal{NP}$-completeness proof is done.

3-SATISFIABILITY (3 SAT)

Input: A Boolean expression E in CNF such that each clause contains exactly 3 literals.

Output: YES if the expression can be satisfied, NO otherwise.

Example 17.1 3 SAT is a special case of SAT. Is 3 SAT easier than SAT? Not if we can prove it to be $\mathcal{NP}$-complete.

Theorem 17.1 *3 SAT is $\mathcal{NP}$-complete.*

Proof: Prove that 3 SAT is in $\mathcal{NP}$: Guess (nondeterministically) truth values for the variables. The correctness of the guess can be verified in polynomial time.

Prove that 3 SAT is $\mathcal{NP}$-hard: We need a polynomial-time reduction from SAT to 3 SAT. Let $\mathbf{E} = C_1 \cdot C_2 \cdot \ldots \cdot C_k$ be any instance of SAT. Our strategy is to replace any clause C_i that does not have exactly three literals with a set of clauses each having exactly three literals. (Recall that a literal can be a variable such as x, or the negation of a variable such as $\overline{x}$.) Let $C_i = x_1 + x_2 + \ldots + x_j$ where $x_1, \ldots, x_j$ are literals.

1. $j = 1$, so $C_i = x_1$. Replace C_i with C_i':

$$(x_1 + y + z) \cdot (x_1 + \overline{y} + z) \cdot (x_1 + y + \overline{z}) \cdot (x_1 + \overline{y} + \overline{z})$$

where y and z are variables not appearing in $\mathbf{E}$. Clearly, C_i' is satisfiable if and only if (x_1) is satisfiable, meaning that x_1 is **true**.

2. $J = 2$, so $C_i = (x_1 + x_2)$. Replace C_i with

$$(x_1 + x_2 + z) \cdot (x_1 + x_2 + \overline{z})$$

where z is a new variable not appearing in $\mathbf{E}$. This new pair of clauses is satisfiable if and only if $(x_1 + x_2)$ is satisfiable, that is, either x_1 or x_2 must be true.

3. $j > 3$. Replace $C_i = (x_1 + x_2 + \cdots + x_j)$ with

$$(x_1 + x_2 + z_1) \cdot (x_3 + \overline{z_1} + z_2) \cdot (x_4 + \overline{z_2} + z_3) \cdot \ldots$$

$$\cdot (x_{j-2} + \overline{z_{j-4}} + z_{j-3}) \cdot (x_{j-1} + x_j + \overline{z_{j-3}})$$

where $z_1, \ldots, z_{j-3}$ are new variables.

After appropriate replacements have been made for each C_i, a Boolean expression results that is an instance of 3 SAT. Each replacement is satisfiable if and only if the original clause is satisfiable. The reduction is clearly polynomial time.

For the first two cases it is fairly easy to see that the original clause is satisfiable if and only if the resulting clauses are satisfiable. For the case were we replaced a clause with more than three literals, consider the following.

1. If E is satisfiable, then E' is satisfiable: Assume x_m is assigned **true**. Then assign $z_t, t \le m - 2$ as **true** and $z_k, t \ge m - 1$ as **false**. Then all clauses in Case (3) are satisfied.

2. If $x_1, x_2, \ldots, x_j$ are all **false**, then $z_1, z_2, \ldots, z_{j-3}$ are all **true**. But then $(x_{j-1} + x_{j-2} + \overline{z_{j-3}})$ is **false**.

$\square$

Next we define the problem VERTEX COVER for use in further examples.

VERTEX COVER:

   Input: A graph $\mathbf{G}$ and an integer k.

   Output: YES if there is a subset $\mathbf{S}$ of the vertices in $\mathbf{G}$ of size k or less such that every edge of $\mathbf{G}$ has at least one of its endpoints in $\mathbf{S}$, and NO otherwise.

Example 17.2 In this example, we make use of a simple conversion between two graph problems.

Theorem 17.2 *VERTEX COVER is $\mathcal{NP}$-complete.*

Proof: Prove that VERTEX COVER is in $\mathcal{NP}$: Simply guess a subset of the graph and determine in polynomial time whether that subset is in fact a vertex cover of size k or less.

Prove that VERTEX COVER is $\mathcal{NP}$-hard: We will assume that K-CLIQUE is already known to be $\mathcal{NP}$-complete. (We will see this proof in the next example. For now, just accept that it is true.)

Given that K-CLIQUE is $\mathcal{NP}$-complete, we need to find a polynomial-time transformation from the input to K-CLIQUE to the input to VERTEX COVER, and another polynomial-time transformation from the output for VERTEX COVER to the output for K-CLIQUE. This turns out to be a simple matter, given the following observation. Consider a graph **G** and a vertex cover **S** on **G**. Denote by **S'** the set of vertices in **G** but not in **S**. There can be no edge connecting any two vertices in **S'** because, if there were, then **S** would not be a vertex cover. Denote by **G'** the inverse graph for **G**, that is, the graph formed from the edges not in **G**. If **S** is of size k, then **S'** forms a clique of size $n - k$ in graph **G'**. Thus, we can reduce K-CLIQUE to VERTEX COVER simply by converting graph **G** to **G'**, and asking if **G'** has a VERTEX COVER of size $n - k$ or smaller. If YES, then there is a clique in **G** of size k; if NO then there is not. □

Example 17.3 So far, our $\mathcal{NP}$-completeness proofs have involved transformations between inputs of the same "type," such as from a Boolean expression to a Boolean expression or from a graph to a graph. Sometimes an $\mathcal{NP}$-completeness proof involves a transformation between types of inputs, as shown next.

Theorem 17.3 *K-CLIQUE is $\mathcal{NP}$-complete.*

Proof: K-CLIQUE is in $\mathcal{NP}$, because we can just guess a collection of k vertices and test in polynomial time if it is a clique. Now we show that K-CLIQUE is $\mathcal{NP}$-hard by using a reduction from SAT. An instance of SAT is a Boolean expression

$$B = C_1 \cdot C_2 \cdot ... \cdot C_m$$

whose clauses we will describe by the notation

$$C_i = y[i, 1] + y[i, 2] + ... + y[i, k_i]$$

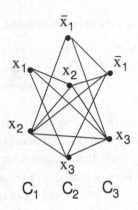

Figure 17.6 The graph generated from Boolean expression $B = (x_1 + x_2) \cdot (\overline{x_1} + x_2 + x_3) \cdot (\overline{x_1} + x_3)$. Literals from the first clause are labeled C1, and literals from the second clause are labeled C2. There is an edge between every pair of vertices except when both vertices represent instances of literals from the same clause, or a negation of the same variable. Thus, the vertex labeled $C1 : y_1$ does not connect to the vertex labeled $C1 : y_2$ (because they are literals in the same clause) or the vertex labeled $C2 : \overline{y_1}$ (because they are opposite values for the same variable).

where k_i is the number of literals in Clause c_i. We will transform this to an instance of K-CLIQUE as follows. We build a graph

$$G = \{v[i,j] | 1 \leq i \leq m, 1 \leq j \leq k_i\},$$

that is, there is a vertex in **G** corresponding to every literal in Boolean expression **B**. We will draw an edge between each pair of vertices $v[i_1, j_1]$ and $v[i_2, j_2]$ unless (1) they are two literals within the same clause ($i_1 = i_2$) or (2) they are opposite values for the same variable (i.e., one is negated and the other is not). Set $k = m$. Figure 17.6 shows an example of this transformation.

B is satisfiable if and only if **G** has a clique of size k or greater. **B** being satisfiable implies that there is a truth assignment such that at least one literal $y[i, j_i]$ is true for each i. If so, then these m literals must correspond to m vertices in a clique of size $k = m$. Conversely, if **G** has a clique of size k or greater, then the clique must have size exactly k (because no two vertices corresponding to literals in the same clause can be in the clique) and there is one vertex $v[i, j_i]$ in the clique for each i. There is a truth assignment making each $y[i, j_i]$ true. That truth assignment satisfies **B**.

We conclude that K-CLIQUE is $\mathcal{NP}$-hard, therefore $\mathcal{NP}$-complete. $\square$

17.2.3   Coping with $\mathcal{NP}$-Complete Problems

Finding that your problem is $\mathcal{NP}$-complete might not mean that you can just forget about it. Traveling salesmen need to find reasonable sales routes regardless of the complexity of the problem. What do you do when faced with an $\mathcal{NP}$-complete problem that you must solve?

There are several techniques to try. One approach is to run only small instances of the problem. For some problems, this is not acceptable. For example, TRAVEL-ING SALESMAN grows so quickly that it cannot be run on modern computers for problem sizes much over 30 cities, which is not an unreasonable problem size for real-life situations. However, some other problems in $\mathcal{NP}$, while requiring exponential time, still grow slowly enough that they allow solutions for problems of a useful size.

Consider the Knapsack problem from Section 16.1.1. We have a dynamic programming algorithm whose cost is $\Theta(nK)$ for n objects being fit into a knapsack of size K. But it turns out that Knapsack is $\mathcal{NP}$-complete. Isn't this a contradiction? Not when we consider the relationship between n and K. How big is K? Input size is typically $O(n \lg K)$ because the item sizes are smaller than K. Thus, $\Theta(nK)$ is exponential on input size.

This dynamic programming algorithm is tractable if the numbers are "reasonable." That is, we can successfully find solutions to the problem when nK is in the thousands. Such an algorithm is called a **pseudo-polynomial** time algorithm. This is different from TRAVELING SALESMAN which cannot possibly be solved when $n = 100$ given current algorithms.

A second approach to handling $\mathcal{NP}$-complete problems is to solve a special instance of the problem that is not so hard. For example, many problems on graphs are $\mathcal{NP}$-complete, but the same problem on certain restricted types of graphs is not as difficult. For example, while the VERTEX COVER and K-CLIQUE problems are $\mathcal{NP}$-complete in general, there are polynomial time solutions for bipartite graphs (i.e., graphs whose vertices can be separated into two subsets such that no pair of vertices within one of the subsets has an edge between them). 2-SATISFIABILITY (where every clause in a Boolean expression has at most two literals) has a polynomial time solution. Several geometric problems require only polynomial time in two dimensions, but are $\mathcal{NP}$-complete in three dimensions or more. KNAPSACK is considered to run in polynomial time if the numbers (and K) are "small." Small here means that they are polynomial on n, the number of items.

In general, if we want to guarantee that we get the correct answer for an $\mathcal{NP}$-complete problem, we potentially need to examine all of the (exponential number of) possible solutions. However, with some organization, we might be able to either examine them quickly, or avoid examining a great many of the possible answers in some cases. For example, Dynamic Programming (Section 16.1) attempts to organize the processing of all the subproblems to a problem so that the work is done efficiently.

If we need to do a brute-force search of the entire solution space, we can use **backtracking** to visit all of the possible solutions organized in a solution tree. For example, SATISFIABILITY has 2^n possible ways to assign truth values to the n variables contained in the Boolean expression being satisfied. We can view this as a tree of solutions by considering that we have a choice of making the first variable `true` or `false`. Thus, we can put all solutions where the first variable is `true` on one side of the tree, and the remaining solutions on the other. We then examine the solutions by moving down one branch of the tree, until we reach a point where we know the solution cannot be correct (such as if the current partial collection of assignments yields an unsatisfiable expression). At this point we backtrack and move back up a node in the tree, and then follow down the alternate branch. If this fails, we know to back up further in the tree as necessary and follow alternate branches, until finally we either find a solution that satisfies the expression or exhaust the tree. In some cases we avoid processing many potential solutions, or find a solution quickly. In others, we end up visiting a large portion of the 2^n possible solutions.

Banch-and-Bounds is an extension of backtracking that applies to **optimization problems** such as TRAVELING SALESMAN where we are trying to find the shortest tour through the cities. We traverse the solution tree as with backtracking. However, we remember the best value found so far. Proceeding down a given branch is equivalent to deciding which order to visit cities. So any node in the solution tree represents some collection of cities visited so far. If the sum of these distances exceeds the best tour found so far, then we know to stop pursuing this branch of the tree. At this point we can immediately back up and take another branch. If we have a quick method for finding a good (but not necessarily best) solution, we can use this as an initial bound value to effectively prune portions of the tree.

Another coping strategy is to find an approximate solution to the problem. There are many approaches to finding approximate solutions. One way is to use a heuristic to solve the problem, that is, an algorithm based on a "rule of thumb" that does not always give the best answer. For example, the TRAVELING SALESMAN problem can be solved approximately by using the heuristic that we start at an arbitrary city and then always proceed to the next unvisited city that is closest. This rarely gives the shortest path, but the solution might be good enough. There are many other heuristics for TRAVELING SALESMAN that do a better job.

Some approximation algorithms have guaranteed performance, such that the answer will be within a certain percentage of the best possible answer. For example, consider this simple heuristic for the VERTEX COVER problem: Let M be a maximal (not necessarily maximum) **matching** in G. A matching pairs vertices (with connecting edges) so that no vertex is paired with more than one partner.

Maximal means to pick as many pairs as possible, selecting them in some order until there are no more available pairs to select. Maximum means the matching that gives the most pairs possible for a given graph. If OPT is the size of a minimum vertex cover, then $|M| \leq 2 \cdot$ OPT because at least one endpoint of every matched edge must be in *any* vertex cover.

A better example of a guaranteed bound on a solution comes from simple heuristics to solve the BIN PACKING problem.

BIN PACKING:
Input: Numbers $x_1, x_2, ..., x_n$ between 0 and 1, and an unlimited supply of bins of size 1 (no bin can hold numbers whose sum exceeds 1).
Output: An assignment of numbers to bins that requires the fewest possible bins.

BIN PACKING in its decision form (i.e., asking if the items can be packed in less than k bins) is known to be $\mathcal{NP}$-complete. One simple heuristic for solving this problem is to use a "first fit" approach. We put the first number in the first bin. We then put the second number in the first bin if it fits, otherwise we put it in the second bin. For each subsequent number, we simply go through the bins in the order we generated them and place the number in the first bin that fits. The number of bins used is no more than twice the sum of the numbers, because every bin (except perhaps one) must be at least half full. However, this "first fit" heuristic can give us a result that is much worse than optimal. Consider the following collection of numbers: 6 of $1/7 + \epsilon$, 6 of $1/3 + \epsilon$, and 6 of $1/2 + \epsilon$, where ϵ is a small, positive number. Properly organized, this requires 6 bins. But if done wrongly, we might end up putting the numbers into 10 bins.

A better heuristic is to use decreasing first fit. This is the same as first fit, except that we keep the bins sorted from most full to least full. Then when deciding where to put the next item, we place it in the fullest bin that can hold it. This is similar to the "best fit" heuristic for memory management discussed in Section 12.3. The significant thing about this heuristic is not just that it tends to give better performance than simple first fit. This decreasing first fit heuristic can be proven to require no more than 11/9 the optimal number of bins. Thus, we have a guarantee on how much inefficiency can result when using the heuristic.

The theory of $\mathcal{NP}$-completeness gives a technique for separating tractable from (probably) intractable problems. Recalling the algorithm for generating algorithms in Section 15.1, we can refine it for problems that we suspect are $\mathcal{NP}$-complete. When faced with a new problem, we might alternate between checking if it is tractable (that is, we try to find a polynomial-time solution) and checking if it is intractable (we try to prove the problem is $\mathcal{NP}$-complete). While proving that some problem is $\mathcal{NP}$-complete does not actually make our upper bound for our algorithm match the lower bound for the problem with certainty, it is nearly as good. Once we realize that a problem is $\mathcal{NP}$-complete, then we know that our next step must either be to redefine the problem to make it easier, or else use one of the "coping" strategies discussed in this section.

17.3 Impossible Problems

Even the best programmer sometimes writes a program that goes into an infinite loop. Of course, when you run a program that has not stopped, you do not know for sure if it is just a slow program or a program in an infinite loop. After "enough time," you shut it down. Wouldn't it be great if your compiler could look at your program and tell you before you run it that it will get into an infinite loop? To be more specific, given a program and a particular input, it would be useful to know if executing the program on that input will result in an infinite loop without actually running the program.

Unfortunately, the **Halting Problem**, as this is called, cannot be solved. There will never be a computer program that can positively determine, for an arbitrary program **P**, if **P** will halt for all input. Nor will there even be a computer program that can positively determine if arbitrary program **P** will halt for a specified input I. How can this be? Programmers look at programs regularly to determine if they will halt. Surely this can be automated. As a warning to those who believe any program can be analyzed in this way, carefully examine the following code fragment before reading on.

```
while (n > 1)
  if (ODD(n))
    n = 3 * n + 1;
  else
    n = n / 2;
```

This is a famous piece of code. The sequence of values that is assigned to n by this code is sometimes called the **Collatz sequence** for input value n. Does this code fragment halt for all values of n? Nobody knows the answer. Every input that has been tried halts. But does it always halt? Note that for this code fragment, because we do not know if it halts, we also do not know an upper bound for its running time. As for the lower bound, we can easily show $\Omega(\log n)$ (see Exercise 3.14).

Personally, I have faith that someday some smart person will completely analyze the Collatz function, proving once and for all that the code fragment halts for all values of n. Doing so may well give us techniques that advance our ability to do algorithm analysis in general. Unfortunately, proofs from **computability** — the branch of computer science that studies what is impossible to do with a computer — compel us to believe that there will always be another bit of program code that we cannot analyze. This comes as a result of the fact that the Halting Problem is unsolvable.

17.3.1 Uncountability

Before proving that the Halting Problem is unsolvable, we first prove that not all functions can be implemented as a computer program. This must be so because the number of programs is much smaller than the number of possible functions.

A set is said to be **countable** (or **countably infinite** if it is a set with an infinite number of members) if every member of the set can be uniquely assigned to a positive integer. A set is said to be **uncountable** (or **uncountably infinite**) if it is not possible to assign every member of the set to its own positive integer.

To understand what is meant when we say "assigned to a positive integer," imagine that there is an infinite row of bins, labeled 1, 2, 3, and so on. Take a set and start placing members of the set into bins, with at most one member per bin. If we can find a way to assign all of the set members to bins, then the set is countable. For example, consider the set of positive even integers 2, 4, and so on. We can assign an integer i to bin $i/2$ (or, if we don't mind skipping some bins, then we can assign even number i to bin i). Thus, the set of even integers is countable. This should be no surprise, because intuitively there are "fewer" positive even integers than there are positive integers, even though both are infinite sets. But there are not really any more positive integers than there are positive even integers, because we can uniquely assign every positive integer to some positive even integer by simply assigning positive integer i to positive even integer $2i$.

On the other hand, the set of all integers is also countable, even though this set appears to be "bigger" than the set of positive integers. This is true because we can assign 0 to positive integer 1, 1 to positive integer 2, -1 to positive integer 3, 2 to positive integer 4, -2 to positive integer 5, and so on. In general, assign positive integer value i to positive integer value $2i$, and assign negative integer value $-i$ to positive integer value $2i + 1$. We will never run out of positive integers to assign, and we know exactly which positive integer every integer is assigned to. Because every integer gets an assignment, the set of integers is countably infinite.

Are the number of programs countable or uncountable? A program can be viewed as simply a string of characters (including special punctuation, spaces, and line breaks). Let us assume that the number of different characters that can appear in a program is P. (Using the ASCII character set, P must be less than 128, but the actual number does not matter). If the number of strings is countable, then surely the number of programs is also countable. We can assign strings to the bins as follows. Assign the null string to the first bin. Now, take all strings of one character, and assign them to the next P bins in "alphabetic" or ASCII code order. Next, take all strings of two characters, and assign them to the next P^2 bins, again in ASCII code order working from left to right. Strings of three characters are likewise assigned to bins, then strings of length four, and so on. In this way, a string of any given length can be assigned to some bin.

By this process, any string of finite length is assigned to some bin. So any program, which is merely a string of finite length, is assigned to some bin. Because all programs are assigned to some bin, the set of all programs is countable. Naturally most of the strings in the bins are not legal programs, but this is irrelevant. All that matters is that the strings that *do* correspond to programs are also in the bins.

Now we consider the number of possible functions. To keep things simple, assume that all functions take a single positive integer as input and yield a single positive integer as output. We will call such functions **integer functions**. A function is simply a mapping from input values to output values. Of course, not all computer programs literally take integers as input and yield integers as output. However, everything that computers read and write is essentially a series of numbers, which may be interpreted as letters or something else. Any useful computer program's input and output can be coded as integer values, so our simple model of computer input and output is sufficiently general to cover all possible computer programs.

We now wish to see if it is possible to assign all of the integer functions to the infinite set of bins. If so, then the number of functions is countable, and it might then be possible to assign every integer function to a program. If the set of integer functions cannot be assigned to bins, then there will be integer functions that must have no corresponding program.

Imagine each integer function as a table with two columns and an infinite number of rows. The first column lists the positive integers starting at 1. The second column lists the output of the function when given the value in the first column as input. Thus, the table explicitly describes the mapping from input to output for each function. Call this a **function table**.

Next we will try to assign function tables to bins. To do so we must order the functions, but it does not matter what order we choose. For example, Bin 1 could store the function that always returns 1 regardless of the input value. Bin 2 could store the function that returns its input. Bin 3 could store the function that doubles its input and adds 5. Bin 4 could store a function for which we can see no simple relationship between input and output.[2] These four functions as assigned to the first four bins are shown in Figure 17.7.

Can we assign every function to a bin? The answer is no, because there is always a way to create a new function that is not in any of the bins. Suppose that somebody presents a way of assigning functions to bins that they claim includes all of the functions. We can build a new function that has not been assigned to

---

[2]There is no requirement for a function to have any discernible relationship between input and output. A function is simply a mapping of inputs to outputs, with no constraint on how the mapping is determined.

	1		2		3		4	5
x	$f_1(x)$	x	$f_2(x)$	x	$f_3(x)$	x	$f_4(x)$	
1	1	1	1	1	7	1	15	
2	1	2	2	2	9	2	1	
3	1	3	3	3	11	3	7	
4	1	4	4	4	13	4	13	
5	1	5	5	5	15	5	2	
6	1	6	6	6	17	6	7	
⋮	⋮	⋮	⋮	⋮	⋮	⋮	⋮	

Figure 17.7 An illustration of assigning functions to bins.

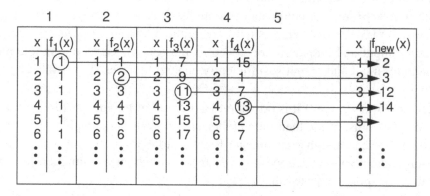

Figure 17.8 Illustration for the argument that the number of integer functions is uncountable.

any bin, as follows. Take the output value for input 1 from the function in the first bin. Call this value $F_1(1)$. Add 1 to it, and assign the result as the output of a new function for input value 1. Regardless of the remaining values assigned to our new function, it must be different from the first function in the table, because the two give different outputs for input 1. Now take the output value for 2 from the second function in the table (known as $F_2(2)$). Add 1 to this value and assign it as the output for 2 in our new function. Thus, our new function must be different from the function of Bin 2, because they will differ at least at the second value. Continue in this manner, assigning $F_{new}(i) = F_i(i) + 1$ for all values i. Thus, the new function must be different from any function F_i at least at position i. This procedure for constructing a new function not already in the table is called **diagonalization**. Because the new function is different from every other function, it must not be in the table. This is true no matter how we try to assign functions to bins, and so the number of integer functions is uncountable. The significance of this is that not all functions can possibly be assigned to programs, so there *must* be functions with no corresponding program. Figure 17.8 illustrates this argument.

17.3.2   The Halting Problem Is Unsolvable

While there might be intellectual appeal to knowing that there exists *some* function that cannot be computed by a computer program, does this mean that there is any such *useful* function? After all, does it really matter if no program can compute a "nonsense" function such as shown in Bin 4 of Figure 17.7? Now we will prove that the Halting Problem cannot be computed by any computer program. The proof is by contradiction.

We begin by assuming that there is a function named **halt** that can solve the Halting Problem. Obviously, it is not possible to write out something that does not exist, but here is a plausible sketch of what a function to solve the Halting Problem might look like if it did exist. Function **halt** takes two inputs: a string representing the source code for a program or function, and another string representing the input that we wish to determine if the input program or function halts on. Function **halt** does some work to make a decision (which is encapsulated into some fictitious function named **PROGRAM_HALTS**). Function **halt** then returns **true** if the input program or function does halt on the given input, and **false** otherwise.

```
bool halt(string prog, string input) {
  if (PROGRAM_HALTS(prog, input))
    return true;
  else
    return false;
}
```

We now will examine two simple functions that clearly can exist because the complete code for them is presented here:

```
// Return true if "prog" halts when given itself as input
bool selfhalt(char *prog) {
  if (halt(prog, prog))
    return true;
  else
    return false;
}

// Return the reverse of what selfhalt returns on "prog"
void contrary(char *prog) {
  if (selfhalt(prog))
    while (true); // Go into an infinite loop
}
```

What happens if we make a program whose sole purpose is to execute the function **contrary** and run that program with itself as input? One possibility is that the call to **selfhalt** returns **true**; that is, **selfhalt** claims that **contrary** will halt when run on itself. In that case, **contrary** goes into an infinite loop (and thus does not halt). On the other hand, if **selfhalt** returns **false**, then **halt** is proclaiming that **contrary** does not halt on itself, and **contrary** then returns, that is, it halts. Thus, **contrary** does the contrary of what **halt** says that it will do.

The action of **contrary** is logically inconsistent with the assumption that **halt** solves the Halting Problem correctly. There are no other assumptions we made that might cause this inconsistency. Thus, by contradiction, we have proved that **halt** cannot solve the Halting Problem correctly, and thus there is no program that can solve the Halting Problem.

Now that we have proved that the Halting Problem is unsolvable, we can use reduction arguments to prove that other problems are also unsolvable. The strategy is to assume the existence of a computer program that solves the problem in question and use that program to solve another problem that is already known to be unsolvable.

Example 17.4 Consider the following variation on the Halting Problem. Given a computer program, will it halt when its input is the empty string? That is, will it halt when it is given no input? To prove that this problem is unsolvable, we will employ a standard technique for computability proofs: Use a computer program to modify another computer program.

Proof: Assume that there is a function **Ehalt** that determines whether a given program halts when given no input. Recall that our proof for the Halting Problem involved functions that took as parameters a string representing a program and another string representing an input. Consider another function **combine** that takes a program P and an input string I as parameters. Function **combine** modifies P to store I as a static variable S and further modifies all calls to input functions within P to instead get their input from S. Call the resulting program P'. It should take no stretch of the imagination to believe that any decent compiler could be modified to take computer programs and input strings and produce a new computer program that has been modified in this way. Now, take P' and feed it to **Ehalt**. If **Ehalt** says that P' will halt, then we know that P would halt on input I. In other words, we now have a procedure for solving the original Halting Problem. The only assumption that we made was the existence of **Ehalt**. Thus, the problem of determining if a program will halt on no input must be unsolvable. □

Example 17.5 For arbitrary program P, does there exist *any* input for which P halts?

Proof: This problem is also uncomputable. Assume that we had a function **Ahalt** that, when given program P as input would determine if there is some input for which P halts. We could modify our compiler (or write a function as part of a program) to take P and some input string w, and modify it so that w is hardcoded inside P, with P reading no input. Call this modified program P'. Now, P' always behaves the same way regardless of its input, because it ignores all input. However, because w is now hardwired inside of P', the behavior we get is that of P when given w as input. So, P' will halt on any arbitrary input if and only if P would halt on input w. We now feed P' to function **Ahalt**. If **Ahalt** could determine that P' halts on some input, then that is the same as determining that P halts on input w. But we know that that is impossible. Therefore, **Ahalt** cannot exist.　　□

There are many things that we would like to have a computer do that are unsolvable. Many of these have to do with program behavior. For example, proving that an arbitrary program is "correct," that is, proving that a program computes a particular function, is a proof regarding program behavior. As such, what can be accomplished is severely limited. Some other unsolvable problems include:

- Does a program halt on every input?
- Does a program compute a particular function?
- Do two programs compute the same function?
- Does a particular line in a program get executed?

This does *not* mean that a computer program cannot be written that works on special cases, possibly even on most programs that we would be interested in checking. For example, some **C** compilers will check if the control expression for a **while** loop is a constant expression that evaluates to **false**. If it is, the compiler will issue a warning that the **while** loop code will never be executed. However, it is not possible to write a computer program that can check for *all* input programs whether a specified line of code will be executed when the program is given some specified input.

Another unsolvable problem is whether a program contains a computer virus. The property "contains a computer virus" is a matter of behavior. Thus, it is not possible to determine positively whether an arbitrary program contains a computer virus. Fortunately, there are many good heuristics for determining if a program is likely to contain a virus, and it is usually possible to determine if a program contains a particular virus, at least for the ones that are now known. Real virus checkers do a pretty good job, but, it will always be possible for malicious people to invent new viruses that no existing virus checker can recognize.

17.4　Further Reading

The classic text on the theory of $\mathcal{NP}$-completeness is *Computers and Intractability: A Guide to the Theory of $\mathcal{NP}$-completeness* by Garey and Johnston [GJ79]. *The Traveling Salesman Problem*, edited by Lawler et al. [LLKS85], discusses many approaches to finding an acceptable solution to this particular $\mathcal{NP}$-complete problem in a reasonable amount of time.

For more information about the Collatz function see "On the Ups and Downs of Hailstone Numbers" by B. Hayes [Hay84], and "The $3x + 1$ Problem and its Generalizations" by J.C. Lagarias [Lag85].

For an introduction to the field of computability and impossible problems, see *Discrete Structures, Logic, and Computability* by James L. Hein [Hei09].

17.5   Exercises

17.1 Consider this algorithm for finding the maximum element in an array: First sort the array and then select the last (maximum) element. What (if anything) does this reduction tell us about the upper and lower bounds to the problem of finding the maximum element in a sequence? Why can we not reduce SORTING to finding the maximum element?

17.2 Use a reduction to prove that squaring an $n \times n$ matrix is just as expensive (asymptotically) as multiplying two $n \times n$ matrices.

17.3 Use a reduction to prove that multiplying two upper triangular $n \times n$ matrices is just as expensive (asymptotically) as multiplying two arbitrary $n \times n$ matrices.

17.4   **(a)** Explain why computing the factorial of n by multiplying all values from 1 to n together is an exponential time algorithm.
    (b) Explain why computing an approximation to the factorial of n by making use of Stirling's formula (see Section 2.2) is a polynomial time algorithm.

17.5 Consider this algorithm for solving the K-CLIQUE problem. First, generate all subsets of the vertices containing exactly k vertices. There are $O(n^k)$ such subsets altogether. Then, check whether any subgraphs induced by these subsets is complete. If this algorithm ran in polynomial time, what would be its significance? Why is this not a polynomial-time algorithm for the K-CLIQUE problem?

17.6 Write the 3 SAT expression obtained from the reduction of SAT to 3 SAT described in Section 17.2.1 for the expression

$$(a + b + \overline{c} + d) \cdot (\overline{d}) \cdot (\overline{b} + \overline{c}) \cdot (\overline{a} + b) \cdot (a + c) \cdot (b).$$

Is this expression satisfiable?

17.7 Draw the graph obtained by the reduction of SAT to the K-CLIQUE problem given in Section 17.2.1 for the expression

$$(a + \overline{b} + c) \cdot (\overline{a} + b + \overline{c}) \cdot (\overline{a} + b + c) \cdot (a + \overline{b} + \overline{c}).$$

Is this expression satisfiable?

17.8 A **Hamiltonian cycle** in graph **G** is a cycle that visits every vertex in the graph exactly once before returning to the start vertex. The problem HAMIL-TONIAN CYCLE asks whether graph **G** does in fact contain a Hamiltonian cycle. Assuming that HAMILTONIAN CYCLE is $\mathcal{NP}$-complete, prove that the decision-problem form of TRAVELING SALESMAN is $\mathcal{NP}$-complete.

17.9 Use the assumption that VERTEX COVER is $\mathcal{NP}$-complete to prove that K-CLIQUE is also $\mathcal{NP}$-complete by finding a polynomial time reduction from VERTEX COVER to K-CLIQUE.

17.10 We define the problem INDEPENDENT SET as follows.

> INDEPENDENT SET
> **Input**: A graph **G** and an integer k.
> **Output**: YES if there is a subset **S** of the vertices in **G** of size k or greater such that no edge connects any two vertices in **S**, and NO other-wise.

Assuming that K-CLIQUE is $\mathcal{NP}$-complete, prove that INDEPENDENT SET is $\mathcal{NP}$-complete.

17.11 Define the problem PARTITION as follows:

> PARTITION
> **Input**: A collection of integers.
> **Output**: YES if the collection can be split into two such that the sum of the integers in each partition sums to the same amount. NO otherwise.

(a) Assuming that PARTITION is $\mathcal{NP}$-complete, prove that the decision form of BIN PACKING is $\mathcal{NP}$-complete.

(b) Assuming that PARTITION is $\mathcal{NP}$-complete, prove that KNAPSACK is $\mathcal{NP}$-complete.

17.12 Imagine that you have a problem **P** that you know is $\mathcal{NP}$-complete. For this problem you have two algorithms to solve it. For each algorithm, some problem instances of **P** run in polynomial time and others run in exponential time (there are lots of heuristic-based algorithms for real $\mathcal{NP}$-complete problems with this behavior). You can't tell beforehand for any given problem instance whether it will run in polynomial or exponential time on either algorithm. However, you do know that for every problem instance, at least one of the two algorithms will solve it in polynomial time.

(a) What should you do?

(b) What is the running time of your solution?

(c) What does it say about the question of $\mathcal{P} = \mathcal{NP}$ if the conditions described in this problem existed?

17.13 Here is another version of the knapsack problem, which we will call EXACT KNAPSACK. Given a set of items each with given integer size, and a knapsack of size integer k, is there a subset of the items which fits exactly within the knapsack?

Assuming that EXACT KNAPSACK is $\mathcal{NP}$-complete, use a reduction argument to prove that KNAPSACK is $\mathcal{NP}$-complete.

17.14 The last paragraph of Section 17.2.3 discusses a strategy for developing a solution to a new problem by alternating between finding a polynomial time solution and proving the problem $\mathcal{NP}$-complete. Refine the "algorithm for designing algorithms" from Section 15.1 to incorporate identifying and dealing with $\mathcal{NP}$-complete problems.

17.15 Prove that the set of real numbers is uncountable. Use a proof similar to the proof in Section 17.3.1 that the set of integer functions is uncountable.

17.16 Prove, using a reduction argument such as given in Section 17.3.2, that the problem of determining if an arbitrary program will print any output is unsolvable.

17.17 Prove, using a reduction argument such as given in Section 17.3.2, that the problem of determining if an arbitrary program executes a particular statement within that program is unsolvable.

17.18 Prove, using a reduction argument such as given in Section 17.3.2, that the problem of determining if two arbitrary programs halt on exactly the same inputs is unsolvable.

17.19 Prove, using a reduction argument such as given in Section 17.3.2, that the problem of determining whether there is some input on which two arbitrary programs will both halt is unsolvable.

17.20 Prove, using a reduction argument such as given in Section 17.3.2, that the problem of determining whether an arbitrary program halts on all inputs is unsolvable.

17.21 Prove, using a reduction argument such as given in Section 17.3.2, that the problem of determining whether an arbitrary program computes a specified function is unsolvable.

17.22 Consider a program named COMP that takes two strings as input. It returns **TRUE** if the strings are the same. It returns **FALSE** if the strings are different. Why doesn't the argument that we used to prove that a program to solve the halting problem does not exist work to prove that COMP does not exist?

17.6 Projects

17.1 Implement VERTEX COVER; that is, given graph **G** and integer k, answer the question of whether or not there is a vertex cover of size k or less. Begin by using a brute-force algorithm that checks all possible sets of vertices of size k to find an acceptable vertex cover, and measure the running time on a number of input graphs. Then try to reduce the running time through the use of any heuristics you can think of. Next, try to find approximate solutions to the problem in the sense of finding the smallest set of vertices that forms a vertex cover.

17.2 Implement KNAPSACK (see Section 16.1). Measure its running time on a number of inputs. What is the largest practical input size for this problem?

17.3 Implement an approximation of TRAVELING SALESMAN; that is, given a graph **G** with costs for all edges, find the cheapest cycle that visits all vertices in **G**. Try various heuristics to find the best approximations for a wide variety of input graphs.

17.4 Write a program that, given a positive integer n as input, prints out the Collatz sequence for that number. What can you say about the types of integers that have long Collatz sequences? What can you say about the length of the Collatz sequence for various types of integers?

PART VI

APPENDIX

A

Utility Functions

Here are various utility functions used by the C++ example programs in this text.

```cpp
// Return true iff "x" is even
inline bool EVEN(int x) { return (x % 2) == 0; }

// Return true iff "x" is odd
inline bool ODD(int x) { return (x % 2) != 0; }

// Assert: If "val" is false, print a message and terminate
// the program
void Assert(bool val, string s) {
  if (!val) { // Assertion failed -- close the program
    cout << "Assertion Failed: " << s << endl;
    exit(-1);
  }
}

// Swap two elements in a generic array
template<typename E>
inline void swap(E A[], int i, int j) {
  E temp = A[i];
  A[i] = A[j];
  A[j] = temp;
}
// Random number generator functions

inline void Randomize() // Seed the generator
  { srand(1); }

// Return a random value in range 0 to n-1
inline int Random(int n)
  { return rand() % (n); }
```

Bibliography

[AG06]   Ken Arnold and James Gosling. *The Java Programming Language*.
          Addison-Wesley, Reading, MA, USA, fourth edition, 2006.

[Aha00]   Dan Aharoni. Cogito, ergo sum! cognitive processes of students deal-
          ing with data structures. In *Proceedings of SIGCSE'00*, pages 26–30,
          ACM Press, March 2000.

[AHU74]   Alfred V. Aho, John E. Hopcroft, and Jeffrey D. Ullman. *The Design
          and Analysis of Computer Algorithms*. Addison-Wesley, Reading, MA,
          1974.

[AHU83]   Alfred V. Aho, John E. Hopcroft, and Jeffrey D. Ullman. *Data Struc-
          tures and Algorithms*. Addison-Wesley, Reading, MA, 1983.

[BB96]   G. Brassard and P. Bratley. *Fundamentals of Algorithmics*. Prentice
          Hall, Upper Saddle River, NJ, 1996.

[Ben75]   John Louis Bentley. Multidimensional binary search trees used for
          associative searching. *Communications of the ACM*, 18(9):509–517,
          September 1975. ISSN: 0001-0782.

[Ben82]   John Louis Bentley. *Writing Efficient Programs*. Prentice Hall, Upper
          Saddle River, NJ, 1982.

[Ben84]   John Louis Bentley. Programming pearls: The back of the envelope.
          Communications of the ACM, 27(3):180–184, March 1984.

[Ben85]   John Louis Bentley. Programming pearls: Thanks, heaps. *Communi-
          cations of the ACM*, 28(3):245–250, March 1985.

[Ben86]   John Louis Bentley. Programming pearls: The envelope is back. *Com-
          munications of the ACM*, 29(3):176–182, March 1986.

[Ben88]   John Bentley. *More Programming Pearls: Confessions of a Coder*.
          Addison-Wesley, Reading, MA, 1988.

[Ben00]   John Bentley. *Programming Pearls*. Addison-Wesley, Reading, MA,
          second edition, 2000.

[BG00]   Sara Baase and Allen Van Gelder. *Computer Algorithms: Introduction
          to Design & Analysis*. Addison-Wesley, Reading, MA, USA, third
          edition, 2000.

[BM85]   John Louis Bentley and Catherine C. McGeoch. Amortized analysis
           of self-organizing sequential search heuristics. *Communications of the
           ACM*, 28(4):404–411, April 1985.

[Bro95]   Frederick P. Brooks. *The Mythical Man-Month: Essays on Software
           Engineering, 25th Anniversary Edition*. Addison-Wesley, Reading,
           MA, 1995.

[BSTW86] John Louis Bentley, Daniel D. Sleator, Robert E. Tarjan, and Victor K.
           Wei. A locally adaptive data compression scheme. *Communications
           of the ACM*, 29(4):320–330, April 1986.

[CLRS09] Thomas H. Cormen, Charles E. Leiserson, Ronald L. Rivest, and Clif-
           ford Stein. *Introduction to Algorithms*. The MIT Press, Cambridge,
           MA, third edition, 2009.

[Com79]   Douglas Comer. The ubiquitous B-tree. *Computing Surveys*,
           11(2):121–137, June 1979.

[DD08]   H.M. Deitel and P.J. Deitel. *C++ How to Program*. Prentice Hall,
           Upper Saddle River, NJ, sixth edition, 2008.

[ECW92]   Vladimir Estivill-Castro and Derick Wood. A survey of adaptive sort-
           ing algorithms. *Computing Surveys*, 24(4):441–476, December 1992.

[ED88]   R.J. Enbody and H.C. Du. Dynamic hashing schemes. *Computing
           Surveys*, 20(2):85–113, June 1988.

[Epp10]   Susanna S. Epp. *Discrete Mathematics with Applications*. Brooks/Cole
           Publishing Company, Pacific Grove, CA, fourth edition, 2010.

[ES90]   Margaret A. Ellis and Bjarne Stroustrup. *The Annotated C++ Refer-
           ence Manual*. Addison-Wesley, Reading, MA, 1990.

[ESS81]   S. C. Eisenstat, M. H. Schultz, and A. H. Sherman. Algorithms and
           data structures for sparse symmetric gaussian elimination. *SIAM Jour-
           nal on Scientific Computing*, 2(2):225–237, June 1981.

[FBY92]   W.B. Frakes and R. Baeza-Yates, editors. *Information Retrieval: Data
           Structures & Algorithms*. Prentice Hall, Upper Saddle River, NJ, 1992.

[FF89]   Daniel P. Friedman and Matthias Felleisen. *The Little LISPer*. Macmil-
           lan Publishing Company, New York, NY, 1989.

[FFBS95] Daniel P. Friedman, Matthias Felleisen, Duane Bibby, and Gerald J.
           Sussman. *The Little Schemer*. The MIT Press, Cambridge, MA, fourth
           edition, 1995.

[FHCD92] Edward A. Fox, Lenwood S. Heath, Q. F. Chen, and Amjad M. Daoud.
           Practical minimal perfect hash functions for large databases. *Commu-
           nications of the ACM*, 35(1):105–121, January 1992.

[FL95]   H. Scott Folger and Steven E. LeBlanc. *Strategies for Creative Prob-
           lem Solving*. Prentice Hall, Upper Saddle River, NJ, 1995.

[FZ98]   M.J. Folk and B. Zoellick. *File Structures: An Object-Oriented Ap-
           proach with C++*. Addison-Wesley, Reading, MA, third edition, 1998.

[GHJV95] Erich Gamma, Richard Helm, Ralph Johnson, and John Vlissides. *Design Patterns: Elements of Reusable Object-Oriented Software.* Addison-Wesley, Reading, MA, 1995.

[GI91]   Zvi Galil and Giuseppe F. Italiano. Data structures and algorithms for disjoint set union problems. *Computing Surveys*, 23(3):319–344, September 1991.

[GJ79]   Michael R. Garey and David S. Johnson. *Computers and Intractability: A Guide to the Theory of NP-Completeness.* W.H. Freeman, New York, NY, 1979.

[GKP94]   Ronald L. Graham, Donald E. Knuth, and Oren Patashnik. *Concrete Mathematics: A Foundation for Computer Science.* Addison-Wesley, Reading, MA, second edition, 1994.

[Gle92]   James Gleick. *Genius: The Life and Science of Richard Feynman.* Vintage, New York, NY, 1992.

[GMS91]   John R. Gilbert, Cleve Moler, and Robert Schreiber. Sparse matrices in MATLAB: Design and implementation. *SIAM Journal on Matrix Analysis and Applications*, 13(1):333–356, 1991.

[Gut84]   Antonin Guttman. R-trees: A dynamic index structure for spatial searching. In B. Yormark, editor, *Annual Meeting ACM SIGMOD*, pages 47–57, Boston, MA, June 1984.

[Hay84]   B. Hayes. Computer recreations: On the ups and downs of hailstone numbers. *Scientific American*, 250(1):10–16, January 1984.

[Hei09]   James L. Hein. *Discrete Structures, Logic, and Computability.* Jones and Bartlett, Sudbury, MA, third edition, 2009.

[Jay90]   Julian Jaynes. *The Origin of Consciousness in the Breakdown of the Bicameral Mind.* Houghton Mifflin, Boston, MA, 1990.

[Kaf98]   Dennis Kafura. *Object-Oriented Software Design and Construction with C++.* Prentice Hall, Upper Saddle River, NJ, 1998.

[Knu94]   Donald E. Knuth. *The Stanford GraphBase.* Addison-Wesley, Reading, MA, 1994.

[Knu97]   Donald E. Knuth. *The Art of Computer Programming: Fundamental Algorithms*, volume 1. Addison-Wesley, Reading, MA, third edition, 1997.

[Knu98]   Donald E. Knuth. *The Art of Computer Programming: Sorting and Searching*, volume 3. Addison-Wesley, Reading, MA, second edition, 1998.

[Koz05]   Charles M. Kozierok. The PC guide. www.pcguide.com, 2005.

[KP99]   Brian W. Kernighan and Rob Pike. *The Practice of Programming.* Addison-Wesley, Reading, MA, 1999.

[Lag85]   J. C. Lagarias. The 3x+1 problem and its generalizations. *The American Mathematical Monthly*, 92(1):3–23, January 1985.

[Lev94]   Marvin Levine. *Effective Problem Solving.* Prentice Hall, Upper Saddle River, NJ, second edition, 1994.

[LLKS85]   E.L. Lawler, J.K. Lenstra, A.H.G. Rinnooy Kan, and D.B. Shmoys, editors. *The Traveling Salesman Problem: A Guided Tour of Combinatorial Optimization.* John Wiley & Sons, New York, NY, 1985.

[Man89]   Udi Manber. *Introduction to Algorithms: A Creative Approach.* Addision-Wesley, Reading, MA, 1989.

[MM04]   Nimrod Megiddo and Dharmendra S. Modha. Outperforming lru with an adaptive replacement cache algorithm. *IEEE Computer*, 37(4):58–65, April 2004.

[MM08]   Zbigniew Michaelewicz and Matthew Michalewicz. *Puzzle-Based Learning: An introduction to critical thinking, mathematics, and problem solving.* Hybrid Publishers, Melbourne, Australia, 2008.

[Pól57]   George Pólya. *How To Solve It.* Princeton University Press, Princeton, NJ, second edition, 1957.

[Pug90]   W. Pugh. Skip lists: A probabilistic alternative to balanced trees. *Communications of the ACM*, 33(6):668–676, June 1990.

[Raw92]   Gregory J.E. Rawlins. *Compared to What? An Introduction to the Analysis of Algorithms.* Computer Science Press, New York, NY, 1992.

[Rie96]   Arthur J. Riel. *Object-Oriented Design Heuristics.* Addison-Wesley, Reading, MA, 1996.

[Rob84]   Fred S. Roberts. *Applied Combinatorics.* Prentice Hall, Upper Saddle River, NJ, 1984.

[Rob86]   Eric S. Roberts. *Thinking Recursively.* John Wiley & Sons, New York, NY, 1986.

[RW94]   Chris Ruemmler and John Wilkes. An introduction to disk drive modeling. *IEEE Computer*, 27(3):17–28, March 1994.

[Sal88]   Betty Salzberg. *File Structures: An Analytic Approach.* Prentice Hall, Upper Saddle River, NJ, 1988.

[Sam06]   Hanan Samet. *Foundations of Multidimensional and Metric Data Structures.* Morgan Kaufmann, San Francisco, CA, 2006.

[SB93]   Clifford A. Shaffer and Patrick R. Brown. A paging scheme for pointer-based quadtrees. In D. Abel and B-C. Ooi, editors, *Advances in Spatial Databases*, pages 89–104, Springer Verlag, Berlin, June 1993.

[Sed80]   Robert Sedgewick. *Quicksort.* Garland Publishing, Inc., New York, NY, 1980.

[Sed11]   Robert Sedgewick. *Algorithms.* Addison-Wesley, Reading, MA, 4th edition, 2011.

[Sel95]   Kevin Self. Technically speaking. *IEEE Spectrum*, 32(2):59, February 1995.

[SH92]   Clifford A. Shaffer and Gregory M. Herb. A real-time robot arm colli-
           sion avoidance system. *IEEE Transactions on Robotics*, 8(2):149–160,
           1992.

[SJH93]   Clifford A. Shaffer, Ramana Juvvadi, and Lenwood S. Heath. A gener-
           alized comparison of quadtree and bintree storage requirements. *Image
           and Vision Computing*, 11(7):402–412, September 1993.

[Ski10]   Steven S. Skiena. *The Algorithm Design Manual*. Springer Verlag,
           New York, NY, second edition, 2010.

[SM83]   Gerard Salton and Michael J. McGill. *Introduction to Modern Infor-
           mation Retrieval*. McGraw-Hill, New York, NY, 1983.

[Sol09]   Daniel Solow. *How to Read and Do Proofs: An Introduction to Math-
           ematical Thought Processes*. John Wiley & Sons, New York, NY, fifth
           edition, 2009.

[ST85]   D.D. Sleator and Robert E. Tarjan. Self-adjusting binary search trees.
           Journal of the ACM, 32:652–686, 1985.

[Sta11a]   William Stallings. *Operating Systems: Internals and Design Princi-
           ples*. Prentice Hall, Upper Saddle River, NJ, seventh edition, 2011.

[Sta11b]   Richard M. Stallman. *GNU Emacs Manual*. Free Software Foundation,
           Cambridge, MA, sixteenth edition, 2011.

[Ste90]   Guy L. Steele. *Common Lisp: The Language*. Digital Press, Bedford,
           MA, second edition, 1990.

[Sto88]   James A. Storer. *Data Compression: Methods and Theory*. Computer
           Science Press, Rockville, MD, 1988.

[Str00]   Bjarne Stroustrup. *The C++ Programming Language, Special Edition*.
           Addison-Wesley, Reading, MA, 2000.

[SU92]   Clifford A. Shaffer and Mahesh T. Ursekar. Large scale editing and
           vector to raster conversion via quadtree spatial indexing. In *Proceed-
           ings of the 5th International Symposium on Spatial Data Handling*,
           pages 505–513, August 1992.

[SW94]   Murali Sitaraman and Bruce W. Weide. Special feature: Component-
           based software using resolve. *Software Engineering Notes*, 19(4):21–
           67, October 1994.

[SWH93]   Murali Sitaraman, Lonnie R. Welch, and Douglas E. Harms. On
           specification of reusable software components. *International Journal
           of Software Engineering and Knowledge Engineering*, 3(2):207–229,
           June 1993.

[Tan06]   Andrew S. Tanenbaum. *Structured Computer Organization*. Prentice
           Hall, Upper Saddle River, NJ, fifth edition, 2006.

[Tar75]   Robert E. Tarjan. On the efficiency of a good but not linear set merging
           algorithm. *Journal of the ACM*, 22(2):215–225, April 1975.

[Wel88]   Dominic Welsh. *Codes and Cryptography*. Oxford University Press, Oxford, 1988.

[Win94]   Patrick Henry Winston. *On to C++*. Addison-Wesley, Reading, MA, 1994.

[WL99]   Arthur Whimbey and Jack Lochhead. *Problem Solving & Comprehension*. Lawrence Erlbaum Associates, Mahwah, NJ, sixth edition, 1999.

[WMB99]   I.H. Witten, A. Moffat, and T.C. Bell. *Managing Gigabytes*. Morgan Kaufmann, second edition, 1999.

[Zei07]   Paul Zeitz. *The Art and Craft of Problem Solving*. John Wiley & Sons, New York, NY, second edition, 2007.

Index

Mathematics-Bestsellers

HANDBOOK OF MATHEMATICAL FUNCTIONS: with Formulas, Graphs, and Mathematical Tables, Edited by Milton Abramowitz and Irene A. Stegun. A classic resource for working with special functions, standard trig, and exponential logarithmic definitions and extensions, it features 29 sets of tables, some to as high as 20 places. 1046pp. 8 x 10 1/2. 0-486-61272-4

ABSTRACT AND CONCRETE CATEGORIES: The Joy of Cats, Jiri Adamek, Horst Herrlich, and George E. Strecker. This up-to-date introductory treatment employs category theory to explore the theory of structures. Its unique approach stresses concrete categories and presents a systematic view of factorization structures. Numerous examples. 1990 edition, updated 2004. 528pp. 6 1/8 x 9 1/4. 0-486-46934-4

MATHEMATICS: Its Content, Methods and Meaning, A. D. Aleksandrov, A. N. Kolmogorov, and M. A. Lavrent'ev. Major survey offers comprehensive, coherent discussions of analytic geometry, algebra, differential equations, calculus of variations, functions of a complex variable, prime numbers, linear and non-Euclidean geometry, topology, functional analysis, more. 1963 edition. 1120pp. 5 3/8 x 8 1/2. 0-486-40916-3

INTRODUCTION TO VECTORS AND TENSORS: Second Edition--Two Volumes Bound as One, Ray M. Bowen and C.-C. Wang. Convenient single-volume compilation of two texts offers both introduction and in-depth survey. Geared toward engineering and science students rather than mathematicians, it focuses on physics and engineering applications. 1976 edition. 560pp. 6 1/2 x 9 1/4. 0-486-46914-X

AN INTRODUCTION TO ORTHOGONAL POLYNOMIALS, Theodore S. Chihara. Concise introduction covers general elementary theory, including the representation theorem and distribution functions, continued fractions and chain sequences, the recurrence formula, special functions, and some specific systems. 1978 edition. 272pp. 5 3/8 x 8 1/2. 0-486-47929-3

ADVANCED MATHEMATICS FOR ENGINEERS AND SCIENTISTS, Paul DuChateau. This primary text and supplemental reference focuses on linear algebra, calculus, and ordinary differential equations. Additional topics include partial differential equations and approximation methods. Includes solved problems. 1992 edition. 400pp. 7 1/2 x 9 1/4. 0-486-47930-7

PARTIAL DIFFERENTIAL EQUATIONS FOR SCIENTISTS AND ENGINEERS, Stanley J. Farlow. Practical text shows how to formulate and solve partial differential equations. Coverage of diffusion-type problems, hyperbolic-type problems, elliptic-type problems, numerical and approximate methods. Solution guide available upon request. 1982 edition. 414pp. 6 1/8 x 9 1/4. 0-486-67620-X

VARIATIONAL PRINCIPLES AND FREE-BOUNDARY PROBLEMS, Avner Friedman. Advanced graduate-level text examines variational methods in partial differential equations and illustrates their applications to free-boundary problems. Features detailed statements of standard theory of elliptic and parabolic operators. 1982 edition. 720pp. 6 1/8 x 9 1/4. 0-486-47853-X

LINEAR ANALYSIS AND REPRESENTATION THEORY, Steven A. Gaal. Unified treatment covers topics from the theory of operators and operator algebras on Hilbert spaces; integration and representation theory for topological groups; and the theory of Lie algebras, Lie groups, and transform groups. 1973 edition. 704pp. 6 1/8 x 9 1/4. 0-486-47851-3

Browse over 9,000 books at www.doverpublications.com

A SURVEY OF INDUSTRIAL MATHEMATICS, Charles R. MacCluer. Students learn how to solve problems they'll encounter in their professional lives with this concise single-volume treatment. It employs MATLAB and other strategies to explore typical industrial problems. 2000 edition. 384pp. 5 3/8 x 8 1/2.   0-486-47702-9

NUMBER SYSTEMS AND THE FOUNDATIONS OF ANALYSIS, Elliott Mendelson. Geared toward undergraduate and beginning graduate students, this study explores natural numbers, integers, rational numbers, real numbers, and complex numbers. Numerous exercises and appendixes supplement the text. 1973 edition. 368pp. 5 3/8 x 8 1/2.   0-486-45792-3

A FIRST LOOK AT NUMERICAL FUNCTIONAL ANALYSIS, W. W. Sawyer. Text by renowned educator shows how problems in numerical analysis lead to concepts of functional analysis. Topics include Banach and Hilbert spaces, contraction mappings, convergence, differentiation and integration, and Euclidean space. 1978 edition. 208pp. 5 3/8 x 8 1/2.   0-486-47882-3

FRACTALS, CHAOS, POWER LAWS: Minutes from an Infinite Paradise, Manfred Schroeder. A fascinating exploration of the connections between chaos theory, physics, biology, and mathematics, this book abounds in award-winning computer graphics, optical illusions, and games that clarify memorable insights into self-similarity. 1992 edition. 448pp. 6 1/8 x 9 1/4.   0-486-47204-3

SET THEORY AND THE CONTINUUM PROBLEM, Raymond M. Smullyan and Melvin Fitting. A lucid, elegant, and complete survey of set theory, this three-part treatment explores axiomatic set theory, the consistency of the continuum hypothesis, and forcing and independence results. 1996 edition. 336pp. 6 x 9.   0-486-47484-4

DYNAMICAL SYSTEMS, Shlomo Sternberg. A pioneer in the field of dynamical systems discusses one-dimensional dynamics, differential equations, random walks, iterated function systems, symbolic dynamics, and Markov chains. Supplementary materials include PowerPoint slides and MATLAB exercises. 2010 edition. 272pp. 6 1/8 x 9 1/4.   0-486-47705-3

ORDINARY DIFFERENTIAL EQUATIONS, Morris Tenenbaum and Harry Pollard. Skillfully organized introductory text examines origin of differential equations, then defines basic terms and outlines general solution of a differential equation. Explores integrating factors; dilution and accretion problems; Laplace Transforms; Newton's Interpolation Formulas, more. 818pp. 5 3/8 x 8 1/2.   0-486-64940-7

MATROID THEORY, D. J. A. Welsh. Text by a noted expert describes standard examples and investigation results, using elementary proofs to develop basic matroid properties before advancing to a more sophisticated treatment. Includes numerous exercises. 1976 edition. 448pp. 5 3/8 x 8 1/2.   0-486-47439-9

THE CONCEPT OF A RIEMANN SURFACE, Hermann Weyl. This classic on the general history of functions combines function theory and geometry, forming the basis of the modern approach to analysis, geometry, and topology. 1955 edition. 208pp. 5 3/8 x 8 1/2.   0-486-47004-0

THE LAPLACE TRANSFORM, David Vernon Widder. This volume focuses on the Laplace and Stieltjes transforms, offering a highly theoretical treatment. Topics include fundamental formulas, the moment problem, monotonic functions, and Tauberian theorems. 1941 edition. 416pp. 5 3/8 x 8 1/2.   0-486-47755-X

Mathematics–Logic and Problem Solving

PERPLEXING PUZZLES AND TANTALIZING TEASERS, Martin Gardner. Ninety-three riddles, mazes, illusions, tricky questions, word and picture puzzles, and other challenges offer hours of entertainment for youngsters. Filled with rib-tickling drawings. Solutions. 224pp. 5 3/8 x 8 1/2.   0-486-25637-5

MY BEST MATHEMATICAL AND LOGIC PUZZLES, Martin Gardner. The noted expert selects 70 of his favorite "short" puzzles. Includes The Returning Explorer, The Mutilated Chessboard, Scrambled Box Tops, and dozens more. Complete solutions included. 96pp. 5 3/8 x 8 1/2.   0-486-28152-3

THE LADY OR THE TIGER?: and Other Logic Puzzles, Raymond M. Smullyan. Created by a renowned puzzle master, these whimsically themed challenges involve paradoxes about probability, time, and change; metapuzzles; and self-referentiality. Nineteen chapters advance in difficulty from relatively simple to highly complex. 1982 edition. 240pp. 5 3/8 x 8 1/2.   0-486-47027-X

SATAN, CANTOR AND INFINITY: Mind-Boggling Puzzles, Raymond M. Smullyan. A renowned mathematician tells stories of knights and knaves in an entertaining look at the logical precepts behind infinity, probability, time, and change. Requires a strong background in mathematics. Complete solutions. 288pp. 5 3/8 x 8 1/2.

    0-486-47036-9

THE RED BOOK OF MATHEMATICAL PROBLEMS, Kenneth S. Williams and Kenneth Hardy. Handy compilation of 100 practice problems, hints and solutions indispensable for students preparing for the William Lowell Putnam and other mathematical competitions. Preface to the First Edition. Sources. 1988 edition. 192pp. 5 3/8 x 8 1/2.   0-486-69415-1

KING ARTHUR IN SEARCH OF HIS DOG AND OTHER CURIOUS PUZZLES, Raymond M. Smullyan. This fanciful, original collection for readers of all ages features arithmetic puzzles, logic problems related to crime detection, and logic and arithmetic puzzles involving King Arthur and his Dogs of the Round Table. 160pp. 5 3/8 x 8 1/2.

    0-486-47435-6

UNDECIDABLE THEORIES: Studies in Logic and the Foundation of Mathematics, Alfred Tarski in collaboration with Andrzej Mostowski and Raphael M. Robinson. This well-known book by the famed logician consists of three treatises: "A General Method in Proofs of Undecidability," "Undecidability and Essential Undecidability in Mathematics," and "Undecidability of the Elementary Theory of Groups." 1953 edition. 112pp. 5 3/8 x 8 1/2.   0-486-47703-7

LOGIC FOR MATHEMATICIANS, J. Barkley Rosser. Examination of essential topics and theorems assumes no background in logic. "Undoubtedly a major addition to the literature of mathematical logic." – *Bulletin of the American Mathematical Society*. 1978 edition. 592pp. 6 1/8 x 9 1/4.   0-486-46898-4

INTRODUCTION TO PROOF IN ABSTRACT MATHEMATICS, Andrew Wohlgemuth. This undergraduate text teaches students what constitutes an acceptable proof, and it develops their ability to do proofs of routine problems as well as those requiring creative insights. 1990 edition. 384pp. 6 1/2 x 9 1/4.   0-486-47854-8

FIRST COURSE IN MATHEMATICAL LOGIC, Patrick Suppes and Shirley Hill. Rigorous introduction is simple enough in presentation and context for wide range of students. Symbolizing sentences; logical inference; truth and validity; truth tables; terms, predicates, universal quantifiers; universal specification and laws of identity; more. 288pp. 5 3/8 x 8 1/2.   0-486-42259-3

Browse over 9,000 books at www.doverpublications.com

Mathematics–Algebra and Calculus

VECTOR CALCULUS, Peter Baxandall and Hans Liebeck. This introductory text offers a rigorous, comprehensive treatment. Classical theorems of vector calculus are amply illustrated with figures, worked examples, physical applications, and exercises with hints and answers. 1986 edition. 560pp. 5 3/8 x 8 1/2.   0-486-46620-5

ADVANCED CALCULUS: An Introduction to Classical Analysis, Louis Brand. A course in analysis that focuses on the functions of a real variable, this text introduces the basic concepts in their simplest setting and illustrates its teachings with numerous examples, theorems, and proofs. 1955 edition. 592pp. 5 3/8 x 8 1/2.   0-486-44548-8

ADVANCED CALCULUS, Avner Friedman. Intended for students who have already completed a one-year course in elementary calculus, this two-part treatment advances from functions of one variable to those of several variables. Solutions. 1971 edition. 432pp. 5 3/8 x 8 1/2.   0-486-45795-8

METHODS OF MATHEMATICS APPLIED TO CALCULUS, PROBABILITY, AND STATISTICS, Richard W. Hamming. This 4-part treatment begins with algebra and analytic geometry and proceeds to an exploration of the calculus of algebraic functions and transcendental functions and applications. 1985 edition. Includes 310 figures and 18 tables. 880pp. 6 1/2 x 9 1/4.   0-486-43945-3

BASIC ALGEBRA I: Second Edition, Nathan Jacobson. A classic text and standard reference for a generation, this volume covers all undergraduate algebra topics, including groups, rings, modules, Galois theory, polynomials, linear algebra, and associative algebra. 1985 edition. 528pp. 6 1/8 x 9 1/4.   0-486-47189-6

BASIC ALGEBRA II: Second Edition, Nathan Jacobson. This classic text and standard reference comprises all subjects of a first-year graduate-level course, including in-depth coverage of groups and polynomials and extensive use of categories and functors. 1989 edition. 704pp. 6 1/8 x 9 1/4.   0-486-47187-X

CALCULUS: An Intuitive and Physical Approach (Second Edition), Morris Kline. Application-oriented introduction relates the subject as closely as possible to science with explorations of the derivative; differentiation and integration of the powers of x; theorems on differentiation, antidifferentiation; the chain rule; trigonometric functions; more. Examples. 1967 edition. 960pp. 6 1/2 x 9 1/4.   0-486-40453-6

ABSTRACT ALGEBRA AND SOLUTION BY RADICALS, John E. Maxfield and Margaret W. Maxfield. Accessible advanced undergraduate-level text starts with groups, rings, fields, and polynomials and advances to Galois theory, radicals and roots of unity, and solution by radicals. Numerous examples, illustrations, exercises, appendixes. 1971 edition. 224pp. 6 1/8 x 9 1/4.   0-486-47723-1

AN INTRODUCTION TO THE THEORY OF LINEAR SPACES, Georgi E. Shilov. Translated by Richard A. Silverman. Introductory treatment offers a clear exposition of algebra, geometry, and analysis as parts of an integrated whole rather than separate subjects. Numerous examples illustrate many different fields, and problems include hints or answers. 1961 edition. 320pp. 5 3/8 x 8 1/2.   0-486-63070-6

LINEAR ALGEBRA, Georgi E. Shilov. Covers determinants, linear spaces, systems of linear equations, linear functions of a vector argument, coordinate transformations, the canonical form of the matrix of a linear operator, bilinear and quadratic forms, and more. 387pp. 5 3/8 x 8 1/2.   0-486-63518-X

Browse over 9,000 books at www.doverpublications.com

Mathematics–Probability and Statistics

BASIC PROBABILITY THEORY, Robert B. Ash. This text emphasizes the probabilistic way of thinking, rather than measure-theoretic concepts. Geared toward advanced undergraduates and graduate students, it features solutions to some of the problems. 1970 edition. 352pp. 5 3/8 x 8 1/2. 0-486-46628-0

PRINCIPLES OF STATISTICS, M. G. Bulmer. Concise description of classical statistics, from basic dice probabilities to modern regression analysis. Equal stress on theory and applications. Moderate difficulty; only basic calculus required. Includes problems with answers. 252pp. 5 5/8 x 8 1/4. 0-486-63760-3

OUTLINE OF BASIC STATISTICS: Dictionary and Formulas, John E. Freund and Frank J. Williams. Handy guide includes a 70-page outline of essential statistical formulas covering grouped and ungrouped data, finite populations, probability, and more, plus over 1,000 clear, concise definitions of statistical terms. 1966 edition. 208pp. 5 3/8 x 8 1/2. 0-486-47769-X

GOOD THINKING: The Foundations of Probability and Its Applications, Irving J. Good. This in-depth treatment of probability theory by a famous British statistician explores Keynesian principles and surveys such topics as Bayesian rationality, corroboration, hypothesis testing, and mathematical tools for induction and simplicity. 1983 edition. 352pp. 5 3/8 x 8 1/2. 0-486-47438-0

INTRODUCTION TO PROBABILITY THEORY WITH CONTEMPORARY APPLICATIONS, Lester L. Helms. Extensive discussions and clear examples, written in plain language, expose students to the rules and methods of probability. Exercises foster problem-solving skills, and all problems feature step-by-step solutions. 1997 edition. 368pp. 6 1/2 x 9 1/4. 0-486-47418-6

CHANCE, LUCK, AND STATISTICS, Horace C. Levinson. In simple, non-technical language, this volume explores the fundamentals governing chance and applies them to sports, government, and business. "Clear and lively ... remarkably accurate." – *Scientific Monthly*. 384pp. 5 3/8 x 8 1/2. 0-486-41997-5

FIFTY CHALLENGING PROBLEMS IN PROBABILITY WITH SOLUTIONS, Frederick Mosteller. Remarkable puzzlers, graded in difficulty, illustrate elementary and advanced aspects of probability. These problems were selected for originality, general interest, or because they demonstrate valuable techniques. Also includes detailed solutions. 88pp. 5 3/8 x 8 1/2. 0-486-65355-2

EXPERIMENTAL STATISTICS, Mary Gibbons Natrella. A handbook for those seeking engineering information and quantitative data for designing, developing, constructing, and testing equipment. Covers the planning of experiments, the analyzing of extreme-value data; and more. 1966 edition. Index. Includes 52 figures and 76 tables. 560pp. 8 3/8 x 11. 0-486-43937-2

STOCHASTIC MODELING: Analysis and Simulation, Barry L. Nelson. Coherent introduction to techniques also offers a guide to the mathematical, numerical, and simulation tools of systems analysis. Includes formulation of models, analysis, and interpretation of results. 1995 edition. 336pp. 6 1/8 x 9 1/4. 0-486-47770-3

INTRODUCTION TO BIOSTATISTICS: Second Edition, Robert R. Sokal and F. James Rohlf. Suitable for undergraduates with a minimal background in mathematics, this introduction ranges from descriptive statistics to fundamental distributions and the testing of hypotheses. Includes numerous worked-out problems and examples. 1987 edition. 384pp. 6 1/8 x 9 1/4. 0-486-46961-1

CATALOG OF DOVER BOOKS

Mathematics–Geometry and Topology

PROBLEMS AND SOLUTIONS IN EUCLIDEAN GEOMETRY, M. N. Aref and William Wernick. Based on classical principles, this book is intended for a second course in Euclidean geometry and can be used as a refresher. More than 200 problems include hints and solutions. 1968 edition. 272pp. 5 3/8 x 8 1/2.   0-486-47720-7

TOPOLOGY OF 3-MANIFOLDS AND RELATED TOPICS, Edited by M. K. Fort, Jr. With a New Introduction by Daniel Silver. Summaries and full reports from a 1961 conference discuss decompositions and subsets of 3-space; n-manifolds; knot theory; the Poincaré conjecture; and periodic maps and isotopies. Familiarity with algebraic topology required. 1962 edition. 272pp. 6 1/8 x 9 1/4.   0-486-47753-3

POINT SET TOPOLOGY, Steven A. Gaal. Suitable for a complete course in topology, this text also functions as a self-contained treatment for independent study. Additional enrichment materials make it equally valuable as a reference. 1964 edition. 336pp. 5 3/8 x 8 1/2.   0-486-47222-1

INVITATION TO GEOMETRY, Z. A. Melzak. Intended for students of many different backgrounds with only a modest knowledge of mathematics, this text features self-contained chapters that can be adapted to several types of geometry courses. 1983 edition. 240pp. 5 3/8 x 8 1/2.   0-486-46626-4

TOPOLOGY AND GEOMETRY FOR PHYSICISTS, Charles Nash and Siddhartha Sen. Written by physicists for physics students, this text assumes no detailed background in topology or geometry. Topics include differential forms, homotopy, homology, cohomology, fiber bundles, connection and covariant derivatives, and Morse theory. 1983 edition. 320pp. 5 3/8 x 8 1/2.   0-486-47852-1

BEYOND GEOMETRY: Classic Papers from Riemann to Einstein, Edited with an Introduction and Notes by Peter Pesic. This is the only English-language collection of these 8 accessible essays. They trace seminal ideas about the foundations of geometry that led to Einstein's general theory of relativity. 224pp. 6 1/8 x 9 1/4. 0-486-45350-2

GEOMETRY FROM EUCLID TO KNOTS, Saul Stahl. This text provides a historical perspective on plane geometry and covers non-neutral Euclidean geometry, circles and regular polygons, projective geometry, symmetries, inversions, informal topology, and more. Includes 1,000 practice problems. Solutions available. 2003 edition. 480pp. 6 1/8 x 9 1/4.   0-486-47459-3

TOPOLOGICAL VECTOR SPACES, DISTRIBUTIONS AND KERNELS, François Trèves. Extending beyond the boundaries of Hilbert and Banach space theory, this text focuses on key aspects of functional analysis, particularly in regard to solving partial differential equations. 1967 edition. 592pp. 5 3/8 x 8 1/2.

0-486-45352-9

INTRODUCTION TO PROJECTIVE GEOMETRY, C. R. Wylie, Jr. This introductory volume offers strong reinforcement for its teachings, with detailed examples and numerous theorems, proofs, and exercises, plus complete answers to all odd-numbered end-of-chapter problems. 1970 edition. 576pp. 6 1/8 x 9 1/4.   0-486-46895-X

FOUNDATIONS OF GEOMETRY, C. R. Wylie, Jr. Geared toward students preparing to teach high school mathematics, this text explores the principles of Euclidean and non-Euclidean geometry and covers both generalities and specifics of the axiomatic method. 1964 edition. 352pp. 6 x 9.   0-486-47214-0

Browse over 9,000 books at www.doverpublications.com